WA 1105069 1

Handbook of Environmental Economics

D1342154

Blackwell Handbooks in Economics

Handbook of International Macroeconomics
Edited by Frederick van der Ploeg

Handbook of Environmental Economics
Edited by Daniel W. Bromley

Handbook of the Economics of Innovation and Technological Change
Edited by Paul Stoneman

Handbook of Applied Econometrics, Vol. 1
Edited by M. Hashem Pesaran and Mike Wickens

Handbook of Environmental Economics

Edited by
Daniel W. Bromley

BLACKWELL
Oxford UK & Cambridge USA

333.72
HAN

To Emery Castle, who has influenced so many of us

Copyright © Basil Blackwell Ltd 1995

First published 1995
Reprinted 1995

Blackwell Publishers Inc.
238 Main Street
Cambridge, Massachusetts 02142
USA

Blackwell Publishers Ltd
108 Cowley Road
Oxford OX4 1JF
UK

All rights reserved. Except for the quotation of short passages for the purposes of criticism and review, no part of this publication may be reproduced, stored in a retrieval system, or transmitted, in any form or by
any means, electronic, mechanical, photocopying, recording or otherwise, without the prior permission of the publisher.

Except in the United States of America, this book is sold subject to the condition that it shall not, by way of trade or otherwise, be lent, re-sold, hired out, or otherwise circulated without the publisher's prior consent in any form of binding or cover other than that in which it is published and without a similar condition including this condition being imposed on the subsequent purchaser.

11050691

Learning Resources
Centre

Library of Congress Cataloging-in-Publication Data

Handbook of environmental economics / edited by Daniel W. Bromley.
  p.   cm.
  Includes bibliographical references and index.
  ISBN 1–55786–506–X. – ISBN 1–55786–641–4 (pbk.)
  1. Environmental economics.   I. Bromley, Daniel W., 1940–
HC79.E5H3285   1995
333.7 – dc20
                                                                94–20714
                                                                CIP

British Library Cataloguing in Publication Data
A CIP catalogue record for this book is available from the British Library.

Typeset in 11 on 13pt Times
by Aarontype Limited, Bristol, England
Printed in Great Britain by Hartnolls Limited, Bodmin, Cornwall

This book is printed on acid-free paper

3/8/96

Contents

Figures

Tables

Contributors

Darius M. Adams is a Professor in the School of Forestry, University of Montana.

Lee G. Anderson is a Professor of Economics and Marine Studies at the College of Marine Studies, University of Delaware.

Giles Atkinson is based at the Centre for Social and Economic Research on the Global Environment (CSERGE), University College London.

Peter Berck is a Professor of Agricultural and Resource Economics at the University of California at Berkeley.

Richard C. Bishop is a Professor in the Department of Agricultural Economics at the University of Wisconsin-Madison.

Nancy E. Bockstael is a Professor in the Department of Agricultural and Resource Economics at the University of Maryland.

Daniel W. Bromley is Anderson-Bascom Professor in the Department of Agricultural Economics at the University of Wisconsin-Madison.

Paul Burrows is based in the Department of Economics at the University of York.

Patricia A. Champ is a Research Assistant in the Department of Agricultural Economics at the University of Wisconsin-Madison.

Jeffrey A. Cochrane is a Research Associate in the Department of Agricultural Economics at the University of Wisconsin-Madison.

Bonnie G. Colby is a Professor in the Department of Agricultural and Resource Economics at the University of Arizona.

Jon M. Conrad is Professor of Resource Economics at Cornell University and a Distinguished Research Fellow at the Centre for Fisheries Economics, Norwegian School of Economics and Business Administration, Bergen.

Michael C. Farmer is based at Ohio State University.

William A. Fischel is a Professor of Economics at Dartmouth College.

A. Myrick Freeman III is based in the Department of Economics at Bowdoin College.

Richard L. Gordon is Professor of Mineral Economics and MICASU University Endowed Fellow at the College of Earth and Mineral Sciences, The Pennsylvania State University.

Theodore Graham-Tomasi is based in the Department of Agricultural Economics at Michigan State University.

Ian Hodge is based in the Department of Land Economy at the University of Cambridge.

Richard Howarth is in the Department of Environmental Studies at the University of California, Santa Cruz.

Jeffrey Krautkraemer is a Professor in the Department of Economics at Washington State University.

Katherine T. McClain is an Assistant Professor in the Department of Mineral Economics at The Pennsylvania State University.

Claire A. Montgomery is Assistant Professor in the School of Forestry, University of Montana.

Richard B. Norgaard is a Professor at the University of California, Berkeley.

Daniel J. Mullarkey is a Research Assistant in the Department of Agricultural Economics at the University of Wisconsin-Madison.

John Pezzey is based in the Department of Economics at University College London.

David Pearce is based at the Centre for Social and Economic Research on the Global Environment (CSERGE), University College London.

Bill Provencher is based in the Department of Agricultural Economics at the University of Wisconsin-Madison.

Alan Randall is a Professor at Ohio State University.

Richard C. Ready is in the Department of Agricultural Economics at the University of Kentucky.

R. Bruce Rettig is a Professor in the Department of Agricultural and Resource Economics at Oregon State University

C. Ford Runge is a Professor in the Departments of Agricultural and Applied Economics, Hubert H. Humphrey Institute of Public Affairs and Department of Forest Resources at the University of Minnesota.

A. Allan Schmid is a Professor in the Department of Agricultural Economics at Michigan State University.

Kathleen Segerson is based in the Department of Economics, University of Connecticut.

T. H. Tietenberg is Christian A. Johnson Distinguished Teaching Professor in the Department of Economics, Colby College.

Michael A. Toman is based at Resources for the Future, Washington, DC.

Arild Vatn is based in the Department of Economics and Social Sciences at the Agricultural University of Norway.

Margaret Walls is based at Resources for the Future, Washington, DC.

Richard T. Woodward is a graduate student in the Department of Agricultural Economics at the University of Wisconsin-Madison.

Part I

Choices and Decisions

1

Choices without Prices without Apologies

Arild Vatn and Daniel W. Bromley

1   On Valuing Environmental Goods and Services

The dominant trend in environmental economics over the past decade has
been an increase in empirical studies to assign monetary values to
environmental goods and services. Given the number and scope of such
studies, one would necessarily conclude that great progress has been made.
While we do not deny the impressive conceptual and empirical progress in
this area, we do not share the enthusiasm of those who would claim that
these valuation efforts have improved the coherence of many environmental decisions. Indeed, the environmental policy problem is difficult and
contentious precisely because environmental goods and services embody
characteristics that present serious complications when choices are made
on the basis of these imputed monetary valuations. The decision problem
is particularly complicated when those monetary valuations are based on
individual values (or prices) elicited by contingent valuation methods.[1] We
are concerned that efforts to derive hypothetical values for the complex
and interrelated attributes of the environment, a process that compresses
this complexity into a simple metric of monetary values, results in an
important loss of information. Our purpose here is to suggest that this
information loss is not randomly distributed and that therefore the process
of assigning monetary values to environmental goods and services
necessarily "twists" the information about their individual and collective
significance.[2] It follows that so-called "contingent valuing," somewhat
paradoxically, may contribute minimally – if at all – to the revelation of
values. Given this, we will argue here that valuing (or pricing) of
environmental goods and services is neither necessary nor sufficient for
coherent and consistent choices about the environment.[3]

To the extent that hypothetical valuing obtains its social legitimacy
(upon which its alleged "necessity" rests) from the claim that only in this

way can society make economically correct decisions, then the loss of information in the process of valuing strips the final metric – the "price" or "value" – of its policy relevance by denying the legitimacy it needs. The claim of necessity in pricing must rest on the coherence of the ultimate product of valuation exercises. The lack of coherence in the resulting metric trumps the claim of necessity. The alleged sufficiency of valuation fares little better. The sufficiency claim rests on the presumption that valuation captures *all* of the information pertinent to any particular environmental choice. Most of what we will say below is directed at undermining this claim.

When pressed, many economists engaged in hypothetical valuation studies will perhaps deny that such pricing is either necessary or sufficient for informed environmental decisions. They will insist, however, that if society wishes to make "efficient" environmental choices there is no substitute for hypothetical valuation (thereby reintroducing a modified "necessity" claim). The ambiguous role of efficiency in social choice has been discussed elsewhere and will not concern us here (Mishan, 1980; Bromley, 1990). Needless to say, the lesser claim for hypothetical valuation – that it infuses environmental choices with the salutary discipline of "efficiency" – is equally undermined by our thesis. After all, if hypothetical prices do not convey the information pertinent to particular choices – and we insist they do not convey that information – how can choices informed by those prices be conducive to "efficiency"?

We base our argument on the fundamental complexity and multiple attributes of environmental goods and services. Some may object and point out that even the most ordinary commodity embodies a multitude of attributes. A loaf of bread is characterized by a constellation of calories, taste, smell, structure, and texture. There is bread for everyday use, bread for feasts, and bread for ceremonies. However, by purchasing bread on a routine basis, one learns about the relations between price and those attributes of bread considered both desirable and undesirable. Moreover, if the "wrong" choice is made on the basis of incomplete information in price, only the consumer knows of the mistake, and bears its consequences.

Even with repeated transactions, there remains the problem of how consumers measure and value all of the pertinent attributes – subsequently to transform them into a single metric. The problem is, in other words, how do individuals map a multiplicity of attributes – mediated by preferences – into one measure? The verb "valuing" describes this information processing activity in which the final product is some *reduced form metric*. In valuing, individuals must weigh each attribute by some standard, and thereby compute one metric reflecting the multitude of characteristics of the object under consideration. The value measure (v^m) is the scalar product of two vectors – one describing the attributes ($a_1, \ldots, a_n$) of the commodity the person recognizes as pertinent and hence valuable, and another vector describing the weighting $(w_1, \ldots, w_n)$ of each attribute reflecting the individual's preferences.

Despite its formal simplicity, this computation process is difficult for most goods. Long experience is required for it to work quickly – and well. Children sent to the bakery for their first bread purchase would not find the process simple. Adults are reminded of this when they undertake the purchase of an automobile. Freeman (1986) comments on this aspect of "preference research" as the opportunity for individuals "to modify their choices in light of what they learn about their preferences and the characteristics of goods" (pp. 150–1).

The calculation process may break down and give rise to information losses for three different reasons. First, losses may arise due to cognitive restrictions. This refers to the difficulty of observing and weighing attributes of the object of choice. We denote this the *cognition problem*. Second, losses will occur if different characteristics of the good are incommensurable. This property means that the chooser cannot easily map disparate attributes – via w – into one dimension. Moreover, if the components of w are regarded as orthogonal, one metric is unable to capture all relevant information. We call this the *incongruity problem*. Finally, there is the *composition problem* – the part–whole dimension. If the attributes of a are dynamically interrelated – either internally or with the attributes of other goods – the computation of v^m is problematical. In practical terms, information problems are created as soon as the value of one attribute depends upon the level of another. As we will see, the above points are of preeminent importance where environmental goods or services are concerned.

There is a second issue that must be addressed as well. We have in mind the important role of the context in which valuing is undertaken and choices are made. As already discussed, the attributes and qualities of goods and services are not immediately or intuitively apprehended or apparent. Preferences are not encoded in human DNA. Rather, preferences are developed or discovered as one goes about choosing. This means that the elicitation context becomes important, and the comprehension of goods and services is simultaneously attached to both vectors above.

These ideas parallel the "constructivist approach" recently suggested by Gregory et al. (1993), and the idea of "preference researched bids" as discussed by Cummings et al. (1986). The issues raised in these works are focused primarily toward how one might elicit values. Our concern is also directed toward the importance of preferences as social constructs – or the "social construction of reality." Societal processes form the context within which individual preferences are both developed and supported. Valuing that fails to recognize the preeminent role of context in preference formation will fail to produce coherent valuation estimates.

We will discuss our concerns about the dominant valuation approaches to collective choices by first addressing the problems related to calculating unidimensional value measures for environmental goods. Next we will turn to a discussion of the various contexts of valuation. We will close with the observation that choices in the realm of the environment are, to a large degree, about choosing alternative development paths.

2   The Process of Value Calculation

As indicated above, the process of transforming a complex of relations into a single metric encounters three different problems – cognition, congruity, and composition.

The cognition problem

The process of individual "valuing" of goods and services entails the selective perception of certain data about the good or service, and a corresponding disregard for other data. There are two issues here. First, there is the issue of observing and understanding those attributes that define a particular good or service. Environmental assets are, to a large extent, characterized by their quintessential invisibility – their *functional transparency*. This transparency creates obvious problems for the valuation process. Second, there is the problem of weighing various attributes. There is evidence that people have restricted capabilities in making *comparisons across scales*. Such discontinuities may explain several of the inconsistencies observed in the valuation literature.

Perception and functional transparency
While it is possible that the environmental good under consideration in hypothetical valuation may be an easily demarcated object, the environment properly comprehended consists of interrelated functions that cannot be casually isolated or separated. Here one might mention a range of services related to (1) the support of life as we know it – exemplified by certain cycles (hydrologic cycle, carbon cycle, nitrogen cycle); (2) the role of ecological diversity; and (3) the interplay between species. As part of essential life-support mechanisms, environmental goods are developed reciprocally over an enormous time span. A continuous trial and error process has shaped a myriad of relations that can best be characterized by their *functional transparency*. Functional transparency means that the precise contribution of a functional element in the ecosystem is not known – indeed is probably unknowable – until it ceases to function. It is through failure that we learn about the critical ecosystem

functions that, while working, are transparent. For instance, nitrogen cycles in wetlands are not obvious until they are destroyed and we then begin to discover the serious implications.

If we relate this to the valuation process, some important problems become apparent. First, the conventional way of learning about the attributes of a good or service – learning by doing – is difficult, not necessarily enlightening, and likely to be very risky. Second, it is indeed problematic to describe the good in such a way that the participants in hypothetical valuation studies have the same feature in mind as they reveal their bids. It is not stretching the point to say that the "resource" in question can be practically anything the respondent – or the researcher – wants it to be.

Valuing across scales

Not all environmental goods are characterized by transparency. For some it is their visual (or other apprehended) properties that are perceived as the most important quality. While this would seem to simplify the valuation problem, there remains the problem of weighing sets of attributes that are very different. There is now evidence that individual respondents have difficulty converting environmental goods and services into monetized units for comparison with other goods. More generally, individuals have difficulties making comparisons *across* different forms of *scales*. Much of the empirical evidence for this comes from the literature on preference reversals (Slovic and Lichtenstein, 1983; Tversky et al., 1990). In essence, the measurement procedure itself influences the resulting measurement.

A number of empirical studies illustrate this problem. One study defined four different groups of students who were presented with pictures showing (1) two conditions for a set of outdoor scenes and (2) two qualities of a set of consumer products (Brown, 1984). Each group was asked to "value" the change in qualities between the amenities and the commodities. Choosing four groups enabled the crossing of two response scales – rating and money – with two different measures of value – importance and willingness to pay (WTP). For the two groups asked to respond on a rating scale (from 1 to 10), the response was generally independent of the measure used. The amenity changes were rated over the commodity changes in both instances. But for those groups asked to respond in dollars, an important difference occurred. Those asked to measure on the basis of importance also gave a higher bid for the amenity changes than for changes in quality of the commodities. For those asked to use WTP as a measure, the conclusion was the opposite.

In reviewing much of the literature on these issues, Gregory et al. (1993) argue that individuals are not accustomed to interpreting environmental goods in monetary terms. That is, the respondents' cognitive beliefs about these values are not easily quantified, especially in monetary terms. The logic of the vector approach discussed above is the presumption that individuals can make extensive comparisons across multiple dimensions. If this is not the case, the vector model offers a seriously flawed heuristic. Tversky argues that it is much simpler to compare the alternatives dimension-by-dimension than it is to evaluate each good across all dimensions and then compare these total assessments.

We see this at work even in regular commodity markets where individuals seem to restrict their calculative comparisons to commodities embodying rather similar attributes. Choices between or among commodity groups seem, by cognitive and computational necessity, to be driven by other considerations. Our view is that such comparisons are driven by learned behavior over previous constellations of attributes and prices. Price-based choices – that is, decisive comparisons – are largely confined to price changes within the same general group of goods or services.

This means that price bids over goods that have never been represented in a monetary form will be plagued with randomness. Gregory et al. note that:

> Environmental values do not exist in any well defined, stable form. Unless the items in question are both simple and familiar – and environmental goods are neither – individuals will construct values heuristically on the basis of the format and context provided by the elicitation setting.
>
> (1993, p. x)

Thus the elicitation procedure may serve as a means to construct preferences rather than merely uncover them.

The elicitation problems related to functional transparency, and a multitude of scales, are compounded by a limited ability to handle situations where risks are involved. Important insights in this field come from the work of Tversky and Kahneman (1986).[4] While part of the problem related to restricted calculation capacity, there is something more fundamental at work attached to the ability to handle uncertainty, and the restricted possibility to build on experience. If agreed rules can be developed, *learned* behavior might solve this problem. As Fishoff (1990) puts it: "Unless the correct behavior is in people's 'repertoire,' there is no way that it can be reinforced by their experience" (pp. 318–19). Douglas (1986), in commenting on the debate about bounded rationality and work by Schotter (1981), argues that there exist societal processes by which individuals try to cope with novel choice problems. Contextual devices – institutions – are constructed to help people through this problem:

> Past experience is encapsulated in an institution's rule so that it acts as a guide to what to expect from the future. The more fully the institutions encode expectations, the more they put uncertainty under control, with the further effect that behavior tends to conform to the institutional matrix.
>
> (Douglas, 1986, p. 48)

The existence of such institutions is no guarantee that they will evolve where and when they are needed. But the above reasoning turns our attention, at least partly, in directions other than the one of eliciting prices.

The incongruity problem

If different attributes of a good are incongruous – that is, attached to orthogonal dimensions – one metric (price) will be unable to capture all relevant information. The *moral aspect* of environmental choices tends to introduce one important basis for such incongruity. In the broader literature, one encounters a range of situations in which individuals are seen to act in ways that differ from the economist's perception of the comparative calculus of the margin. There are many examples where restricted tradeoff possibilities alter perceptions of value. Despite differences in emphasis, Douglas (1966), Douglas and Wildavsky (1982), Kneese and Schulze (1985), Etzioni (1988), and Sagoff (1988, 1993) offer serious explorations of this problem.

Commitment and moral judgments are concepts often attached to those domains where issues about life, quality of life, and personal integrity are at stake (Sen, 1977). These are areas where social norms restrict or reject the commodity fiction.[5] It is clear that environmental issues are dominated by a moral dimension. Edwards (1986), Gregory and McDaniels (1987), Harris et al. (1989), Opaluch and Segerson (1989), Stevens et al. (1991), and Kahneman and Knetsch (1992) discuss this aspect of environmental choices.

Stevens et al. (1991) present standard contingent valuation (CV) results from an evaluation of the importance of enhancing the survival possibilities for different species in New England. Their study shows that "existence value" was the most important reason to support habitat restoration, even for those species with an immediate "use value" (salmon). A majority of their respondents (79 percent) agreed with the statement that "all species of wildlife have a right to live independent of any benefit or harm to people" (p. 396).

Yet, when confronted with hypothetical valuation, the majority of respondents refused to pay.[6] In attempting to understand this behavior, the authors reason that the respondents were "either uncertain about their valuation, believed that wildlife should not be valued in dollar terms, or protested the donation payment vehicle. Moreover, most of those who *would pay* exhibited behavior that appears inconsistent with the neoclassical theory underlying the CVM" (p. 399). They point out that the actual contingent valuation method may have asked people to choose between ordinary goods (income) and a moral principle. They refer to Harper (1989), and to Opaluch and Segerson (1989), who argue that such choices are likely to produce conflict and ambivalence, and that the resulting behavior is likely to be inconsistent with the usual preference assumptions. That is, the hypothetical valuation approach – the questions asked – does not fit the perception of those taking part in the study.

In the Stevens et al. survey, many respondents showed considerable uncertainty about their hypothetical valuation – a finding consistent with the current theme. Since individuals are still in the process of forming their views about environmental goods and services, there is little common understanding, and therefore a paucity of norms, regarding how such issues ought to be framed and evaluated.[7] Certainly the information offered to the respondent may heavily influence the bids.[8]

In the above study, the moral issue is related to the presumed "right" of wildlife to survive, and hence the obvious impertinence of respondents being asked to pay for it individually. Environmental issues raise the question of the "right" to life (or to a certain quality of life) for humans as well as for wildlife – be it now or in the future. The intergenerational question is certainly at the center of this discussion, emphasizing again the moral dimension of environmental choices.

The composition problem

Finally we have the composition problem. Loomis et al. (1991) distinguish five components of value related to natural resources:

> total economic value is made up of five components: (1) onsite recreation use of the resource; (2) commercial use of the resource; (3) an option demand from maintaining the potential to visit the resource in the future; (4) an existence value derived from simply knowing the resource exists in a preserved state; and (5) a bequest value derived by individuals from knowing that future generations will be able to enjoy existence or use of a resource.
>
> (pp. 412–13)

These five components fit well into the standard distinction between *use values* (1 and 2) and *non-use values* (3–5), with "existence value" as the archetype of the latter case. It is illustrative that such a finite – and divisible – list is offered. Further, as is typical for most of the hypothetical valuation literature, there is no component directed specifically toward the *functional aspects* of environmental goods and services.[9]

Indeed, the concept of *functional value* is totally absent in a model that draws the distinction between "use" and "non-use" value. In essence, hypothetical valuation studies have a tendency to describe environmental goods and services in a manner that renders them commodity like. A precise valuation demands a precisely demarcated object. The essence of commodities is that conceptual and definitional boundaries can be drawn around them and property rights can then be attached – or imagined. Polanyi would emphasize that what individuals and societies choose to demarcate as commodities is entirely arbitrary. Indeed, he talks of the *commodity fiction*. Polanyi suggests that as markets evolved in human history it became necessary to regard certain aspects of reality as commodities. After all, markets can only operate where things are – by definition – commodities.[10] The commoditization of land in seventeenth-century Europe, when brought to the Americas with immigration, profoundly clashed with the native American's perception of land. The native American claimed, then as now, that people belong to land, not vice versa.

For the most part, the commoditization of environmental goods can be looked upon as a product of the felt need to value them. It is not immediately obvious to many – other than economists – that environmental goods and services are "commodities." Nor is it apparent to noneconomists why it is necessary to characterize environmental attributes in this way. This disciplinary need to create commodities where they may not, in fact, exist then encounters the reality that some environmental goods may be technically impossible – or perhaps prohibitively expensive – to demarcate and so to "commoditize." A fundamental danger with the commodity fiction is that the commoditized environment thereby becomes a contrived artifact of itself. The "market" exchange becomes one of trading hypothetical dollars (or even real dollars) for the hypothetical (or even real) opportunity to use the commodity for a certain period of time. The respondent is, in effect, renting parts of the ecosystem.

Denying the commodification of the environment forces one to try to comprehend environmental goods and services in a more holistic way – though economists tend to reject holism because it undermines the presumption of the analytical sufficiency of a world usefully defined as consisting of atomistic agents acting on atomistic objects. It is quite possible that much of the hostility arising in the ecological community towards economics (and hypothetical valuation) rests on this aspect of holism.

Three issues arise with respect to hypothetical valuing and the problem of composition. First, in a fully functionalized system, each part must actually be as "valuable" as the whole, and hence the value of any single component cannot be understood – or priced – separately from its contribution to the whole. This means that the idea of continuous tradeoffs among various components has nothing to offer. Tribe (1972) makes the observation:

> the problem . . . relates not merely to undervaluing certain factors but to *reducing entire problems to terms that misstate their underlying structure,* typically collapsing into the task of maximizing some simple quantity an enterprise whose ordering principle is not one of maximization at all.
>
> (p. 97)

Second, ordinary commodities are characterized by their capacity to be exchanged, and their "value" – as measured in prices – is an exchanged value. In these circumstances, the commodity represents a distinct set of attributes over which the use and enjoyment can be defined by, and controlled by, the buyer. The very process of production in an economy is one of transforming disparate factors of production (raw materials) into a constellation of attributes which, taken together, offer usefulness and so command a certain price.

With environmental goods and services this condition is not met. The value of many environmental goods and services is derived from the very act of keeping them working in their existing functional relation. Moreover, environmental goods and services do not exist in discrete units:

> neither natural resources and environmental services as factors of production nor environmental impacts as products of economic activity come in discrete units. The assumptions of the . . . [neoclassical] . . . model are incongruent with the nature of the world. It is ironic that environmental problems in economics are thought of as problems of market failure rather than evidence of the applicable limits of the market model.
>
> (Norgaard, 1984, p. 160)

Third, from a systems perspective, individual components do not acquire their value from their *uniqueness to us as humans*, but rather from their *uniqueness in relation the whole system of which they are a part*. In the standard approach to hypothetical valuation, uniqueness seems to be addressed by the concept of existence value. However, instead of capturing existence as a set of complex relations, the idea of existence value in hypothetical valuation is usually attached to discrete and demarcated segments of the environment that humans find attractive or compelling. Cummings and Harrison (1992) note that it is this kind of uniqueness that actually dominates non-use values as that concept is normally used. Kahneman and Knetsch (1992) capture this notion as well when they argue that: "Indeed, the uniqueness of the valued good is the essence of existence value, as this notion has been discussed since Krutilla (1967)."

A related problem in some hypothetical valuation studies is that the spectacular or the visual tends to dominate the systemic or functional. Bald eagles and grand vistas get much more attention – and hence become more "valuable" – than an ugly fish or the muddy wetland. Lost in all of the attention to species extinction and scenic sunsets is the more fundamental question of which pieces of the environment are essential to long-run sustainability. It seems as if some have come to regard the natural environment as a large zoological garden from which we can select for policy attention those parts that happen to hold our momentary affection. But first we have to "value" it to reassure ourselves that the attention is warranted, or that the attention is "efficient."

3 The Multiple Contexts of Valuation

Valuation of environmental goods and services requires recognition of the multiple contexts within which individuals assign values to such goods and services. Values are context relative. There is no firm point against which one can compare different goods and services. Furthermore, individuals choose social contexts and thereby form the basis for their choices in the absence of prices.

Social norms, individual preferences, and individual values

Consider first the relation between context and value. Two aspects are of relevance: (1) how the context of choice influences individual's preferences; and (2) how the context of choice actually scales or weighs individual values (v^m) in the course of deriving a coherent measure (price or value) across individuals.

Context and individual preferences
While it is true that preferences are associated with the individual, it is also true that social processes play a major role in defining and forming those preferences. From an early age, individuals undergo the internalization of norms and values. Moreover, individual preferences undergo continual evolution as a result of implicit and explicit mechanisms of socialization and control. While Emile Durkheim (1962) and Talcott Parsons (1951) were among the most important contributors to a branch of literature emphasizing continuity, harmony, and solidarity, other writers have stressed differences in interests, class distinctions, and conflict in studying the evolution of norms and values (Marx, 1965; Macpherson, 1985).

It is clear that social norms, conventions, and shared values are necessary components in helping individuals to establish their identity in a community, to provide "reasonable" solutions in certain situations, and to structure or frame necessary choices. There is a duality here to the extent that norms both *enable* individuals to make choices, and norms *constrain* individuals in order to mediate potential conflicts (Giddens, 1976; Etzioni, 1988; Bromley, 1989a). Economists tend to overlook (or dismiss) the contextual framing of individual preferences. However, children are a *tabula rasa* and the values they acquire are the social constructs communicated to them over a range of circumstances. As new issues enter the mental stage, individuals form or solidify their "preferences" as part of the social group to which they closely relate.

From this realization, it follows that the basic challenge in environmental decision making is not measuring, say, individual willingness to pay. Rather, the challenge is one of specifying the conditions for discourse over what is worth "valuing" by individuals – and why that is so. To a very large extent, social context *shapes* individuals and hence environmental "values" in the monetary sense used here.

Context and the weighing of individual values

Social context determines whose interests are to count in the decision process, and to what extent. Preferences already subject to information loss in the process of revelation are once again twisted through contextual mechanisms to influence individual estimates of "value" (the bids in hypothetical valuation studies).

A discussion of this influence of context is, at bottom, a discussion of actual and presumed rights. The so-called Coase theorem denies that the rights structure influences resource allocation and thus prices. But this conclusion rests on a set of strong assumptions more clearly articulated by Coase himself than by many of his more ardent followers (Coase, 1960; Randall, 1974). The most obvious problem here is the reality of non-zero transaction costs – without which economists would have very little to do. Further, the acceptance of the Coase theorem as a guide to policy rests on the assumption of a population with homogeneous and homothetic preferences. Here one enters the domain of income distribution and its obvious effect on prices – be it market prices or bids in hypothetical valuation studies.

It is now well understood that certain environmental costs are not accounted for because the prevailing rights structure allows them to be disregarded. Environmental issues are precisely concerned with the status quo presumption of rights which allow certain costs to go unrecorded (Bromley, 1989b, 1991). This status quo lack of internalization is thought, by some economists, to be optimal. The logic is as follows: Internalization of such external costs will occur when the costs of a change – including transaction costs – become less than the gains of internalization. Until that time, it is alleged that what exists in the status quo must be, by definition, optimal. If it were not optimal, it would change. Demsetz is the most explicit in support of this definitional slip.

The danger in this line of thought, with its strong emphasis on individual bargaining within a given institutional setting, is that such logic conceals the fact that transaction costs are themselves a function of the prevailing institutional setup. That is, not only are *externalities* a function of the status quo institutions, but transaction costs that allow externalities to exist in the first instance – and persist under that most wondrous of Panglossian benedictions, Pareto-irrelevant externalities – are as well. Moreover, an emphasis on individual bargaining ignores the effects related to the distribution of income and the crucial matter of whose interests are to count in the bargaining process.

An equally serious problem arises when a false picture of the institutional setup is used to justify one particular approach to the monetary valuation of environmental goods and services. The evidence is irrefutable that bids based on willingness to accept (WTA) compensation will systematically exceed – often by a large ratio – bids based on willingness to pay (WTP) (Bishop and Heberlein, 1979; Randall and Stoll, 1980; Tversky and Kahneman, 1981; Knetsch and Sinden, 1984; Gregory, 1986; Knetsch, 1990; Hanemann, 1991; Gregory et al., 1993). After reviewing the literature, Gregory concludes that the WTA measures generally seem to exceed the WTP measures by not less than a factor of 3.

Several explanations come to mind. First, income effects may not always be negligible. This will certainly be the case when moral aspects of the environment comprise a nontrivial part of "well-being." Second, the fundamental asymmetry between WTP and WTA arises from the fact that, while WTA is unconstrained in the eyes of the respondent, WTP will always be constrained by existing income.[11] This dimension encompasses the concept of "loss aversion." It is now well known that the value function is steeper for losses than for gains (Tversky and Kahneman, 1986). This alone is sufficient to conclude that WTA will be higher than WTP for related choices. In their work on prospect theory, Tversky and Kahneman emphasize that gains and losses are evaluated – or perceived – on the basis of the status quo situation. Thus *change* from the status quo becomes the important issue, not the absolute level as in ordinary utility theory. This perspective also means that the same future state – or outcome – is valued differently depending on the nature of the existing state.

The third point concerns perceptions of the structure of actual and presumed rights. That is, differences in perceptions of gains and losses arise from differences in the presumed entitlement structure. Simply put, individuals are less inclined to give up something that they perceive to be "theirs." The presumption here is that the individual has a right to something and therefore may be disinclined to offer much in the way of WTP. On the other hand, such *endowment goods* could be expected to have a very high WTA (Thaler, 1980; Bromley, 1989b). If the question of value presupposes that a person has a right to, say, clean air or water, it will be valued differently than if it is supposed that the person does not have this right. In the former case, willingness to accept compensation (WTA) is the relevant approach, while in the latter setting one must inquire about willingness to pay (WTP).

Yet one often sees a distinct preference for WTP measures on the apparent ground that individuals spend their consuming life "bidding for" regular commodities. In this way, by striving to mimic the conventional market behavior of individual consumers, it is apparently thought that environmental goods and services can be made to seem like "ordinary" goods and services. But of course the moral dimension intrudes into the presumed clarity of economic choice. Individuals who imagine with some conviction that, say, their drinking water should be uncontaminated, will be expected to be unimpressed, if not irate, about having to pay to prevent it from becoming even more contaminated. They will often wonder why they should have to pay to obtain a state of nature that existed prior to the advent of chemical runoff caused by someone else. Indeed, they might legitimately wonder why they should not be asked their necessary level of compensation to evince stoicism while the contamination of groundwater continues.

Perhaps the most important point related to the issue of hypothetical valuation is the ambiguous entitlement structures associated with many environmental goods and services. As Gregory and McDaniels (1987) point out, there is often a lack of distinction between compensation and purchase structures, and even if this distinction exists it is often not supported by legal entitlements. Thus confusion may occur in hypothetical valuation studies either because the individual lacks clarity as to the actual entitlement structure, or because the survey instrument presumes a structure different from that presumed by the respondent. The work of Stevens et al. (1991) illustrates this issue.

If the good or service is considered a right for the individual – we call it an *endowment good or service* – then WTA would be the proper approach if hypothetical monetary valuation is to be undertaken. But care must be taken even here. If an individual is asked to "value" wildlife, this may be viewed as an endowments issue – the right of a certain species to exist. But as long as this right is assumed to apply to the species itself, WTA suddenly gets a strong flavor of "bribery." The same reasoning applies to situations where the respondent finds it relevant to take the rights of other humans into consideration. But in situations like this, WTP is not a good measure either. Perhaps the respondent is valuing both his/her own interests and those of others at the same time. Further, we have already seen that there are strong arguments against converting moral commitments into money equivalents.

These insights are helpful in explaining the different types of protest reactions observed in CV studies. Similar reasoning leads Opaluch and Grigalunas (1992) to conclude that one may do better by focusing policy measures on levels of in-kind compensation through natural resource restoration than by attempting to derive hypothetical monetary measures of compensation.

Individual values and social choices

In a new domain of collective choice – and many novel issues relating to the management of environmental goods and services certainly qualify as a new domain – the most basic question concerns the development of societal norms and standards. The collective choice problem is, first of all, about advancing common ways of understanding what the pertinent issues are about. Only then can we develop a basis for collective choice predicated upon the elicitation of individual choice. It is axiomatic – and also well known since Arrow's seminal work – that coherent collective choice cannot be made on the basis of some simple aggregation of individual preferences alone.

That is, because individual preferences are context relative, a fundamental problem becomes which of many "contexts" is pertinent to any particular choice problem, We can actually make a distinction between two kinds of choice processes in society. One concerns decisions from within sets of given values or constraints. The other is about choosing these sets of norms and common values (Sen, 1977; Field, 1979; Bromley, 1989a). As discussed by Elster (1979, 1983), reality is complicated by the interrelatedness of both kinds of choices.

In essence, individuals are both consumers and citizens (Sagoff, 1988), and environmental choices uniquely span both domains. Just as *preferences* count for consumer choice within constraints, *judgments* can be used as the driving concept for citizens choosing basic norms or modifying existing constraints. The distinction is not easily operationalized, but it is nonetheless central to the current discussion. If the choice can be categorized as a "mere" consumer choice, individual preferences and bids are relevant. If choices are about formulating common norms and values, such individual bids have little to offer. Indeed, the concern with strategic behavior in collective action arises from precisely this aspect of choice.

In addition, our approach insists that norms are *instruments* in dealing with certain complex policy issues. These norms and conventions may be understood as having a functional role – or a functional meaning – in the relation between society and, in this case, its natural environment. Douglas is a strong advocate for the view that the decisions of greatest importance are in fact institutionalized – they have a normative form. Concerning the idea of a "just" choice, she writes:

> Justice has nothing to do with isolated cases . . . individuals normally offload such decisions on to institutions. No private ratiocination can find the answer. The most profound decisions about justice are not made by individuals as such, but by individuals within and on behalf of institutions . . . . Choosing rationally, on this argument, is not choosing intermittently among crises or private preferences, but choosing continuously among social institutions.
>
> (1986, p. 124)

Here Douglas also offers a tentative answer to the question of why norms are of such importance in difficult choice settings. If we look at history there is evidence that underlying norms, conventions, and taboos evolve in the human struggle for social order and survival (Lewis, 1986). Marvin Harris is representative of a tradition that sees the basis of such norms lying in the human struggle for mastery over the physical environment. Such norms may be purposely invented, they may have a pure functional explanation, or they may by chosen "by luck" (Elster, 1989).

We would emphasize that valuing environmental goods without taking into account the importance of commitments – or the value-laden character of most issues – is destined to be a biased undertaking. Issues of this kind cannot be resolved through simple aggregation of individual hypothetical bids. Rather, collective discussion is necessary to form a collective understanding, and to construct a coherent basis for choice. There are certainly variations here, for the simple reason that some environmental goods are more "commodity like" than others. That may be the case with many recreational goods. A bid for hunting opportunities among potential hunters may be as trustworthy as any real market price. But as soon as the purview is broadened to other interests attached to, say, wildlife or certain amenities, the object of study loses its defining character as a "commodity" in the ordinary sense.

4   Choice Under the Cloud of Irreversibilities

At bottom, our concern is about environmental choices in the face of the non-trivial possibility that resultant outcomes ordain a devlopment path that is both detrimental and irreversible. Much of the literature handles this issue as a risk problem – a problem of known probabilities over a set of clearly specified outcomes.[12] However useful this mental construct may be to the empirically oriented economist, this characterization will rarely conform to reality. Because of functional transparency, the most important relations are indubitably the ones hampered by unknown probabilities – that is, by pure (Knightian) uncertainty. Since we cannot know the implications of many environmental choices, the main strategy for those not characterized as risk lovers must be to minimize the chance of loss of future opportunities, The characteristics of such a norm – or decision rule – can be illustrated by the *safe minimum standard* (SMS) of conservation (Ciriacy-Wantrup, 1968). It is, admittedly, a fairly coarse norm, and one developed for decisions in the realm of renewable resources with a critical zone.[13]

But even with this kind of decision rule, one is still faced with the difficult task of identifying the level of costs at which the avoidance of future opportunity losses becomes "too expensive" (Bishop, 1978). A determination of this level of "acceptable costs" is necessary, and it is this consideration that will lead to a preservation decision, or a contrary decision. This issue can be handled in different ways.

As developed here, decisive information – or managerial wisdom – cannot be purchased through the simple act of "valuing" potential costs attached to different strategies. In most choices of this kind, the decision is easy if the costs of securing future opportunities can be kept low. The question of "too expensive" becomes of little importance. At the core of this problem, we encounter the search for strategies and development paths that will reduce competition between the "man-made" (internal) economy and the environment, As the problem is characterized here, this seems to be an important way of framing the question.

Ideally, if competition can be avoided, human interaction with the natural environment will not result in any lost opportunity for the future. The environmental goods and service are already "produced" and therefore offer a set – or a constellation – of possible benefits. But certainly, the realization of many benefits may block the realization of others. We cannot have both fancy resorts and undisturbed nature. Still, many uses need not entail competition – or be mutually exclusive. While competition is seldom totally avoided, many losses or risks can be reduced by bringing new options into the choice set. That is, one can search for alternative development paths thereby reducing competition. Often the "market" is unable to bring forward such alternatives.

Examples of existing ways of increasing the choice set are multiple-use strategies securing forestry, wildlife, and recreation. Others are zoning policies where activities with positive external effects are situated together, thereby creating mutual benefits. Those examples are evident, but the idea of combined use can be fertile in a much wider range of issues such as which materials to use in production processes and which material flow patterns to develop. The perspective of deliberately seeking to establish complementarities tends to encourage thinking in "co-evolutionary" terms (Norgaard, 1984). Framing the questions this way opens up the opportunity for important decisions to be made in the absence of guidance from prices. Our primary concern is that by advocating hypothetical valuation (pricing) of environmental goods and services – and then insisting upon benefit–cost analysis built on these hypothetical values – economists have focused analytical attention away from the broader strategies introduced here.

5   Implications

We have raised a number of concerns with the widespread practice of hypothetical valuation of environmental goods and services. To return to an earlier point, the *necessity claim* for such valuation will usually be that consistent and efficient choices demand these values (prices) so that meaningful comparisons with other alternatives – including doing nothing – can be easily undertaken.[14] But this claim of necessity must rest on clear proof that the values (prices) derived from hypothetical valuation studies capture all of the information pertinent to a particular environmental choice. In the absence of such proof, values (prices) from hypothetical valuation studies carry no more normative significance than do competing claims expressed by self-proclaimed interest groups on either side on any particular decision.

Evidence would suggest that a great many "enlightened" choices concerning the environment have been taken in the absence of pricing. Early efforts at disease control through water purification in major urban centers of Europe and America certainly come to mind. Similarly, air pollution programs in these same cities did not await decisive evidence that the citizenry was prepared to pay an aggregate sum in excess of the anticipated "costs" imposed on those whose actions were to be modified.

The dedication of large tracts of the American continent as public domain lands for the eternal enjoyment of all – regardless of their economic situation – is yet another reminder of the historical irrelevance of pricing and valuing of the sort that now seems *de rigueur*. Recent efforts to reduce the chemical contamination of groundwater, and to staunch the loss of millions of tons of valuable topsoil, also suggest that collective choices about the environment need not await definitive proof that aggregated indications of willingness to pay could – if necessary – comprise a sum sufficient to compensate those who imagine that they might lose something of alleged value.

Of course the complaint will be immediately offered that while indeed these programs are probably "worth it," there is no guarantee that drinking water is not now too pure, or that the air over our cities is not too clean, or that groundwater is not too clean, or that there is not too much land devoted to parks and wilderness areas.[15] We grant the point, but immediately dismiss its pertinence for the very argument already advanced. To be less subtle, there is nothing in economics in general – or in hypothetical valuation in particular - that can address the *socially optimal* level of air or water quality, or of land devoted to parks and wilderness (Bromley, 1989a).

The corollary, of course, is that pricing is not sufficient to ensure informed and coherent collective choices about environmental goods and services. We raise the tyranny of the status quo. Because most environmental problems are the result of new technical information about the health effects of certain economic processes – or because the individual and collective "value" of many amenities is itself undergoing continual change in an evolving world – hypothetical valuing and pricing of environmental goods and services necessarily fails to provide decisive information about what is "efficient" and what is "welfare enhancing."

The collective choice problem about environmental goods and services is complex and problematical precisely because it entails aspects of our social existence that defy reduction to the venerable fiction of commodities. Efforts to redefine reality may prove useful in discussing certain aspects of environmental policy in the classroom, but it does not therefore follow that collective choices which reject the commodity fiction are ill-informed, inconsistent, or not in the interest of efficiency. The hypothetical valuation exercise may be its own reward for what it tells us about how individuals value non-ordinary aspects of their lives. But the most fundamental environmental choices will continue to be made without prices – and without apologies.

Notes

We gratefully acknowledge the helpful comments of Richard Bishop, Ron Cummings, Eirik Romstad, Kathy Segerson, and Tom Stevens on earlier drafts. This chapter is drawn extensively from a recent article in the *Journal of Environmental Economics and Management*. We are grateful to that journal and its publisher (Academic Press) for permission to use it here.

1 Throughout we will use "values" and "prices" as carefully as possible to avoid confusion. Some readers will regard "prices" as the empirical manifestation of cleared markets, but we use the term in a more general way to connote per-unit monetary figures assigned by individuals to various parts of the ecosystem. That is, prices are the end product of a process of "valuing" by individuals who are asked to think about their "value" of various environmental goods and services. Their "value" may be in terms of what they would be willing to pay (a price), or what they might demand by way of compensation (a different price).

2 We chose the term "twists" very carefully. Convention would suggest that terms such as "distorts" or "biases" might be used instead. We reject the latter terms because they imply knowledge of some "true" level that we do not believe is known – or knowable.

3 Freeman notes: "On the basis of the familiarity and experience arguments, it appears that the CVM is likely to work best for those kinds of problems where we need it least; that is, where respondents' experience with changes in the level of environmental good have left a record of tradeoffs, substitutions, and so forth which can be the basis of econometric estimates of value. But for those problems for which we need something like the CVM most, that is, where individuals have little or no experience with different levels of the environmental good, CVM appears to be least reliable" (Freeman, 1986, p. 160). Freeman is arguing that in those instances where environmental goods and services are closest to ordinary commodities, hypothetical valuation is most reliable. Where the environmental good or service is not easily commoditized – say in choices concerning entire habitats or particular ecosystems – then hypothetical valuation is of dubious merit.

4 Slovic et al. (1976) is another important reference.

5 The idea of the "commodity fiction" originated with Karl Polanyi. We will elaborate this idea below.

6 In the survey instrument, a reduction in public spending on wildlife restoration in New England was assumed. A private trust was therefore created to compensate for the lack of public funding. The respondents were then asked to offer their bids as a (hypothetical) payment to this fund. The authors point to the possibility that some of

the reactions are due to the view that habitat restoration is a public matter and should not be handled by a private trust.

7   The issue here relates to the CVM instrument in use. The NOAA Panel argues that "external validation of the CV method remains an important issue. A critically important contribution could come from experiments in which state-of-the-art CV studies are employed in contexts where they can in fact be compared with 'real' behavioral willingness to pay for goods that can actually be bought and sold" (Arrow et al., 1993, p. 9). This statement reinforces a point to be made below, That is, hypothetical valuation requires that the environment be fictitiously commoditized so that hypothetical values for those fictitious commodities can then be compared with a more familiar class of commodities bought and sold on a regular basis. This is regarded by the NOAA Panel as "validation." We point out that this particular procedure would "validate" only that the researcher had successfully commoditized the piece of the environment being hypothetically valued, and had then presented it to the respondents as sufficiently commoditized to allow its precise comparison with "regular" commodities. Note that this protocol would not "validate" that the hypothetical value was the true value. Validity, as any logician would remind us, says nothing about truth content.

8   Sagoff (1988) addresses this issue when he raises the question about what is the right amount of information to be given in the survey experiment. That is, how much discussion, deliberation, and "learning" ought to be allowed?

9   Cummings and Harrison (1992) offer their own comments on this particular classification scheme. The NOAA Panel uses the concept of "passive use value" as an alternative to "non-use value." The idea of passive-use value still seems close to our notion of "functional value." However, the NOAA Panel still seems to use the concept within the framework of environmental goods and services as mere commodities. We differ from the NOAA Panel in this important respect.

10   By commodities we do not preclude services that are bought and sold.

11   This is seen most clearly if we consider the status of life. If a person is assumed to have no right to life, one might ask how much the person is willing to pay to secure that right. The bid, in most instances, will be high, but can by no means exceed the presumed present value of all future income. If, on the contrary, the individual is assumed to have a right to life (and not be risk loving), the individual's willingness to accept compensation for a gamble to give up that right would most probably approach infinity.

12   A discussion of this issue can be found in Bishop (1978, 1979), and Smith and Krutilla (1979).

13   The critical zone is the level of harvest or extraction beyond which the future viability of the renewable resource is in doubt.

14   Some will even remind us of Executive Order 12291 requiring that benefits and costs be estimated for governmental regulatory actions.

15   Of course, there will be those who will suggest that those foregoing comparisons ought to be the other way round – drinking water is still too impure, the air is still too dirty, soil erosion is still excessive, and too little land has been devoted to parks and wilderness areas.

References

Arrow, K., Solow, R., Portney, P. R. Leamer, E. E., Radner, R. and Schumam H., 1993: Report of the NOAA Panel on Contingent Valuation. Mimeo, January 11.

Bishop, R. C. 1978: Endangered species and uncertainty: the economics of a safe minimum standard. *American Journal of Agricultural Economics*, 60, 10–18.

Bishop, R. C. 1979: Endangered species, irreversibility, and uncertainty: a reply. *American Journal of Agricultural Economics*, 61, 376–9.

Bishop, R. C. and Heberlein, T. A. 1979: Measuring values of extramarket goods: are indirect measures biased? *American Journal of Agricultural Economics*, 61, 926–30.

Bromley, D. W. 1989a: *Economic Interests and Institutions. The Conceptual Foundations of Public Policy*. Oxford: Basil Blackwell.

Bromley, D. W. 1989b: Entitlements, missing markets, and environmental uncertainty. *Journal of Environmental Economics and Management*, 17, 181–94.

Bromley, D. W. 1990: The ideology of efficiency: searching for a theory of policy analysis. *Journal of Environmental Economics and Management*, 19, 86–107.

Bromley, D. W. 1991: *Environment and Economy: Property Rights and Public Policy*. Oxford: Basil Blackwell.

Brown, T. 1984: The concept of value in resource allocation. *Land Economics*, 60, 231–46.

Ciriacy-Wantrup, S. V. 1968: *Resource Conservation: Economics and Policies*. Berkeley, CA: University of California Press.

Coase, R. H. 1960: The problem of social cost. *Journal of Law and Economics*, 3, 1–44.

Cummings, R. G. and Harrison, G. W. 1992: Identifying and measuring nonuse values for natural and environmental resources: a critical review of the state of the art. Mimeo, Department of Economics, University of New Mexico.

Cummings, R. G., Brookshire, D. S. and Schulze, W. D. 1986: *Valuing Environmental Goods: An Assessment of the Contingent Valuation Method*. Totawa, NJ: Rowman and Allanheld.

Demsetz, H. 1967: Toward a theory of property rights. *American Economic Review*, 57, 347–59.

Douglas, M. 1966: *Purity and Danger: An Analysis of Concepts of Pollution and Taboo*. New York: Praeger.

Douglas, M. 1986: *How Institutions Think*. Syracuse, NY: Syracuse University Press.

Douglas, M. and Wildavsky, A. 1982: *Risk and Culture. An Essay on the Selection of Technical and Environmental Dangers*. Berkeley, CA: University of California Press.

Durkheim, E. 1962: *Rules of Sociological Method*. New York: Free Press. (First published 1895.)

Edwards, S. F. 1986: Ethical preferences and the assessment of existence values: does the neoclassical model fit? *Northeastern Journal of Agricultural and Resource Economics*, 15, 145–50.

Elster, J. 1979: *Ulysses and the Sirens: Studies in Rationality and Irrationality*. Cambridge: Cambridge University Press.

Elster, J. 1983: *Sour Grapes: Studies in the Subversion of Rationality*. Cambridge: Cambridge University Press.

Elster, J. 1989: Social norms and economic theory. *Journal of Economic Perspectives*, 3, 99–117.

Etzioni, A. 1988: *The Moral Dimension: Toward a New Economics*. New York: Free Press.

Field, A. J. 1979: On the explanation of rules using rational choice models. *Journal of Economic Issues*, 13, 49–72.

Fishoff, B. 1990: Understanding long-term environmental risks. *Journal of Risk and Uncertainty*, 3, 315–30.

Freeman, R. 1986: On assessing the state of the art of the contingent valuation method of valuing environmental changes. In R. G. Cummings, D. S. Brookshire and W. D. Schulze (eds), *Valuing Environmental Goods: An Assessment of the Contingent Valuation Method*, Totawa, NJ: Rowman and Allanheld, 148–61.

Giddens, A. 1976: *New Rules of Sociological Method: A Positive Critique of Interpretive Sociologies*. New York: Basic Books.

Gregory, R. 1986: Interpreting measures of economic loss: evidence from contingent valuation and experimental studies. *Journal of Environmental Economics and Management*, 13, 325–37.

Gregory, R. and McDaniels, T. 1987: Valuing environmental losses: what promise does the right measure hold? *Policy Science*, 20, 11–26.

Gregory, R., Lichtenstein, S. and Slovic, P. 1993: Valuing environmental resources: a constructive approach. *Journal of Risk and Uncertainty*, forthcoming.

Hanemann, W. M. 1991: Willingness to pay and willingness to accept: how much can they differ? *American Economic Review*, 81, 635–47.

Harper, C. R. 1989: Rational roots of irrational behavior. *Northeastern Journal of Agricultural and Resource Economics*, 18, 96–7.

Harris, M. 1974: *Cows, Pigs, Wars and Witches: The Riddles of Culture*. New York: Random House.

Harris, M. 1979: *Cultural Materialism: The Struggle for a Science of Culture*. New York: Random House.

Harris, C., Driver, B. L. and McLaughlin, W. J. 1989: Improving the contingent valuation method: a psychological perspective. *Journal of Environmental Economics and Management*, 17, 213–29.

Kahneman, D. and Knetsch, J. L. 1992: Valuing public goods: the purchase of moral satisfaction. *Journal of Environmental Economics and Management*, 22, 57–70.

Kneese, A. V. and Schulze, W. D. 1985: Ethics and environmental economics. In A. V. Kneese and J. L. Sweeney (eds), *Handbook of Natural Resource and Energy Economics*, New York: North-Holland, ch. 5.

Knetsch, J. L. 1990: Environmental policy implications of disparities between willingness to pay and compensation demanded measures of values. *Journal of Environmental Economics and Management*, 18, 227–37.

Knetsch, J. L. and Sinden, J. A. 1984: Willingness to pay and compensation demanded: experimental evidence of an unexpected disparity in measures of value. *Quarterly Journal of Economics*, 99, 507–21.

Krutilla, J. V. 1967: Conservation reconsidered. *American Economic Review*, 57, 787–96.

Lewis, D. 1986: *Convention*. Oxford: Basil Blackwell.

Loomis, J. B., Hanemann, M. and Kanninen, B. 1991: Willingness to pay to protect wetlands and reduce wildlife contamination from agricultural drainage. In A. Dinar and D. Zilberman (eds), *The Economics and Management of Water and Drainage in Agriculture*, Boston, MA: Kluwer Academic, 411–29.

Macpherson, C. B. 1973: *Democratic Theory: Essays in Retrieval*. Oxford: Oxford University Press.

Macpherson, C. B. 1985: *The Rise and Fall of Economic Justice and Other Essays*. Oxford: Oxford University Press.

Marx, K. 1965: *Pre-Capitalist Economic Formations*, ed. by E. J. Hobsbawn. New York: International Publishers.

Mishan, E. J. 1980: How valid are economic evaluations of allocative changes? *Journal of Economic Issues*, 14, 143–61.

Norgaard, R. B. 1984: Coevolutionary development potential. *Land Economics*, 60, 160–73.

Opaluch, J. J. and Grigalunas, T. A. 1992: Ethical principles and personal preferences as determinants of nonuse values: implications for natural resource damage assessments. Staff Paper, University of Rhode Island, Department of Resource Economics, April.

Opaluch, J. J. and Segerson, K. 1989: Rational roots of "irrational" behavior: new theories of economic decision-making. *Northeastern Journal of Agricultural and Resource Economics*, 18, 81–95.

Parsons, T. 1951: *The Social System*. New York: Free Press.

Polanyi, K. 1965: *The Great Transformation*. Boston, MA: Beacon Press.

Randall, A. 1974: Coasian externality theory in a policy context. *Natural Resources Journal*, 14, 35–54.

Randall, A. and Stoll, J. 1980: Consumer's surplus in commodity space. *American Economic Review*, 70, 449–55.

Sagoff, M. 1988: *The Economy of the Earth: Philosophy, Law and Environment*. Cambridge: Cambridge University Press.

Sagoff, M. 1994: Should preferences count? *Land Economics*, 70, 127–44.

Schotter, A. 1981: *The Economic Theory of Social Institutions*. Cambridge, Cambridge University Press.

Sen, A. 1977: Rational fools: a critique of the behavioral foundations of economic theory. *Philosophy and Public Affairs*, 6, 317–44.

Slovic, P. and Lichtenstein, S. 1983: Preference reversals: a broader perspective. *American Economic Review*, 73, 596–605.

Slovic, P., Fischoff, B. and Lichtenstein, S. 1976: Behavioral decision theory. Technical Report DDI-7, Oregon Research Institute, Eugene, OR, September.

Smith, V. K. and Krutilla, J. V. 1979: Endangered species, irreversibilities, and uncertainty: comment. *American Journal of Agricultural Economics*, 61, 371–9.

Stevens, T. H., Echeverria, J., Glass, R. J., Hager, T. and More, T. A. 1991: Measuring the existence value of wildlife: what do CVM estimates really show? *Land Economics*, 67, 390–400.

Thaler, R. 1980: Toward a positive theory of consumer choice. *Journal of Economic Behavior and Organization*, 1, 39–60.

Tribe, L. H. 1972: Policy science: analysis or ideology? *Philosophy and Public Affairs*, 53, 66–110.

Tversky, A. 1969: Intransitivity of preferences. *Psychology Review*, 76, 31–48.

Tversky, A. and Kahneman, D. 1981: The framing of decisions and the psychology of choice. *Science*, 211, 453–8.

Tversky, A. and Kahneman, D. 1986: Rational choice and the framing of decisions. In R. M. Hogarth and M. W. Reder (eds), *Rational Choice: The Contrast Between Economics and Psychology*, Chicago, IL: University of Chicago Press, 67–94.

Tversky, A., Slovic, P. and Kahneman, D. 1990: The causes of preference reversal. *American Economic Review*, 80, 204–17.

2

Benefits, Costs, and the Safe Minimum Standard of Conservation

Alan Randall and Michael C. Farmer

Conservation is the act of setting aside sufficient reserves to satisfy some future-oriented objectives(s). Reasonable people operating from different value systems might disagree about what the objective(s) should be. For many economists, a conservation objective with intuitive appeal is that of sustaining satisfactory levels of consumption for the human population into the indefinite future.

Farmer (1993) has demonstrated conceptually that, with perfect foresight, ideal markets (including intergenerational financial and asset markets) generate powerful incentives for conservation. Nevertheless, he identified conditions – involving, for example, poor initial endowments and niggardly regeneration functions for renewable resources – where purposeful policy would be required to ensure adequate conservation for sustainability. Where foresight is imperfect and markets are incomplete, the list of circumstances that might raise issues of conservation policy would be expanded.

In this chapter, we develop a stylized benefit–cost framework for evaluating conservation projects. Then, we consider the conservation question from the perspective of the major ethical traditions of Western civilization: consequentialism, argument from universal moral principles, and contractarianism. We find reasons to take benefits and costs seriously (even in moral-universalist and contractarian thinking, which one might expect to be hostile to benefit–cost logic). We also find good reasons to impose a constraint requiring a safe minimum standard of conservation (even in consequentialist thinking, which one might expect to be skeptical about a safe minimum standard). The constraint would require that a safe minimum standard of conservation be maintained unless the costs of so doing were intolerably high.

The safe minimum standard is often embraced in the conservation literature, but important questions remain unresolved. We address two of these: what principles might be deduced to guide in setting the standard; and how might one determine the level of cost that would be intolerable? We conclude with a very brief summary of the argument.

1   A Benefit–Cost Analysis Framework

Just as many economists would look first to the market to provide for conservation, so would many economists (but not always the same economists) apply a benefit–cost test to evaluate proposed conservation policies. While, in many applications, there is no shortage of details to engage the analysts, the basic principles of benefit–cost analysis (BCA) are rather straightforward.

Consider a complex environment E producing a vector of services $S(t)$ through time. The production of these services is determined by the attributes $A(t)$ of the environment and the human-controlled factors $X(t)$ applied:

$$S(t) = f[A(t), X(t)] \tag{2.1}$$

The attributes of the environment are themselves the result of interaction between nature and human activity. Where $N(t)$ refers to a vector of natural-systems factors,

$$A(t) = g[N(t), X(t)] \tag{2.2}$$

This completes what might be called the production system. But the economist should never underestimate the effort and the multidisciplinary expertise required to develop quantitative projections of $S(t)$ with the long time horizon relevant for conservation issues.

Each household, $H = 1, \ldots, H$, gains utility from consuming environmental services and ordinary commodities Z. Thus

$$U_h(t) = U_h[S_h(t), Z_h(t)] \tag{2.3}$$

By minimizing expenditures subject to the constraint that household utility be maintained at the baseline level, household valuations for environmental services, $V_h[S_h(t)]$, can be obtained. The value of E, viewed as an asset, is the present value of the service it provides:

$$PV(E) = \sum_{h=1}^{H} \int_{t_0}^{\infty} V_h[S_h(t)] e^{-rt} \, dt \tag{2.4}$$

where r is the discount rate.

Now, consider a project Δ which would change $X(t)$ to $X^\Delta(t)$, thereby changing E to some with-project E^Δ at some cost C^Δ. Environmental attributes would be changed to $A^\Delta(t)$ and environmental services to $S^\Delta(t)$. The net present value of such a project would be

$$PV(\Delta) = PV(E^\Delta - C^\Delta - E) \tag{2.5}$$

This stylized BCA framework enables us to identify the essential characteristics of the benefit–cost criterion. The underlying value system is homocentric, instrumentalist, and welfarist. The environment is regarded as a resource, an instrument for serving human purposes. Humans do the valuing, and value at the household level derives exclusively from the satisfaction of household preferences. Value is aggregated across the households according to the potential Pareto-improvement (PPI) criterion, which is consistent with Benthamite utilitarianism. Since voluntary exchange and contractarian political processes honor the actual Pareto-improvement (PI) criterion, the PPI can be interpreted, albeit with important caveats, in market and contractarian terms.

Proposals are evaluated according to the "with and without" principle (equation (2.5)), which requires that both baseline and with-project conditions be projected into the distant future. Benefits and costs are discounted to reflect the opportunity cost of capital, and expressed in present value terms (equation (2.4)). While the BCA model is presented here in deterministic terms, uncertainty about future conditions and valuation can be addressed readily by expressing the valuations in *ex ante* terms (Smith, 1987; Randall, 1991b).

2   Conservation Decisions: Is the Benefit–Cost Test Enough?

Conservation is, essentially, a process of saving and investment.[1] Rather than saving undifferentiated, fungible capital, we tend to think of conservation as saving natural resources in kind. The urgency of conservation therefore varies across the various kinds of natural resources, depending on factors such as scarcity and the degree to which capital or other natural resources might substitute for the particular resource.

The benefits of conservation

Economics has no monopoly on the general idea of benefits, and other disciplines have made important contributions in recognizing the broad array of beneficial services that natural resources might provide, directly and indirectly, for humans. Since there is enormous variety among natural resources, the array of beneficial services they might provide is also enormous, and it varies widely among the different kinds of natural resources. For enumerating the important kinds of benefits, biodiversity serves as a good example of a natural resource because it provides (at least potentially) most of the important categories of benefits.

To many people, the most immediate reasons for caring about biodiversity are instrumental and utilitarian. A diversity of species in a variety of viable ecosystems serves as an instrument for people seeking to satisfy their needs and preferences. Many of the instrumental services that nature provides for people are obvious: food and fiber from domesticated plants and animals that were bred and selected from wild ancestors; and chemicals and pharmaceutical products with biotic origins.

There are many instances in which biotic resources have proven valuable to people and, together, the total value of these services is enormous. However, the majority of species on this earth are yet to be catalogued and systematically evaluated for their commercial potential. But, since many of those species we know have proven useful, it is reasonable to expect that many of the presently unknown or poorly understood species will turn out to be useful, too (Bishop, 1978). In addition, it is reasonable to expect continued technological progress, although we cannot predict its direction. So, new uses may be discovered for known species not currently thought useful. By standard statistical notions, the usefulness of many species under present technologies suggests a positive probability that literally any species, known or unknown, will eventually prove useful. Thus, we should approach the potential loss of any species with the presumption that its expected value to humans is positive; that is, its preservation is worth something to humans. Nevertheless, this appeal to current and expected future usefulness as commercial raw material is only the beginning.

The knowledge arguments – that species represent a store of genetic information for future use – have been extended to include ethno-biological knowledge. Ecosystems and indigenous human cultures co-evolved in considerable harmony, it is conjectured. This implies that disruption of indigenous cultures by colonists from elsewhere threatens destruction not only of the ecosystem but also of the folk knowledge that enhances its value (Norgaard, 1984, 1988; Southgate, 1988).

In the 1970s, the rapidly growing field of environmental economics established that people have demand for natural systems not only as sources of raw materials but also as amenities. Amenity values include use values and existence values. Use values include aesthetic and recreation values, and in the latter connection it is suggestive to observe that travel is now the fastest growing industry worldwide and adventure travel is the fastest growing segment of the travel industry. Existence value arises from human satisfaction from simply knowing that some desirable thing or state of affairs exists.

The instrumental and utilitarian arguments for preserving biodiversity recognize not only raw material and amenity values, but also ecosystem support services. Natural ecosystems serve as effective assimilators of wastes. In this way, wetlands help purify water, and forests assimilate greenhouse gases and help restore the oxygen balance. Natural ecosystems contribute to water and aid quality objectives. More generally, ecosystems are complex and fragile, and it is a tenet of ecology that everything has its place in the broader scheme of things. Thus, there is a presumption that species are useful not only directly as suppliers of raw materials and amenities but also indirectly for their contribution to ecosystem support. Thus, species that have no conceivable value in providing raw materials and amenities (if there are any) could still be valued for the ecosystem support services they provide to species that are more directly valued.

The ultimate instrumentalist argument – that all species must be preserved because the loss of any would initiate processes leading inexorably to the collapse of the whole ecosystem – seems clearly false. In its place, Ehrlich and Ehrlich (1981) have introduced, by analogy, a statistical argument. Their much-cited rivet popper justifies his continued removal, one-by-one, of rivets from airplane wings by reasoning that the practice must be safe since no planes have been lost yet. There is an obvious logical fallacy in the rivet popper's claim: each successive inconsequential loss of a rivet does not serve to confirm the low probability of the practice causing a crash. Rather, since the initial number of rivets is finite and the number needed for safe operation is smaller yet, each inconsequential rivet removal increases the probability that the next one will be disastrous.

The point of the Ehrlichs' analogy is that one may concede the redundancy that is built into the ecosystem without condoning a cavalier attitude to the piecemeal sacrifice of species. Each inconsequential loss of a species increases the probability that the next one will cause serious problems.

Taken together, these various considerations amount to a convincing argument, in the instrumentalist utilitarian tradition, that preserving biodiversity should be a serious consideration for a society of rational human beings pursuing what are essentially homocentric goals. At the very least, biotic resources are resources to be allocated carefully, rather than squandered or merely wasted. They are to be valued for their amenity services as well as their usefulness as raw materials; use and existence values count; the concept of value encompasses but goes beyond commercial values; ecosystem and environmental support services are recognized; and, where ignorance is rampant, statistical arguments are used to infer positive expected values.

This account of the reasons for valuing biodiversity has broad currency among conservationists, ecologists, and social scientists. It is entirely consistent with standard economic thinking about the benefits of biodiversity, which is scarcely surprising; after all, mainstream economics is a homocentric and utilitarian system of thought. In economics, however, the concept of benefits is counterbalanced by the concept of costs, including opportunity costs. To recognize that biodiversity is beneficial does not, by itself, clinch the economic case for protecting biodiversity. What if the costs outweigh the benefits? Such an outcome is always possible, under benefit–cost thinking, and would do little to promote the case for biodiversity.

In search of a failsafe case for conservation

We suspect that Ehrenfeld (1988) speaks for many preservationists who "would like to see [conservation] find a sound footing outside the slick terrain of the economists and their philosophical allies" (p. 215). For these preservationists, the homocentric, instrumentalist and utilitarian rationale for conservation is slick terrain in that it provides a rationale for valuing biodiversity, but that rationale is anything but failsafe. To avoid the slick terrain, a rationale for preserving biodiversity should not depend on human preferences (which may well be fickle), nor on instrumental arguments (which might be rendered moot by emerging technologies). More fundamentally, Ehrenfeld objects to the very idea of valuing biodiversity in a relative sense: that one can compare its value with that of other good things and adjust society's production and consumption for the better by making tradeoffs at the margin.

If the standard economic approach yields only slick terrain for conservation, it is interesting to consider whether alternative philosophical approaches provide it a more secure footing.

Consequentialist approaches

First, the homocentric, utilitarian approaches are a subset of a broader group of consequentialist theories that claim, loosely speaking, that the rightness of action should be judged by the goodness of its consequences. Consequentialist theories do not have to be homocentric. Bentham was in principle open to the idea that the utility of animals could count; he just could not visualize any obvious way of incorporating it into the utilitarian calculus (1970, p. 311). More generally, utilitarianism evaluates all consequences in terms of their contribution toward preference satisfaction, whereas consequentialism is open to other ways of evaluating consequences.

Clearly, a consequentialist could accord preservation of biodiversity the status of the preeminent value. Then all proposed actions would be evaluated in terms of their effects on biodiversity, and those with the most favorable consequences for biodiversity would be chosen. Other objectives would be subordinated to biodiversity. However, the preeminent-value status of biodiversity is not intuitively obvious. For one important example, many of the world's richest ecosystems and many of the world's poorest people can be found in the tropics. So, it is not surprising that the legitimate human aspiration for improved living conditions frequently clashes with biodiversity objectives in the tropics; and, in such clashes, it is not clear that biodiversity should always win out.

A consequentialist scheme that made biodiversity the preeminent value would avoid the slick terrain, but only at the cost of subordinating other worthy objectives such as enhancing the life prospects of the very worst-off people. Of course, according these other objectives the status of preeminent values, too, would return us to the slick terrain. The primacy of biodiversity cannot be assured in a clash of preeminent values.

Appeals to moral duty

Duty-based moral theories attempt to identify the moral obligations that bind humans, and the morally correct actions these obligations entail. Ehrenfeld (1988) offers a solution to the "slick terrain" problem: "If conservation is to succeed, the public must come to understand the inherent wrongness of the destruction of biological diversity" (p. 215). Clearly, Ehrenfeld's is a duty-based approach: right action is that which respects the moral obligation of human beings to preserve biodiversity.

When several considerations have moral force (cannibalism is morally evil, while self-preservation is morally worthy), clashes among them (under what conditions, if any, would self-preservation justify cannibalism?) can be resolved only via deduction from higher moral principles. The slick terrain can be avoided only by asserting that preservation of biodiversity is a first principle, a trump among moral principles, that defeats all others. Without such an assertation, Ehrenfeld's "inherent wrongness" does not solve his problem. Surely, many would argue that enhancing the life prospects of the worst-off people has moral force at least as powerful as that of protecting biodiversity. Again, biodiversity is on slick terrain.

Contractarian approaches

Contractarians argue that arrangements are justified if they respect the rights of all the affected parties. In duty-based reasoning, "rights" is often used to mean moral claims; one respects rights (in this sense) by observing moral obligations. In contractarian theories, rights are enforceable claims. Change occurs when all affected parties, endowed with enforceable rights, consent to it; without consent, the status quo prevails. While consent justifies change, the lack of consent for change is insufficient to justify the status quo. The starting point (or constitution) must itself be justified directly, typically by arguing that it was (or might have been) chosen by voluntary agreement among all concerned.

Contractarian approaches encounter great difficulties when taken literally. It is difficult to develop convincing arguments that any existing starting point was actually chosen by consent, or that any proposed starting point might be endorsed unanimously by real choosers with diverse interests. Contractarians typically retreat to thought experiments trying to deduce the characteristics of constitutions that might plausibly emerge from voluntary agreement under ideal conditions such as the "veil of ignorance" posited by Rawls (1971).

Contractarians must first determine who is a party to the contract, that is, who counts as a moral agent; and, ideally, they should make this determination in a way that does not unduly influence the outcome of contracting. This presents difficulties, even in the relatively simple case of contracts among contemporaneous humans. Should children, the very old, criminals and incompetents (and by what definitions?), non-citizen immigrants, and those who would like to immigrate be included? The decision about including or excluding these groups is likely to influence how they are treated under the eventual contract. When thinking about intergenerational contracts, the questions get harder because we are dealing with potential future persons. Given that the parties to the contract are choosing among future states of the world which vary in both population and level of living for each generation, it is difficult to choose which potential persons will be admitted to the contract without, in so doing, predetermining the outcome of the contract.

We do not seek to ignore or minimize these difficulties. Nevertheless, in order to move forward, assume a multigenerational Rawlsian contract in which each potential generation of humans is assigned a vote. That way, intragenerational conflicts are suppressed in order to focus on resolving intergenerational conflict. Assuming maximin strategies, the resultant contract would maximize the well-being of the worst-off human generation; and all generations would be bound to a conservation strategy that would achieve that result. We will use this result later in this chapter.

However, this result leaves the fate of biodiversity in the hands of humans who may value it only as an instrument for satisfying human preferences. One could extend the contract, as Norton (1989) suggested, to include all potential generations of all species. The resulting contract would take preservation of biodiversity very seriously. Nevertheless, it is unlikely that this contractarian thought experiment would yield iron-clad constitutional guarantees for biodiversity. If being born into unrelievably miserable circumstances is at least as bad as never being born at all, the commitment to preserving biodiversity would be counterbalanced by a commitment to ensuring a minimally acceptable quality of life for each species-generation born.

The consequentialist case for biodiversity is iron-clad if biodiversity is assigned preeminent value status. Similarly, the duty-based case is failsafe if conservation of biodiversity is the highest of all moral principles, and the contractarian case is secure if all participants in the constitutional process place the survival of all species above all other concerns. Recognition of other co-equal or superior values, moral principles, or individual concerns returns us to the slick terrain. The case for biodiversity is always circumstantial, that is, relative to the possibilities that are available and the strength of completing claims. Ehrenfeld (1988) claimed the high ground by resisting all the circumstantial approaches as mere manifestations of the moral repugnancy of homocentrism. But, his victory is empty, since it depends on first-principle or preeminent value status for biodiversity, and such status is unlikely to survive scrutiny given the powerful appeal of many other candidates.

A strong, but circumstantial, case for conservation

We can do more than deny the viability of a failsafe case for biodiversity. It is possible to work, more affirmatively, toward constructing a strong but defensible circumstantial case.

First consider a duty-based approach. Assume that preserving biodiversity and enhancing the life prospects of the worst-off people are both moral goods. However, the claims of humans trump those of nonhumans. From these moral principles, it can be deduced that humans should make some, but not unlimited, sacrifices for biodiversity. This result endorses the basic idea of a safe minimum standard (SMS) rule: a sufficient area of habitat should be preserved to ensure the survival of each unique species, subspecies, or ecosystem, unless the costs of doing so are intolerably high (Ciriacy-Wantrup, 1968; Bishop, 1978). One could add an additional moral premise – marginal increments in the welfare of people count for less in the case of the already well-off than for those who are currently immiserated – and the implication is that one could identify situations in which the well-off have an obligation to subsidize the SMS in improverished places.

The SMS rule places biodiversity beyond a reach of routine tradeoffs, where to give up 90 cents worth of biodiversity to gain a dollar's worth of ground beef is to make a net gain. It also avoids claiming trump status for biodiversity, permitting some sacrifice of biodiversity in the face of intolerable costs. But it takes intolerable costs to justify relaxation of the SMS.

At this point, consider a utilitarian approach. The benefit–cost approach applies classical utilitarian principles with just one nod toward the value system of mainstream economics. The basic value data in benefit–cost analyses are those of economics – willingness to pay (WTP) for desired changes and willingness to accept (WTA) compensation for changes that are not desired – and as such reflect not only the preferences but also the endowments of the valuer. The rule that benefits and costs be aggregated anonymously, that is, without regard to the identity and welfare status of the gainers and losers, is merely an economic operationalization of Bentham's classic rule of the greatest good for the greatest number. Thus, the benefit–cost approach is (at least) one rather direct and plausible approach to implementing a value system based on preference satisfaction. To the extent that humans value the services that biodiversity provides more than the services that would be forgone in pursuit of biodiversity, the benefit–cost approach would support biodiversity.

One of the more persistent arguments against the benefit–cost approach, and many alternative expressions of utilitarianism, is that preferences may be myopic and human understanding of the technical possibilities – in the Erlich analogy, the consequences of popping each and every possible combination of rivets on the airplane – may be incomplete or mistaken. Not that the benefit–cost approach does worse, in these respects, than other approaches that take citizen opinion seriously. As humans come to comprehend the technology of natural systems and how it limits the performance of anthropogenic technology, this understanding is reflected in a valid benefit–cost analysis. As human preferences extend to the amenity and existence services provided by diverse ecosystems, the valuations that emerge are fully reflected in a valid benefit–cost analysis.

Nevertheless, one must concede that human myopia is a valid concern. How can we be assured that the lure of immediate gratification will not induce us to make decisions that are likely to have very unpleasant consequences later on? Elster (1979) has shown that "binding" behavior – Ulysses bound himself to the mast in advance to prevent himself from doing what he was quite sure he would do in the heat of the moment, that is, steer his ship into the rocky waters separating it from the sirens – is consistent with both rational behavior and utilitarianism. Thus, one logically coherent utilitarian strategy would be to make policy choices on the basis of benefits and costs, but subject always to the constraint that actions we fear we (or future generations of people we care about) will regret are forbidden. Biodiversity issues may be decided by consulting a benefit–cost analysis but subject to a safe minimum standard or similar constraint.[2,3] Net benefits are maximized because benefits are good consequences, and the constraints are imposed because the consequences of not satisfying them are terrible. Again, the SMS constraint would not accord trump status to biodiversity, but would trigger a serious and searching decision process before it could be relaxed.

Let us return momentarily to the duty-based approach. We saw how the SMS could be derived from moral reasoning, but the decision rule was left incomplete. Upon what basis should people decide those many issues that do not threaten the SMS? It is hard to conceive of a plausible moral theory that does not, in the absence of overriding concerns, give a good deal of weight to the satisfaction of human preferences. Thus, we should take seriously a rule that policy issues be decided on the basis of benefits and costs, but always subject to constraints identified by moral reasoning. Net benefits are maximized because human preference satisfaction is morally worthy, and the constraints are imposed because they ensure that higher moral goods can trump preference satisfaction in the event of conflict.

We have argued that a plausible contractarian thought experiment would also identify the SMS constraint as a likely component of a just constitution. Preference satisfaction counts, also, in contractarian thought. However, many contractarians, naturally enough, pursue preference satisfaction via the individualistic routes of free exchange, voluntary taxation, and public decision by consent. The benefit–cost approach emerges from contractarian thinking as a kind of second-best result. If, as may well be the case, the pattern of compensating transfers to achieve voluntary agreement on policy is too complex to be feasible and the transactions costs too high, maximizing net benefits of policy becomes an attractive approach. At least, it assures that the game is positive-sum. In the problem at hand, a plausible contractarian solution is to maximize net benefits (to satisfy preferences) subject to an SMS constraint (because participants in the "veil of ignorance" process would insist on it).

Interestingly, it seems that the same general kind of decision rule – maximize net benefits subject to an SMS constraint – is admissible under consequentialist, duty-based, and contractarian reasoning. We now move to a more detailed consideration of some issues in developing and implementing an SMS-based conservation policy.

3   A Closer Look at the Safe Minimum Standard

Contemporary discussion reveals a wide base of support, across disciplinary lines,[4] for a policy framework based on the SMS. Nevertheless, we find the literature remarkably murky about the details; it is not clear exactly what an SMS-based policy is, or how one would work. Since Ciriacy-Wantrup (1968) and Bishop (1978), economists agree that such a policy would require society to maintain a safe minimum standard of conservation unless the costs of so doing were intolerably high. Our objective here is to explore in a little more depth two basic issues: what principles might guide the setting of the SMS, and how might the intolerable costs be set?

Setting the SMS

In section 2, we used biodiversity as our exemplar of a conservation issue, and biodiversity is well suited to that purpose because it is unusually rich and diverse in the kinds of benefits that might be claimed for it, and in the kinds of reasons that ethicists might entertain for conserving it. Nevertheless, we plan, at this point, to introduce a highly simplified economy in which a single consumption good Y is produced using undifferentiated human-made capital K and a single generic natural resource D. Assume D is renewable, that is, D withheld from production in one period regenerates by the next period. If S_t is the stock of D withheld from production in period t, the regeneration function traces the relationship between S_t and S_{t+1}^a, the amount of D available in the next period. In a two-period diagram, the line of slope unity starting from the origin is diagnostic; at points above that line S_{t+1}^a exceeds S_t so that the natural resource is at least potentially sustainable; but at points below the line, the natural resource will eventually be exhausted even if none of it is used in production (figure 2.1).

Assume perfect foresight and efficient markets in Y, D, and K. An interesting question is whether natural resource "crises" (i.e. situations where scarcity of natural resources threatens the sustainability of adequate consumption levels for the human population) are possible.[5] Assume that

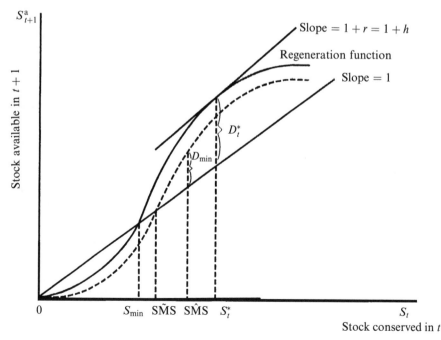

Figure 2.1 Setting the SMS.

D and K are not perfect substitutes and that factor specialization is penalized in production.[6]

Concave regeneration function

If the regeneration function is always concave and lies above the line of slope unity for a range of values of S_t, it will have a steep positive slope near the origin. In this case, the market economy provides very strong defenses against resource crises: the price of D will grow very large as the resource nears exhaustion, and any S_t conserved as a result of this incentive will regenerate generously ($S_{t+1}^a \gg S_t$).

Sigmoid regeneration function

The sustainability question becomes more interesting if the natural resource regeneration function is sigmoid (figure 2.1). If a smaller amount than S_{min} is withheld from production in each period, natural resource exhaustion is inevitable. The optimal stock to carry forward is S_t^*, at which point the steady state efficiency condition $1 + r = 1 + h$ holds (where r is the marginal efficiency of capital and h is the marginal regeneration rate of the natural resource) and D_t^* may be used in production in each period.

Stochastic regeneration   Interpreting S_{min} as the minimum standard of conservation, the idea of a *safe* minimum standard invokes uncertainty. Assume that the regeneration function is stochastic and that its lower bound is traced by the broken curve (figure 2.1). Then, if SM̃S is withheld from production in each period, resource exhaustion will be avoided, even in the worst case with respect to resource regeneration. We take SM̃S as what is meant by the term safe minimum standard in the literature; we would call it the safe minimum standard of *preservation*. One could also identify the safe-S_t^* and safe-D_t^* (not shown in the figure).

Required draws of D   SM̃S sustains the resource (and that may satisfy some conservationists). But we have cast the issue as one of sustaining adequate consumption levels for the human population. Assume that D_{min} is the minimum allocation of natural resources to production that is required to sustain adequate consumption. Let each time period t represent a generation of people. Then, any generation that uses less than D_{min} suffers extreme deprivation (however that is defined). We identify SM̂S (figure 2.1) as the minimum stock withheld from production that will provide D_{min} for each succeeding generation. Draws of D_{min} and regeneration of the stock are guaranteed. SM̂S is the safe minimum standard of conservation. While conservation of SM̂S is *required* to *assure* sustainability, the odds are working in favor of a society that abides by an SM̂S constraint: if regeneration turns out to be better than lower-bound, as it probably will, subsequent generations will be able to use more than D_{min} and/or conserve more than SM̂S.

Why a viable SMS policy must allow for D_{min}

In practical terms, there is a sequenced stream of potential future persons, and the society of people living at any time enjoys a positional dictatorship over future societies. An SM̂S rule requiring present society to conserve resources to avoid exhaustion in some (perhaps distant) future generation is not a sustainable equilibrium outcome; in other words there is no Lockean contract that would bind present society to abide by SM̂S for the benefit of distant future societies. Rather, SM̂S is a commitment that a society might undertake for ethical reasons (and, in section 2, we provide a variety of ethical reasons why some kind of SMS might be a component of a justifiable decision process about conservation).

We have defined D_{min} as the natural resource use necessary to avoid extreme deprivation for the current human society. One would expect a society that inherited a natural resource stock less than SM̂S nevertheless to use at least D_{min}, risking eventual resource exhaustion. To do otherwise would be voluntarily to accept self-sacrifice (to drink from the poisoned cup, as it were) for the benefit of future societies. In practical terms, that seems too much to ask.

Ethical theories offer only limited help here. While many ethical systems would require individual self-sacrifice for the sake of principle or for the good of others, there seems little basis in ethical theory for obliging a society to sacrifice itself for the good of future societies.

We conclude that, in the terms of our analysis, a viable safe minimum standard policy must seek to conserve not SM̃S but SM̂S. That is, it must seek to avoid placing any present or future society in a position where it must choose between sacrificing itself and dooming subsequent societies. In practical terms, an SMS policy would emphasize early warning and early implementation of conservation policies that require only modest sacrifice on the part of each society. Since unilateral withdrawal from any intertemporal contract or obligation is always a possibility, conservationists have a strong interest in keeping the costs of conservation tolerably low.[7]

Defining the intolerable cost

The standard rendition of SMS policy contains an escape clause: "unless the costs of [maintaining the SMS] are intolerably high." Furthermore, our argument (section 2) endorses that escape clause, unless one is prepared to argue that conservation is the concern that trumps all others: the pre-eminent value, the first among moral principles, or the single thing that Rawlsian contractors care about most. Nevertheless one finds the literature rather uninformative about how society might determine what level of cost would be intolerable. To address this question, we will return to the ethical theories introduced in section 2.

Consequentialism

Consequentialists seek, of course, to promote good consequences and avoid bad ones. So, consequentialist arguments hinge on judgements about goodness and badnesses, and consequentialists making different judgements along the way are likely to devise quite different ethical rules.

With this caveat, we suggest that a consequentialist would be inclined to set the level of intolerable cost with some reference to the particulars of each case. There are local and global resource exhaustions and species extinctions and some, we humans would be inclined to judge, are more harmful than others. A plausible consequentialist approach would mimic the "grossly disproportionate" test in environmental restoration and compensation law: the obligation to restore the damaged environment is relaxed if the costs are grossly disproportionate to the value of what is being restored.

A consequentialist SMS policy would be conservative in setting the SMS (choosing at least the SM̂S level of conservation), and would set the intolerable cost at a level larger than but not grossly disproportionate to the worst-case losses from resource exhaustion or extinction. As some critics have noted, this kind of SMS policy is basically a benefit–cost rule with a rather heavy thumb placed systematically on the conservation side of the scales.

Appeals to moral duty

Rules derived from moral duty depend, of course, on what duties are recognized, and where each resides in a hierarchy of duties. There is always the possibility that ethicists taking this approach might set the intolerable cost higher (i.e. make this particular loophole smaller) than would a consequentialist. For example, assume preservation ranks high in the hierarchy of duties. Then a plausible approach would require a living society to accept as a tolerable cost any sacrifice short of extreme deprivation. The intolerable cost would be a requirement that present society use less than D_{min}. It is unlikely that an ethicist appealing to moral duty would set the intolerable cost even higher than that, i.e. would oblige present society voluntarily to decimate itself for the sake of the future.

Contractarianism

Despite the difficulties freely acknowledged in section 2, let us return to the Rawlsian contract among human generations. By standard Rawlsian reasoning, the contract would be very sensitive to the well-being of the worst-off generation.

The reasoning that led us to define SM̂S raises the potential of an intergenerational *Rawlsian dilemma*. Assume society finds itself with the stock of some natural resource below SM̂S: this could happen as a result of low initial endowment, or of scientific ignorance that has permitted unrestrained use of something that turns out to be essential yet in very short supply. If the present society sacrifices itself by drawing less than D_{min} to restore the resource stock to $\hat{SMS}$, it would thereby become the worst-off generation: all subsequent generations would be able to abide by $\hat{SMS}$ and thus sustain adequate consumption levels. If, on the other hand, present society uses D_{min}, it will doom some future society G to being the last. G would be the worst-off generation, or – if one denies our intuition that the society that becomes extinct is worse off than the subsequent societies that are never born – G and all subsequent generations are jointly worst off.

This Rawlsian dilemma is insoluble in Rawlsian terms. We cannot require the present to accept voluntarily the worst-off status in order to avoid thrusting that status on some later generation(s). It follows that, for this Rawlsian contract, the intolerable cost is any requirement that a society use less than D_{min}; such a requirement cannot be justified in Rawlsian terms.

In section 2, we claimed a rather striking convergence – from three rather different ethical stances: consequentialism, appeals to moral principles, and contractarianism – upon a rule that conservation decisions be made by the benefit–cost criterion subject to an SMS constraint. When considering the intolerable cost, some cracks in this consensus emerge.

Consider a conservation decision involving, say, an endangered species or habitat. Assume that society is precommitted to an SMS but that few people really believe that loss of this particular species or habitat will initiate inevitable global ecosystemic collapse. A consequentialist may set the intolerable cost at a level larger than but not grossly disproportionate to the worst-case value of damage from abandoning the SMS. Someone arguing from moral principles may set the intolerable cost much higher: e.g. a cost that would impose extreme deprivation on current human society. The outcome of a multigenerational Rawlsian contract would depend on whether nonhuman species were admitted to the contract. With other species included, the contract might well set the intolerable cost at extreme deprivation for human society. If only humans are parties to the contract, the intolerable cost may be set lower.

In the extreme case – where resource exhaustion would threaten the sustainability of human society – convergence would re-emerge. All three ethical approaches would require each generation in its turn to limit resource use to D_{min} and bear whatever costs that entailed, but none would require sacrifice beyond that.

4 A Very Brief Summary of the Argument

We have argued that benefit–cost analysis provides a rather good accounting of human preference satisfaction and, furthermore, that any coherent moral theory values the satisfaction of human preferences.

However, there are good reasons, from a variety of ethical perspectives, to impose a safe minimum standard of conservation unless the costs of so doing are intolerably high. Thus, a rule to decide natural resources by a benefit–cost criterion but subject to an SMS of conservation would be taken seriously by consequentialists, ethicists who argue from appeals to moral duties, and contractarians.

We then examine two issues that have received relatively little discussion in the literature: how should the SMS be set, and how should the intolerable cost be determined? Our approach to these questions hinges on the definition of sustainability: whereas many conservationists may think of sustaining particular resources, species etc., we follow standard economic thinking by focusing, mostly, on sustaining adequate consumption levels for human populations.

We conclude that the SMS should be set at $\hat{SMS}$, a level of resource stocks higher than many previous authors have implied, in order to provide for continuing human use of natural resources. Furthermore, early warning systems and early implementation of conservation policies make good sense; otherwise, the present society might be confronted with large conservation costs and choose unilaterally to abandon its commitment to the SMS.

Where the conservation issue concerns resources essential to human survival, there is convergence among ethical systems as to the intolerable cost: no living society can be asked reasonably to decimate itself in order to provide sustainable consumption for future generations. Where the issue concerns, say, a species the loss of which would be unlikely to threaten sustainable consumption for humans, the ethical consensus starts to break down. A consequentialist may well define the SMS rule in such a way that it resembles a benefit–cost criterion with a very heavy thumb on the conservation side of the scales. Some ethicists arguing from moral principles may set the intolerable cost at the maximum level, that is, so high as to require society to conserve the species unless so doing would cause extreme deprivation for human society. The outcome of multi-generational Rawlsian contracts may range between these extremes, depending on whether nonhuman species were included in the negotiations.

Finally, we have conducted the whole discussion without reference to human population growth rates and the possibility of investing in technologies to increase the substitutability of human-made capital for natural resources. Consideration of these additional challenges and opportunities would enrich the discussion.

Notes

Our research on these topics was initiated under National Science Foundation Grant BBS8710153 and has continued with support from the Ohio Agricultural Research and Development Center and the National Oceanic and Atmospheric Administration.

1 This section draws heavily upon Randall (1993), which is itself developed from a line of thinking first presented in Randall (1991a).

2 This line of reasoning takes care of a long-standing objection of economists to the SMS: that, in order to adopt the SMS, a rational consumer would need to have kinked indifference curves between biodiversity and the numeraire good. The whole point of the SMS is that it is not a marginal decision but, instead, is a constraint adopted for good reasons.

3 Elster's (1979) "binding behavior" argument is presented in deterministic terms: Ulysses is quite sure that he will be unable to resist temptation when it occurs, so he takes action in advance to prevent himself from responding self-destructively in the heat of the moment. The reader will remember, however, that uncertainty plays a major role in the standard economic rationale for the SMS (e.g. Bishop, 1978). There is no inconsistency. Binding behavior can be extended readily to the case of uncertainty: one might rationally bind oneself in advance to a risk-averse strategy, for fear that one would take unreasonable risks in the heat of the moment.

   Binding behavior may also be a rational defense against the "tyranny of small decisions." Economists tend to slip all too readily, it is often argued (e.g. Norton, 1988), into a framework of optimization at the margin, without keeping track of the aggregate losses of biodiversity that result from a myriad of marginal decisions. An SMS policy would provide a constraint against this kind of "endless chipping away at the margin."

4 Although we must concede that economists, by and large, are more skeptical than many other groups.

5 Farmer (1993) used a three-generation, general equilibrium, overlapping generations model, with fully characterized intergenerational financial and asset markets; but we do not need to elaborate such a model here.

6 Without this assumption, D does not really matter so long as K is accumulating (Solow, 1974).

7 Comments attributed to Interior Secretary Bruce Babbitt (Stevens, 1993) suggest that he was thinking along these lines, as a conceptual basis for the next round of endangered species legislation.

References

Bentham, J. 1970: *An Introduction to the Principles of Morals and Legislation*. Darien, CT: Hafner.

Bishop, R. C. 1978: Economics of endangered species. *American Journal of Agricultural Economics*, 60, 10–18.

Ciriacy-Wantrup, S. von 1968: *Resource Conservation: Economics and Policies*, 3rd edn. Berkeley, CA: University of California Division of Agricultural Sciences.

Ehrenfeld, D. 1988: Why put a value of biodiversity? In E. O. Wilson, (ed.), *Biodiversity*, Washington, DC: National Academy Press, 212–16.

Ehrlich, P. R. and Ehrlich, A. 1981: *Extinction*. New York: Random House.

Elster, J. 1979: *Ulysses and the Sirens*. Cambridge: Cambridge University Press.

Farmer, M. C. 1993: Can markets provide for future generations? Ph.D. dissertation, Ohio State University, Columbus, OH.

Norgaard, R. B. 1984: Coevolutionary development potential. *Land Economics*, 60, 160–73.

Norgaard, R. B. 1988: The rise of the global exchange economy and the loss of biological diversity. In E. O. Wilson (ed.), *Biodiversity*, Washington, DC: National Academy of Press, 206–11.

Norton, B. G. 1988: Commodity, amenity, and morality: the limits of quantification in valuing biodiversity. In E. O. Wilson (ed.), *Biodiversity*, Washington, DC: National Academy Press, 200–5.

Norton, B. G. 1989: Intergenerational equity and environmental decisions: a model using Rawls' veil of ignorance. *Ecological Economics*, 1, 137–59.

Randall, A. 1991a: The economic value of biodiversity. *Ambio: A Journal of the Human Environment*, 20 (2), 64–8.

Randall, A. 1991b: Total and nonuse values. In J. B. Braden and C. D. Kolstad (eds), *Measuring the Demand for Environmental Improvement*, Amsterdam: North-Holland, 303–21.

Randall, A. 1993: Thinking about the value of biodiversity. In K. C. Kim and R. D.; Weaver (eds), *Biodiversity and Landscape*, New York: Cambridge University Press, forthcoming.

Rawls, J. 1971: *A Theory of Justice*. Cambridge, MA: Harvard University Press.

Smith, V. K. 1987: Nonuse values in benefit cost analysis. *Southern Economic Journal*, 54, 19–26.

Solow, Robert, M. 1974: Intergenerational equity and exhaustible resources. *Review of Economic Studies: Symposium on the Economics of Exhaustible Resources*, 41, 29–45.

Southgate, D. 1988: *Efficient Management of Biologically Diverse Tropical Forest*. London Environmental Economics Centre: IIEC/UCL.

Stevens, W. K. 1993: Interior Secretary is pushing a new way to save species. *New York Times*, A1, A11.

3

The Environment and Property Rights Issues

A. Allan Schmid

The ownership of the environment is one of the most contentious issues of our time. Different interest groups vie for control of natural resource opportunities. Do we have either a positive theory and evidence to explain which groups have won historically or a normative theory of which groups should win? A search of the literature will show that different economists give different answers to these questions.

One answer is that people choose and should choose that system and distribution of rights to maximize the total economic product. A variant of this is that the agony of choice can be avoided, for as long as there are markets it does not make any difference who is given the right originally. A contrasting answer is that there is no escape from the burden of moral choice since there is no one set of facts out there from which the correct policy can be deduced.

The following concepts will be reviewed to help understand property rights issues: externalities, transaction costs (including exclusions costs), and common pool resources. These concepts are then applied to choice of rights regimes and alternative legal instruments. The chapter concludes with a discussion of the ability of analysts to provide deterministic solutions to rights conflicts.

Externalities

Natural resources are scarce and some uses are incompatible with others. This means that one person's use affects the welfare of others. The consequence of one person's use is that another user is denied. There is an unavoidable effect external to the user. In this sense, externalities are ubiquitous and reciprocal and the stuff of scarcity and incompatibility.

One textbook definition of externalities is that of an effect on others which is not properly accounted for by the decision maker. This is commonly illustrated with a demand and supply graph for some product such as steel with two marginal cost curves. One is labeled private cost and the higher one is labeled social cost. The implication is that production of steel indicated by the intersection of private cost and demand is too great. If the decision maker had accounted for other costs such as environmental damages, steel output would have been less. To make sense of this, one must talk about property rights.

Property rights are sets of ordered relationships among people that define their opportunities, their exposure to the acts of others, their privileges, and their responsibilities (Schmid, 1987, ch. 1; Bromley, 1989, ch. 7). The transaction is a useful unit of analysis to understand how rights work. It should be emphasized that rights are a relationship among individuals with respect to resources rather than the relationship between an individual and a resource. The latter is the domain of production economics. Rights define the mode of individual participation in resource use decisions and thus are part and parcel of economic power.

Why is any effect of an action taken into account? Why does the steel firm pay for ore and not for the environment? The firm pays when the effect is owned by someone else or the someone else makes a bid to avoid the effect. To own is to be able to create costs for others. Owners act as they wish and, if rights are exchangeable, listen for bids from non-owners to do otherwise. If those who care about the environment are non-owners, they can always make a bid to the steel firm to reduce output. This bid is part of the opportunity cost of steel production and there is only one marginal cost function, not two.

If the environment is owned by environmentalists, the situation is reversed. A steel firm must purchase inputs to steel production from their owners – environmental inputs as well as ore, labor and machines. The firm needs a place to store its waste as well as its steel – the environment is just another factor of production. All inputs have prices as a function of being owned by others.

How then can one say that an action by the steel company has an external effect not properly accounted for? Can this be anything more than a claim that one person rather than the other should be the owner of a particular resource opportunity? Steel firms and enviornmentalists are interdependent and will affect each other regardless of who owns. Cheung (1970, p. 70) following Coase says that "Every economic action has effects." The only choice to be made then is the distribution of ownership. Economists have been careful not to argue for one person's ownership rather than another's because they have no basis for discussing interpersonal welfare distribution. On this view, to find an externality is not to find cause for property right change.

The effect of rights distribution on behavior can be widely observed. A study was made of the interdependence between phosphate processing and citrus growing in Florida (Crocker, 1971). When the phosphate company owned the environment, the company ignored the reduced citrus harvest caused by phosphorus particles on the leaves. The citrus growers did not make any bids to the phosphate company. The law was changed giving ownership to the citrus growers, and then the company began to purchase citrus lands rather than face suits for damage. The interdependence (externality) was there regardless of who owned, only its direction changed. If the phosphate company owned, the citrus growers had reduced harvest because of a missing environmental input. If the citrus growers owned, the phosphate company had to buy a place to put their dust. The company is as surely damaged by the rights and existence of citrus growers as the citrus growers were previously damaged by the rights and existence of phosphate processing.

In the language of welfare economics, the interdependence is internalized by the existence of tradeable ownership rights. If the company owns, they consider the interests of growers to the extent of the growers' bid. If the growers own, they consider the interest of the company to the extent of the company's bid. The externalities are internalized in this sense, but do not go away.

Tourists and other users of nature did not have any explicit ownership rights and were not bought out by the phosphate company. Only later, when the state began to regulate the release of particulates to the atmosphere, did the interests of the environmental users begin to count.

How do US courts decide property rights issues such as the above. A 1970 New York case involved a cement plant which damaged neighboring land owners because of dirt, smoke, and vibration (Boomer v. Atlantic Cement Co., 257 N.E. 2nd 870). The court granted a temporary injunction which would be removed after the cement company paid the plaintiffs' damages. The court noted that third parties may also have been damaged, but since they did not join the suit the court ignored them. It might be hypothesized that the more general public harmed by the cement operation had high transaction costs in organizing to join the suit. (This is explored further below.) The court was of the opinion that a permanent injunction would have been too drastic since it would have resulted in the immediate closing of the plant. This seems unlikely if the parties could negotiate since the plant could buy the air rights from the neighbors if the value to the neighbors was less than the value to the plant.

A dissenting judge argued for a permanent injunction on the ground that the air pollution was a "wrong." While from a technical production function view, the use of air to store dust is not different from any other purchased input necessary to produce cement, this is not always the same in human cognition. Some people regard certain actions as a wrong and not matters of ordinary commerce. Government must decide whose perception counts.

Transaction Costs

There are transaction costs as well as production costs present in any economic activity beyond individual self-sufficiency. To acquire an input controlled by someone else requires effort in negotiation and coordination between buyers and sellers and among buyers (sellers) if a resource serves more than one person simultaneously. Transactions costs can be economized as any other cost. Institutions (rights) can affect the size of transaction costs or the consequences of a given cost.

Consider the above case of phosphate–citrus interdependence. When the phosphate company owned the environment, no bids were forthcoming from the citrus growers. Two reasons are possible: (1) the bid (value) of the growers was less than the reservation price (value) of the phosphate company; or (2) the transaction costs of getting all the growers together to make the bid reduced the effective bid below the company's reservation price. In the first case, the growers' bid is rejected and the "damage" continues and is Pareto irrelevant in the sense that *given* the ownership there is no opportunity via trade to make both parties better off. Pareto irrelevant is not policy irrelevant since location of ownership is politically relevant. In the second case, where transaction costs get in the way of trade, there may be a possibility to reduce them and make both parties better off.

Institutional innovations reducing transaction costs are a source of economic growth because they facilitate wealth-enhancing trade (North, 1990). The polar case of high transaction costs is that created by inalienable rights. Can we then say that use rights are always bad? Not necessarily. Trade is often associated with changed use, and the prohibition of trade is often the instrument which gives effect to those third party interests who prefer the status quo. What appears to be Pareto-better trade between two parties may not be if more parties are relevant. For example, if the citrus growers had an inalienable right to be free of phosphate dust, the phosphate company could not buy out the growers and the environmentalists would enjoy the cleaner nature. It would be possible to achieve the same result by making enviornmentalists joint owners with the citrus growers so that the consent of nature lovers to the bid of the phosphate company would be necessary. Some analysts have a preference for direct ownership interests rather than indirect interests via inalienability and the consequence of transaction costs. But in the political world, a particular group may be able to take advantage of transactions costs when it could not frontally obtain an explicit ownership interest. To argue for alienability or other rights that lower transaction costs between two parties is then to argue that third parties should not count. The boundary of owners whose consent is necessary for change is what rights are all about. Rights determine who can participate in decision making. Note that the result of inalienability and the option for trade can be similar in the case where the environmentalists as joint owners would have rejected the bid of the phosphate company – no change in use (status quo) in both cases.

Return to the case where the transaction cost is inherent in the character of the good and not itself created by institutions. It is costly for large groups to organize a bid for a resource if any person's opportunistic use of the resulting resource cannot be denied. This is the case where the resource is a high exclusion cost good, such as any resource which is costly to fence and deny to non-payers. If the air is free of phosphate particulates, it unavoidably benefits all citrus growers and nature lovers in the area. This is one explanation for the fact that neither group made a bid when the air was owned by the phosphate processors.

The above case illustrates the role of rights distribution in resource use. If the resource is owned by the enviornmentalists and citrus growers, and if the value to them is greater than the bid price of phosphate miners, the resource will be retained. On the other hand, if the environmentalists and citrus growers have to bear the transaction costs of organizing a group bid, their bid may fall short and the resource will be used by the miners.

The location of ownership affects resource use depending on the size of transaction costs relative to the difference in value to the transacting parties. This relationship is now associated with the work of Ronald Coase. The obverse of the above is often called the "Coase rule," namely that if transaction costs are zero the location of ownership makes no difference to resource use. In this limiting case, income can be redistributed without affecting resource use. However, since transaction costs are often significant in environmental problems, the latter obverse expression is of less interest.

There is experimental evidence available on the ability of parties to reach the negotiated agreements necessary to maximize joint gain when transaction costs are zero. One laboratory experiment specified a demand schedule for six buyers and six sellers. In addition each subject incurred monetary damage as a function of the number of units traded (Harrison et al., 1987). This approximates the kind of environmental case where some activity creates damages. The experimenters report that "in relatively sterile and abstract bargaining environments" the parties were able "to identify the social optimum quantity and agree to enforce a voluntary restriction on that quantity" (p. 389). Further experimental results are noted below in the section on common pool resources.

What other policy implications follow from the existence of transaction costs? Some suggest that the resource be given by government to the users who would have paid the most for it gross of transaction costs (Demsetz, 1967). This requires a benefit–cost analysis of the type described in the previous chapter. Classical liberals like James Buchanan would object since the analysts' estimates are not subject to any test of actual individual behavior. In any case, the benefit–cost estimates of willingness to pay are not independent of the distribution of rights. In the case of environmental consumers, previous ownership of income property affects willingness to pay for the environment. A different income distribution might produce a different set of bid and reservation prices.

Where ownership of the resource in question is non-marginal with respect to a person's wealth, the location of ownership affects bid and reservation prices and thus who uses a resource. Poor individuals would pay little or nothing to enhance air and water quality, but might have a positive reservation price if they already owned the resource. Ownership affects the marginal utility of income (Knetsch and Sinden, 1984). It is common to observe that, when people feel they are the rightful owners, they do not want to respond to a question about their willingness to pay. No contingent valuation study can escape the property rights question of whether to measure willingness to pay (which presumes no ownership) and willingness to sell (which presumes ownership).

Groups who want to be on the other end of externality interdependences often seek regulation rather than explicit redistribution of ownership even if instrumentally they come to the same performance. Consider the example of regulation requiring newspapers to contain a percentage of recycled newsprint. This source may be more expensive than virgin material. Is regulation then getting in the way of efficiency? Not if environmentalists "own" a litter-free environment, or the right to be free of the costs of garbage dumps. In this case, newspaper publishers would have to negotiate with all environmentalists to obtain a place to store their used newsprint. It can be imagined that this cost would exceed the extra cost of using recycled material and thus the result of regulation is quite efficient.

On the other hand, if publishers own the environment and can create costs for environmentalists, the nature lovers would have to buy out the publishers. Again transaction costs would be considerable in organizing the bid. The environmentalists might ask government to act as their agent and collect a tax and offer a "subsidy" to those printers who use recycled material. But note that this payment is just like any other payment to a resource owner. A subsidy cannot be defined independently of rights.

In the United States there are constitutional rules which affect choice of institutional change. A direct legislative redistribution is often interpreted by US courts as a "taking" requiring compensation, while if the change is labeled a regulation within the police power, no compensation is required. When rights are disputed, the starting place is often not clear and there is no reference point which defines a taking. New technologies and preferences can make people newly interdependent. Previously, no one bothered to ask whose opportunity counted because they were not conflicting, or the source of interdependence was unknown. When the courts are asked to decide who has the right, they often reason from some precedent. But often there are many precedents to choose from and the appearance of continuity is illusory (Samuels and Mercuro, 1992).

Alienability is attractive because it allows owners to trade for something else they find more valuable. Thus, even the beneficiaries of a publicly owned resource such as air, water, wildlife habitat, or fishing access might prefer to sell (some or all) rather than keep in current use. When such a resource is owned by a group with a unanimity rule it means that the person who places the highest value on the resource determines its use and denies gains to others, if transaction costs are high. Some private contractual rights such as subdivision deed restrictions may be written to require unanimity to change. Some few people may have reservation prices greater than any offer or there may be no practical way to compensate them. People will differ on whether this is reasonable. Courts have to decide whether to uphold private subdivision contracts (even between successors to the original contact). The same question arises when government in managing public lands has to decide if the intense preferences of a few are to count (whether for spotted owls or water quality). The efficient resource use follows only after the question of reasonability is answered.

Guido Calabresi (1985) observes that "what is deemed unreasonable behavior, no less than who is the cheapest avoider of a cost, depends on the valuations put on acts, activities, and beliefs by the whole of our law and not on some objective or scientific notion." He concludes, "what is efficient, or passes a cost–benefit test, is not a 'scientific' notion separated from beliefs and attitudes, and always must respond to the question of whom we wish to make richer or poorer" (p. 69).

Technological change often produces great benefits on the average, but great costs (real or imagined) for some. Examples include pesticides, food preservatives, crop monocultures, pharmaceuticals, transport, and nuclear power. Calabresi calls these "gifts of the evil deity" because, while producing benefits, they may cause death and disability at random.

The toughest property rights case to decide is when future benefits and costs are not predictable. Some of those potentially affected are willing to gamble that benefits will exceed costs while others are risk averse. These preferences are incompatible and not compensable in any practical way. It is not possible to argue for alienability without taking sides. Do future generations or even resources themselves have rights (Swaney, 1987)? This is the way some American Indians would describe the present generation's trustee or fiduciary obligation. However it is expressed, the demands of future generations or resources cannot speak for themselves and, if certain options are kept open for the future, it creates differential benefits (and costs) for present individuals.

Regulation can often be symbolized as righting a wrong. Reducing pollution can take on a moral tone which simply arguing for the interests of one person over another does not. Some may lament the emotional charge attached to pollution or concern for future generations which complicates negotiations. Yet, it is the stuff of cultural learning that prevents opportunistic behavior when exclusion costs are high. People learn to do what is regarded as right without calculating whether they could take what is not theirs. It is a mistake to think of the effectiveness of law as only a matter of bringing costs to bear on individuals. It is also a standard and statement of ideals which become internalized in behavior.

Common Pool Resources

Resources such as ocean fisheries, alpine and desert pastures are high exclusion cost goods and difficult to police and fence. If the prevailing system is one of a free-for-all, no one participant will take into account the effect of her effort on the returns to the efforts of others. This may lead to complete rent dissipation and resource degradation. This is one meaning of externality – failure to maximize the total net value of a resource. Even if one surplus-maximizing person were declared owner of a fishery, she would have difficulty preventing use of the resource outside of any contracts made with some labor and equipment owners.

Regulation and individual ownership are functional equivalents (Cheung, 1970). Both the government and the individual could try to stipulate rates and methods of harvest. Both will be frustrated by the character of the resource and will fail to stipulate and enforce their "rules." Cheung says it is an empirical question whether the government or individuals could do it better. It may cost more – whether public or private – than it is worth to achieve total product maximization. A free-for-all is not ideal, but it must be compared with real possible alternatives.

What is the empirical evidence? Some samples from both experimental and case studies will be noted. People have been assembled and asked to play various games where they have a larger payoff from cooperation than from individual choice independent of others. Hoffman and Spitzer (1985) have tested the Coase rule in the laboratory and generally found that two parties and even larger groups do maximize joint gains from trade. In one experiment, there is a designated controller who may pocket a designated amount. However, the pot is enhanced if the controller can reach agreement with another party on how to split it. This has elements of common pool resource management. Cooperative game theory would predict that subjects would cooperate (manage the pool for maximum net yield) and the controller would divide the rewards with a minimum amount to the other party, and in no case would the controller take less than could be obtained by acting unilaterally. Yet the outcome was always a 50–50 split. Most have learned a standard of fairness which governs these cases. These informal cultural institutions are the matrix in which formal property rights are embedded.

The experiment also varied the manner in which the controller was selected: coin flip or winner of a hash mark game. The winner was labeled "earned right to be controller." The authors regard this as triggering a sense of legitimacy – what they term a Lockean theory of distributive justice. The parties seem to regard the position of controller as justified to a greater extent after playing the hash mark game. In almost all experiments the joint maxima were achieved. In general, about half of the experiments resulted in an equal split and only rarely did the controller receive more than she could have received by unilateral action. But where the game trigger was combined with the moral authority of the position being "earned," the equal split declined sharply and half the time the controller received more than her potential maximum. In real world situations, the moral authority of the controller may be questioned and in fact earn the malevolence of the others as a result of historical violations of standards of fairness.

In ultimatum bargaining experiments one player proposes a split of a pot which is then divided accordingly if the other person accepts. If refused, both receive nothing. Again the 50–50 split was the most common allocation proposed (reported by Frank, 1988, p. 171). In only six of 51 cases did the controller demand more than 90 percent of the total. In five of the six cases where the controller claimed more than 90 percent, the second player refused to play. This suggests that disagreement over distribution can be a barrier to realizing joint gains.

Laboratory experiments may be the only instance of zero transaction costs. The experimenter excludes most sources of transaction costs by bringing the parties together and paying for their time. Most informational deficiencies are excluded since the individual payoff functions are known and the total net payoff is known or easily calculated. The payoff is certain and given rather than something formed in the process of negotiation. The problem is given and exists to be solved. The other person's and group's demand seems a matter of fact rather than raising a question of reasonableness and morality. There is no chance for the parties to become emotionally attached to one or another product such as represented by the dissenting judge in the Boomer case when he labeled pollution as a "wrong." The very structure of the game puts people into their calculating mode rather than their habitual or commitment mode. The game itself becomes an institution. To understand the economics of property rights it is not enough to make a simple assumption of maximizing behavior. Rather, a behavioral economics is required that accounts for actual perceptions and cognitions.

Turning to field studies, the experience in managing oil pools suggests that individual owners of the surface have not coordinated their pumping to maximize net yield (Libecap, 1989). Private solutions were thwarted by the inability of surface owners to agree on how to share the available total gains, and by asymmetric information regarding productivity. Oil on publicly owned land has been managed somewhat better.

The total value of raw land for housing can often be enhanced by leaving some natural features as open space rather than putting a house on each possible lot. Still, even with a subsidy, landowners in the Brandywine valley of Pennsylvania failed to cooperate (Strong, 1975).

On the other side of the ledger, studies of fisheries, pasture, and irrigation system management around the world show many instances where people have agreed to sustainable management without government help (Ostrom, 1990). Ostrom defines common pool resources as having benefits from improvement in the *resource system* which have high exclusion and monitoring cost. The system is subject to joint production up to capacity, but the appropriation of individual *resource units* is incompatible, and yields are uncertain over time and space. The factors found affecting outcomes include "the total number of decision makers, the number of participants minimally necessary to achieve the collective benefit, the discount rate in use, similarities of interests, and the presence of participants with substantial leadership or other assets" (Ostrom, 1990, p. 188). She concludes that destruction of common pool resources is not inevitable, and that neither public nor private solutions are automatic – detail matters.

Rights Regimes and Alternative Legal Instruments

The rights alternatives that have received the most attention are public, private, and common ownership. Some literature refers to any set of rights other than private ownership with full transferability (Furobotn and Pejovich, 1974) as attenuated. But we have seen above that one person's attenuation is often the instrument for another's opportunity. Regulation and court sanctions for interference with private property both limit some people and give opportunities to others. They are functional equivalents and involve a public legitimation. For example, a person who does not build a 40 storey building because of zoning violations or because of threat of court suit of neighbors claiming a tort (nuisance) is equally constrained (attenuated?) by the opportunities of others to enjoy an unimpeded environment.

Regulation as a source of someone's opportunity to enjoy a resource is fundamentally different from a tradeable right in that the non-right holder may not legally offer money in exchange for the right. As has been noted, this may prevent a Pareto-better trade, although, if certain people's high reservation prices are to count, no Pareto-better trade is possible anyway. Regulation and tradeable ownership also differ with respect to transaction costs in protecting the right. If the opportunity protected by a regulation is violated, the public bears the cost of court action, perhaps as a matter of criminal proceeding. If it is a private right, the owners must themselves bring a civil tort action and bear the legal costs which in some instances may make the right worthless and too costly to pursue.

An individual is recognized as a private owner when the state stands ready to issue an injunction if others interfere or to order payment of damages. Both outcomes recognize private property and the basis for market exchange, but provide quite different consequences. If the court is willing to issue an injunction, any non-owner who would like to use the resource must obtain the consent of the owner (even if there are many). This can increase the transaction cost; e.g. in the case of airport noise the developer must buy out each affected property which gives great value to the strategic holdout. In the Florida phosphate case discussed above, when the state indicated that it would enjoin the phosphate firm the firm began to buy citrus land at a price above its present net worth in citrus (Crocker, 1971). Why would the firm pay a premium? The citrus landowners know that the value of the land for waste disposal is greater than for citrus and can bargain for part of the surplus. The farmers can take advantage of the economizing effort by the company to avoid the high transaction costs associated with strategic bargaining.

The payment of court-assessed damages is an alternative to the injunction. In this case, the phosphate firm does not have to reach a prior agreement with the farmers but makes use of the resource and pays afterward as required. This can be referred to as "private condemnation" since it parallels public condemnation where the state need not meet a willing seller. The price set by the court is likely to be less than the firm paid under threat of injunction. Which is the real (efficient) price? Both are real, they just reflect a different distribution of rights. The right to an injunction is equivalent to the farmers being part owners of the phosphate company which would probably be called expropriation by the company. The right to pay damages is equivalent to the company having the right of eminent domain which probably would be called expropriation by the farmers.

Some object to the government exercising eminent domain (Knetsch, 1983). The issue is whether the landowner ever owned the right to take strategic advantage of the government's need for specific sites. The person who stands to make a fortune in a specific case probably is not impressed by the fact that she saved taxes in all the other instances where the public needed land for roads or whatever. The issue is not whether a market test is applied but what one brings to the market. Not being able to sell a strategic position is no different from not being able to sell air quality already owned by environmentalists – the opportunity is simply owned by someone else.

In the case of nuclear power, one can imagine that, if nuclear developers had to get agreement from all of the possibly affected people prior to building, there would be no nuclear power. Even at that, the government had to agree to pay any future damages over a specified amount. The cost of nuclear power is not simply a fact to be calculated but a function of the distribution of rights.

An individual benefits from publicly owned resources according to the administrative rules of use or of leasing. Administrators may be limited by legislation but usually have some discretion, giving opportunity to pursue their own agenda as well as the agenda of various groups in the economy. The uses allowed are not necessarily those that would have won the resource in market bidding. Whether this is bad or good depends on the legitimacy of the income distribution behind the ability to make market bids. The same consequences could be achieved by land reform or direct income transfers, but politically this is more difficult than regulation or, for instance, concessionary leases of mineral or forest resources. Since an institution must be compared with what is possible rather than some ideal, to advocate direct income transfers as the only means of achieving a desired income distribution is either empty or prejudicial support of the status quo. In any case, even the theoretical lump-sum ideal income transfer has transaction costs.

Self-interest of rule makers is inescapable regardless of the type of rule (private or public). Neither judges, legislators, nor administrators are wholly disinterested. All of these make and protect rights. Other procedural rules (rules for making rules) and learned professional standards limit the expression of self-interest of the rights makers. Informal cultural institutions may be more important than formal rules. Simple behavioral assumptions of narrow self-interest are not sufficient to predict performance.

Determinism

It would be analytically convenient if analysts could just add up observable costs and benefits and derive optimal rights. It would avoid the pain of choosing sides and agreeing on income distribution. The idea of choosing rights to maximize total product is attractive. While some would argue that this conception is the very definition of an economic approach, it is not the only one.

Existing costs and benefits are themselves the product of a set of property rights. Thus these costs have implications for rights only if some set of them is held constant (and presumed legitimate) while some marginal change is examined. If rights help determine costs, rights cannot be justified by reference to costs. Welfare economics theorists such as Mishan (1981) are agreed that optimality is not unique. Change the starting place and you change what is efficient. Robin Boadway and Neil Bruce (1984, p. 272) conclude: "To obtain a measure of welfare change in many-consumer economies which serves to rank all alternatives, there appears to be no alternative but to employ a social welfare function. This, of course, was precisely what the compensation test literature was trying to avoid." Consumer sovereignty is an empty slogan without choice of which consumer counts when conflicting with other consumers.

If observation of values thrown up by a particular set of rights cannot itself ground those rights, perhaps the ground (social welfare function) can be supplied by the democratic political process. This prospect was dealt a serious blow by Kenneth Arrow's impossibility theorem even before James Buchanan popularized government failure and bureaucratic self-interest. Different political ideals conflict. Political outcome is affected by choice of voting procedures and boundaries which aggregate the preferences of diverse individuals. Voter sovereignty is an empty slogan without choice of which voter counts when conflicting with other consumers.

If efficiency is derivative from each rights distribution, the dichotomy between equity and efficiency and supposed necessity for tradeoff is misleading. Since each distribution produces a different set of prices, there is a different efficiency associated with each rights set. Kenneth Arrow (1983, p. 26) makes the point by saying, "there is no meaning to total output independent of distribution, that is, of ethical judgments."

Deterministic models have been applied to explain the historical evolution of property rights. An example is John Umbek's (1981) analysis of California gold mining. He characterizes the initial situation as anarchy, as miners rushed to California before any national or state government had mining laws. Choice of rights is conceptualized as a constrained maximization problem with a given production function and relative prices. He assumes selfish wealth maximization and no self-restraint or regard for others. Other people are mere objects to be used as one does a donkey or shovel.

The use of violence is just one item in the production function in Umbek's model. One can use labor combined with land to produce gold or labor to take from others. The choice is simply one of deterministic economizing. "No individual would be willing to accept a contract in which he was assigned property rights of less value than he could obtain by personal violence. Therefore, ignoring the gain from contracting, the distribution of the value of exclusive rights agreed upon by contract must be the same as the distribution resulting from individual violence" (1981, p. 91).

The appearance of a contract and exchange is created by imagining that a person exchanges something of value to avoid the violence of others (goods exchanged to avoid a bad). This is a strange definition of exchange. When a hoodlum says, "Your money or your life," and you hand over your wallet, most people would not call this acquiescence to an exchange of rights. You can obtain a spoil of war by violence, but not a right. A right is the result of an act of self-restraint, not the result of the force of others (Taylor, 1966). It is not clear what a person has to offer to a person exercising superior force, for if they can take the land you have been working, they can take anything else – why call it a trade? Without self-restraint on the part of the person with superior force, the inferior is a slave.

Umbek offers no evidence of one person exchanging a good to avoid a bad. Only the presumed result is observed – namely little violence occurred. How did this come about? As the population of miners increased and gold land became more scarce, the miners in a locality had a meeting where the basis of claims was specified. The miners largely agreed to honor the rights established by majority rule. How shall this be interpreted? Umbek assumes that the capacity for violence was effectively equal. Thus an individual in the minority could calculate that, in a war between the majority and minority, the minority would lose.

An alternative interpretation is that, despite the lack of mining law, people's behavior was embedded in numerous institutions. Most came from places where majority rule was practised. They had learned to regard it as reasonable and fair. The real power of institutions and modes of thought is their ability to rule out some options from active calculation. Most of us do not wake up in the morning and calculate whether we could get away with violence.

As the population of miners increased, these new local "governments" in some cases reduced the size of the claim allowed any one person. Umbek sees this as due to the increased supply of potential violence. Could not it also be seen as self-restraint and an expression of regard for others and fairness? The fact that at some point additional newcomers were left landless does not mean there was no self-restraint. Surely humans sometime adjust their claims on resources given the number of others who are hungry and granted the status of subjects and not objects like shovels. In the world of physical production functions there is no moral anguish, just deductive calculation. This is attractive to some and a horror to others.

Historical observation indicates an interdependence between existing property rights/rules for making rights and the evolution of future rights. People with money and access to government will be able to influence the choice of additional rights. Still, technology, ideals, ideology, and symbols upset any neat trajectory. In previous times people took comfort in reasoning from natural law and various other philosophical justifications (Bromley, 1989, pp. 190–9). These have fewer disciples today, but the demand for psychic balm is no less strong. Many have a preference for those rights which via selective perception appear natural as opposed to rights which are the product of deliberative but messy political contest. It is comforting to find an existing justification for a right rather than to anguish over its creation. The worldwide occurrence of civil war is testimony to our failure to wholly civilize this creative process. The contest for environmental resources is only slightly less intense because natural resources are not just commodities but have the power to evoke a sense of moral outrage and the need to right a wrong. Economists can contribute to reason without being deterministic or foreclosing political debate.

Review

The fundamental propositions of this chapter may be stated as follows.

1   Human interdependence means that freedom and opportunity for one person are exposure and cost to another.
2   Individual property rights and regulating are functionally equivalent in giving opportunities to some and exposures to others.
3   Externalities are ubiquitous and reciprocal.
4   To own is to coerce. Market transactions involve mutual coercion.
5   Government (some collective process) determines who is owner (seller) and who is non-owner (buyer), that is, who can coerce whom. Rights are a public phenomenon.
6   Freedom to contract (market exchange) rests on what individuals bring to the exchange (including learned habitualized self-restraint).
7   The scope of the state equals the scope of human conflict.
8   Rights are antecedent to markets. You cannot exchange what is not publicly acknowledged as yours.
9   Efficiency is not uniquely associated with one set of rights but derivative from each set of rights. This makes the efficiency versus equity dichotomy misleading.
10 Social cost versus private cost conception is value presumptive.
11 Cost is not independent of rights so cannot be a guide to rights. The fundamental choice of any society is whose preferences count, that is, the creation of a social welfare function.

References

Arrow, Kenneth J. 1983: A difficulty in the concept of social welfare. In *Social Choice and Justice*, Collected Papers of Kenneth J. Arrow, Cambridge, MA: Harvard University Press.
Boadway, Robin W. and Bruce, Neil. 1984: *Welfare Economics*. Oxford: Basil Blackwell.

Bromley, Daniel W. 1989: *Economic Interests and Institutions*. Oxford: Basil Blackwell.

Calabresi, Guido. 1985: *Ideals, Beliefs, Attitudes, and the Law*. Syracuse, NY: Syracuse University Press.

Cheung, Steven N. S. 1970: the structure of a contract and the theory of a non-exclusive resource. *Journal of Law and Economics*, 13, 49–70.

Crocker, Thomas D. 1971: Externalities, property rights, and transactions costs: an empirical study. *Journal of Law and Economics*, 14, 451–64.

Demsetz, Harold. 1967: Toward a theory of property rights. *American Economic Review*, 57, 347–73.

Frank, Robert H. 1988: *Passions Within Reason*. New York: Norton.

Furubotn, Erik G. and Pejovich, Svetozar (eds) 1974: *The Economics of Property Rights*. Cambridge, MA: Ballinger.

Harrison, G. W., Hoffman, E., Rutstrom, E. E. and Spitzer, M. L. 1987: Coasian solutions to the externality problem in experimental markets. *Economic Journal*, 97, 388–402.

Hoffman, Elizabeth, and Spitzer, Matthew L. 1985: Entitlements, rights, and fairness: an experimental examination of subjects' concepts of distributive justice. *Journal of Legal Studies*, 14, 259–97.

Knetsch, Jack L. 1983: *Property Rights and Compensation*. Toronto: Butterworth.

Knetsch, Jack L. and Sinden, John A. 1984: Willingness to pay and compensation demanded: experimental evidence of an unexpected disparity in measures of value. *Quarterly Review of Economics*, 99, 507–21.

Libecap, Gary D. 1989: *Contracting for Property Rights*. Cambridge: Cambridge University Press.

Mishan, E. J. 1981: *Introduction to Normative Economics*. New York: Oxford University Press.

North, Douglass C. 1990: *Institutions, Institutional Change and Economic Performance*. Cambridge: Cambridge University Press.

Ostrom, Elinor. 1990: *Governing the Commons*. Cambridge: Cambridge University Press.

Samuels, Warren J. and Mercuro, Nicholas. 1992: The role and resolution of the compensation principle in society: part one and part two. In Warren J. Samuels (ed.), *Essays on the Economic Role of Government*, New York: New York University Press.

Schmid, A. Allan. 1987: *Property, Power, and Public Choice*. New York: Praeger.

Strong, Ann L. 1975: *Private Property and Public Interest: The Brandywine Experience*. Baltimore, MD: Johns Hopkins University Press.

Swaney, James A. 1987: Elements of a neoinstitutional environmental economics. *Journal of Economic Issues*, 21, 1739–79.

Taylor, John F. A. 1966: *The Masks of Society*. New York: Appleton-Century-Crofts.

Umbek, John R. 1981: *A Theory of Property Rights With Application to the California Gold Rush*. Ames, IA: Iowa State University Press.

4

Zoning and the Urban Environment

William A. Fischel

1 Think Globally, Act Globally

The thrust of this chapter is that local zoning laws in the United States provide sufficient protection for local environmental goals, but they are often poorly suited for promoting regional or national goals. The problem with local zoning is that it creates environments that are "too good" locally, which sometimes degrades the economic well-being and perhaps the environmental quality of the larger region. The slogan "Think globally, act locally," may encourage local zoning actions that perversely degrade the environment of a larger area.

A frequently mentioned drawback of municipal zoning is the so-called "beggar thy neighbor" policy of wishing spillovers upon other communities. Dumps and industrial parks are said to be located too frequently on community boundaries, downwind and out of sight of the local voters. The ratio of evidence to assertion on this is surprisingly low, though.

I submit that the more serious drawback of local zoning is its tendency to exclude too much activity, with the result that urban areas are too spread out with respect to residences, employment, and public infrastructure. Spreading out, on balance, probably has undesirable effects on both metropolitan and rural environmental quality. The appropriate reform is not to shift zoning to a higher level of government, since the state and national governments are apt to overlook local problems, but to make local governments in urban areas more responsive to the opportunity cost of unreasonably low density zoning. One way of doing so is to require that local zoning that goes "too far" compensates landowners for their losses.

2   Zoning is Police Power Regulation

Zoning in its narrow sense involves the separation of a political jurisdiction, most commonly a local government, into contiguous geographic zones in which some activities are permitted and others are forbidden or allowed only conditionally. Within each zone, minimum lot size and the maximum (and sometimes minimum) structural dimensions are normally specified for the uses allowed there. Minor exceptions to these requirements are done by zoning boards, whose behavior seems to smooth out the rough edges of zoning but seldom usurps it wholesale (Bryden, 1977).

Zoning is an exercise of the government's "police power," the right to make regulations without having to pay compensation. Zoning is thus nominally unlike eminent domain, in which government takes property but pays for it, and unlike the power to tax, in which owners of property are expected to give resources to the government rather than just refrain from doing certain activities.

The foregoing distinctions in reality are not so neat. Justice Oliver Wendell Holme's opinion in Pennsylvania Coal v. Mahon (1922) constituted judicial notice that police power regulations that go "too far" could amount to an exercise in eminent domain. Newman Baker (1927) and William Anderson (1927) described several cities' attempts to apply zoning by eminent domain, compensating owners for forgone development opportunities. The eminent domain experiment became moot when the US Supreme Court decided Euclid v. Ambler (1926) which held that compensation to landowners for zoning-induced losses was not normally necessary.

In the broader sense used in this chapter, zoning encompasses all locally generated exercises of the police power that pertain to the use of real property. A few of the more common examples, in addition to zoning districts, are (a) subdivision regulations, which impose design and infrastructure requirements on builders; (b) historic preservation ordinances, which restrict the modification of old buildings; (c) special district controls that retard the conversion of wetlands, agricultural land, or environmentally sensitive areas to more intensive uses; and (d) growth controls, which attempt, for a time, to retard overall community development rather than just guiding it to the appropriate zone, by withholding building permits or such essential services as water or sewerage. American constitutional courts of the latter half of the twentieth century have upheld such regulations against property owners' complaints if the regulations are "rationally related" to almost any conceivable public purpose.

3   Zoning is Decentralized

There is an important difference between the study of environmental law at the national level and the study of land use controls at the local level. It is possible to read the text of, say, the Clean Air Act and get a reasonable idea of how the law actually works. It will take some time, and parallel laws and agency history must be read, but nonetheless the researcher interested in it can do the job.

Zoning laws are the environmental laws of local governments. There are upwards of 25,000 general-purpose local governments in the United States, all of which can adopt zoning laws. Most large metropolitan areas have hundreds of local governments. These governments are scattered about 50 states, all of which enact their own legislation concerning what local governments can do.

The ordinances are not brief. The simple ordinance of my hometown of 8000 people contains 85 large pages, and that does not count the subdivision regulations. New York City's zoning ordinance runs to several volumes. Even if a speed-reading scholar tried to get through all local ordinances in a few years, he would be frustrated by the continuing adoption of amendments and, not infrequently, whole new ordinances. What he had read in 1990 might well be outdated by 1995.

To deal with the multitude and mutability of laws, the study of zoning as an environmental institution requires the distillation of some stylized facts. This enterprise is made easier by two conditions. One is that state legislation authorizing local zoning is remarkably similar among the 50 states. This stems from the widespread adoption of the Standard State Zoning Enabling Act (SZEA) promulgated by the US Commerce Department in the 1920s. The SZEA was among the most successful of advisory "model acts" intended to standardize state laws (most others were ignored), and its influence is still perceptible.

The second source of uniformity is that the limits of zoning are often decided by state courts on common law and constitutional law principles that are similar across the states. There are differences in the attitudes of state courts. California is most permissive of local authority, particularly when the locals seek to retard development, while Illinois is probably most protective of developers. But the statutory, common law, and constitutional principles on which court decisions are based, are reasonably uniform. As an example of this uniformity, legal casebook on land use differ in emphasis rather than in coverage or content, and most have little difficulty adapting to a national market for textbooks. (A casebook with broad attention to economic issues is Ellickson and Tarlock (1981).) As another example, Richard Babcock recounted among the many revealing stories of *The Zoning Game* (1966) and *The Zoning Game Revisited*

(Babcock and Sieman, 1985) how his Chicago-based law firm was able to develop a national practice in land use law.

4 Zoning Imposes Many Constraints

One barrier to economists' understanding of zoning has been their tendency to pay exclusive attention to its easily quantifiable rules, such as minimum lot size. This stems from an erroneous analogy of local zoning laws to the federal governments' uniform economic constraints, such as income tax rates or national rules set down by the Environmental Protection Agency. Such an analogy neglects the ability of local authorities to use other regulations as complementary devices and to change the controls if they do not work to their satisfaction. Hence the employment of minimum lot size, the workhorse of local ordinances, as a measure of zoning restrictiveness could lead to dubious inferences. One might expect that, as minimum residential lot sizes increased, developers would substitute land for capital by putting smaller buildings on three acre lots (Henderson, 1985).

Local regulation, however, is not a single-valued constraint on development decisions. It is an obstacle course in which the race director can often raise or lower the barriers after the contest has begun. A commonplace among lawyers is that no one has a vested right to a particular zoning classification. Looked at individually, each zoning barrier may look easy to cross or evade. Collectively, however, the community can wear down the unwelcome developer with procedural delays and by withholding discretionary permits.

As for attempts to pin local governments down by holding them to the master plan that is supposed to guide zoning (but is often adopted long after the first zoning laws), law professor Carol Rose (1983, p. 879) dryly notes that "local governments exhibit a marked talent for evading close examination of the conformity of their regulations to pre-existing plans." Even when courts of law or state legislatures become skeptical of this activity and try to impose limits on it, they are at best partially successful (Briffault, 1990). As judges frequently note, sometimes approvingly and at other times despairingly, the police power is the "least limitable" of all government powers.

Like a carefully engineered drawbridge, zoning is characterized by redundancy. A would-be developer who meets the zoning requirements must often pass site-plan review by the planning commission and, in many states, by other boards concerned about historic districts, wildlife conservation, and wetlands preservation. Having passed muster, the developer may be required to pay numerous fees. Among the more controversial are impact fees, paid to offset the real or supposed derogation of public services caused by the community (Babcock, 1987). Impact fees are a thinly disguised tax, and their widespread use by local governments without having been authorized by state legislatures as a tax indicates the broad authority that zoning confers on local governments.

While one can find the courts in some states hostile to some types of restrictions, it hardly matters in practice. One device can substitute for another. In addition, landowner–developers who, in rare instances, successfully challenge the government's use of an unreasonable regulatory device will seldom receive monetary compensation for their efforts (Ellickson, 1977, p. 490). Only a few courts will even award a building permit for the specific project, let alone court costs and delay damages. The developer must usually go through the local permit process all over again, a prospect that discourages challenges.

5 Zoning Needs a Model of Local Politics

The previous paragraphs suggest despair and hope. There are thousands of different local governments to attend to, each one of them can change the regulation frequently, and the changes are hard to detect in the text of the law. The hope arises from a legal and constitutional framework that is similar across states and their local governments. Most local zoning officials (I have been one in my hometown) could attend a zoning or planning hearing in any part of the country and pick up the issues without much coaching from the locals.

But a similar institutional framework by itself does not help unless one can make some credible generalizations about how the actors in that framework will behave. Thus one needs a theory of the behavior of people who make and remake zoning laws. My theory starts from the political nature of zoning. Appointed zoning boards and professional planning staff have only a small effect on zoning restrictions. The variances, site-plan reviews, and special exceptions that they oversee are undoubtedly important to applicants. But only elected public officials or the voters themselves can actually enact and amend zoning laws. Thus the theory of bureaucracy is not likely to be helpful. One needs a theory of politics.

One might also need a theory of corruption, a by-product of politics. I shall not undertake it here. My impressions from newspaper accounts and from Gardiner and Lyman (1978) are that corruption in zoning is widespread but not large enough to affect overall land use patterns. Some authors have hinted that, from a housing cost perspective, corruption might not be such a bad thing, since it sometimes facilitates housing developments that would otherwise be opposed. As the evidence (discussed below) on zoning and housing cost suggests, such utilitarian corruption is not sufficiently widespread to offset the effect of the restrictions.

6   The Median Voter Model Fits Zoning

The simplest theory of politics is the one children read about in grade school. The majority of voters get what they want. Howard Bowen's (1943) median voter model transformed this simple idea into a statistically estimable proposition. It hypothesizes a predictable relationship between the economic characteristics of potential voters (e.g. their income, sex, education, housing tenure) and their preferences about government policies, such as how much to spend on schools and how restrictive the zoning ordinance ought to be. On this theory elected officials are mere conduits of the median voter's desires.

Modern theories of political economy attempt to disabuse students of the naive model of politics. The voting paradox and Arrow's (1951) theorem undermine the credibility of politics as a rational means of ordering preferences. Economic theories of voter behavior and politics, beginning with Anthony Downs's (1957) rational ignorance and extending through George Stigler's (1971) theory of capture by special interest groups, show why the median voter might not get his or her way. The notion that politics operates "as if" the median voter decided each issue is as hard to swallow as the proposition that legislators operate in a post-electoral Camelot in which they consider only the public interest.

What seems not to have been noticed, however, is that the empirical evidence for the median voter model is a lot stronger than that for the special interest and the public interest models of politics. The empirical evidence comes from employing the median voter approach to estimating demands for *local* public goods (Barr and Davis, 1966; Borcherding and Deacon, 1972; Bergstrom and Goodman, 1973). As a generalization, the median voter model seems to predict local government behavior well (Holcombe, 1989). And, as one might expect, the smaller the unit of government, the better the median voter model seems to work (Bloom and Ladd, 1982; Holtz-Eakin and Rosen, 1989).

There is another reason, besides its being the product of local government politics, why zoning represents what voters want. Unlike most local budget items (except for bond issues), zoning changes are frequently subject to plebiscites (Callies et al., 1991). Plebiscites may take the form of referenda (acts referred to voters by the legislature) or initiatives (laws initiated by people outside the legislature). Even small re-zonings may be subject to direct balloting, and administrative exceptions such as variances and site-plan reviews are always subject to open hearings at which the views of abutters and other neighbors receive considerable attention. Although there are scholars who view zoning as the product of special interest legislation (Denzau and Weingast, 1982), I think that the evidence on zoning suggests the majoritarian problem rather than that of special interests (Levmore, 1991). The problem with zoning is that local voters do get what they want.

7 Homeowners Dominate Suburban Zoning

Saying that local government is responsive to the majority of voters does not tell one what the voters actually want. One could assume they want to maximize utility, but without further specification that assumption yields only tautologies. A more tractable assumption is that voters seek to maximize their wealth, and their votes about zoning are an instrument of wealth maximization (Sonstelie and Portney, 1978; Hochman and Ofek, 1979; Brueckner, 1982). Zoning may be viewed as a communal property right that entitles local voters to the benefits of land use regulation (Nelson, 1977; Fischel, 1978).

Wealth maximization requires a vehicle through which zoning decisions cause an increase (or prevent a decrease) in the voter's wealth. The most obvious means is by property that the voters may own. Zoning can promote a more pleasant environment in the neighborhood or substitute for expenditures that would ordinarily have to be paid by increases in local taxes. Beginning with Wallace Oates's (1969) seminal study of the Tiebout (1956) hypothesis, there is plenty of evidence that pleasant environments and low tax rates are capitalized in the value of residential property in the community. Given the prevalence of owner-occupied housing in most American communities, a reasonable first approximation of zoning policies is that they will be designed to maximize the value of owner-occupied housing in the community. Analyses of local referenda confirm the importance that homeowners place on local land use controls (Dublin et al., 1992).

8 Zoning is Capitalized in Home Values

Protection of home values by zoning is hardly a novel idea. The original zoning laws created a hierarchy of land uses, and owner-occupied housing stood at the top, to be protected from inroads by businesses and other nonconforming land uses. The remarkable persistence of this ideal, which appears in early English common-law decisions (Freeman, 1976), ought to caution reformers against dismissing it lightly.

There is more than history to support the influence of zoning on home values. In 1990, I wrote a short monograph for the Lincoln Institute called

Do Growth Controls Matter? It selectively reviewed and distilled the results of about 80 published studies of the empirical effects of land use controls. One of my conclusions gives support to what I call the good housekeeping theory of zoning: a place for everything, but everything in its place. Nonconforming uses are potentially hazardous to residential house values, and the private means of dealing with them have costs of their own.

I and several others have now debunked the much-cited studies that supposedly show that zoning is not justified because it is hard to find capitalization effects from nonconforming uses in Pittsburgh (Crecine et al., 1967), Rochester (Maser et al., 1977), and Vancouver (Mark and Goldberg, 1986). It is not worth doing again except to note that the censored-sample problem is now well understood. No one should embark on replicating the aforementioned studies without asking what happened to the nonconforming uses that zoning actually prevented. I am sympathetic, however, to comparative studies (mostly by lawyers) that ask whether zoning is the lowest cost way of dealing with the ubiquitous spillovers of urban land uses (Siegan, 1972; Ellickson, 1973; Cappell, 1991).

Finding that spillovers matter does not itself say much about whether zoning regulations matter. Here the best evidence comes from the adoption of novel regulations. My survey found numerous studies of the adoption of growth controls and other novel restrictions on overall community development. Almost all of them show that the new regulations increased the value of existing housing in the community that adopted the regulations. Many of these studies used a sample of communities from California, in which the growth control movement first became widespread in the 1970s. Among the better studies are Frech and Lafferty (1984), which found widely dispersed price increases after the adoption of the California Coastal Zone Commission; Katz and Rosen (1987), which found that San Francisco Bay Area communities that adopted growth controls had prices almost one-third higher than those that did not; and Schwartz et al. (1981), which found smaller but significant price increases from the pioneering growth controls of Petaluma, California.

A less numerous group of studies has looked at the value of undeveloped land when subjected to growth controls. Generally, but not without exception, these studies find that new restrictions reduce the value of undeveloped land. Examples are Knapp's (1985) study of Portland, Oregon, urban growth boundaries; Vaillancourt and Monty's (1985) study of land values subject to Quebec's new agricultural land zoning; and Peterson's (1974) study of Washington, DC, suburban land values during a sewer moratorium. Contrary results are Henneberry and Barrows (1990), who found that rural Wisconsin farmland did not diminish in value when agricultural zoning was adopted, and Beaton and Pollock (1992), who found that new Chesapeake Bay water quality regulations raised existing housing values without devaluing undeveloped land.

The foregoing results generally fit my view of zoning as a device seized upon by homeowner-voters to increase their own property values at the expense of less well represented landowners. Of course, this does not disprove the possibility that real estate developers dominate in those communities that did not adopt growth controls, but if they have, empirical economists have not noticed a trend in that direction. The situations in which undeveloped land values do not seem adversely affected by new restrictions appear to arise in jurisdictions in which landowners are more influential, such as the rural townships studied by Henneberry and Barrows and, as the special interest model would predict, in the Maryland state legislature that adopted the Chesapeake Bay regulations studied by Beaton and Pollock.

9 Re-zoning is Subject to Bargaining

A false implication of analyzing zoning as a means of maximizing homeowners' wealth would be that no nonconforming use should ever be allowed in a residential neighborhood unless it had located there prior to the ordinance and was thereby grandfathered. But such a conclusion mistakes the initial entitlement – the homeowners' right to be free of nonconforming uses – as the final equilibrium. Legal entitlements can be exchanged by those who hold them, and the entitlements that zoning bestows upon local residents can be analyzed in the same way that Professor Coase (1960) suggested would be appropriate for private disputes.

Richard Babcock once remarked that his famous book *The Zoning Game* (1966) was mistitled. It should be *The Re-zoning Game*. The game that I perceive is that local governments re-zone property either to gain more entitlements for themselves or to exchange some of the entitlements they already have for other benefits. Consider an undeveloped tract whose owner is an absentee. The land has just been re-zoned from commercial to its current use, agricultural, so that no development can take place. The owner has just returned from her lawyer's office with a firm opinion. The lawyer believes that the re-zoning cannot be upset by appeal to any statute or constitutional rule, at least not at a cost that justifies the expected increase in the value of the land.

The agricultural re-zoning is an example of the government acquiring an entitlement at a low cost. But it still has an opportunity cost. The landowner may be willing to pay the government to relax at least some of the zoning restrictions in order for her to make a profit. If the local government is a paradigm of the rational agent assumed by economic theory, it will sell those zoning restrictions whose collective value to the community is less than the price the landowner is willing to pay for them.

It is this scenario of exchange of zoning for some other goods that I will explore in the following sections.

10   It is Not Easy to Sell Zoning, Though

My friend Bob Nelson, whose 1977 book pioneered the view of zoning as analogous to private property rights, used to send me newspaper clippings to show that zoning could be sold. A large-scale developer would make an offer well in excess of the market value of the homes in a neighborhood. The neighbors had to all agree to the sale or none would be sold, and they had to support the re-zoning of their property by the relevant county or municipal government. Thus did several shopping centers get built in suburban areas of Atlanta, Georgia, and Washington, DC.

Close, but not quite. The final authority to make the zoning change still rested with the local governing body. The authorities presumably, in the instances in which Nelson's method was successful, were indifferent to which zoning classification applied. But if there had been much opposition outside of the neighborhood, or if the proposed development had been detrimental to the local fiscal situation, it seems more than likely that neighborhood willingness to sell would not have led to a sale.

Exchange does occur, but re-zonings are dispensed gingerly. Facilitating devices such as contract zoning (you do this, then we'll re-zone) are always subject to judicial skepticism when they are not explicitly disallowed (Wegner, 1987). A developer who needs a re-zoning is subject to transaction costs substantially greater than those incurred in obtaining title, financing, and building materials. (The chief exceptions to this are in cities legendary for corruption, but I remain unconvinced that corruption requires more than a parenthetical caveat in a general theory of zoning.)

There are a number of indirect means, however, by which a local government can benefit from a re-zoning. A new shopping center on the former farmfield is likely to generate substantial amounts of property tax revenue. A large factory may generate jobs and higher incomes, although this benefit is not easily internalized by a local government. People outside the jurisdiction are usually apt to benefit from employment gains as much as residents, so that in most communities the net employment benefit will be minor. Only in very isolated communities would the benefit of enhanced consumer opportunities of a shopping center be of much relevance to any single community. Thus fiscal benefits are the most likely currency by which a development-minded landowner might purchase a re-zoning (Fischel, 1975).

The local fiscal benefit issue has a dark (or, depending on your view of the previous process, darker) side. It is as rational for a community to use zoning to avoid fiscal costs as to obtain benefits. Since local governments are obligated to supply a number of human services to their constituents, principally schools but also welfare expenditures, they are inclined to make it difficult to permit people likely to be a net fiscal burden to locate in their jurisdiction. The pursuit of such policies is called "fiscal zoning." Although this process reduces the deadweight loss of the property tax system (Hamilton, 1975), it is often called by the pejorative "exclusionary zoning."

Many planners and social scientists make a distinction between exclusionary zoning and supposedly more benign environmental motivations (Blaesser et al., 1991). The distinction is problematical, though, when zoning is viewed as a community entitlement whose purpose is wealth maximization. The median voter does not care whether his wealth is maximized by keeping the natural landscape pristine or by keeping local property taxes low (Bogart, 1990).

Exclusionary zoning has an important nonfiscal side to it. According to more sophisticated models of local public goods (Bradford et al., 1969), local voters care about more than the direct expenditures that newcomers will occasion. They care also about the characteristics of potential residents, because local service costs may be higher for people with some characteristics than others. The obvious example is families with children and the need for schools, but it extends also to the correlation between lower incomes and higher crime rates, which are not easily set off by additional expenditures on police.

The ubiquitous hostility toward lower-income housing proposals by neighboring homeowners in most American suburbs is not simply a concern about tax rates (Bogart, 1990). Attempts merely to offset the direct fiscal costs of such housing developments (which are often made even more unwelcome by property tax exemptions) do not address these indirect costs. As a result, progress towards *Opening Up the Suburbs*, as Anthony Downs's (1973) advocacy book was entitled, has been painfully slow. More important for the present inquiry, the usual fiscal means by which transactions in zoning are facilitated are often attenuated by attention to other issues. Suburbs may maintain low population densities for reasons that have nothing to do with what are normally considered environmental issues.

11 Impact Fees may Facilitate Exchange

The foregoing section suggested that zoning is not freely alienable through the local jurisdiction. Charging "development exactions" or "impact fees" is an alternative means of collecting some revenue in exchange for re-zonings. Joseph Gyourko (1991) and I (1987) argue that use of these fees can reduce exclusionary zoning and increase the density of development, since they facilitate marginal cost pricing of new development infrastructure. Singell and Lillydahl (1990) indicate that impact fees raise housing prices, but that may reflect a benign internalization of public costs as well as a supply restraint.

The use of exactions grew especially rapidly in California following the passage of Proposition 13 in 1978, which limited local property tax collections to 1 percent, a rate less than half of the average which had previously prevailed. This limitation meant that developments that had formerly paid their own way were now fiscal burdens to their host communities, and the communities attempted to make up the revenue with impact fees and other development charges (Chapman, 1981).

The bald form of such development charges in California looks like a radical change that promoted the sale of zoning. The change is less than it would appear, however, because such fees often simply substituted for property tax payments. Prior to Proposition 13, increased development would generate significantly higher property taxes that would often offset the marginal cost of local services.

However, the use of impact fees is different in one respect. Property tax payments are reasonably predictable for developers and have an important upper limit. Since tax rates must be uniform, the local government must be willing to tax existing members (including the median voter) as well as newcomers. Impact fees have neither characteristic. The chief legal discipline is the requirement that the developer's payment be more or less rationally related to the costs the development imposes on the community. Most courts have ceased imposing much discipline on communities who stretch those boundaries.

The open-ended nature of impact fees makes zoning both more and less fungible than the property tax system. It is more fungible because fees are only loosely connected to community impacts, so that some of the developer's profit may be extracted. This makes the community more interested in bargaining. It is less fungible because the uncertainty of application, particular in multistage projects that require early commitment, makes risk-averse developers shy of beginning in the first place. It is for this reason that development-minded interest groups have promoted the use of formalized "development agreements" in California and other places.

12   The Endowment Effect Retards Transactions

Even if there were no institutional barriers to transactions between would-be developers and local authorities, the endowment effect would reduce the number of trades that would be expected by economic theory. The endowment effect is the reverse side of Adam Smith's observation on the human "propensity to truck, barter and exchange." Many people are reluctant to trade entitlements that they possess. They declare in often-repeated experiments and surveys that their asking price, or willingness to accept payment for something they feel they already own, exceeds by a factor of 2 or 3 their offer price, or willingness to pay for something they do not own (Knetsch, 1989). The disparity between offer price and asking price appears to be even greater for environmental entitlements (Knetsch, 1990; Boyce et al., 1992).

Most experiments have shown that the endowment effect arises even for trivial sums. This rules out the usual explanation for the disparity, which is that owning something makes one wealthier than not owning it, assuming that the entitlement is available without cost. The endowment effect may be enhanced by the effect of wealth on the demand for a pleasant environment, but it exists independently of it.

Evidence that the endowment effect is ubiquitous should assuage anxieties that local governments are apt to give away the store if they could freely trade re-zonings. If local citizens regard the current zoning in their community as the status quo from which they evaluate changes (and one cannot attend a zoning hearing without getting that impression), then they will demand a compensation for surrendering that entitlement that is considerably in excess of the market price, assuming a price could be imputed. As a result, fewer trades from the status quo will occur. The local environment is likely to be better, if the status quo environment is better than developers would leave it, as a result of the endowment effect.

The effect of endowment is much less clear, however, when a novel re-zoning restriction is contemplated. In the previous scenario, the developer sought fewer restrictions and was willing to pay to alter the status quo. But suppose that the community seeks more restrictions on the use of undeveloped land. What if current zoning itself is controversial, so it is not obviously the status quo?

The question is relevant because of the usual evolution of zoning restrictions over time. Rural communities are often loosely zoned or completely unzoned. Rural landowners who want some day to develop are often influential in local politics, and it is hard for planners to convince other citizens in small, rural towns that the cost of setting up zoning is worthwhile when there is nothing but trees and cornfields.

As rural communities develop on the urban fringe, however, they almost invariably become more restrictive in their zoning (Fischel, 1985, p. 67). This is partly because the cost of starting and administering zoning can be shared among more people. But it is mostly because, at least in metropolitan areas, newcomers seldom own any property other than their homes. This sets up a tension between, on the one side, the landowners and their traditional allies who stand to gain from development and, on the other side, suburban (or retirement and vacation) homeowners who see further development as potentially compromising the value of the largest single asset they own, their homes.

When a more restrictive zoning law is contemplated by such a community, what is the status quo from which the endowment effect should be calculated? It is not clear. Landowners may have expected to be able to develop their property, and the loss of this right might be regarded as even larger than the reduction of market value. But new homeowner-residents may have regarded the status quo as being the state of the community when they moved there. The endowment effect presumes that the endowment is clear, and here it is not.

What is clear is that, endowment effect or no, landowners are hardly ever offered even market value of their property when it is devalued by more restrictive zoning laws. Whether they should be paid "just compensation" for such burdens might depend on the transaction costs of making the payment, but it cannot be said that they are owed nothing because those who benefit from the re-zoning were defending the status quo.

13   Love it or Leave it?

The foregoing considerations generally militate against the view that local government zoning is apt to result in local environments that are worse than that which the majority of citizens prefer. Zoning has been around since the 1920s, which implies that most localized nuisances are the joint product of decisions by property owners and the local political process. To suggest that this is a market failure is to beg the question of what constitutes success in a nonutopian world.

To buff the panglossian gloss off of the foregoing statement, let me observe that I am aware of a number of local environments that seem a good deal more polluted and disamenable than I think the majority of citizens who live there would have accepted. This usually happens when the disamenable land use was established prior to urban growth. While it is possible to abate specific nonconforming uses, often with little or no compensation, in practice this is rarely done. Prior use is sometimes regarded as a property entitlement by the courts. More importantly, there is seldom just a single use that degrades local environments, so that upgrading the local environment involves a much larger and more controversial process such as urban renewal.

One might ask why residents move to disamenable locations. Armen Alchian once observed that people must like air pollution because so many people keep moving to Los Angeles, the most polluted large urban area in the United States. If pollution really were at socially excessive levels, why don't people just leave Los Angeles or any other disamenable urban area?

The difficulty with the love-it-or-leave-it approach to pollution is that there may be agglomeration economies that enhance productivity if many people are in close physical proximity to one another. The pull of Los

Angeles or any other large metropolitan area is that wages are higher there. The persistence of higher wages points to the increasing returns from agglomeration economies. People and firms who leave Los Angeles because of the poor air quality impose an external cost of lower productivity on those who remain. Thus if cost-effective measures can be taken to reduce air pollution, Los Angeles might be larger (Henderson, 1974). That will be economically desirable if, because of agglomeration economies in Los Angeles that are greater than those in next-best cities, productivity per worker rises as a result (Tolley, 1974; Henderson, 1988).

Agglomeration economies are also the reason that excessive suburbanization is undesirable. One cost of excessive decentralization – sprawl – is the loss of agglomeration economies. When one firm leaves the downtown or a suburban business center for the cheaper labor (because of lower commuting costs) of the low density suburbs or small towns, it imposes an external cost on the firms that remain. While the departing firm takes into account the losses to itself of not being in the business network, it does not take into account the losses it imposes on other firms by leaving, since total productivity shrinks when the network shrinks. Pushing residents away from the firms by low density land use controls gives the firms extra incentive to break up that old gang of agglomeration benefits.

Technological changes that facilitate communication and exchange without close physical proximity may reduce the advantages of agglomeration economies. It may be that, because of phones, faxes, E-mail and fiber optic communications, decentralization will not reduce productivity. But if this were the case, one would expect to see a long-term decrease in urbanization, not just suburbanization, and there is no such trend. American cities have been spreading outward at least since 1880, but the US population has remained largely urban. Doing highly paid work at home is still unusual, perhaps because inventors have yet to come up with a machine that faxes people together for lunch.

Jane Jacobs (1969) has persuasively described the importance of face-to-face contact in innovative activities such as research and development. An intriguing article by Adam Jaffe (1989) confirms the Jacobs thesis (without apparent knowledge of her work) by finding that close physical proximity of urban universities to businesses increased the number of patents generated by the businesses. The mechanism of transmitting profitable ideas seems to be, as Jaffe puts it, "informal conversations" rather than journal publication.

14   Does Zoning Contribute to Sprawl?

My aforementioned review of empirical studies, *Do Growth Controls Matter* (1990), provides a starting point for the question of whether zoning contributes to sprawl. My survey led me to conclude that growth controls, which are most common in the suburbs, (1) raised prices of existing housing in the towns that adopted new restrictions; (2) lowered the value of undeveloped land subject to the restrictions; and (3) contributed to higher metropolitan area housing prices. The first conclusion supports the idea that homeowners in the suburbs vote for land use policies that increase the value of their own assets, which is the political principle advanced in previous sections of the present chapter. The reduction in undeveloped land prices implies that developers who would have built in the growth-controlled town relocated somewhere else. The higher metropolitan housing costs suggest that the next-best sites were not in perfectly elastic supply. (Higher housing prices are not themselves evidence of inefficiency, since they may reflect better amenities as well as monopoly-like restrictions on supply (Brueckner, 1990; Fischel, 1990, p. 35).)

The question relevant for environmental quality issues is whether the sites to which developers fled are closer to or farther from the centers of metropolitan areas. As I pointed out in my book (Fischel, 1985, ch. 12), it could in principle be either direction, but I gave some reasons for suspecting that the jilted developers headed towards the cornfields and orange groves rather than toward the downtown skyscrapers. Using a theoretical urban model, Michelles White (1975) argued that the effect of suburban growth controls on sprawl was indeterminate, depending on the elasticity of substitution of land for capital.

Like most urban models, White's assumed that the city is not already developed, so that developers face none of the problems of rebuilding in declining neighborhoods of central cities or placating neighbors in the established suburbs. Using more realistic assumptions about the durability of housing, models advanced by William Moss (1977), Stephen Sheppard (1988), and Geoffrey Turnbull (1991) showed that suburban development constraints most probably induce sprawl, making the metropolitan land area larger. The empirical evidence on this, however, is not extensive, in part because of confusion between the process of suburbanization and the result that it obtains.

15   "Leapfrog" Development can Reduce Sprawl

A commonplace among urban planners is that discontiguous development in suburban fringe areas (i.e. leapfrog development) ought to be prevented by a policy that permits only contiguous development. If we consider undeveloped areas around a city as concentric rings A (next to city), B, and C (farthest from city), the idea of the policy is that suburban development should fill in all of ring A, then all of ring B, then all of ring C. The leapfrog pattern of development, in which some development occurs in rings B and C before A gets filled in, should be discouraged, according to this policy. Many modern growth management policies are explicitly motivated to prevent leapfrog development.

Several urban economists have argued, however, that leapfrog-with-infill is actually a benign process, conserving overall land resources and ultimately making for a more dense rather than a less dense city (Ohls and Pines, 1975; Mills, 1981). In other words, leapfrog-with-infill prevents sprawl. The process is explained in the urban economics text by Edwin Mills and Bruce Hamilton (1989, pp. 139–42): land speculators withhold some undeveloped land from economically irreversible commitment to the low density development demanded by the richer suburban pioneers. The speculators later sell their land for higher density development for middle-class homes.

Perhaps because urban economists seem to regard the foregoing argument as self-evident, little empirical evidence has been marshaled in support of it. Richard Peiser (1989) was among the first to present systematic evidence that, where infill does occur, it results in higher density development. He examined subdivisions in the Dallas and Washington metropolitan areas. Newer housing subdivisions on tracts apparently bypassed by the first wave of suburban development were built on smaller lots, that is, at a higher density, than their older neighbors. This is consistent with the theorists' contention that leapfrog-with-infill reduces sprawl. Peiser concludes that "a freely functioning urban land market with discontinuous patterns of development inherently promotes higher density of development . . . by later infill."

A source of confusion is that Peiser, like some others, uses "sprawl," the excessively low density *result*, as a synonym for "leapfrog," the visual metaphor for the *process*. Thus in some places Peiser's defense of leapfrog-with-infill reads as a defense of sprawl. But sprawl could result from any process that involved excessively low density development, whether it involved leapfrog-without-infill or excessively large lots contiguous to existing development.

By examining only actually developed subdivisions rather than all potential sites for infill development, Peiser deliberately ignored the effects of local government growth controls that exclude subdivisions altogether. Anti-growth suburbs often zone large tracts for farmland, wetlands, or open space, or they may impose such unreasonable exactions that development is financially foreclosed. Such areas did not appear in Peiser's sample because he was interested in evaluating a different issue – whether higher or lower densities resulted where infill *was* permitted – rather than finding out where the development foreclosed by growth controls actually ended.

The previous evidence suggests that at least some market forces would work to combat rather than cause sprawl. Yet few observers of American metropolitan areas would deny that they are unusually spread out, often with large amounts of apparently vacant land between central cities and suburban housing developments (Vesterby and Brooks, 1989). American urban density gradients are systematically lower than those of other countries, including the equally wealthy countries of Europe. US urban densities are also lower than those of Canada and Australia, whose open spaces are even wider than our own.

16   Urban Densities may be Lowered by Zoning

An example that supports Peiser's skepticism of anti-leapfrog policies and my contention that growth controls may cause sprawl is offered by George Lefcoe (1990), a University of Southern California planning-law professor and a former Los Angeles County Planning Commissioner. The California Open Space Land Act (Cal. Govt. Code §65561) tries to prevent "premature and unnecessary conversion of open-space land" and "discourage noncontiguous development patterns . . . ." Lefcoe goes on to describe how in practice the anti-leapfrog requirements actually induce greater decentralization.

The law prevented Los Angeles County (which controls the nonurbanized land) from zoning noncontiguous, undeveloped areas for urban densities. It was instead zoned for low density residential to meet open space planning requirements. (The dubious equation of low density development with open space is a separate issue dealt with below.) Areas contiguous to the urbanized area of Los Angeles County that were zoned for high density homes were oversubscribed because the legally mandated population projections that were intended to guide growth were too low. As a result, developers of higher density housing went, in Lefcoe's words, "forum shopping, usually in ever more distant venues . . . . What can't be built in the northern part of Los Angeles County might be acceptable in Lancaster or Palmdale," towns that are even more remote from existing conurbations than the unincorporated parts of the county.

Confirmation of Lefcoe's observations is "Urban sprawl has plans for a move to the desert" (*New York Times*, 16 May 1989, A14:1), describing the proposed development of a remote area of Los Angeles County and attributing it in part to density controls in less remote areas. Claude and Nina Gruen, well-known planning consultants in San Francisco, have also told me that they believe that the rapid growth of Central Valley cities such as Tracy and Stockton is directly caused by the supposedly anti-sprawl growth controls of Bay Area governments. These are just stories, of course, but they suggest an agenda for more systematic research.

There are more formal studies of individual growth control programs that indicate that their net effect is to cause new development to decentralize. A geographical study of Olmstead County, Minnesota (which surrounds Rochester), by Lizbeth Pyle (1985) found that its farmland preservation zoning caused scattered rather than concentrated development. Would sprawl have been worse without the preservation program? Jan Brueckner and David Fansler's (1983) results suggest not. Using data from 1970, which was prior to most growth control and agricultural preservation programs, they found that small and medium-sized urbanized areas surrounded by valuable farmland (like Rochester, MN) had more dense urban development than areas surrounded by low-value rural land. Taken together, these two studies suggest that without the farmland preservation zoning – a mainstay of many local growth controls – there would have been less sprawl. They also give credence to the Minneapolis-area planner who measured the success of his suburban county's farmland preservation program thus: "We're creating problems for the counties that are just outside the metro area. They don't have this type of ordinance, and we're creating a leap frog development effect into these counties" (Toner, 1978, p. 14).

The foregoing studies are supplemented in my mind by the steady accretion of re-zoning stories in which a developer proposes to use her 40-acre tract to put up, say, a hundred single-family homes, pretty much like those already standing in the rest of the community, and ends up building two dozen condominium units (a few earmarked for low-income seniors), a handful of very expensive homes, and donating the rest of the land as open space after years of negotiations with local government agencies and neighborhood groups (Frieden, 1979; Babcock and Siemon, 1985). The condos are probably higher density than the single family homes originally proposed, and local officials might proudly point to that fact as well as their inclusionary aspect. What they do not point to, except in Minneapolis, is the many housing units that have to be built somewhere else.

Although the central cities might have been willing to take the middle-class households who would have lived in the suburb had the developer's original plan gone through, all demographic trends about central cities suggest that the people headed somewhere else (Dynarski, 1986). The central cities' job and housing losses to the suburbs have continued unabated. If developers were headed back to the cities after being frustrated in the suburbs, the trend would seem to be opposite.

17   Is Sprawl Bad for the Environment?

I will not argue that the foregoing connection between local zoning and metropolitan sprawl is more than suggestive of a trend that is likely to be caused by a multitude of factors. Zoning does, however, help explain the persistent puzzle of "wasteful" commuting first pointed out by Bruce Hamilton (1982). I would like the reader to grant my point for the sake of argument, and then ask, so what? Is a sprawling metropolis worse for environmental quality than a more compact one?

Conventional wisdom seems always to answer yes, but there is some iconoclasm on the part of respected scholars. Ben Chinitz (1990) has pointed out, citing Gordon et al. (1989), that sprawl does not necessarily entail more commuting, since jobs are suburbanizing as fast as households. (See also Michelle White (1988) for evidence that commuting among suburban areas is less wasteful than might appear from the monocentric model of cities.) The argument that sprawl is environmentally bad because it interferes with farming falsely supposes that farming is better for the natural environment than suburban development. Even committed environmentalists concede that nature is as dead in the cornfield as under the asphalt. The variety of noncultivated plants and animal species is usually greater in low density suburbs than on farms. Maybe sprawl should be encouraged to give more people access to the natural environment.

It is tough being a two-handed economist. Despite the foregoing concessions, I am not convinced that metropolitan commuting is less than it would be under a more compact urban system. Even if most commuting is suburb to suburb, a more compact development pattern would reduce the distances and the external costs of using automobiles. The chief barrier to making any type of mass transit feasible in metropolitan areas is that the population densities are too low to obtain enough riders (Mills and Hamilton, 1989, ch. 12).

More important, the open land left by suburban sprawl is typically not useful as an environmental amenity or as an ecological resource. Most of the land left undeveloped by growth controls remains in private hands. The public has no access to it, so it is hardly a park. Because at least some uses must be permitted, the pattern of development is seldom spread out enough to nurture animal species that are not tolerant of humans and their domestic animals. (There is some recognition of this among authorities within the Clinton administration, and there are reports of attempts by officials to consolidate ecosystems for endangered species rather than just save one at a time after a species becomes threatened.) The pattern of low density suburban development endemic in most American cities is not, I believe, beneficial to the natural environment.

18   Would Statewide Zoning Improve Things?

Starting in the late 1960s, a number of states began to pass laws that looked similar to local zoning laws (Healy and Rosenberg, 1979). This movement took two forms. One was state preemption of local zoning in selected rural and scenic areas in which there was concern that the local governments in the area were too weak or not inclined to stop development that would threaten the resources. Examples include the creation of New York's Adirondack Park Agency, California's Statewide Coastal Zone Commission, and New Jersey's Pinelands Commission.

The other form of state zoning activity involved setting up state agencies that had the power to review local zoning decisions for, among other things, their environmental consequences. Vermont and Oregon were among the pioneers in creating statewide review of local zoning decisions. These trends were described in a book by Fred Bosselman and David Callies, *The Quiet Revolution in Land Use Control* (1971).

The quiet revolution arrived in a special package – the double-veto arrangement. The higher regulatory agency hardly ever tells a lower level of government that it must accept a development proposal that the locals do not want. A developer climbing up the new regulatory ladders of the quiet revolution can go from no to no, yes to no, and yes to yes, but cannot get from no to yes. As a result, it has in the last 25 years become a lot easier for people outside a community to stop a proposed development than to get one going.

There are exceptions. The Massachusetts Anti-Snob Zoning Law makes localities accept apartment units in some circumstances (Stockman, 1992), and Oregon's Land Conservation and Development Commission has required suburbs close to urbanized areas to zone for higher densities (Morgan, 1984). The ultimate effectiveness of such laws is not clear, but in any case these laws are far less common than the double-veto arrangements.

Allowing a higher level of government to stop a locally desired development is not in principle a bad thing if the development would have imposed substantial net costs beyond the borders of the locality. Intermunicipal spillovers are the most economically persuasive rationale for having a higher layer of land use regulation. But spillovers come in both good and bad forms. A new power plant may create unsightly transmission towers outside the community, but it also creates lower electricity costs that will facilitate regional economic development and perhaps replace an old (and usually grandfathered) polluter. A shopping center may create more traffic on roads in other communities, but it also provides a greater variety of goods for all and may be environmentally superior to piecemeal strip development. A limited-access, arterial highway is often opposed locally, even though it would reduce the congestion and pollution along existing two-lane roads.

As these examples are intended to suggest, it is not obvious that stopping unwanted development in one place makes regional economic or environmental quality any better. I am not arguing that higher-level governments should force local governments to accept things they do not want. Like private individuals whose property is taken by the government, citizens of one locality should be compensated when they have to bear special burdens for the benefit of the region as a whole (O'Hare and Sanderson, 1977). What I am arguing here is that the double-veto system skews the decision away from considering spillover benefits. The nearly exclusive attention to external costs of development has contributed to, among other things, a garbage disposal crisis in a country that has vast amounts of land where no one lives.

19   Property Rights can Help the Environment

Curbing zoning-induced sprawl requires that the people who make the decisions about zoning perceive some opportunity cost of doing so. One is already in place. When property is tightly zoned, developers are willing to pay to have fewer restrictions. The difficulty with this as the sole mechanism is that it creates a potentially endless loop. The community restricts the use of land, the developer pays to get the restrictions removed, and then the community restricts the land again. (This is the "time consistency" problem of Kydland and Prescott (1977).) The problem with this scenario is that without some outside discipline on its future conduct the community can always go back on its promises. Some external discipline on the local government is necessary for it to be able to trade at all.

The curse of sovereignty is that no one else can hold the sovereign to keep its promises. Political theorists and economists have dealt with this in several nonconstitutional ways, including reputation and competition among sovereigns (Taylor, 1985; Grossman and Noh, 1990). But a precondition for competition is that those subject to the sovereign's reneging can at some point remove their assets from his reach. Land is hard to remove from the reach of the government.

An alternative means is to appeal to constitutions, in which some more or less independent source of authority, such as a court of law, enforces the promises. One interpretation of the property and contract-related clauses of the US Constitution is that they are intended to do just that (Epstein, 1985; Holmes, 1988). Enforcement of prior promises enables all parties to gain by facilitating exchange over time.

The takings clause of the US Constitution, which holds that property shall not be taken for public use without just compensation, is an ideal but under-utilized vehicle by which local government can be made to perceive an opportunity cost when it contemplates adopting more than normal restrictions on developable land (Ellickson, 1977). If local governments were subject to having to pay monetary damages for adopting regulations that are abnormally severe, they would only adopt those that local residents were willing to pay for.

The Constitution's contract clause forbids the states from impairing the obligation of contracts. Application of the contract clause to local governments' own dealings about re-zoning would enable them, within the bounds of conscionability, to bargain with developers subject to regulations that are not so extreme as to be judged takings. This allows communities to engage in a wider range of contracts pertaining to the police power than is now usually permitted. The takings clause makes the community perceive an opportunity cost when it contemplates increasing restrictions, while the contract clause allows it to perceive an opportunity cost for restrictions that are not judged to be takings. Normal democratic processes and the endowment effect would, I believe, be sufficient to deter community officials from applying an excessively high discount rate to the benefits of the status quo zoning.

An alternative way of perceiving opportunity cost is to increase the size of the jurisdiction that does the zoning. Here the opportunity cost comes from politics: the outsiders to the community who are excluded by zoning have more of a say in the make-up of state and national legislatures than they do in local legislatures. Thus larger governments are more apt to internalize both costs and benefits of the political process (Danielson, 1976; Komesar, 1978). One problem with the larger legislatures was described above: the process of their involvement has usually been in the form of the double-veto, which, if anything, makes many of the problems of localism worse.

Most economists are also apt to be skeptical of the ability of large legislatures to balance costs and benefits. I am, too, but I must point out that the Constitutional discipline that is the alternative to politics involves equally problematical decision makers. There is nothing in the qualifications of state and federal judges that makes them more likely to correctly balance subtle economic distinctions (Ely, 1980). In this respect, judicial independence from the electorate is a liability rather than an asset, since isolation means that the judges cannot get much relevant information about preferences.

Thus my recommendation is a mix of judicial activism and tolerance. The activism should come in the form of skepticism of *local* government regulation and protection of owners of undeveloped land, who lack realistic influence in local politics and who cannot provide the discipline of taking their assets elsewhere (Fischel, 1991). The tolerance should come in the form of approval of contract zoning when taking issues have been resolved. There are some public–private contracts that are so one-sided that judges should intervene. An example is the condition imposed by regulators in Nollan v. California Coastal Commission (1987) that required a homeowner to grant public access across his land in exchange for a land use permit to build an ordinary-sized house (Fischel, 1988, p. 1588). But, for the most part, voluntary bargaining between developer-landowners and local government officials should be explicitly tolerated and made subject to binding contracts.

The course that I advocate here has been strenuously resisted by environmental advocates, who see in the takings clause a limit on government's ability to control environmental degradation (Bosselman et al., 1973; Williams et al., 1984). But a takings jurisprudence that focused on the behavior of local governments and held their standards up to wider norms would not challenge the ability of state and national officials to act. A standard that focused on parochial decisions by local majorities is more likely to improve the environment of the larger region by promoting more compact development within suburban areas.

References

Anderson, William. 1927: Zoning in Minnesota: eminent domain vs. policy power. *National Municipal Review*, 16 (October), 624–9.

Arrow, Kenneth. 1951: *Social Choice and Individual Values*. New York: Wiley.

Babcock, Richard F. 1966: *The Zoning Game*. Madison, WI: University of Wisconsin Press.

Babcock, Richard F. (ed.) 1987: Exactions: a controversial new source for municipal funds. *Law and Contemporary Problems*, 50 (Winter).

Babcock, Richard F. and Siemon, Charles L. 1985: *The Zoning Game Revisited*. Boston, MA: Oelgeschlager, Gunn and Hahn for Lincoln Institute of Land Policy.

Baker, Newman F. 1927: *Legal Aspects of Zoning*. Chicago, IL: University of Chicago Press.

Barr, J. and Davis, Otto. 1966: An elementary political and economic theory of the expenditures of local governments. *Southern Economic Journal*, 33 (October), 149–65.

Beaton, W. Patrick, and Pollock, Marcus. 1992: Economic impact of growth management policies surrounding the Chesapeake Bay. *Land Economics*, 68 (November), 434–53.

Bergstrom, Theodore C. and Goodman Robert P. 1973: Private demands for public goods. *American Economic Review*, 63 (June), 280–96.

Blaesser, Brian W. and seven others 1991: Advocating affordable housing in New Hampshire: the Amicus Curiae brief of the American Planning Association in Wayne Britton v. Town of Chester. *Washington University Journal of Urban and Contemporary Law*, 40 (Summer–Fall), 3–48.

Bloom, Howard S. and Ladd, Helen F. 1982: Property tax revaluation and tax levy growth. *Journal of Urban Economics*, 11 (January), 73–84.

Bogart, William T. 1990: Property taxation, intergovernmental grants, and housing markets. *Proceedings of the Eighty-Third Annual Conference*, National Tax Association–Tax Institute of America, 122–7.

Borcherding, Thomas, and Deacon, Robert. 1972: The demand for the services of non-federal governments. *American Economic Review*, 62 (December), 891–901.

Bosselman, Fred P. and Callies, David. 1971: *The Quiet Revolution in Land Use Control*. Washington, DC: Council on Environmental Quality.

Bosselman, Fred P., Callies, David, and Banta, John. 1973: *The Taking Issue*. Washington, DC: Council on Environmental Quality.

Bowen, Howard. 1943: The interpretation of voting in the allocation of economic resources. *Quarterly Journal of Economics*, 58 (November), 27–48.

Boyce, Rebecca R., Brown, Thomas C., McClelland, Gary H., Peterson, George L. and Schulze, William D. 1992: An experimental examination of intrinsic values as a source of WTA–WTP disparity. *American Economic Review*, 82 (December), 1366–73.

Bradford, David F., Malt, Richard A. and Oates, Wallace E. 1969: The rising costs of local public services: some evidence and reflections. *National Tax Journal*, 22 (June), 185–202.

Briffault, Richard 1990: Our localism: Part I – the structure of local government law. *Columbia Law Review*, 90 (January), 1–115.

Brueckner, Jan K. 1982: A test for allocative efficiency in the local public sector. *Journal of Public Economics*, 19 (December), 311–21.

Brueckner, Jan K. 1990: Growth controls and land values in an open city. *Land Economics*, 66 (August), 237–48.

Brueckner, Jan K. and Fansler, David A. 1983: The economics of urban sprawl: theory and evidence on the spatial sizes of cities. *Review of Economics and Statistics*, 65 (August), 479–82.

Bryden, David P. 1977: "The Impact of Variances: A Study of Statewide Zoning." *Minnesota Law Review* 61 (May), 769–840.

Callies, David L., Neuffer, Nancy C. and Calibosco, Carlito P. 1991: Ballot box zoning: initiative, referendum and the law. *Washington University Journal of Urban and Contemporary Law*, 39 (Spring}, 53–98.

Cappell, Andrew J. 1991: A walk along willow: patterns of land use coordination in prezoning New Haven. *Yale Law Journal*, 101 (December), 617–42.

Chapman, Jeffrey. 1981: *Proposition 13 and Land Use: A Case Study of Fiscal Limits in California*. Lexington, MA: Lexington Books.

Chinitz, Benjamin. 1990: Growth management: good for the town, bad for the nation? *APA Journal*, 8 (Winter), 3–8.

Coase, Ronald H. 1960: The problem of social cost. *Journal of Law and Economics*, 3 (October), 1–44.

Crecine, John P., Davis, Otto A. and Jackson, John E. 1967: Urban property markets: some empirical results and their implications for municipal zoning. *Journal of Law and Economics*, 10 (October), 79–100.

Danielson, Michael N. 1976: *The Politics of Exclusion*. New York: Columbia University Press.

Denzau, Arthur T. and Weingast, Barry R. 1982: Forward: the political economy of land use regulation. *Urban Law Annual*, 23 (1982), 385–405.

Downs, Anthony. 1957: *An Economic Theory of Democracy*. New York: Harper & Row.

Downs, Anthony. 1973: *Opening Up the Suburbs: An Urban Strategy for America*. New Haven, CT: Yale University Press.

Dublin, Jeffrey, A., Kiewit, D. Roderick, and Noussair, Charles N. 1992: Voting on growth control measures: preferences and strategies. *Economics and Politics*, 4 (July), 191–213.

Dynarski, Mark. 1986: Household formation and suburbanization, 1970–1980. *Journal of Urban Economics*, 19 (January), 71–87.

Ellickson, Robert C. 1973: Alternatives to zoning; covenants, nuisance rules, and fines as land use controls. *University of Chicago Law Review*, 40 (Summer), 681–782.

Ellickson, Robert C. 1977: Suburban growth controls: an economic and legal analysis. *Yale Law Journal*, 86 (January), 385–511.

Ellickson, Robert C. and Tarlock, A. Dan. 1981: *Land Use Controls*. Boston, MA: Little, Brown.

Ely, John Hart. 1980: *Democracy and Distrust: A Theory of Judicial Review*. Cambridge, MA: Harvard University Press.

Epstein, Richard A. 1985: *Takings: Private Property and the Power of Eminent Domain*. Cambridge, MA: Harvard university Press.

Euclid v. Ambler, 272 US 365 (1926).

Fischel, William A. 1975: Fiscal and environmental considerations in the location of firms in suburban communities. In Edwin S. Mills and Wallace E. Oates (eds), *Fiscal Zoning and Land Use Controls*, Lexington, MA: Heath-Lexington Books, 119–74.

Fischel, William A. 1978: A property rights approach to municipal zoning. *Land Economics*, 54 (February), 64–81.

Fischel, William A. 1985: *The Economics of Zoning Laws*. Baltimore, MD: Johns Hopkins University Press.

Fischel, William A. 1987: the economics of land use exactions: a property rights analysis. *Law and Contemporary Problems*, 50 (Winter), 101–13.

Fischel, William A. 1988: Introduction: utilitarian balancing and formalism in takings. *Columbia Law Review*, 88 (December}, 1581–99.

Fischel, William A. 1990: *Do Growth Controls Matter?* Cambridge, MA.: Lincoln Institute of Land Policy.

Fischel, William A. 1991: Exploring the Kozinski paradox: why is more efficient regulation a taking of property? *Chicago-Kent Law Review*, 67 (3), 865–912.

Frech, H. E., III, and Lafferty, Ronald N. 1984: The effect of the California Coastal Commission on housing prices. *Journal of Urban Economics*, 16 (July), 105–23.

Freeman, Alan D. 1976: Give and take: distributing local environmental control through land-use regulation. *Minnesota Law Review*, 60, 883–970.

Frieden, Bernard J. 1979; *the Environmental Protection Hustle*. Cambridge, MA.: MIT Press.

Gardiner, John A. and Lyman, Theodore R. 1978: *Decisions for Sale: Corruption and Reform in Land Use and Building Regulation*. New York: Praeger.

Gordon, Peter, Kumar, Ajay, and Richardson, Harry W. 1989: Congestion, changing metropolitan structure, and city size in the United States. *International Regional Science Review*, 12 (1), 45–56.

Grossman, Herschel I. and Noh, Suk Jae. 1990: A theory of kleptocracy with probabilistic survival and reputation. *Economics and Politics*, 2 (July), 157–71.

Gyourko, Joseph. 1991: Impact fees, exclusionary zoning, and the density of new development. *Journal of Urban Economics*, 30 (September), 242–56.

Hamilton, Bruce W. 1975: Zoning and property taxation in a system of local governments. *Urban Studies*, 12 (June), 205–11.

Hamilton, Bruce W. 1982: Wasteful commuting. *Journal of Political Economy*, 90 (October), 1035–53.

Healy, Robert G. and Rosenberg, John. 1979: *Land Use and the States*, 2nd edn. Baltimore, MD: Johns Hopkins University Press.

Henderson, J. Vernon. 1974: Optimum city size; the external diseconomy question. *Journal of Political Economy*, 82 (March), 373–88.

Henderson, J. Vernon. 1985: The impact of zoning policies which regulate housing quality. *Journal of Urban Economics*, 18 (November), 302–12.

Henderson, J. Vernon. 1988: *Urban Development: Theory Fact and Illusion*. New York: Oxford University Press.

Hennebury, David, and Barrows, Richard. 1990: Capitalization of exclusive agricultural zoning into farmland prices. *Land Economics*, 66 (August), 249–58,.

Hochman, Oded, and Ofek, Haim. 1979: A theory of the behavior of municipal governments: the case of internalizing pollution externalities. *Journal of Urban Economics*, 6 (October), 416–31.

Holcombe, Randall G. 1989: The median voter model in public choice theory. *Public Choice*, 61, 115–25.

Holmes, Stephen. 1988: Precommitment and the paradox of democracy. In Jon Elster and Rune Slagstad (eds), *Constitutionalism and Democracy*, Cambridge: Cambridge University Press.

Holtz-Eakin, Douglas. and Rosen, Harvey S. 1989: the "rationality" of municipal capital spending: evidence from New Jersey. *Regional Science and Urban Economics*, 19 (August), 517–36.

Jacobs, Jane. 1969: *The Economy of Cities*. New York; Random House.

Jaffe, Adam B. 1989: Real effects of academic research. *American Economic Review*, 79 (December), 957–70.

Katz, Lawrence, and Rosen, Kenneth. 1987: The interjurisdictional effects of growth controls on housing prices. *Journal of Law and Economics*, 30 (April), 149-60.

Knapp, Gerrit J. 1985; The price effects of urban growth boundaries in metropolitan Portland, Oregon. *Land Economics*, 61 (February), 28–35.

Knetsch, Jack L. 1989: The endowment effect and evidence of nonreversible indifference curves. *American Economic Review*, 79 (December), 1277–84.

Knetsch, Jack L. 1990: Environmental policy implications of disparities between willingness to pay and compensation demanded measures of values. *Journal of Environmental Economics and Management*, 18 (May), 227–37.

Komesar, Neil K. 1978: Housing, zoning, and the public interest. In Burton A. Weisbrod (ed.), *Public Interest Law*, Berkeley, CA: University of California Press.

Kydland, Finn E. and Prescott, Edward C. 1977; Rules rather than discretion: the inconsistency of optimal plans. *Journal of Political Economy*, 85 (June), 473–92.

Lefcoe, George. 1990: How California state planning requirements restrict market-friendly local governments and legitimize market-hostile ones. Working Paper, University of Southern California Law Center.

Levmore, Saul. 1991: Takings, torts, and special interests. *Virginia Law Review*, 77 (October), 1333–68.

Mark, Jonathan H. and Goldberg, Michael A. 1986: A study of the impacts of zoning on housing values over time. *Journal of Urban Economics*, 20 (November), 254–73.

Maser, Steven, M., Riker, William H. and Rosett, Richard N. 1977: The effects of zoning and externalities of the price of land: an empirical analysis of Monroe County, New York. *Journal of Law and Economics*, 20 (April), 111–32.

Mills, David E. 1981: Growth, speculation and sprawl in a monocentric city. *Journal of Urban Economics*, 10 (September), 201–26.

Mills, Edwin S. and Hamilton, Bruce W. 1989; *Urban Economics*, 4th edn. Glenview, IL: Scott, Foresman.

Morgan, Terry D. 1984: Exclusionary zoning: remedies under Oregon's land use planning program. *Environmental Law*, 14, 779–841.

Moss, William G. 1977: Large lot zoning, property taxes, and metropolitan area. *Journal of Urban Economics*, 4 (October), 408–27.

Nelson, Robert A. 1977: *Zoning and Property Rights*. Cambridge, MA: MIT Press.

Nollan v. California Coastal Commission, 483 US 825 (1987).

Oates, Wallace, E. 1969: The effects of property taxes and local public spending on property values; an empirical study of tax capitalization and the tiebout hypothesis. *Journal of Political Economy*, 77 (November), 957–71.

O'Hare, Michael, and Sanderson, Debra R. 1977: Fair compensation and the boomtown problem. *Urban Law Annual*, 14, 101–33.

Ohls, James C. and Pines, David. 1975: Discontinuous urban development and economic efficiency. *Land Economics*, 51 (August), 224–34.

Peiser, Richard B. 1989: Density and urban sprawl. *Land Economics*, 65 (August), 193–204.

Pennsylvania Coal v. Mahon, 260 US 393 (1922).

Peterson, George E. 1974: Land prices and factor substitution in the metropolitan housing market. Working Paper, Urban Institute, Washington, DC.

Pyle, Lizbeth. 1985: The land market beyond the urban fringe. *Geographical Review*, 75 (January), 32–43.

Rose, Carol M. 1983: Planning and dealing: piecemeal land controls as a problem of local legitimacy. *California Law Review*, 7, 837–912.

Schwartz, Seymour I., Hansen, David E. and Green, Richard. 1981: Suburban growth controls and the price of new housing. *Journal of Environmental Economics and Management*, 8 (December), 303–20.

Sheppard, Stephen. 1988: The qualitative economics of development controls. *Journal of Urban Economics*, 24 (November), 310–30.

Siegan, Bernard H. 1972: *Land Use without Zoning*. Lexington, MA: Heath-Lexington Books.

Singell, Larry D. and Lillydahl, Jane H. 1990: An empirical examination of the effect of impact fees on the housing market. *Land Economics*, 66 (February), 82–92.

Sonstelie, Jon C. and Portney, Paul R. 1978: Profit maximizing communities and the theory of local public expenditure. *Journal of Urban Economics*, 56 (April), 263–77.

Stigler, George J. 1971: The theory of economic regulation. *Bell Journal of Economics*, 2 (Spring), 3–21.

Stockman, Paul K. 1992: Anti-snob zoning in Massachusetts: assessing one attempt at opening the suburbs to affordable housing. *Virginia Law Review*, 78 (March), 535–80.

Taylor, Herb. 1985: Time inconsistency: a potential problem for policymakers. *Business Review of Federal Reserve Bank of Philadelphia* (March–April).

Tiebout, Charles M. 1956: A pure theory of local expenditures. *Journal of Political Economy*, 64 (October), 416–24.

Tolley, George S. 1974: The welfare economics of city bigness. *Journal of Urban Economics*, 1 (July), 324–45.

Toner, William 1978: *Saving Farms and Farmland: A Community Guide*. Chicago, IL: American Society of Planning Officials.

Turnbull, Geoffrey K. 1991. A comparative dynamic analysis of zoning in a growing city. *Journal of Urban Economics*, 29 (March), 235–48.

Vaillancourt, François and Monty, Luc. 1985: The effect of agricultural zoning on land prices, Quebec, 1975–81. *Land Economics*, 61 (February), 36–42.

Vesterby, Marlow and Brooks, Douglas H. 1989: Land use change in fast-growth areas, 1950–1980. In Ralph E. Heimlich (ed.), *Land Use Transition in Urbanizing Areas*, Washington, DC: The Farm Foundation.

Wegner, Judith W. 1987: Moving toward the bargaining table: contract zoning, development agreements, and the theoretical foundations of government land use deals. *North Carolina Law Review*, 65, 957–1038.

White, Michelle J. 1975: The effect of zoning on the size of metropolitan areas. *Journal of Urban Economics*, 5 (April), 219–40.

White, Michelle J. 1988: Urban commuting journeys are not "wasteful." *Journal of Political Economy*, 96 (October), 1097–1110.

Williams, Norman, Jr, Smith, Marlin, Siemon, Charles, Mandelker, Daniel, and Babcock, Richard. 1984: The White River Junction Manifesto. *Vermont Law Review*, 9 (Fall), 193–245.

5

Public Policies for Land Conservation

Ian Hodge

Introduction

Discussions of environmental economics are often based on two general assumptions: first that the focus of concern and hence the objectives of policy are to prevent the production of an environmental bad rather than to promote the provision of an environmental benefit; second that the environmental changes can be quantified in at least some unit, that is, that they are commensurable, even if a satisfactory monetary valuation of the environmental changes proves to be elusive. Public policies for land conservation often occur in circumstances within which these assumptions do not hold. And this has important implications for the forms which land policies take.

Land conservation may be interpreted in two ways. The first is concerned with the maintenance of the productive capacity of the land and the soil. The second relates to a wide range of environmental attributes which are of value to or which impose costs on those other than the owner or occupier. This chapter emphasizes the second of these elements. These environmental attributes thus primarily involve external benefits and costs and commonly have public good characteristics, exhibiting differing degrees of rivalness and excludability (Whitby, 1990). It is important to emphasize the multiple nature of most rural land use, especially in a European context. Practically all land is used for some form of agricultural production, so that landscape, habitat, and recreation are generally a joint product.

In this context, land quality can be assessed within a multiplicity of dimensions. Sometimes an area of land has value primarily because it offers open space within an otherwise built-up environment. Sometimes it is the more detailed attributes of the way in which it is used which are of significance, often because the level of development is relatively low, resulting in the retention of features which have importance for landscape or wildlife. At the same time, many land use attributes impose external costs, perhaps being visually unattractive or allowing leaching of chemicals into water supplies.

The impact of land use on landscape is often an important factor and illustrates some of the difficulties which arise for conservation policy. The appreciation of landscape is especially subjective and opinions vary greatly between observers. In itself this may be no different from the variations in people's appreciation of paintings by Picasso or of the taste of rhubarb. A landscape is composed of many elements, each of which may be thought to add or to detract from the whole. But, perhaps invariably in a valued landscape, the whole is worth more than the sum of the parts. It is the relationship between the components and their associations with history or culture which create the value. However, if the state is to take action in order to control landscape quality, some collective view needs to be taken with respect to the value of particular landscapes. In England, for example, the Countrywise Commission (1987) takes account of these types of factors and the feelings which they evoke in the observer in deciding whether to recommend particular designations. But, in contrast with rhubarb or paintings by Picasso, there is no market within which preferences may be revealed.

This chapter is concerned with public policy mechanisms which seek to influence the externalities associated with the use of land. In practice the range of mechanisms and contexts is extremely broad. We therefore seek here to reflect the range of objectives and mechanisms which can be adopted, drawing particularly on the approaches which have been adopted in the regulation of land use in Europe and in the United Kingdom in particular.

Objectives and Mechanisms

As illustrated in table 5.1, the objectives of intervention may be characterized as falling into three categories: preventing certain types of land use from being implemented, modifying the form of existing land uses, and stimulating land uses which would otherwise not be in place. The latter category includes the maintenance of land uses which would otherwise be replaced by something else. Clearly, in practice, the distinction between a modified land use and a different land use is not clear cut; the intention is simply to represent a greater degree of difference.

Preventing land uses
The most common objective here involves urban containment. Urban sprawl is commonly held to cause external costs. These arise from a concern that the loss of agricultural land may cause a critical constraint on

Table 5.1 Framework for land conservation policies

	Preventing	*Modifying*	*Stimulating*
Regularization	Zoning Development control		
Disincentives		Cross-compliance Tax penalties, planning gain	
Incentives		Tax incentives Environmental contracts	
Land acquisition		Public purchase	

Promoting
  intermediate
  action
		Transfer of
		  development
		  rights
		Convenants
			CARTs

food production at some future date, that low density development tends to raise the costs of service provision and that scattered unplanned development tends to be visually unattractive and to undermine agricultural management where there is a potential for urban development in the future. See for example Hall et al. (1973) for a discussion of the objectives of urban containment.

Modifying land uses
Whether or not broad categories of land use may be prevented, there is often a further concern that, in the absence of control, the characteristics of the ensuing land uses will be undesirable. This may be either in terms of the form of urban land use or in terms of the form of a rural land use. For example, in the absence of control, farming may lead to unacceptable levels of pollution or it may fail to promote a desired quality of landscape or quantity or variety of wildlife.

Stimulating land uses
Finally there is a concern to promote new land uses which lead to the production of public goods. This is probably the least prevalent form of objective. However, the aim to stimulate particular forms of land use is not uncommon. For instance in the United Kingdom there are policies to promote species-rich meadowland, wetlands, and land which is available for public access.

The available mechanisms

Pursuit of these objectives implies a need for a different form of land use policy. Essentially, land uses are controlled either by changing the ownership of property rights or by establishing incentives which lead the existing owners to change their behavior. See Bromley (1991) for a more formal treatment of property rights arrangements. Table 5.1 illustrates a range of options including regulation, disincentives and incentives applied to the landowner or occupier and the acquisition of the land by an agent of the state, and incentives directed through an intermediary.

A critical factor in the choice of instrument concerns whether or not the landowner is considered to hold a right to proceed with the action which the state wishes to prevent or modify. If the owner is deemed to hold the relevant right, then it will be appropriate to make the scheme voluntary or at least to pay compensation for any costs which are imposed by the constraint. For instance, it might be thought desirable to prevent a landowner from proceeding with conventional agriculture in order to create a nature reserve on his land. If it is accepted that he should have the right to farm in the conventional way, the implication is that he should be compensated for being prevented from doing so. On the other hand, a regulation may be passed in order to prevent him from causing pollution, such as allowing hazardous chemicals to leach into water supplies. In this case it would generally be held that a landowner does not have a right to allow this and so no compensation would be paid. While many cases are clear cut, in the context of land conservation they are often controversial. This is discussed further in Hodge (1989).

Regulation involves the separate treatment of individual property rights. Zoning, for instance, operates through the withdrawal of particular property rights from owners within defined localities. This has been discussed in chapter 4. Regulation may be very specific. For instance, in the United Kingdom, Tree Preservation Orders may be used to restrict the owner's rights over individual trees. An alternative approach is to regulate uses on a case-by-case basis, which forms the basis of development control. We return to this example below.

Incentives to existing owners may be either positive or negative. Disincentives may take the form of tax penalties or they may be linked to other policies by means of cross-compliance. In the latter case the disincentive takes the form of a loss of entitlement to some other state payment, particularly to agricultural support payments. But the use of disincentives is relatively rare, particularly in the context of rural land use policy. Policies more commonly offer positive incentives for landowners to take actions favored by the state. One approach is to offer tax relief to owners but this suffers from the disadvantage that owners paying higher levels of tax will tend to have a greater incentive than those paying lower levels, and incentive fluctuates through time with changes in the rates of tax selected for the purposes of macroeconomic management. Thus the incentive to the landowner is unlikely to coincide with the values which are placed on the external benefits which result from his actions. More directly, the state may offer environmental contracts so that in effect it purchases certain environmental services from landowners. This approach is elaborated later.

With public land acquisition, an agent of the state takes control of the entire bundle of rights conventionally associated with landownership. This tends to be an approach only adopted in extreme circumstances, typically where the desired change in land use is so fundamental that the owner would be unable to continue to generate an income, such as where the land is taken for a new road or for a nature reserve.

The final category of mechanism involves a less direct form of intervention and in effect establishes incentives for there to be a change in the ownership of property rights within the private sector. The objective of state action is to promote the ownership of rights by organizations whose objectives coincide with those of the state. As a third example, we consider this option in more detail below.

Development Control

The development control mechanism lies at the center of land use regulation in Britain (see Pearce (1992) for a brief description and assessment of the land use planning system). The approach dates back to legislation introduced in 1947 which in effect nationalized the rights of landowners to develop their land. Once these rights were lost, owners had to apply to the local planning authority for permission if they wanted to undertake building works or major changes in land use. Applications are considered by a local planning committee comprising elected councillors who have to take account of guidance offered by central government and local development plans. In practice some decisions are delegated to professional planners and these professionals may in any case be quite influential in advising elected councillors as to appropriate decisions. Where owners feel aggrieved by a decision, they have the right of appeal to a central government planning inspectorate, which may reverse the local decision.

The system has been the key mechanism in the process of urban containment, protecting agricultural land from urbanization. The policy has been operated particularly strictly in areas of Green Belt which have been defined surrounding many major urban centers, but development in open countryside has also largely been prevented throughout the country except where a landowner can demonstrate that the proposed development is necessary for the purposes of agricultural production. Thus, by most accounts the policy has been effective in giving considerable protection to the countryside (Pearce, 1992).

While there are central government guidelines, development plans, and the possibility of appeal, the system leaves discretion to local commitees to take account of the particular circumstances of each individual application. Thus in concept, costs and benefits can be weighed in every case. It might thus be anticipated that the pattern of development which emerged would reflect closely the interests of the wider community, but that the transactions costs of operating the system would be relatively high.

Not surprisingly, such a detailed degree of interference in individuals' actions is a source of controversy. See for instance criticisms by Evans (1988) and defence by Grant (1988). One major concern is that the planning system has been excessively restrictive. Other concerns have been discussed by Pearce (1987). Restrictions on the supply of land for development have had the effect of raising the prices of both land for housing and housing itself. This in turn has led to higher densities of new development and the re-development of urban areas at higher densities. Also, because of the strict limits on development outside of urban areas, there has been a steady process of in-filling any remaining areas of open space. Evans (1988, p. 28) refers to an environmental swap: maintaining environmental quality in the rural areas at the expense of urban areas. Furthermore, there have been knock-on effects – raising costs of economic activities, damaging international competitiveness, and lowering the rate of investment in industry.

The situation is illustrated in figure 5.1. This shows two types of rent curves. R_{nc} represents the rent on land in urban uses, which declines with distance from the urban center in the absence of development control. R_a represents the rent for agricultural use. This is assumed to remain constant, thus neglecting any possible influence of transport costs or costs imposed on agricultural uses as a result of urban pressures. These two curves indicate that the urban area would extend to the point where R_{nc} and R_a intersect. In practice this would not be a discrete transition; rather, around this margin the values of individual plots of land would vary with specific local circumstances resulting in a reduction in the proportion of the area developed and a reduction in the density of development. The rent curves thus represent the average rent levels at particular distances from the city center.

The introduction of tight controls within an area of Green Belt shifts the rent curve for urban uses to R_{dc}. The Green Belt thus remains predominantly in agricultural use. However, this restriction increases the value of urban uses both within and beyond the Green Belt, represented by the shaded areas *A* and *B* respectively. The effect is emphasized for existing

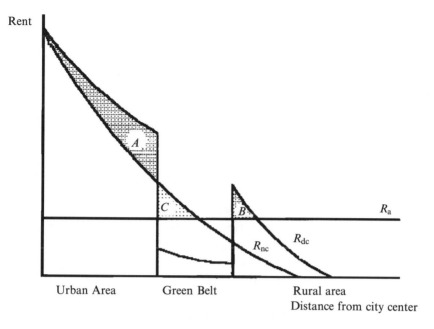

Figure 5.1 Land conservation surrounding urban areas.

property within and close to the Green Belt as a result of the more attractive environment which it tends to promote. These circumstances also generate incentives for the higher densities of urban use referred to earlier. In addition, there is a loss to owners of undeveloped land within the Green Belt, represented by area *C*.

Even outside of the Green Belt, planning permission is restricted and is given on a site-by-site basis. Thus development may be possible within certain categories of land, such as on small sites within settlements or around the edges of expanding towns. Therefore there is considerable difference between the prices of land where development may be possible and those where it is effectively impossible, even at the same distance from the city center. Because of this, planning policy decisions which move land from one category to the other can lead to considerable capital gains. Development land prices are generally from 20 to 200 times the agricultural values, depending upon the development pressures within an area.

The potential capital gains create considerable incentives for rent-seeking behavior, in terms of both attempting to influence decisions on applications for permission to develop individual sites and attempting to influence the development plans which establish the basis against which individual decisions will be taken.

The question of whether the gains accruing to landowners should be recaptured by the state is one which has continued ever since the development control system was introduced. Over the years various schemes have been adopted, such as development land taxes, in order to transfer some of the gain to the state. Most recently, in the absence of any formal tax, planning authorities have been entering into "voluntary" agreements with developers for them to provide benefits in kind to the local community as part of a development proposal. This is referred to as planning gain. Bowers (1992) discusses the economics of this approach.

In practice, of course, an evaluation of the system is fraught with difficulty. Amongst many complications, it is not known whether or not the outcome is socially desirable. Given the intangible nature of many of the factors involved, no satisfactory calculation of the costs and benefits is feasible.

A key issue concerns the representativeness of the planning committee. Every democratic system is imperfect, but there are grounds for particular concern in this context. For instance, certain sections of the population may face particular incentives to get themselves into positions of responsibility. This may be those with a financial interest in promoting development who can exert an influence which may be, perhaps indirectly, to their own financial advantage. Alternatively, local residents may be concerned to restrict the extent of local development in order to preserve the characteristics of their local area. Commonly such people may be better educated and more articulate than those who may be in favor of development for the employment opportunities which it could promote. Thus, those against development may be more effective in influencing local democratic processes, introducing a bias against development.

Environmental Contracts for Countryside Management

The development control system in Britain has had little impact on the way in which agriculture has been practised. Changes within agriculture, such as ploughing up pasture or removing hedges, do not fall within the definition of development as specified in the Town and Country Planning legislation which established the development control process. But there is a further concern that controls which have effect only in respect of land use change would be incapable of generating the necessary incentives to ensure that farmers managed their land in such a way as to maintain a desired environmental quality. Such incentives may be generated through the use of environmental contracts. These take the form of an agreement between a government agency and an individual farmer, under which the farmer agrees to farm in a particular way in return for a payment from the government.

This type of mechanism has now been implemented in a number of ways in the United Kingdom and there are similar arrangements in Germany, France and the Netherlands (OECD, 1988). The first to be widely applied concerned the management of Sites of Special Scientific Interest (SSSIs). Under legislation dating from 1981, owners of SSSIs are notified of Potentially Damaging Operations (PDOs). These are actions which could damage the conservation value of the site, such as cultivation, application of chemicals, burning, or drainage. When an owner proposes to undertake a PDO, he is required to notify the relevant government agency (English Nature in England). This agency may then either give consent or else offer the owner a management agreement under which he would receive compensation payments for not going ahead with the proposed actions. The agreement is essentially voluntary, although in some cases, *in extremis*, the agency does have powers of compulsory purchase if agreement cannot be reached. In practice, this power has very rarely been used, although it remains as a threat in the negotiations. As of March 1991, management agreements covered an area of nearly 49,000 hectares (nearly 120,000 acres) in Great Britain.

A second mechanism of this type applies within designated Environmentally Sensitive Areas (ESAs). This is a policy deriving from European Union legislation and introduced in 1987 under which farmers are offered flat rate annual payments in return for accepting a standard agreement as to how they should manage their land. Agreements which are currently being offered last for ten years. To date 16 ESAs have been designated in England and Wales and a further six have been proposed. By 1992, agreements in ESAs covered over 300,000 acres. Some details relating to the basic tier (i.e. the basic form of agreement) of the South Downs ESA, an area of chalk uplands in the south of England, are shown in table 5.2. This agreement aims to maintain the landscape and grassland on the downs. Other tiers offer agreements to farmers giving higher payments for reverting arable land to chalk downland or to permanent grass. There is also a tier which gives payments to farmers who agree to limit the use of pesticides in strips around the edges of arable fields.

While the approaches on SSSIs and in ESAs are similar, they do have some significant differences. In the case of the SSSIs, each individual site is designated in respect of some particular conservation value with the objective of protecting the best examples of representative habitats. Management agreements are tailored to the specific circumstances and the compensation payment is agreed on a site-by-site basis. In practice, many owners of SSSIs do not have management agreements and some payments are nominal. On the other hand there have also been some extremely large and well publicized payments. Because of the key nature of the sites, the government agency involved is under considerable pressure to protect the site and hence is in a relatively weak bargaining position.

The approach towards ESAs is different. Agreements are available to all farmers within areas which are designated on the basis of broad landscape and habitat objectives. Participants have to opt for one of a

Table 5.2   The South Downs environmentally sensitive area (tier 1)

Purpose: to maintain the South Downs ESA landscape and grassland on the chalk downs

Major conditions:
1 Maintain grassland and do not plough, harrow, level or re-seed the land
2 Graze with cattle or sheep or both but avoid poaching, undergrazing or overgrazing
3 Do not cut grass for hay or silage or top the grass before 16 July
4 Do not apply organic or inorganic fertilizer
5 Do not use fungicides or insecticides
6 Only apply herbicides to control specific weeds by means of spot treatment
7 Maintain stockproof walling and hedges using traditional materials
8 Maintain weatherproof field barns using traditional materials

Payment: £40 per hectare

limited number of standard agreements. While a high participation rate is clearly desired, there is no special pressure to ensure that any particular site is brought into an agreement. There is thus considerably less individual negotiation and no pressure to offer high payments to owners who may otherwise be reluctant to participate. The transactions costs per unit area may thus be expected to be lower, as is the specificity of control. Owners in ESAs do not need to threaten to damage the conservation value of their land in order to become eligible for the payments, as is the case within the SSSIs. In both cases, the objectives of the schemes are determined by government agencies. There is no direct democratic influence.

The discussion is generalized in figure 5.2. AC represents the effect of increasing the level of effort devoted towards targeting policy on particular areas and on establishing detailed prescriptions for the management of individual sites. This is represented in terms of increasing administrative costs. It is assumed that there are diminishing returns to this effort. The line does not pass through the origin, reflecting the value of conservation goods available in the absence of policy administration. I_L and I_H represent indifference curves for different qualities of conservation goods. Because the horizontal axis represents cost, the slope of the indifference curves indicates their price. It is assumed that the price is constant, and so the curves are linear.

The figure indicates different optimal levels of administrative effort for the two qualities of conservation goods. With I_L, a lower level of effort is justified, and such a case is represented by the ESAs where the objective is

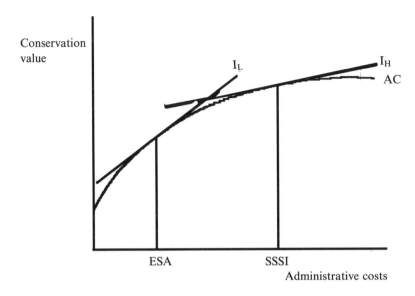

Figure 5.2 Alternative arangement for environmental contracts.

one of relatively general landscape improvement. The value of conservation goods generated by the SSSIs is assumed to be higher, represented by
I_H, and hence a higher level of administrative expenditure is justified. As
suggested by the figure, a whole spectrum of policy mechanisms is possible
and, indeed, some intermediate forms are emerging in the United
Kingdom. For example, a Countryside Stewardship Scheme is also
available which operates on smaller areas than ESAs but which do not
have the particular established conservation values of SSSIs.

It is also evident that a scheme should not be judged in terms of its
administrative costs alone. However, other factors will also affect the level
of administrative costs, some of which may be largely unaffected by
scheme design. For instance, the structure of landholding in the area
affects the administrative costs: it has been found that the administrative
costs of operating the ESAs in the Somerset Levels ESA where there is a
very fragmented landholding pattern are substantially higher than are the
costs of administering management agreements over larger areas of
heather moorland in nearby National Parks (Whittaker et al., 1990).
Colman et al. (1992) and Whitby (1993) discuss the available evidence on
administration costs in more detail.

Other factors are influenced by scheme design. It may be that
alternative policy designs could reduce the cost of the scheme without
significantly reducing the conservation benefit, shifting AC to the left.
One possibility might be for the adoption of competitive tendering. As
the ESA scheme stands, it no doubt pays a substantial number of
farmers who make little or no adjustment to their farming systems and

others may be overcompensated for the costs imposed. There is no incentive for farmers to reveal their willingness to accept compensation for abiding by the requirements of the agreement. On the contrary, there is an incentive not to disclose this figure. It would in principle be possible to call for competitive bids for participation in ESAs and then, assuming that the conservation gains are essentially the same between farms within an ESA, to select farmers with the lowest bids. This type of tendering approach has been adopted in the United States in the Conservation Reserve Program.

Conservation Policy by Intermediary

The achievement of conservation goals can often require detailed information both about the ecology of the habitat being managed and about the agricultural system which is operated within it. In some circumstances, guidelines for management can provide sufficient information for a farmer without a detailed understanding of the ecosystem involved. However, in other circumstances, for instance where habitat is being recreated or where a rare habitat is being protected against external pressures, then a more proactive form of environmental management may be necessary. This would involve a more regular monitoring of the ecosystem and review of the appropriate management responses. This may require a range of skills which are not always available to the particular farmers who happen to be owners of the relevant conservation sites and may be difficult to write into contractual agreements.

A number of private sector organizations have objectives which match quite closely those of the state. This is clearly the case in respect of most charities and includes a variety of conservation bodies, several of which have the provision of conservation goods by means of direct management of land among their objectives. Such organizations are referred to as Conservation, Amenity and Recreation Trusts (CARTs). These are nonprofit-making organizations with the aim of generating wide public benefit through nature conservation and environmental improvement, provision of amenities and opportunities for public recreation, and conservation of landscape heritage.

While most policy mechanisms are directed towards existing owners, an alternative and less direct form of mechanism is therefore for the state to promote the actions of organizations which have objectives in common with those of the state. This may be done in terms of grants for the purchase of land, contributions towards labor costs, and the tax relief generally available to nonprofit organizations.

Where such an organization owns land which is being managed for landscape or wildlife conservation, it will be the residual claimant. As such, it will seek to maximize the value to it of the residual which is left after all costs have been paid. In this case, the value will include the nonmonetary value of the conservation goods. Thus the position is likely to be different from that of a farmer who is persuaded to undertake a particular type of land management in response to the financial incentives offered to him through an environmental contract. The farmer will have an incentive to meet the terms of the contract at minimum cost and it will be necessary for a government agency to monitor such contracts in some detail.

The conservation organization will have an incentive to seek out least-cost ways of generating and protecting the conservation values under its particular circumstances. It will be prepared to trade off costs against conservation gains. In this, the implied price of conservation goods may not be different from that implied in government actions. Therefore such organizations will seek out new methods of achieving conservation goals and will respond to changes in relative prices and technology. This suggests that the conservation organization will require less detailed monitoring than a conventional farmer and that in the longer term it would be likely to develop more cost-effective methods of conservation management.

Conservation organizations may also be more flexible and less bureaucratic than many government agencies given their generally smaller size and the lack of democratic accountability. They may be able to respond more rapidly to opportunities which arise, such as purchasing significant conservation sites when they become available on the market. Such organizations often specialize in particular types of conservation, such as the protection of birds, or may focus their efforts within a particular area. In this way, although they be relatively small organizations, they can build up a level of expertise within their own particular speciality.

Finally, there is an incentive for environmental entrepreneurship. It is particularly difficult for public policies to stimulate the provision of a mix of conservation goods. As represented by the other mechanisms which have been examined here, it is considerably easier to prevent changes from taking place or to stimulate land users to conform to a standard package of measures. However, variety is an important component of the conservation of the countryside. This is in distinct contrast for example to the uniformity which has been engendered by European agricultural support policies which have guaranteed prices for agricultural products.

The creation of variety depends upon some level of entrepreneurship, to bring resources, ideas, and information together, to organize them, and to take risks. In this context, the risk of undertaking unsuccessful projects may lead to a loss of membership and of public sector support, putting the future of the organization at risk. Again, given the public good characteristics of the outputs, the scope for conventional profit-seeking entrepreneurship must be limited.

Private action and the state

It might be argued that the existence of such organizations removes the need for government action at all (e.g. Anderson and Leal, 1991). In a free-market role, such organizations would operate as clubs, acquiring property rights on behalf of their members, funded by member contributions. Certain conditions would need to be met if such organizations can be expected to be effective in providing conservation goods. These include excludability with respect to the benefits provided so that the problem of free-riding can be avoided, homogeneity of membership so that organizations can have clearly defined objectives, and a large number of clubs. See for instance the discussion in Mueller (1989).

In practice these conditions are not met. The objectives often embrace a variety of conservation and leisure aspects (e.g. outdoor recreation, protection of rare habitats and areas of historic interest, lobbying government) which will be valued differentially by different members. As noted earlier, the conservation goods provided often have significant public good characteristics and complete exclusion is rarely possible. This applies quintessentially to the existence benefits arising from their operations but in any case organizations may not always even seek to exclude nonmembers. For instance, many Country Wildlife Trusts (see below) in the United Kingdom do not seek to prevent public access over a significant proportion of their land (Dwyer, 1991). In these circumstances, CARTs cannot be relied upon to provide an optimal level of conservation goods in the absence of government support.

There are of course disadvantages to the indirect implementation of policy in this way. The objectives of the organizations may well not match those of the state precisely. They will respond first to the interests and priorities of their members rather than to the priorities as perceived by government. The degree of matching between the objectives of the organization and those of the government will vary considerably between different sorts of organization and it will often be appropriate for government incentives to be used to influence the way in which they operate as well as the scale of the operation. Thus, the advantages associated with the organization's being the residual claimant may be less clear cut.

Further, small organizations with a largely inactive membership may be susceptible to capture by a subset of the membership which seeks to modify the type of action being taken. Thus the actions taken may not in practice reflect the stated goals of the organization. And even while the objectives may conform to those of the government, the organizations may simply be inefficient. Those people responsible for administration may be well informed about and committed to conservation, but less qualified for and less interested in administration.

Conservation Trusts in Britain

CARTs in Britain represent a significant and growing form of institutional landownership and management in the British Isles, controlling just over 1 million acres. Collectively, CARTs have a combined membership of some 3.1 million (though this double-counts individuals who are members of more than one trust), a staff of over 2000, and a financial turnover approaching £110 million. They are discussed in detail by Dwyer and Hodge (1994).

The National Trust stands out amongst these, accounting for about half of the total turnover. Its properties cover over 570,000 acres and it is one of the largest landowners in the country. It has a membership of 2.2 million. Since the 1930s, the Trust has followed a policy of acquiring large country houses and their estates and it has also played a key role in their preservation. In addition, it has acquired important stretches of countryside and coastline. There is a separate National Trust for Scotland.

Also of significant size is the Royal Society for the Protection of Birds, owning about 180,000 acres. Both of these large organizations were founded over 100 years ago. A third major element, operating at both national and county level, is the network of County Wildlife Trusts affiliated to the Royal Society for Nature Conservation. Together these Trusts own about 140,000 acres (Dwyer, 1991). But in addition there are a growing number of other local and national organizations which operate as CARTs. These are referred to as independent CARTs. Some 122 such CARTs together own or have assumed long-term management responsibility for nearly 125,000 acres of open land in the British Isles (Dwyer and Hodge, 1992). This has risen from about 50,000 acres in 1978.

The role of the state

While not generally recognized as a coherent policy strategy, the state has played a key role in the development of CARTs and is seems inevitable that the scale of the movement would be considerably smaller in the absence of state support. Incomes are drawn from a variety of sources and there is considerable variation between organizations, but financial support is often important. For instance, on average the independent CARTs and the County Wildlife Trusts receive nearly one-third of operational income from the state.

But nonfinancial support is also important. The National Trust stands out as having a special legal status, having powers which are not available to other private organizations in the United Kingdom. First it has the power to hold land inalienably. This means that, under the National Trust Act 1907, property so declared may not be disposed of by the Trust and it may only be acquired compulsorily by the government by consent of Parliament. This places the Trust in an advantageous position with respect to potential donors who will want to be reassured that property given will be preserved. Second, the Trust has a statutory power to covenant land without the requirement which other private organizations have under English law of owning adjoining property. This is equivalent to the powers which organizations have in the United States to enter into conservation easements; they are not available to other private organizations in the United Kingdom.

A particular feature of the growth of independent CARTs in the last ten to 15 years has been CART formation through public sector bodies, either local government or government agency. This has often been undertaken in an effort to distance land management activities from the constraints common to democratic institutions and with the aim that they should become self-financing. CARTs have also been established to manage specific areas of land which had come into local government or government agency ownership, sometimes through planning gain agreements or in association with other functions, such as water supply.

Voluntary organizations are making an increasing contribution to conservation initiatives in the countryside. But they are not doing so on a free-market basis. Their development is substantially dependent upon the state in a variety of ways and their future development depends upon this productive cooperation between the state and the voluntary sector.

Conclusions

There are a variety of different public objectives for land conservation and the policies applied operate in a variety of ways. These all have to include some means whereby policy implementation in some way reflects the demand for the particular public goods which may be generated and some mechanism whereby the necessary objectives can be translated into changes in resource use in practice. The three examples used here differ in each of these respects.

Representing demand

The three examples of policy mechanism illustrated here adopt different methods for representing the demand for the public goods in question. The development control system incorporates democratically elected representatives directly into the decision-making process, subject to a variety of primarily centrally determined constraints. In contrast, the details of the environmental contracts, while subject to consultation, are determined within the government agencies involved, as is the total level of public expenditure to be devoted to them. The third policy mechanism, where policy is operated through an intermediary, takes a much more direct account of the demand for the public goods. A significant component of the decision-making responsibility is delegated to private sector organizations whose membership and private funding directly represent the demand of the public.

All of these approaches may be criticized as not reflecting accurately the wider public interest. But each has some logic in its own particular context. The development control process is an important factor in determining the way in which local communities develop and hence it is appropriate for locally elected representatives to have a say. The objectives for environmental contracts are set at a national level but they represent a more detailed level of decision making than would normally be undertaken by a national legislature. Once the objectives have been chosen, the determination of the conditions for environmental contracts is to a significant extent a technical matter of determining what management actions are necessary. The major government input into the third type of mechanism involves the decision that the objectives of particular organizations do indeed correspond sufficiently closely to those of the government. After this, substantial delegation is necessary in order to allow the organizations the flexibility to engage in some degree of entrepreneurship.

Stimulating supply

The policy mechanisms also adopt quite different approaches to the organization of supply. The first is predicated on the fact that landowners' rights to develop have been taken by the state. It is then generally assumed that there will be sufficient pressures for development that the policy can operate by allowing only that development which is considered to be in the wider interest. One weakness of the approach lies in its limited capacity to stimulate development within depressed local economies.

The establishment of environmental contracts depends upon the relevant government agencies having quite a high level of information. They must identify the opportunities which are available for the provision of public goods and propose the details of the required contracts. The third mechanism generates incentives for the private sector to acquire this type of information. Both of these approaches imply that landowners hold the relevant property rights. These are then acquired on a voluntary basis in the case of the contracts temporarily in agreement with the existing owners; in the case of policy by intermediary the rights are acquired on a permanent basis by the intermediating organization in the open market.

The limits of efficiency measurement

It is not generally possible to make direct comparisons of the efficiency of the various alternatives. As discussed in other chapters, techniques are available for monetary valuation of environmental changes, but in this context, in view of the multiplicity of impacts associated with alternative patterns of land use, it seems unlikely that reliable and generally accepted estimates of benefits will be forthcoming in most cases. There is scope for cost-effectiveness analysis, but care needs to be taken to recognize differences in the nature of the conservation outputs. In practice the formal analysis of these alternative approaches is limited.

However, each of these mechanisms fills a rather different function so that, within any particular area, it is appropriate to develop a package of measures which can influence land uses towards the multiple objectives set for it by society.

Acknowledgment

I am grateful for comments from Martin Whitby on a previous version of this chapter.

References

Anderson, T. L. and Leal, D. R. 1991: *Free Market Environmentalism*. Boulder, CO: Westview Press.

Bowers, J. 1992: The economics of planning gain: a reappraisal. *Urban Studies*, 29 (8), 1329–39.

Bromley, D. W. 1991: *Environment and Economy*. Oxford, Basil Blackwell.

Colman, D., Crabtree, R., Froud, J. and O'Carroll, L. 1992: *Comparative Effectiveness of Conservation Mechanisms*. Manchester: Department of Agricultural Economics, University of Manchester.

Countryside Commission 1987: *Landscape Assessment CCP*. Cheltenham: Countryside Commission.

Dwyer, J. 1991: The County Wildlife Trusts: primary conservation CARTs. Discussion Paper 30, Department of Land Economy, University of Cambridge.

Dwyer, J. and Hodge, I. 1992: The collective management of land for public environmental benefit: an examination of UK Trusts. Discussion Paper 37, Department of Land Economy, University of Cambridge.

Dwyer, J. and Hodge, I. 1994: *Countryside in Trust*. London: Belhaven.

Evans, A. 1988: *No Room! No Room!* Occasional Paper 79, London: Institute of Economic Affairs.

Grant, M. 1988: *Forty Years of Planning Control: The Case for the Defence*, The Denman Lecture. Department of Land Economy, University of Cambridge.

Hall, P., Thomas, R., Gracey, H. and Drewett, R. 1973: *The Containment of Urban England*. London: Allen & Unwin.

Hodge, I. D. 1989: Compensation for nature conservation. *Environment and Planning A*, 27 (7), 1027–36.

Mueller, D. C. 1989: *Public Choice II*. Cambridge: Cambridge University Press.

OECD. 1988: *Agricultural and Environmental Policies: Opportunities for Integration.* Paris, OECD.

Pearce, B. J. 1987: Development control and the development process: an introductory review. In M. L. Harrison and R. Mordey (eds), *Planning Control Philosophies, Prospects and Practice,* London: Croom Helm.

Pearce, B. J. 1992: The effectiveness of the British Land Use Planning System. *Town Planning Review,* 63 (1), 13–28.

Whitby, M. C. 1990: Multiple land use and the market for countryside goods. *Journal of the Royal Agricultural Society of England,* 151, 32–43.

Whitby, M. C. 1993: The UK system for delivery of conservation goods. Paper presented at the Association of Descartes Conference "Agriculture and Society: Directions for Research," Paris.

Whittaker, J., O'Sullivan, P. and McInerney, J. 1990: An economic analysis of management agreements. In N. Hanley (ed.), *Farming and the Countryside: An Economics Analysis of External Costs and Benefits,* Wallingford: CAB International.

Part II

Considering the Future

6

Intergenerational Choices under Global Environmental Change

Richard B. Howarth and Richard B. Norgaard

1 Introduction

Over the course of four decades, economists have sequentially addressed issues of environmental quality as defined by the shifting focus of public opinion: the value of wilderness and recreation in the 1960s and 1970s, the costs of pollution and fossil energy use in the 1970s and 1980s, and the loss of biodiversity and global climate change in the 1980s and 1990s. Three decades ago, environmental issues were viewed as specific, separate, small problems of developed societies that threatened the balance between material affluence and non-market amenities. Today's environmental problems, in contrast, are seen as general, interactive, global transformations that threaten our descendants both materially and aesthetically. This new understanding raises fundamental questions for the theory and practice of environmental economics that challenge the traditional boundaries and conventions of the discipline.

Concerns over the capacity of natural resources to support sustained improvements in human well-being are by no means new to economic analysis. Malthus (1798) and Ricardo (1821) held that agricultural land scarcity implied strict limits on population growth and the development of living standards. Since that time, conservationists have worried that unfettered self-seeking behavior might lead to the overexploitation of resources such as timber and crude oil and undermine long-term economic progress (Marsh, 1864). For the most part, however, economists have expressed skepticism regarding such concerns. Harold Hotelling offered his well-known counterargument in his seminal article of 1931. According to Hotelling, competitive firms would manage exhaustible resource stocks to maximize present-value profits. Competitive extraction paths would therefore match those chosen by a social planner seeking to maximize intertemporal social surplus. Hotelling specifically noted that social and private discount rates must be the same for this result to hold. Subject to this caveat, the equivalence between competitive markets and the work of a rational social planner ostensibly meant that the invisible hand was sufficient and policy intervention inappropriate.

Public concern for resource conservation rose again in the 1950s, when a presidential commission warned that "even a casual assessment" of natural resource availability in the United States "would show many causes for concern" (President's Materials Policy Commission, 1952). This time the counterargument came in the form of an empirical analysis of economic indicators of natural resource scarcity. Barnett and Morse (1963) examined trends in the prices and unit costs of extractive goods (including agricultural, mineral, and forest products) in the United States. They found that the unit cost of extractive output fell by 55 percent between 1870 and 1957. Although the price of forest products increased somewhat over the period, agricultural and mineral prices exhibited no clear long-term trends. These findings suggested that natural resources were becoming less scarce, not more scarce, in an economic sense. The authors argued that technological progress offsets declines in the physical quality and abundance of resource stocks.

This optimistic assessment came under renewed scrutiny in the 1970s when Meadows et al. (1972) argued that exponential growth in resource extraction and environmental degradation could not be sustained through the twenty-first century. According to the authors, fundamental reforms in technology and social institutions would be required to maintain the quality of the physical environment for the benefit of future generations. The response from economists was uniform and emphatic. The model employed by Meadows et al. lacked price feedbacks and other mechanisms through which economic agents could adapt to changing physical conditions. Some argued that the approach constituted "measurement without data" (Nordhaus, 1973) and was therefore wholly unjustified. The findings of Hotelling and Barnett and Morse were brought into the debate, and new developments from the theory of economic growth added a third strand to the argument. By introducing an exhaustible resource to a standard model of intertemporal development, Solow (1974) established that a sustainable consumption level could be achieved, *in principle*, given sufficient substitutability between resource and capital inputs (see Kemp et al. (1984) for a review of the more recent literature).

If resource scarcity and environmental degradation posed no significant threat to the welfare of future generations, then environmental economists could safely abstract from questions of intergenerational fairness and focus squarely on the efficiency of intertemporal resource allocation.[1] Here the potential for intellectual development and practical application was rich indeed, for externalities and related inefficiencies are pervasive in natural resource and environmental management. Barnett and Morse

(1963, ch. 12), for example, called for government intervention to ensure that trends in urbanization, pollution, water supply, and land use did not undermine the progress towards improved living standards made possible by economic growth. The pursuit of this agenda gave rise to impressive developments in the theory of market failure and its application in policy formulation and implementation.

The environmental problems of the 1990s, however, are perceived to be global in scale, pervasive in their effects, and as entailing economic consequences for generations to come. Global climate change, the depletion of stratospheric ozone, and the irreversible loss of biodiversity share characteristics that greatly complicate environmental economic analysis from a welfare-theoretic perspective (Howarth and Monahan, 1992). Actions in today's world entail potential costs on future generations that are inherently unpredictable given the dynamics and complexity of environmental systems. The range of plausible effects, however, includes truly devastating impacts on vulnerable populations. Climate change, for example, could undermine subsistence agriculture in some world regions as well as increase the frequency and severity of tropical storms. Ozone depletion could substantially increase skin cancer fatalities caused by exposure to ultraviolet radiation.

Meanwhile, the three-part reasoning that allowed environmental economists to abstract from issues of intergenerational fairness leaves central questions unresolved. Resource prices turned upwards in the 1960s and 1970s, in contrast with the earlier findings of Barnett and Morse (Slade, 1982: Hall and Hall, 1984). The Hotelling model is based on the assumption of perfect foresight that is often employed but easily questioned (Graham-Tomasi et al., 1986; Norgaard, 1990). The model's power to describe historical data has been cast into doubt by empirical studies (Farrow, 1985).

Neither the Hotelling model nor the optimal growth literature address the question of the institutional mechanisms required to achieve a sustainable future. What institutions would bring private and social discount rates into correspondence to support the Hotelling equivalence result? More generally, what policies would be required to ensure that a sustainable future, which few deny is possible *in principle*,[2] is in fact achieved by the economies of the real world? Perhaps most importantly, today's environmental and social problems are so closely intertwined that they must be addressed jointly if satisfactory solutions are to be found (Norgaard, 1993). With this in mind, the *ceteris paribus* assumption of the dominant partial equilibrium approach is of doubtful utility.

In the face of such concerns, the principle of *sustainable development* has emerged as a unified approach to environmental and development policy. While various interpretations of this criterion have appeared in the literature, a common theme is that current decisions should ensure that members of future generations have access to the resources required to enjoy life opportunities no less satisfactory than our own (World Commission on Environment and Development, 1987).

Some economists maintain that sustainability concerns are adequately addressed through the application of standard cost–benefit techniques. According to this view, the institutions necessary to ensure the internalization of environmental externalities, the efficient management of common property resources, and the efficient allocation of resources over time will preserve critical resources for future utilization. Others argue that efficient resource management is insufficient to ensure a sustainable future. In this emerging view, standard policy evaluation techniques should be supplemented by sustainability constraints to maintain the integrity of natural resource systems (Pearce et al., 1989).

On a conceptual level, this controversy is closely tied to the geometry of the Edgeworth box of general equilibrium analysis (Varian, 1984, pp. 198–203). Cost–benefit analysis is useful in identifying potential Pareto improvements – opportunities to improve the welfare of all while leaving none worse off. The prices and shadow prices on which cost–benefit analysis is based, however, are contingent on the initial endowments held by each agent. Only when endowments are defined so as to achieve an equitable distribution of economic opportunities can the efficient allocation identified by cost–benefit analysis be deemed "optimal" (Bator, 1957).

Figure 6.1 illustrates the extension of this approach to intergenerational resource allocation. In the figure, an allocation is "sustainable" if it lies on or above the 45° line so that future generations are at least as well off as the present. The utility possibility frontier U represents our historic expectation of the tradeoff between the welfare of current and future generations. If this expectation were correct, then each point on the frontier would be efficient. The social optimum would lie at A, the point of tangency between the utility possibility frontier and the social indifference curve W. To achieve this allocation, the current generation would use its share of resources and conserve the rest for future generations.

Suppose, however, that new evidence implied that our historic beliefs about the pace of progress turned out to be overly optimistic so that the actual utility possibility frontier lay on the locus U*. With this in mind, management practices based on the false belief in U might take us to a point like B that was neither sustainable nor efficient. With B as our starting point, some might argue for policies to improve economic efficiency to return us once more to the utility possibility frontier. But the set of allocations that are Pareto superior to B are all unsustainable. Achieving the true optimum at the sustainable point C would therefore require policies not only to improve economic efficiency but also to augment the transfer of assets from present to future generations.

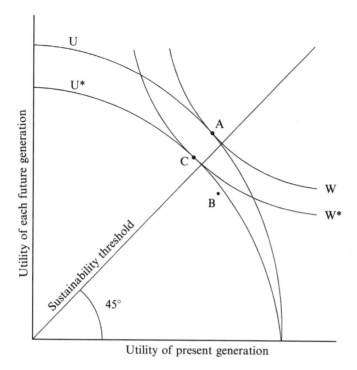

Figure 6.1 Intergenerational utility.

Several key points are already clear from figure 6.1. First, this representation does not rely on the existence of market failures *per se* to explain unsustainability. Second, achieving sustainability might require stronger policies than the Pareto criterion would suggest since the present generation may have to sacrifice to improve living conditions for the future. Third, the solution could not have been deduced through cost–benefit analysis alone since cost–benefit analysis addresses allocative efficiency, not distributional equity. It follows that achieving sustainable development in practice will require careful attention to questions of politics and ethics that by their very nature lie "above" economics.

This representation of the role of intergenerational equity in environmental policy analysis is elaborated in greater detail in this chapter through the development of an overlapping generations model of a society confronted by global climate change. In our model, energy use generates greenhouse gas emissions that impair production activities over the long-term future. The focus on climate change is topical yet reasonably general; elsewhere we have established similar results for models constrained by the availability of exhaustible and renewable resources (Howarth and Norgaard, 1990; Howarth, 1991a, b; Norgaard, 1992). In the following sections we show how environmental externalities, non-market valuation, the discount rate controversy, and the appropriate response to uncertainty are transformed by this framing of intergenerational choices under global environmental change.

2   The Rationale for Overlapping Generations Models

Studies of the allocation of natural resources in an intertemporal setting are often handicapped by assumptions that abstract from the realities of human demographics and the institutional forces that guide economic development. A common device is to assume the existence of a "representative agent" whose life spans from the present to the indefinite future. Typically this agent is characterized by preferences that are additively separable in time with a positive rate of pure time preference. If c_t is taken as her consumption level at dates $t = 0, 1, \ldots$, then her preferences are expressed by the mathematical form $\sum_{t=0}^{\infty} u(c_t)/(1 + \rho)^t$ where $\rho > 0$ and $u(c_t)$ represents the agent's instantaneous utility at each date.

This specification is useful in the analysis of certain problems given its simplicity and mathematical tractability. It is only one of many possible alternatives, however, yet it is often adopted as a criterion for "optimal" resource allocation without much attention to its links to ethical theory. As Page (1977, pp. 156–7) pointed out, "This criterion function, or some variant of it, jumps from the page like Athena from Zeus' brow fully grown. In the usual case it is left to the reader to puzzle out the assumptions underlying it, its interpretations and properties."

The interpretation of the utility discount factor ρ is a matter of special controversy. Some argue that the parameter captures *individuals'* impatience or strict preference for present over future consumption. Others suggest that the discount factor reflects the weight attached to the welfare of present versus future *generations* in social decision making. In reality, the notions of time preference and the distribution of welfare between generations are conceptually distinct (Burton, 1993), yet they are forced into a single parameter given the rough machinery of the model. The very idea of an infinitely lived representative agent is an analytical abstraction with nontrivial implications for economic modeling (Kirman, 1992). In our view, the confusion stemming from this approach may be substantially reduced through the consideration of models that are at once more general and more firmly grounded in economic reality.

We argued in an earlier paper (Howarth and Norgaard, 1990) that the use of single-generation models obscures the relationship between allocative efficiency and intergenerational equity in competitive intertemporal economies. An adequate model for addressing this problem must have at least two essential characteristics.

1   It must consider a sequence of generations with endowments of assets transferred from each generation to the next.

2   These generations must overlap, permitting the competitive exchange of goods and services between them.

Overlapping generations models have become a standard tool in macroeconomic analysis (Blanchard and Fischer, 1989). Their use in natural resource and environmental economics, however, is a relatively recent development. Using an overlapping generations framework, Kemp and Long (1980) illustrated the problem of dynamic inefficiency for an economy constrained by an exhaustible resource. Cropper (1990) examined social willingness to pay to reduce risks to life. Hultkrantz (1991) and Löfgren (1991) considered the problem of optimal forest management using closely similar models. And Burton (1993) illustrated the relationship between intertemporal and intergenerational preferences in natural resource allocation. In this chapter, we examine the integration of economic efficiency and intergenerational equity in an overlapping generations context with a special focus on policy coordination in a competitive economy.

3   Consumer Behavior

Consider an intertemporal economy where a homogeneous consumption/ investment good is produced at a sequence of discrete dates $t = 1, 2, \ldots, T$. Two generations of consumers are alive at each date – the "young" and the "old." To simplify the analysis, we assume that population is constant over time and that each generation consists of n identical individuals. A representative member of generation t lives at dates t and $t + 1$, enjoying the sequential consumption levels C_{yt} in youth and C_{ot+1} in old age.

Young and old individuals each hold one unit of labor that they sell inelastically to the production sector. The young at date t receive a net (positive or negative) income transfer I_{yt} from an exogenous agency – the "government" – while the old receive the net income transfer I_{ot}. The old at date 1 hold an initial endowment of capital K_1. Young individuals of generations $t = 1, 2, \ldots, T$ hold no capital endowments but may invest some portion of their incomes in capital assets (K_{t+1}) to finance consumption in old age. We take the consumption/investment good as numeraire, w_t as the wage rate at date t, and r_t as the interest rate or net return on capital investment. Under these conditions, each generation's budget constraints in youth and old age take the form

$$C_{yt} + K_{t+1} = w_t + I_{yt} \tag{6.1}$$

$$C_{ot+1} = w_{t+1} + (1 + r_{t+1})K_{t+1} + I_{ot+1} \tag{6.2}$$

The income transfers of our model serve two basic purposes. First, they are a means for the government to disperse the revenues raised by taking production activities that generate greenhouse gas emissions in the production sector. Second, they are a tool for redistributing wealth from present to future generations. The assumption that intergenerational asset transfers are specified and enforced by collective institutions may seem curious to some readers. This assumption, however, is not as unnatural as it might appear at first. We know, for example, that local and national governments invest heavily in health care and education for the young. We imagine that the intergenerational transfers of our model represent more than the bequests parents render to their offspring upon death. More broadly, such transfers are meant to capture the full range of benefits that each generation confers on its offspring through public and private institutions. We shall return to the rationale for social provisioning for future generations later in the chapter.

We assume that individuals hold perfect foresight and that the preferences of an individual born at date t may be represented by the utility function $U_t(C_{yt}, C_{ot+1})$ that is concave, differentiable and strictly increasing in consumption. Utility maximization subject to equations (6.1) and (6.2) implies the first-order condition

$$\frac{\partial U_t / \partial C_{yt}}{\partial U_t / \partial C_{ot+1}} = 1 + r_{t+1} \qquad (6.3)$$

that is necessary and sufficient for the attainment of an interior solution.[3] This condition, which is a standard result in the literature, holds that individuals' marginal rate of substitution with respect to consumption in consecutive periods must be equated with the gross return on investment. Individuals are therefore unable to improve their perceived welfare by shifting consumption from one period to another, and the market rate of interest provides an appropriate indicator of marginal time preference, or the increment of consumption an individual would require at date $t + 1$ to willingly give up one unit of consumption at date t.

4 Producer Behavior

So far we have said almost nothing about the technological constraints imposed on the economy. In fact, the model of consumer behavior presented in the preceding section is highly general and may be used to investigate various resource and environmental problems, including the allocation of exhaustible and renewable resources (Howarth and

Norgaard, 1990; Howarth, 1991a, b; Norgaard, 1992). Here we focus on the case where the use of a polluting input ("energy") contributes to a stock externality ("greenhouse gases") that adversely affects production at all future dates by altering global climate (Howarth and Norgaard, 1992).

Suppose that a large number of identical firms produce output using inputs of capital (K_t), labor (L_t), and self-produced energy (E_t) according to the net production function

$$f_t(K_t, L_t, E_t, Q_t) - \alpha E_t \qquad (6.4)$$

The positive constant α represents the unit cost of energy production, and we implicitly assume that there are no limits on cumulative energy use. Q_t is the stock of greenhouse gases in the atmosphere, determined by past energy use according to the recurrence relation

$$Q_{t+1} = \beta(Q_t + \gamma E_t) \qquad (6.5)$$

Some portion of the greenhouse gas stock (GHG stock) is removed from the atmosphere in each period so that $0 < \beta < 1$, and each unit of energy results in the release of $\gamma > 0$ units of greenhouse gases to the atmosphere. The GHG stock has a negative impact on production so that $\partial f_t / \partial Q_t < 0$. Production is zero when all inputs are zero, and f_t is differentiable in all its arguments and concave, increasing, and linearly homogeneous in inputs of capital, labor, and energy. This specification is highly general, accommodating a wide range of possible assumptions regarding technological change and the degree of substitutability between factor inputs.

Because the production function exhibits constant returns to scale, the number of firms is inconsequential to the analysis. It is convenient, however, to set the number of firms equal to n, the number of individuals in each generation. Thus K_t corresponds to the capital endowment held by a representative old individual, the use of labor is $L_t = 2$ at each date, and the GHG stock Q_t is measured in units of pollution per firm. We assume that factor inputs are mobile while savings and investment decisions are managed by the household sector. A representative firm thus purchases inputs and maximizes profits sequentially at each date. The firm takes the GHG stock as fixed, ignoring the impacts of current energy use on future production possibilities. We assume, however, that the government taxes energy at the unit rate v_t to account for the external effects it generates through the GHG stock. The firm's profits may thus be written

$$f_t(K_t, L_t, E_t, Q_t) - r_t K_t - w_t L_t - (\alpha + v_t)E_t \qquad (6.6)$$

Differentiation with respect to each input yields the first-order conditions

$$\frac{\partial f_t}{\partial K_t} = r_t \tag{6.7}$$

$$\frac{\partial f_t}{\partial L_t} = w_t \tag{6.8}$$

$$\frac{\partial f_t}{\partial E_t} = \alpha + v_t \tag{6.9}$$

that are necessary and sufficient for the achievement of an interior solution. These conditions hold that the price of each input is set equal to its marginal product, a standard result from microeconomic theory. Profits are zero because the production function is linearly homogeneous.

5   Energy Taxes and Intergenerational Transfers

An equilibrium is defined for the economy once the government specifies a set of energy taxes and net income transfers that obeys the balanced budget condition $I_{yt} + I_{ot} = v_t E_t$. Under these circumstances, equations (6.1), (6.2), and (6.7)–(6.9) imply that the market for the consumption/investment good clears in each period so that the technical constraint

$$C_{yt} + C_{ot} + (K_{t+1} - K_t) = f_t(K_t, L_t, E_t, Q_t) - \alpha E_t \tag{6.10}$$

is observed. With this in mind, our task is to characterize the welfare properties of competitive equilibria.

We define an allocation as *intergenerationally efficient* if it would be impossible to improve the welfare of one generation without leaving another worse off, that is, if it lies on the utility possibility frontier of figure 6.1. In formal terms, an allocation is efficient if it solves the problem

$$\text{maximize} \sum_{t=0}^{T} \mu_t U_t(\cdot) \tag{6.11}$$

subject to equations (6.5) and (6.10) for some set of constants $\mu_t > 0$ (Takayama, 1985).[4] This problem yields the first-order conditions

$$\frac{\partial U_t / \partial C_{yt}}{\partial U_t / \partial C_{ot+1}} = 1 + \frac{\partial f_{t+1}}{\partial K_{t+1}} \tag{6.12}$$

$$\frac{\partial f_t}{\partial E_t} - \alpha = -\sum_{i=1}^{T-t} \left(\gamma \beta^i \frac{\partial f_{t+i}}{\partial Q_{t+i}} \prod_{j=1}^{i} \frac{1}{1 + \partial f_{t+j} \partial K_{t+j}} \right) \tag{6.13}$$

that are necessary and sufficient for the attainment of an interior solution. A derivation of these results under more general conditions is given in the appendix.

The first condition, which holds that individuals' marginal rate of substitution with respect to consumption at consecutive dates must be equated with the gross return on capital investment, is automatically satisfied given the conditions of utility and profit maximization (equations (6.3) and (6.7)). The implication is that consumption–investment tradeoffs are adequately addressed through the decisions of private individuals with no need for government intervention. Conversely, efficiency requires that government allocation decisions respect the marginal time preference of individuals.

Equation (6.13), however, will be satisfied only if the government taxes energy to account for its external effects through the accumulation of greenhouse gases in the atmosphere. Substitution of equations (6.7) and (6.9) into (6.13) yields the efficient energy tax

$$v_t = - \sum_{i=1}^{T-t} \left(\gamma \beta^i \frac{\partial f_{t+i}}{\partial Q_{t+i}} \prod_{j=1}^{i} \frac{1}{1 + r_{t+j}} \right) \tag{6.14}$$

Here $\gamma \beta^i$ is the marginal increase in the period $t + i$ GHG stock caused by a unit increase in period t energy use, while $-\partial f_{t+i}/\partial Q_{t+i}$ is the marginal loss in period $t + i$ production caused by the GHG stock. The discount factor $\prod_{j=1}^{i} 1/(1 + r_{t+j})$ that is applied to period $t + i$ environmental impacts reduces to the familar $1/(1 + r)^i$ when the discount rate is constant at r.

While the algebra embodied in equation (6.14) is a bit cumbersome, the underlying intuition is readily explained. To achieve a resource allocation that is intergenerationally efficient, the government taxes energy at a rate equal to the marginal present-value costs it imposes on the future economy through its contribution to the GHG stock. The appropriate discount rate is the market rate of interest, equivalent to the subjective marginal rate of time preference that private individuals use to evaluate consumption–investment tradeoffs. With the externality properly internalized, the marginal costs and benefits of energy use are equated in accordance with standard theory.

Note, however, that we have said nothing at all about the distribution of income or well-being between generations. In general, the shadow prices and discount rates that enter into cost–benefit calculations are determined by the transfer of assets from one generation to the next. For the case at hand, the government may use equation (6.14) to achieve an efficient resource allocation subject to the prevailing set of intergenerational asset transfers. The outcome will be socially desirable, however, only if the government chooses the income transfers I_{yt} and I_{ot} in light of social preferences regarding the distribution of welfare between present and future generations.

This point is best illustrated through the consideration of numerical examples. Suppose that the utility function of a representative member of generation t takes the form $U_t = \ln(C_{yt}) + \ln(C_{ot+1})$,[5] while the production function is given by $f_t = (1 - 0.05Q_t^2)L_t^{0.7}K_t^{0.2}E_t^{0.1} - 0.2E_t$. The initial stocks of capital and greenhouse gases are $K_1 = 1$ and $Q_1 = 0.5$. The time horizon is $T = 30$ generations, and the evolution of the GHG stock is governed by $Q_{t+1} = 0.9(Q_t + 0.5E_t)$.

For the sake of argument, we suppose the government seeks to maximize the social welfare function

$$V = \sum_{t=0}^{T} \delta^t U_t(\cdot) \tag{6.15}$$

subject to the technical constraints embodied in equations (6.15) and (6.10). Here $\delta > 0$ is a constant that reflects the relative weight attached to the welfare of future generations. The solution of this problem generates the efficiency conditions described by equations (6.12) and (6.13) plus the additional condition

$$\frac{\partial U_t}{\partial C_{ot+1}} = \delta \frac{\partial U_{t+1}}{\partial C_{yt+1}} \tag{6.16}$$

In accordance with standard arguments (Varian, 1984, pp. 220–4), it may be shown that an optimal allocation may be sustained as a competitive equilibrium given appropriate intergenerational transfers and energy taxes. According to this scheme, I_{yt}, I_{ot}, and v_t are chosen simultaneously for all dates to maximize social welfare.

Figures 6.2 and 6.3 outline the equilibria that arise for two values of δ, 0.45 and 0.90. With $\delta = 0.90$ – the "sustainable future" case – the combined consumption of the young and the old ("total consumption" $= C_{yt} + C_{ot}$) grows steadily over time. This improvement in living conditions requires substantial growth in the capital stock and a doubling of the GHG stock over ten generations. Figure 6.2 traces the development of the net transfer of income from the old to the young ("net income transfer" $= I_{yt} - v_t E_t/2$), or the extra wealth transferred to the young above the level they would receive given the equal division of energy tax revenues amongst young and old individuals. Since the required rate of investment far exceeds the earnings received by the young from sales of labor, the net asset transfer closely mirrors the growth of the capital stock.

Setting δ equal to 0.45 – the "impoverished future" case – yields a sharply different outcome. Under this scenario, total consumption and the capital stock decline steadily over time, and the growth of the GHG stock significantly exceeds the growth that occurs in the "sustainable future." Consumption is dominated by old individuals who pass on a relatively

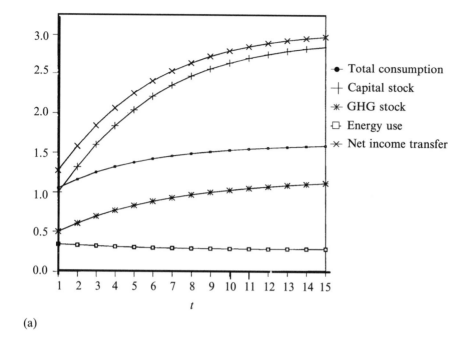

(a)

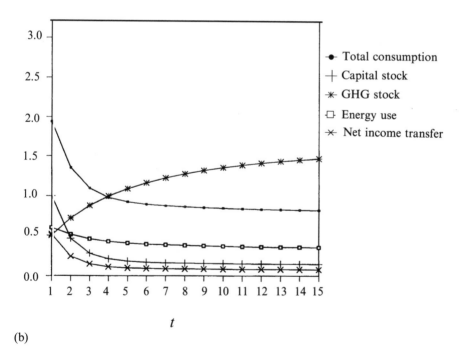

(b)

Figure 6.2   (a) Sustainable future, $\delta = 0.90$; (b) impoverished future, $\delta = 0.45$.

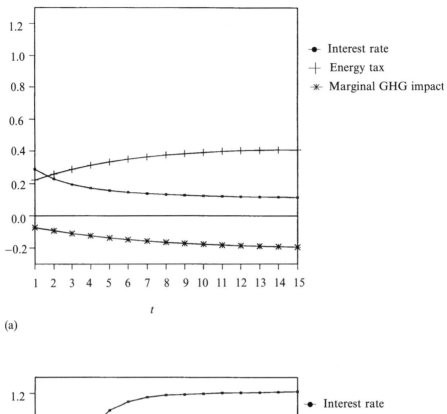

(a)

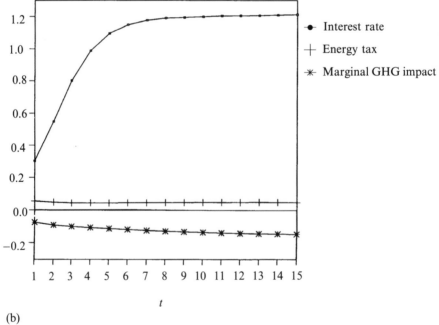

(b)

Figure 6.3   (a) Sustainable future, $\delta = 0.90$; (b) impoverished future, $\delta = 0.45$.

small portion of their wealth to future generations. Thus net intergenerational transfers are close to zero.

We emphasize again that the energy taxes in each scenario conform to the cost–benefit rule given by equation (6.14). The depletion of the capital stock that arises when $\delta = 0.45$, however, results in remarkably high interest rates and hence discount rates for use in cost–benefit analysis (figure 6.3). Moreover, the depressed level of economic activity implies that the marginal economic impacts of the GHG stock ("marginal GHG impact" $= \partial f_t / \partial Q_t$) are smaller in magnitude than when $\delta = 0.90$. Together, high discount rates and low marginal impacts or shadow prices imply low energy taxes and thus higher levels of pollution.

The specific assumptions on which these examples are based were chosen for purely illustrative purposes, and we make no claim that the model is a good approximation to any real-world economic system. Our aim, however, is not to construct a realistic model but rather to illustrate the conceptual relationship between economic efficiency and intergenerational equity as approaches to environmental policy. We have illustrated that cost–benefit techniques may be used to attain an intergenerationally efficient economic future but that the resulting outcome may imply a world of reduced opportunities to members of future generations. Unless cost–benefit analysis is accompanied by criteria that speak to distributional concerns, there is some danger in using it to identify "optimal" government policies.

6   Intergenerational Altruism and Competitive Equilibrium

The analysis so far has assumed that individuals are purely self-interested and that issues of intergenerational fairness are addressed by collective institutions that mandate the transfer of assets from present to future generations. This approach constitutes something of a paradox since the social preferences on which government decisions are based are presumably rooted in the underlying preferences of individuals. Why should the government care about future generations if private individuals do not? And what need is there for government intervention if the altruistic tendencies of private individuals lead them to transfer assets to members of future generations?

A conventional approach to this problem is to assume that members of present and future generations are linked through familial bonds that ensure the transfer of assets from parents to their immediate offspring (Barro, 1974). Suppose, for example, that a representative individual leaves one offspring to the next generation and that her preferences take the form $V_t = U_t(\cdot) + \delta V_{t+1}$ where $0 < \delta < 1$. Under these conditions, each family acts like a long-lived agent seeking to maximize the discounted sum

$\sum_{t=0}^{T} \delta_t U_t(\cdot)$ through consumption–investment decisions. If externalities are properly internalized, the resulting competitive equilibrium corresponds to the path a social planner would choose if she sought to maximize this criterion function subject to the technical constraints imposed on the economy. The outcome is therefore "optimal" in the sense that it maximizes the perceived welfare of a representative member of the present generation, taking into account her concern for her descendants.

Does this result imply that we should be optimistic about the welfare consequences of *laissez-faire* altruism in real-world economies? Consider for the moment that the demographic structure implied by the model – one parent gives rise to a single offspring in the next generation – is seriously at odds with social reality. As Daly and Cobb (1989, p. 39) point out,

> Families endure only by merging and mixing their identities through sexual reproduction, and thus are not independent or well defined over intergenerational time. Your great-great grandchild will also be the great-great grandchild of fifteen other people in the current generation, many of their identities now unknown. Presumably your great-great grandchild's well being will be as much an inheritance from each of these fifteen others as from yourself. Therefore it does not make sense for you to worry too much about your particular descendant, or to take any particular action on his or her behalf.

The intuition contained in this passage may be fleshed out as follows. Suppose we abandon the individualist interpretation of our model and take C_{yt} and C_{ot+1} as the consumption levels of a representative *household* in generation t (Abel and Bernheim, 1991). A household consists of two individuals who share equally in labor, consumption, and economic decision making. Each household leaves two children who join separate households ($i = 1, 2$) in the next generation, and its perceived welfare depends on its own consumption and the welfare of its children's households according to the function

$$V_t = U_t(C_{yt}, C_{ot+1}) + \theta \sum_{i=1}^{2} V_{t+1}^i$$

$$= U_t(C_{yt}, C_{ot+1}) + \sum_{g=1}^{T-t} \sum_{i=1}^{2^g} \theta^g U_{t+g}^i(C_{yt+g}^i, C_{ot+g+1}^i) \qquad (6.17)$$

Here $\theta > 0$ is the relative weight attached to the welfare of each offspring's household, while the index $i = 1, \ldots, 2^g$ denotes the households of descendants born g generations in the future. Let I_{t+1}^i be the income transfer a representative household makes to its offspring in household i. We assume that the government divides the revenues from pollution taxes evenly between households at each date so that each receives the lump sum $v_t E_t/2$. In old age, the household thus enjoys the consumption level

$$C_{ot+1} = w_{t+1} + (1 + r_{t+1})K_{t+1} + \frac{v_{t+1}E_{t+1}}{2} - \sum_{i=1}^{2} I_{t+1}^i \qquad (6.18)$$

while the household of child i consumes

$$C_{yt+1}^i = w_{t+1} + \frac{v_{t+1}E_{t+1}}{2} + I_{t+1}^i + \bar{I}_{t+1}^i - K_{t+2}^i \qquad (6.19)$$

when young. Here $\bar{I}_{t+1}^i$ is the income transfer household i receives from its other set of parents. Taking the actions of others as given, each household seeks to maximize its perceived welfare through its consumption–investment decisions and the transfers it renders to its offspring. Substitution of equations (6.18) and (6.19) into equation (6.17) and differentiation with respect to I_{t+1}^i yields the first-order condition

$$\frac{\partial U_t}{\partial C_{ot+1}} = \frac{\partial U_{t+1}^i}{\partial C_{yt+1}^i} \qquad (6.20)$$

that characterizes intergernerational income transfers in *laissez-faire* equilibria.

This outcome corresponds to the path a social planner would choose if she imposed the condition that the households of each generation were identical and sought to maximize the sum $\sum_{t=0}^{T} \theta^t U_t(\cdot)$ subject to the relevant technical constraints. Note, however, that the perceived welfare of a representative household of generation t may be written

$$V_t = U_t(C_{yt}, C_{ot+1}) + \theta \sum_{i=1}^{2} V_{t+1}^i = \sum_{i=0}^{T-t} (2\theta)^i U_{t+i}(\cdot) \qquad (6.21)$$

when the households of a given generation enjoy identical consumption levels. If the welfare of a representative household were maximized by a social planner, the optimality conditions would thus include

$$\frac{\partial U_t}{\partial C_{ot+1}} = 2\theta \frac{\partial U_{t+1}}{\partial C_{yt+1}} \qquad (6.22)$$

Compared with this outcome, the income transfers effected under decentralized private altruism would underweight the welfare of households living t generations in the future by the factor 2^t.

At this point we see that the choice of the discount factors considered in section 5 was by no means accidental. The "impoverished future" ($\delta = 0.45$) of figure 6.2 would arise for the case at hand if $\theta = 0.45$ and the management of intergenerational transfers was left to the discretion of private households. The "sustainable future" ($\delta = 0.90$) would arise if $\theta = 0.45$ and households were able to join forces and effect intergenerational transfers through public institutions so as to maximize the perceived welfare of a representative household. The cases differ only in the discount factor applied to the welfare of present versus future generations.

As the model is specified, the "sustainable future" is preferred by all present and future households, but the existence of spillover effects weakens the incentive for individual households to render adequate transfers to their children. The problem arises because a household's decision to transfer assets to the household of child i confers indirect benefits on the parents of i's spouse that are not reflected in the structure of private incentives.

The objection might be raised that a remedy could be found in the absence of social intervention. Wouldn't the two sets of parents whose children formed household i collaborate and agree on a set of desired intergenerational transfers I^i_{t+1} and $\bar{I}^i_{t+1}$? In reality, such coordination is impossible because the most crucial intergenerational transfers – the costs of child-rearing and education, for example – are made long before children grow to adulthood and find spouses of their own.

It would be up to society, then, to ensure the effective transmission of wealth from present to future generations. As we noted above, social provisioning for the young is an established fact of modern society. The model under consideration explains why such an approach may be consistent with the private motivations of parents. It should be pointed out, however, that demographic considerations are not the only factor that might suggest a role for public intervention. Suppose, for example, that the altruistic tendencies of present individuals were not limited to their personal descendants but extended more generally to all members of future generations.[6] Then the welfare of future generations would take on the characteristics of a public good, and the intergenerational transfers effected by individuals in the absence of collective action might result in an outcome that all individuals would recognize as unfair to future generations (Marglin, 1963; Sen, 1982; Howarth and Norgaard, in press).

7   Extending the Model to Uncertainty

We have explored the utility of overlapping generations models in analyzing questions of environmental management under certainty. The extension of the approach to uncertainty offers a rich framework for addressing issues such as global climate change, stratospheric ozone depletion, and other long-term environmental problems. The models provide important insights into the interrelationships between time preference, risk aversion, and the problem of intergenerational equity in cases where uncertainty looms large. With this in mind, we recast the basic model of sections 3–5 by introducing a form of technological uncertainty.

Consider the possibility that a pollution control technology will be developed that permits greenhouse gas emissions to be reduced to zero at no net cost.[7] In formal terms, let s_t denote the *state of technology* at date t such that $s_t = 1$ in the absence of pollution control and $s_t = 0$ if the control technology is developed and implemented. The conditional probability that the technology will be available at date $t + 1$ is $\text{pr}(s_{t+1} = 0 \,|\, s_t)$. We assume that $s_0 = 1$ and that upon discovery the technology is used at all future dates so that $\text{pr}(s_{t+1} = 0 \,|\, s_t = 0) = 1$. Under these conditions, the evolution of the GHG stock follows the recurrence relation

$$Q_{t+1} = \beta(Q_t + \gamma s_t E_t) \tag{6.23}$$

that reduces to equation (6.5) in the special case where $s_t = 1$ at every date so that the pollution control technology never becomes available.

Under this formulation, present choices depend on the current state of technology and the stocks of capital and greenhouse gases. These variables in turn depend on the initial capital and GHG stocks and the state of technology in each past period. It follows that the *state of nature* at date t may be fully defined by the vector $S_t = (s_1, \ldots, s_t)$ that may take on any of t values.[8]

To proceed with the analysis it is necessary to make an assumption regarding consumer behavior under uncertainty. We assume that individuals are perfectly informed about current prices and economic conditions and hold *rational expectations* regarding future conditions. Specifically, individuals at date t know the probability of each possible state of nature at date $t + 1$ and the prices and income transfers that would arise under each. Consumer preferences are defined by the expected utility function $E[U_t(C_{yt}, C_{ot+1}) \,|\, S_t]$ that a representative member of generation t seeks to maximize through her choice of consumption and investment at date t subject to her budget constraints (equations (6.1) and (6.2)). This problem yields the first-order condition

$$\frac{\partial E[U_t(\cdot) \,|\, S_t]}{\partial C_{yt}} = E\left[\frac{\partial U_t(\cdot)}{\partial C_{ot+1}}(1 + r_{t+1}) \,|\, S_t\right] \tag{6.24}$$

that is necessary and sufficient for an interior solution (Howarth, 1991a).

Because the behavior of firms may be understood in purely static terms, the introduction of uncertainty adds nothing new to the problem of profit maximization. Equations (6.7)–(6.9) therefore hold without alteration. The introduction of uncertainty, however, considerably complicates the definition and achievement of intergenerational efficiency in a competitive economy. We shall make use of the principle that the sets of individuals born under alternative states of nature at a given date are ethically distinct.

While this notion may seem unintuitive to some readers, in fact it follows from well-established philosophical arguments (Schwartz, 1978; Parfit, 1983; Howarth, 1992). The identities of children depend critically upon the haphazard details of life, including mate selection and the timing of sexual relations. These factors are sensitive to seemingly minor changes in living conditions, and it is therefore apparent that the composition of future generations is contingent on the future development of the economy – different potential futures bring different sets of *potential* persons into actuality.

We define $E[U_t(C_{yt}, C_{ot+1}) \mid S_{ti}]$ as the *conditional welfare* of generation t given that a particular state of nature S_{ti} is realized at date t. This abstraction corresponds to individuals' perceived well-being in contemplating their life prospects when young. Then we shall say that an intergenerational resource allocation is *conditionally efficient* if it is impossible to find an alternative that improves the conditional welfare of one state-contingent generation without leaving another worse off (Howarth, 1991a). In formal terms, an allocation is conditionally efficient if it solves the problem

$$\text{maximize } \mu_0 U_0(C_{o1}) + \sum_{t=1}^{T} \sum_{i=1}^{t} \mu_{ti} E[U_t(\cdot) \mid S_{ti}] \tag{6.25}$$

subject to equations (6.10) and (6.23) for some set of positive constants μ_{ti} (Takayama, 1985). In the case of an interior solution, this problem yields the conditions

$$\frac{\partial E(U_t \mid S_t)}{\partial C_{yt}} = E\left[\frac{\partial U_t}{\partial C_{ot+1}} \left(1 + \frac{\partial f_{t+1}}{\partial K_{t+1}} \right) \middle| S_t \right] \tag{6.26}$$

$$\frac{\partial f_t}{\partial E_t} - \alpha = -\sum_{i=1}^{T-t} E\left(\gamma s_t \beta^i \delta_{t+i} \frac{\partial f_{t+i}}{\partial Q_{t+i}} \middle| S_t \right) \tag{6.27}$$

$$\delta_{t+i} = \prod_{j=1}^{i} \frac{\partial U_{t+j-1}/\partial C_{ot+j}}{E(\partial U_{t+j-1}/\partial C_{yt+j-1} \mid S_{t+j-1})} \tag{6.28}$$

that are necessary and sufficient for the achievement of conditional efficiency. A derivation of these results is given in the appendix.

It is clear from substitution of equation (6.7) into (6.24) that equation (6.26) is satisfied by competitive equilibria. As under perfect foresight, the management of consumption–investment decisions by private individuals is therefore consistent with allocative efficiency in a rational expectations economy. Substitution of equation (6.9) into (6.27) yields the efficient energy tax

$$v_t = -\sum_{i=1}^{T-t} E\left[\gamma s_t \beta^i \delta_{t+i} \frac{\partial f_{t+i}}{\partial Q_{t+i}} \middle| S_t \right] \tag{6.29}$$

This equation holds that the external effects of greenhouse gas emissions on the future economy should be internalized by taxing energy at a rate equal to the expected present-value damage they cause in the form of increased pollution. As under perfect foresight, the $\gamma s_t \beta^i$ term measures the marginal increase in the future GHG stock associated with a unit increase in current energy use, while $-\partial f_{t+i}/\partial Q_{t+i}$ represents the marginal loss in production at each date caused by the stock of greenhouse gases in the atmosphere.

Note, however, that the discount factor δ_{t+i} is variable across states of nature and does not pass outside the expectations operator. This coefficient reflects individuals' marginal preferences regarding consumption tradeoffs over time and across states of nature as determined by their utility functions and life-cycle consumption profiles. In an environment of uncertainty, each potential future is linked to the present by its own contingent discount factor (Debreu, 1959), and it is generally impossible to dissociate the roles of time and risk in the description of individual and social preferences. Only when we abstract away from uncertainty does the tax reduce to the form given by equation (6.14).

Conceptually the calculation of an efficient energy tax using equation (6.29) is a straightforward application of cost–benefit techniques. In practice, however, the calculation requires such exhaustive quantities of information that its operationality is cast into doubt (Howarth and Monahan, 1992). One would need to know not only the probability distribution of contingent futures and the economic conditions that prevail under each, but also the attitude of each successive generation with respect to risk, revealed in this framework by the curvature of the utility functions. It is well recognized that it is generally inappropriate to focus narrowly on expected outcomes in the application of cost–benefit techniques under uncertainty. Good analysis also requires careful attention to the possibility of extreme outcomes and people's willingness to pay to avoid risk (Wilson, 1982).

This last point is underscored by a return to our focus on the relationship between intertemporal efficiency and the distribution of welfare across generations. For the case at hand, the government need not limit its attention to the achievement of efficient resource allocation given fixed intergenerational transfers. More generally, the set of energy taxes and state-contingent income transfers $I_{ot}(S_t)$ and $I_{yt}(S_t)$ might be chosen simultaneously so as to maximize a social welfare function $W(U)$ where

$$U = \{U_0(\cdot), E[U_t(\cdot)\,|\,S_{ti}] : t \in [1, T], i \in [1, t]\} \tag{6.30}$$

is the set of conditional welfare levels. A full discussion of this problem is beyond the scope of the present analysis. It is important to note, however, that this structure allows decision makers to attach great weight to so-called "worst-case" outcomes even when their probabilities are relatively small (Perrings, 1991). Howarth (1991a), for example, outlined a case where state-contingent income transfers were chosen to maximize the welfare of the worst-off state-contingent generation without compromising economic efficiency. Whether such an approach should be construed as "optimal" depends on matters of social ethics that extend beyond the bounds of economic reasoning.

8   Environmental Economics and the Policy Process

In this chapter, we apply the classic framework of welfare economics to analyze issues of allocative efficiency and distributional equity in an intergenerational setting. Given the asymmetries of birth and time, the "endowments" of future generations are effectively specified by their immediate predecessors. Ours is the power to choose the stocks of reproduced capital, natural resources, and other productive assets to transfer to our children's generation. We argue that sustainability is largely a question of ensuring adequate transfers of assets from present to future generations.

Given sufficient intergenerational transfers, cost–benefit analysis may be used to improve the efficiency of resource allocation to the benefit of both present and future persons. But the prices and shadow prices used in cost–benefit analysis – including discount rates and the value of non-market goods – are contingent on the distribution of assets between present and future generations. The discount rate, despite the mystique surrounding its interpretation, is best understood as a market price: the net increment of future consumption individuals demand in exchange for one unit of present consumption. Like other prices, it reflects but does not define the distributional choices made by society.

The use of cost–benefit analysis along an unsustainable path might, as we have seen, point to policies that collectively undermine the ethical objectives embodied in the sustainability criterion. Faced with such a prospect, it might be tempting to adjust discount rates downwards out of concern for the future and simply re-run the analysis. This *ad hoc* approach, however, is inconsistent with the theoretical foundations of cost–benefit analysis and would compromise allocative efficiency without necessarily contributing to sustainability objectives.[9] A more appropriate response would be to augment the transfer of assets from present to future generations. Such transfers would probably drive down interest rates and raise the value of environmental services, but these effects are consequential, not causal.

While this approach to managing the global commons is true to the framework of neoclassical economics, it implies significant changes in the role of economics in environmental policy analysis. The practice of economics has co-evolved with the institutions of politics and governance. The classical economists – notably Smith, Malthus, Mill, and Marx – actively explored the implications of moral values for social decision making. In our own era, this tradition has been carried on by Kenneth Boulding (1978), Amartya Sen (1987), and Mark Sagoff (1988) amongst others. It must be acknowledged, however, that economic reasoning has often been used to defend existing rights structures and social institutions. Adam Smith argued that *laissez-faire* market organization was best suited to achieving the collective interest. Today this ideological stance enjoys wide popularity amongst economists.

In the years following the Second World War, the practice of economics was shaped by the rise of technocracy and the belief that progress would resolve the fundamental problems of social and political life. Economists hoped that economic growth would ameliorate distributional inequalities in the north, while development in the south would alleviate poverty and the residual tensions of the post-colonial period. As governments moved towards "scientific" approaches to decision making, economists complied by providing empirical models well-suited to the management of business cycles. The role of cost–benefit analysis expanded as the public, legislators, and even the courts came to perceive economics as an alternative to the "irrationality" of politics. Since economic growth was thought to imply the general expansion of social and economic opportunities, concern for the future seemed oddly misplaced when more pressing concerns were close at hand.

As a result, applied economics became an exercise in efficiency analysis practised by econocrats on behalf of the public, displacing the moral dimensions of political discourse and democratic processes. Environmental economics flourished during this period with a focus on the important but narrow issues of market failure and allocative efficiency. Today's concern for sustainable development challenges the discipline to build on the strengths of this history while at the same time embracing a more values-sensitive, less technocratic approach.

The practice of economics will probably shift in several ways. Some economists will probably return to a focus on the moral imperatives of social life and the related implications for economic organization. For most, economics will still be about tradeoffs, about helping decision makers understand the relationship between the ends and means of policy. We hope that the quest for "optimality" will give way to a more open-ended approach where economists participate in the political process without claiming special knowledge regarding what is "best" for society.

Some economists will build models that clarify the major choices that lie before us: the tradeoffs between the rich and poor, the north and the south, the present and the future. Those focusing on more specific concerns will pay closer attention to the relationship between micro and macro perspectives – how, for example, would utility regulation need to change if sustainability concerns mandated the reduction of greenhouse gas emissions. Academics will train the next generation of economists to work in each of these new modes. These are very significant changes that will require substantial modifications in the organizational setting of economic practice. We cannot say with confidence what changes will actually occur, but the foregoing transformations appear likely if our concerns about global environmental change and intergenerational equity are reinforced in the decades ahead.

Appendix: Allocative Efficiency under Uncertainty

This appendix presents a derivation of the conditions that characterize conditionally efficient resource allocations under uncertainty. Since the problem of resource allocation under certainty may be interpreted as the special case where $\mathrm{pr}\,(s_t = 1) = 1$ at each date, the derivation also holds for the basic model of sections 3–5.

It is helpful to distinguish explicitly between the values variables take on under alternative states of nature. Let $S_{ti(j)}$ and S_{t+1j} be successive states of nature at dates t and $t+1$. The $i(j)$ subscript indicates that, given knowledge of conditions at a particular date, conditions for each past date are also known. We use the indices j and $i(j)$ to denote the state of nature under which each variable is determined (Howarth, 1991a). The Lagrangian for the conditional efficiency problem may thus be written

$$
\begin{aligned}
\mathcal{L} = {} & \mu_0 U_0(C_{o1}) + \sum_{t=1}^{T-1}\sum_{i=1}^{t}\mu_{ti}E[U_t(C_{yt}, C_{ot+1})|S_{ti}] + \sum_{t=1}^{T}\mu_{Ti}U_T(C_{yTi}) \\
& + \sum_{t=1}^{T}\sum_{j=1}^{t}\lambda_{1tj}[f_t(K_{ti(j)}, L_j, E_{tj}, Q_{ti(j)}) \\
& \quad - \alpha E_{tj} - C_{ytj} - C_{otj} - K_{t+1j} + K_{ti(j)}] \\
& + \sum_{t=1}^{T}\sum_{j=1}^{t}\lambda_{2tj}[\beta(Q_{ti(j)} + \gamma s_{tj}E_{tj}) - Q_{ti+1j}]
\end{aligned}
\tag{A6.1}
$$

where

$$
\frac{\partial \mathcal{L}}{\partial C_{yti}} = \mu_{ti}\frac{\partial E(U_t \mid S_{ti})}{\partial C_{yti}} - \lambda_{1ti} = 0
\tag{A6.2}
$$

$$
\frac{\partial \mathcal{L}}{\partial C_{ot+1j}} = \mu_{ti(j)}\,\mathrm{pr}\,(S_{t+1j}|S_{ti(j)})\frac{\partial U_{tj}}{\partial C_{ot+1j}} - \lambda_{1t+1j} = 0
\tag{A6.3}
$$

$$\frac{\partial \mathscr{L}}{\partial K_{t+1i}} = \sum_{j|i} \lambda_{1t+1j} \left(1 + \frac{\partial f_{t+1j}}{\partial K_{t+1i}} \right) - \lambda_{1ti} = 0 \qquad (A.64)$$

$$\frac{\partial \mathscr{L}}{\partial E_{ti}} = \lambda_{1ti} \left(\frac{\partial f_{ti}}{\partial E_{ti}} - \alpha \right) + \lambda_{2ti}\beta\gamma s_{ti} = 0 \qquad (A.65)$$

$$\frac{\partial \mathscr{L}}{\partial Q_{t+1i}} = \sum_{j|i} \left(\lambda_{1t+1j} \frac{\partial f_{t+1j}}{\partial Q_{t+1i}} + \lambda_{2t+1j}\beta \right) - \lambda_{2ti} = 0 \qquad (A.66)$$

that are necessary and sufficient for the achievement of an interior solution. With algebraic manipulation, these conditions reduce to the form given in the text. Because the economy does not extend beyond date T, λ_{1T+1j} and λ_{2T+1j} drop out of the equations; it follows that $K_{T+1} = 0$ and $\partial f_{Ti}/\partial E_{Ti} = \alpha$.

Notes

This work was sponsored in part by the US Environmental Protection Agency and the Stockholm Environment Institute through the Department of Energy under Contract DE-AC03-76SF00098.

1 This assumes of course that issues of fairness between contemporaries are adequately addressed. See Bryant and Mohai (1992) for a discussion of this problem.
2 Even Meadows et al. (1972, p. 29) held that it would be possible to "establish a condition of ecological and economic stability that is sustainable far into the future . . . so that the basic material needs of each person on earth are satisfied and each person has an equal opportunity to realize his individual human potential."
3 Throughout the chapter we focus on interior solutions, where the values of all variables are strictly positive. Corner solutions may be formally ruled out given sufficiently strong technical assumptions, e.g. if $U_t(C_{yt}, C_{ot+1})$ is greater than $U_t(0, C_{ot+1})$, $U_t(C_{yt}, 0)$, and $U_t(0,0)$ whenever C_{yt} and C_{ot+1} are each positive.
4 Note that generation 0 (the old at date 1) and generation T enjoy consumption in only one period each. We represent their preferences by the utility functions $U_0(C_{o1})$ and $U_T(C_{yT})$ that are increasing and concave.
5 The utility functions for generations 0 and T are $U_0 = \ln(C_{o1})$ and $U_T = \ln(C_{yT})$.
6 This possibility should not be dismissed out of hand. The authors, for example, know numerous individuals who plan never to have children and yet profess great sympathy for the fate of posterity.
7 This assumption is readily generalized to allow for uncertainty regarding the rate of technological change and the environmental impacts of greenhouse gas emissions. See Howarth (1991a).
8 In period $t = 4$, for example, S_t may take on the values $(1, 1, 1, 1)$, $(1, 1, 1, 0)$, $(1, 1, 0, 0)$, $(1, 0, 0, 0)$. Other possibilities are ruled out by the assumption that the pollution control technology is available at all dates after it is discovered.
9 One *might* use distributional weights to balance costs and benefits accruing to present and future generations (Little and Mirlees, 1968; Harberger, 1978). But identifying the "correct" set of weights involves ethical commitments that must be generated by the

political process. Moreover, consistency demands that the cost and benefits accruing to the members of a particular generation be weighed according to individuals' marginal time preference as revealed by prevailing interest rates. We are therefore not convinced that the use of distributional weights constitutes a useful approach to policy analysis.

References

Abel, A. B. and Bernheim, B. D. 1991: Fiscal policy with impure integenerational altruism. *Econometrica*, 59 (November), 1687–1711.

Barnett, H. J. and Morse, C. 1963: *Scarcity and Growth – The Economics of Natural Resource Availability*. Baltimore, MD: Johns Hopkins University Press.

Barro, R. 1974: Are government bonds net wealth? *Journal of Political Economy*, 82 (November), 1095–1117.

Bator, F. 1957: The simple analytics of welfare maximization. *American Economic Review*, 47 (March), 22–59.

Blanchard, O. J. and Fischer, S. 1989: *Lectures on Macroeconomics*. Cambridge, MA: MIT Press.

Boulding, K. E. 1978: *Ecodynamics: A New Theory of Societal Evolution*. Beverley Hills, CA: Sage.

Bryant, B. and Mohai, P. 1992: *Race and the Incidence of Environmental Hazards: A Time for Discourse*. Boulder, CO: Westview Press.

Burton, P. S. 1993: Intertemporal preferences and intergenerational equity considerations in optimal resource harvesting. *Journal of Environmental Economics nd Management*, 24 (March), 119–32.

Cropper, M. 1990: Valuing risks to life. *Journal of Environmental Economics and Management*, 19 (September), 160–74.

Daly, H. E. and Cobb, J. B. 1989: *For the Common Good – Redirecting the Economy Toward Community, the Environment, and a Sustainable Future*. Boston, MA: Beacon Press.

Debreu, G. 1959: *Theory of Value*. New York: Wiley.

Farrow, S. 1985: Testing the efficiency of extraction from a stock resource. *Journal of Political Economy*, 93 (June), 452–87.

Graham-Tomasi, T., Runge, C. F. and Hyde, W. F. 1986; Foresight and expectations in models of natural resource markets. *Land Economics*, 62 (August), 234–49.

Hall, D. C. and Hall, J. V. 1984: Concepts and measures of natural resource scarcity with a summary of recent trends. *Journal of Environmental Economics and Management*, 11 (December), 363–79.

Harberger, A. C. 1978: On the use of distributional weights in social cost–benefit analysis. *Journal of Political Economy*, 86 (April), S87–S120.

Hotelling, H. 1931: The economics of exhaustible resources. *Journal of Political Economy*, 39 (April), 137–75.

Howarth, R. B. 1991a: Intergenerational competitive equilibria under technological uncertainty and an exhaustible resource constraint. *Journal of Environmental Economics and Management*, 21 (November), 225–43.

Howarth, R. B. 1991b: Intertemporal equilibria and exhaustible resources: an overlapping generations approach. *Ecological Economics*, 4 (December), 237–52.

Howarth, R. B. 1992: Intergenerational justice and the chain of obligation. *Environmental Values*, 1 (Summer), 133–40.

Howarth, R. B. and Monahan, P. A. 1992: *Economics, Ethics, and Climate Policy*. Lawrence Berkeley Laboratory, LBL-33230.

Howarth, R. B. and Norgaard, R. B. 1990: Intergenerational resource rights, efficiency, and social optimality. *Land Economics*, 66 (February), 1–11.

Howarth, R. B. and Norgaard, R. B. 1992: Environmental valuation under sustainable development. *American Economic Review*, 82 (May), 473–7.

Howarth, R. B. and Norgaard, R. B. In press. Integenerational transfers and the social discount rate. *Environmental and Resource Economics*, forthcoming.

Hultkrantz, L. 1991: Forestry and the bequest motive. *Journal of Environmental Economics and Management*, 22 (March), 164–77.

Kemp, M. C. and Long N. V. 1980: The underexploitation of natural resources: a model with overlapping generations. In M. C. Kemp and N. V. Long (eds), *Exhaustible Resources, Optimality and Trade*, Amsterdam: North-Holland.

Kemp, M. C., Long, N. V. and Shimomura, K. 1984: The problem of survival: a closed economy. In M. C. Kemp and N. V. Long (eds), *Essays in the Economics of Exhaustible Resources*, Amsterdam: North-Holland.

Kirman, A. P. 1992: Whom or what does the representative individual represent? *Journal of Economic Perspectives*, 6 (Spring): 117–36.

Little, I. and Mirlees, J. 1968: *Manual of Industrial Project Analysis*, vol. II. Paris: Organization for Economic Cooperation and Development.

Löfgren, K. G. 1991: Another reconciliation between economists and forestry experts: OLG-arguments. *Environmental and Resource Economics*, 1, 83–95.

Malthus, T. R. 1978: *An Essay of Population*. London: Ward, Lock.

Marglin, S. A. 1963: The social rate of discount and the optimal rate of investment. *Quarterly Journal of Economics*, 77 (February), 95–111.

Marsh, G. P. 1864: *Man and Nature, or Physical Geography as Modified by Human Action*. Cambridge, MA: Harvard University Press (copyright 1965).

Meadows, D. H., Meadows, D. L., Randers, J. and Behrens, W. W. 1972: *The Limits to Growth*. New York: Signet.

Nordhaus, W. D. 1973: World dynamics – measurement without data. *Economic Journal*, 82 (December), 1156–83.

Norgaard, R. B. 1990: Economic indicators of resource scarcity: a critical essay. *Journal of Environmental Economics and Management*, 19 (July), 19–25.

Norgaard, R. B. 1992: *Sustainability and the Economics of Assuring Assets for Future Generations*. WPS 832, Washington, DC: World Bank.

Norgaard, R. B. 1993: The coevolution of economic and environmental systems and the emergence of unsustainability. In R. W. England (ed.), *Evolutionary Concepts in Contemporary Economics*, Ann Arbor, MI: University of Michigan Press.

Page, T. 1977: *Conservation and Economic Efficiency*. Baltimore, MD: Johns Hopkins University Press.

Parfit, D. 1983: Energy policy and the further future. In D. MacLean and P. G. Brown (eds), *Energy and the Future*, Totowa, NJ: Rowman & Littlefield.

Pearce, D. Markandya, A. and Barbier, E. 1989: *Blueprint for a Green Economy*. London: Earthscan.

Perrings, C. 1991: Reserved rationality and the precautionary principle: technological change, time and uncertainty in environmental decision making. In R. Constanza (ed.), *Ecological Economics: The Science and Management of Sustainability*, New York: Columbia University Press.

President's Materials Policy Commission. 1952; *Resources for Freedom*, vol. I: *Foundations for Growth and Security*. Washington, DC: Government Printing Office.

Ricardo, D. 1821: *The Principles of Political Economy and Taxation*, 3rd edn. London: G. Bell.

Sagoff, M. 1988: *Economy of the Earth: Philosophy, Law, and the Environment*. New York: Cambridge University Press.

Schwartz, T. 1978: Obligations to posterity. In R. I. Sikora and B. Barry (eds), *Obligations to Future Generations*, Philadelphia, PA: Temple University Press.

Sen, A. K. 1982; Approaches to the choice of discount rates for social benefit–cost analysis. In R. C. Lind (ed.), *Discounting for Time and Risk in Energy Policy*, Washington, DC: Resources for the Future.

Sen, A. K. 1987: *On Ethics and Economics*. New York: Basil Blackwell.

Slade, M. E. 1982; Trends in natural-resource commodity prices: an analysis of the time domain. *Journal of Environmental Economics and Management*, 9 (June), 122–37.

Solow, R. M. 1974: Integenerational equity and exhaustible resources. *Review of Economic Studies*, 41 (Symposium), 29–45.

Takayama, A. 1985: *Mathematical Economics*, 2nd edn. New York: Cambridge University Press.

Varian, H. 1984: *Microeconomic Analysis*, 2nd edn. New York: Norton.

Wilson, R., 1982: Risk measurement of public projects. In R. Lind (ed.), *Discounting for Time and Risk in Energy Policy*, Washington, DC: Resources for the Future.

World Commission on Environment and Development. 1987: *Our Common Future*. Oxford: Oxford University Press.

7

Neoclassical Economic Growth Theory and "Sustainability"

Michael A. Toman, John Pezzey, and
Jeffrey Krautkraemer

1 Introduction

The issue of "sustainability" figures prominently in contemporary discussions of natural resource and environmental management and economic development. However, the concept is not easily defined and is interpreted differently by economists, ecologists, philosophers, and others. Even among economists there are significant differences of interpretation. Some treat sustainability as not much more than another way of espousing economic efficiency in the management of services derived from the natural endowment.[1] Others claim that conventional economic efficiency criteria are inadequate for addressing sustainability concerns (see, for example, Norgaard, 1988; Daly and Cobb, 1989; and a number of the essays in Costanza, 1991). Solow (1993a, b) takes a more middle ground position, acknowledging the significance of intergenerational equity in sustainability, but largely emphasizing conventional efficiency criteria.

Our aims in this chapter are to identify the issues that seem to be most salient in formal economic analysis of sustainability, and to review economic growth theory involving natural resources and the environment that bears on these issues. In the latter effort we focus mostly on literature within the methodological mainstream of neoclassical economics, though the studies do not always maintain all the common assumptions of neoclassical theory. We do not attempt the more daunting task of systematically reviewing the methodological critiques of neoclassical theory, though the discussion of basic sustainability issues in the next section briefly summarizes some of the criticisms and provides numerous references. Nor do we attempt to cover all of the non-neoclassical modeling strategies that can and are being used (particularly by European economists) to address sustainability issues.

In addition, our review of the theoretical literature on economic progress and the natural environment focuses on studies in which population is exogenous. Clearly mutual interactions among population, economic progress, and the natural endowment are a central element of the sustainability debate. However, a review of the endogenous population literature is beyond the scope of this chapter.[2] We also focus on sustainability from the perspective of a single society rather than multiple social groupings. Finally, we focus here exclusively on theoretical issues, leaving to others in this volume the task of assessing how sustainability can be gauged in practice. However, our discussion in section 3 below has relevance for empirical work in this area.

In the next section we draw together arguments from economics, ecology, and philosophy to briefly describe what seem to be the most important issues in addressing sustainability. Armed with this characterization, we then review several categories of studies related to economic advance, natural resource use, and environmental preservation over time. We include both representative agent models and overlapping generations models in the review. The concluding section of the chapter summarizes our discussion and offers an overall assessment of the literature.

2   Sustainability: Basic Issues

While there is not a "textbook" definition of sustainability that commands widespread agreement, it is clear that a central issue is concern for the well-being of future generations in the face of growing pressure on the natural environment to provide a range of valued services (extractable materials, waste absorption, ecological system resilience, aesthetics).[3] A second issue, given a concern for future well-being, is the capacity for the economic system to substitute other forms of wealth for diminution of "natural capital" – the total repository of service capacities from the natural environment – in order to maintain the welfare of future generations. We consider these issues of intergenerational equity and resource substitutability in turn.

Intergenerational fairness

The debate over the connections between intergenerational equity and economic theory is long-standing and often confusing (see Kneese and Schulze (1985) for a good summary of the critique by economists). The conventional present-value approach in economic valuation is seen by many critics as putting too much weight on the welfare of the current generation. This approach seeks to make the sum of discounted net benefits across generations as large as possible, whether or not the current generation makes any efforts to compensate its descendants for prospective future damages resulting from current resource use. Critics of the approach sometimes argue that the emphasis on efficiency in economic analysis is misplaced, and that an appropriate strategy for increasing the attention placed on future generations is to lower discount rates.

The issue is more complicated than these criticisms would indicate. To understand the issues more clearly, we must first distinguish theories of value and fairness that are basically individualistic from theories that are more "organic," placing greater emphasis on the rights or welfare of the community at large. Arguments for the protection of the well-being of the human species as a whole, and of the ecosystems that surround it, are particularly common in the literature on environmental values (see, for example, Leopold, 1949: Lovelock, 1988; Callicott, 1989; Norton, 1982, 1986, 1989; Page, 1983, 1991, 1992). These arguments are a provocative challenge to economic reasoning that inherently treats the individual as the unit of analysis. However, because our focus in this chapter is on economic theory and sustainability, we limit our attention in what follows to individualistic constructs. Our approach also assumes that welfare, broadly defined, is a meaningful and relevant criterion. Critics have suggested that welfare is an inadequate or even meaningless indicator (Sen, 1982; Parfit, 1983b; Sagoff, 1988; Norton, 1992).

Within this domain, we can start with the broad concept of intergenerational economic efficiency given by the Pareto principle as a basic criterion for all intergenerational resource allocations. There are an infinite number of welfare allocations that are consistent with inter-temporal Pareto efficiency (Page, 1988). We must discriminate among these allocations using some intergenerational social welfare function (ISWF) that reflects the values associated with intergenerational fairness.[4]

The conventional approach of maximizing the present value of generational welfare is one possible ISWF. We shall henceforth refer to this criterion as *PV-optimality* to distinguish it from other allocations that also are efficient in the Pareto sense. One alternative to PV-optimality is to maximize the present value of welfare *subject to some form of rigid side constraint of justice*. The most familiar approach in this class derives from *Rawls's (1971) maximin criterion*, based on the maximization of the welfare level of the least well-off generation. This approach has been studied extensively in the context of economic growth models with natural resources, as discussed in the next section. Even if each generation is concerned only with the welfare of its immediate descendants, a recognition that our descendants also will be concerned about their descendants' welfare can give rise to an intertemporal "chain of obligation" to more distant generations that is akin to the maximin principle (Howarth, 1992). This can be thought of as a justice side constraint in that individuals are required to take a broader view of the well-being of their descendants than in the standard bequest model. Pezzey (1989) considers a more flexible constraint requiring only that *future utility be nondecreasing* (see also Riley, 1980). Asheim (1991) derives a similar criterion from a more basic set of social fairness axioms that extend the maximin framework.[5]

A relatively common theme in this line of argument is that individuals are more than just narrow welfare maximizers; they are citizens as well as consumers. It is in the former role that they agree to the specified justice constraints. However, there are both theoretical and practical difficulties in defining and assigning rights to (potential) members of future generations (see, for example, Golding, 1972; Passmore, 1974; Barry, 1977; Parfit, 1983a; Baier, 1984; Broome, 1992).

Another disadvantage of this approach is the framing of justice concerns as a side constraint in the ISWF. It would be desirable to represent sustainability concerns as properties of the ISWF itself, rather than as side constraints. In principle this could be done by *building a "sustainability function" into the ISWF* which adds a positive but finite social value for any future satisfying some posited sustainability condition. In practice, the properties of such a function are difficult to specify. The side constraint approach is a special case with an infinite penalty for violating the constraint and zero value in moving closer to it without satisfying it. A smoother formulation that allows *some tradeoffs between intergenerational concern and other social goods* might be a closer reflection of current political concerns, and might come closer to satisfying utilitarian philosophers like Broome (1992) who have argued against sustainability concepts. In a sense, this approach would come full circle back to PV-optimality, but with a vastly expanded set of arguments in the present-value calculation (including intergenerational concern) relative to conventional practice.

One hybrid approach that combines tradeoffs with more rigid side constraints is a "two-tier" approach to resource management (Page, 1983, 1991; Norton, 1984, 1992; Randall, 1986; Toman, 1992). Given a positive association among the scale of potential damage to natural capital, the degree of irreversibility, and the harm to future generations, the two-tier approach posits a fuzzy, societally determined dividing line where smaller-scale, more reversible threats are addressed primarily by conventional economic efficiency criteria while larger-scale, less reversible threats are more subject to *a priori* "constitution-like" constraints.

Resource substitutability

The other fundamental issue in discussions of sustainability, as noted above, concerns the capacity to substitute other forms of wealth for natural capital in order to maintain utility as natural capital is depleted or degraded from greater use. Sustainability in the sense of maintaining acceptable levels of welfare over time is concerned with the capacity of the natural environment and other social assets to provide the desired intertemporal welfare streams. The development of natural environments could disrupt the provision of services available from natural environments. If substitution possibilities are high enough this natural disruption gives no concern provided society's total savings rate is high enough to produce sustainable welfare paths. However, the converse also is true: if substitution possibilities are limited, then intergenerational equity concerns give rise to a special need for safeguarding natural capital.

The substitution issue goes beyond substituting technological progress (human and knowledge capital) or investment (built capital) for depletion of mineral and energy resources, as important as this set of substitution questions is. Substitution also involves the ability to offset a diminished capacity of the natural environment to provide waste absorption, ecological system maintenance, and aesthetic services. Questions about substitutions and technical progress versus thresholds and catastrophe risks are especially relevant when addressing large-scale damages to natural systems whose ecological functions remain poorly understood.[6]

As discussed further in the next section, the literature on depletable resources and economic progress shows that a relatively substantial capacity to substitute other inputs for diminished natural capital services is needed to maintain consumption of final goods and services over time. In the context of the familiar constant elasticity of substitution (CES) class of production functions, isoquants must be asymptotic to the axes (substitution elasticity, 1) or intersect the axes (substitution elasticity greater than 1) of input space. The difficulty with these conditions is that they seem to be inconsistent with physical laws.[7] Since the first law of thermodynamics requires conservation of mass and energy, the implication that, for example, the economy could run on zero or a vanishingly small quantity of energy is problematic. It seems more plausible to assume minimum input requirements and a bounded average product of material and energy inputs (as with a CES function with elasticity less than 1), thus eventually limiting total output to a level consistent with the capacity of renewable resource inputs. Materials balance also raises the specter of congested waste sinks as total demand for goods and services grows. In addition, dissipation of production potential (implied by the second law of thermodynamics) may limit long-term production, though here the argument is more controversial. A key issue is the capacity of technological progress to continue without bound, and the capacity of humans to keep up with perpetually accelerating technical change.[8]

Given potential nonsubstitutabilities between services derived from natural capital and other productive inputs, a complete sustainability criterion must address the flow of natural capital services as well as intergenerational fairness. One way this can be done is to retain the focus on utility, as in the previous paragraph, and represent nonsubstitutabilities in the production constraints that determine society's opportunity set. Alternatively, one can emphasize directly the preservation of "adequate" natural capital service flows. In dealing with these issues the concepts of "weak sustainability" and "strong sustainability" are often invoked, though these terms can be interpreted in various ways. An interpretation that refers directly to substitution among different production inputs is found in Pearce and Atkinson (1993) and Victor (1991). In this interpretation, if natural capital and other capital are substitutable then the weak sustainability criterion of preserving aggregate capital can be applied, but if there are limits on substitution then the strong sustainability criterion of preserving natural capital may be relevant. Another interpretation of weak and strong sustainability, one with an intertemporal element, is found in Barbier et al. (1990). These authors treat strong sustainability as requiring that net damages to environmental capital be nonpositive along the whole time path of resource exploitation, while weak sustainability requires only that the present value of damages be nonpositive; both of these definitions allow for some substitutability among various capital inputs.

Exactly how a sustainability criterion can best be formulated from these elements remains a subject for further research. For our purposes, the emphasis on both intergenerational fairness and natural capital services is sufficient to provide a frame for reviewing relevant contributions from the literature on economic progress and the natural environment.

3   Resource Use, Economic Growth, and Intergenerational Equity

Basic theory

From the mid-1970s through the early 1980s, a substantial literature developed that addressed (1) the nature of optimal economic growth paths, according to the utilitarian present-value criterion, with depletable resources; (2) the feasibility of sustained or growing per-capita consumption paths, whether such paths are present-value-maximizing or the result of an intergenerational fairness rule; and (3) the means through which such consumption paths might be achieved in practice. The term sustainability is rarely invoked in these earlier papers, but it is clear that the literature bears directly on the issues raised in the previous section.

Almost all of the papers under consideration here are based on extensions of the basic one-sector model of growth in which a depletable resource is also an input to production (along with labor and capital services).[9] The models fall into the representative agent category, with a central planner seeking to maximize the present value of a utility function whose argument is per-capita consumption (in section 4 we consider more complex utility specifications). As noted above, to avoid terminological confusion we will refer to outcomes under the present-value criterion as PV-optimal to distinguish them from optimal outcomes under other social welfare criteria or outcomes that simply are Pareto efficient. Consistent with the standard approach in growth theory, aggregate production technology in the studies being considered is assumed to be neoclassical with constant returns to scale; many results depend on the further assumption that technology shows CES.

The three papers by Dasgupta and Heal (1974), Solow (1974), and Stiglitz (1974) exemplify the contribution of this literature. Taken together, these papers deliver a number of conclusions. To present these conclusions, some notation is helpful. Let $\delta > 0$ denote a positive but constant rate of social time preference in the planner's objective function. Let $\rho \geq 0$ denote the asymptotic marginal product of capital as depletable resource use falls to zero and the capital–resource ratio increases without bound. Let $n \geq 0$ denote a constant exponential rate of population growth, and let $m \geq 0$ denote a constant exponential rate of technical progress (described more precisely below). Finally, let σ denote the elasticity of substitution between capital services and the resource.

Using this notation, we can draw the following conclusions from the three papers cited in the previous paragraph, at least with CES production.

1 If $m = 0$, then constant or growing consumption over time along a PV-optimal path occurs if and only if $\rho > \delta + n$.

2 However, it is feasible to have constant or increasing consumption and utility across generations if $\sigma \geq 1$, that is, if capital services are sufficiently substitutable for the depletable resource. If $\sigma > 1$ the result holds since output is possible even without the resource. If $\sigma = 1$ (a Cobb—Douglas technology), it must also be the case that $n = 0$ and that the share of total output going to capital must exceed the share of output going to the resource.[10]

3 Ever-increasing technical progress can, in theory, substantially alleviate resource constraints. For example, Stiglitz (1974) shows in the Cobb–Douglas case that sustained growth in per-capita consumption and thus utility can be feasible or even PV-optimal with growing population provided that m/γ is sufficiently large, where γ is the income share of the resource and m is the rate of factor-neutral progress. Intuitively, this follows from the fact that with Cobb–Douglas production m/γ can be thought of as the rate of resource-augmenting technical change.[11]

Stiglitz does not examine the case where $\sigma < 1$, but sustained consumption and utility are also possible in this case if the rate of resource-augmenting progress is high enough. This leaves open the question of whether it is realistic to make such a conception of progress that squeezes a constant flow of final consumption services out of an ever-shrinking flow of resource service inputs.[12]

Thus, consumption and utility along a PV-optimal path will be harshly intergenerationally inequitable if technical progress and the marginal productivity of capital are limited. Even the feasibility of sustained consumption requires a minimum degree of technical progress or factor substitutability. These conditions are sobering when one recalls the materials balance objections to CES production specifications with $\sigma \geq 1$ noted in the previous section. If $\sigma < 1$ then the average product of the resource is uniformly bounded and cumulative total output of the economy over the whole planning horizon is bounded by the product of the maximal average product of the resource and the initial resource stock. Clearly sustained consumption and utility are impossible in this case in the absence of technical progress.[13] Sustained consumption and utility are possible with a renewable backstop resource, though with a bounded average product of the resource the level of sustainable final consumption will be bounded above by a number that reflects the maximum sustainable flow of renewable resource services.

Sustainability, income accounting, and the reinvestment of resource rents

Models of resource–capital tradeoffs have been used to study a question of special policy interest: given that a society wants a sustainable consumption path over time while depleting its stock of nonrenewable resources, how rapid should investment in (human-made) capital be? An empirical aspect of this question is how national income accounting data can be used to evaluate the sustainability effects of different investment plans.

Hartwick (1977) shows that in a simple model with Cobb–Douglas technology, constant population, and a larger share of national output going to pay for the services of nondepreciable capital than for depletable resources, providing that it is feasible always to invest exactly the Hotelling scarcity rents from the depletable resource, then such investment results in constant consumption over time. This investment regime is now known as Hartwick's rule. Three qualifications immediately apply, however. First, the precise form of the rule will vary in more general economies, as shown by Hartwick (1978), Dixit et al. (1980), and Dasgupta and Mitra (1983), among others. Second, the rule is generally satisfied only when a continuous policy incentive is deliberately created; for example, along a

PV-optimal path it will not generally be true. Third, although Solow (1974) shows that a constant-consumption path is feasible for a Cobb–Douglas economy provided that initial consumption and resource extraction are not too high, the feasibility of Hartwick's rule is not generally guaranteed. In particular, it might lead to exhaustion of the resource stock in finite time, in which case consumption could not be maintained.

Hartwick's rule has been advocated as a prescription for sustainability, not just a condition of it, by several authors, notably Solow (1986) and Maler (1991). In particular, it is argued that following Hartwick's rule will maintain the value of total national wealth (natural and human-made) constant when appropriate shadow prices are used for valuation; and that the sustained consumption in this case can be seen as equal to net national product at these shadow prices, given zero aggregate value of investment under Hartwick's rule.

There are at least two objections, however, to this use of Hartwick's rule as prescription, not just characterization. The first is the problem of feasibility already noted. Second, and more troubling, is that Asheim (1994) and Pezzey (1994) have independently shown that an economy in which current investment exceeds the level of resource rent is not necessarily able to sustain its current level of utility by following Hartwick's rule (i.e. setting investment equal to resource rent) from now onwards. Both authors offer the counterexample that, during a certain finite period on the PV-optimal development path of a Cobb–Douglas economy with a large initial resource endowment relative to capital, investment exceeds the resource rent, and yet the maximum sustainable level of consumption starting from any time during that period is well below the current PV-optimal consumption level. The intuitive explanation is that the PV-optimal path is depleting the resource stock too fast for sustainability, causing the current resource price and hence the rent to be low relative to the sustainable outcome, so that even full investment of such rent will not ensure enough capital formation for sustainability.

The studies by Asheim and Pezzey point out an inherent flaw in using prices estimated under unsustainable conditions (even if, as in these studies, standard environmental externalities are assumed to have been fully taken into account). This poses a problem for estimating empirical measures of sustainable national income. Only by measuring resource rents using shadow prices *which reflect the sustainability constraint* (including the constraint of the remaining levels of resource stocks) will Hartwick's rule provide a correct guide to sustainability, indicating for example the unsustainability of the PV-optimal path discussed above. But estimating these shadow prices is even harder, and subject to greater uncertainty (e.g. regarding future resource discoveries and technical change), than any of the existing empirical efforts in resource accounting.[14]

Endogenous growth and sustainability

Recently interest in growth theory has been renewed by extensions of the standard model to include features referred to collectively as "endogenous growth" influences. Prominent examples include accumulations of human capital or investments in infrastructure that in some way provide increasing returns, so that such activities can cause acceleration in the expansion of economic activity (Romer, 1986, 1990; Lucas, 1988; Barro, 1990; Grossman and Helpman, 1992). Endogenous growth models are also finding their way into the resources and environment literature, though such applications are still at a fairly early stage and relatively little literature is published yet (for a recent review see Gastaldo and Ragot, 1994).

It would be fairly straightforward in principle to introduce endogenous growth factors into the Dasgupta–Heal–Solow–Stiglitz framework discussed in this section. Such factors would provide yet another channel in which resource-based limits to growth could be overcome in the theory. However, our earlier comments about the basic growth-with-resources model also apply to such extensions: if one assumes from the start that there are such substitution possibilities, the growth paths derived from the theory will be consistent with those assumptions. This leaves open the question of whether the indicated assumptions about substitution are appropriate.

4   "Stock Effects" and Preservation of Natural Capital

A second important strand of literature relevant to sustainability concerns the preservation of natural capital, given that natural capital provides valuable services in preserved states as well as extracted resource inputs. Thus, the issue of preservation is an important component in the overall debate on sustainability. The papers reviewed in this section do not impose the requirement that natural capital be preserved on ethical or ecological grounds. Instead, they seek to identify conditions under which at least partial preservation is part of a PV-optimal or a maximin program. The level of preservation is endogenous and may be large or small.

Amenity values and stock preservation

A simple way to capture the value of preserved environments in a growth model with a nonrenewable resource is to include the resource stock in the utility function. This is appropriate if the provision of "amenity" services for preserved environments is positively related to the stock of preserved natural environments, and if the stock of natural environments declines with the extraction of natural resources. In this framework, there is preservation asymptotically if and only if the resource is not completely exhausted.

Perhaps the earliest attribution of utility to the resource stock is by Vousden (1973) who includes the resource stock to represent an unspecified "conservation motive." This conservation motive reduces the rate of depletion of the resource stock. Whether or not it is desirable to consume all of the resource stock along a PV-optimal path depends upon the rate of discount relative to the marginal rate of substitution between consumption and amenity services. Since the latter depends upon what happens to the marginal utility of consumption as resource extraction goes to zero, the PV-optimality of permanent preservation depends in turn upon what happens to consumption as resource extraction goes to zero. If resource extraction is essential in producing the consumption good and the marginal utility of consumption becomes infinite as consumption use goes to zero, then it is PV-optimal to consume all of the resource stock. If there are alternative sources of the consumption good, then it may be desirable to preserve some of the resource stock along a PV-optimal path permanently.

The importance of maintaining the level of consumption carries over to more complex models. As noted previously, technological progress and capital–resource substitution are two ways in which an economy might maintain consumption in the presence of an essential nonrenewable resource. Krautkraemer (1985) examines the impact of these factors on the permanent preservation of natural environments. Preventing consumption from falling to zero is a necessary condition for permanent preservation to be PV-optimal since the marginal value of the extractive resource input becomes infinite as the level of consumption falls to zero. In this case, it can never be PV-optimal to leave some of the resource behind.[15]

Krautkraemer shows that if the society's initial capital stock is large enough and capital is sufficiently productive and substitutable for the depletable resource, some permanent preservation is desirable along a PV-optimal path. Under these conditions sustained consumption growth and preservation are not incompatible. The proof of this proposition assumes a CES production function with elasticity substitution greater than unity, which has problematic material-balance implications as noted previously. Krautkraemer also shows that it may be PV-optimal to exhaust the resource stock even if the marginal value of consumption is declining to zero because of growth in consumption from technological progress or from capital accumulation.[16] The incentive to exhaust the resource derives from the fact that the same forces which cause consumption growth also raise the marginal value product of the resource.

The prospects for permanent preservation of natural environments along a PV-optimal path are better if there is an upper bound on both the marginal value of the consumption output and the marginal productivity of the depletable resource input. This occurs if there is an alternative source of either consumption or resource input. Renewable resources and backstop technologies are ways in which a positive flow of consumption can be maintained without a perpetually increasing marginal product of the resource. In the case of a renewable resource, the PV-optimal path can lead to a steady state with a positive stock of depletable resource and preserved amenities (Krautkraemer, 1982). There can be multiple steady states depending upon the initial point. It is possible that a capital-rich economy would move to a steady state with a positive resource stock while a capital-poor economy would exhaust both its capital and resource stocks (Krautkraemer, 1982).

A backstop resource technology places an upper bound on the marginal productivity of the nonrenewable resource. If the marginal product of capital is greater than the rate of discount when the backstop becomes cost-competitive, then some permanent preservation can be PV-optimal (Krautkraemer, 1986). The steady state level of environmental preservation can be positively or negatively related to the rate of discount, depending upon the output shares of capital and the resource input (Krautkraemer, 1988).

Barrett (1992) examines a model in which a flow of consumption continues to be derived from developed land after resources have been extracted. Such a situation would occur with the conversion of virgin forest land to agricultural use. The case for permanent preservation is strengthened because the economy can sustain its level of consumption without the extractive resource. In essence, the flow of consumption from developed land is like a backstop technology.

As noted, the feasibility of sustainable growth in consumption does not imply that permanent preservation is PV-optimal. The rate of discount plays a critical role in capital–resource growth models since it determines the asymptotic rate of growth of the economy (Dasgupta and Heal, 1974). It is possible that a high rate of discount will bring about exhaustion of resource stocks, deterioration of the environment, and the steady decline of the economy along a PV-optimal path even when it is technologically feasible to sustain both the level of consumption and the quality of the environment (Krautraemer, 1985; Pezzey, 1989). The discount rate can affect the mix of assets as well as the size of the bequest to the future, so it is possible that a lower rate of discount will result in a more rapid depletion of some environmental and natural resource assets (Farzin, 1984: Krautkraemer, 1988).

Models with pollution effects

Pollution and environmental assets also have been incorporated in a number of studies on PV-optimal and maximum growth (Keeler et al.,

1972; Plourde, 1972; d'Arge and Kogiku, 1973; Forster, 1973; Asako, 1980; Becker, 1982; Heal, 1982; Tahvonen and Kuuluvainen, 1993). Pollution can enter the model in a variety of ways – as a stock (level of ambient quality), or as a flow (rate of emission). It can be a by-product of consumption and/or production and it can be an argument of either the production function, the utility function, or both. Pollution can be controlled through the choice of production processes or through the allocation of resources to the clean-up of effluents (see Klassen and Opschoor (1991) for further discussion).

Because of the diversity of modeling possibilities, the literature has produced a wide variety of sometimes disparate results. In most cases (e.g. Forster, 1973), the economy following a PV-optimal path approaches a steady state equilibrium in which the marginal value of consumption is equal to the marginal cost of production, including the environmental cost of pollution. In models which include both a pollution stock and a capital stock, there can be more than one PV-optimal steady state equilibrium (Heal, 1982). The PV-optimal steady state levels of pollution and consumption may depend upon the initial position of the economy. A capital-rich economy may move towards a relatively clean steady state environment while a less endowed economy may choose to pursue a lower level of abatement activity in order to allocate capital to the production of consumption goods. However, if the available technology allows sufficient capacity to substitute capital-intensive but lower-emission techniques as pollution accumulates, a unique PV-optimal steady state will exist (Tahvonen and Kuuluvainen, 1993) and the rich–poor dichotomy described above is avoided.[17]

5 Models of Sustainability

In this section we consider some recent literature in which sustainability is an explicit focus. The section is divided into three parts. We first consider representative agent models in which only one type of agent (whether infinitely lived or finitely lived) exists at any moment. We then consider overlapping generations (OLG) models, and finally models that focus on the preservation of natural capital.

Sustainability with representative agents

A PV-optimal path in a neoclassical growth model generally will have declining per-capita utility over time when the cost of deferring utility into the future, as indicated by the utility discount rate, exceeds the benefit of delayed utility. This benefit will depend on the productivity of capital (which indicates the benefit of savings), the rate of technical progress (more may be gotten out of resource consumption in the future), and the rate at which current resource use and overall production degrade the environment.

This observation about PV-optimal programs lies behind the work of Pezzey (1989), who analyzes sustainability as a societally determined constraint that per-capita utility not decrease over time. With this criterion, Pezzey examines sustainability in some simple, steady state models of nonrenewable resource depletion and capital–resource substitution in which too low a rate of technical progress leads to unsustainable PV-optimal paths, and government policies such as subsidies for resource conservation can combine with some technical progress to induce sustainable outcomes. Pezzey also notes that even if the government internalizes externalities from environmental degradation (such as the stock effects in the models of Krautkraemer and others discussed in the previous section), the result need not be a nondeclining utility path. Thus, sustainability policies and policies for efficient use of environmental resources are conceptually distinct. Moreover, since interest rates are endogenous in an economy with capital–resource substitution, they may rise or fall as the utility path moves closer to satisfying the sustainability constraint. This indicates that simply attempting to manipulate interest rates is not likely to be a useful sustainability policy. Pezzey's analysis of a simple agrarian economy suggests that reduced population growth rates, improved input productivity, and improved initial endowments through foreign aid could help promote sustainability.

Asheim (1988) and Pezzey (1994) study sustainability in the context of the Dasgupta–Heal (1974) economy reviewed in section 3. In this economy there is no technical progress and the productivity of capital, which motivates saving, decreases as the natural resource input is depleted. Asheim and Pezzey show that the path of maximum present value of utility subject to the nondeclining utility constraint, which Pezzey calls the "opsustimal path," generally has two phases: an initial finite phase of rising consumption and utility, followed by a perpetuity of constant consumption. Consistent with the discussion in section 3, it can be shown that the first phase is absent if the marginal product of capital if always less than the utility discount rate, while the phase of constant consumption (when the sustainability constraint is binding) never occurs if the marginal product of capital always remains above the utility discount rate (as pointed out previously, this assumption may be problematic). Simulation experiments by Pezzey show that opsustimal consumption during the first phase may exceed PV-optimal consumption, and that during the second phase the constant rate of opsustimal consumption may exceed the maximin consumption that a purely egalitarian society would have chosen at the outset. The latter point reflects the relatively low consumption in the early part of the first phase relative to the maximin path, allowing for capital accumulation that benefits future generations.

Pezzey (1994) then examines policies for achieving the opsustimal outcome in a decentralized economy. A consumption tax that declines over time, thereby directly stimulating savings especially earlier on, can achieve a sustainable path. However, neither a resource extraction tax nor a resource conservation subsidy can succeed in inducing sustainability in the absence of technical progress. These policies can maintain the marginal product of capital and thus the level of savings only with a rising rate of resource depletion over time, and this is impossible with a finite resource stock. This suggests that *if* capital–resource substitution is possible, savings policies are likely to promote sustainability better than policies for the preservation of natural capital.

In Pezzey's analyses the societally dictated constraint of nondeclining utility is taken as given. Asheim (1988) shows that the two-phase path is the only one that provides a time-consistent solution to the problem of maximizing the minimum present value of utility for any starting date.[18] Asheim (1991) further shows that, in any economy where deferring utility yields some productivity benefit, any "just" consumption path must be both efficient and nondeclining. Here a "just" path is defined by Asheim essentially as one which is not overtaken by any other path in terms of total *undiscounted* consumption and the equality of the allocation of consumption over time. Equality of the temporal allocation is in turn defined in a fairly subtle fashion (involving the existence of a bistochastic matrix).

These fairly difficult results provide an important link between the assumption of a nondeclining utility constraint and more fundamental ethical principles. However, they do not resolve the dilemma identified in section 2 as to how an ISWF should reflect concerns of intergenerational equity. The criteria used by Asheim, with a heavy emphasis on long-term intergenerational equity, clearly do not exhaust the set of plausible ISWFs. In particular, advocates of PV-optimality will fail to be persuaded that Asheim's arguments justify the imposition of a strict nondeclining utility constraint.

Intergenerational equity among overlapping generations

Howarth and/or Norgaard have written several papers showing how the distribution of resource rights or transfers among successive overlapping generations affects intergenerational equity (Howarth and Norgaard, 1990, 1992, 1993; Howarth, 1991a, b; Norgaard, 1992). The analysis rests on several basic assumptions.

1   There is a closed economy with a structure of overlapping generations. Generation t lives for two periods and seeks to maximize utility $U_t(C_{t1}, C_{t2})$, where C_{t1} is its consumption in period t when it is young and C_{t2} is its consumption in period $t + 1$ when it is old;[19] individuals in any generation are identical, so no issues of intragenerational equity are considered.

2   There is an ISWF $W(U_1, U_2, \ldots, U_t, \ldots)$ which society (as represented by its government) wants to maximize; this function may be the utilitarian present-value criterion or some other formulation.

3   A set of resource or income transfers from earlier to later generations can be made to reflect intergenerational social values.

4   There are competitive resource, goods, and labor markets in which the young of generation t trade with the old of generation $t - 1$ during period t, treating their resource or income transfers as given endowments.

A basic result in all the papers is a simple but powerful intergenerational extension of a standard result in welfare economics: "The choice of distribution of income is the same as the choice of a reallocation of endowments, and this in turn is equivalent to choosing a particular welfare function" (Varian, 1984, p. 209). Along paths seen as optimal from the standpoint of the current generation, in which that generation holds all property rights, there will be some intergenerational transfers (in the form of conserved natural resources or accumulated human-made capital) because of the current generation's concern for its own future. However, these transfers will not in general lead to an optimal distribution of welfare over time as indicated by the ISWF. The set of intergenerational property rights which enables competition to maximize social welfare will generally entail future generations "owning" some property.[20]

Howarth and Norgaard (1990) illustrate this result for an economy with a nonrenewable resource but no productive capacity, and Howarth (1991a) extends it to an economy with production and investment where intergenerational transfers are made using the produced good rather than the resource. Howarth (1991b) introduces uncertainty by considering alternative future states of nature, say $i = 1, \ldots, N$. He shows that treating generations born into these alternative possible states of nature at time t as ethically distinct, and hence setting $U_t = \min(U_{t1}, \ldots, U_{tN})$ in the ISWF, generally will require more risk-averse resource transfers to maximize social welfare W than if the more conventional expected utility assumption is made where U_t is the expected value of the U_{ti} over all the states of nature.

In Howarth and Norgaard (1992) the focus shifts from nonrenewable resources to cumulative pollution; they show that both the efficient pollution tax (i.e. the value of the environment) and interest rate both depend on the ISWF chosen. Howarth and Norgaard (1993) show that including the concern that individuals in a generation may privately feel for the utility of their own children, or of the whole next generation, does not avoid the basic result of the earlier studies. Such private altruism may still result in transfers between generations which are insufficient to allow the social optimum to be reached. Both papers show, in a straightforward application of the basic result given above, that internalizing environmental or intergenerational externalities will not necessarily achieve intergenerational equity, echoing a result in Pezzey (1989).

While Howarth and Norgaard are among the leading exponents of OLG models in sustainability analysis, they are by no means alone. Another example of this approach is given by Mourmouras (1993), who compares competitive and maximin equilibria in OLG models with renewable resources and waste accumulation. He shows in particular that when intertemporal markets to mediate waste flows do not exist, future generations may be unfairly disadvantaged and the government may need to pursue both tax and expenditure/debt policies to compensate for the missing markets.

The focus on intertemporal social preference orderings, particularly in Howarth and Norgaard's work, spotlights again the issue of how an ISWF should be specified. Howarth and Norgaard indicate a preference for a more egalitarian, maximin formulation, $W = \min(U_1, U_2, \ldots)$. Howarth (1992) derives this ISWF from an ethical maximin principle between just parents and children. They do not formally consider the efficiency-with-nondeclining-utility approach suggested by Pezzey (1989), which allows utility to rise over time. Instead, Howarth and Norgaard (1992) illustrate a case where maximizing the discounted utilitarian ISWF $W(U_1, U_2, \ldots, U_t, \ldots) = \Sigma_t U_t/(1 + \delta)^t, \delta > 0$, achieves sustainability only if the discount rate δ is low enough to give sufficient weight to the well-being of future generations.

There is also an important special case not covered by Howarth and Norgaard in which the same discount factor is used in both the ISWF and a within-generation utility function which includes private altruism, e.g. $W = \Sigma_t U_t/(1 + \delta)^t$ and $U_t = \ln(C_{t1}) + \ln(C_{t2})/(1 + \delta) + U_{t+1}/(1 + \delta)$. In this special case, endowing the first generation with all resource rights and maximizing all the U_ts through "social efficiency" – competition plus internalizing all externalities, but no socially mandated intergenerational transfers – does achieve social optimality, at least in the two-generation case (and probably more generally). Neoclassical economists would perhaps attach considerable weight to this special case, since it is arguably the only one where the ISWF is derived from individual within-generation preferences. Many philosophers, on the other hand, would claim that there is no reason to expect such a derivation, and that a maximin or sustainability-constrained ISWF is ethically more defensible. This leaves the debate over ISWFs where it belongs, in the realm of ethics rather than economics.

Sustainability and the preservation of non-substitutable natural capital

Barbier and Markandya (1990) consider a model in which natural capital is not freely substitutable by human-made capital. Their analysis therefore begins with the need to maintain some minimum positive level of natural capital in order to prevent ecological catastrophe (which of course would also destroy human utility), as opposed to relying only on a sustainability ethic. Barbier and Markandya start with the problem of maximizing discounted utility which depends on consumption and natural capital, $U = U(C, E)$ where E represents natural capital. This specification is similar to the amenity preservation studies reviewed in section 4. This maximization is carried out subject to preventing E from falling below the threshold where catastrophe occurs. The dynamic evolution of natural capital over time satisfies $\dot{E} = g(C, E)$ with $\partial g / \partial C < 0$ and $\partial g / \partial E > 0$ (provided E exceeds the threshold level). This relationship is derived from more basic materials-balance assumptions about how resource extraction and waste discharges affect environmental quality.

The behavior of the functions g and U as E approaches the threshold level is not fully spelled out. This makes it difficult to infer how unsustainable the PV-optimal outcome might be. Moreover, at the level of generality presented in the paper some important results (e.g. the presence of multiple equilibria) are conjectured rather than proved. Nevertheless, the analysis does further illustrate important potential differences between efficient and sustainable outcomes.

The main conclusions are that, if there are multiple equilibria, maximizing discounted utility may lead to catastrophe if the initial level of E is less than a critical value (above the threshold); and a higher discount rate increases the critical value, thus making catastrophe more likely. These conclusions are similar to those reported by Krautkraemer (1985, 1986, 1988), though in his studies the effect of a change in the discount rate is more ambiguous and there is no environmental threshold. The argument highlights an important point: while it might be suggested that conventional efficiency criteria (competitive markets, internalization of externalities) would prevent E from falling below the critical level, if market failures have caused E to fall below the threshold then invoking efficiency criteria alone will not achieve sustainability. This point is important to keep in mind when evaluating calls for improved economic efficiency in the use of natural resources and the environment by developing countries (see, for example, World Bank, 1992): such actions may well be necessary for sustainability, but they may also not be sufficient. The main policy implication is that foreign aid or some other policy which enables the natural resource base in an environmentally very poor country to recover can make the difference between individuals in a country being so poor that they "optimally" drive themselves to environmental catastrophe, and wealthy enough for the "optimal" path to achieve an environmentally sustainable state.

One other paper that can be put in this category is Common and Perrings (1992). These authors compare economic sustainability in terms of nondecreasing aggregate wealth with ecological sustainability in terms of preserving key attributes of complex natural functions. Their discussion provides a rationale for emphasizing preservation of natural capital broadly defined to include a range of ecological functions as a necessary condition for economic sustainability. Their analysis also highlights the difficulties in integrating realistic natural constraints on production possibilities into an economic model. In addition, they highlight the large distance between economic and ecological conceptions of sustainability.

6   Concluding Remarks

Our review of theoretical literature based on intertemporal models of resource use and capital accumulation indicates that, while these models provide only stylized descriptions of economic progress and economy–environment interactions, the literature nonetheless can contribute to an understanding of sustainability. The lessons drawn from this literature depend in part on the assumptions one makes. Those who believe in the capacity of substitution and innovation to address any problem of natural capital scarcity take comfort in the analyses that highlight the potency of substitution and innovation under certain conditions. Those who question the realism of these conditions will take a less sanguine view, emphasizing the importance of technical progress but also the relevance of constraints on renewable input flows.

We believe that one of the most important lessons to be drawn from the literature surveyed here is that sustainability is not synonymous with or automatically achieved by efficiency in the conventional sense of maximizing the present value of utility over time. Along such a program, the total rate of savings expressed in both accumulation of built capital and maintenance of natural capital may be too low to maintain or expand utility, even if substitution and innovation possibilities are favorable. If these possibilities are less favorable then the maintenance of natural capital becomes even more important in anticipating the basic interests of future generations.

It follows that the usual prescriptions for internalizing externalities and correcting market failures, while perhaps necessary for sustainability, are not sufficient. Sustainability is perfectly consistent with intertemporal Pareto efficiency and intergenerational justice as expressed in other intertemporal social welfare criteria, but achieving sustainability would require different degrees and direction of collective intervention than the conventional prescriptions. In this regard, the proposition that sustainability may be more likely for economies with significant endowments of built capital than for capital-poorer societies seems particularly relevant since it points to a role for distribution policies as well as conventional efficiency policies for achieving sustainability.

Because of the stylized nature of the models reviewed here, it is easy to identify potentially fruitful extensions. Actually carrying out these extensions is another matter, however. One obvious direction is toward incorporating somewhat greater realism and detail in the representation of ecological production possibilities and constraints, thereby narrowing the gap between ecological and economic sustainability. This requires in particular a more complex stochastic framework, in contrast to the deterministic analyses reviewed here.

A second, related research direction would involve a more systematic exploration of the relationship between scale and sustainability, particularly in an international context. Sustainability criteria and constraints depend partly on the scale of impacts under consideration. Sustainability at the village, national, and global levels will not be the same. Substitution possibilities will be different. Moreover, citizens of one country can affect the sustainability of others both through trade in goods and through transboundary environmental spillovers. These interactions generate complex interdependences of different countries' sustainability policies.

It would be also profitable to examine the influences on individual and societal values in order to understand better the preferences of the current generation and the prospective values of future generations whose interests figure so prominently in sustainability. However, purely logical or axiomatic philosophical reasoning can never settle the question of what kinds of sustainability preferences society *should* have. Only the crude test of popularity ultimately can settle the issue. Moreover, while it is desirable to have a better understanding of how different sustainability criteria can be derived from particular individual preference orderings, it is important to bear in mind that our knowledge of individual preferences for sustainability remains limited, social decision rules are not just mechanical products of individual utility functions, and some controversy remains over whether the issue should be couched in terms of preferences.

Finally, this chapter has looked at sustainability only in a single society which in some sense has a unified social objective, whatever that may be; but the real world comprises scores of different societies, be they tribes, nations or supranational groupings. Since cultural attitudes towards sustainability (including philosophical views about intergenerational equity) in such groups are to some degree inherited, they are shaped by the course of history. Such attitudes will inevitably be different in groups which have expanded rapidly by exploiting nonrenewable resources than in groups with nearly static territories and technologies. This may explain, for example, why material progress rather than sustainability has been the unquestioned overall aim of Western societies until very recently, and why a shift toward greater emphasis in sustainability will encounter resistance (see Pezzey, 1992, for further discussion). Much remains to be done in understanding issues like this, which transcend the standard disciplinary boundaries of economics.

Notes

The authors are grateful to Geir Asheim, Edward Barbier, Richard Howarth, David Pearce, and Tom Tietenberg for helpful advice during the preparation of this chapter. The chapter also benefited from the assistance of Mary Elizabeth Calhoon and Kay Murphy. Pezzey's research was supported by award L320-27-3002 from the UK Economic and Social Research Council. Toman's research was supported in part by grant R82-1386-010 from the US Environmental Protection Agency.

1 See, for example, Dasgupta and Maler (1991). This itself would be no small accomplishment given the current inefficiencies of resource use throughout the world (World Bank, 1992).

2 Dasgupta (1993, ch. 12) provides an excellent survey of population issues; see also Mitra (1983).

3 The often-cited report of the World Commission on Environment and Development (1987, p. 43) describes sustainable development as "development that meets the needs of the present without compromising the ability of future generations to meet their own needs."

4 It is worth pointing out that, even in a conventional utilitarian framework, Pareto efficiency need not imply uniform discounting of utilities, particularly in the context of intertemporal public goods (Sandler and Smith, 1976, 1977, 1982; Bishop, 1977; Cabe, 1982). It is also possible to assume a low or zero time preference rate on ethical grounds and still set the discount rate to reflect the rate of growth of productive capacity and the declining marginal utility of consumption as income grows (Page, 1977; Pearce, 1983; Burton, 1993). In addition, intergenerational concerns in individual utility functions can be represented with bequest concerns. Such bequests could include compensation for irreversible damages (valued as described in Krutilla (1967) and Krutilla and Fisher (1985)), assuming such compensation is feasible.

5 Justice constraints also figure prominently in many noneconomic writings that argue for an intergenerational stewardship obligation (see, for example, Weiss, 1989). These arguments tend to emphasize assessment of natural capital itself over utility, an emphasis also found in the economic writings of Barbier et al. (1990).

6 Lying behind these questions are exceedingly complex empirical issues (Pezzey, 1992).

7 For discussion of physical limits see Ayres and Kneese (1969), Kneese et al. (1971), Perrings (1986), Anderson (1987), and Gross and Veendorp (1990).

8 For discussion of these issues see Ayres and Miller (1980), Baumol (1986), Lozada (1991), Young (1991), Amir (1992), and Pezzey (1992).

9 Some of the models generalize technology to consider multiple capital services.

10 There is an upper bound on the size of the consumption flow that can be sustained in this case.

11 It is certainly open to question in the case of energy inputs since there clearly are thermodynamic limits to energy efficiency.

12 A similar issue arises in connection with the recent paper by van Geldrop and Withagen (1993), in which the authors assume that any damages to natural capital can be offset by renewal or compensatory investments.

13 While sustained consumption is feasible with $\sigma = 1$ it is not optimal, since $\rho = 0$ in this case.

14 Hartwick's rule must also be modified when the substitutability of resources and capital assumed in the Hartwick analysis does not hold. As discussed by El-Serafy (1989) and von Amsberg (1992), when natural capital is singled out for preservation more stringent investment requirements must be met.

15 Krautkraemer assumes that the marginal utility of amenities is bounded even as the resource stock and amenities from locations where the resource is found to go to zero. This can be justified by assuming that there is a "backstop" source of amenities at some minimal level from environments that have not been disturbed by resource depletion. This assumption is reasonable for amenity losses associated directly with extraction, but it may be more difficult to maintain when the issue is disamenities from global pollution accumulation.

16 Even if the amenity value does not prevent exhaustion of the resource stock, it does lead to greater conservation of the resource in that extraction is deferred to the future.

17 The potential variation in dynamic models increases dramatically when both an exhaustible resource and an environmental asset are incorporated in the model. As one might expect, a resource–environmental quality model generates pessimistic results unless more attractive features, such as a backstop technology, recycling, or capital or renewable resource substitutions are also included. d'Arge and Kogiku (1973) examine a model in which a nonrenewable resource is used in production and pollution is a by-product of production. In this model, the economy is unable to sustain itself permanently, even with recycling. More optimistic results are obtained when capital accumulation is included in the model (Asako, 1980).

18 Riley (1980) also uses a social criterion based on the present value of utility available from any specified starting date onwards, but he basically restricts attention to paths which make this criterion nondeclining without concern for maximization of the criterion. By assuming a somewhat unusual specification of energy technology, he shows that, if the initial energy endowment is large enough, the current generation's own selfish present-value-maximizing plan will lead to too rapid energy use compared with the just (nondeclining) outcome, at least until technical progress relaxes the resource stock constraint by making renewable energy competitive.

19 In Howarth and Norgaard (1990) utility depends directly on resource depletion and labor services.

20 The argument that intergenerational equity issues can be assessed by intergenerational reallocations of property rights has been criticized in a recent paper by Randall and Farmer (1993). These authors argue that, when the two-generation analyses of Howarth and Norgaard are generalized to a setting with three or more generations, a more Coasian kind of result obtains: equilibrium is less sensitive to the initial distribution of property rights.

References

Amir, S. 1992: The environmental cost of sustainable welfare. RFF Discussion Paper QE92-17-Rev, Resources for the Future, Washington, DC.

von Amsberg, J. 1992: The economic evaluation of natural capital depletion: an application of the sustainability principle. Draft manuscript, University of British Columbia, Faculty of Commerce and Business Administration, Vancouver, BC, January 31.

Anderson, C. L. 1987: The production process: inputs and wastes. *Journal of Environmental Economics and Management*, 14 (1) (March), 1–12.

d'Arge, R. and Kogiku, K. 1973: Economic growth and the environment. *Review of Economic Studies*, 40 (1) (January), 61–77.

Asako, K. 1980: Economic growth and environmental pollution under the max–min principle. *Journal of Environmental Economics and Management*, 7, (2) (June), 157–83.

Asheim, G. B. 1988: Rawlsian intergenerational justice as a markov-perfect equilibrium in a resource technology. *Review of Economic Studies*, 55 (3) (July), 469–84.

Asheim, G. B. 1991: Unjust intergenerational allocations. *Journal of Economic Theory*, 54 (2) (August), 350–71.

Asheim, G. B. 1994: New national product as an indicator of sustainability. *Scandinavian Journal of Economics*, forthcoming.

Ayres, R. U. and Kneese, A. V. 1969: Production, consumption, and externalities. *American Economic Review*, 69 (3) (June), 282–97.

Ayres, R. U. and Miller, S. 1980: The role of technological change. *Journal of Environmental Economics and Management*, 7 (4) (December), 353–71.

Baier, A. 1984: For the sake of future generations. In T. Regan (ed.), *Earthbound: New Introductory Essays in Environmental Ethics*, New York: Random House.

Barbier, E. B. and Markandya, A. 1990: The conditions for achieving environmentally sustainable development. *European Economic Review*, 34 (2–3) (May), 659–69.

Barbier, E. B., Markandya, A. and Pearce, D. W. 1990: Environmental sustainability and cost-benefit analysis. *Environment and Planning A*, 22 (9) (September), 1259–66.

Barrett, S. 1992: Economic growth and environmental preservation. *Journal of Environmental Economics and Management*, 23 (3) (November), 289–300.

Barro, R. J. 1990: Government spending in a simple model of endogenous growth. *Journal of Political Economy*, 98 (5) (October), 103–25.

Barry, B. 1977: Justice between generations. In P. M. S. Hacker and S. J. Raz (eds), *Law, Morality, and Society: Essays in Honour of H. L. A. Hart*, Oxford: Clarendon.

Baumol, W. J. 1986: On the possibility of continuing expansion of finite resources. *Kyklos*, 39 (2), 167–79.

Becker, R. A. 1982: Intergenerational equity: the capital–environment trade-off. *Journal of Environmental Economics and Management*, 9 (2) (June), 165–85.

Bishop, R. C. 1977: Intertemporal and intergenerational Pareto efficiency: a comment. *Journal of Environmental Economics and Management*, 4 (3) (September), 247–57.

Broome, J. 1992: *Counting the Cost of Global Warming*. Cambridge: White Horse Press.

Burton, P. S. 1993: Intertemporal preferences and intergenerational equity considerations in optimal resource harvesting. *Journal of Environmental Economics and Management*, 24 (2) (March), 119–32.

Cabe, R. A. 1982: Intertemporal and intergenerational Pareto efficiency: an extended theorem. *Journal of Environmental Economics and Management*, 9 (4) (December), 355–60.

Callicott, J. B. 1989: *In Defense of the Land Ethic*. Albany, NY: State University of New York Press.

Common, M. and Perrings, C. 1992: Towards an ecological economics of sustainability. *Ecological Economics*, 6 (1) (July), 7–34.

Costanza, R. (ed.) 1991: *Ecological Economics: The Science and Management of Sustainability*. New York: Columbia University Press.

Daly, H. and Cobb, J. 1989: *For the Common Good*. Boston, MA: Beacon Press.

Dasgupta, P. S. 1993: The population problem. In *An Enquiry into Well-Being and Destitution*, Oxford: Clarendon.

Dasgupta, P. S. and Heal, G. M. 1974: The optimal depletion of exhaustible resources. In *Review of Economic Studies Symposium on the Economics of Exhaustible Resources*, Edinburgh: Longman, 3–28.

Dasgupta, P. S. and Maler, K.-G. 1991: The environment and emerging development issues. In *Proceedings of the World Bank Annual Conference on Development Economics 1990*, Washington, DC: World Bank.

Dasgupta, S. and Mitra, T. 1983: Intergenerational equity and efficient allocation of exhaustible resources. *International Economic Review*, 24 (1) (February), 133–53.

Dixit, A., Hammond, P. and Hoel, M. 1980: On Hartwick's rule for regular maximin paths of capital accumulation and resource depletion. *Review of Economic Studies*, 47 (3) (April), 551–6.

El-Serafy, S. 1989: The proper calculation of income from depletable natural resources. In Y. J. Ahmad, S. el Serafy and E. Lutz (eds), *Environmental Accounting for Sustainable Development*, Washington, DC: World Bank.

Farzin, Y. H. 1984: The effect of the discount rate on depletion of exhaustible resources. *Journal of Political Economy*, 92 (5) (October), 841–51.

Forster, B. 1973: Optimal consumption planning in a polluted environment. *Economic Record*, 49 (128) (December), 534–45.

Gastaldo, S. and Ragot, L. 1994: Une approche du développement soutenable par les modèles de croissance endogène. In *Models of Sustainable Development: Exclusive or Complementary Approaches to Sustainability*, vol. 1, Papers presented at a conference at the University of Paris, March.

van Geldrop, J. and Withagen, C. 1993: Natural capital and sustainability. Draft manuscript, Department of Mathematics and Computing Science, Eindhoven University of Technology.

Golding, Martin P. 1972: Obligations to future generations. *The Monist*, 56 (1), 85–99.

Gross, L. S. and Veendorp, E. C. H. 1990: Growth with exhaustible resources and a materials-balance production function. *Natural Resource Modeling*, 4 (1) (Winter), 77–94.

Grossman, G. M. and Helpman, E. 1992: *Innovation and Growth in the Global Economy*. Cambridge, MA: MIT Press.

Hartwick, J. M. 1977: Intergenerational equity and the investing of rents from exhaustible resources. *American Economic Review*, 67 (5) (December), 972–4.

Hartwick, J. M. 1978: Exploitation of many deposits of an exhaustible resource. *Econometrica*, 46 (1) (January), 201–17.

Heal, G. H. 1982: The use of common property resources. In V. K. Smith and J. V. Krutilla (eds.) *Explorations in Natural Resource Economics*, Baltimore, MD: Johns Hopkins University Press for Resources for the Future.

Howarth, R. B. 1991a: Intergenerational competitive equilibria under technological uncertainty and an exhaustible resource constraint. *Journal of Environmental Economics and Management*, 21 (3) (November), 225–43.

Howarth, R. B. 1991b: Intertemporal equilibria and exhaustible resources: an overlapping generations approach. *Ecological Economics*, 4 (3) (December), 237–52.

Howarth, R. B. 1992: Intergenerational justice and the chain of obligation. *Environmental Values*, 1 (2) (Summer), 133–40.

Howarth, R. B. and Norgaard, R. B. 1990: Intergenerational resource rights, efficiency and social optimality. *Land Economics*, 66 (1) (February), 1–11.

Howarth, R. B. and Norgaard, R. B. 1992: Environmental valuation under sustainability. *American Economic Review*, 82 (2) (May), 473–7.

Howarth, R. B. and Norgaard, R. B. 1993: Intergenerational transfers and the social discount rate. *Environmental and Resource Economics*, 3 (4) (August), 337–58.

Keeler, E., Spence, M. and Zeckhauser, R. 1972: The optimal control of pollution. *Journal of Economic Theory*, 4 (1) (February), 19–34.

Klassen, G. A. J. and Opschoor, J. B. 1991: Methodological and ideological options. *Ecological Economics*, 4 (2) (November), 93–115.

Kneese, A. V. and Schulze, W. D. 1985: Ethics and environmental economics. In A. V. Kneese and J. L. Sweeney (eds), *Handbook of Natural Resource and Energy Economics*, vol. 1, Amsterdam: North-Holland.

Kneese, A. V., Ayres, R. and d'Arge, R. 1971: *Economics and the Environment*. Baltimore, MD: Johns Hopkins University Press for Resources for the Future.

Krautkraemer, J. A. 1982: Optimal growth, resource amenities and the extraction of natural resources. Unpublished Ph.D. Dissertation, Stanford University.

Krautkraemer, J. A. 1985: Optimal growth, resource amenities and the preservation of natural environments. *Review of Economic Studies*, 52 (1) (January), 153–70.

Krautkraemer, J. A. 1986: Optimal depletion with resource amenities and a backstop technology. *Resources and Energy*, 8 (2) (June), 133–49.

Krautkraemer, J. A. 1988: The rate of discount and the preservation of natural environments. *Natural Resource Modeling*, 2 (3) (Winter), 421–37.

Krutilla, J. V. 1967: Conservation reconsidered. *American Economic Review*, 54 (4) (September), 777–86.

Krutilla, J. V. and Fisher, A. C. 1985: *The Economics of Natural Environments: Studies in the Valuation of Commodity and Amenity Resources*, 2nd edn. Washington, DC: Resources for the Future.

Leopold, A. 1949: *A Sand County Almanac*. New York: Oxford University Press.

Lovelock, J. 1988: *The Ages of Gaia*. New York: Norton.

Lozada, G. A. 1991: Why the entropy law is relevant to the economics of natural resource scarcity. Draft manuscript, Energy and Resources Group, University of California, Berkeley, October.

Lucas, R. E. 1988: On the mechanics of economic development. *Journal of Monetary Economics*, 22 (1), 3–42.

Maler, K.-G. 1991: National accounts and environmental resources. *Environmental and Resource Economics*, 1 (1), 1–16.

Mitra, T. 1983: Limits on population growth under exhaustible resource constraints. *International Economic Review*, 24 (1) (February), 155–68.

Mourmouras, A. 1993: Conservationist government policies and intergenerational equity in an overlapping generations model with renewable resources. *Journal of Public Economics*, 51 (2) (June), 249–68.

Norgaard, R. B. 1988: Sustainable development: a co-evolutionary view. *Futures*, 20 (6) (December), 606–20.

Norgaard, R. B. 1992: Sustainability and the economics of assuring assets for future generations. Working Paper WPS 832, World Bank, Washington, DC.

Norton, B. G. 1982: Environmental ethics and the rights of future generations. *Environmental Ethics*, 4 (4) (Winter), 319–30.

Norton, B. G. 1984: Environmental ethics and weak anthropocentrism. *Environmental Ethics*, 6 (2) (Summer), 131–48.

Norton, B. G. 1986: On the inherent danger of undervaluing species. In B. G. Norton (ed.), *The Preservation of Species*, Princeton, NJ: Princeton University Press.

Norton, B. G. 1989: Intergenerational equity and environmental decisions: a model using Rawls' veil of ignorance. *Ecological Economics*, 1 (2) (May), 137–59.

Norton, B. G. 1992: *Toward Unity Among Environmentalists*. New York: Oxford University Press.

Page, T. 1977: *Conservation and Economic Efficiency*. Baltimore, MD: Johns Hopkins University Press for Resources for the Future.

Page, T. 1983: Intergenerational justice as opportunity. In D. MacLean and P. G. Brown (eds), *Energy and the Future*, Totowa, NJ: Rowman & Littlefield.

Page T. 1988: Intergenerational equity and the social rate of discount. In V. Kerry Smith (ed.), *Environmental Resources and Applied Welfare Economics*, Washington, DC: Resources for the Future.

Page T. 1991: Substainability and the problem of valuation. In R. Costanza (ed.), *Ecological Economics; the Science and Management of Sustainability*, New York: Columbia University Press.

Page T. 1992: Environmental existentialism. In R. Costanza, B. G. Norton, and B. D. Haskell (eds), *Ecosystem Health New Goals for Environmental Management*, Washington, DC: Island Press, 97–123.

Parfit, D. 1983a: Energy policy and the further future: the identity problem. In D. MacLean and P. G. Brown (eds), *Energy and the Future*, Totowa, NJ: Rowman & Littlefield.

Parfit, D. 1983b: Energy policy and the further future: the social discount rate. In D. MacLean and P. G. Brown (eds), *Energy and the Future*, Totowa, NJ: Rowman & Littlefield.

Passmore, J. 1974: *Man's Responsibility for Nature*. New York: Scribner's.

Pearce, D. W. 1983: Ethics, irreversibility, future generations and the social rate of discount. *International Journal of Environmental Studies*, 21 (1), 67–86.

Pearce, D. W. and Atkinson, G. D. 1993: Capital theory and the measurement of sustainable development: some empirical evidence. *Ecological Economics*, 8 (2) (October), 103–8.

Perrings, C. 1986: Conservation of mass and instability in a dynamic economy–environment system. *Journal of Environmental Economics and Management*, 13 (3) (September), 199–211.

Pezzey, J. 1989: *Economic Analysis of Sustainable Growth and Sustainable Development*, Environment Department Working Paper 15. Washington, DC: World Bank, March. Now reprinted as Pezzey. J. 1992: *Sustainable Development Concepts: An Economic Analysis*, World Bank Environment Paper 2.

Pezzey, J. 1992: Sustainability: an interdisciplinary guide. *Environmental Values*, 1 (March), 321–62.

Pezzey, J. 1994: The optimal sustainable depletion of nonrenewable resources. Draft manuscript, Department of Economics, University College London, March.

Plourde, C. G. 1972: A model of waste accumulation and disposal. *Canadian Journal of Economics*, 5 (1) (February), 199–25.

Randall, A. 1986: Human preferences, economics, and the preservation of species. In B. G. Norton (ed.), *The Preservation of Species*, Princeton, NJ: Princeton University Press.

Randall, A. and Farmer, M. C. 1993: Policies for sustainability: lessons from an overlapping generations model. Draft manuscript, Ohio State University, Columbus, OH, January 25.

Rawls, J. 1971: *A Theory of Justice*. Cambridge, MA: Harvard University Press.

Riley, J. G. 1980: The just rate of depletion of a natural resource. *Journal of Environmental Economics and Management*, 7 (3) (September), 291–307.

Romer, P. M. 1986: Increasing returns and long-run growth. *Journal of Political Economy*, 94 (5) (October), 1002–37.

Romer, P. M. 1990: Endogenous technological change. *Journal of Political Economy*, 4 (3) (September), 252–7.

Sagoff, M. 1988: *The Economy of the Earth*. New York: Cambridge University Press.

Sandler, T. and Smith, V. K. 1976: Intertemporal and intergenerational Pareto efficiency. *Journal of Environmental Economics and Management*, 2 (3) (February), 151–9.

Sandler, T. and Smith, V. K. 1977: Intertemporal and intergenerational Pareto efficiency revisited. *Journal of Environmental Economics and Management*, 4 (3) (September), 252–7.

Sandler, T. and Smith, V. K. 1982: Intertemporal and intergenerational Pareto efficiency: a reconsideration of recent extensions. *Journal of Environmental Economics and Management*, 9 (4) (December), 361–5.

Sen, A. K. 1982: Approaches to the choice of discount rates for social benefit–cost analysis. In Robert C. Lind et al. (eds), *Discounting for Time and Risk in Energy Policy*, Washington, DC: Resources for the Future, 325–53.

Solow, R. M. 1974: Intergenerational equity and exhaustible resources. *Review of Economic Studies, Symposium on the Economics of Exhaustible Resources*, vol. 41. Edinburgh: Longman, 29–45.

Solow, R. M. 1986: On the intergenerational allocation of natural resources. *Scandinavian Journal of Economics*, 88, 141–9.

Solow, R. M. 1993a: An almost practical step toward sustainability. *Resources Policy*, 19 (30) (September), 162–72.

Solow, R. M. 1993b: Sustainability: an economist's perspective. In R. Dorfman and N. Dorfman (eds), *Selected Readings in Environmental Economics*, 3rd edn, New York: Norton.

Stiglitz, J. 1974: Growth with exhaustible natural resources: efficient and optimal growth paths. *Review of Economic Studies, Symposium on the Economics of Exhaustible Resources*, vol. 41. Edinburgh, Longman, 123–37.

Tahvonen, O. and Kuuluvainen, J. 1993: Economic growth, pollution, and renewable resources. *Journal of Environmental Economics and Management*, 24 (2) (March), 101–18.

Toman, M. A. 1992: The difficulty in defining sustainability. In J. Darmstadter (ed.), *Global Development and the Environment: Perspectives on Sustainability*, Washington, DC: Resources for the Future.

Varian, H. 1984: *Microeconomic Analysis*, 2nd edn. New York: Norton.

Victor, P. A. 1991: Indicators of sustainable development: some lessons from capital theory. *Ecological Economics*, 4 (3) (December), 191–214.

Vousden, N. 1973: Basic theoretical issues in resource depletion. *Journal of Economic Theory*, 6 (2) (April) 126–43.

Weiss, E. B. 1989: *In Fairness to Future Generations*. Dobbs Ferry, NY: Transnational Publishers.

World Bank. 1992: *World Development Report 1992: Development and the Environment*. New York: Oxford University Press.

World Commission on Environment and Development (WCED). 1987: *Our Common Future*. New York: Oxford University Press.

Young, J. T. 1991: Is the entropy law relevant to the economics of natural resource scarcity? *Journal of Environmental Economics and Management*, 21 (2) (September), 169–79.

8

Measuring Sustainable Development

David Pearce and Giles Atkinson

1 Introduction

"Sustainable development" was the subject of the World Commission of Environment and Development's report *Our Common Future* (WCED, 1987) and the focus of the "Earth Summit" in Rio de Janeiro in June 1992. Discussion has centered on

- defining sustainable development,
- determining the conditions for achieving sustainable development,
- measuring sustainable development, that is, determining whether a nation or the global economy is on or off a sustainable development path.

This chapter is concerned with the third issue – measuring sustainability. We propose a simple measure of what we call "weak sustainability" and present a simple yet intuitive sustainability index. This measure is assessed in the light of arguments regarding "strong sustainability" and the concept of critical natural capital. Finally, further qualifications and extensions are examined, notably the role of international trade and technological progress in modifying any index.

2 Defining Sustainable Development

Definitions of sustainable development abound (Pezzey, 1989). *Economic* definitions have tended to focus on sustainable development as nondeclining per-capita human well-being over time (Pearce et al., 1989, 1990). Nondeclining well-being is an intertemporal *equity* principle rather than an *efficiency* principle. It is well known that maximization of future utility streams is consistent with eventually declining utility (Dasgupta and Heal, 1979; Pezzey, 1989). As such, sustainability is potentially inconsistent with a conventional cost–benefit approach since it denies the possibility that greater net benefits now can be secured at the expense of the future – actual not potential compensation must apply. Attempts to modify cost–benefit analysis for sustainability are in their infancy. One approach has been suggested by Barbier et al. (1990). Our concern in this chapter, however, is sustainability at the macroeconomic level.

3   Conditions for Sustainability

Various authors have established a relationship between sustainability, defined as nondeclining utility, and the underlying capital stock. Hartwick (1977) has shown that this corresponds to a requirement to invest the rents from nonrenewable resource use. Thus, a nation relying heavily on a nonrenewable natural resource such as oil should reinvest the rents from the exploitation of that resource if it is to achieve constant real consumption over time. The "Hartwick rule" has been reflected in the political economy of oil and gas in Norway, the Netherlands and the United Kingdom, where the criticism has been that resource rents have been consumed rather than reinvested (e.g. Forsyth, 1986). Solow (1986) has shown that Hartwick's rule can be interpreted as a requirement to "keep capital intact." To achieve constant real consumption through time (the lower bound of sustainability) it is necessary to keep the underlying capital stock constant. Much of the import of the Hartwick–Solow analysis had already been captured in an important and often neglected work by Page (1977). Moreover, the flow of consumption that can be sustained without reducing capital corresponds to Hicks' definition of income (Hicks, 1946). Thus, the line of analysis from Hicks through Page, Hartwick, and Solow establishes the "constant capital" rule.

Capital assets take three forms:

1   man-made capital (or, in much of the literature, "reproducible capital") in the conventional sense of machines, buildings, and roads etc. – this we denote K_M;
2   human capital – the stock of knowledge and skills, denoted here by K_H;
3   "natural capital" – K_N. In terms of the growth theory literature K_N appears as "natural resources." However, it is important to construe K_N more widely. It is far more than the stock of energy and mineral assets. It includes all renewable resources and "quasi-renewables" such as tropical forests, the ozone layer, the atmospheric carbon cycle etc. Any natural asset yielding a flow of ecological services with economic values over time (and all ecological services are likely to have economic values) is natural capital.

The Hicks–Page–Hartwick–Solow rule (henceforth HPHS) thus becomes a requirement that the value of the net change in the total capital stock (K) must be equal to or greater than zero:

$$\frac{dK}{dt} = \dot{K} = \frac{d(K_M + K_N + K_H)}{dt} \geq 0 \tag{8.1}$$

where $K = K_M + K_N + K_H$. From this we can take a simple short-cut to an intuitive rule for sustainability. We know that net capital accumulation can be expressed as

$$\dot{K} = S(t) - \delta K(t) \tag{8.2}$$

where $S(t)$ is gross savings and δ is depreciation on overall capital stock. Combining (8.1) and (8.2) the condition for sustainability becomes

$$S(t) - \delta K(t) \geq 0 \tag{8.3}$$

Decomposing K into its three main components, this becomes

$$S(t) - \delta_M K_M(t) - \delta_H K_H(t) - \delta_N K_N(t) \geq 0 \tag{8.4}$$

For current purposes we assume $\delta_H = 0$, that is, knowledge and skills do not "depreciate." Obviously, if $\delta_H \neq 0$ the sustainability criterion presented here will alter. If we assume knowledge and skills are specific to an individual, depreciation occurs through either death or obsolescence.[1] There are nonrival public good aspects of knowledge and it is therefore not entirely the private property of any particular individual, in the conventional sense of human capital theory (Romer, 1990). If this is the case then the stock of knowledge will always be increasing (d'Arge et al., 1991). However, depreciation may still occur through obsolescence (Solow, 1992). Depreciation might also occur in other ways such as the loss of indigenous skills and knowledge (e.g. through displacement of tribes, loss of ancient crafts etc.). Such considerations are important to understanding development issues but actual measurement presents immense difficulties.

Dropping time and dividing through by income Y gives

$$\frac{S}{Y} - \frac{\delta_M K_M}{Y} - \frac{\delta_N K_N}{Y} \geq 0 \tag{8.5}$$

Inequality (8.5) is our basic condition for sustainability. It is an intuitive zero-order rule for determining whether a country is on or off a sustainable development path at any one point in time.

4   Weak and Strong Sustainability and Criticality

Inequality (8.5) is also a "weak sustainability" rule. It assumes substitution possibilities between the component parts of capital. It is therefore wholly consistent with "running down" the stock of natural capital provided that the proceeds are reinvested, as per the HPHS rule. It is a generalized capacity to produce that can be passed to future generations rather than any specific component of K (Solow, 1992). On this basis, we can express "compensation" to future generations in terms of a savings rule.

This conclusion has evolved from models where sufficient substitutability is usually assumed *a priori*. Empirical evidence for this, in so far as it exists, is usually based on a narrow definition of K_N, which understates the full importance of natural capital to human well-being. This is particularly crucial, as the feasibility of the substitutability assumption depends upon the relative shares of K_N and K_M (Stiglitz, 1979).[2]

Much of the ecological literature denies this substitutability, at least across some classes of natural capital. Of particular interest are the "life support" functions of ecosystems, e.g. maintenance of carbon balance, hydrologic cycles, nutrient cycles etc. Economists have not so far achieved much success in capturing all ecosystem functions, despite considerable progress in function valuation using the concept of total economic value (TEV) (Randall, 1991). Future losses will be underestimated and any measurement of compensation will potentially be seriously incomplete. The suspicion also remains that there is more to the total value of an ecosystem than the sum of the values of individual functions. If so, then substitutability is open to question.

Asymmetries between K_M and K_N also suggest a stronger focus on K_N than is permitted by the weak sustainability approach. Thus K_M is *reversible*: the capital stock can be increased and decreased within limits. K_N will comprise some assets which are *technically irreversible* and others which are *feasibly irreversible*. Thus extinct species cannot be recreated. Global warming is very likely to be feasibly irreversible, that is, the conditions for technical reversibility are unlikely to arise in practice (owing to growing population and economic growth).

Uncertainty also differentiates K_N and K_M. Whereas knowledge about current machines tends to be complete, knowledge about environmental assets is seriously incomplete. For example, out of a possible 5 to 10 million species in the world, only 1.4 million have been identified (Wilson, 1986; Swanson, 1991). The precise way in which the carbon and hydrological cycles work is not known. Whilst uncertainty will undoubtedly decline through time, the natural world remains imperfectly understood. Assuming risk aversion, there is good reason not to reduce K_N unless the benefits from doing so are known and are substantial. This is akin to the safe minimum standards (SMS) principle of Ciriacy-Wantrup (1952) and Bishop (1978).

Finally, there is increasing evidence for *loss aversion* with respect to natural capital. Contingent valuation studies have repeatedly shown discrepancies between willingness to pay and willingness to accept which cannot be explained by income effects (Gregory, 1986). This in turn has been argued to reflect an "endowment effect" whereby there is a vested interest in maintaining the *status quo* with respect to environmental assets (Knetsch, 1989). These arguments stress the nonsubstitutability in the utility function. Much of the substitutability debate has been interpreted as a basic dispute over the appropriate specification of the production function (Ruttan, 1991). Musu and Lines (1993) drawing on Krautkraemer (1985) also stress the utility value of natural capital. In addition to measuring the losses in terms of production, the direct loss in utility must also inferred if true compensation is to be found (Beltratti, 1993).

For these reasons we believe the weak sustainability rule is limited in scope, and the *combination* of these strong sustainability characteristics needs to be emphasized, as opposed to their presence in isolation. A strong sustainability rule would require that K_N be held constant (or increasing) within the more general constraint that K be constant (or increasing). Note that implicit in such an aggregation is an assumption of perfect substitution between the components that make up total K_N. No particular component is essential in the provision of critical (e.g. ecosystem) functions. Given the heterogeneity of natural capital, we might expect these components to have widely differing total economic values. We describe that natural capital which has such characteristics as to imply a high TEV and hence nonsubstitutability as exhibiting *criticality*. It is this critical natural capital (K_N^*) that is constrained to be nondecreasing under an alternative strong sustainability rule. The use of the remaining components of natural capital can then be analyzed according to a weak sustainability approach. The remaining K_N can be substituted for K_M *provided* that a full evaluation of costs and benefits in a distortion-free context warrants it. As is well known, distortions such as market and intervention failure themselves contribute to major biases against conservation of K_N (see Pearce, 1993a). Identification of K_N^* will be complex, although some critical functions are capable of identification, such as basic biogeochemical functions (Schulze and Mooney, 1993; Pearce et al., 1994). In addition, it may be the very diversity of natural capital that is of value, giving to the ecological concepts of stability and resilience (Common and Perrings, 1992; Conway, 1993). Uncertainties surrounding the identity of K_N^*, combined with the other strong sustainability arguments noted above, should urge a more precautionary approach.

5   Measuring Sustainable Development

A sustainability index

Inequality (8.5) provides us with a *sustainability indicator* of the form

$$Z = \frac{S}{Y} - \frac{\delta_M K_M}{Y} - \frac{\delta_N K_N}{Y} \qquad (8.6)$$

where Z is a sustainability index. The value of Z must be either zero or positive to ensure sustainability. This approach is (in principle) complementary to environmentally adjusted national accounts, that is, conventional economic aggregates "corrected" for environmental concerns. In those exercises, inputed values of $\delta_M K_M(t)$ and $\delta_N K_N(t)$ are subtracted from gross domestic product (GDP) to arrive at net domestic product (NDP) (see, for example, Bartelmus et al., 1991). In turn, NDP has been interpreted as indicating sustainable income in the Hicksian sense – the interest on the capital stock of a nation (Bojo et al., 1990). In the present chapter, by emphasizing the level of gross savings, we are in effect asking the question: how much of this income was *actually consumed*?

The definition of natural capital depreciation

Natural resource depreciation (δ_N) takes two main forms – depletion and degradation. These can be broadly interpreted as (scarcity) *rent*, arising from depleting or degrading the environmental asset in question. The importance here is that δ_N can then be interpreted as the amount to be reinvested to maintain capital intact, on the basis of the HPHS rule. Many of the methodological issues relating to the measurement of these values are still unresolved (Hamilton, 1993: Hamilton et al., 1993). Thus, the estimates that we have collated here are derived from several differing methods. The validity of each as an approximation of natural capital depreciation will be a question of degree. For present purposes we treat all under the umbrella of "natural capital depreciation." A brief outline of these various methods is given below.

Resource depletion
For a nonrenewable resource, the (Hotelling) rent is equivalent to the market price of the resource minus the marginal costs of extraction. Total (Hotelling) rent is this rent multiplied by the units of the resource extracted.[3] This method can also be extended to the depletion of renewable resources (i.e. exploitation net of an allowance for natural regeneration).

In practice, needless to say, valuation is less precise. In particular, marginal cost information is largely unavailable, so that typically empirical studies have used data on average costs (AC) as a proxy. However, where the costs (MC) of extracting the marginal unit of the resource are increasing over time due to variations in quality, it is usually envisaged that MC > AC. Hence, the rent (to be reinvested) may be overstated (Hartwick and Hageman, 1991).

Environmental degradation
Environmental degradation refers to the degradation of environmental quality, as in the case of air or water pollution. The correct measure of

depreciation here is the change in the (present) value of the flow of environmental services. In turn, this might be inferred from the marginal value to consumers of receiving an additional unit of pollution (Hartwick, 1990; Mäler, 1991). The question then is how to measure these (non-marketed) values. One route is via direct valuation techniques such as revealed or stated preference methods. The prices obtained by such methods can also be used as inputs in indirect valuation methods.

However, any systematic use of these methods is not yet possible despite considerable progress made in valuation techniques (Mäler, 1991). Other methods do exist, but in many cases these are a proxy for actual damage values. The United Nations Statistical Office (UNSO) advocates a particular method to measure the cost of returning the environment to the level of quality prevailing at the beginning of the accounting period or to some specified standard (Bartelmus et al., 1991). Lastly, environmental defensive expenditures represent the expenditures actually incurred in mitigating adverse changes in environmental quality. As such it has been suggested that they offer some indication of the magnitude of actual environmental damage.

Results: are national economies sustainable?

In what follows we use the weak sustainability rule, but provide an indication of how a strong rule might apply. Condition (8.6) produces a deviation measure from borderline or marginal sustainability in the form of Z. A negative value of Z might be interpreted as indicating the "effort" needed to get back to sustainability relative to national income. It might be claimed that any country could allow some deviation from the requirement to maintain capital intact over short periods. However, if this behavior occurs for any significant time period then the sustainability of current economic activity is called into question (Hennings, 1990). Obviously, a country that consistently behaves in a way that "registers" negative values of Z will risk this outcome. Barbier et al. (1990) consider two criteria: sustainability for all time periods (t) or sustainability to be fulfilled over a prespecified time horizon long term.[4] In terms of a requirement for a sustainability index Z this implies

$$\sum_t Z \geq 0 \quad \forall t \quad \text{or} \quad \sum_t Z \geq 0 \tag{8.7}$$

For present purposes, we illustrate a sustainability index where $Z \geq 0$ in any one period. Table 8.1 shows estimates of the component parts of Z for 22 countries. The results, while preliminary, nonetheless provide some useful insights, indicating that even on a weak sustainability rule many countries are unlikely to pass a sustainability test.

In total, eight of the 22 countries shown in table 8.1 fail to satisfy the rule in condition (8.6). Some of these countries are as one would expect: Madagascar, Ethiopia, and Burkina Faso for example. Indeed, Mali clearly fails on the basis of a negative savings ratio without any reference to environmental degradation. However, a relatively high positive savings ratio need not be any guarantee of weak sustainability. This can be seen with reference to Mexico, Nigeria, and Papua New Guinea. For the United States, the values shown in table 8.1 are taken from the year 1981. This emphasizes the essentially static nature of Z at the present stage. It should be noted that the US savings ratio declined

Table 8.1   Testing for sustainable development: an economy is sustainable if it saves more than the depreciation on its man-made and natural capital

	S/Y	$-$ σ_M/Y	$-$ σ_M/Y	$=$ Z
Sustainable economies				
Brazil	20	7	10	+3
Costa Rica	26	3	8	+15
Czechoslovakia	30	10	7	+13
Finland	28	15	2	+11
Germany (pre-unification)	26	12	4	+10
Hungary	26	10	5	+11
Japan	33	14	2	+17
Netherlands	25	10	1	+14
Poland	30	11	3	+16
United States	18	12	3	+3
Zimbabwe	24	10	5	+9
Marginally sustainable				
Mexico	24	12	12	0
Philippines	15	11	4	0
United Kingdom	18	12	6	0
Unsustainable				
Burkina Faso	2	1	10	−9
Ethiopia	3	1	9	−7
Indonesia	20	5	17	−2
Madagascar	8	1	16	−9
Malawi	8	7	4	−3
Mali	−4	4	6	−14
Nigeria	15	3	17	−5
Papua New Guinea	15	9	7	−1

to around 12 percent per annum during the remainder of the 1980s (World Bank, 1991). Hence, if the per annum values of δ_M and δ_N remained constant throughout this period then Z would become negative, indicating nonsustainability. The United Kingdom's apparent position of marginal sustainability is attributable to imputed pollution damages and the rents that accrued due to the exploitation of North Sea oil and natural gas discoveries. The consumption of these rents is reflected in a relatively low savings ratio. This is in contrast to other examples of developed countries shown in the table: the Netherlands, Japan and Germany. In all, we find that half the countries surveyed are sustainable in the sense defined here (assuming of course that savings are invested efficiently).

We have already defined a possible strong sustainability rule. This might operate such that

$$\frac{\delta_N K_N}{Y} \leq 0 \qquad (8.8)$$

This states that the stock of natural capital should be nondecreasing. The substitution possibilities permitted in the weak test are denied. Condition (8.8) is not a savings rule in that natural capital cannot be simply run down and built up. Even if a country is "comfortably" satisfying a weak sustainability criterion, development will not be sustainable as it is a strong rule that is the relevant constraint on present behavior. In effect, any positive value of $\delta_N K_N / Y$ is unsustainable. Table 8.1 reveals that all 22 countries would fail this test, although a wide range of values for $\delta_N K_N / Y$ is shown (reflecting in part the variety and incompleteness of the data).

From an economic perspective, the criticality of K_N should be reflected in a relatively high shadow price for environmental services where, in principle, rents will capture known technological and substitution possibilities (Born, 1992). In turn, if natural capital is being run down this will give rise to large values for $\delta_N K_N / Y$, reflecting the full scale of losses to future generations. In the case of no substitution possibilities then, potentially, these losses approach infinity. A weak sustainability criterion is impossible to fulfill by definition in this context. Whilst not being an absolute indication of TEV, results from monetary valuation studies can provide some indication of the value of K_N. Adger and Whitby (1993) have examined some of these non-marketed values in the context of the land use sector in the United Kingdom. By placing values on various environmental services, using for example stated preference techniques, it is shown that an adjusted output is significantly in excess of marketed output. Although an incomplete picture, the difference is substantial – in the region of 25 percent.

6 Qualifications

International trade issues

Any single country could have a value of $\delta_N K_N \leq 0$ by importing the natural resources it requires. A weak sustainability rule might then suggest that the exporter may permit these reductions in K_N as long as the rents are reinvested. The onus of "responsibility" for reinvesting the value of this depreciation – whether in domestic or foreign assets – is on the exporter. However, this conclusion does not concur with the intuition that the importer is "importing sustainability" (Pearce et al., 1989).

Asheim (1986) has shown how Hartwick's rule may lose validity when extended to the open economy and trade in nonrenewable resources. It can be shown, on similar reasoning, that the operation of Hotelling's rule gives the exporting country "income" over time akin to a capital gain. Given the specification of the model, the resource exporter can consume the proceeds of its exports forever, maintaining constant consumption. The onus is now on the resource importer to invest in alternative forms of capital in order to sustain its own consumption. This is because, over time, this nation will be importing a declining quantity of the resource. It is deceptive to say that the importer is importing sustainability in this story.

An alternative proposition emerges from Proops (1992). The starting point is conceptually the same in that we have to distinguish between resources used by an economy and resources used for an economy in terms of final use. This is achieved by examining intercountry or regional trade flows in an expanded national accounting framework. In this way, a value representing an adjustment to a known "closed economy" $\delta_M K_N / Y$ can be found.[5]

On these terms, a country that currently uses little of its own resources but imports resources from another country might be unsustainable even though on our first (closed economy) rule it would look sustainable. Conversely we might find the opposite result for the resource exporter. Thus, an examination of the two sets of results – closed economy and open economy – would reveal strikingly different conclusions. It remains to be seen whether the "adjusted open economy" rent (or depreciation on natural capital) of the resource importer can be interpreted as "compensation" from the importer to the exporter for final use of the resource. If so, it is a measure of the outward investment flows necessary to secure sustainability in the exporting country. Hence, this has more in common with the idea of "importing sustainability."

Capital accumulation and technological change

Over time, an economy might accumulate capital and by doing so increase the level of well-being that can be sustained in the future (Hennings, 1990).

The present generation is foregoing consumption possibilities in order to shift the economy onto a "higher" development path. However, within a "Rawlsian" intergenerational equity criterion of constant well-being over time these efforts are disallowed (Beltratti, 1993). Alternatively, it is consistent with sustainable development as we have interpreted it, where we define constant human well-being as the lower bound of sustainability. In other words, future generations are entitled to the same or more (but no less) well-being than the current generation. In the terms defined here we would find $Z > 0$. A positive value of Z under these conditions implies a surplus of savings over the requirement to keep capital intact, that is, net savings are positive.

A "constant capital" rule that aims to maintain constant a flow of well-being discounts the possibility of technological change. The relevance is that, in the event of technological change, a constant capital stock would leave future generations with higher well-being than present generations, as the capital stock is more productive. If lower bound ("Rawlsian") sustainability is thought to be desirable, then technological change would be consistent with a *declining* capital stock and negative net saving (Solow, 1974). However, as both Hartwick and Solow point out, sustainability requires that technological change should exceed population growth. Put another way, technological change permits a declining capital stock only to the extent that this change exceeds (some function of) population growth. This might be interpreted as a second "rule of thumb" to a savings rule. Hence, the possibility of technological change should not be interpreted as negating the need to investigate and develop the idea of constant capital rules. Given the difficulties of predicting technological change, this appears to be a reasonable proposition, although the outcome might appear somewhat pessimistic (Dasgupta and Heal, 1979).[6]

In traditional models of economic growth it was assumed that technological change was determined outside the economic system. In the long run, due to diminishing returns, capital accumulation could only influence the level of development and not the rate of growth. The latter was given by this *exogenous* technological change (and population growth). Endogenous growth theory suggests that technological change and therefore economic growth are endogenous variables, determined as a result of the decisions of maximizing firms and individuals (e.g. Romer, 1990; Stern, 1991; Shaw, 1992).

If technological change is attributable to economic variables then it will respond in part to relative prices and in particular expected profitability, in the same way as these price movements determine pure technical substitution between factors. This is similar to Hayami and Ruttan's (1971) model of demand-induced innovation and the idea of resource-augmenting technical progress in general. It therefore becomes even more crucial for the appropriate valuation of environmental assets if natural-capital-conserving technological progress is to come about.

5 Conclusions

Significant progress has been made in defining terms and determining the conditions for sustainable development. The challenge now is to focus on measurement and hence to develop sustainability indicators (Victor, 1991; Solow, 1992; Pearce and Atkinson, 1993). In this chapter we have shown how the challenge might be taken up on the basis of a sustainability savings rule and the collation of data regarding the depreciation of capital. The latter component must be suitably expanded to encompass the use of the environment, achieved by embracing the concept of natural capital. The criterion we have employed is a weak sustainability rule. We do not wish to suggest that this is the only (or indeed the most desirable) way to proceed with measurement. It does, however, provide some "first-order" insights into the issues involved and offers a starting point in order to develop stronger criteria. A strong sustainability indicator would involve identifying and measuring "critical" natural capital or maintaining intact some aggregate measure of natural capital, where any positive depreciation would be a sign of nonsustainability. Both approaches involve natural capital measurement and, although this may not be able to capture all the economic functions of ecological systems, we argue strongly that efforts to monetize the values of those functions will yield important insights into the measurement of sustainable development.

Notes

We wish to thank John Proops for collaboration on the general idea of measuring sustainability. The normal disclaimers apply. We wish to acknowledge financial assistance of the UK Overseas Development Administration (ODA), but the opinions expressed are ours alone and must not be taken as representing the views of the ODA or any other UK government agency. CSERGE is a designated research center of the UK Economic and Social Research Council (ESRC).

1 This assumes that there is no significant depreciation of skills and knowledge during the individual's lifetime (Kennedy and Thirlwall, 1972).
2 For example, in a Cobb–Douglas (constant returns to scale) production function, Euler's theorem tells us that the elasticities on the inputs K_M and K_N correspond to the factor shares of capital and resources (respectively a and b). Dasgupta and Heal (1979) speculate that a might approximate 0.20 and b 0.05. That is, resource rents are 5 percent of total measured output. The possibility of a sustainable path requires $a > b$.
3 Known stocks of nonrenewable resources are augmented by discoveries. No consensus as to the valuation of these finds exists. One method values the discovery at the full value of the rent (Repetto, 1989; Hartwick, 1990). Hamilton (1993) argues that this is incorrect and can lead to extremely perverse results. An appropriate adjustment is the marginal costs of exploration.

4   The actual problem considered was sustainability in cost–benefit analysis where the two variants were (strong) sustainability in each period or sustainability over the project life.

5   The sustainability indicator in Proops and Atkinson (1994) is slightly different from the criterion presented in this chapter, that is,

$$s \geq b + \frac{\delta a}{r}$$

where b is the share of resources (i.e. rents) in output, a is capital's share in output, δ is depreciation on the man-made capital stock, and r is the rate of return on capital. Formally, b is equivalent to our $\delta_N K_N / Y$.

6   It is worth pointing out that technological change is not necessarily "progress" in that new developments can bring "novelty" in the form of unforeseen costs in addition to benefits, e.g. CFCs (Faber and Proops, 1990).

Sources for values of δ_N

Brazil: Seroa da Motta, R. and Young, C. 1991: Natural resources and national accounts: sustainable income from mineral extraction. Mimeo, Instituto de Pesquisa Econômica Aplicada (IPEA), Rio de Janeiro.

Brazil: Seroa da Motta, R. and May, P. H. 1992: Loss in forest resource values due to agricultural land conversion in Brazil. Mimeo, IPEA, Rio de Janeiro.

Brazil: Seroa da Motta, R., Mendes, A., Mendes, F. and Young, C. 1992: Environmental damages and services due to household water use. Mimeo, IPEA, Rio de Janeiro.

Burkina Faso: Lallement, D. 1990: *Burkina Faso: Economic Issues in Renewable Natural Resource Management*. Agricultural Operations, Sahelian Department, Africa Region, World Bank.

Costa Rica: Soloranza, R. 1991: *Accounts Overdue: Natural Resource Depreciation in Costa Rica*. Washington, DC: World Resources Institute.

Czechoslovakia: Wilczynski, P. 1990: *Czechoslovakia: Environmental Economics – Finance*. Europe Department, World Bank.

Ethiopa: Newcombe, K. 1989: An economic justification for rural afforestation; the case of Ethiopa. In G. Schramm and J. Warford (eds), *Environmental Management and Economic Development*, Baltimore, MD: Johns Hopkins University Press.

Finland: Offerström, T. 1992: Evaluating the environmental impact of road traffic emissions in monetary terms using indirect valuation methods. Mimeo, Swedish School of Economics.

Germany: Pearce, D. W. 1991: German studies of environmental damage. Mimeo, Centre for Social and Economic Research on the Global Environment (CSERGE), London.

Hungary: World Bank. 1990: *Hungary – Environmental Issues*. Washington, DC: World Bank.

Indonesia: Repetto, R. 1989: *Wasting Assets*. Washington, DC: World Resources Institute.

Japan: Uno, K. 1991: Economic growth and environmental change in Japan: net national welfare and beyond. In Archibugi and P. Nijkamp (eds), *Ecology and Economics: Towards Sustainable Development*, Dordrecht: Kluwer.

Madagascar: World Bank. 1988: *Madagascar – Environmental Action Plan*. Washington, DC: World Bank.

Malawi: Bishop, J. 1990: *The Cost of Soil Erosion in Malawi*. Report to Malawi Country Operations Department, World Bank.

Mali: Bishop, J. and Allen, J. 1989: *The On-Site Costs of Soil Erosion in Mali*. Environment Department Working Paper 21, World Bank, Washington, DC.

Mexico: Van Tongeren, J., Schweinfest, S., Lutz, E., Luna, M. Gomez and Guillen, F. 1991: *Integrated Environmental and Economic Accounting: A Case Study for Mexico.* Environment Working Paper 50, World Bank, Washington, DC.

Netherlands: Opschoor, J. 1986: A review of monetary estimates of benefits of environmental improvement in the Netherlands. OECD Seminar, Avignon.

Nigeria: World Bank. 1990: *Towards the Development of an Environmental Action Plan for Nigeria.* Washington, DC: World Bank.

Papua New Guinea: Bartelmus, P., Lutz, E. and Schweinfest, S. *Integrated Environmental and Economic Accounting: A Case Study for Papua New Guinea.* Environment Department Working Paper, World Bank, Washington, DC.

Philippines: Cruz, W. and Repetto, R. 1992: *Environmental Effects of Stabilisation and Structural Adjustment Programs: The Philippines Case.* Washington, DC: World Resources Institute.

Poland: Hughes, G. 1992: *The Costs of Environmental Damage in Poland: Methodology.* Washington, DC: World Bank.

United Kingdom: Bryant, C. and Cook, P. 1992: Environmental accounting. *Economic Trends,* 469, 99–122.

United States: Freeman, A. 1990: Air and water pollution control: a benefit–cost assessment. In P. Portney (ed.), *Public Policies for Environmental Protection,* Washington, DC: Resources for the Future.

Zimbabwe: Adger, N. 1992: Accounting for natural resource degradation in Zimbabwe. CSERGE Working Paper GEC92-32, CSERGE, University of East Anglia and University College London.

References

Adger, N. and Whitby, M. 1993: Natural resource accounting in the land-use sector: theory and practice. *European Review of Agricultural Economics,* 20, 77–97.

d'Arge, R. C., Norgaard, R. B., Olson, M. and Somerville, R. 1991: Economic growth, sustainability and the environment. *Contemporary Policy Issues,* 9 (1), 1–23.

Asheim, G. 1986: Hartwick's rule in open economics. *Canadian Journal of Economics,* 86, 395–402.

Barbier, E. B., Markandya, A. and Pearce, D. W. 1990: Environmental sustainability and cost–benefit analysis. *Environment and Planning,* 22, 1259–66.

Bartelmus, P., Stahmer, C. and Van Tongeren, J. 1991: Integrated environmental and economic accounting: framework for a SNA satellite system. *Review of Income and Wealth,* 37 (2), 111–48.

Beltratti, A. 1993: Sustainable growth: analytical models, policy implications and measurements. Paper presented to the Conference of the European Economics Association, Oriel College, Oxford.

Bishop, R. 1978: Endangered species and uncertainty: the economics of a safe minimum standard. *American Journal of Agricultural Economics,* 60, 10–13.

Bojo, J., Mäler, K.-G. and Unemo, L. 1990: *Environment and Development: An Economic Approach.* Dordrecht: Kluwer.

Born, A. 1992: Development of natural resource accounts: physical and monetary accounts for crude oil and natural gas reserves in Alberta. Environmental Discussion Paper 11, Statistics Canada, Ottawa.

Ciriacy-Wantrup, S. V. 1952: *Resource Conservation: Economics and Policies.* Berkeley, CA: University of California Press.

Common, M. and Perrings, C. 1992: Towards an ecological economics of sustainability. *Ecological Economics,* 6 (1), 7–34.

Conway, G. R. 1993: Sustainability in agricultural development: trade-offs with productivity, stability and equitability. *Journal for Farming Systems Research and Extensions,* forthcoming.

Dasgupta, P. and Heal, D. 1979: *Economic Theory and Exhaustible Resources.* London: Cambridge University Press.

Faber, M. and Proops, J. L. R. 1990. *Evolution, Time, Production and the Environment.* Heidelberg: Springer.

Forsyth, P. J. 1986: Booming sectors and structural change in Australia and Britain: a comparison. In J. P. Neary and S. Van Wijnbergen (eds), *Natural Resources and the Natural Economy,* Oxford: Basil Blackwell.

Gregory, R. 1986: Interpreting measures of economic loss: evidence from contingent valuation and experimental studies. *Journal of Environmental Economics and Management,* 13, 325–37.

Hamilton, K. 1991: Proposed treatment of the environment and natural resources in the national accounts. Discussion Paper 7, National Accounts and Environment Division, Statistics Canada, Ottawa.

Hamilton, K. 1993: Resource depletion, discoveries and net national product. Mimeo, Centre for Social and Economic Research on the Global Environment, UCL and UEA.

Hamilton, K., Pearce, D. W., Atkinson, G., Gomez-Lobo, A. and Young, C. 1993: *The Policy Implications of Environmental and Resource Accounting.* Report to the World Bank, Washington, DC.

Hartwick, J. M. 1977: Intergenerational equity and the investing of rents from exhaustible resources. *American Economic Review,* 66, 972–4.

Hartwick, J. M. 1990: National accounting and economic depreciation. *Journal of Public Economics,* 43, 291–304.

Hartwick, J. M. and Hageman, A. P. 1991: Economic depreciation of mineral stocks and the contribution of El Serafy. Divisional Working Paper 27, Environment Department, World Bank, Washington, DC.

Hayami, Y. and Ruttan, V. 1971: *Agricultural Development: An International Perspective.* Baltimore, MD, and London: Johns Hopkins University Press.

Hennings, K. H. 1990: Maintaining capital intact. In J. Eatwell, M. Milgate and P. Newman (eds), *Capital Theory,* London and Basingstoke: Macmillan.

Hicks, J. R. 1946: *Value and Capital,* 2nd edn. Oxford; Oxford University Press.

Kennedy, C. and Thirwall, A. P. 1972: Surveys in applied economics: technical progress. *Economic Journal,* 82, 11–72.

Knetsch, J. 1989: The endowment effect and evidence of nonreversible indifference curves. *American Economic Review,* 79, 1277–84.

Krautkraemer, J. A. 1985: Optimal growth, resource amenities and the preservation of natural environments. *Review of Economic Studies,* 153–70.

Mäler, K.-G. 1991: National accounts and environmental resources. *Environmental and Resource Economics,* 1, 1–15.

Musu, I. and Lines, M. 1993: Endogenous growth and environmental preservation. Paper presented to the Conference of the European Economics Association, Oriel College, Oxford.

Page, T. 1977: *Conservation and Economic Efficiency,* Baltimore, MD: Johns Hopkins University Press.

Pearce, D. W. 1993a: *North South Transfers and the Capture of Global Environmental Value.* Oregon State University, Oregon, forthcoming.

Pearce, D. W. 1993b. Sustainable development. In D. W. Pearce (ed.), *Ecological Economics: Essays in the Theory and Practice of Environmental Economics,* London: Edward Elgar, forthcoming.

Pearce, D. W. and Atkinson, G. 1993: Capital theory and the measurement of weak sustainability. *Ecological Economics,* 8, 103–8.

Pearce, D. W., Barbier, E. B. and Markandya, A. 1990: *Sustainable Development.* London: Earthscan.

Pearce, D. W., Atkinson, G. D. and Dubourg, W. R. 1994: The economics of sustainable development. *Annual Review of Energy and Environment,* 19, 457–74.

Pezzey, J. 1989: Economic analysis of sustainable growth and sustainable development. Environment Department Working Paper 15, World Bank, Washington, DC

Proops, J. L. R. 1992: A sustainability criterion when there is international trade. Mimeo, University of Keele, Keele.

Proops, J. L. R. and Atkinson, G. 1994: A practical sustainability criterion when there is international trade. CSERGE Working Paper GEC 94-05, Centre for Social and Economic Research on the Global Environment (CSERGE), University College London and University of East Anglia.

Randall, A. 1991: Total and non-use values. In J. Braben and C. Kolstad (eds), *Measuring the Demand for Environmental Quality,* Amsterdam: North-Holland.

Repetto, R., Magrath, W., Wells, M., Beer, C. and Rossini, F. 1989: *Wasting Assets: Natural Resources in the National Accounts,* Washington, DC: World Resources Institute.

Romer, P. M. 1990: Endogenous technological change. *Journal of Political Economy,* 98, S71–S102.

Ruttan, V. 1991: Sustainable growth in agricultural production: poetry, policy and science. CREDIT Research Paper 91/13, University of Nottingham.

Schulze, E.-D. and Mooney, H. A. (eds) 1993: *Biodiversity and Ecosystem Functions,* Ecological Studies 99. Berlin: Springer.

Sefton, J. A. and Weale, M. R. 1992: The net national product and exhaustible resources: the effects of foreign trade. Mimeo, Department of Applied Economics, University of Cambridge.

Shaw, G. K. 1992: Policy implications of endogenous growth theory. *Economic Journal,* 102, 611–21.

Solow, R. M. 1974: Intergenerational equity and exhaustible resources. *Review of Economic Studies Symposium.*

Solow, R. M. 1986: On the intergenerational allocation of natural resources. *Scandinavian Journal of Economics,* 88, 141–9.

Solow, R. M. 1992: An almost practical step toward sustainability. Paper presented to 'Resources for the Future' (RFF), Washington, DC, in *Resources Policy,* forthcoming.

Stern, N. 1991: The determinants of growth. *Economic Journal,* 101, 122–33.

Stiglitz, J. E. 1979: A neoclassical analysis of the economics of natural resources. In V. K. Smith (ed.), *Scarcity and Growth Revisited,* Washington, DC: Resources for the Future.

Swanson, T. 1991: Conserving biological diversity. In D. W. Pearce (ed.), *Blueprint 2: Greening the World Economy,* London: Earthscan.

Victor, P. 1991: Indicators of sustainable development: some lessons from capital theory. *Ecological Economics,* 4, 191–213.

WCED. 1987: *Our Common Future.* World Commission on Environment and Development, Oxford: Oxford University Press.

Wilson, E. O. (ed.) 1986: *Biodiversity.* Washington, DC: National Academy.

World Bank. 1991: *World Tables 1991.* Washington, DC: World Bank.

9

Nonrenewable Resource Supply: Theory and Practice

Michael A. Toman and Margaret Walls

1 Introduction

The analysis of nonrenewable resource supply behavior has generated one of the largest literatures within natural resource and environmental economics. That literature can be divided into two fairly distinct phases. The first phase, coming shortly on the heels of the first oil shocks in late 1973, involved a rediscovery of the Hotelling (1931) model for efficient depletion of a fixed homogeneous resource stock. The now familiar "Hotelling rule" governing such depletion is that net price – price less marginal extraction cost – should rise at the rate of interest in order for producers to be indifferent to the timing of extraction and in order for *in situ* reserves to be competitive asset holdings (Solow, 1974). Because the resource is homogeneous it is completely exhausted.

There was an explosion of studies based on this model in the 1970s, with many applications not just to resource extraction but also to development of "backstop" resources, investment in research and development, effects of uncertainties, the nature of market equilibrium with resource depletion, and intergenerational equity (see Dasgupta and Heal (1979) for a comprehensive summary). This framework continues to be used right up to the present. However, its assumptions fly in the face of the facts about nonrenewable resources, which are heterogeneous and can be augmented by exploration, and the implication of complete exhaustion is neither realistic nor innocuous for policy analysis.

The 1970s also saw the publication of a number of empirical studies of resource supply, particularly as applied to petroleum supply in the United States. Most (though not all) of the petroleum studies in this period derive from the model first published by Franklin Fisher (1964). The Fisher model is an *ad hoc* econometric model of exploration that seeks to explain three basic components: the rate of exploratory drilling, the success ratio (proportion of wells with commercial quantities of petroleum discoveries), and the average size of a commercial discovery. The product of these variables gives total additions to reserves. During the 1970s, the Fisher model was considerably elaborated upon to include a more complex description of exploration and equations for post-discovery development investment and extraction (see especially Pindyck, 1974). Unfortunately, these models proved to be disappointing in their power to explain observed supply behavior: small changes in specification produces large changes in sign, size, and significance of coefficients, and the models did not predict well.

In this chapter we review the second wave of theoretical and empirical studies of nonrenewable resource supply that began in the late 1970s, in response to perceived shortfalls in previous approaches.[1] In the theoretical review we emphasize developments built around models with hetero-geneous reserves and exploration that add to the realism of the conceptual models. In the empirical review we address the emergence of the rational expectations econometric method, particularly in petroleum applications, and the potential for integrating contemporary econometric practice with the information provided by geologists. Cutting across both elements of our review is an interest in the consistency or gaps between theory and practice. How capable are theoretical models in addressing important real-world aspects of resource supply, and where do they fall short? How does theory help guide empirical practice and vice versa? What is the state of the empirical art? How can both theory and practice be improved, both separately and jointly?

The next section of the chapter sketches the conceptual resource supply model developed by Pindyck (1978), which we view as a watershed in the theoretical literature. Section 3 reviews a number of extensions in the literature since Pindyck's article, as well as important remaining open questions. Section 4 turns to recent developments in the econometric resource supply literature, with particular emphasis on rational expecta-tions modeling. This section also discusses the integration of econometric geologic modeling.

2   The Pindyck Resource Supply Model[2]

Pindyck's (1978) model is a deterministic, continuous-time description of joint decisions to extract from and add to reserves over time using optimal control techniques. Variants of the model describe the behavior of a representative competitive firm, a competitive market outcome, and monopoly behavior. Our focus here is on the competitive case; we discuss market structure issues in the next section. We also focus on the single-output version of the model, though it can be readily extended to joint products like oil and gas (Pindyck, 1982).

To fix notation,[3] let q be the rate of resource extraction, R the stock of reserves available for extraction, y the rate of exploratory effort, z the cumulative new discoveries, $C(q, R)$ the cost of extraction, $D(y)$ the cost of exploratory effort, $F(y, z)$ the rate of new reserve additions, p the price of extracted output, $V'(q)$ the marginal market value of the resource (the inverse demand curve), and r the constant intertemporal discount rate.[4]

Given these definitions, it follows that per-period profit for a competitive producer is given by

$$\pi = pq - C(q, R) - D(y) \tag{9.1}$$

while the resource stock variables R and z evolve according to

$$\dot{R} = -q + F(y, z) \tag{9.2}$$

$$\dot{z} = F(y, z) \tag{9.3}$$

The optimization problem for the individual firm can then be stated as

$$\max \int_0^\infty e^{-rt} \pi \, dt$$

subject to (9.2) , (9.3), and the obvious nonnegatives including $R(t) \geq 0$ for all t.[5] The market equilibrium can be characterized by the same problem once $V'(q)$ is substituted for p in (9.1).

The dependence of extraction cost on R captures the idea that, as reserves decline, extraction cost is likely to rise; thus we assume $C_R < 0$ and $C_{qR} < 0$.[6] This in turn causes extraction to slow as reserves are diminished so that they are economically exhausted before physical exhaustion looms. We return to this point in the next section of the chapter. Pindyck actually assumes an important special case of the extraction cost function,

$$C(q, R) = qg(R) \tag{9.4}$$

where $g(R)$ is the unit cost of extraction and $g' < 0$. It is also assumed that, the greater the volume of cumulative past discoveries, the lower the productivity of additional exploratory effort since (at least on average) the largest and best sites are likely to be discovered first. Thus we assume $F_z < 0$ and $F_{yz} < 0$. This formulation also comes in for some scrutiny in the next section. Note that additions to reserves in this model do not directly appear in the profit function (9.1), but they indirectly benefit the producer since they retard the depletion effect on extraction cost in view of (9.2).

The Pindyck model contains many desirable attributes. It describes both production and reserve additions as well as dynamic interactions between these stages of the supply process. Those dynamic interactions derive from the presence of stock effects at both stages of the supply process. A wide variety of individual and market behavior patterns are consistent with the theory. While this is frustrating from a purely conceptual standpoint, it indicates the richness of the framework. In particular, if the marginal cost of exploratory effort initially is low and reserve additions are substantial, the extraction rate may rise before ultimately falling. This yields a U-shaped price path rather than the inexorable rise under Hotelling's rule (see the appendix).

3   Theoretical Extensions and Open Questions

The Pindyck (1978) model described in the previous section provides a useful point of departure for a number of extensions that further advance the theory toward a more realistic description of supply behavior. In this section we briefly review extensions and open questions concerned with (A) applications to hard rock minerals, (B) other issues related to the specification of cost functions, (C) investment in capacity, (D) uncertainty, (E) market structure considerations, and (F) the effects of tax policy. No attempt is made to provide a comprehensive set of references; instead, selected papers are cited that seem to illustrate the basic points (and provide leads to the rest of the literature).

Minerals applications

The cost structure of the Pindyck model treats the level of remaining reserves as the indicator of geological/geophysical conditions determining extraction cost for each deposit. As Krautkraemer (1988) observes, this may not be appropriate for hard rock minerals (as opposed to fugacious oil and gas). Hard rock minerals have a fixed spatial distribution of concentration in the earth's crust. Treating reserves as the indicator of cost assumes that it is possible to extract all the highest-concentration ore first, then rework the deposit to take out the next-lower grade, and so on. This is not possible in many cases.

To address this, Krautkraemer reformulates the mining problem to make the distance traveled down the axis of an ore deposit and the radius of each "plug" taken from the deposit the choice variables. The depletion effect in this setting shows up in the limited length of the ore body and, potentially, the rise in cost (for a given plug size) as one moves along (or down) this axis in the ore body. Under the special case of no such effects on cost, Krautkraemer derives conditions under which a rise in refined metal price will lower the cutoff grade (the minimum concentration ore taken). The conditions require some restriction of the cost function, and general results do not appear to be available (particularly when cost does rise with distance into the ore body).

Cost function specifications

As noted above, the cost structure of the Pindyck model is based upon the assumptions that extraction cost rises as reserves are depleted, and that discovery cost rises as the stock of undiscovered sites decreases and the sites remaining are lower in "quality." Livernois and Uhler (1987) argue that the assumption of a negative correlation between extraction cost and reserves is appropriate only on the intensive margin, the level of the individual deposit (see also Uhler, 1979). The two assumptions about extraction cost and discovery cost stated above are contradictory at the aggregate level when one considers both the intensive and extensive margins of activity. If, they note, reserves discovered later in time are lower in quality, why wouldn't we expect extraction costs to rise with new reserve additions on the extensive margin? They address this by making the extraction cost function a function not only of reserve size but also of cumulative exploratory effort or cumulative discoveries. Each discovery along the sequence experiences rising costs as reserves are depleted; and cost rises, holding constant the reserve stock, as activity moves along the extensive margin.[7]

This is a partial resolution of the issue, but problems remain. As Swierzbinski and Mendelsohn (1989) observe, the Pindyck approach and, by extension, the Livernois–Uhler modification assume a smooth progression from higher to lower quality sites. If one relaxes this assumption then extraction cost will depend on the whole distribution of site-specific characteristics influencing costs, not just on summary statics like total reserve volume. This is a troubling observation since, given the uncertainty surrounding the discovery process, we would not expect smooth progression from better to worse sites. The Swierzbinski–Mendelsohn analysis suggests that considerable further work is needed to understand the microfoundations of the industry cost function, a task that has obvious relevance for empirical work with industry data.[8]

Practical problems also arise in characterizing the exploration depletion effect. Exploration effort generates valuable information that can lower the cost of future exploration, even if the particular effort is unsuccessful (Peterson, 1978; Polasky, 1992). The net result may be declining cost with cumulative effort, at least until the resource base is reasonably well delineated. More generally, the uncertainties associated with exploration mean that a rising cost with cumulative exploration effort can be viewed only as a long-term average trend. All of these observations point to the need for a better understanding of the stochastic nature of the discovery process.

Capacity investment

As Lasserre (1985) points out, most of the literature on nonrenewable resource supply including the Pindyck model does not deal explicitly with capital as a productive input and the consequences of constraints on the rate of investment or disinvestment. This is an unfortunate omission since resource industries are highly capital intensive. Working with a simple Hotelling cake-eating model extended to include investment behavior as well as extraction, Lasserre shows that the technical or economic constraints on investment (adjustment costs) may considerably alter the predictions of the standard model in which capital is assumed to be fully malleable and instantaneously, costlessly adjustable. In particular, output may grow (and market price decline) over an initial period of capital buildup before output ultimately declines (and capital becomes redundant if investment is irreversible) because of a rising scarcity rent from resource exhaustion. Similarly, Powell and Oren (1989) show that when there are adjustment costs to expanding production capacity for a "backstop" resource, the socially efficient investment path will have a buildup of "excess" backstop capacity before it is used. While these analyses apply models without stock effects in the cost functions, it seems likely that the results generalize to investments in depletable resource capacity with depletion effects.

This line of reasoning raises questions about the nature of market equilibrium and the degree to which that equilibrium approximates a socially efficient outcome that do not appear to have been adequately explored in the literature. To illustrate, while social efficiency may require a period of capacity buildup prior to use, for an individual competitive producer any capacity investment is sunk and, *ex post*, the best strategy is producing until price equals marginal extraction cost (including user cost). On the other hand, if price equals marginal extraction cost (including user cost) then firms cannot cover fixed costs. These are issues that have been addressed within the contemporary literature on contestable markets, and application of these concepts to depletable resources would be a useful addition to the resources literature.

Uncertainty

The literature on Hotelling cake-eating models considers a number of what might be called "point" uncertainty issues such as uncertainty over the size of the reserve to be exhausted or the cost of a future backstop technology.[9] Pindyck (1980) extends uncertainty analysis by introducing "dynamic" uncertainty into his 1978 model of extraction and exploration with stock effects. The model describes uncertainty about future resources prices, reserves, and costs at any moment in time with a dynamic specification of stochastic shocks. Because Pindyck's model is formulated in continuous time he uses continuous stochastic diffusion processes (so-called Ito processes) such as have been applied in the finance literature. These processes are the continuous-time analogues of time series models of stochastic shocks used in dynamic econometric modeling.

Using the stochastic diffusion model, Pindyck characterizes the expected value of the difference between optimizing decision paths with the stochastic shocks and decision paths in a "certainty-equivalent" formulation where the dynamic processes for the evolution of price or reserves are deterministic. In general, the two outcomes will not be the same because optimizing decisions will be influenced by the variances of the shocks, not just their average values. This will be the case even with risk-neutral actors, as Pindyck assumes.

To illustrate the reasoning, suppose that the marginal cost of extraction $g(R)$ is a convex function of the reserve stock R. Suppose that reserves evolve stochastically because of uncertainties about the marginal product of exploratory effort. To take a simple case, suppose that reserves may be either ΔR above or below a mean value (which changes over time with depletion and discoveries). Under these conditions, the expected sizes of future marginal costs will be larger than marginal costs if reserves remained at their expected values (a consequence of Jensen's inequality). This in turn will lead producers to deplete reserves faster under uncertainty than along the certainty-equivalent path.

This line of argument illustrates the difficulty of addressing uncertainty in resource supply decisions in practice, notwithstanding the theoretical advance in Pindyck's analysis. Generally, both the models Pindyck considers and their discrete-time analogues do not generate concrete decision rules that can be estimated econometrically. An exception is the linear-quadratic model, where the profit function is linear in stock and shock variables and quadratic in the decision variables. In this setting, however, there is no difference between the optimizing decision rules and their certainty-equivalent counterparts. Thus, gaining analytical tractability requires a considerable restriction in how the presence of uncertainty affects behavior.

Market structure

There is an extensive analysis of how monopolization or oligopolization of the resource base might affect the time path of extraction in cake-eating models. The main result of these studies is that "monopoly is a friend of conservation." Initially extraction under monopoly will be lower than with competition, and price will be higher; subsequently, with larger remaining reserves than under competition, the monopolist will produce more than the competitive outcome. This outcome with crossing output paths derives directly from the exhaustion constraint.

To extend the analysis to incomplete exhaustion, Eswaran and Lewis (1984) consider a model in which the unit cost of extraction for each firm is independent of the share of total industry reserves possessed by the firm.

This assumption is made so that the comparison of competitive and concentrated outcomes depends only on behavioral differences, not on an assumed technological advantage from concentrated or dispersed reserve ownership. With this model, Eswaran and Lewis show that ultimate cumulative extraction by the industry is *independent* of the structure of the market. This follows from the transversality condition and the assumption on extraction cost just discussed. If ultimate cumulative extraction is the same for all market structures and extraction is initially slower under a more concentrated structure, then the concentrated structure must generate more rapid output in later periods. Again, these results depend on the assumed cost structure. This analysis also does not address how noncompetitive behavior might alter the time path of additions to reserves.[10]

Tax policy

The analysis of tax policy in the cake-eating model is very similar to the comparison of competitive and monopoly outcomes just described.[11] With a tax on resource extraction output will initially decline, but subsequently output will be higher than in the no-tax case in order to satisfy the exhaustion constraint. This will be true for fixed or *ad valorem* taxes.

The analysis is much more complex with incomplete exhaustion. Generally we would expect a tax to reduce cumulative extraction or, equivalently, to raise the cutoff grade. This is a direct consequence of the transversality condition (Conrad and Hool, 1984; see also Krautkraemer, 1990). The effect on the time path of output is more difficult to ascertain since the effects will depend on the time path of the tax and on how the tax affects the user cost of extraction. To illustrate, a tax that is expected to accelerate sharply in the future could raise current extraction because, in effect, it lowers the user cost of current extraction. On the other hand, Slade (1984) uses a simulation model with econometrically estimated parameters to show that the time-invariant taxation of resource extraction generally causes extraction in all periods to fall.

The literature on tax policy and nonrenewable resources has been extended significantly by Deacon (1993), who considers the joint effects of taxation on exploration and production in the context of the US petroleum industry. Starting with a variant of the Pindyck model discussed above, Deacon resorts to a simulation model with econometrically estimated parameters to cut through the theoretical ambiguities of this more complex but realistic framework. Deacon finds that taxes on the petroleum industry generally lead to both "high-grading" (the rendering of some exploration and production opportunities as subeconomic) and some tilting of exploration and production activity toward the future. A property tax (applied to the value of mineral rights) is an exception in that it dampens exploration while also accelerating depletion, as producers seek to reduce tax liabilities.

4   Econometric Models of Oil and Gas Supply

Capturing the richness of a theoretical structure is difficult in any empirical endeavor. In the case of modeling nonrenewable resource supply, the problems are compounded by the need to deal with the intertemporal aspects, the inherent geologic and economic uncertainties in the supply process, and a general paucity of spatially and temporally disaggregated data. These problems are illustrated by a review of the empirical literature on oil and gas supply.[12]

As described in section 1, early empirical oil and gas supply models generally were unsatisfactory. In part this was because they were not based on a theoretical model of nonrenewable resource supply that incorporated uncertainty and because the results from the models, both estimated elasticities and forecasts, varied widely.[13] Moreover, the models ignored the lessons about the supply process learned years earlier by petroleum geologists and engineers.

1 There is regularity in the discovery process in a region – as cumulative exploratory drilling proceeds, average discovery sizes decline.[14]

2 Reservoir pressure determines production rates: declining pressure as production proceeds leads to lower production rates, and changes in prices or costs alter the economic life of the reservoir but do not otherwise significantly change the pattern of production over time (McCray, 1975).

The Pindyck theoretical model described in section 2 above is consistent with geologists' findings for the discovery process but is unnecessarily complicated, from their point of view, in describing production.

Subsequently models by Griffin and Moroney (1985) and Deacon et al. (1990) incorporated some of the geologists' and engineers' lessons and generally developed more detailed descriptions of oil and gas supply. For example, they explicitly modeled each phase of the supply process (exploration, development, and production), used more detailed and disaggregated data than previous models,[15] and included geologic trends in both the discoveries and production equations. On the other hand, the models still suffered from some shortcomings, including the lack of an explicit theoretical underpinning and no satisfying treatment of uncertainty. The equations describing exploration behavior, for example, were almost as *ad hoc* as the early Fisher-type models.

Rational expectations econometric analyses

Progress was made in the late 1980s with the application of "rational expectations econometric" (REE) techniques to oil and gas.[16] Three studies that use this approach are Epple (1985), Hendricks and Novales (1987), and Walls (1989). The REE approach is derived explicitly from a model of optimal decision making under uncertainty. It requires a careful specification of the uncertainties facing the producer, and it allows the analyst to identify from the estimating equations properties of the "deep" structural parameters – those parameters representing the technology of oil and gas supply and the stochastic processes driving exogenous variables. These deep parameters are what ultimately must be understood for reliable forecasting and policy analysis.

In the Hendricks and Novales model and the Walls model, an exploration firm chooses the number of exploratory wells to drill in each period to maximize the expected discounted net present value from exploration. In the Walls model, discovering additional barrels becomes more costly for the firm as its drilling proceeds; this is captured in the model by having the firm's exploration costs rise with cumulative drilling. Dynamics in the Hendricks and Novales model take the form of adjustment costs rather than a depletion effect – exploration costs rise if drilling in the current period varies significantly upward or downward from drilling in the previous period.

The outcome of the exploration process in both of the models is an oil discovery, and discoveries are governed by a stochastic process. In the Walls model, these stochastic discoveries vary directly with the level of exploration undertaken, and the marginal value of a discovery, which depends on the wellhead price of oil, operating and development costs, and relevant taxes, is stochastic as well. The outcome of the optimization process is a set of econometrically estimable equations – one describing the aggregate number of exploratory wells drilled, one describing the marginal value of a discovery, and one describing average discovery sizes. Because parameters from the firm's exploration cost function and the marginal discovery value and average discovery size equations appear in the exploratory wells equation, the set of equations must be estimated jointly in order to obtain consistent estimates of the model's structural parameters.

Hendricks and Novales use a generalized method of moments estimation procedure (see Hansen, 1982; Hansen and Singleton, 1982) that does not require explicit specification of the processes governing stochastic variables. Consistent parameter estimates are obtained from this simpler estimation approach, but the impacts of changes in the stochastic processes – such as a tax change or other price shock – cannot be analyzed since the forms of those stochastic processes are not specified. Hendricks and Novales estimate their model using annual data from Alberta.

Walls is able to use her model to address changes in the stochastic processes, such as the impacts on US drilling and discoveries of the 1986 oil price collapse (see Walls, 1989) and the impacts of an oil import fee (see Walls, 1991). On the other hand, the system estimation technique required for the model depends on the availability of a large number of degrees of freedom. Walls obtains these degrees of freedom by using monthly aggregate US data but monthly estimates of new discoveries must be interpolated from annual data. It is unclear how this interpolation might be affecting the model's results.

The Epple model focuses on estimating discoveries directly rather than exploratory drilling. His cost function for discoveries has costs rising as cumulative discoveries rise. Epple uses annual aggregate US data and simplifies the processes governing stochastic variables in the model so that a two-stage estimation procedure can be used instead of a system estimation procedure as in Walls. There may be a problem with estimating discoveries directly rather than drilling since the former are a stochastic output of the exploration process and exploratory drilling is the variable over which the firm has direct control.

The advantage of the REE approach is the clear link between a theory of the firm's dynamic behavior under uncertainty and the econometric equations of the model. Uncertainty is captured in a satisfying way in that expectations of future exogenous variables are formed rationally; *ad hoc* representations such as adaptive expectations, which some of the earlier models had used (see Deacon et al., 1990, for example), are avoided. Geologic trends are captured in the Walls and Epple models since exploration costs rise with cumulative exploratory drilling or with cumulative discoveries.

Moreover, the impacts of price shocks on the structure of the model can be analyzed. An oil import fee, for example, changes the stochastic process governing oil prices in a way that can be measured; the impact on the structural parameters of the model can then be assessed; and finally, the reduced form parameters – parameters of the exploratory drilling equation in the Walls model – are changed as a result. The final forecasts of drilling behavior and discoveries incorporate these parameter changes. In the more *ad hoc* frameworks, an import fee would simply change the price variable in the drilling equation but not the parameters of that equation. In principle, forecasts from REE models should be more accurate than those from *ad hoc* specifications because of the incorporation of parameter changes. Walls (1989) finds some evidence to support this when she simulates the impacts of the 1986 oil price shock.

For all of these positive features of the REE models, there also are a number of drawbacks. In order to obtain a closed form solution to the maximization problem and readily estimable econometric equations, the linear-quadratic structure is necessary. This means that only expected values of stochastic variables matter to the exploration firm and not variances or any higher moments. Even this simplified specification can be mathematically complicated if one wishes to capture at least some of the most important features of the oil and gas supply process. As they stand, these models do not possess the level of detail of, say, the Griffin and Moroney and Deacon et al. models.

The estimation results from the three REE models suggest that the linear-quadratic structure may be too restrictive. All three models get negative signs on the intercept term of the (linear) marginal cost of drilling equation (or, in Epple's case, marginal cost of discoveries equation), implying that total exploration costs at low levels of exploration are actually negative. Such a finding can come, of course, from fitting a straight line to a function that actually increases at an increasing rate. The irony, as Epple and Londregan (1993) point out, is that without the link to the underlying theoretical structure no problem with the estimation results would have been perceived. It is only because the estimated reduced form parameters are understood to be functions of the underlying structural parameters, one of which is the intercept of the marginal cost function, that the problem is recognized.

Another problem with REE models, as mentioned above, is the large number of degrees of freedom necessary in order to estimate them. It is difficult to come by spatially disaggregated data that are available over a sufficiently long period of time.

"Hybrid" approaches

One promising possibility for future research to overcome problems with existing approaches is a geologic/econometric "hybrid" approach that, like the REE models, uses a stochastic dynamic model of firm behavior as its starting point. A hybrid model incorporates features of the geologists' discovery process models, but unlike most of the geologic models it has a more explicit economic component and uses econometric techniques to estimate hypothesized relationships based on historical data. Examples of hybrid applications are given by Attanasi et al. (1980)[17] and Walls (forthcoming). Both studies model exploratory effort – either wells drilled or total expenditures – as a function of economic variables and discoveries as a function of cumulative past exploratory effort. The latter takes the following form:

$$F(W) = \bar{F}(1 - e^{\theta W}) \tag{9.5}$$

where W is cumulative exploratory drilling, $F(W)$ is cumulative discoveries made by drilling W wells, $\bar{F} > 0$ is "ultimate" discoveries – discoveries made as the number of cumulative wells drilled approaches infinity – and θ is a parameter to be estimated. Differentiating (9.5) with respect to W yields

$$F' = -\bar{F}\theta\, e^{\theta W} \qquad (9.6)$$

F', the "discovery rate," is positive as long as θ is negative and $\bar{F}$ is positive; but the second derivative of (9.5) is negative, indicating that the discovery rate declines as drilling proceeds.

In Walls's (forthcoming) application to the Gulf of Mexico Outer Continental Shelf, estimates of $\bar{F}$ and θ are obtained by taking logs of both sides of (9.6) and econometrically estimating the equation based on historical data. In Attanasi et al.'s analysis of the Denver Basin, in an approach typical of most of the pure discovery process models, the estimates of $\bar{F}$ and θ are based on geologists' knowledge of the region; the exploratory drilling equation is the only econometrically estimated component of their model. In both of the studies, results from the discovery process equation feed into the exploration equation, since expected discoveries are a component of the expected payoff from drilling exploratory wells.[18]

Neither of the two models base their econometric equations on an explicit dynamic optimization model that incorporates uncertainty. Because the discovery process component is inherently nonlinear, to do so would almost certainly mean leaving the linear-quadratic structure of the existing REE models for something more general. Nonetheless, we feel that this is the approach that should be pursued in future research. Although solutions to nonlinear models are more complicated because they are based on numerical methods, a variety of approaches are becoming available.[19] Most of the approaches rely on quadratic approximations to more general structures. One possibility for incorporating a discovery process equation in a dynamic objective function is to linearly approximate equation (9.5). Parameter estimates from the geologic literature could then be used to calibrate the model in order to get around the identification problem that might arise from introducing more parameters. Approximation techniques in combination with calibration have been used by Kydland and Prescott (1982).

In addition to this marrying of the discovery process approach with econometric supply analysis, future models should focus on describing the full supply process – exploration, development, and production – to develop a better understanding of the links between the stages. It would also be instructive to see application of the models to more spatially disaggregated data, assuming such data can be developed. An advantage of the discovery process component is its more realistic description of discoveries in a particular petroleum reservoir or basin; whether this carries over to more aggregated data is unclear.

Econometric supply models have come a long way since Fisher's pioneering work in the mid-1960s. Further improvements will come through an even better link between the economics and geology of nonrenewable resource supply.

Appendix: The Pindyck Model

To characterize solutions to the maximization problem formulated by Pindyck form the Hamiltonian

$$H = e^{-rt}\pi + \lambda[-q + F(y, z)] + \mu F(y, z) \tag{A9.1}$$

where λ is the costate corresponding to R and μ is the costate corresponding to z. These variables satisfy

$$\dot{\lambda} = -H_R = e^{-rt}C_R \tag{A9.2}$$

$$\dot{\mu} = -H_z = -(\lambda + \mu)F_z \tag{A9.3}$$

Since we are assuming that $R > 0$ for all t (the exhaustion constraint is nonbinding), the transversality condition implies that λ goes to zero and (A9.2) can be integrated to yield

$$\lambda(t) = \int_t^\infty e^{-rt}C_R \, dt > 0 \tag{A9.4}$$

As indicated by (A9.4), λ is the *user cost of depletion*, the present value of future cost increases caused by more rapid resource depletion at date t: it is also the shadow price of new reserve additions that counteract depletion.

To interpret the shadow price μ, it is helpful to consider the first-order conditions for optimizing choices of the decision variables q and y. Assuming interior solutions, we have

$$H_q = e^{-rt}(p - C_q) - \lambda = 0 \tag{A9.5}$$

$$H_y = -e^{-rt}D' + (\lambda + \mu)F_y = 0 \tag{A9.6}$$

We have already noted that λ can be interpreted as the user cost of depletion, so (A9.5) simply states that the price of extracted output should equal the full marginal cost of extraction.[20] Rearranging (A9.6), we have

$$\lambda = e^{-rt}D'/F_y - \mu \tag{A9.7}$$

The first term on the right-hand side of (A9.7) can be interpreted as the direct marginal cost of reserve additions (since the numerator is the rate of cost increase with an increase in effort y while the denominator is the rate of increase of discoveries with increasing y). It can be shown that $\mu > 0$ is the *user cost of reserve additions*, reflecting the fact that an increase in discoveries today raises cumulative discoveries z in all future periods and retards the productivity of future exploratory effort (since $F_z < 0$). This intuition is consistent with (A9.3), which states that the rate of change in exploration user cost over time is equal to the rate of decrease in effort productivity from current reserve additions multiplied by the *net* shadow of additions, $\lambda + \mu$. In integral form, (A9.3) says that μ equals the present value of future decreases in reserve additions from current additions, where each future decrement in discoveries is valued at $\lambda + \mu$.

To analyze the decision paths, differentiate the first-order conditions (A9.5) and (A9.6) with respect to time, using the adjoint equations (A9.2) and (A9.3) and invoking the multiplicative cost specification $C = qg(R)$ plus the market-clearing condition $p = V'(q)$. The results are

$$\dot{q} = \frac{r(p - C_q) + qFg'}{V''} \tag{A9.8}$$

$$\dot{y} = \frac{rD' + (D'/F_y)(F_{yz}F - F_yF_z) + C_RF_y}{D'' - D'F_{yy}/F_y} \tag{A9.9}$$

From (A9.8) it follows that if R initially is large, so user cost $p - C_R$ is small, and if the marginal cost of reserve additions initially is low so that F is large, then $\dot{q} > 0$ and $\dot{p} < 0$. However, as the depletion effect in exploration retards reserve additions, and the user cost of extraction correspondingly rises, $\dot{q} < 0$ and $\dot{p} > 0$. This possible U-shaped outcome is in sharp contrast to the prediction of inexorable price increase in the simple Hotelling model.

Equation (A9.9) is somewhat harder to interpret in that several cases must be considered. If marginal cost of reserve additions D'/F_y is small then the second term on the right-hand side is small and the sign of $\dot{y}$ depends on the importance of the extraction depletion effect $C_R = qg'$. If this effect also is small then we would expect y to be small initially but to increase as extensive extraction depletes reserves. This is consistent with (A9.9), which predicts $\dot{y} > 0$ under the assumed conditions.[21] Even if the marginal cost of reserve additions is not small initially, if initial reserves are large and additions F are small (and C_R also is small) then the numerator on the right-hand side of (A9.9) is dominated by $D'(r - F_z) > 0$. If the extraction depletion effect is large, on the other hand, we would expect a retarding of extraction and a corresponding retarding of exploratory effort. Finally, as marginal reserve additions cost grows from the exploration depletion effect and F falls off, the second term on the right-hand side again helps to make $\dot{y}$ large – the rate of decline in exploratory effort will moderate as effort falls off toward zero.[22]

Notes

1 Some theoretical papers prior to the late 1970s also reflected a broader perspective than the Hotelling rule; see, for example, Gordon (1967), Burt and Cummings (1970), and Kuller and Cummings (1974).

2 Several other important papers appeared around the time of the transition from the simple Hotelling framework to more complex models. Peterson's (1978) is quite similar to Pindyck's, though Peterson treats discoveries as the decision variable in the exploration stage of the supply while Pindyck focuses on exploratory effort. The interpretation of Peterson's first-order conditions is somewhat more transparent, but Pindyck's model is closer to being operational. The earlier paper by Levhari and Liviatan (1970) focuses only on extraction but clearly describes the difference between a cake-eating framework and one with stock-dependent costs and incomplete physical exhaustion.

3 The notation presented here differs in some ways from that used in Pindyck's article.

4 The assumption of a constant discount rate is expositionally convenient, but the model is readily generalized to variable discount rates over time.

5 Here we are setting the upper limit of integration in the integral, the terminal date, equal to infinity. In doing so we are also assuming, consistent with the long-run focus of the model, that $C(0, R) = 0$ – there are no quasi-fixed costs. A more careful derivation would allow the terminal date T to be a choice variable and derive conditions for $T = \infty$.

6 It may seem troublesome to index the cost function by a variable – *in situ* reserves – that is unobservable to the firm. This is done here only as a theoretical convenience; we could restate the cost function as $C(q, x)$ where x is cumulative extraction minus cumulative new discoveries and $C_x > 0$. This maneuver conceals the deeper lingering question of how to deal with incomplete information about the cost structure. We address this issue in the next section and in subsequent discussions of empirical methods.

7 A useful extension of the model would incorporate both exploration effort along the extensive margin and exploration/development effort along the intensive margin that expends the stock of available reserves and helps hold down extraction cost. We consider the capacity investment problem further below.

8 See also Livernois (1987). Aggregation problems are magnified by joint products.

9 The more sophisticated of these analyses considers sequential decision making in which expectations about the random outcome (e.g. date of backstop availability) get updated over time. See Pindyck (1980) for a brief review.

10 The relevance of noncompetitive supply theory to empirical supply behavior also remains to be demonstrated. For petroleum, simple models of cartel or oligopoly behavior do not appear to be adequate to describe the behavior of the Organization of Petroleum Exporting Countries (see the papers in Griffin and Teece (1982) for a review of the literature).

11 Taxes are by no means the only economic policy of interest when analyzing nonrenewable resource supply. Lewis and Slade (1985) show that a price control can be analyzed in the same way as a tax (they also examine a number of tax effects). Open access problems also have been examined in many papers (e.g. Eswaran and Lewis, 1985). However, many of these studies do not reflect actual institutions in place to regulate the externalities or to allocate publicly managed resources (e.g. McDonald, 1971, 1979).

12 There is much larger and more advanced body of empirical work on oil and gas supply than on the supply of other types of nonrenewable resources. Thus we choose to limit our focus to papers on oil and gas.

13 See, for example, Pindyck's (1974) reestimation of the Erickson and Spann (1971) model and Neri's (1977) comparison of the MacAvoy and Pindyck (1973) model with a model used by the American Gas Association. For discussions and critiques of the Fisher-type models, see Epple and Londregan (1993).

14 See Arps and Roberts (1958) for the classic exposition and Attanasi et al. (1981) for a general discussion of the methodology.

15 Deacon et al. (1990) use field-level data from California, for example.

16 See the volumes edited by Lucas and Sargent (1981) for applications of the REE approach in macroeconomics. See Sargent (1981) for an exposition of the basic modeling structure. The motivation for the approach in macroeconomics arose from the contention by Lucas (1976) that the poor performance of macroeconomic forecasts was due to the lack of a formal relationship between individual dynamic optimizing behavior and traditional econometric forecasting methods – the same complaint that we make here about models of oil and gas supply.

17 The same model is described in slightly less detail in Attanasi (1979).

18 The US Department of Energy/Energy Information Administration's PROLOG model (see DOE/EIA, 1988) uses a kind of hybrid approach, but it lacks this feature of a link between the two components.

19 See the ten articles in a special issue of *Journal of Business and Economic Statistics* (1990) and see Taylor and Uhlig (1990) for a comparison of results from the models; see also Novales (1990).

20 With multiplicative cost function $C = qg(R)$, H_q is linear in q and, strictly speaking, either $q = 0$ *or* $q = q_{max}$ where q_{max} is some exogenously specified capacity constraint. (The notion of endogenous capacity is discussed in the next section.) However, in the market version of the model market-clearing implies the "singular" solution where price is equal to marginal cost.

21 Note that the denominator on the right-hand side of (A9.8) is positive given the standard assumptions that $D'' \geq 0$ and $F_{yy} < 0$.

22 Pindyck shows that exploratory effort generally will cease before extraction terminates, unless the marginal cost of reserve additions happens to have a zero intercept term (which seems unlikely).

References

Arps, J. J. and Roberts, T. G. 1958: Economics of drilling for cretaceous oil on east flank of Denver–Julesburg basin. *Bulletin of American Association of Petroleum Geologist*, 42 (11) (November), 2459–67.

Attanasi, Emil D. 1979: The nature of firm expectations in petroleum exploration. *Land Economics*, 55 (3) (August), 299–312.

Attanasi, Emil D., Drew, L. J. and Schuenemeyer, J. H. 1980: *Petroleum-resource Appraisal and Discovery Rate Forecasting in Partially Explored Regions – An Application to Supply Modeling*, Geological Survey Professional Paper 1138-C. Washington, DC: US Government Printing Office.

Attanasi, Emil D., Drew, L. J. and Root, D. H. 1981: Physical variables and the petroleum discovery process. In James Ramsey (ed.), *The Economics of Exploration for Energy Resources*, Greenwich, CT: JAI Press.

Burt, O. and Cummings, R. 1970: Production and investment in natural resource industries. *American Economic Review*, 60 (4) (September), 576–90.

Conrad, Robert and Hool, Bryce. 1984: Intertemporal extraction of mineral resources under variable tax rates. *Land Economics*, 60 (4) (November), 319–27.

Dasgupta, P. S. and Heal, G. M. 1979: *Economic Theory and Exhaustible Resources.* Cambridge: Cambridge University Press.

Deacon, Robert T. 1993: Taxation, depletion, and welfare: a simulation study of the U.S. petroleum resource. *Journal of Environmental Economics and Management*, 24 (2) (March), 159–87.

Deacon, Robert, DeCanio, Stephen J., Frech, H. E., III, and Johnson, M. B. 1990: *Taxing Energy: An Economic Analysis of the Crude Oil Severance Tax.* New York: Holmes & Meyer.

Epple, Dennis. 1985: The econometrics of exhaustible resource supply: a theory and an application. In Thomas J. Sargent (ed.), *Energy Foresight and Strategy*, Washington, DC: Resources for the Future.

Epple, Dennis, and Londregan, John. 1993: Strategies for modeling exhaustible resource supply. In A. V. Kneese and J. L. Sweeney (eds), *Handbook of Natural Resource and Energy Economics*, vol. 3, Amsterdam: Elsevier.

Erickson, Edward W. and Spann, Robert M. 1971: Supply response in a regulated industry: the case of natural gas. *Bell Journal of Economics and Management Science*, 2 (1) (Spring), 94–121.

Eswaran, Mukesh and Lewis, Tracy R. 1984: Ultimate recovery of an exhaustible resource under different market structures. *Journal of Environmental Economics and Management*, 11 (1) (March), 55–69.

Eswaran, Mukesh and Lewis, Tracy R. 1985: Exhaustible resources and alternative equilibrium concepts. *Canadian Journal of Economics*, 18 (3) (April), 459–73.

Fisher, Franklin M. 1964; *Supply and Costs in the U.S. Petroleum Industry: Two Econometric Studies.* Baltimore, MD: Johns Hopkins University Press for Resources for the Future.

Gordon, Richard L. 1967: A reinterpretation of the pure theory of exhaustion. *Journal of Political Economy*, 75 (3) (June), 274–86.

Griffin, James M. and Moroney, John R. 1985: The economic impact of severance taxes: results from an economic model of the Texas oil and gas industry. Report to the Texas Mid Continent Oil and Gas Association.

Griffin, James M. and Teece, D. 1982; *OPEC Behavior and World Oil Prices.* London: Allen & Unwin.

Hansen, Lars Peter. 1982: Large sample properties of generalized method of moments estimator. *Econometrica*, 50 (4), 1029–53.

Hansen, Lars Peter, and Sargent, Thomas J. 1981: Formulating and estimating dynamic linear rational expectations models. In Robert E. Lucas, Jr and Thomas J. Sargent (eds), *Rational Expectations and Econometric Practice*, Minneapolis, MN: University of Minnesota Press.

Hansen, Lars Peter and Singleton, K. J. 1982: Generalized instrumental variables estimation of nonlinear rational expectations models. *Econometrics*, 50 (5) (September), 1269–86.

Hendricks, Kenneth and Novales, Alfonso 1987: Estimation of dynamic investment functions in oil exploration. Draft manuscript.

Hotelling, H. 1931: The economics of exhaustible resources. *Journal of Political Economy*, 39 (2) (April), 137–75.

Journal of Business and Economic Statistics. 1990: Ten articles on solving nonlinear rational expectations models. *Journal of Business and Economic Statistics*, 8 (1) (January), 1–52.

Krautkraemer, Jeffrey A. 1988: The cutoff grade and the theory of extraction. *Canadian Journal of Economics*, 21 (1) (February), 146–60.

Krautkraemer, Jeffrey A. 1990: Taxation, ore quality selection, and the depletion of a heterogeneous deposit of a nonrenewable resource. *Journal of Environmental Economics and Management*, 18 (2) (March), 120–35.

Kuller, R. and Cummings, R. 1974: An economic model of production and investment for petroleum reservoirs. *American Economic Review*, 64 (1) (March), 66–79.

Kydland, Finn E. and Prescott, Edward C. 1982: Time to build and aggregate fluctuations. *Econometrica*, 50 (6) (November), 1345–70.

Lasserre, Pierre. 1985: Exhaustible resource extraction with capital. In Anthony Scott (ed.), *Progress in Natural Resource Economics: Essays in Resource Analysis by Members of the Programme in Natural Resource Economics (PNRE) at the University of British Columbia*, Oxford: Clarendon, 176–94.

Levhari, D. and Liviatan, N. 1977: Notes on Hotelling's economics of exhaustible resources. *Canadian Journal of Economics*, 10 (1) (Autumn), 111–20.

Lewis, Tracy R. and Slade, Margaret. 1985: The effects of price controls, taxes, and subsidies on exhaustible resource production. In Anthony Scott (ed.), *Progress in Natural Resource Economics: Essays in Resource Analysis by Members of the Programme in Natural Resource Economics (PNRE) at the University of British Columbia*, Oxford: Clarendon, 203–26.

Livernois, John R. 1987: Empirical evidence on the characteristics of extractive technologies: the case of oil. *Journal of Environmental Economics and Management*, 14 (1) (March), 72–86.

Livernois, John R. and Uhler, Russell S. 1987: Extraction costs and the economics of nonrenewable resources. *Journal of Political Economy*, 95 (1) (February), 195–203.

Lucas, Robert E., Jr 1976: Econometric policy evaluation: a critique. In K. Brunner and A. H. Meltzer (eds), *The Philips Curve and Labor Markets*, Carnegie-Rochester Conference Series on Public Policy, Amsterdam: North-Holland.

Lucas, Robert E., Jr, and Sargent, Thomas J. (eds) 1981: *Rational Expectations and Econometric Practice*. Minneapolis, MN: University of Minnesota Press.

MacAvoy, Paul W. and Pindyck, Robert S. 1973: Alternative regulatory policies for dealing with the natural gas shortage. *Bell Journal of Economics and Management Science*, 4 (2) (Autumn), 454–98.

McCray, Arthur W. 1975: *Petroleum Evaluations and Economic Decisions*. Englewood Cliffs, NJ: Prentice-Hall.

McDonald, S. L. 1971: *Petroleum Conservation in the United States: An Economic Analysis*. Baltimore, MD: Johns Hopkins University Press for Resources for the Future.

McDonald, S. L. 1979: *The Leasing of Federal Lands for Fossil Fuels Production*. Baltimore, MD: Johns Hopkins University Press for Resources for the Future.

Neri, John A. 1977: An evaluation of two alternative supply models of natural gas. *Bell Journal of Economics*, 8 (Spring), 289–302.

Novales, Alfonso. 1990: Solving nonlinear rational expectations models: a stochastic equilibrium model of interest rates. *Econometrica*, 58 (1) (January), 93–111.

Peterson, F. M. 1978: A model of mining and exploring for exhaustible resources. *Journal of Environmental Economics and Management*, 5 (3) (September), 236–51.

Pindyck, Robert S. 1974: The regulatory implications of three alternative econometric supply models of natural gas. *Bell Journal of Economics*, 5 (2) (Autumn), 633–45.

Pindyck, Robert S. 1978: The optimal exploration and production of nonrenewable resources. *Journal of Political Economy*, 86 (5) (October), 841–61.

Pindyck, Robert S. 1980: Uncertainty and exhaustible resource markets. *Journal of Political Economy*, 88 (6) (December), 1203–25.

Pindyck, Robert S. 1982: Jointly produced exhaustible resources. *Journal of Environmental Economics and Management*, 9 (4) (December), 291–303.

Polasky, Stephen. 1992: The private and social value of information: exploration for exhaustible resources. *Journal of Environmental Economics and Management*, 23 (1) (July) 1–21.

Powell, Stephen G. and Oren, Shmuel S. 1989: The transition to non-depletable energy: social planning and market models of capacity expansion. *Operations Research*, 37 (3) (May–June), 373–83.

Sargent, Thomas J. 1981: Interpreting economic time series. *Journal of Political Economy*, 89 (2), 213–48.

Slade, Margaret E. 1984: Tax policy and the supply of exhaustible resources: theory and practice. *Land Economics*, 60 (2) (May), 133–47.

Solow, Robert M. 1974: The economics of resources or the resources of economics. *American Economic Review*, 64 (2) (May), 1–14.

Swierzbinski, Joseph E. and Mendelsohn, Robert, 1989: Exploration and exhaustible resources: the microfoundations of aggregate models. *International Economic Review*, 30 (1) (February), 175–86.

Taylor, John B. and Uhlig, Harald. 1990: Solving nonlinear stochastic growth models: a comparison of alternative solution methods. *Journal of Business and Economic Statistics*, 8 (1) (January), 1–18.

Uhler, R. S. 1979: The rate of petroleum exploration and extraction. In R. S. Pindyck (ed.), *Advances in the Economics of Energy and Resources*, vol. 2, Greenwich, CT: JAI Press.

US Department of Energy, Information Administration (EIA). 1988: *Model Methodology and Data Description of the Production of Onshore Lower-48 Oil and Gas Model.* Washington, DC: EIA, September.

Walls, Margaret A. 1989: Forecasting oil market behavior: rational expectations analysis of price shocks. Discussion Paper EM87-03, Resources for the Future, Washington, DC, February.

Walls, Margaret A. 1991: Dynamic firm behavior and regional deadweight losses from a U.S. oil import fee. *Southern Economics Journal*, 57 (3) (January).

Walls, Margaret A. Forthcoming: Using a "hybrid" approach to model oil and gas supply: a case study of the Gulf of Mexico outer continental shelf. *Land Economics*.

10

Empirical Consequences of the Hotelling Principle

Peter Berck

The theory of natural resources leads to testable predictions about prices and quantities in resource markets. These tests stem from viewing a natural resource as a capital asset. They are subject to the same problems and caveats as all other tests of asset pricing. In addition, they often suffer from an inability to observe directly the asset prices of interest. The results from such testing are mixed.

The Basic Model

To see how the basic resource theory can be tested, it is best to start with the basic resource model. In the basic model, it is assumed that all variables present and future are known with certainty. The model can most easily be analyzed as conditions for equilibrium in a capital market for the unextracted resource, in a flow market for a resource product, and in the processing market for making the product from the unextracted resource.[1]

The capital market clears when the price of the unextracted resource at time t, λ_t, increases at a rate r_t, which is the risk-adjusted interest rate:

$$\lambda_{t+1} = \lambda_t(1 + r_t) \qquad (10.1)$$

With constant r, the solution to the difference equation for λ is

$$\lambda = \lambda_0(1 + r)^t \qquad (10.1')$$

Equation (10.1) assures that the resource owners are maximizing present-value profits by their extraction paths, at least during the extraction period. If there is an end to the planning horizon or extraction period T, then the price of the resource at that time cannot change discontinuously. That is, holding the resource for an instant longer than T cannot produce capital gains or losses, at least in expectation. In the basic model, the extraction period is assumed to be infinitely long. Profit maximization then implies that no resource should be left at the end of time. Equivalently, all of the resource is used eventually:

$$x(0) = \sum_{t=0}^{\infty} q(t) \qquad (10.2)$$

Equations (10.1) and (10.2) together are the capital market equilibrium conditions. They ensure that no higher present-value profits can be made from the resource stock.

The third condition is that the price of the resource product equals the cost of the raw resource plus the marginal cost of converting the raw resource into that product. It ensures profit maximization in the processing industry. For example, the price of concentrated nickel ore in rail cars should equal the value of unmined nickel ore plus the marginal costs of mining and concentrating it:

$$p_t = \mathrm{mc}_t + \lambda_t \qquad (10.3)$$

The fourth equilibrium condition is that the market for the resource product clears or that the supply and demand for the product are equal. Letting $Q(p, z)$ be the demand curve where the z are demand shift variables,

$$q(t) = Q[p(t), z] \qquad (10.4)$$

The theory described in (10.1)–(10.4) differs from the theory for any other good only in its assumption that there is always storage of the raw resource. For comparison, the stock of cars at dealers and in factory inventory is often just sufficient to facilitate trade. The stocks are held because there is value in facilitating trade. Such stocks are called working stocks. Only when there is an unexpected downturn in the economy are there stocks beyond the working stocks. In those times, cars are often discounted, which is to say that their price is expected to rise (at the rate which reflects holding costs and interest). The discounts help to work off the excess inventory and, eventually, the industry returns to holding only working stocks. What is special about a natural resource is that stocks, well beyond working stocks, are held all of the time. The holding of stocks does not depend upon demand conditions. Since natural resource stocks provide no service by being held (such as the working stocks of cars at dealers), owners can only be compensated for holding them (rather than, say, a Treasury bill) by a price increase. Therefore, the price of a natural resource must always be rising, while the price of an ordinary good only need increase after an unexpected demand shortfall. The unique part of the resource theory is the consequence of stock holding (equation (10.1)), that resource rents always rise at a rate sufficient to compensate their owners for holding them rather than another asset. In the basic model, that rate is the rate of interest. Since it is continuous stock holding and continuous price increase that are unique to resource theory, any test of the theory must make use of this information.

Inherent Problems in Testing for Capital Market Equilibrium

There are two types of problems inherent in testing resource theory as embodied in realistic versions of equation (10.1). It is hard to observe λ, and it is unclear what constitutes a rejection of a realistic version of (10.1).

For almost all resources, there is no time series evidence on λ. There is only evidence on p. Thus, tests are performed on p (for instance, the test that p will rise eventually) or tests are performed on the implied λ. The implied λ is found from some other equation, typically $\lambda = p - mc$.

Second, and perhaps worse, there is no definitive empirical characterization of an "asset." One set of characterizations depends upon market efficiency and concentrates on the unconditional predictability of future prices. Another set depends on relation to market indexes and concentrates on conditional predictability. Neither set of characterizations proves to be definitive.

Equation (10.1) is the most common theoretical assumption using unconditional predictability. It is called unconditional because it uses only information available at time t to predict λ_{t+1}. In (10.1'), there is a constant interest rate. In nominal terms, it is absurd. In real terms, it is simply untrue. Nevertheless, it is a common assumption in empirical work. However, there are two valid empirical counterparts of equation (10.1), both of which assert that the rate of return on holding a resource, λ_{t+1}/λ_t, is best predicted by an appropriate interest rate. If λ is in nominal terms, then r_t needs to be in nominal terms as well. The empirical implementation of r_t is an estimated risk premium plus the rate of interest on a fixed asset, such as a Treasury obligation. Since the nominal rate of return on fixed obligations is observable, there is no problem with implementation as far as equation (10.1) is concerned. The problem is pushed onto equation (10.2). The demand curve estimates need to be done in real terms, which requires an estimate of future inflation so as to get an estimate of future real prices.

The alternative is to estimate (10.1) in real terms. Now the question is how to choose a real rate. In stochastic form equation (10.1) asserts that $E(\lambda_{t+1}/\lambda_t) = 1 + r_t$. (Less generally, $\lambda_{t+1}/\lambda_t = 1 + r_t + \varepsilon$, where ε is a normal error term.) The decision to hold a resource or other asset for the period t to $t + 1$ is made at t, so the relevant decision variables need to be known at t. The rate of inflation is not known at t. Taking a nominal rate of interest and subtracting the realized rate of inflation gives an *ex post* measure of the real interest rate. Being observed only after asset decisions are made, an *ex post* rate can have no relevance to the *ex ante* decision of how much resource to hold or sell and no relevance to equation (10.1). One must use an *ex ante* real rate of interest. There are several possible ways to get an *ex ante* real rate of interest. The most direct is to estimate an autoregressive integrated moving average (ARIMA) model for the rate of inflation (see Cecchetti, 1989, for an example). The predicted rate of inflation is then subtracted from the nominal rate to get the *ex ante* real rate. Mishkin (1981) recovers the *ex ante* real rate from a regression of the realized real rate on the nominal interest rate and money variables. In order to keep the estimation in real terms, an equation could be added for predicting the real rate. For instance, $r_t = a_0 + a_1 r_{t-1} + a_2 r_{t-2} + \cdots + \psi$, where ψ is an error term and the a are parameters. (In order to approximate an ARIMA process reasonably, the degree of the lag polynomial needs to be no more than about the cubed root of the number of observations.) Adding this predictive equation for r to the system, or acknowledging in any other way that r is not perfectly known, introduces an errors-in-variables problem.

With a good definition of r, tests of $E(\lambda_{t+1}/\lambda_t) = 1 + r_t$ are most easily made by showing that better predictors cannot be constructed. Given the *ex ante* real rate, other interest rates, the demand shift variables z, and past rates of return $\lambda_{t+1-i}/\lambda_{t-i}$ should be of no help in predicting the rate of return. This is the notion of market efficiency, at least in its empirical version. One could proceed in a fashion similar to that done with stock-market data and see if the return from holding the resource n periods after some date, ρ_{t+n}, was correlated with the return to holding the resource n periods before the date, ρ_{t-n}. Fama and French (1988) did this for stock-market returns and found a negative correlation at a lag on the order of three to five years. Since the stock market as a whole exhibits violations of the rules for pure assets, it is surely futile to see whether a real asset also violates those rules.

A second view of assets is that they perform like other assets. That is, if the rate of return s_t is known on the Standard & Poor (S&P) 500 the rate of return could be guessed for the asset at hand. Since this estimate uses the realized rate of return, it is conditional on information observed at $t + 1$, which is very different from using only information observed up until t. A form of equation (10.1) that uses this type of information is $\lambda_{t+1}/\lambda_t = (1 - \beta)r_t + \beta s_t + \varepsilon$. This is the capital asset pricing model (CAPM). One rejects this characterization if the error terms are autocorrelated or if other variables are also important. There are many other possible parameterizations of asset equations, however (the arbitrage pricing model and consumption-based capital asset pricing model come readily to mind). Adjusting rates of return for taxes and inflation[2] are also potential empirical trouble spots so that any rejection of a pricing equation could be taken as evidence for one pricing model over another rather than a rejection of the statement that the resource is an asset. On the other hand, finding a β of reasonable size and lack of autocorrelation would be a sign that the resource in question does not behave much differently from other assets.

In summary, empirical versions of equation (10.1) suffer from problems that the basic theory model does not address. Resource prices need to be observed, and they generally are not. Interest rates need to be real *ex ante* rates (or inflation needs to be forecast elsewhere in the model). Testing "Hotelling" then comes down to testing whether the resource in question has the properties ascribed to financial assets. Market efficiency is one such property. However, showing that the resource market is not efficient will not settle the matter, because many financial markets are not efficient. (At least there is substantial empirical evidence against efficiency.) Since it is difficult to declare that stock-market prices act like the textbook example of an asset, it is very unlikely that resource prices, which are prices of real, not financial, assets, will behave any better. Estimating a capital market pricing model may, at least, show whether the resource price behaves as other assets, relative to the S&P 500. These two fundamental problems (unobservability and lack of a clear asset test) need to be kept in mind when evaluating all empirical tests of the Hotelling hypothesis.

Direct tests of λ and p

Barnett and Morse (1963) performed some of the first tests of Hotelling's rule. What they found was basically disturbing. Prices fell. The data at hand were resource prices (i.e. an index of iron ingot prices, prices for metallic copper and silver, and so on). There was only one price series on the resource itself, and those were prices of timber.

Timber is unique in that it is sold while still standing, often at open outcry auctions and with reasonably (but not perfectly) standardized terms. Standing timber that is sold is called stumpage. Stumpage sales, particularly US government stumpage sales, gave only series on λ_t rather than p_t. Many authors have estimated capital asset pricing model equations using such series (Redmond and Cubbage, 1988). The overall finding is that one can estimate some types of asset pricing model using timber, though there is disturbing sensitivity to specification and period. Timber appears to be an "asset," but its high value in its raw form and the organized market make it unique. All other resources on which there are easily available time series have time series on p.

Slade (1982) clearly articulated the rationale of testing whether or not p will rise. Her version of (10.1)–(10.4) included a cost function for making a product from a raw resource, $c(q, x, t)$, that depended upon remaining reserves x and technical progress, parameterized through time t. The standard assumption in the literature is that costs increase as remaining reserves decrease, because the least cost of extraction reserves are mined first. Abstracting from this stock effect, substituting (10.3) into (10.1), and rearranging gives

$$p_t = (1+r)p_{t-1} + mc_t - (1+r)mc_{t-1} \qquad (10.5)$$

Prices can fall (even while λ rises!) as long as technical progress makes marginal cost (mc) fall fast enough. Figure 10.1 shows the price series for iron, and it is definitely falling at the beginning of this century. Considerable other research confirms that there was large technical progress during that period (Berck, 1978). Given that extraction and processing costs are bounded below by zero and that rents are rising at an exponential rate, it is expected that sooner or later $p = mc + \lambda$ will rise.

That supposition can be defeated in several ways. The rent could be zero because the resource in question is in effectively infinite supply. (When a rent of zero rises at the rate of interest, it is still zero, so it never dominates the effects of costs.) More empirically, the ratio of annual use to economic reserves could be quite large. It is suspected that this is true of iron and lead because of their great abundance. Asbestos deposits are also likely to be in this category because of environmental constraints. If the work of Meadows et al. (1972) is taken seriously, the energy minerals may also have no intrinsic rent, because air pollution controls will curtail their use before scarcity does.

Given that costs of extraction are falling, due to technical progress, observing increasing prices is evidence for increasing resource rents. While this is not as strong as asserting that they rise at rate r (or at some rate related to the S&P 500), it is evidence that asset market considerations are important for natural resource markets. It is a weak test.

The standard form for such a test is to see whether the real prices of iron ingots and other basic mineral products rise. (Inflation will make nominal prices rise whether or not there are asset market considerations.) When Slade (1982) performed her tests on real prices, she used the then current technology of fitting the observed series with a quadratic trend with autoregressive error. Indeed, such a model "fits" the iron series shown in Figure 10.1. All the t statistics are over 2.0, R^2 is 0.69, and the autocorrelation parameter is 0.60, which wold appear to be quite far from unity. The model predicts a U-shaped price path with prices rising in Slade's post-sample period of 1977 onward. Re-estimating the same model with data until 1985 (the end of this particular series) gives similar results. Using this trend model, the chance that prices in the year 2000 will be higher than they were in 1985 is 99.92 percent, which is certainly an affirmation of the theory that prices will almost certainly rise.

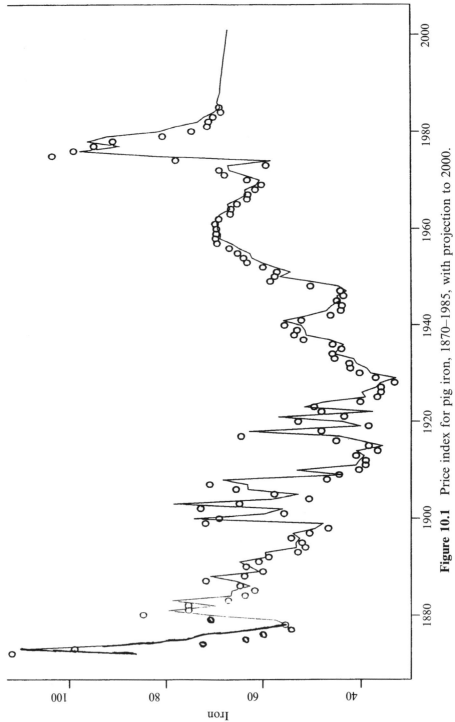

Figure 10.1 Price index for pig iron, 1870–1985, with projection to 2000.

There are two major reasons to believe that the case for rising prices is overstated by these results. First, the parameters of the quadratic trend model change with the period of estimation. For instance, if one estimates the model with two subperiods, from 1870 to 1919 and from 1920 to 1985, then the parameters from the first subperiod estimation are not equal to the parameters from the second subperiod estimation. The appropriate test is a likelihood ratio test, and it rejects the equality at the 0.001 level.

The second reason to doubt the prediction is that the series may be stationary around a stochastic trend rather than a deterministic one. This is the problem of spurious regression (Nelson and Kang, 1981). A random walk can very often be fitted with a deterministic trend, and the fitted regression will have all of the proper regression statistics. It will also be totally wrong. The tests for a stochastic trend are unit root tests. The appropriate one for testing a unit root in the possible presence of a quadratic trend is the Lagrange multiplier test of Schmidt and Phillips (1992). The test does not reject a unit root at the 10 percent level (or 0.05 or 0.01 level) for iron prices. If the true model were the quadratic trend with autocorrelation correction model, there is about a 70 percent probability that the test would reject a unit root. A Dickey–Fuller (1981) test also does not reject a trendless unit root model. From these tests, and others, the conclusion is that the most appropriate univariate representation of these data is an ARIMA model integrated of order 1. The solid line in figure 10.1 is the fitted ARIMA model. The ARIMA model prediction is that there is a 60 percent chance that prices in the year 2000 will be higher than they are today. The same procedure was tried for seven other nontimber resources, and the chance that any of these will increase in price lies between 45 percent and 72 percent. This is much weaker evidence for the "rents matter" hypothesis than would be obtained using a deterministic trend model.

Stock-dependent costs

With some reworking, equation (10.3), the equilibrium condition for the extractive industry, can shed light on resource rent, though not on capital markets. Another way of stating that a resource is exhausted is to say that the costs of extracting it become very large as the remaining stock becomes small. Good quality deposits then earn rents because they are easier to extract than bad quality deposits and because the underlying resource provides some good or service cheaper than the next best way of producing that good or service. The theoretical model by Hartwick (1978) provides a thorough explanation of this type of model, while the following explanation hits only a few of the points.

The natural expression for the supply of extractive effort is that the price *p* of the semiprocessed product (concentrated ore or ingots, for instance) equal the marginal cost mc of producing that product from ore *in situ* plus the value λ of the ore *in situ*. In a resource model with many deposits, extractors will endeavor to find the easiest to extract (lowest cost) deposits first. As each deposit comes closer to exhaustion, the cost of removing ore from it should rise. (In the limit, where the deposit is exhausted, the marginal cost of extraction will be infinite, so this result is guaranteed.) These two observations suggest that a marginal cost of extraction function for a particular deposit should have the form $mc(q, n, x_t)$ where *q* is quantity extracted per year, *n* is the number of deposits discovered before the deposit in question, and x_t is the amount remaining in the deposit.

Marginal cost is expected to increase in *q* and *n* and decrease in *x*. Livernois and Uhler (1987) tested a cost function of this form for a cross-section of 166 Canadian oil wells that were producing in 1976. He found that costs do increase when stock decreases.

Indirect tests using $p - mc$

Indirect tests of the "Hotelling hypothesis" use an equation, such as price (or marginal revenue, mr) less marginal extraction cost to measure the unobservable resource rent λ. The set-up for this class of statistical models comes down to two equations (or at least two types of equations). A capital equilibrium equation (10.1) links the unobserved rent at time *t* to the unobserved rent at time $t + 1$. The measurement equation gives the unknown, $λ_t$, in terms of observable or estimable quantities, such as $p - mc$. The general strategy is to substitute $p - mc$ or $mr - mc$ for λ in equation (10.1). The equation then contains mc_t and mc_{t+1}, which are observable.

One of the earliest serious indirect tests of the Hotelling capital market hypothesis is Stollery's (1983) paper on nickel. It makes use of a remarkable data set on the nickel industry. Stollery obtained the operating history of Inco, a publicly traded company and a near monopolist in the production of nickel. Because Inco is publicly traded, there are stock-market data on the value of the firm and the rate of return on the firm's stock in capital market equilibrium.

Stollery proceeded in stages. First he estimated a demand equation for nickel and a production function for mining nickel. From these he found mr and mc. Rent was estimated as $mr - mc$. The costs were corrected for grade differences and technical progress in mining (which was nil over the estimation period). The estimated values for rent were then treated as data (not observations with error) and used in an estimation of the capital market rule (10.1). The parameter to be estimated was the interest rate *r*.

The recovered estimate of the interest rate from this procedure was compared with an estimate of the required rate of return from a CAPM. Since the two estimates were not dissimilar, the exercise was seen as confirming the theory. The unobservable rents do rise at the rate of interest.

The estimation of the capital market equation includes proper correction for grade changes and variables for changes in income and a substitute (stainless steel) which were interpreted as proxies for the intercept of the demand curve, commonly called the choke price. Going back to basics, λ grows at the rate of interest and gives a whole family of possible rent paths. Setting $\lambda(T)$ (where T is the time of exhaustion) equal to the price of a substitute, P_s, determines which one of these paths is the correct path. The capital market equilibrium asserts that $(1 + r)\lambda_t$ is the best predictor of λ_{t+1}, given the information available at t. The estimated equation uses the change in price of stainless steel, which is to say that it uses the price of stainless steel at $t + 1$. Thus, Stollery's estimated equation mixes the strict capital market concept of equation (10.1) with information on the whole structure of the problem. The paper is quite clear about the assumption of expectations regarding the future, namely that a change in the price of stainless steel today translates into an expected change in the price of stainless steel many years from today. This need to proxy beliefs about the future with current information is necessary in any structural estimation of resource markets, as will be shown below.

Halvorsen and Smith (1991) use the implicit resource price from a restricted cost function to measure λ. Let β be a vector of parameters that will ultimately be estimated. Let $c(q, h, w; \beta)$ be the cost of producing final product q (concentrated ore) from extraction h with other input prices w. The function $c(q, h, w)$ is a restricted cost function for producing q. Letting λ be the price of extraction (raw ore, *in situ*), the unrestricted cost function for producing concentrated ore is the solution to

$$c(q, \lambda, w) = \min_h c(q, h, w; \beta) - \lambda h \qquad (10.6)$$

The first-order condition for this minimization is used as a measurement equation for λ:

$$\frac{\partial c(q, h, w; \beta)}{\partial h} = \lambda + \nu \qquad (10.7)$$

where ν is an error term. Twice substituting the measurement equation into the capital equilibrium condition and adding an error term ω gives the capital equation to be estimated:

$$\frac{\partial c(q_{t+1}, h_{t+1}, w_{t+1}; \beta_0)}{\partial h} - \nu_{t+1} = \left[\frac{\partial c(q_t, h_t, w_t; \beta_0)}{\partial h} - \nu_t \right] (1 + r_t) + \omega_{t+1}$$

$$(10.8)$$

Assuming that ν is zero (i.e. marginal cost perfectly measures rent), the equation includes only observables and can be estimated. Since there are data on costs of processing, c_t, there is another way to estimate β, namely direct estimation of the cost function:

$$c_t = c(q_t, h_t, w_t; \beta_1) + \varepsilon_t \qquad (10.9)$$

(Halvorsen and Smith also estimate the factor demand equations in share form, which increases efficiency and does not change the nature of the argument.) The null hypothesis is that the estimate of the parameter vector β is the same in the direct estimation of the restricted cost function as it is in equation (10.8), the modified capital market equilibrium equation. That is, $H_0: \beta_0 = \beta_1$.

Halvorsen and Smith's (1991) data were aggregate Canadian metallic ore production from 1954 to 1974. The data included the extraction, h, as well as the concentrated ore production, q, which was then presumably further refined. Prices of capital and labor constituted w, and the restricted cost function was further extended to include technical progress (more exactly time) and cumulative extraction, $x_0 - x_t$. The equations were estimated, and the hypothesis test rejected H_0.

The authors then point out a number of qualifications to their results, including the use of aggregate data (rather than data on a specific mineral) and the possibility that the capital market equation was inadequately general. The use of *ex post* real rates of interest as opposed to *ex ante* real rates, the assumption of no measurement error in λ, and the use of a pretest to prune down the number of variables in the almost translog cost function should be added to their list. Of these empirical problems, the use of aggregate data and the underlying problem of what it means to test equation (10.1) seem to be the most important.

Devarajan and Fisher (1982), writing a more theoretical piece on exploration in natural resources, find that the resource rent is also equal to the marginal cost of finding more of a resource (i.e. to marginal exploration cost). Thus, marginal exploration cost is also a measure of resource rent.

A Reduced Form Approach

The solution of (10.1)–(10.4) gives an equation (the Hotelling reduced form). For simplicity, assume that marginal costs mc and the real *ex ante* rate of interest r are constant. Since λ increases according to equation (10.1) at rate $1 + r$ per period, $p(i)$ for $i \geq t$ is given by

$$p_i = (p_t - \mathrm{mc})(1 + r)^{i-t} + \mathrm{mc} \qquad (10.10)$$

Inserting the demand curve into equation (10.2), the adding up constraint, and using the expression for p_i just derived gives

$$x_t = \sum_{i=t}^{\infty} Q[(p_t - \text{mc})(1 + r)^{i-t} + \text{mc}, z_i] \qquad (10.11)$$

This equation plainly involves future demand-shift variables z_i. Let those variables be forecast according to some function $f(z_t)$ of the current variables.

$$x_t = \sum_{i=t}^{\infty} Q[(p_t - \text{mc})(1 + r)^{i-t} + \text{mc}, f(z_t)] \qquad (10.12)$$

Solving the above equation for p_t gives the reduced form

$$p_t = p(x_t, z_t, r, \text{mc}) \qquad (10.13)$$

The reduced form equation can be found empirically in two different ways. The first is simply to estimate a reasonably general (e.g. translog) ordinary least squares regression of p on x, z, r, and mc. This form implies little about the theory. Exactly the same reduced form results from positing a one-period supply and demand for the resource. The second method is to estimate the demand equation (e.g. by a two-stage least squares almost translog function) and then perform the steps listed above to derive the function $p_t = p(\ldots)$. If the theory is true, the two results should be the same.

When one cannot carry out the summation called for in (10.12), then it is still possible to perform the required test by working on the derivatives and elasticities of the reduced form and demand equations. First, we derive a property of the Hotelling reduced form and see if it is true using the parameter estimates from a demand equation. Again, let $p = \lambda + \text{mc} = \lambda_0(1 + r)^t + \text{mc}$ be the product price and approximate the demand curve for product by the translog function:

$$\ln Q = -\alpha \ln p + \beta(\ln p)^2 + \gamma \ln p \ln z + \delta(\ln z)^2 + \phi \qquad (10.14)$$

Recall the feasibility condition $x = \sum Q$ and take the derivative of this identity with respect to p. Substitute the translog expression for dQ/dp, substitute $d\lambda/dt = dp/dt$, and use the inverse function theorem to rearrange the result to get

$$\frac{d\lambda}{dx} = \left[\sum \frac{Q(-\alpha + 2\beta \ln p + \gamma \ln z)}{\lambda_0 + \text{mc}(1 + r)^{-t}} \right]^{-1} \qquad (10.15)$$

Since the demand elasticity is given by

$$\varepsilon(t) = -\alpha + 2\beta \ln p + \gamma \ln z < 0 \qquad (10.16)$$

and p is increasing over time, $d\varepsilon/dt$ has the sign of β. The relevant case is where $\beta < 0$. Making the assumption that $\beta < 0$ and using the definition of ε,

$$\sum \frac{Q\varepsilon}{\lambda_0 + mc(1 + r)^{-t}} < \varepsilon(0) \sum \frac{Q}{\lambda_0 + mc(1 + r)^{-t}} \tag{10.17}$$

Note that mc is less than $mc(1 + r)^{-t}$, the summation of Q is x, and $\varepsilon(0)$ is negative. Combining these facts gives the inequality

$$\varepsilon(0) \sum \frac{Q}{\lambda_0 + mc(1 + r)^{-t}} < \varepsilon(0) \frac{x}{\lambda_0 + mc} \tag{10.18}$$

The two inequalities above combine to yield

$$\sum \frac{Q\varepsilon}{\lambda_0 + mc(1 + r)^{-t}} < \varepsilon(0) \frac{x}{\lambda_0 + mc} \tag{10.19}$$

Recalling the expression for $d\lambda/dt$ gives

$$\frac{d\lambda}{dx} > \left[\varepsilon(0) \frac{x}{\lambda_0 + mc} \right]^{-1} \tag{10.20}$$

which can be rearranged to give

$$\frac{d\lambda}{dx} \frac{x}{\lambda_0 + mc} > [(\varepsilon(0)]^{-1} \tag{10.21}$$

The left-hand side of the above inequality is just the reduced form estimate of the inventory elasticity of price. The right-hand side is the demand elasticity of price estimated from the demand equation. Thus, the inequality is a restriction on the elasticities estimated from two separate translog equations. The inequality can be tested by estimating the equations as a system and comparing the likelihood of the constrained and unconstrained estimates of the parameters.

Using a time series of prices on redwood stumpage, these equations were estimated and the test described above was performed. The null is that the inventory elasticity is *less* than $1/\varepsilon$. A Wald test rejects that null (and therefore accepts the theory) at the 99 percent level of significance (see Berck and Bentley (1988) for more background on redwood as a resource).

The Valuation Approach

The simplest approach of all to testing the Hotelling theory is the valuation approach. Popularized and used as a rigorous test by Miller and Upton (1985), this argument was made in the Federal courts in both of the Redwood Park Taking cases (1968 and 1978) and probably in many other cases involving the valuation of natural resources. Mathematically, the argument is trivial: $E(\lambda_{t+n}) = \lambda_t(1 + r)^n$. This is equation (10.1). In legal terms, it asserts that the discount rate a firm uses for its capital decisions (i.e. its marginal cost of capital) is exactly the same as the rate at which it believes the price of its resource will increase. Let $\{q_t\}$ be any proposed extraction profile that exhausts stock x_0. The present value of any extraction plan is $PV_t = \sum_{i=t}^{\infty} \lambda_i(1 + r)^{t-i}q_i$. On substituting $\lambda_t(1 + r)^{i-t}$ for λ_i and summing one gets $\lambda_t x_t$, regardless of choice of path $\{q_t\}$. In other words, if the firm thought that it could get a better present-value price in some future period, then it would not extract today. It would wait for the future period. Since the real-world firms all plan to extract in every period, the present-value benefit of extraction must be constant and equal to the benefit of period t extraction, λ_t. Hence, today's price for the resource is the correct price and no discounts (or additions) need be made because the deposit can only be extracted over a prolonged length of time. Miller and Upton called this the Hotelling valuation principle and tested it with a cross-section of oil properties. They found that (except for very small properties, which they excluded) the stock-market value of a property was its Hotelling value, $x_0 \lambda_0$. Size of deposit had no effect on value.

The same type of analysis with redwood stumpage prices has been done, with a slightly different conclusion (see Berck (1988) for more details). By using a smoother rather than a linear or quadratic function of deposit size and including small sales, it was found that there was a steep increase in value from the very small sizes up to reasonable sizes. Very large sizes had a slight discount but were significant only at the 33 percent level. The result on small sizes is explained by set-up costs. There are fixed appraisal and equipment moving costs incurred regardless of size. The discount for the very large sizes could either be a statistical artifact or it could represent difficulty in assembling the capital needed to make a very large deal.

On a theoretical level, a different result could be derived from the valuation principle in a number of ways. Allowing for shut-down, abandonment, and positing definite fixed operational costs gives the Brannan and Schwartz (1985) model in which the option of operating is valuable. Rather trivially, a known but not operated deposit cannot be valued in this fashion, because its nonoperation indicates that it has more value in future than in current extraction.

Despite all the disclaimers, the empirical evidence on Hotelling's valuation principle favors (10.1)–(10.4) as a parsimonious description of the data.

The Maximum Likelihood Kalman Filter

Since one cannot observe the actual price of a resource *in situ*, it is natural to use a statistic that one can observe as a proxy. That is the approach used by both Stollery (1983) and Halvorsen and Smith (1991). However, once one has decided to use a proxy, it is important to recognize that it is a proxy and not the variable itself. It is also desirable to produce the best possible proxy. The statistical method most easily applicable to this problem is the maximum likelihood Kalman filter. This section explains the filter and makes some suggestions as to how it can be used in a test of the theory of resources.

The method depends upon the capital equation (10.1) and processing equation (10.3) of the general model. An explicitly uncertain version of these equations is

$$\lambda_{t+1} = \lambda_t(1 + r_t + \beta_{00}) + z_t\beta_0 + \omega_t \qquad (10.1'')$$

The variable ω_t is a mean zero normal error term with variance W. All error terms in this model are assumed independent of all other errors and serially uncorrelated. Taking r as an appropriate *ex ante* real rate, β_{00} is the risk premium. For simplicity, most of the rest of this discussion will treat β_{00} as zero. The variable z is any other variable which might influence the capital equation, but is observed at time t. It could be current inflation, housing starts, or lagged return on the resource, for instance. It could not be the return on any asset (such as the S&P 500) taken from period t to $t + 1$, because that cannot be observed at t. A reasonable version of the hypothesis that the resource is a capital good would be that $\beta_0 = 0$ for any contemporaneous variable z. More narrowly, if z would not help predict the S&P 500, then it should not help predict λ either.

The second equation of this model is a measurement equation, in this case the processing equilibrium equation.

$$p_t = \mathrm{mc}(\beta_1, z_{1t}) + \lambda_t + \nu_t \qquad (10.3')$$

The random error ν_t is distributed normal with mean zero and variance V. Equation (10.3') is called a measurement equation because the dependent variables are observable and depend on the unobservable rent λ. The parameter vector β_1 and variables z_1 are just the parameters and variables of the marginal cost function. Assume that the marginal cost function is linear and that the variables z_1 are known in time to be used to predict p_t.

Typically, all variables are observed except rent λ and the parameters $\beta = (\beta_0, \beta_1)$ are estimated.

Estimation with unknown rent

The parameters of the equations representing the simple resource model can be estimated by a combination of the Kalman filter and maximum likelihood. The presentation in Meinhold and Singpurwalla (1983) is followed. More standard and more detailed explications can be found in Harvey (1981) or Gelb (1974).

Equation (10.1) is called a state equation because it describes the evolution of the unobservable state variable, rent. Its value is never known. The best estimate of rent at time t, given all observations (on p and z) up to and including $t - 1$, is denoted $\lambda_{t|t-1}$. This is shorthand for a normal random variate with mean $\hat{\lambda}_{t|t-1}$ and variance $L_{t|t-1}$. Then p_t and z_t are observed. This new information leads to a revised estimate of the rent. This new best estimate, given information through time t, is denoted $\lambda_{t|t}$; and it is, again, a normal random variate with mean $\hat{\lambda}_{t|t}$ and variance $L_{t|t}$. Given β, W, and V_y, or estimates of them, the Kalman filter is an algorithm to determine $\lambda_{t|t}$ when one knows $\lambda_{t-1|t-1}$ and realizations of the variables p_t and z_t which depend on λ_t. The filter also gives the variance of $\lambda_{t|t}$, denoted $L_{t|t}$, which is determined from $L_{t-1|t-1}$, z_t, and p_t.

Assume that $\hat{\lambda}_0$ and $L_{0|0}$ are the mean and variance of λ at time zero. The filter will give an estimate $\lambda_{1|1}$ in terms of $\lambda_{0|0}$ and the observable variables. The process can be repeated indefinitely, giving estimates of λ_{t+1} in terms of the estimates of λ_t and the observable variables at t.

At time $t - 1$, which is to say before $(p, x)_t$ are observed, the estimate of λ_t, called $\lambda_{t|t-1}$, is $(1 + r_t)\lambda_{t-1|t-1} + z_0\beta_0 + w$. Its mean is $\beta_0 z_0 + (1 + r_t)\hat{\lambda}_{t-1|t-1}$. Its variance is $W + (1 + r_t)L_{t-1|t-1}(1 + r_t)$. The latter term is the contribution of the randomness of $\lambda_{t-1|t-1}$ to the randomness of $\lambda_{t|t-1}$. For later use, let this variance be called R_t.

Since $\lambda_{t|t-1}$ summarizes the beliefs about λ prior to observing p and z, it is a prior expectation in the Bayesian sense.

At $t - 1$, the best estimate of p_t comes from equation (10.3'):

$$p_{t|t-1} = mc_t + \lambda_{t|t-1} + v_t \tag{10.22}$$

The point forecast of p_t is just its mean:

$$\hat{p}_{t|t-1} = mc_t + \hat{\lambda}_{t|t-1} \tag{10.23}$$

From the two previous expressions, define the error in predicting p as the normal random variate

$$e_{t|t-1} = p_t - \hat{p}_{t|t-1} = \lambda_{t|t-1} - \hat{\lambda}_{t|t-1} + v_t \tag{10.24}$$

where $E(e_{t|t-1}) = 0$. The variance of the prediction error in price is $V + R_t$, where V is the variance in the error of the processing equation. One other statistic that will be needed is the covariance of $e_{t|t-1}$ and $\lambda_{t|t-1}$:

$$\text{cov}(\lambda_{t|t-1}, e_{t|t-1}) = E[(e_{t|t-1} - 0)(\lambda_{t|t-1} - \hat{\lambda}_{t|t-1})] = R_t \tag{10.25}$$

where $E( )$ is the expectation operator. The variables $\lambda_{t|t-1}$ and $e_{t|t-1}$ are correlated normal random variates, so they are jointly normal with the following distribution:

$$\begin{pmatrix} e_{t|t-1} \\ \lambda_{t|t-1} \end{pmatrix} = N\left[\begin{pmatrix} 0 \\ \hat{\lambda}_{t|t-1} \end{pmatrix}, \begin{pmatrix} V + R_t & R_t \\ R_t & R_t \end{pmatrix} \right] \tag{10.26}$$

Since observing the error in predicting price is the same as observing price, the posterior distribution of λ (which is $\lambda_{t|t}$) is just the same as $(\lambda_{t|t-1}|e_t)$ or the conditional distribution of $\lambda_{t|t-1}$, given the observed error e_t. To summarize, equation (10.26) gives the joint distribution of the normal variates $e_{t|t-1}$ and $\lambda_{t|t-1}$. The conditional distribution of $\lambda_{t|t-1}$, given $e_{t|t-1}$, is sought. The conditional distribution for a joint normal can be found in a standard text or in the article by Meinhold and Singpurwalla (1983). From the formula for the conditional distribution, $\lambda_{t|t}$ is normally distributed with mean and variance given by

$$\hat{\lambda}_{t|t} = b_0 z_0 + (1 + r_t)\hat{\lambda}_{t-1|t-1} + R_t(V + R_t)^{-1} e_t$$

$$L_{t|t} = R_t - R_t(V + R_t)^{-1} R_t \tag{10.27}$$

The pair of equations (10.27) gives the rule, called the Kalman filter, to get from an estimate of rent at time t to an estimate of rent at time $t + 1$. The new estimate includes the observation of product price at time $t + 1$. Since this rule can be applied recursively, for any set of parameters β and any $\lambda_{0|0}$ and $L_{0|0}$, all $\lambda_{t|t}$ can be calculated by use of the rule. The calculation is simply the algebra of conditional expectations and nothing more.[3]

Equations (10.1″) and (10.3′) are jointly estimated by maximum likelihood. Likelihood is always the likelihood of what one observes, so it is the likelihood of observing p_t given the parameters (β, λ_0, L_0) and exogenous variables (z). The parameters are ultimately chosen to maximize the likelihood function, which is the product of the likelihood of the T observations.

A typical observation consists of p_t and $\hat{\lambda}_{t|t-1}$. The likelihood of p is the same as $mc_t + \lambda_{t|t-1} + v_y$ which is a normal variate with mean $mc_t + \hat{\lambda}_{t|t-1}$ and variance $V + R_t$. Letting u_t be the observed residual $u_t = p_t - mc_t + \hat{\lambda}_{t|t-1}$, the likelihood of the ith observation is

$$\mathcal{L}_t = \frac{1}{[2\pi(R_t + V)]^{1/2}} \exp[-u_t(V + R_t)^{-1} u_t] \tag{10.28}$$

The likelihood of the sample is just $\mathcal{L}(\lambda_{0|0}, L_{0|0}, \beta, V, W) = \prod_{t=1,T} \mathcal{L}_t$, which is the likelihood of observing all T observations of y. In practice, for any set of parameters, $\mathcal{L}$ is evaluated by first using the filter to find all the λs and Ls. The λs and Ls are used to calculate R_t and u_t. Finally, the $\mathcal{L}_t$ are calculated and multiplied together for $t = 1, \ldots, T$ (or the logs of $\mathcal{L}_t$ are summed) to get the likelihood function.

The methods used by other authors set the observation error R in the likelihood function equal to zero and use an inefficient estimator of λ. In filter terms, Stollery (1983) uses only the contemporaneous observation equation to find the estimate of λ. This is not the best estimate because it does not take into account the information that λ grows at the rate of interest. In his estimation of the implied interest rate in the capital market equation, he uses his derived λs as data rather than as estimates. The general belief is that the resulting errors-in-variables equation should bias the coefficients downward, that is, that his estimate of r might be too low! Halvorsen and Smith (1991) also use contemporaneous information only in their estimate of λ and abstract from the errors-in-variables problem.

There are two tests possible with the method advocated here. First, the variables z_0 should not influence the estimate of λ unless they belong in a capital market equation. Lagged values of λ and variables that enter the demand equation, such as industrial production, should no more help to predict λ than they should help to predict the stock market. This observation leads to likelihood ratio tests on $\beta_0 = 0$. The second method of testing is very similar to what Stollery did. Compare the rate of return $r_t + \beta_{00}$ estimated by this model with the rate of return estimates from a CAPM. Note that there are two differences between the capital equation (10.1) and the CAPM: the CAPM uses the firm's stock price, while (10.1) does not; the CAPM uses the realized return on the S&P, which is only known at $t + 1$, while equation (10.1) is limited to information available at t.

Conclusion

In order to test Hotelling's natural resource model, what makes that model different from other possible models for equilibrium in resource markets needs to be defined first. One modern interpretation of the Hotelling model is that it asserts that capital market considerations are paramount in the pricing of natural resources. There are then two major problems with "testing" the theory.

The first problem is that the price of the capital good, resource *in situ*, is not normally observed. Either work with the product price, which may well be dominated by processing costs, or infer the *in situ* price from an estimated (observation) equation. Both methods have their inherent pitfalls. If the *in situ* price is a small part of the observed product price, which is all that is observed, then one is left looking for a very small effect. (How much is learnable about gnat behavior by observing elephants?) It is not surprising that direct observation of metals and minerals prices gives little evidence on Hotelling. Indirect methods of observation encounter the econometric problem of errors in variables. The Kalman filter method gives a way to correct for the fact that $p - mc$ is not the resource rent – it is only an estimate of the resource rent. Other errors-in-variables methods are also possible.

The second problem with testing Hotelling cannot be overcome with better data or better econometric tricks. There is no version of the capital market equilibrium, equation (10.1), whose rejection would cause all economists to reject the notion that capital effects matter. Real assets, those that lack standardization, are costly to assay and take time to sell and are not supposed to perform even as well as the S&P. Even financial assets, such as the S&P 500, do not perfectly follow the rules that economists have set out for them. The literature of late concentrates on autocorrelation of returns, excess volatility, and too high a risk premium for equities over riskless assets. With these puzzles in the performance of the quintessential financial asset, there is little chance of turning up behavior in the price of a natural resource that is so bizarre as to constitute proof that resource prices are not asset market related. On the other hand, it is quite easy to reject some overly strong versions of equation (10.1). The situation is much the same as when Barnett and Morse (1963) first investigated prices: there is clear evidence for capital market considerations in only a few resources and much murkier evidence for the rest. Whether capital market considerations are important for any given resource remains an empirical matter.

Notes

1 Hotelling (1931) set the problem up as a calculus of variations problem and showed that the surplus maximizing and competitive outcomes were the same.
2 See Feldstein (1980) for the importance of these adjustments for the land and gold markets, particularly in the inflationary late 1970s.
3 Kalman's derivation of this rule shows that it gives the minimum mean square error estimates of λ. Since normal likelihoods will be estimated, the normality of the λs rather than their approximation properties is emphasized. See Gelb (1974) or Harvey (1981) for an explanation that follows Kalman.

References

Barnett, H. J., and Morse, C. 1963: *Scarcity and Growth*. Baltimore, MD: Johns Hopkins University Press.
Berck, Peter. 1978. Hard driving and efficiency: iron production in 1890. *Journal of Economic History*, 38 (December), 879–900.
Berck, Peter. 1988: Adjusting prices for volume: a test of the Hotelling valuation principle. Working Paper 480, Department of Agricultural and Resource Economics, University of California, Berkeley.
Berck, Peter, and Bentley, William R. 1988: Hotelling's theory, enhancement, and the taking of the Redwood National Park. Working Paper 456, Department of Agricultural and Resource Economics, University of California, Berkeley.
Brannan, M. and Schwartz, E. 1985: Evaluating natural resource investments. *Journal of Business*, 58, 135–57.
Cecchetti, Stephen G. 1989: Prices during the Great Depression: was the deflation of 1930–32 really unanticipated. NBER Working Paper 3174, November.
Devarajan, Shantayanan, and Fisher, Anthony C. 1982: Exploration and scarcity. *Journal of Political Economy*, 90 (December), 1279–90.

Dickey, D. A. and Fuller, W. A. 1981: Likelihood ratio statistics for autoregressive time series with a unit root. *Econometrica*, 49, 1057–72.

Fama, Eugene, and French, Kenneth.1988: Permanent and temporary components of stock prices. *Journal of Political Economy*, 96 (April), 246–73.

Feldstein, M. 1980: Inflation, tax rules, and the prices of land and gold. *Journal of Public Economics*, 14 (December), 309–17.

Gelb, A. 1974: *Applied Optimal Estimation*. Analytic Sciences Foundation, Cambridge, MA: MIT Press.

Halvorsen, Robert, and Smith, Tim R. 1991: Test of the theory of exhaustible resources. *Quarterly Journal of Economics*, 106 (February), 123–40.

Hartwick, John. 1978: Exploitation of many deposits on an exhaustible resource. *Econometrica*, 46, 201–18.

Harvey, A. C. 1981: *Time Series Models*. New York: Halsted Press.

Hotelling, Harold, 1931: The economics of exhaustible resources. *Journal of Political Economy*, 39, 137–75.

Livernois, John, and Uhler, Russell. 1987: Extraction costs and the economics of nonrenewable resources. *Journal of Political Economy*, 95, 195–203.

Meadows, D. H. et al. 1972: *Limits to Growth*. New York: Universe Books.

Meinhold, R. J. and Singpurwalla, N. D. 1983: Understanding the Kalman filter. *American Statistician*, 37 (May), 123–7.

Miller, M. H. and Upton, C. W. 1985: A test of the Hotelling valuation principle. *Journal of Political Economy*, 93, 1–25.

Mishkin, Frederic. 1981: The real interest rate: an empirical investigation. In K. Brunner and A. Meltzer (eds), *The Costs and Consequences of Inflation*, Carnegie Rochester Conference Series on Public Policy 15, Amsterdam: North-Holland, 151–200.

Nelson, Charles R. and Kang, Heejoon. 1981: Spurious periodicity in inappropriately detrended time series. *Econometrica*, 49, 741–51.

Redmond, C. H. and Cubbage, F. W. 1988: Portfolio risk and returns from timber asset investments. *Land Economics*, 58, 34–51.

Schmidt, Peter, and Phillips, Peter C. B. 1992: LM tests for a unit root in the presence of a deterministic trend. *Oxford Bulletin of Economics and Statistics*, 54, 257–87.

Slade, Margaret E. 1982: Trends in natural resource commodity prices: an analysis of the time domain. *Journal of Environmental Economics and Management*, 9 (June), 122–37.

Stollery, K. R. 1983: Mineral depletion with cost as the extraction limit: a model applied to the behavior of prices in the nickel industry. *Journal of Environmental Economics and Management*, 10, 151–65.

11
Recycling Programs

Katherine T. McClain

1 Introduction

Municipal solid waste (MSW) has been called many things but not, until recently, a resource. However, with per-capita waste generation approaching 4.5 pounds per day, many now regard it as an important resource, even though most waste products are still consigned to the municipal solid waste stream at the end of their useful life. The entrance of non-virgin, reusable materials into raw material markets has changed the nature of those markets and the meaning of nonrenewable, and to ignore the success of some recyclables[1] and the potential of others is shortsighted. Recycling has spawned the creation of a new resource market with several economic issues to address and whose economic viability is as yet unclear. The focus of this chapter will be those economic issues and some of the policy responses to them.

 MSW includes durable goods, nondurable goods, containers and packaging, food scraps, yard trimmings, and other inorganic wastes. It originates from residential sources (houses, duplexes, apartments), commercial sources (office buildings, stores, hotels, airports), institutional sources (schools, prisons, hospitals), and industrial sources (packaging and office waste from factories but not waste from industrial processes) (Environmental Protection Agency (EPA), 1992, p. ES-2). It does not include construction debris, sludge, or combustion ash, although all may be found in landfills and incinerators and may be recyclable in part. The Environmental Protection Agency estimates that the United States produced more than 195 million tons of MSW in 1990, more than double the 88 million tons produced in 1960 (EPA, 1992, p. 2-2). Much of the increase can be attributed to the increasing population, but even per-capita waste generation has nearly doubled, from 2.7 pounds per person per day in 1960 to 4.3 in 1990. This increase is expected to continue and with it the need for effective waste management.

Until recently, waste management depended mainly on the ability and desires of local governments. The US government first entered solid waste management with the passage of the 1965 Solid Waste Disposal Act (SWDA) authorizing research grants to states. That was followed by three pivotal events in 1970. First, the SWDA was amended by the Resource Recovery Act to require the federal government to issue waste disposal guidelines. Second, the Clean Air Act was passed, which – while not directed at waste management practices – indirectly forced the closure of many incinerators and stopped the open burning of waste through its restrictions on emissions. Finally, the first Earth Day was held in 1970, focusing public attention on environmental issues in general and several aspects of waste disposal in particular, including recycling. The first bottle bill followed in Oregon in 1971.

The first legislation that required a significant federal role was the 1976 Resource Conservation and Recovery Act (RCRA). Commonly thought to address only hazardous wastes, it also emphasized the conservation of resources, particularly energy, and named recycling as the preferred MSW management alternative. Subsequent reauthorization of the Act further emphasized the role of recycling and essentially established the integrated waste management approach and hierarchy most commonly employed today.

Integrated waste management calls for not a single disposal approach but a combination of methods specifically tailored to individual communities. Each community is free to choose whatever methods are most effective for its needs (although suggested federal recycling legislation may – and some state legislation does – restrict this freedom), but a preferential ranking of alternatives is widely recognized. Source reduction and reuse (not using something or using the same product more than once without reprocessing) are most preferred because both reduce the amount of waste generated. Newer packaging approaches (e.g. smaller compact disc boxes) and refillable containers fall into this category. Recycling and composting are next. These processes take products that would have become waste and turn them into other useful products, thus preventing their entrance into the waste stream. Closed-loop recycling, where the recovered product is reprocessed into the same product again (as in aluminum cans), is less common but preferred to open-loop recycling, where the recovered product becomes another product (a glass bottle becomes glasphalt). The least preferred alternatives are incineration and landfills. Incineration used to be considered more environmentally benign than landfilling, and if accompanied by energy generation a better use of resources. However, doubts have recently arisen over the emission of dioxins (which result from burning some polymers) and ash disposal.

Source reduction is difficult to measure and probably hard to achieve on a large scale at the local level. Community officials have instead turned to recycling to help alleviate the growing quantity of MSW they face. The remainder of this chapter focuses on the rise of recycling as a waste management alternative and its economic viability. We then consider the status of the markets for recyclables and conclude by looking at the nature of the policy approaches thus far employed.

2 The Rise of Recycling

Tables 11.1, 11.2, and 11.3 show the generation and recovery of MSW and materials discarded from 1960 through 1990 (EPA, 1992, pp. 2-1 to 2-3). The growth in the generation of MSW has been tremendous, and while recycling efforts have been increasing since the 1970s the amount of MSW landfilled increased by 137 percent from 1960 to 1990. Per-capita daily generation grew from 2.7 pounds in 1960 to 4.3 pounds in 1990. Table 11.2 reveals that recycling is becoming successful at diverting products from the waste stream. This growing success, and the increase of per-capita waste generated, can largely be traced to five social, political, and economic factors.

Increased social pressure for more environmentally benign human activities
Environmental awareness in the United States heightened in the 1960s, culminating with the first Earth Day and the first piece of major federal environmental legislation, the Clean Air Act. Trash was regarded as "bad" and recycling and composting as natural and "good," even though misconceptions can be harbored about what is technologically or economically feasible. At the same time, the 1970s oil embargo and subsequent oil and gas shortage focused attention on the finite nature of some raw materials. And although experts disagree over the likelihood or extent of resource shortages, the events of the early 1970s may have contributed psychologically to the public outcry to reuse nonrenewable resources.

Scientific knowledge of the environment and the effects of modern lifestyles on it was accumulating at this time, along with technological breakthroughs that allowed environmental damages to be measured more precisely. This new understanding of the impacts of landfills and incineration on groundwater and air pollution created social pressure for increased regulation, more restrictive waste disposal, and more recycling.

Lifestyle changes that led to increased generation of MSW
Lifestyles have changed dramatically in the last 50 years and more material per person must be disposed of than ever before, escalating pressure on local governments to manage waste disposal more effectively. At the

Table 11.1 Materials generated[a] in the municipal waste stream, 1960–90 (in millions of tons and percentage of total generation)

Materials	1960	1965	1970	1975	1980	1985	1990
				Millions of tons			
Paper and paperboard	29.9	38.0	44.2	43.0	54.7	61.5	73.3
Glass	6.7	8.7	12.7	13.5	15.0	13.2	13.2
Metals							
Ferrous	9.9	10.1	12.6	12.3	11.6	10.9	12.3
Aluminum	0.4	0.5	0.8	1.1	1.8	2.3	2.7
Other nonferrous	0.2	0.5	0.7	0.9	1.1	1.0	1.2
Total metals	10.5	11.1	14.1	14.3	14.5	14.2	16.2
Plastics	0.4	1.4	3.1	4.5	7.8	11.6	16.2
Rubber and leather	2.0	2.6	3.2	3.9	4.3	3.8	4.6
Textiles	1.7	1.9	2.0	2.2	2.6	2.8	5.6
Wood	3.0	3.5	4.0	4.4	6.7	8.2	12.3
Other	0.1	0.3	0.8	1.7	2.9	3.4	3.2
Total materials in products	54.3	67.5	84.1	87.5	108.5	118.7	144.6
Other wastes							
Food wastes	12.2	12.7	12.8	13.4	13.2	13.2	13.2
Yard trimmings	20.0	21.6	23.2	25.2	27.5	30.0	35.0
Miscellaneous inorganic wastes	1.3	1.6	1.8	2.0	2.2	2.5	2.9
Total other wastes	33.5	35.9	37.8	40.6	42.9	45.7	51.1
Total MSW generated (weight)	87.8	103.4	121.9	128.1	151.4	164.4	195.7
				Percentage of total generation			
Paper and paperboard	34.1	36.8	36.3	33.6	36.1	37.4	37.5
Glass	7.6	8.4	10.4	10.5	9.9	8.0	6.7
Metals							
Ferrous	11.3	9.8	10.3	9.6	7.7	6.6	6.3
Aluminum	0.5	0.5	0.7	0.9	1.2	1.4	1.4
Other nonferrous	0.2	0.5	0.6	0.7	0.7	0.6	0.6
Total metals	12.0	10.7	11.6	11.2	9.6	8.6	8.3
Plastics	0.5	1.4	2.5	3.5	5.2	7.1	8.3
Rubber and leather	2.3	2.5	2.6	3.0	2.8	2.3	2.4
Textiles	1.9	1.8	1.6	1.7	1.7	1.7	2.9
Wood	3.4	3.4	3.3	3.4	4.4	5.0	6.3
Other	0.1	0.3	0.7	1.3	1.9	2.1	1.6
Total material in products	61.8	65.3	69.0	68.3	71.7	72.2	73.9
Other wastes							
Food wastes	13.9	12.3	10.5	10.5	8.7	8.0	6.7
Yard trimmings	22.8	20.9	19.0	19.7	18.2	18.2	17.9
Miscellaneous inorganic wastes	1.5	1.5	1.5	1.6	1.5	1.5	1.5
Total other wastes	38.2	34.7	31.0	31.7	28.3	27.8	26.1
Total MSW generated (%)	100.0	100.0	100.0	100.0	100.0	100.0	100.0

[a]Generation before materials recovery or combustion. Does not include construction and demolition debris, industrial process wastes, or certain other Subtitle D wastes. Details may not add to totals due to rounding.
Source: EPA Doc. 530-R-92-019

Table 11.2 Recovery[a] of municipal solid waste, 1960–90 (in milions of tons and percentage of total generation of each product)

Materials	1960	1965	1970	1975	1980	1985	1990
			Millions of tons				
Paper and paperboard	5.4	5.7	7.4	8.2	11.9	13.1	20.9
Glass	0.1	0.1	0.2	0.4	0.8	1.0	2.6
Metals							
Ferrous	0.1	0.1	0.1	0.2	0.4	0.4	1.9
Aluminum	Neg.	Neg.	Neg.	0.1	0.3	0.6	1.0
Other nonferrous	Neg.	0.3	0.3	0.4	0.5	0.5	0.8
Total metals	0.1	0.4	0.4	0.7	1.2	1.5	3.7
Plastics	Neg.	Neg.	Neg.	Neg.	Neg.	0.1	0.4
Rubber and leather	0.3	0.3	0.3	0.2	0.1	0.2	0.2
Textiles	Neg.	Neg.	Neg.	Neg.	Neg.	Neg.	0.2
Wood	Neg.	Neg.	Neg.	Neg.	Neg.	Neg.	0.4
Other[b]	Neg.	0.3	0.3	0.4	0.5	0.5	0.8
Total materials in products	5.9	6.8	8.6	9.9	14.5	16.4	29.2
Other wastes							
Food wastes	Neg.	Neg.	Neg.	Neg.	Neg.	Neg.	Neg.
Yard trimmings	Neg.	Neg.	Neg.	Neg.	Neg.	Neg.	4.2
Miscellaneous inorganic wastes	Neg.	Neg.	Neg.	Neg.	Neg.	Neg.	Neg.
Total other wastes	Neg.	Neg.	Neg.	Neg.	Neg.	Neg.	4.2
Total MSW recovered (weight)	5.9	6.8	8.6	9.9	14.5	16.4	33.4
			Percentage of total generation				
Paper and paperboard	18.1	15.0	16.7	19.1	21.8	21.3	28.6
Glass	1.5	1.1	1.6	3.0	5.3	7.6	19.9
Metals							
Ferrous	1.0	1.0	0.8	1.6	3.4	3.7	15.4
Aluminum	Neg.	Neg.	Neg.	9.1	16.7	26.1	38.1
Other nonferrous	Neg.	60.0	42.9	44.4	45.5	50.0	67.7
Total metals	1.0	3.6	2.8	4.9	8.3	10.6	23.0
Plastics	Neg.	Neg.	Neg.	Neg.	Neg.	0.9	2.2
Rubber and leather	15.0	11.5	9.4	5.1	2.3	5.3	4.4
Textiles	Neg.	Neg.	Neg.	Neg.	Neg.	Neg.	4.3
Wood	Neg.	Neg.	Neg.	Neg.	Neg.	Neg.	3.2
Other	Neg.	100.0	37.5	23.5	17.2	14.7	23.8
Total material in products	10.9	10.1	10.2	11.3	13.4	13.8	20.2
Other wastes							
Food wastes	Neg.	Neg.	Neg.	Neg.	Neg.	Neg.	Neg.
Yard trimmings	Neg.	Neg.	Neg.	Neg.	Neg.	Neg.	12.0
Miscellaneous inorganic wastes	Neg.	Neg.	Neg.	Neg.	Neg.	Neg.	Neg.
Total other wastes	Neg.	Neg.	Neg.	Neg.	Neg.	Neg.	8.2
Total MSW recovered (%)	6.7	6.6	7.1	7.7	9.6	10.0	17.1

[a]Recovery of postconsumer wastes for recycling and composting; does not include converting/fabrication scrap.
[b]Recovery of electrolytes in batteries; probably not recycled.
Details may not add to totals due to rounding.
Neg., negligible (less than 0.05 percent of 50,000 tons).
Source: EPA Doc. 530-R-92-019

Table 11.3 Materials discarded[a] in the municipal waste stream, 1960–90 (in millions of tons and percentage of total discards)

Materials	1960	1965	1970	1975	1980	1985	1990
	Millions of tons						
Paper and paperboard	24.5	32.3	36.8	34.8	42.8	48.4	52.4
Glass	6.6	8.6	12.5	13.1	14.2	12.2	10.6
Metals							
Ferrous	9.8	10.0	12.5	12.1	11.2	10.5	10.4
Aluminum	0.4	0.5	0.8	1.0	1.5	1.7	1.6
Other nonferrous	0.2	0.2	0.4	0.5	0.6	0.5	0.4
Total metals	10.4	10.7	13.7	13.6	13.3	12.7	12.5
Plastics	0.4	1.4	3.1	4.5	7.8	11.5	15.9
Rubber and leather	1.7	2.3	2.9	3.7	4.2	3.6	4.4
Textiles	1.7	1.9	2.0	2.2	2.6	2.8	5.3
Wood	3.0	3.5	4.0	4.4	6.7	8.2	11.9
Other	0.1	0.0	0.5	1.3	2.4	2.9	2.4
Total materials in products	48.4	60.7	75.5	77.6	94.0	102.3	115.4
Other wastes							
Food wastes	12.2	12.7	12.8	13.4	13.2	13.2	13.2
Yard trimmings	20.0	21.6	23.2	25.2	27.5	30.0	30.8
Miscellaneous inorganic wastes	1.3	1.6	1.8	2.0	2.2	2.5	2.9
Total other wastes	33.5	35.9	37.8	40.6	42.9	45.7	46.9
Total MSW discarded (weight)	81.9	96.6	113.3	118.2	136.9	148.0	162.3
	Percentage of total generation						
Paper and paperboard	29.9	33.4	32.5	29.4	31.3	32.7	32.3
Glass	8.1	8.9	11.0	11.1	10.4	8.2	6.5
Metals							
Ferrous	12.0	10.4	11.0	10.2	8.2	7.1	6.4
Aluminum	0.5	0.5	0.7	0.8	1.1	1.1	1.0
Other nonferrous	0.2	0.2	0.4	0.4	0.4	0.3	0.2
Total metals	12.7	11.1	12.1	11.5	9.7	8.6	7.7
Plastics	0.5	1.4	2.7	3.8	5.7	7.8	9.8
Rubber and leather	2.1	2.4	2.6	3.1	3.1	2.4	2.7
Textiles	2.1	2.0	1.8	1.9	1.9	1.9	3.3
Wood	3.7	3.6	3.5	3.7	4.9	5.5	7.3
Other	0.1	0.0	0.4	1.1	1.8	2.0	1.5
Total material in products	59.1	62.8	66.6	65.7	68.7	69.1	71.1
Other wastes							
Food wastes	14.9	13.1	11.3	11.3	9.6	8.9	8.1
Yard trimmings	24.4	22.4	20.5	21.3	20.1	20.3	19.0
Miscellaneous inorganic wastes	1.6	1.7	1.6	1.7	1.6	1.7	1.8
Total other wastes	40.9	37.2	33.4	34.3	31.3	30.9	28.9
Total MSW discarded (%)	100.0	100.0	100.0	100.0	100.0	100.0	100.0

[a]Discards after materials and compost recovery. Does not include construction and demolition debris, industrial process wastes, or certain other Subtitle D wastes. Details may not add to totals due to rounding.
Source: EPA Doc. 530-R-92-019

residential level, smaller families and an increase in the elderly population living alone means less bulk purchasing and more products packaged in single or small-serving portions. The increase of women's participation in the labor force and the arrival of the microwave have led to a greater reliance on prepared foods that usually are more heavily packaged than staples. Products are also more intensively packaged for advertising, security, and to prevent theft. The weight of containers and packaging has increased steadily since 1970, although its percentage of MSW has fallen slightly due to the substitution of lighter materials for heavier materials (plastics and aluminum for glass and steel). Overall, containers and packaging account for about 33 percent of total waste generation (EPA, 1992, p. 2-33).

Another substantial part of the increase comes from nondurable paper and paperboard products (which account for approximately 21 percent of MSW (EPA, 1992, p. 2-32)) including newspapers, office paper, magazines, third class mail, and telephone books. The introduction of the copier machine and personal computers into the business world, and the increasing use of third class mail for advertising, have played a major role in the increase. The weight of discarded office paper alone has quadrupled since 1960.

Finally, the emergence of a "consumer society" is revealed in the growing disposal of durable goods. Major appliances, furniture and rugs, rubber tires, and lead acid batteries are rarely recycled or otherwise recovered. By weight their disposal tripled from 1960 to 1990.

These trends in consumption habits and changes in lifestyles have meant the generation of more waste. As existing landfills neared capacity, and as new landfills became difficult to site, local officials turned to recycling to reduce the volume of waste.

Shortage of adequate disposal space
Several factors contributed to a growing shortage of landfill capacity in the 1970s and 1980s. Air pollution regulations in the Clean Air Act closed many incinerators and stopped the open burning of solid waste at a time when small, single community incinerators were not uncommon, forcing many municipalities to seek disposal alternatives. Then, in 1979, the EPA banned the open dumping of solid waste and began to issue a series of regulations affecting the design and operation of new and existing landfills and the management of the methane they produce. The new regulations and the growing quantities of waste needing disposal forced 70 percent of existing landfills to close between 1978 and 1988 (Lund, 1993, p. 1.4). New landfills became more expensive to build and acceptable locations that met EPA regulations on such factors as nearness to groundwater and soil type became more difficult to find. Transportation to distant existing landfills was sometimes cheaper than the costs of siting and opening a new facility.

Even when acceptable locations for new landfills and incinerators could be identified, community opposition to their construction became and remains formidable. Local residents are more knowledgeable of the potential negative health effects associated with these facilities (e.g. groundwater contamination or cancer-causing air pollutants, although the scientific evidence on their severity is not unanimous), as well as the nuisance of living nearby. Studies show that residential property values and appreciation rates fall in the vicinity of landfills, hazardous waste sites, and incinerators (see, for example, Kiel and McClain, 1994a, b), further fueling resident's concerns. New landfills are also frequently quite large (serving several communities) and residents are becoming less willing to shoulder the burden of living near a landfill while the benefits accrue to a broader public, even when the host community may receive preferential disposal fees. These factors have all contributed to the emergence of the not-in-my-backyard syndrome and increased the difficulty and cost of constructing new landfill capacity.

Recycling is becoming more viable economically
The combination of escalating tipping fees and siting costs and new markets for recyclables have made recycling economically viable for some communities. As landfill space became more scarce, the cost per ton of disposal (the tipping fee) rose. This effect was most pronounced in the east, where the shortage was most acute. In 1989, the tipping fee in Hollywood, Florida, was $38 per ton. By 1991, that fee had risen to $62.50 (Lund, 1993, p. 12.17). Fees in metropolitan areas can be even higher. The borough of Park Ridge, New Jersey, pays $98 dollars per ton and the city of Garfield, New Jersey, pays $124 per ton (Lund, 1993, p. 12.12). At the same time, markets for recyclables were opening up, providing an outlet for the collected material. Although the revenues from the sale of recyclables could be small or even negligible, as long as the net cost of operating the recycling program was less than the tipping fees, local officials found recycling an attractive alternative to existing or future landfills and incinerators.

As an example, tables 11.4 and 11.5 illustrate the benefits to Wellesley, Massachusetts, of their recycling program. Wellesley is an affluent suburb of Boston with a population of 27,000. The town does not provide house-to-house waste collection but does provide a Recycling and Disposal Facility (RDF) which includes a transfer station, compost area, and recycling center. Ninety-two percent of the residents use the RDF (the remainder contract with private waste haulers). Composting began prior to 1969 and the source-separated recycling center opened in 1971. Eighty-two percent of households recycled 24.5 percent of Wellesley's solid waste in 1989.

Because the cost of the recycling program to the town is low (since the town pays no collection or separating costs) and participation is high, the

Table 11.4   Savings per ton by recycling, Wellesley, Massachusetts

	FY1988	*FY1991 estimated*
Avoided cost of burying or burning	$52/ton	$100/ton
Sale of recyclables (average)	$25/ton	$10/ton
Gross benefit (lines 1 + 2)	$77/ton	$110/ton
Cost of recycling program	$15/ton	$20/ton
Net benefit of recycling (lines 3 − 4)	$62/ton	$90/ton

financial benefit of the program was over $200,000 in 1989, mostly from avoided tipping fees. The actual revenue from the sale of its recyclables was $79,684 and the cost of operating the program about $50,000, so the town not only avoided tipping fees but collected about $30,000 as well. Other communities have also found recycling programs beneficial (see, for example, Powell, 1989).

New technological advances have made widespread recycling possible
Scientific advances in the last two decades have expanded both the nature and the quantity of materials that can be recycled. Communities have been able to divert more classes of material from their waste stream and more frequently sell the material. The technology for using recyclable glass in the production of new glass has long been well known. Aluminum beverage cans have been successfully recycled into new beverage cans for two decades. But while newsprint has been collected and recycled in sizable quantities since the 1960s, it was usually refabricated into chipboard and cardboard rather than newsprint or other paper. Newspaper publishers maintained that recycled paper lacked the tensile properties needed for high speed presses, and the original recycled papers were not a bright

Table 11.5   Financial recycling results, Wellesley, Massachusetts

	Recycling financial benefit				
	FY87	*FY88*	*FY89*	*FY90*	*FY91*
Sale of recyclables	$72,246	$76,468	$75,453	$69,580	$72,090
Sale of compost	N/A	N/A	1,160	8,979	10,815
Avoided transfer haul costs	122,929	152,328	211,959	285,816	273,670
Gross benefit	$195,175	$288,796	$291,643	$364,375	$356,575
Recycling expenses	35,116	42,791	49,085	57,521	88,183
Compost expenses	N/A	N/A	N/A	10,300	37,659
Recycling net benefit	$160,059	$186,005	£242,558	$296,554	$230,733

enough white to meet office paper demand. Recent advances in recycled paper technology have alleviated these problems and created an additional demand for used office and mixed paper.

Advances in plastics recycling have been even more dramatic. Plastics were rarely recycled until the late 1980s, when small quantities of polyethylene terephthalate (PET) soda bottles and high density polyethylene (HDPE) milk jugs were collected and refabricated into plastic lumber and fiberfill. Since then, plastics manufacturers have developed methods to manufacture new soda bottles from a feedstock containing some recycled PET and have also begun to recycle other plastics such as polystyrene (Styrofoam), polyvinyl chloride (PVC), and low density polyethylenes (LDPE). Current research focuses on separating polymers into individual monomers to recover their inherent chemical value and on separating commingled polymers. Automated methods are also being developed to sort mixed post-consumer plastics by their resin types and colors.

Progress has also been made in collection and separation technologies. New co-collection trucks that simultaneously pick up trash and recyclables have cut collection costs in half for Loveland, Colorado (personal communication). Researchers are also attempting to place identifiable chemical markers in all plastics that would be recognized by automated photospectrometers (Wood et al., 1991).

The combination of more waste, fewer places to put it, and increasingly available secondary markets have contributed to the rising popularity of recycling. But its eventual success depends not only on successfully collecting materials but also on finding buyers and fabricators for the materials.

3 The Markets for Recyclables

In order for community recycling programs to be an effective alternative to landfills and incinerators, the markets for secondary materials need to become more established and stable. Finding these secondary markets is not an easy task. Many public works officials and transfer facility managers spend a large portion of their time looking for potential buyers offering the best price for their recyclables. The markets for these commodities are not well organized and prices can change on a daily basis. A well-known example is the 1990 supply glut of old newspapers on the east coast. As community recycling programs became more common, the quantity of collected newspapers overwhelmed the capacity of paper mills capable of using recyclable feedstock. Even if that capacity was available, the demand for recycled paper was weak. As a result, the price for old newsprint plummeted, at times to the point where communities had to pay to have their collected newspaper hauled away. Stories were also reported of other collected recyclables that were eventually landfilled because no buyers could be found. Market disequilibria such as these plague the recyclables market.

The supply of recyclables

Secondary material suitable for reuse in production processes comes from two sources. Pre-consumer waste is generated during industrial processes and is usually recycled on-site rather than traded in the secondary market. Post-consumer waste is generally collected by community programs and sold either to scrap and salvage dealers or directly to manufacturers who can utilize a recyclable feedstock. Typically, communities and dealers do not have long-term agreements and communities are not always guaranteed a buyer or anticipated price.

Several factors have inhibited the smooth functioning of the supply side of this market. First, producers need to be assured of a steady stream of recyclable materials if they are to invest in manufacturing capacity that uses recyclables. In general, the production technology and the equipment required differ depending on the feedstock; a mix of virgin raw materials and recyclable materials cannot be accepted by equipment designed only for virgin materials, nor can the input feedstock alternate between the two. Predicting the quantity a community will collect of a given recyclable is difficult and historically manufacturers have been reluctant to build new capacity that would rely on an uncertain stream of recyclable materials. Since communities were not assured of a buyer and faced volatile prices and revenues, they in turn were reluctant to invest in collecting the materials.

This circle has been difficult to break, but the disposal crisis provided a strong incentive for communities to recycle regularly, and producers have responded to the growing and steady supply by adding new capacity. Some communities are also joining together into collection and marketing associations to market their recyclables and assure industry of a steady supply, like the 20 southwestern communities of the Southwest Public Recycling Association (Weddle, 1992). Industry has taken steps to ensure a steady supply by operating their own collection programs or cooperating with others. Huntsman and Dow have formed a partnership with the National Park Service to recycle National Park waste (Hoffman, 1991) and Wellman is working with the waste hauler Browning-Ferris Industries (BFI) to gather post-consumer plastic waste (Wood et al., 1991).

A community's disposal alternatives may impede steady collection and supply. In some regions of the country, particularly the midwest and southwest, landfill capacity is adequate and the cost of landfilling is low enough that recycling programs cannot economically compete. Some also believe that incinerators can hamper recycling efforts because they compete directly for the same feedstock (Commoner, 1991). An incinerator operates most profitably at or near capacity. If the waste stream is reduced through recycling, that capacity may not be reached. The local government of Warrent County, New Jersey, attributed the weekly $59,000 losses of its incinerator to the passage of a state law requiring 25 percent recycling. They were forced to reimburse the incinerator's builder and operator for its losses (Young, 1991, p. 20).

Collection and transportation costs can inhibit the development of recycling programs. Drop-off centers for separated wastes are inexpensive to operate but not always effective. Curbside programs either accept commingled materials or require source separation by the household. These programs have fairly high participation rates. Seattle has achieved 88 percent participation on its north side and 74 percent on its south side (Kourik, 1990). Seventy-five percent of households in Charlotte, North Carolina, participate in their voluntary curbside program (Chandler, 1992). The drawbacks to curbside programs, however, are the collection costs. In 1992 Charlotte and the surrounding Mecklenburg County spent $6.2 million on recycling collection and processing (Chandler, 1992, p. 16). Longmeadow, Massachusetts, recycled 24 percent of its waste, spending $68,000 on the collection of 1615 tons of recyclables later sold for $30,460 (thus avoiding a $34 per ton tipping fee (Powell, 1989)). As communities become more rural and widespread, the collection fees can overwhelm the economic success of the programs, although transportation hubs may overcome this drawback (McDonald, 1992). High labor requirements for collection, separation, and initial processing (e.g. baling) can also be inhibiting in areas of high wages. Peterborough, New Hampshire, spends $97,000 per year on labor costs to recycle 935 tons, or 73 percent of their waste stream (personal communication).

Processing and transportation costs add another layer of expense. Most collected materials need further processing before they are acceptable to manufacturers. The materials must be sorted and free of contamination, and then baled and transported to buyers and manufacturers who may be quite distant from the community. These additional expenses make recycling less attractive in rural areas and areas distant from manufacturers.

The demand for recyclables

Like most industrial raw materials, the demand for recyclable materials is a derived demand. Consumers demand final goods and from production of those goods demand is derived for industrial raw materials. For recycling to be successful, markets must be found for recyclables and so in turn markets for recycled products. Finding markets for recycled products is typically called "closing the loop."

Finding those markets has not been easy. For many years, consumers resisted purchasing recycled products, perceiving them as inferior or used. In some instances those fears were justified, as with early recycled paper. Technological advances have overcome numerous problems and many recycled products are now indiscernible from their virgin counterparts, although some misperceptions persist. Social pressure to "buy green" has raised demand and producers have found advertising products as "recycled" or "recyclable" a successful marketing tool.

A greater barrier to successfully shifting demand towards recycled products is their price. Many recycled products are more expensive than their virgin substitutes. In 1989 virgin office paper sold for $39.25 per carton in the Boston area while recycled office paper cost $46.00. In 1993, recycled paper cost $10.35 more than virgin paper in central Pennsylvania. The higher prices partially result from the added separation, collection, processing, and transportation costs, and possibly because recycled production has not yet achieved economies of scale on the same scope as virgin production.

More importantly, recycled products are generally more expensive because recyclable raw materials are often more expensive as well. Intuitively recyclable raw materials should sell for less than virgin materials because they are partially processed. Reprocessing some recyclables also uses less energy than processing virgin raw materials. Aluminum produced from recycled metal uses 20 times less electricity than aluminum produced from bauxite (Chandler, 1983, p. 24), and virgin aluminum does generally sell for a 15 or 20 cent premium (Topfer, 1991, p. SR8). But repelletized plastic is more costly than virgin plastic. Virgin injection grade HDPE sold for 31 to 33 cents per pound in 1992 while the price for recycled HDPE pellet ranged from the low 30 to mid 40 cents (Peterkofsky, 1992, pp. 5, 21). Some maintain that the price of virgin plastic must clear 40 cents per pound before recycled plastic can effectively compete with it, and some polymer buyers believe recycled resin should sell at a 10 percent discount to virgin resin to compensate for quality differences (Loesel, 1991, p. SR3).

Several factors account for this paradox. Some virgin materials and energy are subsidized. The US government owns a significant amount of the country's softwood forests and leases large areas, regardless of pulp demand and sometimes below cost (Chandler, 1983, p. 20). Recyclables also bring lower prices because of quality and contamination problems. A single green bottle can ruin a batch of clear glass, and old newspaper buyers will no longer accept bales that contain paper of any other kind. The fight against contamination is a constant challenge for community recycling programs and raises the costs of the programs while it lowers the price the recyclables can bring. Plastics are especially difficult to separate cleanly. Finally, the recycling process involves extra production stages that may create unrecyclable or hazardous residues requiring disposal. Paper de-inking creates an unusable sludge sometimes containing heavy metals. The recycling process may also require other scarce resources whose cost must be considered when measuring the net benefit of recycling. Recycling paper requires large quantities of water which may impede its recycling in the southwest.

Equilibrium

Ideally, a market equilibrium evolves as the supply of a good is matched by its demand. For recyclables, supply and demand have often been unbalanced, as in the 1990 old newspaper glut. Local governments were quick to enact recycling legislation following the landfill crisis, but demand and capacity for recyclables were inadequate for the burgeoning supplies. Prices were highly volatile as a result.

The market for recyclables is also highly regional, and in some sense would better be described as several submarkets. Regional landfill availability strongly affects the nature and extent of local recycling programs and thus the regional supply of recyclables. At the same time, producers are not evenly dispersed across the country. Denver is approximately 800 miles from the nearest paper mill recyclable feedstock capacity and thus faces substantial transportation costs. International markets for recyclables also unevenly affect regions. The United States accounts for 85 percent of net international sales of waste paper (Chandler, 1983, p. 19) but most of that trade occurs between the west coast and the Pacific Rim nations. West coast processors typically receive $30 to $40 more per ton than processors in the northeast. During 1990 the price of old newspaper dropped below zero in New York but was $30 in San Francisco (Alexander, 1992, p. 31).

Recycling markets are still relatively young and will continue to evolve over time. Some market distortions have led to policy intervention, the subject of the next section.

4 Policy Approaches

Local, state, and federal governments have all passed waste disposal legislation. Early regulations addressed the negative externalities associated with various disposal methods – air pollution controls on incinerators, and liners for landfills. In the 1980s, legislation began to be directed at controlling the disposal of the waste stream. Massachusetts placed a moratorium on incinerator construction pending a comprehensive state waste plan; Rhode Island made recycling mandatory statewide; and many local communities passed recycling legislation. In the 1990s attention shifted towards legislation that encourages the demand for recyclables, including tax credits and minimum content laws. Many states and courts are also considering legislation governing the sensitive area of interstate transportation of solid waste. At the federal level, RCRA reauthorization will probably include several new statutes, among them interim recycling goals, requirements for state waste management plans, the creation of a national information clearinghouse, and the creation of a products and packaging board. Taxes on virgin materials, plastic container labeling, and additional minimum content laws may also be voted upon.

Legislation on recyclables can be divided according to those laws that affect the supply of recyclables and those that encourage their demand. The legislation can then be further divided between command-and-control legislation, which requires a certain set of prescribed actions, or legislation that provides economic incentives for certain behaviors.

In principle, command-and-control legislation can achieve a social optimum if the government applies the right policy tool at the correct level, in practice a difficult if not impossible task. The difficulties arise from inadequate information, crude regulatory instruments, enforcement problems, and the haphazardness of burdens (Dorfman and Dorfman, 1977, p. 31). The government lacks data on firm marginal costs, public willingness to pay, and the most economical method to achieve a desired effect (only individual firms would know). Enforcement requires constant monitoring and a system of penalties. Regulations impose the same blanket criterion on every source, a situation found to be inefficient (Johnson, 1967) and inequitable. In short, command-and-control regulation is not usually an optimal policy alternative, although it does outperform the uncontrolled market in many situations.

A variety of economic inducements, including taxes, subsidies, credits, marketable permits, and variable fees, have been used or considered in waste-related legislation. All attempt to achieve an efficient solution by allowing individual producers and consumers wide discretion. Some are aimed at internalizing waste management costs otherwise ignored by producers and consumers, while others address public finance issues that undervalue the cost of waste disposal (Alexander, 1992, p. 33). In terms of efficiency, economic measures will provide an incentive to improve the situation in the most cost-effective way. However, in order to achieve total efficiency, the tax or policy instrument must be set at the level where the cost of further prevention just equals the amount sufferers would be willing to pay for that additional prevention. Finding that correct level is a difficult task.

The regulating body is essentially left with three choices: do nothing, use command-and-control legislation to achieve a desired result but not necessarily in the most efficient way, or use more efficient economic inducements whose level of abatement will be difficult to predict. The best decision will depend on the characteristics of the problem at hand. In general, policy experts prefer economic approaches over direct regulation (Dorfman and Dorfman, 1977, p. 37).

On the supply side of the market, 39 states and the District of Columbia use some sort of comand-and-control recycling law. These laws fall into three categories. Twenty states require recycling plans although not necessarily recycling. Twelve states require local governments to offer citizens the opportunity to recycle, while seven states require source separation and collection of one or more materials (Miller, 1993). Other direct regulation laws include disposal bans on designated recyclables (e.g. oil, tires, and lead acid batteries), product bans (e.g. six pack yokes and mixed resin food and beverage containers), and plastics coding.

A variety of innovative economic incentives have been enacted. Bottle bills have resurfaced and some state legislatures are exploring other types of advanced disposal fees. Variable fees on garbage and recyclables are common. Individuals pay a certain fee on garbage disposal, usually by volume, and no fee or a lower fee on recyclables, creating an incentive for residents to recycle as much as possible and throw away as little as possible. These schemes have been very successful. Other economic incentives have been grants and low interest loans to groups who organize and encourage recycling and a sales tax on waste collection and disposal services.

On the demand side, minimum content laws and procurement policies are the most commonly used command-and-control practices. Thirteen states have minimum content legislation covering newspaper, glass, telephone directories, and plastics and 11 others have voluntary minimum content agreements on newsprint (Miller, 1993). Thirty-five states have procurement laws requiring state offices to purchase some percentage of recycled products or use recycled products in state-funded projects. California and Oregon have extended their minimum content legislation to require that certain containers and packaging be reusable or refillable a specified number of times.

At least 27 states use tax credits to encourage the production of recycled products. Most provide some kind of income, sales, or property tax credit for the purchase of equipment or facilities used for processing recyclable materials or producing recycled products. Other economic incentives include grants to agencies, groups, and market development efforts promoting the use and sale of recycled products, and taxes or lower subsidies on raw materials. Policymakers have also begun to study the practicality and effectiveness of marketable permits in this arena.

Many of the legislative approaches have met with criticism. Bottle bills induce individuals to return cans to redemption centers rather than to municipal facilities, where they are instrumental in the economic success of recycling programs. Some complain that long-term goals are arbitrarily set and not based on technologically or economically feasible levels (Wood et al., 1991) and may conflict with other raw material standards (Hoffman, 1991). Others maintain that national or state-wide standards may be inappropriate at the local level because of the highly regional nature of the market for recyclables. Connecticut has found glass and aluminum recycling successful but not newspaper, while newspaper recycling in Oregon is profitable but glass recycling is not (Franke, 1992). Finally, some of the market distortions may be the result of situations beyond the scope of realistic policy options, such as international markets and exchange rates.

5 Conclusion

Recycling is a feasible part of the waste disposal hierarchy for some materials. As the markets for recyclable materials mature, it will become economically feasible for other materials as well. More accurately valuing the price of waste disposal and internalizing waste management costs will also make recycling a more attractive alternative.

The EPA estimates that without additional source reduction, per-capita waste generation in the year 2000 will be 5 percent higher than 1990 levels. This amounts to an additional 26.3 million tons of waste *per year* (EPA, 1992, p. ES-3). Most experts feel that 30 percent of the waste stream can be recycled by 2000, up from 17 percent in 1990, provided that demand for recyclables continues to grow and stabilize. Even with successful recycling, landfills will continue to fill up, but instead of the 81 percent of MSW waste landfilled in 1980, recycling combined with increasing combustion levels will leave less than half to be landfilled in 2000 (Franklin and Franklin, 1992). Recycling is not the sole solution to the problem of solid waste disposal, but it will play an increasingly important role.

Notes

I would like to thank Greg Adams and Jorn Aabakken for their excellent research assistance. Any errors are my own.

1   Recyclable refers to products or packaging able to be collected, separated, or otherwise recovered from the solid waste stream for use in the form of raw materials in the manufacture or assembly of a new product. In contrast, a recycled product is made from materials that have been recovered or otherwise diverted from the solid waste stream, either during the manufacturing process (pre-consumer) or after consumer use (post-consumer) (*EPA Journal*, 1992, vol. 18).

References

Alexander, Michael. 1992: The challenge of markets. *EPA Journal*, 18 (3) (July–August), 29–33.

Chandler, Liz. 1992: A tale of one city: making recycling a top priority in Charlotte, North Carolina. *EPA Journal*, 18 (3) (July–August), 15–17.

Chandler, William, U. 1983: Materials recycling: the virtue of necessity. Worldwatch Paper 56, Worldwatch Institute, Washington, DC.

Commoner, Barry. 1991: *Making Peace With The Planet*. New York: Pantheon.

Dorfman, Robert, and Dorfman, Nancy. 1977: *Economics of the Environment*. New York: Norton.

Earle, Ralph. 1990: Northeast promotes recycling markets. *Journal of State Government*, 63 (July–September), 64–6.

Environmental Protection Agency. 1992: *Characterization of Municipal Solid Waste in the United States: 1992 Update*. EPA/530-R-92-019, July.

Franke, Randall. 1992: Recycling laws may tie hands. *American City and County*, 107 (6) (May), 18.

Franklin, William, and Franklin, Marjorie. 1992: Putting the crusade into perspective. *EPA Journal*, 18 (3) (July–August), 7–13.

Hoffman, John. 1991: Showdown time. *Chemical Marketing Reporter*, 240 (September 9), SR18–SR21.

Johnson, Edward. 1967: A study in the economics of water quality management. *Water Resources Research*, 3 (Second Quarter), 291–306.

Kiel, Katherine, and McClain, Katherine. 1994a: House prices during siting decision stages: the case of an incinerator from rumor through operation. *Journal of Environmental Economics and Management*, forthcoming.

Kiel, Katherine, and McClain, Katherine. 1994b: The effects of an incinerator siting on housing appreciation rates. *Journal of Urban Economics*, forthcoming.

Kourik, Robert. 1990: What's so great about Seattle? *Garbage*, 2 (6), 24–31.

Loesel, Andrew. 1991: Boxed in by green. *Chemical Marketing Reporter*, 239 (April 8), SR3–SR5.

Lund, Herbert, F. 1993: *The McGraw-Hill Recycling Handbook*. New York: McGraw-Hill.

McDonald, Lisa. 1992: A preliminary analysis of the feasibility of marketing for secondary fibers within EPA region VIII. Working Paper 92-1, Department of Mineral Economics, Colorado School of Mines.

Miller, Chaz. 1993: Recycling in the States. *Waste Age*, 24 (3) 26–34.

Peterkofsky, David. 1992: Recycling units running, but big questions remain. *Chemical Marketing Reporter*, 241 (8), 5, 21.

Powell, Jerry. 1989: Recycling is cheaper: the Massachusetts experience. *Resource Recycling* (October), 37, 61.

Topfer, Kurt. 1991: Secondary thoughts. *Chemical Marketing Reporter*, 240 (September 9), SR5, SR8.

Weddle, Bruce R. 1992: Collection: the first step. *EPA Journal*, 18 (3) (July–August), 19–22.

Wood, Andrew, Chynoweth, Emma, Rotman, David and Kiesche, Elizabeth. 1991: Plastics makers recycle for new growth. *Chemicalweek*, 149 (December 18–25), 28–43.

Young, John E. 1991: Discarding the throwaway society. Worldwatch Paper 101, Worldwatch Institute, Washington, DC.

Part III

Environmental Quality

12

Nonconvexities and the Theory of External Costs

Paul Burrows

1 Conventional Theory of External Costs

1.1 Introduction

There is now an extensive literature exploring the efficiency characteristics of markets which contain producers or consumers who generate external costs (e.g. such harmful effects as the damage costs caused by the emission of pollutants) that are borne by other producers or consumers. This research has provided the foundations for the economic theory of pollution control policy, the purpose of which is to predict the efficiency consequences of alternative instruments for pollution control.[1] An important element in all this research has been the notion of external costs, which specifies the form of the interdependence between those who create the harmful effects and those who suffer from them, two groups I shall refer to as the polluters and the victims.

There has emerged a form of presentation of the theory of external costs which, because it is widely used, can be called the "conventional theory." This conventional theory adopts a number of assumptions that have important implications for the predictions made about the effects of pollution control policies. One of these assumptions concerns the nature of the relationship between the level of pollution emissions and the amount of harm, or damage cost, that results. As we shall see in section 1.3, the total damage cost function is conventionally assumed to be convex. But in the last 20 years or so a number of economists have questioned this convexity assumption, and have claimed that the real-world damage cost functions may take a form that would cast serious doubt on the policy recommendations that emerge from the conventional theory.

The aims of this chapter are

1   to explain why anyone would claim that the conventionally assumed convex damage cost function is unrealistic, and
2   to consider whether or not the existence of nonconvex damage costs would have serious consequences for the design of pollution control policies.

In sections 2, 3, and 4 respectively we will look at nonconvexities relating to the external costs imposed on production, the external costs on people, and the self-defense activities of pollution victims. But first, in the remainder of section 1, it is necessary to provide a reasonably clear definition of external costs, and to outline those parts of the conventional theory that are relevant to the analysis of the nonconvexity issue.

1.2   Defining external costs

The following is a definition which conveys the essential characteristics of an external cost:

> An external cost exists when either a production activity or a consumption activity causes a direct loss of utility to another consumer, or an increase in production cost to another producer, which does not enter the decision calculus of the controller of the activity (the polluter).

Such external costs will occur when the polluter is willing to disregard them and when there is no legal obligation to take them into account. The absence of a legal obligation means that the polluter has no externally imposed incentive, financial or otherwise, to balance the benefits of the activity against the harm to others that the external cost represents, in deciding the design and the extent of production or consumption activity. If such an incentive were introduced it would have the effect of internalizing the otherwise-external costs, that is, it would make them a part of the polluter's decision calculus.

There are two aspects of the above definition that deserve a brief clarification. First, the use of the word "direct" is intended to concentrate attention on costs which result from a sensitivity of one activity to another, usually a physical sensitivity, and to exclude the wide range of market indterdependences which operate through the price mechanism.[2] Second, the definition does not say whether the imposition of the external cost is accidental or deliberate. Some economists have sought to limit the notion of external costs to accidental cases.[3] The reason for this is not entirely clear to me, but one thing does seem certain: a very large number of pollution sources are regular activities rather than accidental events. One could, of course, claim that a factory owner does not intend the emissions from production to harm others, but it is stretching the definition of "accident" to say that the consequences of regular emissions are accidental. Even accidents, such as the grounding of oil tankers, often include a degree of negligence which obscures the distinction between accidental and deliberate. To limit external costs by excluding the deliberate imposition of harm does seem too restrictive, and it is not, I believe, the way most economists use the term. However, our external cost theory will not address the subset of deliberate harms comprising those in which the polluter gains pleasure from the fact that others are harmed, as distinct from gaining pleasure (or saving cost) from not having to alter some activity to prevent the harm.

1.3 A résumé of the conventional theory of external cost

Let us go through a checklist of the elements of the conventional theory that will prove to be relevant to the analysis of the nonconvexity issue in sections 2, 3, and 4, using a simple example to illustrate the conventional reasoning. Think of a case of pollution which displays the following characteristics:

(a) It is a production-on-production case; that is, the polluter is one firm (A) whose emissions (pollution) from production damage the production of another firm (the victim, firm B).[4]
(b) The external cost is imposed unilaterally, that is, firm A damages firm B's production, but B does not harm A.
(c) There is no prospect of negotiation between A and B.
(d) Both firms are profit maximizers, and they operate in competitive goods and factor markets. They utilize fixed technologies, which means that the polluter can abate pollution only by cutting output level, since there is a fixed ratio between A's output, q^A, and the level of pollution, E^A.
(e) Total (external) damage cost is a *positive strictly convex function* of the level of pollution, and therefore of the level of firm A's output.[5] This means that the marginal damage cost (MDC) rises at each upward step in the level of A's output (see figure 12.1(b)). It is usually assumed that marginal damage cost approaches zero as the polluter's output tends to zero. But as the polluter raises output, for each extra unit of that output the victim, firm B, suffers an increasing marginal loss of output, that is, the marginal *physical* damage increases with rises in q^A. At the same time each extra unit of firm B's output that is lost was more profitable than the previous unit, that is, the *value* of the marginal physical damage also increases with rises in q^A. Combining increasing marginal physical damage and increasing value of marginal physical damage implies the convex marginal damage cost curve.
(f) Total abatement cost is a positive convex function of the level of pollution abatement, and by implication is a *negative convex function* of the level of pollution up to some level of pollution where total

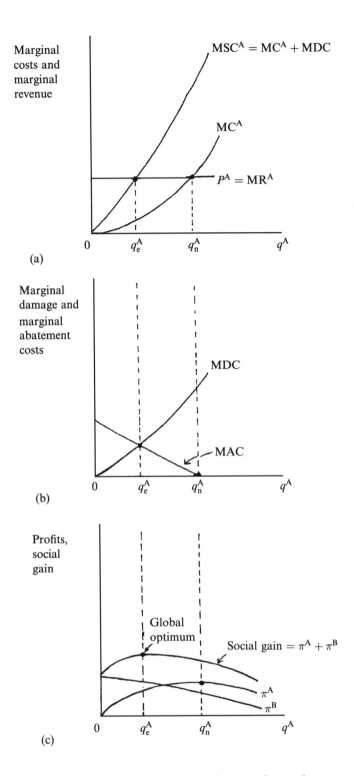

Figure 12.1 Global optimum in conventional external cost theory.

abatement cost is zero.[6] This means that starting from a position of zero abatement, that is, from firm A's profit maximizing output q_n^A in figures 12.1(a) and 12.1(b), the marginal cost of abating pollution rises at each step in the level of A's reduction in pollution and therefore at each downward step in A's output starting from q_n^A. (Therefore, the rising marginal abatement cost is seen by viewing the MAC curve in figure 12.1(b) from right to left.)

(g) The pollution victim, firm B, is assumed to choose the socially efficient level of *its* output.[7] The meaning of "socially efficient" will be explained below.

Using this description of a pollution case we can briefly present the conventional predictions of the impact of external costs, and of the effects of internalizing such costs. If the polluter, firm A, ignores the external cost then it will choose the output level q_n^A at which marginal private cost equals marginal revenue, $MC^A = MR^A$ in figure 12.1(a). This minimizes abatement costs at zero in figure 12.1(b), and maximizes profit π^A in figure 12.1(c). Note that the profit curves for both firms in figure 12.1(c) are concave, which follows from the convexity of the relevant cost functions, given that marginal revenue is constant for both firms. The profit level of the pollution victim, shown by the π^B curve in figure 12.1(c), is a concave negative function of the output of the polluter, q^A.

While the output level q_n^A maximizes the polluter's own profit level, society would prefer to judge the efficiency of the polluter's activity on the basis of the net value (profit) of the polluter's output *together with* the damage cost (loss of firm B's profit) it brings about. We shall call the sum of the profits of the polluter and the victim, $\pi^A + \pi^B$, the *social gain* from the two activities together. The strictly concave social gain curve, shown in figure 12.1(c), has an interior peak which is the global optimum.[8] Such an interior optimum is guaranteed given the assumptions of the conventional theory as stated in (a)–(g) above. Increasing the polluter's output from $q_A = 0$ to q_e^A raises the social gain because the damage cost created by each unit increase in q^A is less than the abatement cost avoided ($MAC > MDC$ from 0 to q_e^A in figure 12.1(b)). But further increases in q^A above q_e^A reduce the social gain because for each of these unit increases in q^A the damage cost created exceeds the abatement cost avoided ($MAC < MDC$ at outputs above q_e^A in figure 12.1(b)). Consequently the polluter's output q_e^A can be said to be socially efficient.

The maximization of the social gain from the outputs of firm A and firm B can be achieved if the polluter is compelled to bear the full marginal social cost of its production, MSC^A, which is the sum of the marginal private cost, MC^A, and marginal damage cost, MDC, in figure 12.1(a). Firm A will then choose output q_e^A because this maximizes profit net of damage cost. The output level q_e^A is characterized by $P^A = MSC^A$ and, by implication, by marginal abatement cost equal to marginal damage cost in figure 12.1(b). These two equalities are alternative versions of the first-order condition for an extremum of the social gain curve. The convexity of the marginal private cost and marginal damage cost curves ensures that the second-order sufficient condition for the extremum to be a maximum

$$\frac{d^2(\pi^A + \pi^B)}{d(q^A)^2} < 0$$

is satisfied.[9]

Central to this analysis is the concavity of the two firms' profit functions, represented formally as follows:

$$\pi^A = \pi^A(q^A) \frac{d\pi^A}{dq^A} \gtreqless 0 \text{ as } q^A \lesseqgtr q_n^A$$

$$\frac{d^2\pi^A}{d(q^A)^2} < 0$$

$$\pi^B = \pi^B(q^A, q^B) \frac{\partial\pi^B}{\partial q^B} \gtreqless 0 \text{ as } q^B \lesseqgtr q_n^B$$

(where q_n^B is B's profit-maximizing output),

$$\frac{\partial\pi^B}{\partial q^A} < 0$$

$$\frac{\partial\pi^B}{\partial(q^B)^2}, \frac{\partial^2\pi^B}{\partial(q^B)^2} < 0$$

Table 12.1 makes explicit the conventional convexity assumptions that are associated with these concave profit functions: this will be a useful point of reference when we turn to the arguments in the "nonconvexity" literature. In the table the first column states the function concerned, the second shows it graphically, the third states the convexity or concavity assumed, the fourth states the implied derivatives, and the fifth describes the slope and how the slope changes from left to right. In the second column $f(x)$ is used as a shorthand for the function; for example, in the case of a production function for the polluting firm A (row 1), $f(x)$ would be $q^A = q^A(L^A, K^A)$ where L^A and K^A are firm A's labor and capital inputs. So $f(x) = q^A$, the firm's output, and x represents any of the explanatory variables on the right-hand side, L^A and K^A in this case. In the fourth column this shorthand is extended by writing the first and second derivatives respectively as $f'(x)$ and $f''(x)$; so $f'(x)$ is $\partial q^A / \partial L^A$ or $\partial q^A / \partial K^A$

Table 12.1 Convexity assumptions of the conventional theory

Function	Curve shape	Convexity or concavity of function[a]	First and second derivatives	Slope and change in slope left to right
(1) Production and utility functions	$f(x)$	Strictly concave	$f'(x) > 0$ $f''(x) < 0$	Slope positive and getting flatter
(2) Total damage cost function	$f(x)$	Strictly convex	$f'(x) > 0$ $f''(x) > 0$	Slope positive and getting steeper
(3) Total abatement cost function	$f(x)$	Strictly convex	$f'(x) < 0$ $f''(x) > 0$	Slope negative and getting flatter
(4) Profit functions $f(x)$ (a) As function of firm's *own* output	$f(x)$	Strictly concave	$f'(x) \gtrless 0$ $f''(x) < 0$	Up to peak slope positive and getting flatter; after peak, slope negative and getting steeper
(b) Victim's profit as function of *polluter's* output	$f(x)$	Strictly concave	$f'(x) < 0$ $f''(x) < 0$	Slope negative and getting steeper
(5) Social gain $(\pi^A + \pi^B)$ function	$f(x)$	Strictly concave	$f'(x) \gtrless 0$ $f''(x) < 0$	Slope positive and getting flatter up to global optimum, thereafter negative and getting steeper

[a]The borderline, linear case is ignored (see note 5).

in the production function case, and $f''(x)$ is $\partial^2 q^A/\partial(L^A)^2$ or $\partial^2 q^A/\partial(K^A)^2$. Thus, the $f'(x) > 0$ and $f''(x) < 0$ assumptions are interpreted as the production function displaying positive but diminishing marginal products of the two inputs labor and capital. The production function for the victim firm B will include, in addition to B's use of labor and capital, a negative input represented by the output of the polluter, q^A. For this variable the function is assumed to take the form $f'(x) < 0, f''(x) < 0$ which means that the marginal *loss* of firm B's output, as q^A rises, is always positive and increasing.

The characteristics of the conventional theory of external cost that are on display in table 12.1 can be summarized as convex cost functions and concave production (or utility), profit, and social gain functions.

While in principle the peak of the social gain curve can be attained through perfectly internalizing the external cost, in practice there are a number of obstacles to such an idealized policy.[10] The government may, for example, have information only on the damage costs and abatement costs associated with small changes in pollution levels from the status quo. Starting from a no-policy position, q_n^A in figure 12.1, the government may therefore only be able to estimate the change in the social gain *in the locality of* q_n^A, because knowledge of the global characteristics of the social gain curve is beyond its reach. This has led some observers to advocate iterative taxes or regulated standards which make stepwise adjustments in the pollution level. Each downward step of the myopic iteration would be evaluated on the basis of *marginal* cost–benefit analysis: a step is taken only if marginal damage cost exceeds marginal abatement cost. If a step passes this test on the basis of local information the government knows it is moving *upwards* on the social gain curve. Given the assumptions of the conventional theory, a sequence of such steps would eventually lead to the single, interior peak of the curve, the global optimum.

2   Nonconvexity and External Costs on Production

2.1   Some preliminary points on the "nonconvexity" issue

It is clear from table 12.1 that the conventional theory assumes some functions to be convex, others to be concave. The "nonconvexity" issue we shall be concerned with relates to the convexity of the damage cost function, so references to nonconvexity henceforth should be interpreted in this particular way.[11]

It will prove to be important to distinguish between the *existence* of a nonconvexity in the damage cost function and the *relevance* of such a nonconvexity. A nonconvexity *exists* when the function fails, at any point, to meet the requirements of convexity. Intuitively this means a nonconvexity exists if the curve representing the function (second column in table 12.1) is not everywhere smooth and upward sloping with an ever-increasing gradient as we move left to right. Formally, it exists if at any point $f''(x) < 0$.

A nonconvexity will be described as *relevant* only if its position in the range of the polluter's output, q^A, is such that it would fall in the path of, *and block*, a myopic iteration policy from the status quo point, q_n^A, to the globally efficient pollution level, q_e^A, in figure 12.1. As we shall see, a convergence of the iteration on the global optimum can be blocked only if a nonconvexity which exists at the microlevel is transmitted as a local peak in the *aggregate* social gain curve (aggregation across all pollution victims), *and if* this local peak is generated by a pollution level which lies in the policy-relevant range.

It is therefore apparent that the subsequent analysis will need to explore the basis of the suggestions that nonconvexities exist, but it will also need to consider whether any nonconvexities that do exist are policy relevant, for nonconvexities that exist but are not policy relevant need not keep us awake at night.

Curiously the claims that have been made concerning the importance of nonconvexities as an obstacle to pollution control policy have not been based on analyses which do establish both their existence *and* their relevance. On the contrary, there has been a surprising tendency to jump from a demonstration that a nonconvexity may exist to assertions that it is a serious obstacle to policy.[12]

2.2 Three theories suggesting the existence of nonconvexity

Three different theories have been offered to rationalize the existence of a nonconvexity somewhere in the damage cost function when the pollution victims are firms:

1 a firm shut-down theory,
2 a pollution saturation theory, and
3 a theory of the multiplicative interdependence between firms' production functions.

Firm shut-down

Consider the effect of increasing pollution exposure on the production decision of the victim firm, B. In the earlier analysis (see figure 12.1(c)) it was assumed that as the polluter's output rises the profit level of firm B continually declines. The shut-down theory consists of the rather obvious point that this cannot continue indefinitely: there must be a level of firm

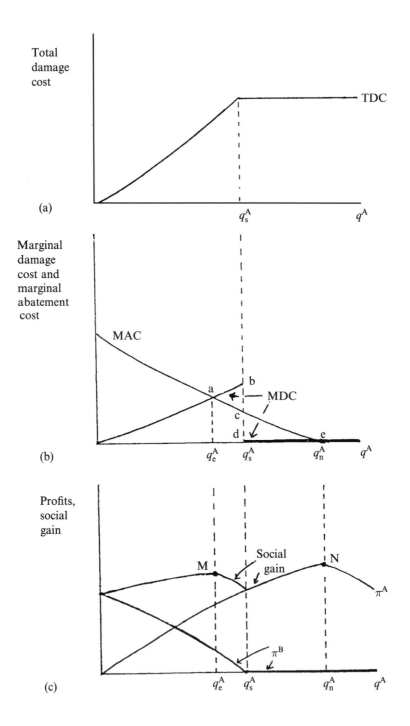

Figure 12.2 Sharp nonconvexity in the firm shut-down theory.

A's output, q_s^A, and hence of pollution, at which firm B's profits fall to zero and the firm goes out of business. There exists a sharp nonconvexity at q_s^A. The term sharp nonconvexity refers to the abrupt change of gradient of the total damage cost curve in figure 12.2(a) at q_s^A. Above q_s^A there is zero physical damage, so marginal damage cost (MDC) is zero, as shown in figure 12.2(b), and the total damage cost curve has zero gradient. Clearly the conventional convexity assumption is violated, and the nonconvexity of the total damage cost curve is associated with a nonconcavity of the victim's profit curve, π^B, at q_s^A in figure 12.2(c).

The relevance of a sharp nonconvexity to iterative policy depends partly upon whether q_s^A lies in the policy-relevant range of the polluter's output q_e^A to q_n^A. If q_s^A lies *above* q_n^A then the conventional analysis applies: the damage cost function is convex below q_n^A and the social gain curve has a single interior peak at q_e^A. In this case an iteration from q_n^A to q_e^A is not affected by the policy-irrelevant shut-down nonconvexity.[13] In fact since the profit-maximizing polluter will not pollute above q_n^A, even in the absence of policy, the shut-down is merely a theoretical possibility which will not occur.

The situation where q_s^A lies *below* the no-policy starting point q_n^A can be divided into two cases.

(a) Point M is a *local* peak of the social gain curve (figure 12.2) but because the excess of abatement cost over (zero) damage cost in the range $q_s^A \rightarrow q_n^A$ (the area ced in figure 12.2(b)) is greater than the excess of damage cost over abatement cost in the range $q_e^A \rightarrow q_s^A$ (area abc), it is socially efficient for firm B to shut down. The no-policy starting point q_n^A is the global optimum, point N on the social gain curve being the highest peak. The iterative policy will take no step from q_n^A, since just below this point MAC > MDC. Again the nonconvexity is not policy-relevant.

(b) The nonconvexity remains below the no-policy point q_n^A, but the configuration of marginal damage cost and marginal abatement cost is such that the second quadrant of figure 12.2 should be redrawn with abc > ced. In that case the local peak M at q_e^A would become the global optimum, the higher of the two peaks, and N would be reduced to a lower local peak. The starting point for policy is point N at q_n^A, but the iterative procedure would take no steps to pollution levels lower than q_n^A, because MAC > MDC just below q_n^A. Consequently the policy fails to achieve the global optimum, due to the policy-relevant nonconvexity and to the limitation of the policy decision to local information on the pollution levels near q_n^A. It is worth noting, however, that the policy does not make the situation *worse* than the no-policy position, since no move is made; the effect of the nonconvexity is to impose a social opportunity loss.

In general, the shut-down nonconvexity either does not prevent an iteration to the global optimum or it does block such a policy sequence but does not worsen the situation compared with the no-policy state. There is no danger that the policy will actually worsen matters by moving us on a downward path from the local peak on the social gain curve.

This argument is strengthened when the shut-down nonconvexity is placed in a macroeconomic context, which the proponents of the shut-down theory have not done. The main point that emerges from an analysis which aggregates the damage costs across a large number of victim firms is that the shut-down of individual victim firms does not necessarily imply a discontinuity, or even a downward-sloping segment, in the aggregate marginal damage cost curve.

If all victim firms had the same marginal damage cost curves then naturally we would expect the aggregate marginal damage cost curve to display a sharp nonconvexity at the one pollution level that brings about the shut-down of all the victim firms. In this implausible case the analysis of the shut-down nonconvexity at the micro level could be carried over to the macro level. But it can be shown that if there is diversity between firms in their sensitivity to pollution then individual firm shut-downs will occur at different pollution levels, and this spread of response, when there are many victim firms, can leave intact the convexity of the *aggregate* damage cost function.[14] Such diversity seems realistic since firms differ both in their profitability and in the costs of defensive actions, quite apart from the fact that some productive activities are physically more vulnerable to pollutants than others are.[15] Those who have used the shut-down nonconvexity in their claim that nonconvexities are an important obstacle to policy have offered no empirical support for such a proposition.

Saturation

The shut-down of a pollution-affected firm means that extra units of pollution cause no extra physical damage. But even without a shut-down it is possible that extra units of pollution do not always cause *increasing* marginal damage cost. In other words, seriously damaged victim firms may experience a decline in damage *at the margin* before they reach the shut-down point. In this case there is no guarantee that the total damage cost function is strictly convex over the whole range of pollution levels below the shut-down point.

Let q_R^A be the polluter's output at which the marginal damage cost ceases to rise as pollution increases, shown as a point of inflection in the total damage cost curve in figure 12.3(a). At this point the gradient of the curve begins to decline, and the associated marginal damage cost curve in figure 12.3(b) has a negative slope above q_R^A. The "smooth nonconvexity" of the total damage cost curve at q_R^A is reflected as a point of inflection also in the victim firms' profit function, π^B in figure 12.3(c).

As with the shut-down nonconvexity, the implications for policy depend upon the positions of the marginal damage cost and marginal abatement cost curves. Four cases can be distinguished.

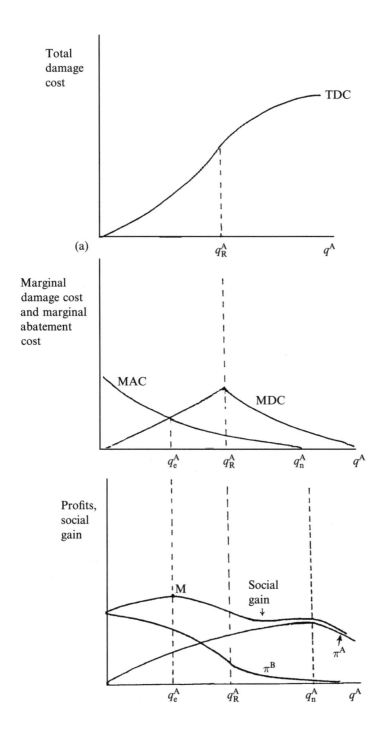

Figure 12.3 Smooth nonconvexity in the saturation theory.

(a) If $q_R^A > q_n^A$ (not shown in the figures), that is, the nonconvexity lies above the no-policy starting point, the nonconvexity is policy irrelevant.

(b) If $q_R^A > q_n^A$ but MDC > MAC in the range from q_n^A down to the interior peak M at q_e^A, as in figure 12.3(b), the nonconvexity does not block a policy iteration to the global optimum. Again the nonconvexity is policy irrelevant.

(c) With $q_R^A > q_n^A$ the downward-sloping section of the marginal damage cost curve may be steep enough for MDC to fall below MAC somewhere in the pollution range q_n^A down to q_e^A. An example of this is shown in figure 12.4. The case shown is one in which the excess of MDC over MAC for some pollution units (the two black areas) is less than the excess of MAC over MDC for other units (the hatched area). The implied social gain curve in quadrant (b) has interior local peaks at M and N, of which N is the global optimum at q_q^A. A myopic iteration starting from q_n^A will take us to the global optimum, since MDC > MAC in the range q_n^A down to q_q^A; so again the nonconvexity is not policy relevant.

(d) The one case of saturation nonconvexity which *is* policy relevant is when the size of the black areas exceeds the size of the hatched area (if figure 12.4 were redrawn). The social gain curve would have two interior local peaks, M and N, but this time M, at q_e^A, would be the higher one, the global optimum. The iteration from q_n^A to q_q^A would still be made (as in case (c)), but the excess of MAC over MDC in the pollution range from q_q^A down to q_e^A would block the further progress to the global optimum M. The iteration does *increase* efficiency over the no-policy starting point at q_n^A, but the nonconvexity in this case creates the social opportunity loss of failing to reach point M.

There are a number of reasons for doubting whether saturation nonconvexities at the individual victim firm level will generally carry over to nonconvexities of the total damage cost curves aggregated across large numbers of victim firms.[16] As in the shut-down case a diversity of firms' sensitivities can ensure macro convexity, as can an increase in the number of firms affected as the pollution level rises.

The conclusion on the saturation nonconvexity is similar to the one we reached on shut-down nonconvexity. The existence of such a nonconvexity does not guarantee policy relevance; and the claim that it poses a serious problem for pollution control policy can only be substantiated if the prevalence of declining marginal damage can be established empirically for particular real-world pollution cases.[17]

Multiplicative interdependence

There is a third possible source of nonconvexity in the damage cost function for victim firms that proves to be technically more complex than the previous two sources, and which I will only attempt to summarize here.[18] The essential feature of the model used to represent this third

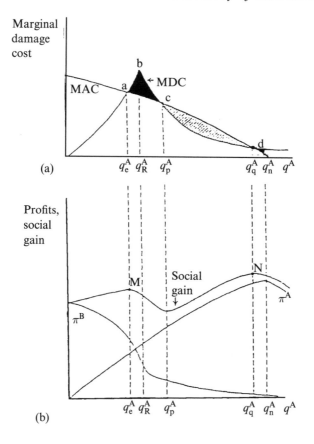

Figure 12.4 Policy relevance of nonconvexity in the saturation theory.

source is that the size of the total damage cost depends upon the *multiple* of the outputs of the polluter and of the victim firm. In particular, if w is a parameter that measures the strength of the externality the total damage cost TDC is $wq^A q^B$.

So, if $q^A = 0$ and the victim produces undisturbed at q_n^B, or if the victim does not produce at all, $q^B = 0$, while the polluter produces freely at q_n^A, then TDC $= 0$. In between these extreme outcomes total damage cost depends upon the multiple $q^A q^B$. As originally presented, the model assumed a resource constraint where the resources available are used either by firm A or by firm B, and A's and B's outputs are reciprocally related.[19] Thus, as the polluter's output q^A rises the victim's output q^B falls. There will consequently be some intermediate output at which the multiple $q^A q^B$ is maximized and, given w constant at different levels of the polluter's output, total damage cost is maximized as well. If w is large enough, and the total damage cost at any level of q^A is therefore great enough, this nonconvex total image cost function with an interior peak will result in the system operating not on a concave social gain curve (Social gain (no

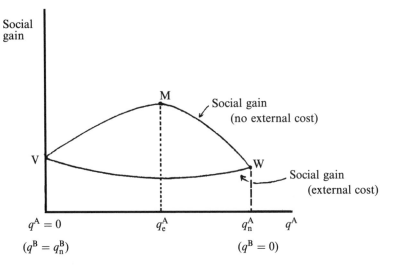

Figure 12.5 The effect of nonconvexity in the case of multiplicative interdependence.

external cost) in figure 12.5) but on a convex curve (Social gain (external cost)). The vertical distance between the two social gain curves represents the total damage cost at different levels of q^A, given that the victim's output q^B falls as q^A rises.

The effect of the external cost, with w large and constant, is to eliminate the previous interior peak M as the global optimum and to replace it with a corner optimum either at V or at W in figure 12.5. As the curves are drawn, V is socially preferable to W, but the reverse would be true if the social value of q_n^A were greater than the social value of q_n^B. Thus, V is the optimum when it is socially efficient for the polluter A not to produce, and W is the optimum when it is socially efficient for the victim firm B not to produce.

Clearly two cases need to be considered in the analysis of a myopic iterative policy.

(a) V is the global optimum, W a local peak. The nonconvexity obviously lies between the no-policy starting point W and the global optimum, V. The nature of the damage cost function is such that total damage cost *increases* for reductions in the polluter's output just below q_n^A and such steps would not be taken with positive marginal abatement cost. The nonconvexity is policy relevant, and the iterative policy does not get started, so that although it does not improve the situation neither does it reduce efficiency.
(b) W is the global optimum, V a local peak. Since the global optimum occurs where the polluter is free to pollute the nonconvexity is not policy relevant.

This theory of multiplicative interdependence relies upon some strong assumptions that cast doubt upon its generality. First, the damage cost function is of a very specific form whose empirical significance has not been established. Second, the theory requires the parameter w, which measures the strength of the externality, to be constant for all levels of pollution. Yet a case can be made for treating w as a positive function of the polluter's output. If this argument were accepted it can be shown that instead of creating a global convexity of the social gain curve the multiplicative interdependence would imply that the social gain curve is only *locally* convex. The external cost would generate a convexity in the social gain function only at those high levels of polluter's output for which w is large enough. The total damage cost curve would then be nonconvex at the upper end, and the analysis of the policy consequences of the nonconvexity would (mostly) parallel the analysis previously presented for the shut-down and saturation nonconvexities. The conclusions from such an analysis would be as follows.[20]

(a) The model of multiplicative interdependence does not establish the policy relevance of a nonconvexity; it establishes only the possibility of the existence of a nonconvexity.
(b) Even in those cases where the local nonconvexity would block an iteration to the global optimum, usually this involves an opportunity loss rather than any policy-induced movement further *away* from the global optimum.

These two conclusions represent a fair summary of the consequences of nonconvexities relating to external costs on production from all of the three sources, firm shut-down, saturation, and multiplicative interdependence.

3 Nonconvexity and External Costs on Consumption

Some of the most important external costs relate to the harm suffered by people as a result of their exposure to pollutants. Economists tend to classify such harm as external costs on *consumption*, but I prefer to use the term "external costs on *people*" to remind us that harm can be experienced even when we are not engaged in any particular consumption activity. Despite the obvious importance of this class of externality the nonconvexity literature has tended to be dominated by the case of external costs on production.

Two reasons have been offered for expecting that the total damage cost function which represents the harm suffered by people may not be convex:

1 a consumer-withdrawal theory, and
2 the existence of nonconvex preferences concerning the quality of life.

Consumer withdrawal

Consider the consequences of a pollutant that affects the use of a particular consumption good, such as the loss of pleasure from using one's garden because of the smell from a nearby chemical factory. The consumer's preference for garden use, relative to alternative uses of one's time and income, is clearly altered by the pollutant. The consumer's reaction to this can take either, or both, of two forms:

(a) gradually withdraw from the use of the product, so as to mitigate the effect of the external cost that is reducing the quality of the product;
(b) at some pollution level, stop using the consumption good altogether.

The effect that these possible reactions by the consumer will have on the convexity of the total damage cost function will now be explained, and we shall see that analytically reaction (a) parallels the saturation theory discussed earlier and reaction (b) parallels the shut-down theory.

When a consumer is exposed to a pollutant that affects the use of a product, the *quality* of the product effectively is reduced. Increases in the pollution level cause the quality to decline further, and this marginal quality decline is the marginal physical damage. If the consumer does *not* reduce consumption of the good then the total damage cost function will be convex *if* the consumer's preferences are convex in relation to product quality and *if* marginal physical damage increases as pollution increases.[21] These two conditions are assumed to hold in the conventional theory.

Return now to the withdrawal theory. What happens to convexity of the total damage cost function under reaction (a) above? The effect of the increases in the level of pollution is to push the product to lower and lower levels of quality, and the loss of quality is increasingly valuable at the margin (convex preferences). But as the consumer responds by gradually withdrawing from the use of the product there is, as pollution rises, less and less of the product left for the pollution to reduce in quality (analogous to the earlier saturation case). Consequently, if the withdrawal is rapid enough increasing pollution may cause further damage at the margin (through quality decline) that is less serious because fewer units of consumption are affected. That is, the marginal physical damage may decline. However, this does not guarantee that the convexity of the total damage cost function is violated. Strongly convex preferences may still ensure that the *value* of the marginal damage continues to rise as pollution increases.[22]

Eventually, of course, the consumer whose consumption good is decreasing in quality as a result of its exposure to increasing levels of pollution may give up the ghost and terminate consumption of the product (reaction (b) above). This is the consumption equivalent of the firm shut-down case. Once this termination point is reached marginal damage cost falls to zero, a sharp nonconvexity of the damage cost function.[23]

The evaluation of the consumer-withdrawal theory runs on lines parallel to the evaluation of the saturation and firm shut-down theories, so it can be presented fairly briefly. First, the theory establishes only the possibility of the existence of a local nonconvexity at the micro, individual consumer level. That the possible nonconvexity is local rather than global is self-evident in the case of consumption termination. But in the case of gradual withdrawal also, the nonconvexity would be restricted to some ranges of the pollution levels *unless* the consumer perceived the decline in quality, and adjusted consumption, from the very first unit of pollution. Global nonconvexity could occur only if from the first unit of pollution upwards the decline in quality led to a sufficient withdrawal of consumption to offset the convexity of consumer preferences. If the nonconvexity is only local then it will be policy relevant only if it lies in the path of an iteration from the no-policy starting point to the global optimum.

Second, the theory relies upon the assumption that withdrawal is a feasible option. This is not unreasonable when a pollutant is fairly product specific – that is, reduces the quality of some goods but not others. But many pollutants that affect people are either not very product specific or are specific to certain goods which consumers cannot easily withdraw from (such as air and water). For example, if the air quality in a town is poor it is not feasible to stop breathing it unless one can move jobs and residence to a town with a better air quality, and this is clearly not feasible for most inhabitants.

Third, the existence of a micro nonconvexity does not necessarily imply a macro nonconvexity at that pollution level. As the emissions of a pollutant increase the tendency of some consumers to withdraw may be offset by the expansion of the number of consumers who suffer damage, so that the aggregate marginal damage cost continues to rise. Once again the nonconvexity will prove a serious obstacle to an interactive policy only if it is reflected as a nonconvexity in the aggregate curve *and* this lies on the policy-relevant range of pollution levels. Whether these conditions prevail for particular types of pollution will need to be established empirically.

Nonconvex preferences

A quite different rationale for a nonconvex total damage cost function for pollution that harms people relies upon the proposition that preferences are not always convex. The argument is that in the main external costs relate to the deterioration of the quality of life (such as one's appreciation of a beautiful view)[24] and that people's preferences with respect to the quality of life are *inherently* nonconvex. With nonconvex preferences of this kind improvements in the quality of life yield increasing rather than diminishing marginal utility. Consequently successive declines in the quality (e.g. the quality of the view) due to increases in pollution are of lower and lower marginal value.

If nonconvex preferences are inserted into an otherwise conventionally formulated marginal damage cost function, then a negative slope becomes a possibility, although the existence of nonconvex preferences alone is not a sufficient condition for this result.[25]

It is important to notice that, in one respect, this rationale is different from any of the theories of nonconvexity we have considered before. It is not being suggested in this case that the nonconvexity of preferences is *caused* by the external costs; rather the problem relates to the consequences of pre-existing nonconvex preferences for the design of pollution control policy. If such preferences were pervasive clearly the implications for microeconomic analyses of government policies would extend far beyond the design of pollution control policies.

The question of the convexity of preferences has been considered a number of times in the last 30 years or so, as economists have sought to establish the degree of significance that can be attached to some fairly obvious counterexamples to the conventional convexity assumption.[26] The counterexamples have ranged from a consumer who prefers not to mix his drinks or the color of his socks, to the gourmet who prefers not to mix tripe à la mode de Caen with filet de sole Marguéry. While concave indifference curves cannot be ruled out on *a priori* grounds, doubt has nevertheless been cast on the significance of nonconvex preferences both at the level of the individual consumer and, *a fortiori*, in the aggregate. As far as the individual's preferences are concerned, it can be shown that a consumer who pursues the plausible objective of maximizing *average* level of enjoyment over many periods, subject to an average-income flow constraint within which funds can be redistributed between periods, will have convex preferences.[27] Furthermore, it is established that even where smooth nonconvexities do exist in individual indifference maps, they do not necessarily imply nonconvex aggregate preferences for large *groups* of consumers.[28] In particular, with a dispersion of incomes and tastes within the group, nonconvex individual preferences aggregate to strictly convex group preferences.

There is one final reason for doubting that nonconvex preferences generate nonconvex total damage cost functions for many of the major pollutants. Even if the nonconvexity of preferences were conceded in relation to the aesthetic elements of pollution damage (e.g. the possibility that "people do not prefer two moderately beautiful views to one extremely beautiful view"[29]), preferences surely are not nonconvex in relation to the risk of damage to health or to the destruction of human life. Pollution control policies will inevitably be based on the belief that a risk-averse population will have convex preferences with respect to the risk to life and limb.[30]

4 Nonconvexity and Self-Defense by Victims

Throughout the discussion so far it has been assumed that total damage cost is the sum of the harms suffered by firms or people exposed to pollution. Implicitly it has also been assumed that there is only one way to reduce these harms, namely for the polluter to reduce the level of emissions. But for some types of pollution this may not be realistic because it is feasible for the victims themselves to alleviate the harm that results from a given level of emissions. Sound-insulation to reduce noise nuisance and filters to reduce water impurities are examples of the defensive activities available to pollution victims. For those pollution cases in which self-defense is a feasible strategy we need to reinterpret the total damage cost function. For any unit of pollution the damage cost it causes is the lower of the cost of harm if no defense is attempted and of the cost of undertaking such a defense. So, for a particular unit of pollution, if the cost to the victim of preventing the harm is lower than the harm itself would be, then the damage cost for that unit is the cost to the victim of the defensive activity against it.

Once the total damage cost function is reinterpreted in this way it becomes apparent that defensive activities may be a source of nonconvexity of the damage cost function.[31] This is shown in the first part of figure 12.6.[32] The upward-sloping MDC^H curve, the marginal cost of the harm if not prevented by defensive measures, reflects the conventional convexity assumption. Consider the defensive activity available to the pollution victim who is exposed to a pollution level E_n^A. At E_n^A the marginal damage cost would be high if the harm were suffered, but the victim can reduce the harm by neutralizing the last (E_n^Ath) unit of pollution at a marginal cost close to zero. This is shown by the fact that the marginal cost of defense (MCD) curve is close to the horizontal axis just below E_n^A. Defending even further, the victim can neutralize extra units of pollution, moving further down from E_n^A, but only at an increasing marginal cost of defense – the MCD curve is rising as the victim moves to the left in figure 12.6(a). The extension of his defensive activity reduces the *effective* pollution level. Once this has been reduced to E_b^A it does not pay the victim to defend further: $MDC^H < MCD$ below E_b^A. The newly interpreted marginal damage cost curve comprises the lower segments of the MDC^H curve and the marginal cost of defense curve, MCD, shown as the solid-line, kinked curve in figure 12.6(a). The result is a smooth nonconvexity at E_b^A (an inflection point in the newly interpreted total damage cost curve, not shown).

Let us explore the implications of a nonconvexity created by self-defense activity. First, we will initially adopt the assumption, used by Oates in his analysis, that units of abatement by the polluter must precede units of alleviation by the victim.[33] If there are 10 units of pollution emitted and

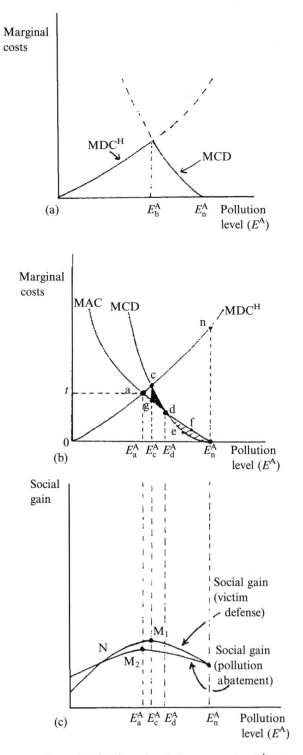

Figure 12.6 Nonconvexity and self-defense by victims, assuming E_n^Aedf > acd.

the polluter abates to 5 units, it is possible for the victim then to alleviate the effects of the remaining 5 units. But if there are 10 units emitted and the victim alleviates the effects of 5 of them, it is not possible for the polluter then to concentrate on eliminating the remaining 5, because reducing emissions must *start* from the tenth unit which is no longer harmful. This leads Oates to assume that polluter abatement must precede victim defense if abatement is to play any role in pollution control.

It will be instructive to consider Oates's description of the consequences of self-defense by the victim, and then to mention some amendments to his analysis that are needed to clarify the policy significance of the nonconvexity. Oates's presentation centers on figure 12.6(b), in which the MDC^H, MCD and MAC curves are respectively the marginal cost of harm at different pollution levels in the absence of self-defense by the victim, the marginal cost of defensive activity, and the marginal cost of polluter abatement. He makes two points in interpreting the situation in figure 12.6(b).

1　A *sequence* of polluter abatement followed by victim self-defense would not provide an efficient solution. Imagine, for example, that the polluter abated from E_n^A and E_d^A, and then the victim alleviated pollution further from E_d^A to E_c^A. The hatched area shows the excess of abatement cost over self-defense costs for the pollution units E_n^A to E_d^A, and the black area shows the excess of defense cost over abatement cost for the units E_d^A to E_c^A.[34]

2　This suggests that the efficient solution will involve using *either* polluter abatement *or* victim defense alone. Abatement alone, from E_n^A to E_a^A, would yield a social gain of E_n^Afdan, represented by a move upwards on the social gain curve for polluter abatement from N to M_2 in figure 12.6(c). Victim defense alone, on the other hand, would result in a social gain of E_n^Aedcn as the victim neutralizes pollution from E_n^A to E_c^A; this gain is shown by the move from N to M_1 in figure 12.6(c). Clearly, the element of social gain represented by area acd is achievable *only* through polluter abatement, and the element of social gain represented by area E_n^Aedf is achievable *only* through victim defense. If E_n^Aedf > acd, as has been assumed in figures 12.6(b) and 12.6(c), then the pollution level E_c^A is the global optimum (conditional upon victim defense being employed); but if the reverse were true then the pollution level E_a^A would be the global optimum (conditional upon polluter abatement being employed). The problem that the existence of these two local optima poses for pollution control policy, Oates suggests, is that Pigovian tax (emissions charge) of 0*t* in figure 12.6(b) will take us to the local optimum, M_2 at E_a^A, through polluter abatement alone. But unless the control agency knows that acd > E_n^Aedf it cannot be sure it has achieved the global optimum. In addition, a myopic iteration, based on the local information requirement that MDC > MAC for each step, will proceed to E_a^A, but again it does not guarantee the attainment of the global optimum.

The first point to notice about this analysis is that it does not include a claim that policy, whether a charge of $0t$ or an iteration from E_n^A, will lead to a social *loss*, since either E_a^A or E_c^A is more socially efficient than the assumed no-policy starting point E_n^A. However, there is some doubt as to whether it is correct, when self-defense is feasible, to assume E_n^A to be the starting point for policy. It is surely arguable that, if a policy of pollution control is implemented some time after the exposure of victims to pollution has started, then the victims will *already* have introduced the defensive measures that would make E_c^A the prevailing *effective* level of pollution. How does this affect the conclusion concerning the consequences of either imposing a charge of $0t$, or pursuing a policy iteration in which each unit of pollution emitted is abated if $\text{MAC} > \text{MDC}^H$ for that unit? The answer is that it may weaken further the case for such a policy. To see why this is so, consider a policy that induces polluter abatement even when the victims have already moved to point c in figure 12.6(b). The pollution units up to E_n^A are still being emitted when the policy is introduced, and each unit of abatement from E_n^A to E_a^A will still be undertaken even though some of those units (E_n^A to E_c^A) are no longer harmful. This sequence of course violates Oates's assumption that polluter abatement cannot follow after victim self-defense. However, there appears to be no technical reason to assume that abatement cannot begin *from* E_n^A even though the victims have already reduced their *exposure* to the units of pollution being emitted. What is the net social gain, or loss, that the policy now generates? It depends on the nature of the self-defense activity that the victim has undertaken.

1   If the defense mechanism, once installed, offers *continuing* protection, then in effect the abatement policy offers an additional net social gain of acg on the units of abatement from E_c^A to E_a^A, but at the cost, $E_c^A \text{gf} E_n^A$, of the whole abatement from E_n^A to E_c^A which yields no return because these units have already been made harmless. Evidently the policy could yield a net social *loss* in these circumstances.

2   If the cost of self-defense must be incurred again and again in successive periods for the protection to be maintained, then in effect the policymaker *can* regard E_n^A as the no-policy starting point because it is not inevitable that the victims will reduce the effective pollution from E_n^A to E_c^A in the periods following the implementation of the policy. In this case the Oates analysis seems appropriate, and the availability of efficient victim self-defense implies that a control policy that induces polluter abatement will *improve* social efficiency to a local optimum, which may or may not be the global optimum.

How serious an obstacle to policy the victim's self-defense activities represent will depend upon the agency's ability to identify the reduction in actual cost incurred by the victim (as distinct from reduction in the hypothetical harm suffered by a victim who does not undertake defensive measures) that is achieved by each successive unit of pollution abatement. In principle the risk of implementing a policy that created a social loss could be eliminated if the agency were able to use the more sophisticated criterion "abate a unit of pollution only if MAC is lower than the *smaller* of the marginal cost of harm suffered and the marginal cost of victim defense." This would prevent the loss-creating iteration described in case 1 above, because the first steps below E_n^A would not be taken since they involved MAC > MCD.

Finally, a moment's reflection suggests that a nonconvexity caused by the victim's defense activity need not be policy relevant. With the cost configuration used in figure 12.6(b), achievement of the global optimum is thwarted *only if* achieving E_c^A through victim defense alone is optimal, and if the agency induces polluter abatement by basing its iteration upon the hypothetical harm represented by the MDC^H curve rather than upon the correctly defined externality represented by the cost of defense that the pollution imposes on the victim. What is more, other cost configurations may represent the situation for some pollutants. For example, assume that victim defense costs must be repeated each period for the protection to be effective (case 2) and that the MAC and MDC curves in figure 12.6(b) are *reversed*. Then an iteration that induced polluter abatement from E_n^A down to E_c^A because MAC < MDC^H, followed by victim defense which neutralized the further pollution units from E_c^A to E_a^A, would be *sure* to improve social efficiency. This follows from the fact that MAC < MCD < MDC^H in the range E_n^A to E_d^A, MAC < MDC^H in the range E_d^A to E_c^A, and MCD < MDC^H in the range E_c^A to E_a^A. However, the globally optimal adjustment, which is polluter abatement from E_n^A to E_d^A followed by victim defense from E_d^A to E_a^A (for which MCD < MAC), would be achieved only if the more sophisticated iteration criterion (p. 21) could be employed.

5   Conclusion

This chapter has reviewed the consequences of nonconvexities in damage cost functions which derive from a variety of sources. A theme has emerged which is common to all of these sources, namely that the nonconvexity is a potentially serious obstacle to policy only if it is policy relevant. But even with policy-relevant nonconvexities, iterative policies do not necessarily cause a social *loss*. In quite a high proportion of the analytically identifiable cases, the policy-relevant nonconvexity blocks an iteration to the global optimum but the policy nevertheless yields a social gain. Whether control policies will cause a social loss in practice depends upon whether the analytically exceptional social loss cases turn out to be the *empirically* relevant ones.

Notes

1 A good recent survey of the field is Cropper and Oates (1992). For a thorough, formal textbook presentation of the major issues see Baumol and Oates (1988); a nonmathematical presentation can be found in Burrows (1979).

2 See Burrows (1979, p. 9) and Baumol and Oates (1988, pp. 29–31).

3 For example, Mishan (1969, pp. 342–3) and Baumol and Oates (1988, p. 17). Contrast Burrows (1979, pp. 10–12).

4 In many respects the implications of the analysis are similar for cases that involve firms harming consumers or consumers harming other consumers. See Dick (1974, chs 3 and 4).

5 A strictly convex function of one variable is represented graphically as a U-shaped curve (or part of such a curve) which is convex when viewed from the horizontal axis. See Chiang (1984, pp. 241–4) for a lucid explanation of convex and concave (inverse U-shaped) functions.

   For simplicity, throughout the linear cases will be ignored and *strict* convexity or concavity will be assumed. Generally the conventional theory can work with non-strict ("weak") convexity of the damage cost function. That is, linear damage costs do not pose a problem for the conventional theory.

6 For a fuller explanation of abatement costs, which includes a discussion of the abatement cost curve relating to abatement through changes in technology, see Burrows (1979, ch. 2, section 3).

7 This is a rather strong assumption which is used here merely to simplify the exposition. It is better to recognize the interdependence of the output choices of the two firms, as in Burrows (1979, section 3.1.2).

8 If marginal damage cost does not approach zero at $q^A = 0$ (see assumption (e) above), a corner (non-interior) peak becomes a possibility. See Burrows (1979, pp. 172–3).

9 On the second derivative test for an extremum see Chiang (1984, ch. 9, section 4).

10 See Baumol and Oates (1988, ch. 11), Burrows (1979, ch. 4).

11 It would probably be more elegant and consistent to relate the "nonconvexity" to the characteristics of the underlying production and preference *sets*, but I have come to feel that the problems raised by the nonconvexity issue are most easily understood if we can relate them to the assumed shapes of the *functions*. See Rothenberg (1960, pp. 435–6) and Chiang (1984, pp. 348–52).

12 See Burrows (1986, pp. 103–4) for a number of quotations in support of this point. The authors quoted there are Baumol (1972), Baumol and Oates (1975), Starrett and Zeckhauser (1974), Gould (1977), and Dasgupta and Heal (1979). The recent survey by Cropper and Oates (1992, p. 685) seems to make a similar jump.

13 This case is not shown in the diagrams. It can be found in figure 1 in Burrows (1986, p. 105).

14 On the derivation of the aggregate MDC curve see Burrows (1986, pp. 106–9).

15 For example, Nordhaus (1991, p. 931) discusses the variations in the impact of global warming across industries.

16 These are discussed in Burrows (1986, pp. 112–14).

17 Repetto (1987, pp. 13–14) claims that nonconvexities are empirically important, but he does not address the question of policy relevance. His analysis of the case of interactions between nitrogen oxides and hydrocarbon emissions in forming atmospheric ozone shows that the relationships between changes in *either one* of the two pollutants and the atmospheric ozone concentration are likely to be nonconvex. His analysis does not, however, extend to establishing the characteristics of the total damage cost function (which would require evidence on the damage consequences of increases in ozone concentration).

18 See Baumol and Oates (1988, ch. 8) for an analysis of the existence of the nonconvexity, and Burrows (1986, pp. 114–22) for an analysis of its policy relevance.

19 For simplicity I have assumed that if firm A uses all the resources it can produce q_n^A and this maximizes its profit, or if B uses all the resources it can produce q_n^B and this maximizes its profit in the absence of the externality.

20 See Burrows (1986, pp. 117–22).

21 We can use Slater's (1975) model to identify the determinants of the change in the slope of the total damage cost curve. Assume that the consumer's utility function is

$$U = U(y, z)$$

where y is the quantity of good consumed and z is the quality of good, outside the individual's control. Where a change in the pollution level E affects the quality of the good the slope of the marginal damage cost function (with λ representing the constant marginal utility of income) is

$$\frac{d}{dE}MDC = -\frac{1}{\lambda}\left[\frac{d^2 U}{dz^2}\left(\frac{dz}{dE}\right)^2 + \frac{dU}{dz}\frac{d^2 z}{dE^2}\right]$$

$$[1] \quad [2] \quad\quad [3]\ [4]$$

in which

term [1] is negative *if* preferences over quality are convex (i.e. when the marginal utility of quality rises as quality falls)

term [2] is positive, the square of marginal physical damage

term [3] is positive, the marginal utility of quality

term [4] is negative *if* the marginal physical damage increases as pollution increases (i.e. if quality declines at an increasing rate as E rises)

Under the conventional assumptions of convex preferences and increasing marginal physical damage, [1] and [4] both negative, the above expression is positive, so the total damage cost function is convex.

22 Using the expression for the slope of the marginal damage cost function in note 21, we can see that term [4] being positive is not sufficient for $dMDC/dE < 0$, especially if term [1] is strongly negative.

23 With $dz/dE = 0$ and $d^2 z/dE^2 = 0$ the marginal damage cost goes to zero, and $dMDC/dE = 0$ (from the expression in note 21) after termination.

24 Slater (1975, p. 868).

25 In the expression in note 21 let term [1] be positive, nonconvex preferences, while [2] and [3] are positive and [4] is negative. Then $dMDC/dE$ will be negative only if the nonconvexity of preferences is *strong*.

26 See, for example, Gorman (1957), Farrell (1959), Arrow and Hahn (1971), Green (1976), and Deaton and Muellbauer (1980).

27 Gorman (1957, pp. 43–5).

28 See Farrell (1959), Rothenberg (1960), Starr (1969), and Sondermann (1975).

29 Slater (1975, p. 868).

30 Yaari (1965) provides evidence in support of the assumption that preferences over risky outcomes are convex. On the relationship between risk aversion and convexity see Green (1976, ch. 15).

31 See Shibata and Winrich (1983) and Oates (1983).

32 For brevity the analysis will concentrate here on the marginal curves and the social gain curves; hopefully the reader is by now sufficiently familiar with the associations between the marginal and total damage cost curves, and between the damage and abatement cost curves, to complete the analysis for him/herself.

33 Oates (1983, p. 371).

34 Oates actually considers victim defense down to E_a^A, but this further alleviation of harm would not be chosen by the victim because $\text{MCD} > \text{MDC}^H$ below E_c^A.

References

Arrow, K. J. and Hahn, F. H. 1971: *General Competitive Analysis*. San Francisco, CA: Holden-Day.

Baumol, W. J. 1972: On taxation and the control of externalities. *American Economic Review*, 62 (June), 307–22.

Baumol, W. J. and Oates, W. E. 1975: *The Theory of Environmental Policy*. Englewood Cliffs, NJ: Prentice-Hall.

Baumol, W. J. and Oates, W. E. 1988: *The Theory of Environmental Policy*, 2nd edn. Cambridge: Cambridge University Press.

Burrows, P. 1979: *The Economic Theory of Pollution Control*. Oxford: Martin Robertson.

Burrows, P. 1986: Nonconvexity induced by external costs on production: theoretical curio or policy dilemma? *Journal of Environmental Economics and Management*, 13 (June), 101–28.

Chiang, A. C. 1984: *Fundamental Methods of Mathematical Economics*, 3rd edn. Tokyo: McGraw-Hill.

Cropper, M. L. and Oates, W. E. 1992: Environmental economics: a survey. *Journal of Economic Literature*, 30 (June), 675–740.

Dasgupta, P. S. and Heal, G. M. 1979: *Economic theory and Exhaustible Resources*. Cambridge: Cambridge Economic Handbooks.

Deaton, A. and Muelbauer, J. 1980: *Economics and Consumer Behaviour*. Cambridge: Cambridge University Press.

Dick, D. T. 1974: *Pollution, Congestion and Nuisance*. Lexington, MA: Lexington Books.

Farrell, M. T. 1959: The convexity assumption in the theory competitive markets. *Journal of Political Economy*, 67 (August), 377–91.

Gorman, W. M. 1957: Convex indifference curves and diminishing marginal utility. *Journal of Political Economy*, 65 (1), 40–50.

Gould, J. R. 1977: Total conditions in the analysis of external effects. *Economic Journal*, 87 (September), 558–64.

Green, H. A. J. 1976: *Consumer Theory*. London: Macmillan.

Mishan, E. J. 1969: *Welfare Economics: An Assessment*. Amsterdam: North-Holland.

Nordhaus, W. D. 1991: To slow or not to slow: the economics of the greenhouse effect. *Economic Journal*, 101 (July), 920–37.

Oates, W. E. 1983: The regulation of externalities: efficient behaviour by sources and victims. *Public Finance*, 38 (3): 362–75.

Repetto, R. 1987: The policy implications of non-convex environmental damages: a smog control case study. *Journal of Environmental Economics and Management*, 14 (March), 13–29.

Rothenberg, J. 1960: Non-convexity, aggregation and Pareto optimality. *Journal of Political Economy*, 68 (October), 435–68.

Shibata, H. and Winrich, J. S. 1983: Control of pollution when the offended defend themselves. *Economica*, 50 (November), 425–37.

Slater, M. 1975: The quality of life and the shape of marginal loss curves. *Economic Journal*, 85 (December), 864–72.

Sondermann, D. 1975: Smoothing demand by aggregation. *Journal of Mathematical Economics*, 2, 201–24.

Starr, R. 1969: Quasi-equilibria in markets with nonconvex preferences. *Econometrica*, 37 (January), 25–38.

Starrett, D. A. and Zeckhauser, R. 1974: Treating external diseconomies – markets or taxes? In J. W. Pratt (ed.), *Statistical and Mathematical Aspects of Pollution Problems*, New York: Marcel Dekker.

Yaari, M. E. 1965: Convexity in the theory of choice under risk. *Quarterly Journal of Economics*, 79 (May), 278–90.

13

Liability and Penalty Structures in Policy Design

Kathleen Segerson

Introduction

Most of the literature on the use of market incentives to allocate environmental resources has focused on the use of tax-like policies (such as emission taxes and deposits) or permit trading policies (including "bubble" and "offset" policies).[1] These policies can create an effective "market" for environmental resources when polluters' activities are observable so that payments based on that behavior can be determined. An alternative approach, which does not require that polluters' behavior be monitored, is the imposition of legal liability for damages resulting from that behavior.[2] For example, imposition of strict liability, which requires polluters to pay for damages resulting from their activities, creates a "market" for certain resources by placing a price on consumption of those resources (the creation of damages). It is a contingent price, however, in the sense that, rather than paying *ex ante* for expected damages, polluters are required to pay for damages only when (and if) they occur.[3]

Liability for environmental damages can be imposed either statutorily or under the common law. Under common law, both nuisance law and property law have been used to prevent environmental damages or secure compensation for them (Baram, 1982; Developments in the Law: Toxic Waste Generation, 1986; Dewees, 1992). In addition, liability for environmental damages has been imposed under a number of statutes, including the Comprehensive Environmental Response, Liability, and Compensation Act (CERCLA), the Rivers and Harbors Act, the Clean Water Act, and the Outer Continental Shelf Lands Act (Opaluch, 1984).[4] Liability has been used primarily for stochastic pollution problems, where damages are accidental (rather than simply incidental, as, for example, with continuous emissions of air pollutants). Examples include chemical spills, oil spills, landfill leaching, and other forms of groundwater contamination.

Questions regarding the efficiency of relying on legal liability to allocate resources can take several forms. For example, one could ask what legal rules lead to efficient private decisions given the response of individuals to the rule. This question is the focus of much of the theoretical literature on liability rules. The basic approach used in addressing this question is (i) to define socially efficient decisions (usually as decisions that minimize total social costs, including prevention costs, expected damages, and possibly litigation costs), (ii) to set up a theoretical model of private decisions under alternative legal rules, and (iii) to compare the predicted responses of individuals to the socially efficient outcomes.

While economic theory can be used to define an efficient liability rule, actual outcomes of the legal process (and the precedents they create) are based on decisions made by judges and juries. To the extent that these decisions are based on factors other than economic efficiency, the rules as actually applied will differ from the efficient rules. A second question of interest is thus whether over time actual legal rules tend toward efficient rules, given the workings of the legal system. The literature addressing this question focuses on the role of precedent in legal decisions and the factors that tend to change precedents over time.[5]

Finally, even if an efficient rule is being applied, there is still a question of whether imposition of the rule is actually affecting private decisions regarding prevention as predicted by theory. In practice, the incentive effects of liability are imperfect and incomplete. Even under an efficient rule, the actual price paid for consuming an environmental resource is often less than the full social cost due to imperfections in the legal system. These include failure to impose liability on responsible parties (because of uncertainty over causation, statutes of limitation, or high legal fees) and payments that fall short of actual damages (because of asset limitations or difficulties in proving the full extent of damages). Reliance on liability to allocate environmental resources should thus hinge on whether, given the limitation of the legal system, liability can still create an effective market for otherwise unpriced environmental goods. This is primarily an empirical question of the extent to which changes in liability in fact lead to desired changes in behavior. To date, this question has received considerably less attention than the other two.[6] Yet, it is the crux of the argument that the legal system effectively establishes a market that can lead to efficient resource allocation.

This chapter provides an introduction to the role of legal liability in inducing efficient pollution abatement. Since most of the literature on the economic effects of liability has been theoretical, we focus here on theory as well. However, as noted above, reliance on liability as an alternative (or even a complement) to more traditional policy approaches should be based on empirical evidence of the effectiveness of liability in providing abatement incentives.

Overview of Alternative Legal Rules: Prices versus Sanctions

In general, economists look to pricing mechanisms, such as Pigovian taxes or tradeable permits, to allocate environmental resources. In the context of legal liability, the main type of "price" rule is strict liability, under which a responsible party is held liable for damages regardless of the amount of care exercised in undertaking the externality-generating activity.[7] The main alternative to strict liability is a negligence rule,[8] under which a responsible party would be held liable for damages only if it failed to comply with the "due standard of care" regarding the activity that led to damages.[9] In contrast to strict liability, which effectively imposes a payment for doing what is permitted, liability under negligence can be viewed as a "sanction" or punishment imposed for doing what is forbidden (Cooter, 1984). The distinction between strict liability and negligence is also similar to the distinction between taxes and regulation (prices versus quantities) in standard models of pollution control.[10]

While standard models of pollution control focus on the decisions of the polluters, in many cases it may also be possible for the victims to take steps to reduce the level of damages they might suffer. Such avoidance or mitigation behavior may be an important part of damage reduction. For example, in cases of groundwater contamination, victims can use alternative sources such as bottled water. Failure to do so could increase the overall level of damages suffered. Some legal rules recognize the potential of victims to undertake avoidance behavior, and couple injurer liability with a defense of contributory negligence. Under such a defense, the injurer's liability (under either strict liability or a negligence rule) hinges on the victim having undertaken appropriate avoidance behavior. In other words, if the victim did not satisfy the due standard of care for avoidance behavior, then the injurer will not be held liable for damages regardless of his care level.[11]

Factors Affecting Efficiency of Alternative Rules

When analyzing the efficiency of alternative legal rules, it is necessary to delineate explicitly the nature of the setting in which environmental damages occur. Several distinctions are important. The first is between cases where there is a contractual relationship between the polluter and the victim and those where there is not such a relationship. Examples where a contractual relationship does exist are workplace accidents, where the firm is the injurer and the employee is the victim, and consumer product accidents, where the producer is the injurer and the consumer is the victim. No such relationship exists in cases of third party damages, such as when neighboring households suffer from groundwater contaminated by a nearby hazardous waste dump. The existence of a contractual relationship creates a mechanism for shifting costs between the two parties, which can affect the role that liability plays in providing incentives for care.

The second necessary distinction is between cases of unilateral care, where only the polluter's actions affect damages, and those of bilateral care, where the victim can also take steps to reduce the level of damages.[12] As noted above, avoidance behavior by victims can be an important part of damage reduction. In such cases, the legal rule needs to be designed to create incentives for both the polluter and the victim to exercise care. In cases of unilateral care, victim incentives are not relevant.

Finally, it is necessary to identify whether the level of damages is affected only by the amount of care undertaken (by the polluter and possibly the victim) or by both the amount of care and the level of the activity (or the output level). For example, in the context of groundwater contamination from agricultural pesticides, the total level of contamination is generally affected by both the care taken in applying pesticides and the total amount applied. When output can affect damages as well, then the liability rule needs to be designed to provide efficient incentives not only for care but for the choice of the activity/output level as well.

The following sections summarize the efficiency of strict liability and negligence and compare these rules to a Pigovian tax under different assumptions regarding the three factors listed above.[13] We simply sketch the nature of the results and the models used to derive them, with an emphasis on some basic principles relating to the above factors that underlie all of the results.[14]

Third Party Damages

When there is no contractual relationship between the polluter and the victim, the two parties interact only through the damage function. We start with the simplest case of unilateral care with damages affected only by care levels.

Unilateral care

Assume that, if the polluter chooses a care level x (measured in dollars), then with probability $p(x)$ the victim will suffer damages of $D(x)$, where $p'(x) < 0$ and $D'(x) < 0$.[15] The socially efficient choice of x (x^*) then minimizes total social costs $x + p(x)D(x)$.[16,17] If the sufficient second-order conditions are met, then x^* is defined by the first-order condition

$$1 + p'D + pD' = 0 \qquad (13.1)$$

The polluter, on the other hand, chooses a level of x that minimizes $x + p(x)L(x)$, where $L(x)$ is the polluter's liability payment if damages occur and he chose a care level x.[18] Under a strict liability rule, the polluter is liable for all damages that occur, that is, $L(x) = D(x)$ for all x. Clearly, under such a rule, private costs equal social costs and the polluter is induced to choose the efficient level of care. Thus, strict liability is similar to a Pigovian tax in that it forces the firm to internalize the social costs of its actions.

Similarly, the firm can be induced to choose the efficient care level under a properly designed negligence rule as well. Under a negligence rule, $L(x)$ takes the form

$$L(x) = D(x) \quad \text{if } x < x_s$$
$$L(x) = 0 \qquad \text{if } x \geq x_s \tag{13.2}$$

where x_s is the due standard of care. If the due standard is set equal to the efficient level of care x^*, then in minimizing private costs the firm will choose x^*.[19] This can be seen from figure 13.1, where the bold line indicates the firm's private costs under the negligence rule. The liability payment in (13.2) creates a discontinuity in these costs at the due standard. With $x_s = x^*$, the cost-minimizing choice for the firm is x^*. Thus, the firm is induced to choose the efficient level of care. This is analogous to a regulatory context in which the penalty for failure to comply with the regulation is sufficiently high to induce compliance.

Thus, in the case of unilateral care where only care affects damages, either a strict liability rule or a negligence rule can be used in lieu of a Pigovian tax to induce efficient pollution control. However, when the assumptions of this simple case are relaxed, differences among the approaches exist. These are summarized below.

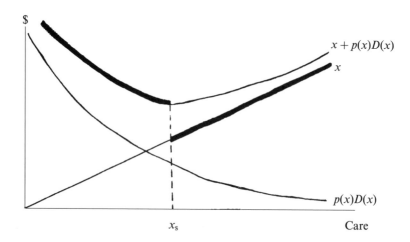

Figure 13.1   Choosing the efficient level of care.

Choice of activity/output levels

While Pigovian taxes provide efficient marginal incentives regarding pollution abatement, it is well known that in the long run they create the correct entry/exit incentives only if marginal damages are constant (over the relevant range for the firm) so that total tax payments equal total damages (Spulber, 1985). Similarly, in the context of liability, efficient incentives regarding whether or not to engage in an activity, or, equivalently, the level at which to engage in it, require that the injurer face the full social costs of engaging in the activity.[20]

To see this, let q be the output or activity level of the injurer and reinterpret x and D to be the care level and damages per unit of output. Let $B(q)$ be the benefits from the production of q and let $c(x)$ be the per-unit production costs.[21] Then the socially efficient choice of q (q^*) solves

$$\max B(q) - [c(x^*) + p(x^*)D(x^*)]q \qquad (13.3)$$

With an interior solution and appropriate second-order conditions, q^* satisfies the first-order condition

$$B'(q) - [c(x^*) + p(x^*)D(x^*)] = 0 \qquad (13.4)$$

Given q^*, the efficient entry condition becomes

$$B(q^*) - [c(x^*) + p(x^*)D(x^*)]q^* \geq 0 \qquad (13.5)$$

Injuries should continue to enter (be active) up to the point that (13.5) holds as an equality.

The polluter, on the other hand, chooses q to maximize net private benefits $B(q) - [c(x) + p(x)L(x)]q$, where again $L(x)$ is its liability payment if damages occur. Clearly, in the absence of any penalty conditional on the choice of q, the polluter's choice of q will be efficient if and only if $L(x) = D(x)$. Since under a strict liability rule polluters pay the full amount of damages for all x, this rule will induce an efficient choice of activity level. In other words, since polluters bear the full social costs of all of their actions (choice of care and activity level), those choices will be efficient. Note that, unlike in the case of Pigovian taxes, efficiency results here even if marginal damages are not constant since under strict liability total payments are equated to total damages (rather than simply equating marginal payments to marginal damages).

Under a negligence rule, however, the choice of q will not be efficient if negligence is defined only in terms of care levels (Polinsky, 1980a). If properly designed, the negligence rule will induce polluters to be non-negligent regarding their care levels and thus in equilibrium they will not be liable for damages, that is, they will not pay the total social costs of their actions. As a result, they will choose a level of q that is too high. This is similar to the result that under a regulatory approach where polluters do not pay for residual damages total industry output will be too large. In other words, because total private costs are less than total social costs, under perfect competition the equilibrium price will be too low and the equilibrium number of firms will be too high.

Bilateral care (victim incentives)

In cases of bilateral care, where victims can engage in avoidance or mitigation behavior, consideration must be given to the effect that alternative policies have on victim incentives. Under a system of Pigovian taxes, any victim compensation must be lump sum in order to preserve the victim's incentive to choose the efficient level of avoidance or care (Baumol and Oates, 1988). In particular, not compensating victims at all will preserve efficient victim incentives. Since Pigovian taxes collected by the government are not necessarily used for victim compensation, this instrument has the asymmetry property that ensures efficient incentives for both the polluter and the victim (Baumol and Oates, 1988).

In contrast, under common law liability rules, payments made by the injurer are generally by definition used for victim compensation.[22] In other words, aside from legal fees, there is a one-to-one correspondence between the amount paid by the polluter and the amount received by the victim. While these payments act as lump-sum transfers (and thus have no efficiency effects) in the case of unilateral care, when victims can take steps to mitigate damages, compensation reduces the incentive for victims to do so.

The ability of victims to mitigate damages can be incorporated into the simple model outlined above by replacing $D(x)$ and $L(x)$ with $D(x, y)$ and $L(x, y)$ respectively, where y is the level of prevention or mitigation undertaken by the victim. If y is measured in dollars, then the socially efficient level of y minimizes (simultaneously with x) $x + y + p(x)D(x, y)$. However, a victim would choose y to minimize his private net costs, given by $y + p(x)[D(x, y) - L(x, y)]$. Clearly, if $D(x, y) = L(x, y)$, that is, if polluters are liable for all damages under strict liability, then victims will chose $y = 0$, which will generally be less than the socially efficient level. Thus, while a strict liability rule creates efficient incentives for polluters to take care, it provides inefficient victim incentives. Effectively, since strict liability provides a form of insurance for victims, it creates a moral hazard problem.

However, strict liability can induce efficient victim incentives if it is coupled with a defense of contributory negligence. In this case, the victim will not receive any compensation if $y < y^*$.[23] Using an argument similar to the one above for the negligence rule, it can easily be shown that the contributory negligence defense will induce the victim to be non-negligent. Given this, the polluter will bear the full accident costs and, as a result, choose the efficient care and activity levels. Thus, a rule of strict liability with a defense of contributory negligence will induce efficient care by both the polluter and the victim. Note, however, that, because in equilibrium victims will not bear any accident costs, they will choose an inefficient activity level.

In contrast, victim incentives to take care would be efficient under a negligence rule even without the contributory negligence defense. Since if properly designed the negligence rule will induce the polluter to be non-negligent, in equilibrium no payments will be made to the victim. Thus, in equilibrium the victim will bear all residual damages. This induces the victim to choose the efficient level of care. In addition, victims would choose an efficient activity level because in equilibrium they bear all damages themselves. Thus, both care and activity levels of victims are efficient under a simple negligence rule.

Table 13.1 summarizes the efficiency results thus far, which apply to bilateral care cases where both care levels and activity levels can affect the level of damages.[24] If marginal damages are constant, then the Pigovian tax ensures efficiency of all decisions of both the polluter and the victim. In contrast, when imposition of liability implies that payments from the injurer go directly to the victim as compensation for damages, then none of the liability rules ensures efficient incentives for all decisions. However, if injurer payments and victim compensation can be decoupled so that there is not a one-to-one relationship between the two, as in some statutory applications of liability, then strict liability can theoretically replicate the efficiency properties of the Pigovian tax and ensure efficient decisions by all parties. Nonetheless, even if payments by injurers are not used for victim compensation, some important differences between using liability and Pigovian taxes for internalizing externalities remain.

Uncertainty of payment

Under a Pigovian tax, the injurer's payment is certain in the sense that it is known and payable at the time that the injurer engages in the externality-

Table 13.1 Efficiency of alternative rules

	Pigovian tax	Strict liability	Strict liability with contributory negligence	Negligence
Polluter care	Efficient	Efficient	Efficient	Efficient
Polluter activity	Efficient if MD constant	Efficient	Efficient	Not efficient
Victim care	Efficient	Not efficient	Efficient	Efficient
Victim activity	Efficient	Not efficient	Not efficient	Efficient

generating activity. Thus, the injurer must make the tax payments "up-front." If he does not, he will not be able to engage in the activity. In contrast, under strict liability, payment is not made at the initial time of the activity. As a result, the probability of actually paying damages *ex post* may be less than one.

There are a number of reasons why polluters may never end up paying for the damages resulting from their activities.[25] For example, in most liability contexts the external effects of the activity are generally uncertain at the time that the injurer engages in the activity. When external effects are uncertain, it may be difficult to prove that a given polluter was responsible for some observed damage. For example, it is generally difficult to prove that exposure to a given substance was the cause of an observed cancer. This is particularly true with long latency periods where the damages are not apparent until many years after exposure. To the extent that the difficulty of proving causation prevents responsible parties from being held liable, the incentive effects of liability are reduced.

The probability that the responsible party will be held liable for the full amount of damages may be less than one for other reasons as well. For example, the polluter may have limited assets that prevent full payment or may be judgment-proof for other reasons. Alternatively, victims may not bring suit if legal fees are high and/or damages are widely dispersed across individuals (Shavell, 1982b). If the polluter perceives the probability of a successful suit to be less than one for any of these reasons, then even under strict liability he will not fully internalize the social costs of his activity. However, if the expected damages are known, then use of an *ex ante* tax based on expected damages would internalize those costs.

Risk allocation

In most analyses of environmental problems, all parties are assumed to be risk neutral, implying that the allocation of risk has no welfare implications. However, with stochastic pollution events where the level of damages can be substantial, parties are likely to be risk averse. With risk aversion, the allocation of risk has efficiency effects.

Under a Pigovian tax approach where tax payments are based on expected damages, polluters bear no risk since tax payments are known *ex ante*. Victims, on the other hand, do bear risks since they receive no compensation for the damages they incur. A similar allocation of risks exists under a negligence rule.[26] Non-negligent polluters face no liability and hence no risk,[27] while uncompensated victims bear the full risk. In contrast, under a strict liability rule where injurer payments go directly to victims as compensation, injurers bear the full risk since their ultimate liability is unknown *ex ante*. The compensation under strict liability provides insurance for victims, leaving them bearing no residual risk.

Whether it is more efficient for polluters or victims to bear the risks associated with stochastic damages depends on how risk averse the two parties are and the availability of mechanisms to ensure against those risks. In general, if both parties are risk averse and insurance is not available, then a tradeoff between risk-sharing and incentives will exist and a first-best outcome will not be achievable (Shavell, 1982a).

Contractual Relationships

The conclusions regarding the efficiency of alternative liability rules discussed above apply when there is no contractual relationship between the injurer and the victim. In some cases, however, a contractual relationship will exist in the sense that one party buys a good or service from the other. The price paid for that good or service then provides a mechanism for shifting costs from one party to the other. An obvious example of a direct relationship between polluter and victim is an employer–employee relationship in a hazardous industry, where (at least in theory) costs can be shifted through changes in the wage rate. In other cases, the contractual relationship is between two parties who might be held liable for damages to a third party, as, for example, when both a producer and a user of a good share liability for damages to a bystander.

The existence of a contractual relationship has implications for the impact of alternative assignments of liability. In particular, if costs can be perfectly shifted forward (from the seller to the buyer) or backward (from the buyer to the seller) through changes in the price, then decisions regarding output and care are in theory independent of the assignment of liability.[26] In addition, as long as together the buyer and the seller bear the full amount of damages (regardless or how it is distributed between them), those decisions will be efficient. However, this "irrelevance result" requires that victims correctly perceive risks and, in cases where the buyer's choices of care and output affect damages, that sellers be able to tailor prices to those choices.

Unilateral care

To see the role of the contractual relationship, consider first the case of unilateral care where only the polluter's decisions affect damages. Assume the polluter is the seller of the good. Let P be the market price of the good and let s be the share of damages borne by the polluter/seller. Clearly, if $s = 0$ the polluter is not liable for any damages associated with consumption or use of the good, while $s = 1$ corresponds to a strict liability rule where polluters are responsible for all damages. The polluter then chooses care and output levels (x and q) to

$$\max Pq - [c(x) + p(x)sD(x)]q \qquad (13.6)$$

where the other variables are defined above.

Likewise, the victim will choose a consumption level where price is equal to marginal benefit of consumption of the good net of any damages as a result of that consumption. Let $U(q)$ be the marginal gross benefit from consumption. Then consumer demand is determined by

$$P = U(q) - p(x)(1 - s)D(x) \qquad (13.7)$$

where $1 - s$ is the share of uncompensated damages borne by the victim. Clearly, when $s < 1$, the expected damages from consuming a unit of the good shift the consumer's demand curve (willingness to pay) downward.

Given (13.7), the polluter's choice problem can be rewritten as

$$\max [U(q) - p(x)(1 - s)D(x)]q - [c(x) + p(x)sD(x)]q$$

$$= U(q)q - [c(x) + p(x)D(x)]q \qquad (13.8)$$

Clearly, since (13.8) is independent of s, the polluter's choices of both x and q are independent of the amount of liability borne directly. In other words, the polluter effectively bears the full social costs of his actions either directly (through strict liability for the full amount of damages) or indirectly (through a reduction in the price received for his product). Thus, he chooses the efficient levels of both care and output for all s. In particular, his decisions will be efficient under a rule of strict liability ($s = 1$) or a rule of no liability ($s = 0$). Using the same basic principle of cost shifting, it can easily be shown that efficiency would result from use of a negligence rule as well.

Note, however, that in order for perfect shifting to occur the victim must correctly perceive risks. Specifically, the formulation in (13.7) assumes that victims correctly perceive expected damages and thus correctly shift their demand curves to reflect uncompensated damages. This requires that victims know the care level of the seller from which they are buying. In the presence of victim misperceptions, a strict liability rule would still lead to efficient incentives since there are no uncompensated damages. However, any rule where $s < 1$, including a negligence rule, will no longer be efficient.[29]

Bilateral care

Consider next the case of bilateral care where care by the victim can also affect damages, that is, $D = D(x, y)$. The polluter's problem can still be written as (13.6), with $D(x, y)$ replacing $D(x)$. However, the victim now chooses q and y to

$$\max \int_0^q U(Q)\,dQ - [P - y - p(x)(1 - s)D(x, y)]q \qquad (13.9)$$

Differentiating (13.9) with respect to q to determine the demand curve and substituting the result into (13.6) allows the polluter's choice problem to be written as

$$\max\ [U(q) - y]q - [c(x) + p(x)D(x, y)]q \qquad (13.10)$$

Thus, the results regarding the polluter's behavior are the same as before. In particular, the choices of output and care are efficient for all s, given the victim's choice of y. The question is then whether the victim's care level will be efficient as well.

The answer to this question depends on whether the seller can tailor the price to the care level of the victim. In equilibrium, price equals marginal cost, that is,

$$P = c(x) + p(x)sD(x, y) \qquad (13.11)$$

If the seller can observe y and the equilibrium price reflects the victim's actual choice of y, then (13.11) will hold for the actual choice of y. Knowing this, the victim will expect the price he pays to reflect his choice of care and will therefore substitute (13.11) into (13.9) when choosing y. With this substitution, the victim's objective function becomes

$$\max \int_0^q U(Q)\,dQ - [c(x) - y - p(x)D(x, y)]q \qquad (13.12)$$

which is clearly independent of s. Thus, with prices tailored to the victim's care level, the victim's choices will be efficient regardless of the assignment of liability.

However, if the seller cannot observe y, then (13.11) will not hold for the actual choice of y. In this case, the victim will perceive P to be constant, that is, independent of the actual choice of y. With a constant price in (13.9), the victim will choose an inefficient level of care whenever $s > 0$. In this case, the inefficiency results from the inability of the seller to shift costs onto the buyer through an appropriate shift in his supply curve. In this sense, it can be viewed as a case of seller "misperceptions."

Multiple Polluters or "Joint Torts"

As noted above, in many cases the damages from a given activity are affected by the actions of more than one party, such as the polluter and the victim. It is also possible, however, for the other party to be another polluter, as when the actions of two (or more) polluters combine to create damages in a nonseparable way. For example, if several generators have dumped hazardous waste into a given landfill, then it is the combined activities of the generators that create a single potential for contamination that cannot be separated into damages attributable to any one polluter.[30] In terms of the simple model above, damages would be given by $D(x, z)$, where z is the care (or activity) level of another polluter.[31]

When the actions of polluters combine to create damages in this way, a potential inter-polluter externality exists.[32] A pricing system must be established that ensures that each polluter internalizes the full costs of his actions. This is ensured if each pays a price equal to his incremental damages, where incremental damages for polluter i are the difference between damages when i engages in the activity and damages when he does not. Such a scheme can be implemented by requiring each polluter to pay the full amount of damages less a fixed"credit" equal to the damages that would have occurred in his absence.[33] This scheme ensures that each polluter pays the full amount at the margin (thus eliminating the moral hazard problem associated with fixed sharing rules) but adjusts total costs in such a way that the correct long-run entry/exit incentives are retained.

While the above scheme ensures efficiency, there is in general no guarantee that total payments by all polluters will equal total damages. Due to synergisms, they can be more or less than total damages. In practice, however, total payments cannot exceed damages and the court must determine the allocation of liability across parties. If the court has some basis for apportioning costs (such as the shares of total waste contributed by each polluter), then it can use that as a means of allocating responsibility for damages. Alternatively, a principle known as "joint and several liability" has been used, under which the court can apportion damages across responsible parties or hold a single party responsible for the full amount of damages, regardless of his relative contribution.[34] Under the principle of "contribution," the targeted party is then free to seek reimbursement from the other parties, but the initial responsibility for damages is borne by him alone. If the other responsible parties are judgement-proof, that is, unable to pay, then the burden remains with the party initially targeted.

There are alternative forms that a joint and several liability rule can take. Kornhauser and Revesz (1989) have shown that a negligence-based joint and several liability rule is generally preferred to the existing apportionment rules used under strict liability, at least with regard to the choice of care. The rationale follows the logic of the results discussed above. Under a negligence rule, the prospect of being held liable for the entire amount of damages if negligent is sufficient inducement to parties to choose the efficient level of care. However, sharing under a strict liability-based apportionment rule creates a moral hazard problem that is similar to the problem created by strict liability in cases of bilateral care. Because parties do not bear the full social costs of their actions, they undertake too little care. In addition, the impact of joint and several liability depends on whether contribution is allowed and, in the context of CERCLA, on the litigation strategy followed by the government (Kornhauser and Revesz, 1989; Tietenberg, 1989).

Applications

While the above discussion has focused on general theoretical results regarding the efficiency of alternative rules, these results have a number of interesting policy implications. This section briefly describes some of the policy contexts in which the above models have been applied and shows how the general results can be used to guide public policy regarding environmental quality.

Oil spills

Oils spills are a frequent type of environmental accident and can result in large-scale damages, as exemplified by the Exxon Valdez spill. Several statutes impose strict liability for cleanup and damages on the responsible companies (Grigalunas and Opaluch, 1988). This is consistent with the theory discussed above, as shown by Cohen (1987) and Polinsky and Shavell (1992). Oil spills are an example of a predominantly unilateral accident with third party damages, where those damages can depend on both the care and the activity level of the polluter. In such a context, victim incentives are not an important concern and a strict liability rule will induce efficient care and activity/output levels, as well as efficient expenditures on cleanup. A negligence rule, on the other hand, will lead to too much output. In addition, a negligence rule imposes larger informational costs, since it requires monitoring of firms' actions to determine whether the firm was negligent and reduces the incentive to improve safety technology. However, when potential liability is large relative to the size of the firm's assets, then use of a negligence rule can reduce the probability of bankruptcy, which in turn increases the firm's incentive to avoid spills.

Farmer liability for groundwater contamination

Within the last decade, the discovery of agricultural pesticides in groundwater has led to concern about the environmental effects of these chemicals. However, because these products are approved for use by federal agencies and they are now a part of "normal" farming practices, there is also concern about holding farmers liable for groundwater contamination that results from their use. As a result, farmers have been granted exemptions from general liability requirements under CERCLA and some state laws (Mill, 1992).

The principles discussed above have been used to analyze the effect that farmer exemptions from liability for groundwater contamination will have on incentives (Segerson, 1990; Mill, 1992). If contamination is viewed simply as a case of third party damages, where the farmer is the injurer and the neighboring household is the victim, then the above analysis suggests that liability exemptions (i.e. imposing no liability on farmers) will lead to inefficient incentives for farmers to adjust both their care and their use levels, unless alternative mechanisms (such as regulation) can be used to ensure efficient incentives.[35]

However, it is likely that, if farmers are exempted from liability, responsibility for damages would revert to the manufacturer of the pesticide. Since the farmer and the manufacturer have a contractual relationship, there is the possibility of cost shifting between the two parties. In particular, if liability is imposed on manufacturers, they can shift some of the associated cost onto farmers through an increase in the pesticide price. As shown above, this will induce efficient decisions regarding the output or use level of pesticides. Thus, even if farmers do not face any direct liability for contamination from pesticides, their consumption level would be efficient. However, farmer exemptions may not induce efficient care by farmers. if manufacturers cannot tailor the price of their products to the care levels of the individual farmers, then they will have no mechanism for shifting the costs of insufficient care back to the farmer. It may be possible to induce efficient care by farmers, though, by making the exemption contingent on non-negligent use of the pesticide or coupling it with extensive regulation of pesticide applications.

Liability transfers

Many forms of environmental pollution involve a polluted site where some activity has contaminated the land or water on or near the site. Examples include contamination from waste disposal, from application of chemicals (e.g. pesticides) to the land, or from industrial "fallout" such as emissions that settle quickly or crumbling lead paint. In such cases, responsibility for cleanup often falls on the owner of the site and, if the site is sold, some or all of the liability can be transferred to the new owner. For example, CERCLA imposes cleanup liability on "potentially responsible parties," which include both past and present owners of the site. This category has been interpreted broadly enough to include lenders who loaned money to the owner, using the site as collateral, and subsequently served as a financial advisor to the owner or actually acquired the site through foreclosure. This potential for "lender liability" raised obvious concerns within the lending community, leading to recent regulations limiting lenders' exposure.

The efficiency implications of these transfers of liability to subsequent owners and lenders have been analyzed using a simple model of property transfers (Segerson, 1992, 1993). Since there is a contractual relationship between the buyer and the seller and between the owner and the lender, there is a mechanism for shifting costs between the two parties (through changes in the price of the land or in the interest rate). Thus, if shifting is perfect, liability transfers will have no efficiency effects since any changes in the allocation of liability will simply get capitalized (positively or negatively) into the price (or interest rate).

In practice, however, perfect shifting is unlikely to occur. One reason is the long time lags between the time contamination occurs, the time the land is sold, and the time cleanup is required. For example, in many cases, current contamination is the result of activities undertaken decades ago. With such long lags, the possibility that one or more of the parties will be judgment-proof at the time that cleanup is required increases. If these probabilities differ across the parties, due, for example, to differences in the nature, size, or assets of the party, then perfect shifting will not occur and the assignment of liability can affect buy/sell and abatement incentives. In such cases, whether liability transfers increase or reduce efficiency depends on the relative likelihoods that the parties will be judgment-proof.

Another reason that perfect shifting may not occur is imperfect information about the extent of the contamination of the land. For example, if there are buyer misperceptions or asymmetric information about the level of contamination, then buyers will not be able to adjust their willingness to pay to reflect the actual level of contamination and as a result perfect capitalization will again not occur. These information problems can create inefficiencies when liability is transferred from one party to another.

Industrial accidents

The now-famous Bhopal chemical release exemplifies the potentially devastating effects that industrial accidents can have. Such accidents often result from a combination of workers' actions (such as failure to follow proper operating procedures) and the firm's policies regarding safety equipment and procedures. Under civil proceedings, fines and penalties can be levied on the individual workers involved, the executive officers or managers, or the corporate entity. In addition, if criminal charges are filed, then incarceration of workers or executives can be sought.

The efficiency effects of alternative fine and incarceration policies have been examined by Segerson and Tietenberg (1992a, b) and Polinsky and Shavell (1993). Because of the contractual relationship between workers and the firm, there is the potential for shifting costs between the two through changes in the wage rate. If perfect shifting can occur, then fines on individuals and fines on the firm (corporate fines) are perfect substitutes. However, perfect shifting requires that the firm be able to monitor the workers' actions and/or base wages on the environmental consequences of those actions. In addition, when firm-level decisions also affect accidents, then the worker must be able to demand a higher wage when faced with a higher risk of environmental damages and thus higher penalties.

In practice, the conditions for perfect shifting (full observability and wage flexibility) may often not be satisfied. Long lag times in the discovery of environmental consequences or inflexibility in wage contracts may prevent wages from reflecting the risk of penalties. If wages are unrelated to safety considerations, then the problem reduces to one of joint torts between unrelated parties since no shifting can occur.

Incarceration is a possible substitute for, or complement to, the use of financial penalties. Since incarceration generates social costs that do not exist with fines (namely, the cost of running prisons), fines are generally preferred. However, in cases where imperfections in the legal system and imperfect shifting prevent efficiency through the use of fines alone, incarceration can promote efficiency. However, as shown by Segerson and Tietenberg (1992a), an incarceration rule based on negligence principles, where an individual would be subject to incarceration only if negligent, is preferred to one based on strict liability principles. The reason is that, as discussed above, a properly designed negligence rule will induce parties to be non-negligent. Thus, while there is the threat of incarceration, in theory no actual incarceration occurs, thereby saving on social costs. The preference for a negligence-based rule is also consistent with actual practice, since incarceration is generally limited to criminal convictions and presumably criminal behavior would be deemed negligent as well.

Summary and Conclusion

Legal liability has been used increasingly as a means of internalizing external environmental costs. Liability can take the form of payment to compensate victims for damages (as, for example, under common law) or payment of fines or damages to government agencies (as under many statutorily imposed liability rules or enforcement mechanisms). The two main types of rules are a strict liability rule and a negligence rule, where either can be coupled with a defense of contributory negligence. The efficiency effects of these rules depend upon whether there is a contractual relationship between the parties involved and whether victim incentives and output levels are important determinants of damages. In theory, if polluter payments are not used for direct victim compensation, then the use of liability can replicate the efficiency properties of Pigovian taxes that have led to strong support of such taxes by many economists, without the need to monitor behavior continuously. Since monitoring is difficult for many actions that contribute to environmental pollution, liability may be a more effective means of controlling such actions.

Nonetheless, there is reason for caution in advocating reliance on liability as a sole or even primary means of controlling environmental externalities. While there is some evidence that individuals and firms change their behavior in response to potential liability, liability acts only indirectly to affect behavior. Given the imperfections in the legal system, particularly the possibility that responsible parties will not be successfully sued for the full amount of damages, this indirect effect may be incomplete. In addition, when potential damages are large, as they are in many environmental externalities, use of liability (particularly strict liability) can impose large risks on firms that would not exist under a regulatory or *ex ante* Pigovian tax approach. For these reasons, it seems desirable to view liability as a complement to rather than a substitute for more traditional policies for controlling environmental externalities.

Notes

1 See, for example, Bohm and Russell (1985) for a discussion of traditional policies for controlling environmental externalities.
2 In some cases, liability may be viewed as a complement to rather than a substitute for Pigovian taxes or regulation. In fact, in many cases (such as workplace safety, consumer product safety, and hazardous waste disposal) liability is imposed on top of an extensive set of regulatory standards. See White and Wittman (1983), Shavell (1984a, b), Segerson (1986, 1987), and Johnson and Ulen (1986) for discussions of the use of regulation versus liability in controlling externalities.
3 We focus here on liability rules rather than property rules. See Bromley (1978) and Polinsky (1980b) for discussions of the distinctions between these approaches.
4 Of these, liability under CECLA has received the most attention. See "Developments in the Law: Toxic Waste Litigation" (1986) for a detailed description of CERCLA liability.
5 See, for example, Priest (1977), Rubin (1977), Goodman (1978), Cooter et al. (1979), and Blume and Rubinfeld (1982).
6 For limited evidence on the relationship between liability and prevention incentives, see Chelius (1976), Fishback (1987), and Ehrenberg (1988) for workplace safety, Higgins (1978) and Priest (1988) for product safety, Landes (1982) for motor vehicle accidents, Opaluch and Grigalunas (1984) for offshore oil leasing, and Ringleb and Wiggins (1990) for latent injuries.

7   Note that under strict liability the party must still somehow be "responsible" for the injury in order to be held liable. The notion of responsibility that is applied can vary, however. For example, in products liability, a party can be held responsible for damages if he was the producer of the product *and* it was defective. In other words, simply being the producer is not sufficient. (Holding producers responsible for damages from products that were not defective is referred to as "absolute liability.") In contrast, under CERCLA, producers of hazardous waste become potentially responsible parties simply by generating the waste.

8   Historically, negligence was the standard rule applied to tort cases. The use of strict liability was limited to damages from "ultra-hazardous" activities (e.g. blasting). It is only recently that the scope of strict liability has been expanded to other areas such as products liability (Epstein, 1980) and pollution liability (Opaluch, 1984).

9   In theoretical models of negligence, the due standard of care is generally assumed to be the efficient care level (e.g. Shavell 1980, 1987). In practice, however, the standard of care to which an injurer is held under the negligence rule can vary significantly. See Craswell and Calfee (1986) for the implications of uncertainty regarding the level standard of care.

10   In many ways, payment of liability under a negligence standard can be viewed as payment of a fine for failure to comply with a regulation or, more generally, for engaging in some undesirable activity. Likewise, payment under a strict liability rule can be viewed as payment of a fine for causing some undesirable effect. See Polinsky and Shavell (1984) and Segerson and Tietenberg (1992b) for analyses of the use of fines to control undesirable behavior, Cohen (1987) for a discussion of fines for undesirable events (oil spills), and Russell et al. (1986) for a general review of enforcement in the context of environmental law.

11   Because of the "all or nothing" nature of the contributory negligence defense, some states have substituted a defense of comparative negligence, under which negligent behavior by the victim reduces but does not eliminate the injurer's liability. See Rubinfeld (1987) for a discussion of comparative negligence.

12   There is also a distinction between unilateral risk, where only the victim suffers damages, and bilateral risk, where both the injurer and the victim suffer damages from their combined actions (Arlen, 1990). However, since with most environmental risks the victim's actions do not in turn impose damages on the polluter, we do not consider cases of bilateral risk here.

13   Other differences among the approaches are discussed in the references cited in note 2.

14   Details regarding many of the efficiency results are discussed in Brown (1973), Green (1976), Shavell (1980, 1987), and the references cited therein.

15   This allows the injurer's choice of care to affect both the probability of damages occurring and their magnitude. For example, the care taken in disposing of hazardous waste can affect both the probability of contaminating water supplies and the level of contamination that might occur.

16   This assumes risk neutrality (constant marginal utility of income) or that independent income distribution mechanisms are available. When such mechanisms are not available, then the liability rule must simultaneously try to achieve cost minimization and income distribution goals. See Miceli and Segerson (1993) for a discussion of efficient care in this context.

17   Throughout we ignore litigation costs. See Shavell (1982b) for a discussion of efficiency in the presence of litigation costs.

18   We assume here and throughout that parties are risk neutral. The implications of risk aversion are discussed briefly below. For a more detailed discussion, see Shavell (1982a).

19   The firm will not necessarily choose x^* if x_s exceeds x^*. In other words, if the due standard is set too high above the efficient level of care, the firm may choose to be negligent.

20   Alternatively, efficient activity levels could be induced by imposing sufficiently high penalties for failure to choose efficient levels. For example, if negligence could be defined in terms of choice of both care and activity level, then a negligence rule could induce efficient choices of both. However, in practice, negligence is generally defined only in terms of care levels.

21   Defining care and damages in this way implies that the care level can be chosen independently of the output level. The efficient level of care then simply minimizes per-unit costs, $c(x) + p(x)D(x)$. The results below would differ somewhat under a more general specification.

22   This is not true under statutorily imposed liability where payments are made to the government rather than to individuals, as, for example, under CERCLA. In addition, if liability takes the form of fines or penalties imposed on polluters, then victim compensation does not occur. Liability of this form is similar to simple enforcement schemes that impose penalties for accidents that occur or for failure to comply with regulations. See note 10.

23   With contributory negligence, it is important to distinguish between cases of simultaneous choice (where both parties choose their care levels simultaneously) and cases of sequential choice (where one party chooses first and the other party reacts). In cases of sequential choice, the due standard of care for the reacting party (generally the victim) could be defined in terms of either the efficient choice by the first party or the first party's actual choice. When defined in terms of actual choice, the first party can act strategically to shift some of the burden of care onto the second party. We consider here only the case of simultaneous choice. See Shavell (1983) for a detailed discussion of the sequential choice problem.

24   While not discussed in the text, the results for a negligence rule with a defense of contributory negligence would be the same as for a simple negligence rule. The defense would ensure that victims were non-negligent, implying that negligent injurers would be liable for damages. This potential liability would induce injurers to be non-negligent as well, leaving victims to bear all damages themselves, as under a simple negligence rule.

25   See Baram (1982), "Developments in the Law: Toxic Waste Litigation" (1986), and Dewees (1992) for general discussions of the implications of these issues, and Shavell (1984a) for a formal model incorporating some of them. Note, however, that efficiency can be restored by making injurer payments (awards) greater than damages when there is a successful suit, so that expected payments still equal expected damages. This is one rationale for the imposition of punitive damages.

26   If the government couples a Pigovian tax or negligence approach with a victim compensation fund, then, if the fund fully compensated for damages, the victim would not bear any risk. See Trauberman (1981) for a discussion of the use of victim compensation funds.

27   This assumes that the polluter knows the standard of care to which he will be held at the time he makes his care decision. In practice, the due standard of care may be uncertain. See Craswell and Calfee (1986) for a related discussion.

28   This result is analogous to the well-known result in public finance that the effect of an excise tax is independent of whether the buyer or the seller of the taxed good is legally responsible for paying the tax.

29   See Shavell (1980) and Polinsky and Rogerson (1983) for discussions of the impacts of misperceptions.

30   The difficulty in attributing damages to any one polluter may be due to true synergisms or to uncertainty about the source of a given pollutant.

31   Of course, it is possible that the victim's actions would still affect damages, in which case damages would be given by $D(x, y, z)$. Since victim incentives have been discussed above, we focus here on damages affected only by the actions of the two polluters.

32   This assumes that the polluters do not have a contractual relationship with each other. If a contractual relationship exists, then the externality can be internalized through the price. See the discussion above.

33   See Segerson (1988) for a discussion of such a pricing scheme using Pigovian-type taxes on ambient environmental quality and Miceli and Segerson (1991) for a similar scheme using a strict liability rule. Other mechanisms for solving the "moral hazard in teams" problem have been suggested as well, often in the context of nonpoint source water pollution. (See Meran and Schwalbe (1987) for a survey.) However, these mechanisms are not linked to legal institutions or doctrines.

34   For example, courts have interpreted CERCLA as imposing joint and several strict liability on potentially responsible parties. In principle, joint and several liability could also be coupled with a negligence rule.

35   Of course, other motivations, such as stewardship and avoidance of waste, may provide some incentives for undertaking care.

References

Arlen, Jennifer H. 1990: Re-examining liability rules when injurers as well as victims suffer losses. *International Review of Law and Economics*, 10, 233–9.

Baram, Michael S. 1982: *Alternatives to Regulation: Managing Risks to Health, Safety, and the Environment*. Lexington, MA: Heath.

Baumol, William J. and Oates, Wallace E. 1988: *The Theory of Environmental Policy*. Cambridge: Cambridge University Press.

Blume, Lawrence E. and Ribinfeld, Daniel L. 1982: The dynamics of the legal process. *Journal of Legal Studies*, 11, 405–19.

Bohm, Peter, and Russell, Clifford S. 1985: Comparative analysis of alternative policy instruments. In Allen V. Kneese and James L. Sweeney (eds), *Handbook of Natural Resource and Environmental Economics*, vol. I, Amsterdam: North Holland.

Bromley, Daniel W. 1978: Property rules, liability rules, and environmental economics. *Journal of Economic Issues,* 12, 43–60.

Brown, John Prather. 1973: Toward an economic theory of liability. *Journal of Legal Studies*, 2, 323–49.

Chelius, James R. 1976: Liability for industrial accidents: a comparison of negligence and strict liability systems. *Journal of Legal Studies*, 5, 293–309.

Cohen, Mark A. 1987: Optimal enforcement strategy to prevent oil spills: an application of a principal–agent model with moral hazard. *Journal of Law and Economics*, 30, 23–51.

Cooter, Robert. 1984: Prices and sanctions. *Columbia Law Review,* 84, 1523–60.

Cooter, Robert, Kornhauser, Lewis, and Lane, David. 1979: Liability rules, limited information and the role of precedent. *Bell Journal of Economics*, 10, 366–73.

Craswell, Richard, and Calfee, John E. 1986: Deterrence and uncertain legal standards. *Journal of Law, Economics and Organization*, 2, 279–303.

Developments in the law: toxic waste generation. 1986: *Harvard Law Review*, 99, 1458–1661.

Dewees, Donald. 1992: Tort law and the deterrence of environmental pollution. In T. H. Tietenberg (ed.), *Innovation in Environmental Policy: Economic and Legal Aspects of Recent Developments in Environmental Enforcement and Liability*, Cheltenham: Edward Elgar.

Ehrenberg, Ronald G. 1988: Workers' compensation, wages, and the risk of injury. In John F. Burton, Jr (ed.), *New Perspectives in Workers' Compensation*, Ithaca, NY: Cornell University ILR Press.

Epstein, Richard. 1980: *Modern Products Liability Law*. Westport, CT: Quorum.

Fishback, Price V. 1987: Liability rules and accident prevention in the workplace: empirical evidence from the early twentieth century. *Journal of Legal Studies*, 16, 305–28.

Goodman, John C. 1978: An economic theory of the evolution of the common law. *Journal of Legal Studies*, 7, 393–406.

Green, Jerry. 1976: On the optimal structure of liability laws. *Bell Journal of Economics*, 7, 553–74.

Grigalunas, Thomas A. and Opaluch, James J. 1988: Assessing liability for damages under CERCLA: a new approch for providing incentives for pollution avoidance? *Natural Resources Journal*, 28, 509–33.

Higgins, Richard S. 1978: Producers' liability and product-related accidents. *Journal of Legal Studies*, 7, 299–321.

Johnson, Gary V. and Ulen, Thomas S. 1986: Designing public policy toward hazardous waste: the role of administrative regulations and legal libaility rules. *American Journal of Agricultural Economics*, 68, 1266–71.

Kornhauser, Lewis A. and Revesz, Richard L. 1989: Sharing damages among multiple tortfeasors. *Yale Law Journal*, 98, 831–84.

Landes, Elisabeth M. 1982: Insurance, liability, and accidents: a theoretical and empirical investigation of the effects of no-fault accidents. *Journal of Law and Economics*, 25, 49–65.

Meran, G. and Schwalbe, U. 1987: Pollution control and collective penalties. *Journal of Institutional and Theoretical Economics*, 143, 616–29.

Miceli, Thomas J. and Segerson, Kathleen 1991: Joint liability in torts: marginal and inframarginal efficiency. *International Review of Law and Economics*, 11, 235–49.

Miceli, Thomas J. and Segerson, Kathleen 1993: Defining efficient care: the role of income distribution. Working Paper, Department of Economics, University of Connecticut.

Mill, John W. 1992: Agricultural chemical contamination of groundwater: an economic analysis of alternative liability rules. *University of Illinois Law Review*, 1991, 1135–67.

Opaluch, James J. 1984: The use of liability rules in controlling hazardous waste accidents: theory and practice. *Northeastern Journal of Agricultural and Resource Economics*, 14, 210–17.

Opaluch, James J. and Grigalunas, Thomas A. 1984: Controlling stochastic pollution events through liability rules: some evidence from OCS leasing. *Rand Journal of Economics*, 15, 142–51.

Polinsky, A. Mitchell. 1980a: Strict liability vs. negligence in a market setting. *American Economic Review*, 70, 363–7.

Polinsky, A. Mitchell. 1980b: On the choice between property rules and liability rules. *Economic Inquiry*, 18, 233–46.

Polinsky, A. Mitchell, and Rogerson, W. P. 1983: Product liability, consumer misperceptions, and market power. *Bell Journal of Economics*, 14, 581–9.

Polinsky, A. Mitchell, and Shavell, Steven 1984: The optimal use of fines and imprisonment. *Journal of Public Economics*, 24, 89–99.

Polinsky, A. Mitchell, and Shavell, Steven 1992: Optimal cleanup and liability after environmentally harmful discharges. Stanford Law School Working Paper 99.

Polinsky, A. Mitchell, and Shavell, Steven 1993: Should employees be subject to fines and imprisonment given the existence of corporate liability? *International Review of Law and Economics*, forthcoming.

Priest, George L. 1977: The common law process and the selection of efficient rules. *Journal of Legal Studies*, 6, 65–83.

Priest, George L. 1988: Products liability law and the accident rate. In R. E. Litan and C. Winston (eds), *Liability: Perspectives and Policy*, Washington, DC: Brookings Institution.

Ringleb, A. H. and Wiggins, S. N. 1990: Liability and large-scale, long-term hazards. *Journal of Political Economy*, 98, 574–95.

Rubin, Paul H. 1977: Why is the common law efficient? *Journal of Legal Studies*, 6, 51–63.

Rubinefeld, Daniel L. 1987: The efficiency of comparative negligence. *Journal of Legal Studies*, 16, 375–94.

Russell, Clifford S., Harrington, Winston, and Vaughan, William J. 1986: *Enforcing Pollution Control Laws*. Washington, DC: Resources for the Future.

Segerson, Kathleen. 1986: Risk sharing in the design of environmental policy. *American Journal of Agricultural Economics*, 68, 1261–5.

Segerson, Kathleen. 1987: Risk-sharing and liability in the control of stochastic externalities. *Marine Resource Economics*, 4, 175–92.

Segerson, Kathleen. 1988: Uncertainty and incentives for nonpoint pollution control. *Journal of Environmental Economics and Management*, 15, 87–98.

Segerson, Kathleen. 1990: Liability for groundwater contamination from pesticides. *Journal of Environmental Economics and Management*, 19, 227–43.

Segerson, Kathleen. 1992: Property transfers and environmental pollution: incentive effects of alternative policies. Working Paper, Department of Economics, University of Connecticut.

Segerson, Kathleen. 1993: Liability transfers: An economic assessment of buyer and lender liability. *Journal of Environmental Economics and Management*, forthcoming.

Segerson, Kathleen, and Tietenberg, Tom. 1992a: The structure of penalities in environmental enforcement: an economic analysis. *Journal of Environmental Economics and Management*, 23, 179–200.

Segerson, Kathleen, and Tietenberg, Tom. 1992b: Defining efficient sanctions. In T. H. Tietenberg (ed.), *Innovation in Environmental Policy: Economic and Legal Aspects of Recent Developments in Environmental Enforcement and Liability*, Cheltenham: Edward Elgar.

Shavell, Steven. 1980: Strict liability versus negligence. *Journal of Legal Studies*, 9, 1–25.

Shavell, Steven. 1982a: On liability and insurance. *Bell Journal of Economics*, 13, 120–32.

Shavell, Steven. 1982b: The social versus private incentive to bring suit in a costly legal system. *Journal of Legal Studies*, 11, 333–9.

Shavell, Steven. 1983: Torts in which victim and injurer act sequentially. *Journal of Law and Economics*, 26, 589–612.

Shavell, Steven. 1984a: A model of the optimal use of liability and safety regulation. *Rand Journal of Economics*, 15, 271–80.

Shavell, Steven. 1984b: Liability for harm vs. regulation of safety. *Journal of Legal Studies*, 13, 357–74.

Shavell, Steven. 1987: *Economic Analysis of Accident Law*. Cambridge, MA: Harvard University Press.

Spulber, Daniel F. 1985: Effluent regulation and long-run optimality. *Journal of Environmental Economics and Management*, 12, 103–16.

Tietenberg, Tom H. 1989: Indivisible toxic torts: the economics of joint and several liability. *Land Economics*, 65, 305–19.

Trauberman, Jeffrey. 1981: Compensating victims of tox substances pollution: an analysis of existing federal statutes. *Harvard Environmental Law Review*, 5, 1–29.

White, Michele J. and Wittman, Donald. 1983: A comparison of taxes, regulation, and liability rules under imperfect information. *Journal of Legal Studies*, 12, 413–25.

14

A Bargaining Framework for the Global Commons

Daniel W. Bromley and Jeffrey A. Cochrane

We are interested in this chapter with environmental problems that fall within the domain of the global commons (Bromley and Cochrane, 1993). The issue in the global commons is that global environmental problems persist because the actions of some individuals or governments in one location hold important implications for individuals and governments in other locations. Or, to put it somewhat differently, individual (and state) *interests* in one region of the globe are threatened by the status quo use of certain natural resources. It follows, logically, that there are global environmental *policy* problems because adversely affected individuals (and governments) have subsequently attempted to influence these activities in far-off places – either for certain self-interested reasons or because of genuine concern for the sustainability of life on earth over the long run.

We are here concerned to develop a framework with which to analyze such global environmental problems, with the policy objective of crafting a resource management regime that will *align the incentives* of those who for whatever reason seek a change in the status quo (i.e. those who will benefit from a change in the resource management regime) and those who find the status quo quite to their liking (i.e. those who will be adversely affected by a change in the status quo). Such an incentive realignment will, *inter alia*, align the interests of the two parties to this particular environmental policy problem. Incentive alignment is, in a phrase, *the policy problem*; one must find ways to align interests through realigning incentives for individual and group behaviors.

The Empirical Problem

For illustrative purposes, we focus here on one particular global environmental problem – greenhouse gas emissions, and the world's forests. The linkage between the earth's atmosphere and forests is direct and allegedly critical to sustaining life on earth. The issue is one of the interests of one group counterpoised to the interests of another. Those who harvest trees in the Amazon forest, for example, and those who wish to clear land for settlement stand united against the interests of those who would protect the forests for their own sake or because life as we know it cannot otherwise continue.

The problem is truly global in scope. For example, it has been estimated that "South and Southeast Asia contribute about 25 percent of the carbon dioxide emissions caused by burning wood, or about 6 percent of total CO_2 emissions" (Archer and Ichord, 1989, p. 13). Having said that, we must note that the industrial world, with its fossil-fuel-driven factories and automobiles, is a major contributor to the total annual production of greenhouse gases. In the starkest possible terms, it is not unreasonable to suggest that the wealthy citizens of the industrial north wish the Amazonian "lungs of the earth" to be protected, the better to process carbon dioxide production arising from our self-indulgent lifestyle. In less polite language, tropical forests comprise a free waste-processing facility for the rich – whether in Japan, Europe, or North America. It is crucial to understand how the lifestyle of the industrialized north impacts upon the nature and extent of problems faced in the tropics.

Human activities in the industrialized world result in the generation of large quantities of greenhouse gases. The tropical forests serve an important function of processing much of that production. However, land uses in the agrarian tropics threaten the sustainability of much of that forest cover. And so land use decisions in the agrarian nations are seen to be linked to activities in the industrialized nations of the world. In economic terms, current energy consumption practices in the industrialized world impose demands on the biosphere's resource services, and land use activities in the tropics threaten the sustainability of those resource services. Those in the industrialized north have an interest in protecting tropical forests as a means to process the large and increasing production of greenhouse gases.

The problem in simplified terms can be seen in figure 14.1. In 14.1(a), Gs represents total production of greenhouse gases from agrarian countries located generally in the southern hemisphere, while Gn represents total production of greenhouse gases from the more industrialized economies primarily in Europe, North America, Japan. For simplicity we will refer to these two general zones as North and South, or symbolically as N and S.

G^* represents the level of total production of greenhouse gases that will not change the chemistry of the atmosphere; call G^* the sustainable level of greenhouse gases. The figure depicts the production of gases from the industrial nations holding constant over the relevant time horizon. The figure also depicts the production of greenhouse gases in the agrarian

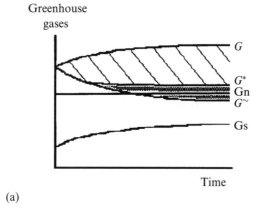

(a)

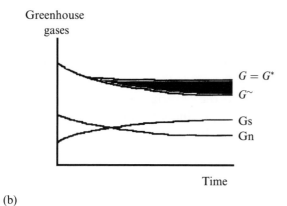

(b)

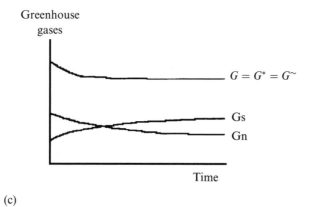

(c)

Figure 14.1   Greenhouse gas emissions over time.

South increasing as those nations undertake economic advance, as factories become more prevalent, and as automobiles become more ubiquitous. Without significant technical change in the developing world, increased reliance on fossil fuels there holds serious implications for total loadings of carbon gases. For instance:

> China's ratio of CO_2 emissions to gross national product (GNP) is roughly five times that of Japan.... If China were to achieve even 60% of Japanese efficiency and carbon intensity levels in its new energy-producing and energy-consuming infrastructure, it could improve this ratio substantially in a relatively short time. The one major hurdle is obtaining the technical information, management assistance, and capital required to promote more efficient and less polluting supply and use of energy and other natural resources.
>
> (Nitze, 1990, p. 608)

The line labeled G shows the total production of greenhouse gases over time (where $G = \text{Gn} + \text{Gs}$). The diagonal-lined region in figure 14.1(a) shows the excess production of gases with respect to the earth's assimilative capacity ($G > G^*$). Here one sees the threat to both the industrialized North and the agrarian South. Efforts by an international body to impose a global production limit at G^* would meet opposition from the citizens of the industrialized nations because it would threaten their lifestyle; they would argue that it is the increased production from the newly industrialized nations of the agrarian South that has "created the problem." Similarly, a limit on total production is of considerable concern to those in the agrarian South because it would mean that the allocation of the total production would give the more favorable situation to the industrialized North; citizens here would argue that the rich wish to impose a limit on their (the southerner's) industrial ambitions.

There is something even more ominous in figure 14.1(a). The line $G^\sim$ traces out the earth's assimilative capacity for greenhouse gases under the assumption that tropical forests are cleared and burned as part of the industrialization of the agrarian South. That is, G^* is no longer the long-run sustainable capacity to process greenhouse gases; the assimilative capacity is now driven down to $G^\sim$ by the clearing of Amazonian forests. The dotted region in 14.1(a) shows the processing deficit that results from changes in land use in the agrarian nations of the South. Together, the two marked areas in the figure – between G and $G^\sim$ – indicate the excess atmospheric loadings of greenhouse gases of potential significance for global climate change.

In figure 14.1(b) we illustrate a policy setting in which excess production is eliminated by a program in which the industrialized North reduces total production of greenhouse gases at the same rate as the newly industrializing agrarian South increases its total production. In this setting the total production of greenhouse gases from the two regions matches the predicted assimilative capacity for greenhouse gases ($G = G^*$). But notice that as the South industrializes it reduces the forest cover such that the actual processing capacity is less than the predicted processing capacity ($G^\sim < G^* = G$); a processing deficit still exists. Also notice that, as drawn, the industrialized North, because of stricter environmental policies, has brought its total production of greenhouse gases below that in the newly industrialized South.

In figure 14.1(c) we drop the assumption of massive forest clearing in the industrializing South, or we assume that compensating reforestation occurs in the north, so G^* remains the assimilative capacity for greenhouse gases and total global production is brought in line with that capacity. The hard part, of course, remains. And that concerns how to restructure the international resource management regime such that the happy results of 14.1(c) are realized. There are two aspects of this challenge. First, there is the problem in obtaining agreement between these two artificial regions "North" and "South." That is difficult enough. The second problem will concern changing behaviors of individuals within the two regions. We prefer to avoid here a discussion of divergent interests among countries in the two regions and so will regard the "North" (N) as one state and the "South" (S) as another. This simplification does not change the nature of the basic bargaining problem, but it certainly simplifies it by reducing the number of units in the policy hierarchy.

To simplify somewhat further, the policy problem of the global commons is to find a set of incentives that will perfectly align the interests of individuals in the two regions under consideration here – North and South. That alignment of interests will, in fact, manifest itself in terms of a convergence of individual choices that will reduce two tendencies. The first tendency is the one that threatens the earth's capacity to process greenhouse gases. In this chapter we will regard the world's forests as essential to that global assimilative capacity. For simplicity we will generally focus on the problem of deforestation in the South, though there is no technical reason why a compensating reforestation could not occur in the North. The second tendency is the one that threatens to increase the total production of greenhouse gases in both regions of the world. Notice that individuals in both regions are inextricably linked by the physical aspects of atmospheric chemistry – more production of greenhouse gases by individuals in the North (or in the South for that matter) places an ever-increasing economic value on the role of forests.

Put somewhat differently, with a higher total production of greenhouse gases in both hemispheres, a reduced assimilative capacity will impose greater costs on the world in terms of accelerated climate change. Or, to avert that climate change, the two regions will be forced to undertake expensive alternatives to the processing capacity of the forests. Thus, continued reduction of the Amazonian forest with total production of greenhouse gases held constant, and without any compensating reforestation outside the Amazon, would carry nontrivial costs as well.

Notice our assumption that the tropical and other forests provide a resource service at a cost significantly less than the service could be provided through any alternative technology. The only "cost" of using the forests is that we must preserve them intact. The cost then becomes the alternative uses of the forested area rendered impossible because of the presence of the forest. We are abstracting from the role of tropical forests as important assets in their own right, quite apart from their role as processors of greenhouse gases.

The policy problem requires the introduction of some action-forcing event. For in the absence of this event there is no reason why the status quo resource management regime could not continue despite increasing evidence of higher concentrations of greenhouse gases. This particular decision problem will begin with the assumption that one of the governments (either N or S) determines that it is desirable to stabilize the production of greenhouse gases such that total production is brought into balance with the earth's processing capacity. This is shown in figure 14.1(c) where $G = G^*$. This decision could be arrived at autonomously by the government of one of the countries, or it could be "forced" upon that government by a rising political force of individuals within the country. We note that in November 1990 in Geneva a number of governments of the industrialized world, for whatever reason, agreed to stabilize total production of greenhouse gases.

Agency Theory and Bilateral Negotiations

It will prove helpful to apply the economic model of agency to this problem of the global commons. The usual examples in agency theory concern the problems of team production where monitoring costs of individual effort are high. Also, the employment contract – whether or not there is a team – is the essence of a principal–agent problem. In what follows we will apply agency theory both to the relationship between individuals and the state and to the relationship between one state and another.

The logic for this approach is straightforward. The essence of the state is to define a choice domain for atomistic decision makers such that the aggregate of millions of independent choices is seen to be in the "public interest" – whatever that is defined to be. All of the celebration of Smithian *laissez-faire* unfortunately abstracts from the ineluctable fact that markets cannot function without a clear and precise articulation of who owns what (property rights), who may do what to whom (civil and criminal law), and who must pay whom to have their interest protected (again, property rights and the law of contract). So called "free markets" are clearly not free of collective definition of the range of choice open to market participants, and it distorts analysis of public policy to imagine otherwise (Bromley, 1989).

Assume that it is the government of N that seeks a new *resource management regime* to accomplish sustainable production of greenhouse gases as in figure 14.1(c). In agency theory we talk of the *principal* and of the *agent*. It is the problem for the principal to establish an incentive regime that will align the interests of the agent with those of the principal. Consider a simple example. A family may wish to have its garden weeded by a teenager but will be away for three weeks while the task is to be accomplished. The owner of the garden is the principal, the teenager is the agent. The owner's problem is to design an incentive scheme that will align the interests of the teenage with the owner's interests. Put somewhat more directly, the gardener wishes to design a system of compensation to the teenager such that she will behave exactly as the owner wishes in carrying out the task.

Imagine the garden owner says to the teenager: "I will pay you $1.00 per day to weed my garden. When I return in three weeks I expect to find the garden free of weeds. I will then pay you for the total days you worked." It should be obvious that there is an *incentive alignment problem* inherent in this scheme. The gardener's interests are to have the garden weeded at the least possible cost. The teenager's interests are to earn as much money as possible from this transaction. One does not have to assume complete dishonesty to imagine that the youngster has a strong incentive to inflate, even if a little, the actual time it took to weed the garden. It is also possible that the aggressiveness with which she carries out the weeding will tend to be influenced by this payment scheme; she may report days worked honestly, but how hard did she actually work during those days? This payment scheme leaves the gardener bearing all the uncertainty.

An alternative payment scheme, though most impractical, would be to pay her "piece rate," that is, per weed pulled. The monitoring costs of this approach are clearly prohibitive. The obvious compromise is to pay her for the entire job. Under this scheme both the teenager and the owner of the garden share a little of the uncertainty. The gardener must estimate, from his own experience, how many hours the job might take. The teenager must calculate the same thing. In order for her to maximize her earnings per hour, the teenager has an incentive to work fast. However, the gardener has an incentive not underestimate the time it will take – otherwise the teenager will not accept the job, or if she does accept it she may work so fast as to be careless. A compromise is reached that aligns the interests of both. The gardener's interest is in having a weed-free garden and having paid a "reasonable price" for it; the teenager's interest is in earning her "opportunity wage" yet being able to undertake the weeding with enough slack to make sure that the job is well done. It should come as no surprise that many such services – leaf raking, house painting, and vegetable harvesting come immediately to mind – operate precisely on this basis. The policy problem in garden weeding is to align the interests of the principal and the agent. Agency theory is concerned with precisely this problem, whether applied to gardeners, home owners, the owners of large firms, or state governments.

To return to the global commons problem, consider the government of N which in fact faces two "agency" problems. The first is to induce its own citizens to alter their behavior with respect to activities pertinent to the production of greenhouse gases. Call this the *domestic policy problem* for N. The second agency problem concerns the government of S. That is, how can the government of N induce the government of S to alter the choice environment for the individual citizens (individual decision makers) in S? Call this the *international policy problem*. Notice that, in fact, this is a *hierarchical agency problem* in which there are two "agents" – the government of S, and the citizens in S. That is, the government of N is the principal with respect to its own citizens as well as with respect to the government of S. Notice that the government of S, in addition to being an agent with respect to the government of N, is itself a principal with respect to its own citizens (who are, in turn, agents to the government of S).

Within this hierarchical problem, we assign to the government of N the role of ultimate principal, recognizing that wealth affords N greater freedom in action on the world stage. Thus the action-forcing event that leads to a policy initiative is assumed most likely to be found in N. This event may be the discovery and revelation by scientists in N that trends in the levels of greenhouse gases in the atmosphere have serious implications for life, particularly in the industrialized world. This revelation forces the issue to the forefront of public attention in N, resulting in the declaration by the government of N that it seeks to change the status quo ante resource management regime in which greenhouse gases are produced in abundance.

While there may be general public concern about the production of greenhouse gases, this problem is assumed here to be of scant significance to many of the *individual* citizens of both N and S. This is because the actions of any single individual contribute only minimally to the problem. It is the cumulative effect that is of concern, but there is no great incentive for any particular individual to alter behavior. Indeed, there may be strong incentives in other directions, particularly in S where the government may be committed to a policy of increased economic development at the expense of the tropical forests (and their processing services), a policy that would also increase the production of greenhouse gases through accelerated industrialization.

As the principal in this principal–agent problem, the government of N is faced not only with the challenge of modifying atomistic choices within N, but also of doing the same within S. The difference, however, lies in the relative inability of the government of N to develop direct policies to modify behavior in S. Generally, in the absence of direct physical force by N against S, the government of N may only develop policies that affect S at the border, and must work through the government of S on any policies that require enforcement or other action within the borders of S. The government of N is therefore faced with both a domestic and an international problem.

The Domestic Policy Problem

Initially, certain individual actors in N are free to behave in a way that is in total disregard for the interests of others in N who care about the total production of greenhouse gases. In more formal language, we would say that those who are concerned about high production of greenhouse gases have *no rights*, while those well served by the status quo resource management regime have *privilege* (Bromley, 1991). By privilege we mean individuals are able to act without regard for the interest of others. Should those alarmed about greenhouse gases go to court to prevent continued emissions the court would say, in effect, "sorry, there is no law against the production of greenhouse gases. You have *no right* to seek relief."

Another way to put the status quo ante resource management regime is to note that the air is an *open access resource* in which anyone who wishes to partake of its services may do so freely and without restraint. The costs that arise from the emission of greenhouse gases are of scant concern to those responsible for such emissions. Of course, some of the citizens in N are concerned about such emissions and have undertaken to pressure their government to change the status quo ante resource regime. As noted, the court sent them away with the assertion that they had no right to prevent such emissions.

With respect to greenhouse gas emissions, the domestic policy problem can be defined in terms of a change in the resource regime over air such that those now in a situation of *no right* acquire a *right* and those now with *privilege* are given, instead, *duty*. That is, the legal structure of the economy is altered such that those with privilege over air emissions acquire a duty to consider the harm their emissions are causing others. The state intervenes in the "public interest," however that may be defined in the political arena. For example, the state may establish limits on gas emissions, or ban them altogether. It may require that compensation be paid in the event that greenhouse gases are emitted, perhaps in the form of taxes paid to the general treasury. The state may also offer subsidies to encourage the transition to cleaner technologies. In the language of resource regimes, through these various actions the state creates rights and corresponding duties: a right to be free of emissions and a duty to refrain from emitting them, a right to compensation and a duty to pay it, a right to receive funds for the purchase of cleaner equipment and a duty to make those funds available in the form of taxes. In each case the aim of government is to alter the structure of the resource regime so as to realign incentives and encourage particular actions.

Consider the example of air emissions policy in California, which incorporates a variety of measures to realign incentives. A ceiling on greenhouse gas emissions was established for firms, but the government permitted firms to meet this ceiling in a variety of ways. The Amoco oil company was able to delay reduction in its own emissions by purchasing older, heavily polluting automobiles from individuals. This enabled the individuals to purchase more modern, cleaner cars. By eliminating Amoco's privilege to emit greenhouse gases, and by replacing that privilege with a duty to respect newly established rights to be free of such gases, the government recreated the economic environment in which Amoco operated. The government did not, however, simplify specify the levels of gases to be emitted by particular Amoco factories. Instead, it specified a broad emissions limit that Amoco was free to meet in a variety of ways. Amoco found it less expensive under this regime to encourage the elimination of emissions from older polluting automobiles than to refit its refineries. The objective of the government was met at a presumably lower cost to firms and individuals than would have been the case had the government simply mandated that all emissions reductions take place in Amoco factories.

In the agency examples of the preceding section, the principal was able to manipulate the actions of the agent by offering or withholding payments of particular forms. It was the form of payment that was of particular interest, since by altering the form of payment the principal was able to minimize the costs of monitoring and enforcement. In domestic policy, the government of N is faced with a similar problem. While it can enact a new resource regime with new rights and duties, the form of this regime will have important implications for monitoring and enforcement. Consider a hypothetical example in which the government fails to give adequate attention to monitoring and enforcement costs. Suppose government requires individuals to stop driving their automobiles once a particular quantity of emissions in a given year has been emitted. The advantages of cheating, particularly for the poor who could not easily afford to purchase cleaner cars, would be great. To enforce such a regime, the government would need meters on every vehicle, inspections to ensure that vehicles were not operated beyond the mandated limit, and additional inspections to ensure that vehicle operators did not tamper with emissions meters. Clearly such a regime would be prohibitively costly and therefore untenable.

As an alternative to emissions management at the level of each individual vehicle owner, government might enact a regime that alters incentive at the level of the vehicle manufacturer. Consider the example of mandated catalytic converters on automobiles in the United States. Government requires these devices to be installed at the factory to reduce emissions, and the presence of the devices can easily be monitored before vehicles are delivered to consumers. Of course the monitoring and enforcement problem is not completely eliminated. Not only must frequent inspection of exhaust be part of the new regime, but the government may also levy stiff fines on those who disconnect (or tamper with) their vehicle's catalytic converter. These inspections and litigations entail costs that must be paid to maintain the resource regime.

The International Policy Problem

Two general strategies are available to N at the international level. One involves the creation of an overarching authority that can mandate and enforce policies in both N and S. The authority of this supra-state would supersede that of the governments of N and S, and the policy actions available to this supra-state would be little different from those envisioned in the preceding section. The hierarchical nature of the agency problem would be eliminated, since this overarching authority would not need to work through the governments of N and S but could presumably implement policies directly affecting individuals in both states. Of course the present nonexistence of such a supra-state, and the difficulties faced by such international bodies as the United Nations, is testimony to the difficulties of establishing an authority to which presently largely sovereign states would be willing to yield their sovereignty.

In the absence of a supra-state authority, the problem of the global commons remains hierarchical. In order to effect changes in the behavior of individuals in S, the government of N has little recourse but to work through the government of S. The methods amenable to domestic policy generally are not available. New methods of incentive alignment must be found. The policies within N must be coordinated with policies between N and S, giving additional consideration to the problems S will then face in implementing such policies at the level of its own citizens. We consider two aspects of this problem, the first having to do with efficiency concerns and the second related to a feasible hierarchical bargaining solution.

Efficiency

In figure 14.2 we consider the relationship between actions in N and S. Consider figure 14.2(a). Here we show, as in Figure 14.1, the earth's sustainable assimilative capacity for greenhouse gases, G^*. The curve Gn shows the emissions trajectory in N assuming that effective domestic policies are instituted. Notice that the policy path in N is a function of the policy path in S, and vice versa. That is, if the total production of greenhouse gases (G^*) has been identified as the policy target, then it follows, by definition, that $Gs^*|Gn = G^* - Gn$, where Gs^* is the policy target level of greenhouse gas production in S and G^* is fixed because the area of tropical and other forests remains constant at its current level. We will assume for now that an integral part of any policy agreement between N and S entails maintenance of the earth's present assimilative capacity at present levels through preservation of existing forests, and we therefore leave it to others to argue the questionable merits of reliance upon "backstop" technologies that might replace the earth's forests. We also assume for the moment that S responds to the emissions level of N in order to meet the policy objective G^*, leaving aside for the moment why S might be inclined to do so.

The distance G^*-Gn between the two curves in figure 14.2(a) represents the assimilative capacity for greenhouse gases that is available for use by individuals in S. Notice that, should the government of N undertake a more lax policy with respect to greenhouse gases, then the production path Gn' becomes relevant. The obvious implication is that total production of greenhouse gases from S must be significantly less under Gn' than would be possible were Gn followed in N. That is, total "allowable" production of greenhouse gases from S is not given by

$$Gs^*|Gn' = G^* - Gn'$$

where Gn' $\geq$ Gn.

These two situations are plotted in figure 14.2(b) as $Gs^*|Gn$ and as $Gs^*|Gn'$. These two functions suggest a policy domain for the two governments. If we think of the function Gn' as depicting the most lax feasible policy outcome in N, and the function Gn as depicting the most severe yet still feasible policy outcome in N, then these two outcomes represent, in essence, the range of bargaining open to the government of N in its discussions with the government of S. By similar logic, the government of S will regard the two functions $Gs^*|Gn$ and $Gs^*|Gn'$ as defining its own bargaining domain, given the two constraints that (i) the total area of tropical and other forests remains at its current level and (ii) S responds to N in order to met the G^* policy.

Another way to regard this bargaining domain between $Gs^*|Gn$ and $Gs^*|Gn'$ is to consider the difference in costs that will fall upon individuals

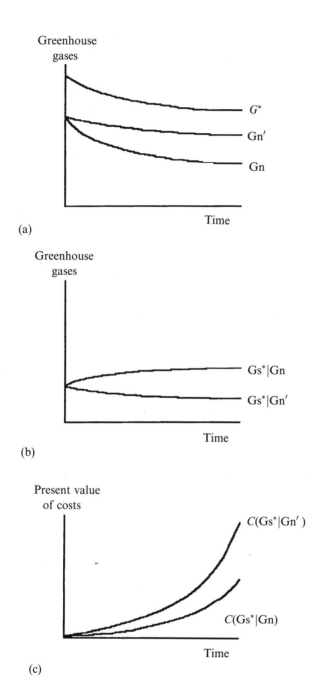

Figure 14.2 The international dimension of greenhouse gas emissions.

in S should the governments of both N and S attempt to establish a resource management regime in S as a function of Gn' rather than as a function of Gn. We show that extra cost in figure 14.2(c). We may expect that this magnitude represents the *minimum willingness to accept compensation* on the part of the government of S for adopting a sustainable resource management regime with respect to greenhouse gases. That is, if the government of S is to preserve the area of topical forests, and also to induce or require its citizens to reduce the production of greenhouse gases, then it will insist that the government of N recognize the magnitude of its costs from pursuing a more stringent policy functionally related to the domestic policy that N itself pursues.

Notice in figure 14.2(c) that $C(Gs^*|Gn)$, the lower of the two curves, represents the baseline costs within S of maintaining the tropical forests in their rather pristine condition to provide resource services for processing greenhouse gases. This lower-cost scenario is based on the assumption of a Gn emissions policy in N, so that S is required to absorb the costs of preserving its forests but can pursue a lax policy toward its own greenhouse gas emissions. If, however, N pursues a less stringent emissions policy of Gn', then S will be forced to absorb higher costs of controlling its own emissions in order to meet the overall emissions policy of G^*. These higher costs in S are represented by the upper curve in figure 14.2(c). The difference in costs is the extra amount S is likely to demand from N if the government of N fails to impose upon its own citizens a strict regime to reduce emissions, that is, if N fails to do all it can to solve the problem of greenhouse gas emissions.

The bargaining domain for the governments of both N and S is constructed in figure 14.3. In 14.3(a) we show the present-valued costs of various levels of reduction in the total loadings (production) of greenhouse gases from S. Notice that, as greenhouse gas emissions are permitted to increase along the horizontal axis, the present-valued cost of emissions reduction decreases along the vertical axis. We have also indicated the fixed cost to S of maintaining its tropical forests at a level Ts. In 14.3(b) we show the same relationship for N, though N is assumed not to incur costs of maintaining its own forests. The sustainable emissions policy G^* is indicated for both states and is a function of the forest cover Ts. Thus, if we were to alter the level of forest cover in S, then the positioning of G^* would also have to change.

The relationship between figures 14.2 and 14.3 is critical for policy formulation between N and S with respect to the global commons. This can be seen by placing figures 14.3(a) and 14.3(b) together. Figure 14.3(a) is simply inverted and placed on top of 14.3(b) such that the cost curves are tangent and such that the horizontal dimension is equal to the policy limit G^*; the reason for associating the two panels in this fashion will become clear shortly. Along the lower abscissa (NG^*), the far right point (G^*)

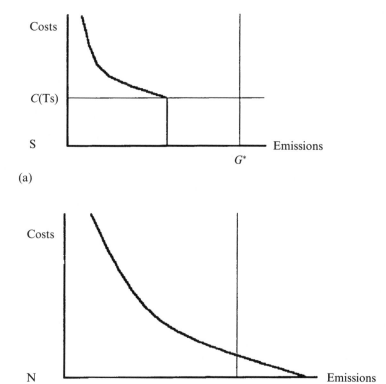

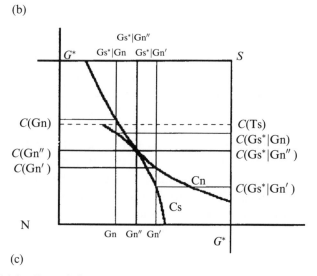

Figure 14.3 Bargaining over reductions in greenhouse gas emissions.

shows the situation if N were able to use all of the assimilative capacity for greenhouse gases without the individuals in S having any access to that assimilative capacity. Similarly, along the upper abscissa (SG*)we see the situation again at G^* if S were able to use the entire assimilative capacity of the atmosphere without any loadings from N. The left and right ordinates show, respectively, the present-valued costs to N and S from reductions in their citizens' production of greenhouse gases.

We can next consider the two levels of production of greenhouse gases within N from before. We continue to assume that S will maintain its forests at a level Ts as in 14.3(a), now represented by the broken horizontal line in 14.3(c). We also continue to assume that S will respond to emissions from N so as to meet the policy objective G^*. Thus emissions from S are determined by emissions from N. If N pursues a rather lax greenhouse gas policy, earlier referred to as Gn′, it will require S to pursue a very restrictive policy of Gs*|Gn′ with implied costs for S of C(Gs*|Gn′). This domestic policy regime is very expensive for S (reading down along the right ordinate), but cheap for N (reading up along the left ordinate), since N's costs will be only C(Gn′). Alternatively, should N pursue a more restrictive domestic policy regime, one earlier referred to as Gn, then N's costs will be much higher, C(Gn), while costs to S will be considerably less, C(Gs*|Gn).

The cooperative efficient policy to pursue is the one in which the marginal (*not total*) costs of reduction in loadings are the same between the two countries. Here efficiency is defined to be that level of emissions in the two states where neither is willing to pay the other the amount required to induce the other to reduce emissions further. Since the curves Cn and Cs are the total costs of abatement of loadings, we know that their slopes are the marginal cost of abatement of greenhouse gases. We also know there is a unique point at which the slopes of Cn and Cs are identical when G^* is satisfied (i.e. along a vertical line through the box). This is also the point of tangency between Cn and Cs when 14.3(a) and 14.3(b) are aligned as we have done in 14.3(c). That point yields the efficient level of reduced production of greenhouse gases for the two states. For N the efficient level of loadings (or, conversely, of abatement) is at Gn″ and hence the efficient level for reductions in loadings in S is at Gs*|Gn″. Here the costs for N are given by C(Gn″), while the costs to S are given by C(Gs*|Gn″). There is no other possible allocation of loadings and abatement between the two countries that will produce a lower total cost. Of course "efficiency" as determined here is silent with respect to the capacity of each of the two regions to incur these costs of reduced loadings.

Feasibility

And this brings us back to our hierarchical principal–agent problem. We have repeatedly assumed that S will adhere to a policy of maintaining its forests at a level Ts, and will also respond to N's emissions level in order to satisfy the policy G^*. But it may not be in the interest of S to do so unless some further action on the part of N is forthcoming.

We assume that N is the principal in seeking a new resource management regime more to its liking, and that the government of S is the agent. But of course the government of S is also the principal *vis-à-vis* its own citizens. The nascent resource management regime, in which N must induce the citizens and government of S to incur costs of $C(Gs|Gn'')$, requires some sustainable agreement whereby N can count on S making sure that its new environmental policies both sustain the tropical forests and also induce or require its citizens to reduce their aggregate production of greenhouse gases.

As noted earlier, unlike domestic policy for N (or for S), in international policy there is no authority system that can force the government of S to abide by the interests of the government of N. But of course the two governments have mutual interests, and the problem here is to explore the nature and extent of those interests. Let us assume that the government of S has scant interest in the preservation of tropical biomass. To preserve such expanses of forest may deprive the government of the chance to earn large amounts of foreign exchange. It may also force the government to undertake other economic development policies to address the problems of landless peasants clamoring for new land. Indeed, to preserve the tropical forests may require the government of S to expropriate the large estates of wealthy ranchers and then to redistribute such lands to the landless. The tropical frontier provides, as it were, a "safety valve" allowing the government of S to offer land to the poor without having to confront the landed gentry.

Preserving the present tropical forest cover is largely an objective of the principal, not the agent. The problem is that the forest of interest to the principal (N) lies within the sovereign territory of the agent (S), though of course it must be remembered that this "problem" would not be so pressing had the principal not already largely eliminated its own domestic forests. We have assumed that there is no compulsion within S to preserve the forest at the level Ts specified in figures 14.3(a) and 14.3(c). We reproduce figure 14.3(c) as figure 14.4(a) but with the addition of a new lower level of tropical forest cover, Ts−, to be maintained by S. The government of N could induce S to preserve its forests at the higher level Ts through payments of $C(Ts) - C(Ts-)$. A further payment of $C(Gs^*|Gn'') - C(Ts)$ would also be required to induce S to reduce emissions to the efficient level, here assuming that S would otherwise be unwilling to undertake any emissions reduction measures. Finally, N would incur costs of $C(Gn'')$ to induce or compel its own citizens to reduce emissions to the efficient sustainable level.

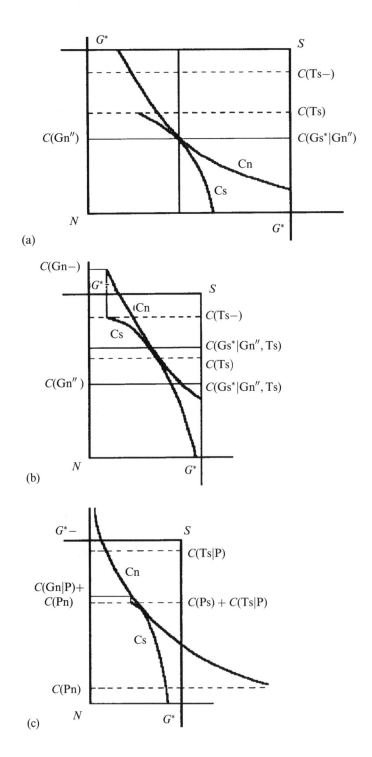

Figure 14.4 Enhanced forest preservation in the tropics.

Figure 14.4(b) indicates the outcome if a policy of payments to S by N is not adopted. Without payments, S permits deforestation to occur until Ts−. Because of the reduced forest cover, emissions can only be sustained at a level $G^{*}-$, which results in a policy-domain box of smaller dimensions. To achieve its objective of sustainability in emissions without any payments to S, N must now incur costs of $C(Gn-)$ to induce its own citizens to reduce emissions. Note that if $C(Gn-)$ is greater than $C(Gs^{*}|Gn'') - C(Ts-) + C(Gn'')$, then it would behoove N to induce S to preserve its forests. Of course we could have as easily drawn 14.4(b) such that the cost curve for S intersected the $C(Ts-)$ line outside of the box, that is, such that, without payments from N, S alone would emit more than the sustainable quantity of greenhouse gases. The latter scenario would presumably have much harsher consequences for N, perhaps requiring N to institute a policy of reforestation to compensate.

The government of N need not rely exclusively on policies of inducement toward S, however. Figure 14.4(c) portrays a punitive policy, perhaps including trade sanctions, imposed by N on S if S refuses to preserve its forests without inducements. Under the assumption that the volume of trade with S is fairly inconsequential to N but of great importance to S, the panel suggests high costs of $C(Ps)$ to S from the sanctions but only the smaller costs of $C(Pn)$ to N. Note the assumption implicit in the drawing of 14.4(c) that S would preserve even less forest once sanctions are imposed, further reducing the dimensions of the policy-domain box. We have abstracted from numerous additional costs that might fall upon N from this further reduction in tropical forest cover, such as any intrinsic or existence value of the forest to citizens of N, or any pharmaceutical value that might eventually obtain from destroyed species. These additional costs weaken the credibility of N's threat of punitive sanctions. The costs of this policy of sanctions to N (if imposed) are at least $C(Pn) + C(Gn|P)$, since it is assumed that S will not cooperate with N while sanctions are in force. The hope of N, of course, must be that its threat is credible. S would then find it advantageous to avoid punitive sanctions by preserving its forests voluntarily, while N would incur little if any cost. To the extent that N is likely to incur great costs of its own in imposing sanctions on S, the threat to S is likely not to be perceived as credible.

All things considered, the policy suggested by figure 14.3 seems the most palatable, since it preserves the forest and entails a normatively plausible transfer of funds from the wealthy N to the presumably less-wealthy S. It is also the path that preserves the earth's diminishing forests at present levels, and thus takes into account a wide variety of benefits – intrinsic, pharmaceutical, and others – that accrue to all the earth's citizens when those forests are maintained. It surely does not seem unreasonable to suppose that the government of S might seek a substantial increase in

economic assistance so as to promote economic opportunities for its
landless poor. That is, foreign assistance may be useful in making the
seemingly difficult choice between expropriating haciendas and savaging
the forest. Similarly, if preserving the forests implies confronting the
powerful timber concessionaires then it is quite possible that payments
from N could be used to redirect these contractors into other lines of work.

It may happen, of course, that the domain of mutual interests is too
restricted to accomplish what the principal (N) seeks; perhaps the political
pressure on the government of S to continue its timber concessions is simply
too overwhelming to be overcome by payments (or policy concessions)
from N. If the exported timber from such practices is being imported into
N, the solution is straightforward. The government of N could simply
decide to ban exports from S, which would be consistent with the scenario
proposed in figure 14.4(c). If, however, the timber is exported to a third
country, then the government of N will need to involve that third region in
the negotiations. Such punitive policies are the last resort for the simple
reason that they tend to create "winners" and "losers." The essence of long-
run international policy is to seek outcomes that allow all governments to
interpret their new position as that of a "winner."

Agency Theory and the Global Commons

Agency theory provides a set of organizing concepts that allow us to
formulate the essence of the policy problem in the global commons. We see
the important difference between domestic policy in the two states, and we
see how the international sphere is informed by – indeed defined by – the
domestic component of the two states. The interests of the principal drive
the bargaining process, and yet we see that the domain for new
institutional arrangements is, in reality, entirely dependent upon the
interests and importance of the individual citizens of the two polities. It is a
mistake to imagine that governments simply order their citizens around;
indeed the failures of the economy in the former USSR suggest that, unless
governments get the incentives right, atomistic behavior can be positively
counterproductive.

The policy problem in the global commons is to realign interests
through the redesign of domestic and international institutional arrangements such that new behaviors result. It is not a matter of *directing*
individual decision makers, for such a regime requires enormous
monitoring costs. These monitoring costs are made necessary by the
very powerful incentives for defection from the newly imposed regime. A
dirigiste approach will certainly fail.

Rather, the ideal policy is one that incorporates policies of inducements
as much as possible in order to modify, at the margin, atomistic behaviors

among millions of individuals. When such behaviors of relevance for the production and processing of greenhouse gases are correctly modified, then the problem of the global commons will be solved. There is no magic wand that will produce a new international regime, nor is there (at present) some all-powerful supra-state to impose a new institutional regime that will reach down into the daily lives of millions of individuals on the farms and emerging industrial centers of the South or in the cities of the already industrialized North. There is only the long process of changing incentives in order to alter atomistic choices.

In the authoritative work on international regimes, Young talks of three possible origins of regimes formation: (i) spontaneous; (ii) negotiated; and (iii) imposed (Young, 1989). The discussion here has focused on the second and third of these. It is entirely possible that the governments of N and S would come to the same realization regarding the seriousness of greenhouse gases, and hence commence to reformulate domestic policies accordingly. This would represent the spontaneous case. That case is not very interesting for the problems of the global commons because it suggests that the problem of greenhouse gases would be rather immediately recognized by governments and solved autonomously. While this would be a wonderful situation, it is also not very realistic. What makes it unlikely is that independent states have very different interests in how their citizens behave with respect to the natural environment and hence the global commons. So the second two sources – negotiation and imposition – are much the more likely. These two classes of the origins of international regimes have comprised the essence of the approach followed here.

Young also points to the obvious result that negotiated and imposed regimes will ordinarily stand up better to the temptations offered by changing circumstances. After all, spontaneous regimes are only as durable as the separate calculations of the interests of the respective parties. In that sense then, the approach taken here, based on agency theory, seems to offer a conceptual guide to the problems of the global commons.

Note

Parts of this chapter are based on a longer paper in the *International Journal of Environment and Pollution*, 3 (4) (1993), 250–68.

References

Archer, R. and Ichord, R. 1989: Global warming and climate change: role of the Asia Near East region. Paper prepared for the Agency for International Development, Washington, DC.

Bromley, Daniel W. 1989: *Economic Interests and Institutions: the Conceptual Foundations of Public Policy*. Oxford: Basil Blackwell.

Bromley, Daniel W. 1991: *Environment and Economy: Property Rights and Public Policy*. Oxford: Basil Blackwell.

Bromley, Daniel W. and Cochrane, Jeffrey A. 1993: Understanding the global commons. Working Paper, Environmental and Natural Resources Policy and Training Project, USAID, Washington, DC.

Nitze, William A. 1990: A proposed structure for an international conventions on climate change. *Science*, 249 (August 10), 607–8.

Young, Oran R. 1989: *International Cooperation: Building Regimes for Natural Resource and the Environment*. Ithaca, NY: Cornell University Press.

15

Transferable Discharge Permits and Global Warming

T. H. Tietenberg

Introduction

The tradeable permit approach to pollution control was first introduced in the United States and has received its most vigorous application there. Beginning in 1975, burgeoning costs associated with the rigidities inherent in its traditional predominantly legal approach to controlling air pollution led the US Environmental Protection Agency (EPA) to begin experimenting with a transferable permit approach now known as the emissions trading program. Since that time the tradeable permit concept has been applied to several new areas of environmental policy and is currently being proposed for several more.

Support for the use of this market approach to environmental control has clearly grown in the United States, as reflected in the favorable treatment it has received in the popular business and environmental press. Some public interest environmental organizations, most notably the Environmental Defense Fund, have even adopted tradeable permit approaches as a core part of their strategy for protecting the environment. As described below the tradeable permit approach is also now being used to control local pollution within other nations and even to control transborder pollution problems.

Our knowledge about tradeable permits has grown rapidly in the two decades in which it has received serious analytical attention. Not only have the theoretical models become more focused and the empirical work more detailed, but we have now had over a decade of experience with several limited, but operational, versions of this approach. It seems a propitious time to stand back and to organize what we have learned about this practical and promising approach to pollution control.

This chapter draws upon economic theory, empirical studies, and actual experience with implementing the various versions of tradeable permit programs to provide a brief overview of some of the major lessons which are instructive in crafting a similar approach tailored to the control of greenhouse gases.[1] Some of the proposed extensions to new settings will also be discussed to suggest the range of applicability.[2]

The Current Experience

Protecting stratospheric ozone

The ozone shield in the stratosphere protects humans from harmful ultraviolet radiation. Current evidence suggests that this shield is being depleted by man-made chemicals such as chlorofluorocarbons (CFCs) and halogens and the resulting increase in ultraviolet rays raises the incidence of both skin cancer and damage to eyesight. These gases also contribute to global warming.

Responding to the ozone depletion threat 24 nations signed the Montreal Protocol during September 1988. According to this agreement signatory nations were to restrict their production and consumption of the chief responsible gases to 50 percent of 1986 levels by June 30, 1998. Soon after the Protocol was signed new evidence suggested that it had not gone far enough; the damage was apparently increasing more rapidly than previously thought. In response some 59 nations signed a new ozone agreement at a conference in London in July 1990. This agreement called for the complete phaseout of halons and CFCs by the end of this century. Moreover two other destructive chemicals – carbon tetrachloride and methyl chloroform – were added to the Protocol and are scheduled to be eliminated by 2000 and 2005 respectively. Limited transfers of the production allowances across national borders is allowed by the agreement.

An important component of this new agreement was the establishment of a special $240 million fund to help poorer countries switch away from ozone-depleting chemicals to more expensive but less harmful substitutes. This was an important breakthrough because without this assistance the use of ozone-depleting chemicals was expected to rise dramatically in the developing countries. In China, for example, by 1980 only one out of ten households owned a refrigerator. (Refrigerators use ozone-depleting chemicals both as a coolant and as a blowing agent in the insulating foam that makes up the walls.) The government plans for every kitchen in China to be equipped with a refrigerator by 2000. This fund establishes an important precedent for including developing countries in the process of controlling global warming.

Applications in the United States

Conventional air pollutants

Stripped to its essentials, the foundation of the US approach to pollution control is based upon a traditional command-and-control regulatory system. Ambient standards, which establish the highest allowable concentration of the pollutant in the ambient air or water for each conventional pollutant, represent the targets of this approach. To reach these targets emission or effluent standards (legal discharge ceilings) are imposed on a large number of specific discharge points such as stacks, vents, outfalls, or storage tanks. Following a survey of the technological options of control, the control authority selects a favored control technology and calculates the amount of discharge reduction achievable by that technology as the basis for setting the emission or effluent standard. Technologies yielding larger amounts of control (and hence supporting more stringent standards) are selected for emitters in areas where it is very difficult to meet the ambient standard and for new emitters. The responsibility for defining and enforcing these standards is shared in legislatively specified ways between the national government and the various state governments.

In an attempt to inject more flexibility into the manner in which the objectives of the Clean Air Act are met during the last half of the 1970s the US EPA created what has now become known as the emissions trading program.[3] The program attempts to facilitate compliance by allowing sources a much wider range of choice in how they satisfy their legal pollution control responsibilities than is possible in the command-and-control approach. Any source choosing to reduce emissions at any discharge point by more than is required by its emission standard can apply to the control authority for certification of the excess control as an "emission reduction credit" (ERC). Defined in terms of a specific amount of a particular pollutant, the certified emissions reduction credit can be used to satisfy emission standards at other (presumably more expensive to control) discharge points controlled by the creating source or it can be sold to other sources. By making these credits transferable, the EPA has allowed sources to find the cheapest means of satisfying their requirements, even if the cheapest means are under the control of another firm. The ERC is the currency used in emissions trading, while the offset, bubble, emissions banking and netting policies govern how this currency can be stored and spent.[4]

The offset policy requires major new or expanding sources in "nonattainment" areas (those areas with air quality worse than the ambient standards) to secure sufficient offsetting emission reductions (through the acquisition of ERCs) from existing firms that the air is cleaner after their entry or expansion than before.[5] Prior to this policy no new firms were allowed to enter nonattainment areas on the grounds that they would interfere with attaining the ambient standards. By introducing the offset policy EPA allowed economic growth to continue while ensuring progress toward attainment.

The bubble policy receives its unusual name from the fact that it treats multiple emission points controlled by existing emitters (as opposed to those expanding or entering an area for the first time) as if they were enclosed in a bubble. Under this policy only the total emissions of each pollutant leaving the bubble are regulated. While the total leaving the bubble must be no larger than the total permitted by adding up all the corresponding emission standards within the bubble (and, as a result of recent changes in the rules, must be 20 percent lower), emitters are free to control some discharge points less than dictated by the corresponding emission standard as long as sufficient compensating ERCs are obtained from other discharge points within the bubble. In essence sources are free to choose the mix of control among the discharge points as long as the overall emission reduction requirements are satisfied. Multi-plant bubbles are allowed, opening the possibility for trading ERCs among very different kinds of emitters.

Netting allows modifying or expanding sources (but not new sources) to escape from the need to meet the requirements of the rather stringent new source review process (including the need to acquire offsets) so long as any net increase in emissions (counting any ERCs earned elsewhere in the plant) is below an established threshold. In so far as it allows firms to escape particular regulatory requirements by using ERCs to remain under the threshold which triggers applicability, netting is more properly considered regulatory relief than regulatory reform.

Emissions banking, the final component, allows firms to store certified ERCs for subsequent use in the offset, bubble or netting programs or for sale to others. The banking component provides key institutional support for the program by serving as an easily accessed storehouse of credits available for sale and as a means of facilitating trades when the credit demands and supplies are not perfectly synchronized in time.

Lead in gasoline

Since the inception of the emissions trading program, the transferable discharge permit concept has been applied in a number of new, rather different, areas. One application involved a program to facilitate a rapid transition to the widespread availability of unleaded gasoline.

A main concern of EPA in issuing these regulations was the rigidity of the intermediate deadlines used to implement the phasedown. While some refiners could meet early deadlines with ease, others could do so only at a significant increase in cost. Recognizing that meeting the goal did not require every refiner to meet every deadline, EPA initiated the lead banking program to provide additional flexibility in meeting the regulations.

While not a part of the emissions trading program discussed above, the lead banking program does share some design similarities with it. Under this program, refiners reducing lead more than required by the applicable standard in each quarter of the year could bank the credits for use or sale in some subsequent quarter. Banked credits were fully transferable among refiners.

The lead banking program, though plagued by less-than-perfect implementation procedures, eased the transition to the new, more stringent regulatory regime.[6] Refiners had an incentive to respond quickly because reductions in lead undertaken prior to the deadlines became valuable under this new program. Acquiring these credits made it possible for other refiners to comply with the deadlines, even in the face of equipment failures or acts of God; fighting the deadlines in court, the traditional response, was unnecessary. Designed purely as a means of facilitating the transition to this new regime, the lead banking program ended as scheduled on December 31, 1987.

The lead banking program shows how transferable discharge permit systems can be used to facilitate the transition to stricter regulatory regimes. By providing more flexibility coupled with incentives for meeting the deadlines early, it respects differences in the capabilities of polluters to meet stringent deadlines without sacrificing the overall environmental objectives. Since deadlines will be an essential part of any international approach to controlling global warming, this is a useful attribute.

Ozone-depleting chemicals

On August 12, 1988, the US EPA issued regulations implementing a transferable discharge permit system to achieve the US targeted reductions.[7] According to these regulations all major US producers and consumers of the controlled substances were allocated baseline allowances using 1986 levels as the basis for the pro-ration. Each producer and consumer is allowed 100 percent of this baseline allowance for each year before July 1, 1993, 80 percent between July 1, 1993, and June 30, 1998, and 50 percent of the baseline allowance after June 30, 1998. These allowances are transferable within producer and consumer categories and, as noted above, production allowances can be transferred across international borders to producers in other signatory nations provided that the transaction is approved by EPA and results in the appropriate changes in the buyer and seller production allowances in their respective countries. Production allowances can be augmented by demonstrating the safe destruction of an equivalent amount of controlled substances by approved means, but so far no means have been approved.

Confronted with scientific evidence that the reduction in CFC use mandated by the Montreal Protocol might not be sufficiently stringent, concerned about the excess profits to which the allowance holders would be entitled,[8] and seeking new sources of revenue to counteract a growing budget deficit, the US Congress complemented this transferable discharge permit approach with a special tax on ozone-depleting chemicals.[9] The amount of the tax per pound of the chemical sold or used is equal to a base tax multiplied by an "ozone-depleting factor" specific to each chemical. These factors range from a low of 0.8 for CFC-113 to 10.0 for Halon-1301. The base tax rates rise from $1.37 in 1991 to $2.65 in 1994, with further annual increases of 45 cents each year after that.

One of the useful lessons for controlling global warming from this application is that it demonstrates the complementarity of using transferable entitlements in conjunction with fees. When used together, both are allowed to fulfill the roles for which they are best suited – permits produce the desired control of quantitites emitted, while fees raise revenue.

Water pollution[10]

Virtually all water pollution control policy in the United States has been focused on point sources – large identifiable polluters emitting effluents from specific discharge points. As the controls on point sources have been tightened, nonpoint sources (such as the overflow from urban storm sewers or the runoff from farms) become responsible for a larger share of the remaining pollution. Although nonpoint sources are responsible for the largest proportion of the remaining problem, they are notoriously difficult to regulate by traditional means.

Because the marginal cost of controlling nonpoint sources is now considerably lower than the marginal cost of securing further reductions from point sources, ways of bringing nonpoint sources under control are of great interest. One result of this attention has been the introduction of an option to trade waste reduction permits between point and nonpoint sources for bodies of water where further control is required.

Three examples of this approach have occurred, two of them in Colorado. The Lake Dillon Watershed, a primary source of water for Denver, Colorado, the Cherry Creek Reservoir, an important recreation area near Denver, and the Tar-Pimlico Basin in North Carolina have all instituted programs to allow point sources to meet their nutrient loading reduction responsibilities by securing additional requirements from nonpoint sources.[11]

The nonpoint source application demonstrates how a transferable discharge permit system can reduce costs by bringing previously unregulated sources under regulation. By coupling economic incentives for controlling new sources with procedures forcing traders to bear a rather heavy burden of proof in demonstrating the magnitude and enforceability of the proposed reductions, regulators can spread the control burden over a larger number of sources (thereby reducing compliance cost) while assuring the integrity of the process. The similarity between controlling the unregulated nonpoint water pollution sources and the problems associated with bringing sources in less developed countries under control make the lessons learned from these applications of particular importance in global warming control.

Tradeable permits have also been used in mitigating the effects of wetlands destruction in some ten states.[12] Both federal and state regulations require any developments in wetlands to minimize the adverse effects. In the case that on-site remedies are considered insufficient, credits toward the requirements can be demonstrated either by the enhancement of existing marshes or the creation of new marshes. In either case those responsible for the mitigation activities can bank the credits (usually defined in "habitat units") for subsequent sale or use.

Acid rain

Perhaps the most sophisticated version of the emissions trading concept has also been incorporated into the US approach for achieving further reductions in pollutants contributing to acid rain from electric utilities.[13] Under this innovative approach allowances to emit sulfur oxides will be allocated to older plants; the number of allowances will be restricted to ensure a reduction of 10 million tons in emissions from 1980 levels.[14] Although these allowances are defined for a specific calendar year and cannot be used prior to that year, the Clean Air Act (as amended 1990) contains provisions for carrying unused allowances forward into the next year. Unused allowances are transferable among the affected sources. Any plant reducing emissions more than required by its initial allocation of allowances could transfer the unused allowances to other plants or even to environmental groups. These acquired allowances can be used (i) by the owners of the purchasing source to ensure that its emissions do not exceed the levels permitted by the allowances (allocated plus acquired) that it holds, or (ii) by environmental groups as a means of improving air quality beyond the requirements of the Act.[15] The Act even anticipates the possibility of interpollutant trading between sulfur and nitrogen oxides by asking for a study of its feasibility.[16]

The acid rain application is particularly interesting because the acid rain tradeable allowances treat sulfur oxides in the same manner as greenhouse gases would be treated in a global transferable permit market designed to control warming – they can be traded on a one-for-one basis. The expectations for a vigorous market in these acid rain allowances are sufficiently high that a spot market in these allowances already exists and the Chicago Board of Trade has opened a forward market. This is an important development. As the institutional market structure for handling these credits becomes more sophisticated, the transaction costs and uncertainty associated with the trades are reduced. As these impediments to smooth trading are removed, actual trading systems move closer to realizing the high expectations suggested by economic theory.

Applications outside the United States

Germany[17]

The Federal Republic of Germany has used a limited form of transferable discharge permits for a number of years. Under this program plant operators are allowed to deviate from strict standards, provided that ambient air concentrations are reduced. The first program (governed by the plant renewal clause) allows new plants seeking to locate in areas where allowable ambient concentrations have been exceeded to acquire emission offsets from the renovation or renewal of old plants; without these compensating reductions the establishment of new plants in these areas would not be allowed. In the second program authorities can deviate from the new licensing procedure required for plants undergoing a renewal provided greater reductions are achieved from the proposed deviation (including the acquisition of offsets) than would have been achieved from the follow-up order. One unique characteristic of the German program is that it does not force the offsetting reductions to be for the same pollutant; reductions of other pollutants can serve as offsets provided they have comparable effects on the environment.

Canada[18]

An intra-utility form of trading (similar to the US bubble concept) is already allowed in Ontario. The utility involved is required to meet an aggregate emissions cap, but is given great flexibility in how it chooses to fulfill that responsibility.

Canada is currently investigating the use of transferable permits in two new contexts. The first application would allow trading NO_x and VOC (volatile organic carbon) credits within each of Canada's three ozone nonattainment areas (Vancouver, Ontario and Quebec, and southern New Brunswick). The second application would involve SO_2 trading.

Chile

To combat serious air pollution Santiago, Chile, has introduced two transferable permits schemes. The first is used to control particulates from industrial sources. Trading of permits is used to provide greater flexibility in meeting new, stricter standards. The second was used to reduce mobile source particulates from diesel engines. Since Santiago was plagued with a large number of heavily polluting vehicles with little or no coordinated service, permits to operate mass-transit vehicles were required and were auctioned off. However, instead of auctioning them off in terms of price, they were auctioned off in terms of quality of service. Suppliers bid for the permits in terms of the service which they would provide (including the polluting characteristics of the vehicles). Apparently the scheme has worked well as service has improved and pollution has declined.

Lessons

Lessons from theory

Theory can help us to understand the characteristics of this economic approach in the most favorable circumstances for its use and to assist in the process of designing the instruments for maximum effectiveness. Several conclusions follow:

1. *Assuming all participants are cost-minimizers, a "well-defined" transferable discharge permit market could cost-effectively allocate the control responsibility for meeting a predefined pollution target among the various pollution sources despite incomplete information on the control possibilities by the regulatory authorities.* The intuition behind this conclusion is not difficult to grasp. Cost-minimizing firms seek to minimize the sum of permit costs and control costs. Minimization will occur when the marginal cost of control is set equal to the permit price. Since all sources will be setting their marginal control costs equal to the same price, a permit market will equalize marginal control costs across all discharge points, precisely the condition required for cost-effectiveness.[19] In essence, sources needing extra emission reduction either as a precondition to entering an area or to meet emissions standards can purchase transferable permits from sources with the lowest marginal costs of control.

   Though derived in the rarified world of theory, the practical importance of this should not be underestimated. Transferable permits offer a unique opportunity for regulators to solve a fundamental dilemma. Control authorities usually want to allocate the responsibility for control cost-effectively, but they rarely have the information required to achieve this objective. Transferable permits create a system of incentives in which those who have the best knowledge about control opportunities – the environmental managers for the industries – are encouraged to use that knowledge to achieve environmental objectives at minimum cost. Information barriers do not preclude effective regulation.

2. *Transferable permits encourage more technological progress in pollution control than the command-and-control system.*[20] Traditional command-and-control policies usually base standards on technologies known to the regulators. Meeting those standards can be accomplished simply by

adopting the identified technology. Adopters have little incentive to search for superior technologies.

With transferable permits, adopters not only have an incentive to search for new technologies that reduce the cost of compliance of meeting the mandated standard, they have an incentive to search for technologies that can reduce emissions more than required by the standard. Selling the emission reduction credits (or unused allowances) produces revenue which can be used to finance the new technologies.

3. *As long as markets are competitive and transactions costs are low, the trading benchmark in an emissions trading approach does not affect the ultimate cost-effective allocation of control responsibility. When markets are noncompetitive or transactions costs are high, however, the final allocation of control responsibility is affected.*[21]

Once the control authority has decided how much pollution of each type will be allowed, it must then decide how to allocate the permits among the sources. In theory permits can either be auctioned off, with the sources purchasing them from the control authority at the market-clearing price, or be allocated among existing sources free of charge based on some regulatory distribution rule. The theorem suggests that either approach will ultimately result in a cost-effective allocation of the control responsibility among the various polluters as long as they are all price-takers, transactions costs are low, and the permits are freely transferable. Even when the permits are randomly distributed without cost among existing sources, the after-market in which firms can sell excess permits and purchase additional ones corrects any problems with the initial allocation. This is a significant finding because it implies that under the right conditions the initial allocation can be used to pursue distributional goals without interfering with cost-effectiveness. This is a particularly noteworthy characteristic in view of the potential role for incorporating transfers to developing countries in any permanent solution to the global warming problem. As long as transaction costs are very low, and there are many buyers and sellers, negotiators can choose any particular initial allocation of greenhouse gas quotas without placing the overall goal of cost-effectiveness in jeopardy. No such flexibility exists for the traditional approach of nontransferable quotas.

When firms are price-setters rather than price-takers, however, cost-effectiveness will only be achieved if the control authority initially allocates the permits so that a cost-effective allocation would be achieved even in the absence of any trading. For all other initial permit distributions an active market would exist, offering the opportunity for price-setting behavior. The larger is the deviation of the initial allocation of permits to a single price-setting source, the larger is the likelihood for that source to exercise market power.[22]

Similar problems exist when transaction costs are high. High transaction costs can preclude or reduce trading by diminishing the gains from trade. When the costs of consummating the transaction exceed the potential gains, the incentive to participate in the market is lost.

Lessons from empirical research

1. *A vast majority, though not all, of the relevant empirical studies have found the control costs to be substantially higher with the regulatory command-and-control system than with the least-cost means of allocating the control responsibility.*[23] While theory tells us unambiguously that the command-and-control system will not be cost-effective except by coincidence, it cannot tell us the magnitude of the excess costs. The empirical work adds the important information that the excess costs have typically been very large. This is an important finding because it provides the motivation for introducing a reform program; the potential social gains (in terms of reduced control cost) from breaking away from the status quo are sufficient to justify the trouble. Although the typical estimates of the excess costs attributable to a command-and-control system overstate the cost savings that would be achieved by even a completely unrestricted permit market (a point discussed in more detail below), the general conclusion that the potential cost savings from adopting market-based approaches are large remains accurate even after correcting for overstatement. Preliminary studies of the use of transferable permits for global warming indicate that large cost savings could be achieved in that use as well.[24]

2. *Only a transferable entitlement system that allocates permits free of charge to sources on the basis of their historic emission rate would guarantee that existing sources would be no worse off than they would be under a command-and-control system imposing the same degree of control. The financial outlays associated with acquiring allowances or ERCs in an auction market (or a comparable emissions charge) would be sufficiently large that sources would typically have lower financial burdens with the traditional command-and-control approach than with these particular economic incentive approaches.*[25] *The exception is a zero-revenue auction.*[26]

From the point of view of the source required to control its emissions, two components of financial burden are significant: (i) control costs; and (ii) expenditures on permits. While only the former represent real resource costs to society as a whole (the latter are merely transferred from one group in society to another), to the source both represent a financial burden. The empirical evidence suggests that when an auction market is used to distribute permits (or, equivalently, when all uncontrolled emissions are subject to an emissions tax) the permit expenditures (tax revenue) would frequently be larger in magnitude than the control costs; the sources would spend more on permits (or pay more in taxes) than they would on the control equipment.

Under the traditional command-and-control system firms make no financial outlays to the government. Although control costs are necessarily higher with the command-and-control system than with a transferable discharge permit system, they are not so high as to outweigh the additional financial outlays required in an auction market permit system (or an emissions tax system). For this reason existing sources understandably oppose distributing permits by an auction market despite its social appeal, unless the revenue derived is used in a manner which is approved by the sources and the sources with which it competes are required to absorb similar expenses.

3. *While it is clear from theory that larger trading areas and larger numbers of traders offer the best opportunities for larger potential cost savings in a transferable entitlement program, some empirical work suggests that substantial savings can be achieved even when the trading areas and the number of potential trades are rather small. This is an important point because it suggests that even very limited steps toward a transferable permit system could be beneficial.*

Sometimes political considerations mandate a limited transferable permit program. Whether large trading areas and large numbers of traders are essential for the effective use of this policy is therefore of some relevance. The amount of cost savings achieved by any permit market would be a function of the size of the area within which the permits may be traded and the number of traders. In general, larger trading areas and larger numbers of traders increase the potential cost savings due to the wider set of cost reduction opportunities made available. The empirical question is how sensitive the cost estimates are to these components.

One study of utilities in the United States found that even allowing a plant to trade among discharge points within that plant could save from 30 to 60 percent of the costs of complying with new sulfur oxide reduction regulations, compared with a situation where no trading whatsoever was permitted.[27] Expanding the trading possibilities to other utilities within the same state permitted a further reduction of 20 percent, while allowing inter-state trading permitted another 15 percent reduction in costs. If this study is replicated in other circumstances, it would appear that even small trading areas offer the opportunity for significant cost reduction.[28]

4. *Although only a few studies of the empirical impact of market power on the cost-effectiveness of transferable permit markets have been accomplished, their results are consistent with a finding that market power does not seem to have a large effect on regional control costs in most realistic situations.*[29]

Under favorable circumstances for the exploitation of market power, the available evidence suggests that, while price manipulation in auction permit markets could have a rather large impact on regional financial burden, it would under normal circumstances have a rather small effect on control costs. Estimates typically suggest that control costs would rise by less than 1 percent if market power were exercised by one or more firms.

The effects of market power depend on whether the permits are distributed by auction or distributed free of charge. In an auction market the price-setting source reduces its financial burden by purchasing fewer permits than otherwise in order to drive the price down. To compensate for the fewer number of permits purchased, the price-setting source must spend more on controlling its own pollution, limiting the gains from price manipulation.

Within the class of free distribution rules, some rules create a larger potential for strategic price behavior than others. In general the larger the divergence between the number of permits received by the price-searching source and the cost-effective number of permits, the larger the potential for market power. When allocated an excess of permits by the control authority, price-searching firms can exercise power on the selling side of the market, and when allocated too few permits, they can exercise power on the buying side of the market.

According to the existing studies it takes a rather considerable divergence from the cost-effective allocation of permits to produce much difference in regional control costs. Since most realistic rules used to distribute permits are estimated to affect control costs to such a small degree, the deviations from the least-cost allocation caused by market power pale in comparison with the much larger potential cost reductions achievable by implementing a transferable permit system.[30]

Lessons from implementation

Although comprehensive data on the effects of the various transferable permit programs do not exist because no one has yet collected information in a systematic way, some of the major aspects of the experience are clear.

1. *The transferable permit programs in the United States have gone through a considerable evolution since their inception in the 1970s. Starting with a*

very limited system which only remotely resembled the theoretical concept, the program has evolved to the point where the newest program, the sulfur allowances, is expected to approximate a true transferable permit market rather closely.

Rather than establishing a vigorous market with well-defined prices as envisioned by early proponents, the early emissions trading programs involved negotiated trades between sources, individually supervised and approved by regulatory agencies on a case-by-case basis. This program was a complement to, rather than a substitute for, the traditional command-and-control approach.

Experience with the program has instilled confidence in it among the major participants. Air pollution regulators, who were once very opposed to transferable permits, have become a major source of support for the sulfur allowance program and were instrumental in its design. Environmental groups have also begun to lend their support.

2. *The existing programs in the United States have lowered compliance costs while improving air quality.* The program has unquestionably and substantially reduced the costs of complying with the requirements of the Clean Air Act. Most estimates place the accumulated capital savings for all components of the program at over $10 billion. This does not include the recurring savings in operating cost.[31]

Somewhere between 7000 and 12,000 trading transactions have been consummated. Each of these transactions was voluntary and for the participants represented an improvement over the traditional regulatory approach. Several of these transactions involved the introduction of innovative control technologies.

Though designed primarily to reduce the compliance costs of achieving predefined environmental goals, the emissions trading program has also produced an improvement in air quality. Facilitating compliance with the pollution control acts by making compliance cheaper and easier has been one avenue for improving air quality. Trading has increased the possible means for compliance and polluting sources have responded. Other avenues by which emissions trading have improved air quality include (i) providing a basis for more stringent standards; (ii) encouraging banked emissions reduction credits; and (iii) developing trading rules which extract an "improvement premium."

In the negotiations over the sulfur allowance program it became clear that utility representatives were more willing to accept a larger reduction of sulfur oxides once it was specified that allowance trading was going to be allowed. Since introducing trading lowers the cost of compliance (making it easier to reach any given target reduction), larger target reductions could be reached with a lower financial burden than would have been possible with a pure command-and-control approach. Allowing trading increased the political acceptability of larger reductions.

Banking not only provides incentives to create credits for future use, it also provides an incentive for some credits to remain unused. While normal credits are used to justify emissions, the pollutant flows justified by banked credits are not being emitted. This reduction in actual emissions represents an improvement in air quality for as long as the credits remain banked.

Finally, the emissions trading program has opted to improve air quality by requiring trading ratios in excess of 1:1. For example, buyers must typically acquire 120 percent of the entitlements they actually intend to use. If a facility wishes to use credits to justify a 10-ton reduction, they must actually purchase 12 tons. The extra 2 tons represent an improvement in air quality.[32]

The demonstrated ability of transferable permit programs to lower compliance costs is particularly relevant for international attempts to control global warming. Not only would lower compliance costs make it more likely that countries would sign an agreement, but it makes it more likely that signatories will comply. In the international arena, where enforcement and monitoring is so difficult, that is a very important point.

Designing a Greenhouse Gas Trading System

Key characteristics of the system

The list of controlled substances

Creating a workable transferable permit system must begin with agreement on the substances that will be subject to the entitlement system. What gases would be involved?

Though a comprehensive approach incorporating all greenhouse gases allows the global warming objective to be achieved with the widest selection of options, reducing the cost of achieving any given target,[33] in the harsh realities associated with implementing a workable global system of control, practical solutions dominate less practical solutions, even those which may appear superior in theory.[34] Carbon dioxide is much easier to monitor and to document than other gases such as methane.[35] Since an effective transferable permit system presumes a capability to calculate the effects of various control strategies on emissions, incorporating all sources of all greenhouse gases from the beginning would run the significant risk that fraudulent trades could result – trades that appear to involve equivalent reductions in greenhouse gases but in fact do not.

Fortunately starting with a system based on carbon dioxide does not preclude its subsequent expansion to include other greenhouse gases. The decision to incorporate other gases could be made on a case-by-case basis. Reductions in other greenhouse gases would be tradeable contingent on a demonstration that the effect of the proposed reductions on global warming would be equivalent, even considering all the associated monitoring and enforcement problems. Some sources of other greenhouse gases can already meet this test; others cannot. While those meeting the test could be incorporated immediately into the system, incorporation of the others would await a demonstration of this capability.

The entitlement

Though as a practical matter entitlements can be imposed at any stage in the life-cycle of a greenhouse gas (extraction or production, consumption or emission), all other things being equal, entitlements defined in terms of emissions would be preferred; this would produce the most cost-effective outcome. With an emissions target the tendency of the market to seek the least-cost means of control would be focused on reducing emissions, which, of course, is the ultimate objective.[36] But all other things are never equal, so intervening in other stages of the life-cycle can become a viable, if less desirable, alternative.[37] Different entitlement systems could be established for the case of carbon dioxide emissions from fossil fuels. Requiring entitlements for fossil fuels as they are extracted, as they move through the wholesale distribution channels, as they are sold to final consumers, or as the emissions are injected into the atmosphere by the combustion source are all possible points of control.

To facilitate a market in permits, the implied entitlement should be defined in terms of a homogeneous unit such as a ton of carbon dioxide emissions. To the extent that the entitlement involves another gas or an activity other than emission, the results must be translated back into a "ton of carbon dioxide equivalent."

Entitlement duration

Entitlements would be dated in annual terms – 1991, 1992 etc. – and could be used during the specified year or after, but not before. Each permit would allow a specified number of tons of emissions. Once the amount authorized by the permit had been emitted, the entitlement would become worthless.

Global emission targets

The first step in establishing any tradeable permit system is to define the allowable emission levels of controlled greenhouse gases for the signatory nations. Typically these emission targets would be a function of time, recognizing both the tendencies for growth to increase emissions and the relative ease of securing reductions from new rather than old technologies.

Substantial reductions are easier to secure in the long run as production technologies change than in the short run where old production technologies are rather locked in. The emission targets would have to strike a compromise between these two offsetting tendencies.

International initial allocation

Once the allowable emission targets have been defined, the next step is to allocate these targets among the signatory countries.[38] That presumably would be handled by international negotiations. Whatever allocations result, the importance of making these allocations transferable cannot be overemphasized. Not only would transferability provide the basis for an international flow of funds from the industrial to the less developed countries, it could well facilitate the acceptance of lower quota limits by the industrialized nations.[39] Lower quota limits by the industrialized nations would increase the likelihood that more of the less industrialized countries would participate in the agreement, since, for a given aggregate reduction, it would increase the share of future allowable emissions available for them.

Domestic complementary policies

How individual signatory governments would meet their authorized emission target would be left to them. Some might choose to use a traditional regulatory system, while others might choose to use emissions charges. The effective functioning of a tradeable carbon dioxide entitlement system does not presume or require any particular choice.

The private trading variant

Transferable permit systems could be designed where all trades took place exclusively between governments, exclusively between private parties, or with some mix of the two. Exclusive government trading could be initiated whenever actual greenhouse gas emissions were lower than allowed by the treaty in some countries and higher than allowed in others. Tradeable permits could be created by a generous treaty definition of "allowable" emissions, by certified reductions in either controlled or uncontrolled greenhouse gases, or by certified increases in greenhouse gas absorption capabilities.

Governments could choose to facilitate the participation of trades by private organizations by allocating their entitlements among the various competing sources within their borders.[40] In theory permits could either be auctioned off, with the sources purchasing them from their respective governments at the market-clearing price, or distributed to each source on the basis of some allocation rule (typically historical use). Theory suggests that either approach will ultimately result in a cost-effective allocation of the control responsibility among the various polluters as long as they are all price-takers, transactions costs are low, and the permits are fully transferable. *Any* free distribution of permits among existing sources is compatible with cost-effectiveness because the after-market in which firms can buy or sell permits eliminates any excess costs associated with the initial allocation. This highly significant result implies that, *under the right conditions*, governments can use this initial allocation to pursue within-country distributional goals without interfering with cost-effectiveness.

Both free distribution and the auction market have significant disadvantages. A main disadvantage of the free distribution approach is that it does not generate any revenue for the government. A main disadvantage of the auction approach is that it raises the financial burden of the polluting firms, a significant deterrent in an increasingly competitive global market.

The middle ground between these two domestic distribution approaches can be exploited to produce a workable alternative. The government could allocate the permits on a free distribution basis but charge an annual fee to those receiving them.[41] Because this fee would be lower than the auction price, it would put less of a financial burden on the polluters than a full auction market. Yet the ability to collect an annual fee would make it possible for governments to derive some revenue from the system – revenue that could be used to undertake monitoring and enforcement efforts. The ability to collect this revenue could well serve even to increase the attractiveness of becoming a signatory nation.

Once completed, the initial within-country allocation of permits would serve as a baseline for trades of controlled substances. The permits would define allowable emissions of greenhouse gases; any certified reductions from that baseline would entitle the bearer to sell the excess to another party seeking to justify a larger allowable emission level than the one to which it would otherwise be authorized.

Entitlement supply
Once the initial allocation has been completed, it is necessary to decide the conditions under which the supply of permits could be expanded. The general rule is that supply increases should not undermine the goal of reduced global warming.

One possible source of permit supply is provided by participants who undertake activities which absorb or destroy greenhouse gases. Currently, for example, it is possible to destroy CFCs so that they do not contribute to global warming. By allowing the certified destruction of greenhouse gases to create entitlements, the development of destruction techniques and capability would be encouraged.

Another source of entitlement expansion could come about from the development of new greenhouse gas absorption capabilities. The most obvious example is the development of new biomass plantations to sequester carbon through photosynthesis or, perhaps, saving forests scheduled for burning (thereby preventing the liberation of the sequestered carbon). Allowing these offsetting activities to create new entitlements provides a powerful inducement for them to be undertaken and therefore is a desirable objective. However, this path is not without its problems.

Generally only offsetting activities which go beyond some prespecified baseline qualify for entitlements. The baseline establishes the "normal" or "expected" amount of planting or harvesting activity. Without the baseline it would be possible for a country, for example, to threaten to burn all its forest for the sake of acquiring valuable global warming entitlements once they could be convinced not to carry out their threat. In essence, without a properly defined baseline, incentives for counter-productive strategic behavior are introduced.

While the within-country initial allocation of permits would auto-matically define a trading baseline for controlled substances in signatory nations, it does not define a baseline for uncontrolled greenhouse gases or for emission reductions from nonsignatory nations or from activities which could sequester greenhouse gases. Although this baseline would have to be separately defined, it could be determined on a case-by-case basis. Trades involving these activities would only be approved upon completion of the certification process (described below in the section on monitoring and enforcement). Determining the appropriate baseline would be a normal component of the certification process.

Trading rules

Once the entitlement system is defined and the initial allocation of permits has been completed, the rules governing trades must be determined. How are the trading ratios determined?

For global gases same-pollutant trades should normally take place at a one-to-one ratio. For example, a 1-ton emission permit originally held by a source in country X should, when sold, entitle the acquiring trader to a 1-ton emission in any country.[42]

Interpollutant trades would not generally be conducted on a one-for-one basis because the different greenhouse gases do not have the same affect on global warming. The trading ratios for interpollutant trades should reflect the relative contributions of the gases. The objective should be to ensure that global warming would not be adversely affected by the trade.

Ideally it would be possible to develop a table of equivalences, which would be published and available to all traders in advance. Unfortunately any such table would necessarily represent a simplification of the atmospheric chemistry involved in global warming. In particular since the reactions take place at markedly different rates, the contribution of each gas to global warming is a function of time. Reductions in some gases would have a more immediate impact than others.[43] The practical implication of these chemical reactions for policy is that the relative contribution of any two gases to global warming is not a constant. And the construction of a table of equivalences presumes that the relative contribution can be expressed as a constant.

Some proposed trades would necessarily involve some uncertainty. Suppose, for example, that the contribution of some particular greenhouse gas to global warming was not known with precision or that the capability to monitor emissions would be less than perfect (introducing the possibility that post-trade emissions would in fact be higher than expected). As an alternative to banning all such trades, one way to confront and to deal realistically with this uncertainty is to account for it in the trading ratios.

When the proposed trade involves some uncertainty about the effects, "worst case" trading ratios can be used. Suppose, for example, that the ability to monitor emissions from a new source is accurate only within 50 percent of the actual. This trade could be permitted as long as twice as much reduction of this gas was required compared with a case in which monitoring was perfect. Adjusting trading ratios as a response to uncertainty offers regulators a considerable amount of discretionary flexibility.

The clearinghouse and banking function

The global greenhouse trading system should involve a provision for a clearinghouse to provide a centralized location for permit transactions. With a clearinghouse, potential purchasers do not have to spend excessive amounts of time and resources searching out potential trades; they merely have to check the clearinghouse.

Entitlement banks should provide a safe haven for certified but unused credits. In terms of the security they offer the depositor, banked permits should be considered the equivalent of permits in use. One problem that has arisen in the American system of emissions trading is that some of the permits held in banks (which in that program are controlled by the states) were confiscated as a means of quickly improving air quality. Confiscation, of course, had the unintended, but nonetheless very real, effect of destroying any incentive for firms to create banked credits. Regulatory authorities should not be allowed to confiscate banked credits if the proper incentives are to be maintained. Further air quality improvements can be secured while maintaining the integrity of banked permits, a topic discussed below.

Leasing

Leasing recognizes and responds to the temporal variability in the need for permits, a point that has special validity in the greenhouse gas context.

As an inducement to the participation of developing countries in a comprehensive global warming agreement, the initial international allocation of permits is likely to grant a surplus to the developing countries. This surplus would provide an opportunity to earn revenue (from trading those surplus permits to the industrialized nations) and an opportunity to create a permit reserve to facilitate and accommodate future economic growth. Unfortunately outright sale of the permits can exploit only one of these opportunities; it would provide revenue only by selling permits from the reserve.

Leasing provides an opportunity to fulfill simultaneously both objectives. Leased permits are transferred to a new owner for a fixed, prespecified period of time. (In other words a nation could lease some portion of its 1991–4 entitlements but retain the 1995 and subsequent entitlements.) This arrangement would work well for both the industrialized and developing countries. Because restructuring the industrial system takes time, the industrialized nations could use leased permits to buy time while the restructuring takes place. Meanwhile the developing countries would be receiving much needed revenue from the leased permits. As the developing countries needs for permits to support economic growth grew, they could retain the later entitlements as a guaranteed source. Leasing would facilitate the transition to a new sustainable regime of energy use in both the developing and the industrialized world.

Special design issues

The special circumstances associated with establishing a global version of a tradeable permit system for greenhouse gases give rise to some potential pitfalls. By anticipating these problems it is possible to design the system to avoid them or to mitigate their importance.

Market power
Market power can exist in permit markets on either the buyer or the seller side. When traders attempt to control the price (rather than react to the market-determined price), the cost-effectiveness of the system can be affected.[44]

The degree to which market power can be exercised either internationally or, if the private variant is chosen, domestically is a function of how permits are initially allocated. The larger is the share of the initial allocation of permits to colluding sources, the larger is the potential deviation of ultimate control costs from the least-cost allocation. When the colluding sources are initially allocated an excess of permits, higher control costs can be inflicted on others by withholding some permits from the market. When colluding sources are initially allocated a deficiency of permits, however, to reduce prices they must necessarily bear higher control cost as the means of reducing demand for the permits.

The evidence suggests that market power has rarely been a problem in existing uses of tradeable permits and is not expected to be much of a problem in a global permit market either. Successful cartels are difficult to establish and maintain for any commodity, and greenhouse gas permits would not be an exception. Successful cartelization on the seller side depends upon an ability to capture a substantial proportion of the supply of permits available for sale. All other things being equal, the larger the supply which falls outside the control of the cartel, the lower the cartel's ability to wield its influence.

Because this would be a global market, the number of potential buyers and sellers is very large indeed. The market would not be thin. Since market power can only arise whenever either the buying activity or the selling activity is concentrated in the hands of a few nations, as long as the baseline (initial allocation) is defined in such a way as to create a large number of buyers and sellers, cartelization is unlikely.

Even if the initial allocation does not precipitate a large number of buyers and sellers, the number can be increased by other means. For example, allowing new credits to be created by the certified destruction of greenhouse gases, and by certified increases in greenhouse gas absorption capabilities, creates alternative supplies of permits. Allowing both international trades and the participation of private sources in these trades would also increase the number of traders.

Finally, as Grubb and Sibenius (1992) point out, the ultimate protection against the accumulation of market power is the capability all nations have to withdraw from the agreement. Any nation or group of nations which has been damaged by a cartelization of global warming permits can simply withdraw from the agreement and be unconstrained in their emissions. The right of withdrawal provides a significant check on the benefits of cartelization.

Changing control needs

It is necessary to build into a global greenhouse permit system a process for change. With as much uncertainty as currently exists with respect to global warming, change is inevitable. Yet modifications in the system, if not implemented carefully, have the potential to undermine the system. Tradeable permit systems depend on permit holders having secure ownership rights. Insecure property rights undermine the incentive to invest in the activities that free up permits for sale. Can the desire constantly to incorporate change be made compatible with the desire to preserve sufficient security for the permits?

Fortunately, compatibility is possible. To the extent that the change can be anticipated it should be announced in advance. If initial permit allocations turn out, in retrospect, to be too high over the long run and further reductions are necessary, the schedule of further reductions should be published in advance. Uncertainty is reduced when the changes are known in advance.

Second, even when the ultimate changes are not known in advance, it is possible to have a stable process for incorporating those changes. Reviews of the aggregate emission target should be conducted on a periodic, announced schedule. The process and criteria for deciding whether a change is needed and, if so, how large a change is needed should be made transparent to interested parties.

Finally the *process* for incorporating changes should be known in advance even if the nature of the changes cannot be. Suppose the latest scientific evidence suggests that further emission reductions are necessary. In general all permits, whether banked or in use to justify emissions, should be reduced proportionately or the changes should be taken out of the growth increment. Government should *not* confiscate banked credits just because they are handy.

Hoarding

In the emissions trading program developed in the United States, fewer trades have taken place than expected. In part this is due to the fact that some sources have hoarded created credits; instead of selling them, they have retained them for possible future use. The effect has been thinner markets and fewer trades than might otherwise have been possible. Would hoarding plague a global market in greenhouse entitlements? If so, what can be done to counteract it?

The key to assessing the likelihood of hoarding in a global market is to understand the motivations that give rise to hoarding behavior. Hoarding is a response to risk and it intensifies the very problem to which it is a response. Faced with the risk that future permits might not be available for sale, firms creating credits retain them to preserve their future options should they decide to expand operations.

Price risk is one specific incentive for hoarding. Prices were individually negotiated and were subject to considerable variability depending on the available supply of credits. Because emissions trading transactions have taken place in local markets with few buyers and sellers, demand and supply conditions could change rather quickly; a large number of participants, the precondition for a stable and smoothly functioning market, was not present.[45]

Is this likely to be a problem for a global market? Probably not. Its global scope would provide a large number of participants on both the buyer and the seller side of the market. Thin markets would be much less of a problem even for within-country trades.

Certain design features of the global system also mitigate against the occurrence of hoarding. Allowing permit supply to be increased by the development of greenhouse gas absorption or destruction activities provides an alternative source of permits. Facilitating the transboundary flow of permits would also contribute to the type of vigorous market that destroys the preconditions for hoarding.

Recent developments in the markets for the sulfur allowances in the US acid rain reduction program also provide some hope for reducing the risk associated with both the availability and price of future permits. A spot market for these allowances already exists. In the United States the Chicago Board of Trade has established a forward market for these allowances during 1991–2 and subsequently even plans a futures market. Large brokerage firms have shown some interest in participating.

Organized markets for future contracts, which have existed for well over a hundred years, bring together those who want to minimize their risk with those who are willing to take the risk for a price.[46] An active futures market affords an opportunity for purchasers to lock in the future price and availability of permits, thus eliminating the need to hoard as a hedge against this risk.

The evolution of these financial markets is an important complement to the evolution of the cost-effective control of greenhouse gases. They facilitate trades by revealing prices and by reducing the risk associated with investments to reduce greenhouse gases.

Other financial devices are also being developed to facilitate the evolution of this system by reducing risk. In the United States, for example, insurance pools are currently being set up to allow the utilities to pool their risks. Since penalties associated with violating the sulfur standards are rather severe, utilities selling permits run the risk that some future unanticipated event (such as an equipment malfunction) could make them vulnerable to a penalty assessment. The traditional strategy to deal with this contingency is to hold more permits than necessary. With an insurance pool utilities would band together to share the costs of penalties levied for truly unanticipated events, providing greater security for permit sellers. Greater security translates into a greater willingness to sell.

Implementing a Greenhouse Gas Trading System

While implementing a global entitlement system to control greenhouse gases is in the narrow sense an unprecedented event, in the broader sense a large number of international precedents exist.[47] While this is not the appropriate place to review, or even summarize, these precedents, it is important to realize that most of the individual steps involved have been undertaken before in the context of one or more international agreements.

Initial steps

An international system for controlling greenhouse gases must evolve slowly over time. The initial steps will necessarily be small as the parties will be hesitant to undertake large commitments.[48]

As long as the initial steps are consistent with the evolution of a cost-effective and equitable system, a slow moving process can be an advantage rather than a disadvantage. Starting small gives both the institutions and the parties a chance to adjust and to become familiar with the system. Since most initial efforts will be precedent setting, it will take time to work them out. Once the precedents have been established, however, the process will become smoother, quicker and better able to handle a larger number of participants, gases and permit trades.

Institutions will evolve along with attitudes. The clearinghouse and bank will be able to develop effective procedures for processing permit transactions. Signatory nations will become better at tracking and reporting emissions. Nonsignatory nations will learn how to participate in the process from the outside and become familiar with the advantages of being a signatory. Maturation of the associated financial markets will lay the groundwork for reducing the transactions costs associated with trading, a process that has already been triggered by the US sulfur allowance program.

Evolving to a more complete system

Beginning with a simple system with the understanding that it could evolve to a more complete system presumes some knowledge about the more complete system. Otherwise the process might well start down a path that could ultimately lead in a rather different direction. What would a more complete system look like?

The rules governing a more complicated system represent a natural evolution of the simple system by opening the agreement to more signatories, by facilitating the expansion of coverage to all greenhouse gases, and by providing the framework for tighter certification, monitoring, and enforcement procedures. While initially the limited system would necessarily be based primarily on trust, as the system evolved more complete monitoring and enforcement procedures could be developed.

Monitoring and enforcement

Although it would be inappropriate to attempt to catalogue all the monitoring and enforcement activities that would be associated with each of the unique sources of greenhouse gases, it is essential that general monitoring and enforcement strategies be identified as well as the institutional requirements to implement them. In this section we undertake that task, paying particular attention to the relative roles for private organizations, nations, and international agencies.

Monitoring
Nations which contain the individual pollution sources would have the major responsibility for monitoring and enforcing the activities of those sources. Ample precedent for this approach has been established by previous international agreements.[49]

Self-reporting of their emission levels by the sources to national enforcement agencies would be the key to the system supplemented by cross-checks provided by other sources of data. A standard practice in environmental regulation, self-reporting has the virtue that it is relatively inexpensive, and when backed by the appropriate sanctions for misrepresentation it provides remarkably accurate information.[50]

A combination of suitably defined effluent standards coupled with monitoring reports that directly reveal the compliance status of the source has proved in the United States to be an effective enforcement vehicle not only for EPA but for private enforcers as well. Citizens have access to the discharge monitoring reports, and the courts have generally accepted the information contained in them as proof of violations in enforcement actions brought by private parties.[51] By allowing citizens to use these reports as the basis for their claims, monitoring reports have significantly reduced the cost of both public and private enforcement activities.[52] The discharge monitoring report approach has proven so successful for the control of water pollution in the United States that it was incorporated into air pollution control legislation in 1991.[53]

Private monitoring has also become an important check of the self-reporting system. Many bodies of water in the United States are now protected and monitored by private associations of citizens concerned about that particular body of water. One increasingly typical activity of these voluntary, privately financed associations is hiring a full time "riverkeeper" or "harborkeeper" to monitor polluting activities continuously on that body of water and to monitor the water quality itself. Successful legal actions brought against municipalities and other polluters along the Hudson River in New York State have not only been a powerful force for cleaning it up but have established some institutional and legal precedents now being followed in other parts of the country.

Computer systems and software have now advanced to the point where it has become relatively easy to develop automated systems to aggregate and to integrate all these reports, to compare them with alternative sources of data for purposes of validation, and to identify and prioritize suspected cases of noncompliance for action.[54] Both the requisite hardware and software could easily be transferred to nations who sought them.

The direct measurement of emissions is expensive, but fortunately it is also unnecessary. Because of the close link between the carbon content of the fuel and the amount of carbon dioxide emissions, monitoring the flow of fuels is not a bad proxy for monitoring emissions.[55] This is an important point because monitoring the flow of fuels is much easier than monitoring emissions. While record-keeping systems are already in place to keep track of the flow of carbon-based fuels across international borders, no counterpart exists for emissions.

Individual governments would also have a responsibility for ensuring that all greenhouse gas trades are integrated into their emissions inventory. To ensure that their national allocations square with their emissions, all governments would at least have to be notified of trades. Depending on the wishes of the treaty negotiators, national approval of transboundary trades may or may not be required.

How would these monitoring and enforcement activities be financed? Private entitles could pay a fee to the government for each permit received. This revenue could be used to finance the record-keeping and surveillance necessary to run the system. Even fees which are too low to have any significant incentive effects have the potential to generate considerable revenue.

A smaller but important monitoring role would be reserved for the newly designated international monitoring authority. One department in this organization would be set aside to receive the individual country reports, to integrate them with estimates of emission levels for the nonsignatory countries, to validate these country estimates in so far as possible by cross-checking with independent sources, and to match reported achievements with treaty obligations on a country-by-country basis. This organization would then issue an annual report containing the country-by-country compliance information, a summary of progress toward the overall global warming goals, and recommendations for the future.

While this type of *ex post* monitoring would clearly not be appropriate for all environmental problems (particularly those posing immediate health risk), it does seem appropriate for controlling greenhouse gases. Given the rather long lags which characterize the gap between the emission of greenhouse gases and the perceived effects of the higher concentration, the delays associated with *ex post* monitoring seem inconsequential.[56]

Enforcement

What works at the national level would not work or even be necessary in the international context. Oversight of the national enforcers requires a rather different approach. As Professor Louis Henkin puts it in his book *How Nations Behave* despite some conspicuous departures, *"almost all nations observe almost all principles of international law and almost all of their obligations almost all of the time"* (emphasis in the original).[57]

Compliance with the norms of international law by the nation-states subject to those laws is driven less by the economic motivations that tend to drive profit-making firms than by the desire to be a part of maintaining a stable, dynamic equilibrium in international relations. This basic tendency can certainly be reinforced by an appropriately designed global warming agreement; rules universally perceived as fair are more likely to be obeyed than rules perceived as unfair.

It can also be reinforced by instituting what Chayes and Chayes (1991, pp. 290–304) call the principles of "accountability" and "transparency." According to these principles governments should be held accountable for their behavior by rendering their performance transparent to scrutiny by the international community. Requiring the submission of, and making public, the annual reports to the international monitoring authority would provide the foundation for applying these principles.

Skeptics are likely to suggest that public awareness of noncompliance is not a sufficient condition for compliance. That may be true, but it is also true that the power of public awareness should not be underestimated. In the United States, for example, many toxic air pollutants had not been regulated prior to the passage of the 1990 Clean Air Act Amendments. The Emergency Planning and Community Right-to-Know Act of 1986, however, required some 20,000 plants to report annual emissions of 320 potentially carcinogenic chemicals. These reports were then made available to the public. Publicized by newspapers and environmental groups, they became a rallying point for action. Even before the discussions about increasing the regulation of these substances became serious, businesses were beginning to make significant reductions in toxic emissions to counter the adverse publicity. A 39 percent reduction in toxic emissions has already been achieved by Monsanto. Dow Chemical plans a 50 percent reduction by 1995; and DuPont plans a 63 percent reduction.[58]

An alternative to taking legal action against a noncomplying party is provided by defining a complaint process to make all noncompliance transparent and to hold responsible parties accountable. One model of this approach, for example, is provided by the 1957 Rome Treaty establishing the European Economic Community.[59] Article 155 of that Treaty designated the EEC Commission responsible for implementing the Treaty's provisions and Article 169 empowers it to initiate proceedings against any noncomplying party.

The proceedings involve four stages. In the first step "letters of formal notice" are sent by the Commission to member states believed to be in violation of an EEC environmental directive. In the second step the member state is given the opportunity to respond to the notice, filing any information with the Commission that it believes supports its position. In the third step the Commission issues a "reasoned opinion" confirming the infringement or dismissing the case. Finally, should noncompliance continue, the EEC has the authority to initiate legal proceedings before the European Court of Justice.

Private actions are an important component of this process. As Sand (1991, p. 272) puts it:

> What may be the most significant feature of this procedure, however, is mentioned nowhere in the treaty and evolved only gradually in the course of its implementation: more than half of the infringement proceedings initiated against member states were based not upon the commission's own monitoring of compliance but on citizen complaints – from private individuals, associations (such as Greenpeace and Friends of the Earth), or entire municipalities.

This mechanism has apparently been successful not only in encouraging complaints but in encouraging compliance as well.[60] The increasing role for public-interest, nongovernmental organizations in the process of monitoring and enforcement in international law offers a wide range of new opportunities for enhancing the degree of compliance with international agreements.[61]

Three aspects of the Rome Treaty experience are particularly worth noting. First, the process of filing and publicizing complaints is by itself a powerful force for compliance. Second, affording standing to public-interest nongovernmental organizations considerably strengthens a monitoring and enforcement regime based upon transparency and accountability. Finally, the process of putting in place an international regime for enforcement is likely to be an evolutionary process. The first steps will be hesitant and will no doubt prove frustrating for those who seek to transfer the traditional national model of sanctions into an international setting. Nonetheless experience shows that transparency and accountability can be powerful enforcement principles which can provide a foundation for action. Should further action become necessary, these initial steps will pave the way for a further strengthening of the procedures.[62]

As with monitoring, the primary responsibility for enforcing the allocations held by individual sources would fall on the countries containing the regulated source. Countries would naturally be able to choose their own set of enforcement strategies but the menu of possibilities is growing rapidly. Many conventional and some unconventional strategies exist for encouraging these sources to comply.[63]

Notes

This chapter is an updated and revised version of a research report originally written for the United Nations. See United Nations Conference on Trade and Development (1992) for the report on that project.

1   In the limited space permitted in this chapter only a few highlights can be illustrated. All the details of the proofs and the empirical work can be found in the references listed at the end. For a comprehensive summary of this work see Tietenberg (1980, 1985, 1990), Dudek and Palmisano (1988), and Hahn and Hester (1989).

2   For other treatments of this issue see Bertram (1992), Haites (1991), Dudek and LeBlanc (1990), and Grubb (1989).

3   The impetus for most of the US trading programs in air pollution control has come from the federal government. Though states have the ultimate responsibility for implementing them, the programs have largely been designed and authorized at the national level. Recently that has begun to change as states have begun to take the initiative. The largest example is the RECLAIM program in California which is designed to use permit trading to control the precursors of smog. Other states are likely to follow the California lead soon.

4   The details of this policy can be found in "Emissions Trading Policy Statement" 51 *Federal Register* (December 4, 1986): 43829. This document is based upon a decade of experience with the program. For a description of its evolution see Tietenberg (1986).

5   Offsets are also required for major modifications in areas which have attained the standards if the modifications jeopardize attainment.

6   For some of the details of the program as well as a description of some of the implementation difficulties see Nussbaum (1992).

7   *Federal Register* (August 12, 1988): 30598. The final rules governing transfer of import and production allowances are in 54 *Federal Register* (February 9, 1989): 6376. These rules have been consolidated in 40 *Code of Federal Regulations* 82.

8   Since the demand for these allowances is quite inelastic, supply restrictions increase revenue. By allocating allowances to the seven major domestic producers of CFCs and halons, EPA was concerned that its regulation would result in sizable windfall profits (estimated to be in the billions of dollars) for those producers.

9   Ozone-depleting chemicals are defined in the Act as CFC-11, CFC-12, CFC-113, CFC-114, CFC-115, Halon-1211, Halon-1301, and Halon-2402. See 103 Stat 2365.

10   For more details on these programs see Carlin (1992).

11   Primarily these involve the reduction of phosphorus, but in the Tar-Pimlico Basin nitrogen is involved as well.

12   According to Carlin (1992, pp. 5–17) more than 35 wetlands mitigation banks currently function in those ten states.

13   This title was included in the Clean Air Act Amendments of 1990, which became law on November 15, 1990. See 104 Stat 2584. For an analysis of the application of the emissions trading concept to acid rain see Atkinson (1983), Raufer and Feldman (1984), Oates and McGartland (1985), Feldman and Raufer (1987), and Tietenberg (1989).

14   A relatively small number of allowances are also made available through a zero-revenue auction run for the EPA by the Chicago Board of Trade. This component was designed to alleviate fears that new, independent power producers would be unable to secure the allowances they would need to commence production.

15   One such trade to a public-interest group has already taken place. Northeast Utilities of Connecticut donated to the American Lung Association the company's right to emit 10,000 tons of sulfur allowances (valued at some $3 million). The company was expected to be able to take a tax deduction for the transfer.

16   104 Stat 2591.

17   Opschoor and Vos (1989, pp. 97–8).

18   The information in this section was derived from a telephone conversation with Erik Haites, a principal with Barakat & Chamberlin, the consulting firm involved in examining the feasibility of these proposals.

19   It should be noted that while the allocation is cost-effective, it is not necessarily efficient. It would only be efficient if the predetermined target happened to coincide with the efficient amount of pollution. Nothing guarantees this outcome.

20   Milliman and Prince (1989).

21   See Hahn (1984) for the mathematical treatment of this point. Further discussions can be found in Tietenberg (1985) and Misiolek and Elder (1989).

22   When a price-setting source is initially allocated more than its cost-effective allocation, it can inflict higher control costs on others by withholding some permits from the market. When a price-setting source is initially allocated fewer permits than would be justified by its cost-effective responsibility, however, it can exercise power on the buyer side of the market.

23   These studies are surveyed and compared in Tietenberg (1985).

24   See, for example, Manne and Richels (1992, p. 99).

25   See Atkinson and Tietenberg (1982, 1984), Hahn (1984), Harrison (1983), Krupnick (1986), Lyon (1982), Palmer et al. 1980), Roach et al. (1981), Seskin et al. (1983), and Shapiro and Warhit (1983) for the individual studies and Tietenberg (1985) for a summary of the evidence.

26   The zero-revenue auction was first proposed in Hahn and Noll (1982, p. 141). Essentially sources are required to put some proportion of their allowances up for sale in the auction and they receive the resulting revenue. A small zero-revenue auction is a component of the US sulfur allowance program.

27   ICF Resources Inc. (1989).

28   As indicated below, the fact that so many emissions trades have actually taken place within the same plant or among contiguous plants provides some confirmation for this result.

29   For individual studies see de Lucia (1974), Hahn (1984), and Maloney and Yandle (1984). For a survey of the evidence see Tietenberg (1985).

30   Strategic price behavior is not the only potential source of market power problems. Firms could conceivably use permit markets to drive competitors out of business. See Misiolek and Elder (1989). For an analysis which concludes that this problem is relatively rare, and can be dealt with on a case-by-case basis should it arise, see Tietenberg (1985).

31   For detailed evaluations see Tietenberg (1985, 1990), Dudek and Palmisano (1988), Hahn (1989), and Hahn and Hester (1989).

32   Notice that unlike the introduction of banking and the encouragement of greater compliance, this source of improved air quality extracts a cost-effectiveness penalty. Using trading ratios to produce better air quality leads to fewer trades and lower cost savings.

33   For a strong articulation of this point of view see the discussion in Stewart and Wiener (1991) and US Department of Justice (1991).

34   Richard Elliot Benedick, one of the negotiators of the Montreal Protocol, also suggests that an early insistence on a comprehensive approach could be quite

counterproductive by "bogging down the negotiators and unneccessarily prolonging the entire process." See Benedick (1991, p. 11).

35   A comprehensive treatment of this point of view is presented in Swart (1992). Victor (1991) also suggests that a comprehensive approach is impractical, given the uncertainty of monitoring gases other than CO_2.

36   If the ratio of emissions to produced substance is controllable, then focusing on production provides no incentives to reduce this ratio, even when that may be the preferred method of emission reduction. This problem has arisen with the Montreal Protocol, since it controls production and consumption rather than emissions. This structure provided inefficient incentives for signatory countries to test suggested technologies or to develop new technologies for the recovery and destruction of the controlled substances. See Bohm (1991).

37   In the Montreal Protocol, for example, the allowances of controlled substances are defined in terms of production and consumption rather than emissions.

38   In theory the permits could be allocated directly to private sources, skipping the allocation among nations altogether. Since a tradeable permit system is likely to be implemented through a treaty signed by nations, an initial allocation of permits to the nations is the most likely outcome of that process.

39   Acceptance of a low quota limit is likely because making the permits transferable opens a larger supply of emission-reducing options, thereby reducing the cost of compliance. This was the case in the negotiations over the sulfur allowance program described above. Bohm (1992) also points out that making the permits transferable allows the less developed countries to negotiate and get larger initial quotas than they otherwise would.

40   It could also reserve some proportion, known typically as the growth increment, to accommodate expected future growth. This growth increment could be used to encourage the development of new employment-generating activities by providing entitlements at below market prices.

41   An alternative approach, suggested in Kågeson (1991), envisions allocating 80 percent of the permits by a grandfathering approach and the remaining 20 percent by an auction approach. His study focused on the limited objective of implementing a greenhouse gas permit system only among the EU countries.

42   The problem is complemented somewhat when the greenhouse gases also have local effects. In this case the local effects can be handled by local regulations. No trade violating a local regulation would be permitted.

43   For example, a 1 part per million concentration of methane at a point in time contributes 26 times more to global warming than an equivalent amount of CO_2, but the atmospheric lifetime of CO_2 is 10 to 20 times longer.

44   Only if the control authority initially allocates the permits so that a cost-effective allocation would be achieved even in the absence of any trading will the possibility of market power be completely eliminated. In this special case cost-effectiveness would be achieved even in the presence of market power on either the buyer or the seller side because no trading would take place, eliminating the possibility of exploiting any market power.

45   The effect of this type of sequential trading is modeled and analyzed in Atkinson and Tietenberg (1991).

46   For an examination of futures markets in general see Carlton (1984).

47   Levi (1991), for example, notes the striking parallels between the requirements for a greenhouse gas permit system and the arrangements which grew out of the Bretton Woods Agreement of 1944. Some of the specific aspects of global warming believed to have direct parallels in the situation facing the Bretton Woods negotiators are the

need (i) to structure an agreement such that both developed and developing countries would find it in their interest to participate; (ii) to balance emissions reductions with efforts to increase absorption capacity; (iii) to provide technical assistance to countries too poor or too small to know the most efficient way to contribute to atmospheric improvement; (iv) to monitor aggregate and individual country achievements and punish offenders; and (v) to have the means to follow a well-defined path of net reduction in greenhouse gas emissions so as to achieve climatic stability.

48   For examples of proposals for initial steps see Dudek and LeBlanc (1990) and Roland (1991).

49   Since 1973, for example, the Washington Convention on International Trade in Endangered Species of Wild Fauna and Flora has established worldwide trade controls based on a permit system administered completely by the individual nations. For other examples see Sand (1991, pp. 259–61).

50   In the United States virtually all environmental statutes now make the falsification of these environmental compliance reports a criminal offense with the responsible individual subject to personal fines and imprisonment. For further details see Segerson and Tietenberg (1992).

51   See Student Public Interest Research Group v. Fritzsch, Dodge & Olcott, Inc. 579 F. Supp at 1538.

52   For an analysis of the determinants and effects of supplementing public enforcement with private enforcement as revealed by the US experience see Naysnerski and Tietenberg (1992).

53   Section 504 of the 1991 Amendments to the Clean Air Act require facilities to certify that they are in compliance with all applicable regulations and permit conditions. These certifications are similar to the discharge monitoring reports required under the Clean Water Act, and they are also subject to sanctions for false or improper certification. See Unterberger (1991, p. 1636).

54   The nature of the system used to support the US lead trading system is described in Nussbaum (1992). Kete (1992) describes in some detail the system currently being developed to support the sulfur oxide trading system that is an integral part of the US approach to reducing acid rain.

55   It is not a perfect proxy, however. Since combustion is the source of the carbon dioxide emissions, oil used for lubrication does not pose the same problem as oil used as a fuel. As a practical matter this can be handled by giving production facilities a credit for all oil sold for lubrication.

56   This point is developed in Haites (1991).

57   Cited in Chayes and Chayes (1991, p. 289).

58   Howe (1991, p. 35).

59   Sand (1991) describes this custodial procedure as "one of the most important means of enforcing EEC environmental standards."

60   The number of complaints rose from 10 in 1982 to 460 in 1989. One complaint by a citizen of the United Kingdom against his own government ultimately led to an investigation that resulted in infringement proceedings against seven member states (Sand, 1991, p. 272).

61   For an examination of the successful roles public-interest nongovernmental organizations have already played in shaping, monitoring, and enforcing international environmental law as well as a vision suggesting a greatly enhanced role in the future see Sands (1989).

62   Many observers believe that harmonizing the competing claims of protecting the global environment and protecting national sovereignty will require the development

of an enforcement process in stages. For one view of how this might be done in two phases see Holley (1991, pp. 82–95).

63   For a description of some of these innovative strategies and how they work in practice see the enforcement essays in Tietenberg (1992).

References

Atkinson, Scott, E. 1983: Marketable pollution permits and acid rain externalities. *Canadian Journal of Economics*, 16 (November), 704–22.

Atkinson, Scott, E. and Tietenberg, T. H. 1982: The empirical properties of two classes of designs for transferable discharge permit markets. *Journal of Environmental Economics and Management*, 9 (June), 101–21.

Atkinson, Scott, E. and Tietenberg, T. H. 1984: Approaches for reaching ambient standards in non-attainment areas: financial burden and efficiency considerations. *Land Economics*, 60 (May), 148–59.

Atkinson, Scott, E. and Tietenberg, T. H. 1991: Market failure in incentive-based regulation: the case of emissions trading. *Journal of Environmental Economics and Management*, 21 (1), 17–31.

Benedick, R. E. 1991: Lessons from the "ozone hole." In R. E. Benedick et al. (eds), *Greenhouse Warming: Negotiating a Global Regime*, Washington, DC: World Resources Institute.

Bertram, G. 1992: tradeable emission permits and the control of greenhouse gases. *Journal of Development Studies*, 28 (3), 423–46.

Bohm, P. 1991: Implications of imperfect competition on fossil fuel markets comparing a global carbon tax and globally tradeable CO_2 quotas. University of Stockholm Working Paper, June.

Bohm, P. 1992: Distributional implications of allowing international trade in CO_2 emission quotas. *The World Economy*, 15 (1), 107–14.

Carlin, A. 1992: *The United States Experience With Economic Incentives to Control Environmental Pollution*. Washington, DC: US Environmental Protection Agency, Report 230-R-92-001, July.

Carlton, Dennis W. 1984: Futures markets: their purpose, their history, their growth, their successes and failures. *Journal of Futures Markets*, 4 (3), 237–71.

Chayes, A. and Chayes, A. H. 1991: Adjustment and compliance processes in international regulatory regimes. In *Preserving the Global Environment: The Challenge of Shared Leadership*, New York: Norton.

Dudek, D. J. and LeBlanc, A. 1990: Offsetting new CO_2 emissions: a rational first step. *Contemporary Policy Issues*, 8 (3), 29–42.

Dudek, D. J. and Palmisano, J. 1988: Emissions Trading: why is this thoroughbred hobbled? *Columbia Journal of Environmental Law*, 13 (2), 217–56.

Feldman, Stephen L. and Raufer, Robert K. 1987: *Emissions Trading and Acid Rain Implementing a Market Approach to Pollution Control*. Totowa, NJ: Rowman & Littlefield.

Grubb, M. 1989: *The Greenhouse Effect: Negotiating Targets*. London: Royal Institute of International Affairs.

Grubb, M. and Sibenius, J. K. 1992: Participation, allocation and adaptability in international tradeable emissions permit systems for greenhouse gas control. In Tom Jones and Jan Corfee-Morlot (eds), *Climate Change: Designing a Tradeable Permit System*, Paris: Organization for Economic Co-operation and Development, 185–227.

Hahn, R. W. 1984: Market power and transferable property rights. *Quarterly Journal of Economics*, 99 (4), 753–65.

Hahn, R. W. 1989: Economic prescriptions for environmental problems: how the patient followed the doctor's orders. *Journal of Economic Perspectives*, 3 (2) 95–114.

Hahn, R. W. and Hester, G. L. 1989: Where did all the markets go? An analysis of EPA's emission trading program. *Yale Journal of Regulation*, 6 (1), 109–53.

Hahn, R. W. and Noll, R. G. 1982: Designing a market for tradeable emission permits. In *Reform of Environmental Regulation*, Cambridge, MA: Ballinger, 199-46.

Haites, E. 1991: Tradeable allowances and carbon taxes: cost-effective policy responses to global warming. *Energy Studies Review*, 3 (1), 1–19.

Harrison, David, Jr. 1983: Case study 1: The regulation of aircraft noise. In Thomas C. Schelling (ed.), *Incentives for Environmental Protection*, Cambridge, MA: MIT Press.

Holley, S. E. 1991: Global warming: construction and enforcement of an international accord. *Stanford Environmental Law Journal*, 10, 44–96.

Howe, C. W. 1991: An evaluation of US air and water policies. *Environment*, 33 (September), 10–15, 34–6.

ICF Resources Inc. 1989: Economic, environmental, and coal market impacts of SO_2 emissions trading under alternative acid rain control proposals. Report prepared for the Regulatory Innovations Staff, USEPA, March.

Kågeson, Per. 1991: *Economic Instruments for Reducing Western European Carbon Dioxide Emission*. Stockholm: Swedish Environmental Advisory Council, Ministry of the Environment, June 7.

Kete, N. 1992: the U.S. acid rain control allowance trading system. In Tom Jones and Jan Corfee-Morlot (eds), *Climate Change: Designing a Tradeable Permit System*, Paris: Organization for Economic Co-operation and Development, 69–93.

Krupnick, Alan J. 1986: Costs of alternative policies for the control of nitrogen dioxide in Baltimore. *Journal of Environmental Economics and Management*, 13 (June), 189–97.

Levi, Maurice D. 1991: Borrowing from international financial organizations: learning from Bretton Woods for dealing with global warming. University of British Columbia Working Paper, January.

de Lucia, Russell J. 1974: An evaluation of marketable effluent permit systems. Report No. EPA-600/5-74-030 to the US Environmental Protection Agency, September.

Lyon, Randolph M. 1982: Auctions and alternative procedures for allocating pollution rights. *Land Economics*, 58 (February), 16–32.

Maloney, Michael T. and Yandle, Bruce. 1984: Estimation of the cost of air pollution control regulation. *Journal of Environmental Economics and Management*, 11 (November), 244–63.

Manne, Alan S. and Richels, Richard G. 1992: *Buying Greenhouse Insurance: The Economic Costs of CO_2 Emission Limits*, Cambridge, MA: MIT Press.

Milliman, Scott R. and Prince, Raymond. 1989: Firm incentives to promote technological change in pollution control. *Journal of Environmental Economics and Management*, 17 (November), 247–65.

Misiolek, Walter S. and Elder, Harold W. 1989: Exclusionary manipulation of markets for pollution rights. *Journal of Environmental Economics and Management*, 16 (March), 156–66.

Naysnerski, Wendy, and Tietenberg, Tom. 1992: Private enforcement of environmental law. *Land Economics*, 68 (1), 28–48.

Nussbaum, B. 1992: Phasing down lead in gasoline in the U.S.: mandates, incentives, trading and banking. In Tom Jones and Jan Corfee-Morlot (eds), *Climate Change: Designing a Tradeable Permit System*, Paris: Organization for Economic Co-operation and Development, 21–34.

Oates, W. E. and McGartland, A. M. 1985: Marketable pollution permits and acid rain externalities: a comment and some further evidence. *Canadian Journal of Economics*, 18 (August), 668–75.

Opschoor, J. B. and Vos, H. B. 1989: *The Application of Economic Instruments for Environmental Protection in OECD Countries*. Paris: Organization for Economic Co-operation and Development.

Palmer, Adele R., Mooz, William E., Quinn, Timothy H. and Wolf, Kathleen A. 1980: Economic implications of regulating chlorofluorocarbon emissions from nonaerosol applications. Report #R-2524-EPA prepared for the US Environmental Protection Agency by the Rand Corporation, June.

Raufer, Roger K. and Feldman, Stephen L. 1984: Emissions trading and what it may mean for acid deposition. *Public Utilities Fortnightly*, 114 (August 16), 17–25.

Roach, Fred., Kolstad, Charles., Kneese, Allen V., Tobin, Richard, and Williams, Michael. 1981: Alternative air quality policy options in the four corners region. *Southwestern Review*, 1 (Summer), 29–58.

Roland, K. 1991: An international clearinghouse for greenhouse gas entitlements: some issues for Norwegian negotiators. A draft memo from ECON Energi, Oslo.

Sand, P. H. 1991: International cooperation: the environmental experience. In Jessica Tuchman Mathews (ed.), *Preserving the Global Environment: The Challenge of Shared Leadership*, New York: Norton.

Sands, P. J. 1989: The environment, community and international law. *Harvard International Law Journal*, 30 (Spring) 393–420.

Segerson, Kathleen, and Tietenberg, Tom. 1992: Defining efficient sanctions. In T. H. Tietenberg (ed.), *Innovation in Environmental Policy*, Cheltenham: Edward Elgar, 53–73.

Seskin, Eugene P., Anderson, Robert J., and Reid, Robert O. 1983: An empirical analysis of economic strategies for controlling air pollution. *Journal of Environmental Economics and Management*, 10 (June), 112–24.

Shapiro, M. and Warhit, E. 1983: Marketable permits: the case of chlorofluorocarbons. *Natural Resource Journal*, 23 (5), 577–91.

Stewart, R. B. and Wiener, J. B. 1991: A comprehensive approach to climate change. *The American Enterprise*, 75–80.

Swart, R. 1992: Greenhouse gas emissions trading: defining the commodity. In Tom Jones and Jan Corfee-Morlot (eds), *Climate Change: Designing a Tradeable Permit System*, Paris: Organization for Economic Co-operation and Development, 137–66.

Tietenberg, T. H. 1980: Transferable discharge permits and the control of stationary source air pollution: a survey and synthesis. *Land Economics*, 56 (November), 391–416.

Tietenberg, T. H. 1985: *Emissions Trading: An Exercise in Reforming Pollution Policy*. Washington, DC: Resources for the Future.

Tietenberg, T. H. 1986: Uncommon sense: the program to reform pollution control policy. In *Regulatory Reform: What Actually Happened*, Boston, MA: Little, Brown.

Tietenberg, T. H. 1989: Acid rain reduction credits. *Challenge*, 32 (March–April), 25–9.

Tietenberg, T. H. 1990: Economic instruments for environmental regulation. *Oxford Review of Economic Policy*, 6 (Spring), 17–33.

Tietenberg, T. H. 1992: *Innovation in Environmental Policy: Economic and Legal Aspects of Recent Developments in Liability and Enforcement*. Cheltingham: Edward Elgar.

United Nations Conference on Trade and Development. 1992: *Combatting Global Warming: Study on a Global System of Tradeable Carbon Emission Entitlements*. Geneva: United Nations.

Unterberger, Glenn L. 1991: Citizen enforcement suits: putting Gwaltney to rest and setting sights on the Clean Air Act. *Environmental Reporter: Analysis and Perspective* (4 January), 1631–6.

US Department of Justice. 1991: *A Comprehensive Approach to Addressing Potential Climate Change*. Washington, DC: US Department of Justice.

Victor, D. G. 1991: Limits of market-based strategies for slowing global warming: the case of tradeable permits. *Policy Sciences*, 24 (2), 199–222.

16

Trade, Pollution, and Environmental Protection

C. Ford Runge

Introduction: Trade, Pollution, and Environmental Quality

In the 1980s and 1990s air pollution, acid rain, and global warming became major items on the international agenda, as environmental issues moved beyond domestic policy.[1] This shift reflects growing recognition of the global impact of economic development and the rising problem of international externalities, as hazards spill over national borders and affect the oceans, air, and climate. But just as environmental risks flow through the world's biosphere, so they also flow through the world economy – and threaten to disrupt it. Environmental risks tend to concentrate in those countries with the least regulation. Some regulatory differences exist among countries at the same stage of development, but in the world as a whole the flow of environmental and health risks runs from the north to the developing nations of the south. The mechanism of this flow is trade.

At the same time, growing consumer concerns about environmental quality and pollution in the north are prompting more attention to environmental hazards from imported products, particularly food. As a result, domestic interests and other producers seeking protection from foreign competition are finding a new source of support in the environmental and consumer movements. Import restrictions, when presented as a public health measure, gain a legitimacy that they might not otherwise enjoy.

These events suggest the new realities created by uneven environmental and health regulation and their links to trade. When nations exchange goods and services, they also trade environmental and health risks. These risks are the opposite of services – they are environmental and health *disservices* traded across national borders. This trade in disservices is an emerging source of tension in trade negotiations. The United States and other signatories to the General Agreement on Tariffs and Trade (GATT) are committed to pursuing more open borders in the ongoing Uruguay Round of trade negotiations. But as national health, safety, and environmental regulations grow in importance, different national regulatory priorities pose several related problems for trade and development. These differences have been especially obvious in negotiations over the North American Free Trade Agreement (NAFTA).

In both NAFTA and GATT negotiations, charges have been made that groups in some countries seek to gain competitive advantage over foreign producers by moving production to sites where environmental regulations are less strict. Alternatively, environmental claims have disguised protectionism, as the environment is used as an excuse to keep out imported products. Producers may also try to export products that threaten the health of consumers in foreign countries. All such actions could do unnecessary harm to *both* environmental quality and world trade unless new international arrangements are devised to resolve the problems.

The Chapter in Review

Five main issues dominate the debate over trade, pollution, and the environment, and will serve as the focus of this chapter. The first is how best to capture the interactions of environmental and trade measures from an analytical and modeling standpoint. The second is the potential environmental impact of trade liberalization, both in the regional context of NAFTA and in the global trade talks continuing in GATT. The third is the possible use of environmental measures as nontariff barriers to trade. The fourth is the relationship between trade agreements under NAFTA and GATT and the variety of international environmental agreements (IEAs), such as the Montreal Protocol agreement to protect atmospheric ozone. Finally, a variety of institutional issues present themselves as challenges to policymakers.

For professional economists, the first challenge is an analytical one: how to blend the theory of externalities with international trade theory in a way which allows comparisons of both environmental and trade impacts. Currently, approaches to the problem are evolving from partial equilibrium models toward more general equilibrium approaches. Here we will adopt the simpler, but revealing, partial framework.

The second and most politically charged issue is the concern that trade liberalization, whether in NAFTA or under GATT, will lead to increased levels of environmental damages. There are numerous facets of this concern, which has been expressed strongly by a variety of environmental groups and members of Congress. One is the role of trade in allocating economic activities among countries, some of which are polluting, some of which are not. Overall, trade promotes specialization and efficiency, but may also create incentives to export pollution itself. Many environmental concerns also derive from the fact that, as trade expands, "scale effects" may cause added pollution. Scale effects are the result of increases in the quantity of goods and services moving within countries and across borders, due to the fact that increases in trade lead to greater transportation needs, higher levels of manufacturing output, and general increases in the demand for raw and processed products which can impose greater wear and tear on natural ecosystems. Among these possible scale effects are increasing consumption of nonrenewable natural resources including fossil fuels, minerals, and old-growth forests, and increasing levels of air and water pollution. A particularly striking example often cited by environmental groups is the pollution found in the rapidly growing border region between Mexico and the United States (Golden, 1993). It has also been suggested that differences in environmental standards, especially between north and south, will create "pollution havens" for firms and industries seeking less regulatory oversight, as the composition of goods and services changes. Trade also affects the technologies employed in various countries. Finally, trade may induce policy shifts, either in favor of improved environmental quality or in the opposite direction.

In contrast to the environmental community's concern over the impacts of more liberal trade, those most directly involved in trade have tended to focus more on a third main issue, the potential for protectionism disguised as environmental action. This can occur when a country or trading bloc protests internal markets in the name of environmental health or safety – for example the European Union's decision to ban the import of beef from cattle treated with certain growth hormones. It can also occur when higher levels of environmental standards are used to bar market access to goods and services produced under lower levels of regulation, especially by developing countries. The fundamental issue concerns the ability to distinguish legitimate environmental measures, which may well distort trade, from those which are not only trade distorting but have little basis from an environmental standpoint. Developing such criteria involves complex legal, scientific, and institutional issues.

The fourth issue involves the relationship between trade agreements and IEAs. In the last decade, a variety of new international agreements have been negotiated in response to global environmental challenges such as ozone depletion, species extinction, the protection of Antarctica, and international management of the oceans. The Rio Conference on Environment and Development, held in June 1992, resulted in a broad new mandate for environmental action, Agenda 21, together with the creation of a new UN Commission on Sustainable Development. Some of these agreements call on their signatories to refrain from trade in certain goods or processes. In the recent NAFTA negotiations, for example, a tri-national commission was created with apparent authority over trade with damaging environmental effects. This commission has authority apart from the GATT and the existing GATT dispute resolution process. The question is: how are international environmental accords to be balanced with existing or new trade obligations? What body of international law, and which international institutions, should exercise authority over the intersection between multilateral environmental and trade policy?

Finally are a variety of institutional challenges for policymakers. The increasingly competitive trade relations between the United States, the European Community, and Japan are one axis along which institutional issues arise. In some respects, the high income countries of the north are increasingly alike in placing relatively greater value on environmental quality. But these economies are also locked in a high stakes game of competition for global markets, and their governments face domestic pressures to loosen regulatory oversight. Even given their similarities, differences exist in the north not only in scientific and environmental standards but in culture and social norms, which will continually confront efforts to harmonize environmental regulations. The gap between the environmental regulations along the north–south axis is even wider, accentuating problems of harmonization. The NAFTA negotiations reflect these differences in microcosm, with Mexico attempting rapidly to upgrade its environmental regulations in order to satisfy fears in the United States and Canada. How global institutions and domestic policies are altered to deal with these problems will determine how effectively trade and environmental issues will be confronted in the years ahead.

Analytical Issues

The analysis of pollution and environmental quality in an international context poses a variety of challenges. The traditional analytical treatment of pollution in a closed economy (absent trade) involves externalities theory in which one agent imposes external costs on others in ways unreflected by market prices. This "wedge" between market prices and a shadow price reflecting the external effect can be corrected through a Pigovian tax-sum-subsidy scheme. The complexity of doing this depends in turn on the nature of the external effect.[2] Equivalently, property rights may be redefined and assigned (subject to the costs of these transactions) in such a way that the external effect is made attributable to those who are responsible for it, thus internalizing it (as when two firms are merged). Generalizing from the case of an externality imposed on a few agents, any negative effect imposed on a group of others may be modeled as a public "bad," so that the theory of public goods and bads applies (Mishan, 1971). In cases of a "pure" public bad, external costs are imposed in such a way that all agents consume the same amount of the bad (e.g. a given level of pollution, such as particulates in the air). The dilemma is that while each agent consumes the same amount, individual willingness to pay to reduce the negative effect is *not* the same. This stands in contrast to the pure private good (or bad) in which each agent pays the same amount but the quantity consumed differs depending on individual preferences (see Samuelson, 1954). It is the capacity to misrepresent one's willingness to pay in the case of public goods or bads which leads to the classic "free-rider" problem. In the case of pollution, an individual may understate or overstate his or her true willingness to pay for cleanup, since the price mechanism does not reveal true preferences (Sandler, 1992, ch. 2).

An alternative and analytically convenient formulation is to treat an external effect from the point of view of a producer rather than a consumer, as an input into production (see Antle and Just, 1992). Here, the analytical consequences depend on how pollution affects the production technology of the firm, rather than the consumers' preferences. While the effect of the externality will be valued by the firm at the margin in a (negative) shadow price, this shadow price typically will not correspond to a market price because the market fails to capture its negative impact.

The already complicated situation arising from these market failures is made even more so when the economy is opened to trade. When negative external effects and bads are traded internationally along with goods, or when they enter as negative inputs into international production processes, what has changed analytically is that the effect is "transboundary" in nature (Livingston et al., 1993). Its transboundary nature complicates its resolution. A traditional tax-cum-subsidy scheme in a closed economy, for example, presumes that an authority exists which can levy taxes or pay subsidies, or can redefine and reassign property rights. But when one or more nations are involved, and an international authority capable of levying and enforcing such measures is absent, then the national governments must coordinate their actions. This international coordination problem aggravates the tendency of firms or individuals to free-ride by shirking responsibility for the external effect or public bad, since costs are borne in part or in whole by foreign individuals and firms and become the concern of foreign governments. A classic example is the attempt by the United States and Canada to develop a coordinated approach to acid rain arising from US emissions of sulfur dioxide (SO_2) (Mohen, 1988). There are also important terms of trade effects arising from transboundary externalities, so that the trading interests of nations will be affected by actions taken to regulate them (Brown et al., 1993). These terms of trade effects arise from both the costs and benefits of internalizing the environmental externality.

Given these complexities, the attempt to integrate externalities theory with the neoclassical theory of international trade is relatively recent (Merrifield, 1988; Krutilla, 1991; Anderson, 1992; Antle and Just, 1992).

Here we will develop a simple partial equilibrium approach, following Anderson (1992).[3] Consider a small country facing both market failures and the prospect of trade liberalization, in which its own actions do not affect the rest of the world.[4] The small country produces or consumes a commodity, such as corn, in which an externality results from the failure of the market to account for the impact of corn production or consumption on the natural environment. An example of a production externality might be soil erosion which reduces the productivity of agricultural lands and lowers water quality. An example of a consumption externality might be water pollution from farm chemicals which raises the risk of water-borne disease (Sullivan et al., 1992). The result of the externality is to drive a "wedge" between private and social costs of production, reflected in the divergence of S and S' in figure 16.1. These alternative supply curves measure marginal private and social costs, respectively. The demand curve D measures marginal private benefits. The price axis refers to the price of corn relative to all other prices in the economy, which remain constant throughout.

In this case, OQ is the level of corn production without either (i) international trade or (ii) measures to "internalize" environmental impacts such as erosion. Production occurs at point e, the intersection of *private* marginal benefits and costs. Net *social* welfare is given as the sum of producer and consumer surplus minus the social costs of the external effect, or abe − ade. Now assume that the country shifts from autarchy (no trade) to open trade. If OP_0 is the prevailing international (border) price, as in figure 16.1(a), production will fall to OQ_m, consumption will rise to OC_m and Q_mC_m units of corn will be imported. Net social welfare is now abfg − ahg, and the welfare gain is defgh. This gain from trade is both positive and greater than it would have been if no externality had existed in the form of erosion by the shaded area degh. In effect, the country benefits because it imports corn more cheaply than it can produce it, and benefits by reducing soil erosion as well. Imports are "substitutes" for erosion.

On the other hand, suppose OP_1 is the prevailing international (border) price, as in figure 16.1(b). The country would thus become a net exporter of C_xQ_x units of corn if it moved to open trade. Net social welfare would be abik − amk, so the welfare effect of trade liberalization without any action to internalize the effects of erosion would be eik − edmk, which could be a net gain or net loss, depending on the relative magnitude of the *gain* from trade versus the *loss* from increased erosion as production expanded from Q to Q_x.

Several propositions follow from this analysis. The first is that liberalizing trade in a good with adverse environmental impacts which are left uncontrolled improves a small country's welfare if following liberalization it imports the good; but if it exports it, the negative environmental effects are subtracted from the gains from trade and the welfare effect is ambiguous. By importing the polluting good, a country

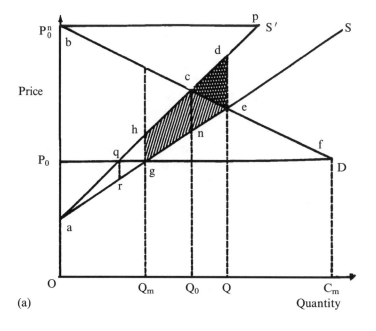

(a)

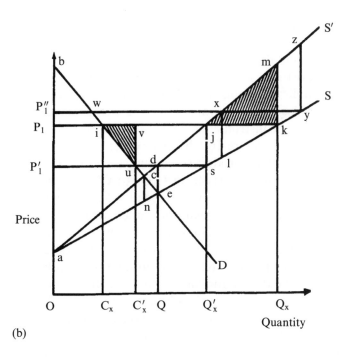

(b)

Figure 16.1 Effects of opening up a small economy to trade in a product whose production is pollutive; (a) importable; (b) exportable.
Source: Anderson, 1992, p. 28.

lets some other country worry about its polluting properties. By exporting it, it continues to face the social cost of these externalities in the home market.

Now suppose that instead of leaving erosion uncontrolled the small country *combined* trade reform with an environmental policy intervention sufficient to internalize the externality. Such an intervention could take the form of a tax, charge, or equivalent regulation or change in property rights.[5] Given such an environmental policy intervention, the gain from trade liberalization is qcf in figure 16.1(a) and cij in figure 16.1(b), depending on whether corn is imported or exported. In contrast to the situation in which no environmental intervention occurs, *this is a net gain in either the importing or exporting case.*

It is important to note, however, that without environmental intervention the benefits of liberalization for the exporter would be even greater, by cde. Hence, an incentive exists for net exporters to forgo environmental interventions because the benefits from trade are reduced somewhat by the production declines resulting from such environmental policy interventions. In this restricted sense, it is accurate to say that environmental interventions reduce an exporting nation's "competitiveness." But the larger loss is in net welfare, in that *without* such interventions it is not clear that expanded exports will improve net welfare at all. However, whether a small country is an importer *or* an exporter, there is a welfare gain from trade provided that a targeted (nearly optimal) environmental policy is introduced.

A third proposition concerns the relative efficacy of trade and environmental policy instruments. Suppose that instead of targeted environmental policy interventions aimed at erosion control, it was proposed to use a trade instrument such as an export tax aimed at the same target. This is shown in figure 16.1(b). An export tax could be used equal to is to lower the price producers receive from P_1 to P'_1, reducing production and lowering exports from C_xQ_x to $C'_xQ'_x$. This would lower the marginal cost of production to a level equivalent to an environmental intervention, producing a welfare gain of shaded area jmk. But the export tax causes consumers to pay P'_1P_1 below the opportunity cost of OP_1, leading to a deadweight welfare loss due to excess domestic consumption $C_xC'_x$, equal to the shaded are iuv. Hence, using a trade policy instrument reduces environmental degradation as much as an environmental tax set at the same rate, but at higher cost. Trade instruments can thus be used to reduce environmental degradation by a given amount, but they will generally improve welfare less than a more direct intervention at the source of the environmental pollution, and may even worsen welfare.

Moving from the small to the large country case, it is possible that the liberalization and/or environmental policies undertaken will affect world prices, so that the price lines in figures 16.1(a) and 16.1(b) are no longer horizontal. Moreover, the environmental policies and polluting activities of large countries such as the United States or the European Union will have global impacts, spilling over and ultimately back into home markets and welfare. Finally, policy changes in large countries may have demonstration or leadership effects on other countries.

In summary, the welfare effects of liberalizing trade are ambiguous if environmental externalities are left uncontrolled; but if they are largely internalized by an appropriately targeted environmental policy, the joint "liberalization effect" and "environmental effect" on welfare is positive. Simple welfare analysis thus offers a rudimentary analytical foundation for issues in trade and the environment. At an empirical level, however, there is still very little understanding of the effects of trade liberalization on the environment, and how different commodities and countries will be affected. Trade liberalization is also unlikely to be total or all inclusive, so that distortions and adverse environmental impacts will remain. This analytical exercise demonstrates an important overriding lesson: environmental externalities influence the welfare outcomes of trade; and trade influences the way in which externalities are borne and resolved. This interdependence requires further analysis, not only at the level of theory but in terms of recent experience and empirical research.

The Environmental Impacts of Trade

The impacts of trade on environmental quality have been an important focus of opposition to trade liberalization, especially in the context of NAFTA and the Uruguay Round of GATT. However, most claims about the negative environmental impacts of trade liberalization have been based on limited evidence. In fact, the impacts of trade on the environment vary greatly in degree and by location. In agriculture, for example, there is evidence that reducing subsidies and trade distortions would often help to reduce environmental damages by lowering fertilizer and pesticide use and increasing the efficiency with which soil and water resources are used (Runge, 1990; Harold and Runge, 1993).

In the industrial border region of Mexico,[6] by contrast, limited investment in wastewater treatment and hazardous waste disposal has created serious environmental damages resulting from foreign investments. These damages reflect a failure to address the environmental externalities of larger scale United States–Mexico trade. Yet the NAFTA process has also brought these problems to wider attention, stimulating new environmental investments and the enforcement of stricter standards that would be less likely under a situation of no trade. These investments are part of the trade impacts of NAFTA's environmental "side agreement"; stricter standards will be overseen by the North American

Commission on the Environment (NACE), an institutional by-product of trade liberalization. As trade growth raises incomes, demands for a cleaner environment also tend to rise, and new regulatory constraints induce technological innovations which are more environmentally benign (Runge, 1987; Grossman and Krueger, 1991).

Five separate impacts of trade growth on the environment may be distinguished: (i) on allocative efficiency; (ii) on scale; (iii) on the composition of output; (iv) on technology; (v) on policy. The overall effect of trade on the environment is the sum of these separate impacts, which may be positive or negative depending on the case examined.

Allocative efficiency

Since Adam Smith (1776) first analyzed the impact of trade on production, it has been observed that greater allocative efficiency results when countries specialize in producing those things for which they have a natural advantage and then trade with other nations for other products, rather than attempting to produce all of the products in demand at home. Formalized as the theory of comparative advantage, it predicts that countries will utilize their natural and human resources in such a way that abundant resources will be used more in the production of goods and services than scarce resources, which will be conserved. To the extent that these "factor proportions" rule, trade will promote allocative efficiency by inducing patterns of production which are less wasteful than if every country tried to produce a full range of goods and services itself.

In this sense, more open trade leads to higher levels of economic satisfaction than inward-looking policies closed to trade, and reduces waste of scarce resources. This efficiency in production and exchange means that, for a given endowment of resources, trade will be less wasteful than autarchy, the absence of trade. The best empirical evidence of the wastefulness arising from closed economies comes from Eastern Europe and the former Soviet Union, where "self-sufficiency" often justified widespread environmental destruction (Boyd, 1993). Less dramatic, but substantial, environmental damage has resulted from the European Union's drive for self-sufficiency in agriculture (Hartmann and Matthews, 1993). However, the exercise of comparative advantage and more open trade is itself not inconsistent with overexploitation of *globally* scarce resources. If country A is endowed with locally abundant resources S and trades them to country B in return for locally abundant resources W, it may still be true that S or W, while locally abundant, are globally scarce and would be better conserved than traded. The former Soviet Union, to take a recent example, has offered opportunities to Western game hunters to hunt a variety of globally endangered species, at prices driven low by foreign currency scarcity and internal competition (Schapiro, 1993). If these hunting opportunities are traded because of their relative abundance in the Soviet Union, it does not diminish the fact that they deplete globally scarce endangered species.[7] The relative efficiency of comparative advantage and trade is just that: relative.

Scale

Granting the allocative efficiency of trade relative to no trade, there is still little question that the scale of economic activity in a world with no trade would probably be much lower, and in this limited sense would impose less wear and tear on the environment. As a mental experiment, such a world would somewhat resemble turning back the clock three or four hundred years, eliminating rail and road transportation based on hydrocarbon fuels, international air travel and transport, and returning largely to locally based agricultural subsistence. Obviously, it is not possible to turn back the clock; and eliminating trade in the face of today's population levels would probably lead to a global economic and ecological catastrophe as a population many times that of three or four centuries ago attempted unsuccessfully to revert to local subsistence. The role of increased trade in supporting income growth per capita and thus supporting higher levels of employment for growing populations is clear. In the United States, for example, it is estimated that without the growth in US exports (which doubled between 1985 and 1992) the 1990–3 recession would have been twice as deep, with 100 percent higher levels of unemployment than in fact occurred. Trade growth has been especially notable with developing countries. US export sales to developing countries, according to the US Department of Commerce, rose to £167 billion in 1992, up to 145 percent from 1991, largely offsetting weak demand from Japan and the European Union. Exports to developing countries increased in 1992 to 37 percent of total, up from 32 percent in 1990 (Greenhouse, 1993).

As this trade growth increases gross domestic product (GDP) per capita, does the scale of economic activity do damage to the environment in the same or similar proportions? The question of *scale* can be thought of in the following sense: as growth in GDP per capita occurs (due in part to trade), does pollution increase at the same rate, a decreasing rate, or an increasing rate, or does it actually decrease? Grossman and Krueger (1991) report evidence that, when a cross-section of countries was studied over time, pollution measured by particulates and SO_2 increased at a decreasing rate with GDP per capita up to a threshold of about US$5000 a year and then decreased, although the total began increasing again at higher income levels (figure 16.2). This nonlinear relationship between the scale of

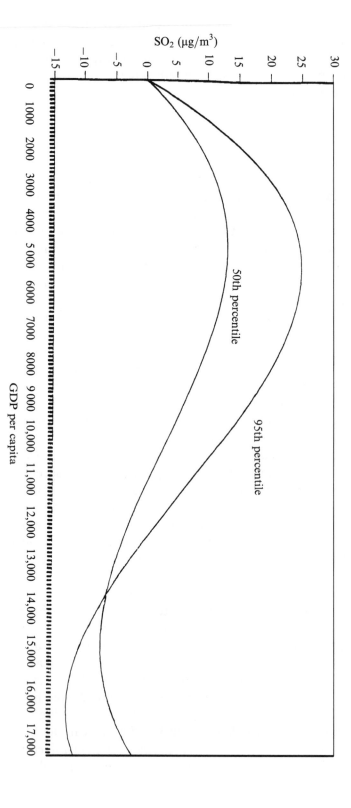

Figure 16.2 SO$_2$ versus GDP per capita.

Source: Grossman and Krueger, 1991, p. 42.

economic activity and the level of pollution suggests that other forces are at work, influencing how growth due in part to trade affects levels of environmental quality. These include the composition of output, technology, and policy decisions.

Composition of output

Environmental impacts of trade due to the composition of output can occur when increases in GDP lead to reduced heavy manufacturers with large levels of pollution and shifts to higher levels of services with lower levels of pollution. This change in the composition of output may influence total pollution levels, offsetting some of the scale effects of economic growth through trade. The relative growth of the services versus the manufacturing sector in the higher income nations, coupled with their decreasing per capita levels of certain pollutants, suggests that shifts in the composition of output may play a role (see Dean, 1992).

Technology

A fourth way in which trade may affect the environment is through induced technological innovations. As increased value is given to environmental quality with increases in income, markets for "green" technologies may develop and grow. These environmental technologies (such as wastewater treatment or materials recycling) may also be accompanied by changes in traditional technologies (such as shifts toward more energy-efficient and less polluting steel production) which lower the overall level of residuals and hazards from manufacturing processes. Some companies have found that new waste reduction technologies are highly profitable. In 1986, for example, Dow Chemical launched its Waste Reduction Always Pays (WRAP) program, credited with saving millions of dollars. Similar efforts are under way at other companies, including Minnesota Mining and Manufacturing (3-M) and Shell Oil (Rice, 1993). These experiences suggest that incentives for environmentally beneficial technological innovation may be greater at larger, more integrated manufacturing firms.

Policy

All of the environmental effects of trade discussed above, whether arising from allocative efficiency, scale, composition of output, or technology, operate in the context of government policies. Indeed, there is reason to believe that without the increasing stringency of environmental regulation many of the incentives to alter the character and methods of production so as to reduce waste and pollution would be far weaker. While trade may encourage greater allocative efficiency, the negative scale effects of economic growth on the environment are only offset by composition and technology to a degree largely determine by the regulatory framework. It is the political will to impose such discipline on environmental externalities which ensures that trade liberalization is ultimately welfare enhancing. In the United States, for example, since 1986 the Environmental Protection Agency (EPA) has required a Toxic Release Inventory (TRI) in which plants of 10,000 US manufacturers report annual releases from their facilities into the air, ground, and water of some 317 toxic chemicals. These include asbestos, freon, and PCBs, as well as 20 toxic chemical categories such as lead compounds. As this list continues to grow, companies and the public have an increasing basis to "keep score," utilizing measures such as TRI releases per dollar of sales. Dow Chemical, for example, eliminated practices of injecting hazardous wastes underground before the TRI began, reducing this ratio, while Du Pont failed to do so (Rice, 1993, p. 115). On the one hand, this regulatory framework creates a quantitive basis for reducing emissions. On the other hand, it can create incentives to move production to foreign plants where such oversight is less stringent.

Total effects

The sum of these effects of trade on the environment may be positive or negative, depending on the industry or pollutant involved. Schematically, we can think of trade as inducing allocative efficiency, which in turn leads to economic growth and increased GDP per capita, with attendant negative scale effects. These scale effects may lead to increases in demands for environment protection and policies to accomplish this protection, inducing changing output composition and production technologies which in turn diminish negative externalities (table 16.1). However, in many cases this chain of events is broken by failures to develop and enforce regulations leading to the internalization of externalities. Where demands

Table 16.1 Trade impacts on the environment

Trade → allocative efficiency (+) →growth in GDP/capita
→ scale effects (−) → demand for environmental protection
→ change in policy → change in composition (+) → change in technology (+)

The plus sign denotes positive and the minus sign negative environmental impacts.

for environmental protection are not expressed or heard, as in many poor developing countries, changes in policy leading to changes in composition and technology may not occur.

This was the situation until relatively recently in Mexico, However, one of the most interesting and potentially beneficial consequences of the NAFTA has been to help induce institutional changes both in Mexico and under the trilateral "side-agreement" to NAFTA. These changes will help to develop more stringent levels of environmental protection and enforcement in Mexico as well as in the United States and Canada. This "environmental conditionality" represents an important new chapter in the evolution of institutional responses to the interaction of trade and environment (see Runge, 1994). We turn now to the opposite side of the trade–environment nexus – the impact of domestic environmental regulations on trade, and their role as disguised forms of trade protection.

Environmental Measures and Trade Burdens

When domestic environmental measures lead to claims of *trade* harm, it is generally because a burden has been imposed on individuals or firms seeking to export or import goods or services in the name of domestic (and sometimes global) environmental protection. The question is whether the environmental measure is justified primarily as a form of necessary environmental protection or is a disguised restriction to trade, in which harmful trade effects loom proportionately larger than beneficial environmental effects.

The issue of whether a government environmental regulation is a nontariff trade barrier is a question face domestically by the states in America under the commerce clause of the US Constitution and by the 12 member states in the European Union under the Treaty of Rome. Such questions typically break down into two parts. (i) Does the measure create a burden on trade? (ii) Is the burden justifies by the environmental benefits of the regulation? From a legal perspective the apparent burden imposed on trade is a "gateway concept." If a burden appears to be present, it opens the way to further inquiry as to its justification, in which its benefits for the environment are weighed against its harm to trade (Hudec and Farber, 1992). If "no burden" is found, then the trade effects of the regulation are not at issue (table 16.2).

While nearly all environmental regulations impose some differential burdens on commercial transactions, to be trade related this differential must exist between some foreign producers and their domestic competition. The differential may be relatively easy to see, as when foreign products are subjected to obviously different standards compared with domestic products. Under Section 337 of the 1930 Trade Act, for example,

Table 16.2   The impact of environmental measures on trade

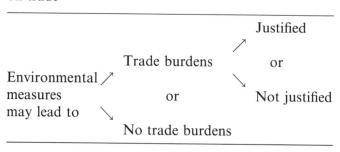

certain trade cases for foreign violators are heard before the International Trade Commission (ITC), while cases against US firms charged with similar violations are sent to US courts. In general, going before the ITC is regarded as more burdensome to the defendant. Not every differential rule clearly constitutes a burden, however, even though domestic and foreign products are treated differently. Inspections of auto safety glass at US auto manufacturers' factories are different from inspections of foreign vehicles' windshields at the border, but the border inspections do not appear to create a differential burden.

Less obvious are standards which appear neutral on their face but have a differential impact on foreign and domestic products. Provisions of the 1985 Farm Bill sought to apply sanitary processing and inspection standards to chicken from outside the United States that were "the same" as those standard used domestically ("the same" standards were substituted for previous language by members of Congress to Arkansas). The previous language had called for foreign standards "at least equal to" those used domestically. In a case brought before the federal court for the Southern District of Mississippi, the language calling for "the same" standard was upheld, despite warnings from the Department of Agriculture that "such a definitional finding would augur dire foreign trade implications . . . ."[8]

Overall, balancing legal and economic judgments must be made in order to extend the regulation of environmental risk into the international arena. Where trade measures led to environmental risks, these risks can be remedied through regulations. However, many such risks are not subject to regulations in the home market and may require negotiations with other countries, whether bilaterally or trilaterally as in NAFTA or multilaterally through international agreements. Where environmental actions lead to trade distortion, then the burden on trade must be assessed in relation to the environmental benefits, to determine if the trade burden is justified. Again, the decision that a trade-distorting environmental regulation is justified cannot be wholly unilateral. Consultation and agreement with other countries is likely to be necessary.

Environment–Trade Interactions: The Montreal Protocol

As the number of IEAs has grown in recent years, new questions have arisen concerning the relationship between these agreements and existing or future trade obligations in GATT (see Wirth, 1992). First, there is the question of whether countries are *parties or non-parties* to the treaties, such as the Montreal Protocol affecting chlorofluorocarbon and halon emissions damaging to atmospheric ozone. The Montreal Protocol, signed in 1987 and amended by the London Amendments in 1990, commits the signatory parties to study the feasibility of a ban applied to nonmember countries against imports of products made with a process that uses the ozone-depleting chemicals, as well as various other actions affecting trade in these products. In January 1993, for example, signatories were scheduled to ban the export of these substances to non-parties.[9] However, fewer than 20 countries were signatories by 1992, whereas over 100 countries are signatories to the GATT Articles. If countries are parties to GATT, with all of the *trade* obligations that this implies, and are also parties to the Montreal Protocol, with all of the *environmental* obligations this implies, then what if these obligations conflict? Alternatively, what if countries who have signed the Montreal Protocol take trade actions to ban imports from countries who have *not* signed the Protocol? Clearly, principles must be established to determine matters of priority and consistency.

In addition to the question of obligations under various treaties to which countries are pledged, there is the question of *"extrajurisdictionality,"* or whether countries have rights to impose trade measures in response to the environmental policies of other countries. This issue has come to the forefront with the United States–Mexico dispute over whether the United States can, under GATT, ban imports of tuna caught with fishing methods which kill dolphins in the process, even if these actions are taken outside the territorial jurisdiction of the United States.

A third question, related to the first two, is the legal *standing* of IEAs versus GATT obligations. While the Vienna Convention on the Law of Treaties provides general rules on the relationship of successive treaties, notably that the treaty "later in time" prevails,[10] the rule applies only where the two treaties address the same subject matter. In the case of a party to both the Montreal Protocol and GATT, for example, the section of the Protocol banning imports of substances produced with ozone-depleting chemicals would prevail over any inconsistent provisions of GATT (assuming the GATT Articles are considered a treaty). While the "later in time" rule of the Vienna Convention allows subsequent environmental agreements to "trump" trade obligations, some feel it may make it too easy to override trade rules in the name of these objectives (Housman, 1992, p. 3). In cases in which a country is not a party to the

IEA, the Vienna Convention (Article 34) states that an IEA that is later in time cannot bind non-party states without their consent, unless the treaty rules become customary international law (see Jackson, 1992).

In response to this lack of definition and clarity, some leading authorities have proposed a "waiver" for IEAs, at least temporarily, until better definitions and understanding can be worked out. A waiver limited to, say, five years could include specific current IEAs and provide for future ones as well. In addition to the Montreal Protocol, such a waiver might initially include two other major environmental agreements – the Convention on International Trade in Endangered Species of Wild Flora and Fauna,[11] and the Basel Convention on the Control of Transboundary Movements of Hazardous Wastes and Their Disposal.[12]

In summary, there is currently no consensus on the complicated intermeshing of trade obligations and IEAs. The critical questions include treatment of *parties and non-parties*, the reach of *extraterritorial* actions to protect the environment, the *standing* of IEAs versus GATT obligations, and the issue of a *waiver* for IEAs until some of these questions can be answered more clearly and definitively.

Institutional Issues

As the twentieth century draws to a close, two global trends are converging. The first, and most powerful, is the increasing integration of the world economy and the resulting interdependence of domestic and international policies affecting trade in goods and services. This trend creates both greater trade frictions and greater opportunities to develop mutually beneficial trading relationships. It also tests the rules of trade developed under the auspices of GATT and regional trading arrangements such as the European Union and NAFTA.

The second global trend is the increasing value placed on protection of the environment, and the need for national and international policies of environmental preservation to minimize the bads and disservices that trade can bring. Despite differences in the emphasis given to the environment in the north versus the south, there is little doubt that environmental issues will continue to dominate international discussion, including north–south dialogues, in the years ahead, especially given the transformation and diminished security threats posed by east–west relations.

These two global trends are now intertwining in complex ways. These complexities have been the subject of this chapter. Yet despite the many technical issues involved, an important and simple complementarity also exists (Repetto, 1993). In much the same way that international trade rules have evolved inside and outside of GATT in response to global economic interdependence, so new international environmental rules are now evolving in response to global environmental interdependence. Out of this mutual evolution an opportunity arises to *link* the objectives of market integration with environmental protection. Curiously, because the gap between environmental standards in the north and south is so great, it is precisely along the north–south axis that the opportunity for such linkage is also greatest.

In the same way that differences in resource endowments create gains from trade between dissimilar nations, so differences in levels of development and environmental protection can create complementaries built on incentives to exchange market access to the north in return for commitments to raise environmental standards in the south. The essential bargain in the making is to link one of the primary objectives of the Uruguay Round of GATT (more open market access) with the objective of raised levels of environmental protection. This is precisely what the negotiations over an environmental side-agreement to NAFTA have reflected: a promise of access to the markets of North America in return for a commitment to environmental improvements and enforcement. What the NAFTA experience suggests most clearly, however, is that trade rules alone are inadequate to the task: *environmental rules* are also required. And where such rules are developed, new *institutions* will be required to monitor and enforce them.

For more than a decade, the United States has relinquished its role as a leader in international environmental affairs while continuing aggressively to pursue both regional and multilateral trade agreements. The consequence has been to open it to criticism that freer trade was being pursued without regard to its environmental consequences. Restoring balance in the relationship between free trade and a protected environment now requires that the United States undertake comparable efforts to create new rules for international environmental policy. In many respects, the opportunity to take the lead in this arena fits naturally with the redefinition of international security resulting from the end of the Cold War.

Both trade and the environment have emerged in the post-Cold War era as issues of primary importance, leading to a new sense of international security, defined in economic and ecological terms (Mathews, 1989). Yet until recently ecological security has often been regarded as competitive with economic prosperity, creating an either/or proposition for policy-makers. While tradeoffs will often be necessary between environmental quality and unrestrained trade, it is increasingly clear that many areas of complementarity exist as well (see Freeman, 1992). In order to exploit this complementarity, it will be necessary to develop rules and incentives for environmental protection at both national and international levels which accomplish their objectives with a few burdens for market forces as is feasible; conversely, market expansion must proceed within constraints which protect nations from the negative externalities of economic activity.

In this process, the United States will need to take the lead, as reflected in negotiations over an environmental side-agreement to NAFTA. Despite progress in the European Union on both economic and environmental grounds, the unified Europe and new European leadership promoted early in the decade has not emerged (see Krause, 1991). Japan, clearly a powerful force in trade and a leader in some areas of environmental control technologies, has not yet fully embraced the Uruguay Round goals of market access and the Rio Conference objective of global environmental improvement. By contrast, NAFTA and its side-agreements, if successful, offer in microcosm precisely the sort of complementarity between trade liberalization and environmental protection possible on a global scale.

There is unlikely to be so lasting a set of institutional issues and challenges for this and future governments than to achieve a new balance between trade and environmental interests, both north and south. In contrast to the balance of destructive forces which has dominated negotiations between nations in the postwar era, this new balance is one of welfare improvements from both economic and environmental sources. To achieve such an equilibrium would reward the welfare of this generation, and generations to come, with continued prosperity and improved environmental quality.

Notes

This chapter was presented in draft form at the conference "Environmental Policy with Economic and Political Integration: The European Community and the United States," September 30–October 1, 1993. University of Illinois at Urbana-Champaign. My thanks to Judy Berdahl for help in preparation.

1   The material in this section draws on C. Ford Runge (1990, 1994).
2   Marchand and Russell (1973), following Davis and Whinston (1962), for example, show that, if an external effect is not additively separable in its arguments, then a constant Pigovian tax or subsidy is infeasible: the tax-cum-subsidy must vary at the margin. See Marchard and Russell (1973) and Davis and Whinston (1962).
3   This approach is based in part on Anderson (1992).
4   The assumptions underlying the model include the usual ones of partial equilibrium analysis in a trade setting (see Houck, 1986), augmented by standard externalities theory. While subject to criticism by advocates of empirical general equilibrium analysis (see Hazilla and Kopp, 1990; Merrifield, 1988), the approach is sufficient for clarifying analytical issues of relevance to public and environmental policy. Among the key underlying assumptions are that transactions costs prevent spontaneous negotiated "internalization" of the external effect, ruling out a "Coasian" solution; that taxes-cum-subsidies are lump sum (nondistorting); that the externality can be accurately measured; that it is a "product" rather than "process" externality; that all curves are linear and that the externality begins with the first unit of production; and that the marginal benefit and cost curves fully incorporate feedback effects from the rest of the economy. See Anderson (1992).
5   See Lloyd (1992). The "equivalence" of these measures is of course not guaranteed in practice as discussed in Baumol and Oates (1975). The effect of such a policy would be to eliminate the "wedge" between S' *and* S, so that marginal social costs of production

would equal marginal social benefits. In the case of no trade, such intervention would be equivalent to a tax of cn per unit, which would reduce corn production from OQ to OQ_0 in figure 16.1(a). The welfare benefit from internalizing the externality would be the shaded area cde, due to the reduced erosion resulting from the production fall. From a welfare perspective, we can thus isolate a welfare improvement due to the "environmental effect" of targeted enironmental intervention, assuming no "liberalization effect."

6 This area is often referred to as the "maquiladora sector." A maquiladora is a foreign-owned plant in Mexico subject to duty-free import of raw materials, in which finished products are exported duty free except for value added in Mexico. See McKeith (1991).

7 Valentin Ilyachenko, chief of the International Department of Conventions and Licenses in the Russian Ministry of Ecology in Moscow, noted competition such "that the prices for foreign hunters are actually going down. You can pay the equivalent of a VCR in the West for a Russian brown bear." He continues, "we have the same problem with animal trophies as we have with our rare religious icons being sold on the streets of Moscow and St Petersburg. As the prices for a hunt get lower and lower, we are trading off our natural resources for next to nothing" (Schapiro, 1993, p. 24).

8 *International Trade Reporter*, May 27, 1992 (Mississippi Poultry Association Inc. v. Madigan, No. J91-0086(W), DC SMiss 4/23/92).

9 The Montreal Protocol on Substances that Deplete the Ozone Layer, *adopted and opened for signature* September 16, 1987, reprinted in 26 I.L.M. 1541 (1987) (entered into force January 1, 1989). See US Congress, Office of Technology Assessment, chapter 3, pp. 42–6.

10 Vienna Convention of the Law of Treaties, opened for signature May 23, 1969, UN Doc. A/COIF. 39/27, 8 I.L.M. 679, Article 30, 8 I.L.M. at 691. For a general discussion, see Housman and Zaelke (1992).

11 The Convention of International Trade in Endangered Species of Wild Flora and Fauna, March 3, 1973, 27 U.S.T. 1087, T.I.A.S. No. 8249, 993 U.N.T.S. 243.

12 The Basel Convention on the Control of Transboundary Movements of Hazardous Wastes and Their Disposal, adopted and opened for signature March 22, 1989, reprinted in UNEP/I.G. 80/3, 28 I.L.M. 649 (1989) (entered into force May 1992).

References

Anderson, K. 1992: The standard welfare economics of policies affecting trade and the environment. In K. Anderson and R. Blackhurst (eds), *The Greening of World Trade Issues*, Ann Arbor, MI: University of Michigan Press, 25–48.

Antle, J. M. and Just, R. E. 1992: Conceptual and empirical foundations for agricultural-environmental policy analysis. *Journal of Environmental Quality*, 21, 307–16.

Basel Convention on the Control of Transboundary Movements of Hazardous Wastes and Their Disposal 1989: Adopted and opened for signature March 22; reprinted in UNEP/I.G. 80/3, 28 I.L.M. 649 (1989) (entered into force May 1992).

Baumol, W. J. and Oates, W. E. 1975; *The Theory of Environmental Policy: Externalities, Public Outlays, and the Quality of Life.* Englewood Cliffs, NJ: Prentice Hall.

Broadway, R. W. and Bruce, N. 1984: *Welfare Economics.* New York: Basil Blackwell.

Boyd, James. 1993: The allocation of environmental liabilities in central and Eastern Europe. *Resources for the Future*, 112 (Summer), 1–6.

Brown, D. K., Deardorff, A. V. and Stern, R. M. 1993: International labor standards and trade: a theoretical analysis. University of Michigan, July 23.

Convention on International Trade in Endangered Species of Wild flora and Fauna, March 3, 1973: 27 U.S.T. 1087, T.I.A.S. No. 8249, 993 U.N.T.S. 243.

Davis, O. A. and Whinston, A. B. 1962: Externalities, welfare, and the theory of games. *Journal of Political Economy*, 70, 241–62.

Dean, Judith M. 1992: trade and the environment: a survey of the literature. In Patrick Low (ed.), *International Trade and the Environment*, World Bank Discussion Paper 159, Washington, DC: World Bank, 27.

Freeman, Orville L. 1992: Perspectives and prospects. *Agricultural History*, 66 (2) (Spring), 3–11.

Golden, Tim. 1993: A history of pollution in Mexico casts cloud over trade accord. *New York Times* (August 16), A-1.

Greenhouse, Steven. 1993: Surge in growth in Third World gives an economic lift to U.S. *New York Times* (August 19), A-1.

Grossman, Gene M. and Krueger, Alan B. 1991: Environmental impacts of a North American free trade agreement. Woodrow Wilson Institute for Public Affairs. Princeton University, October 8.

Harold, Courtney and Runge, C. Ford. 1993: GATT and the environment: policy research needs. *American Journal of Agricultural Economics*, 75 (August), 789–93.

Hartmann, Monika and Matthews, Alan. 1993: Sustainable agriculture in the European Community: the role of policy., *Forum for Applied Research and Public Policy*, forthcoming.

Hazilla, M. and Kopp, R. J. 1990: social cost of environmental quality regulations a general equilibrium analysis., *Journal of Political Economy*, 98 (4), 853–73.

Houck, J. P. 1986: *The Elements of Agricultural Trade Policies.* New York: Macmillan.

Housman, Robert. 1992: The interaction of international trade and environmental agreements. Center for International Environmental Law, Washington DC, June 1, p. 3.

Housman, Robert F. and Zaelke, D. 1992: Trade, environment and sustainable development: a primer. *Hastings International and Comparative Law Review*, 15 (Summer), 535–612.

Hudec, Robert and Farber, Daniel. 1992: Distinguishing environmental measures from trade barriers. Workshop on International Economic Policy, University of Minnesota, November 17,

International Trade Reporter. 1992: Mississippi Poultry Association Inc. v. Madigan, No. J91-0086(W), DC SMiss 4/23/92, May 27.

Jackson, John H. 1992: World trade rules and environmental policies: congruence or conflict? *Washington and Lee Law Review*, 49 (4) (Fall), 1227–78.

Krause, Axel. 1991: *Inside the New Europe.* New York: Harper Collins.

Krutilla, K. 1991: Environmental regulation in an open economy. *Journal of Environmental Economics and Management*, 20, 127–42.

Livingston, Marie L., von Witzke, Harald and Hausner, Ulrich. 1993: The political economy of international pollution. Center for International Food and Agricultural Policy, St Paul, MN.

Lloyd, Peter J. 1992: The problem of optimal environmental policy choice. In K. Anderson and R. Blackhurst (eds), *The Greening of World Trade Issues*, Ann Arbor, MI: University of Michigan Press, 49–72.

Marchand, J. R. and Russell, K. P. 1973: Externalities, liability, separability and resource allocation. *American Economic Review*, 63 (September), 611–20.

Mathews, Jessica Tuchman. 1989: Redefining security. *Foreign Affairs*, 68 (2) (Spring), 162–77.

McKeith, Malissa H. 1991: The environment and free trade: meeting halfway at the Mexican border. *Pacific Basin Law Journal*, 10 (1), 183–211.

Merrifield, J. D. 1988: The impact of selected abatement strategies on transnational pollution, the terms of trade, and factor rewards; a general equilibrium approach. *Journal of Environmental Economics and Management*, 15, 259–84.

Mishan, Ezra, J. 1971: the postwar literature on externalities: an interpretive essay. *Journal of Economic Literature*, 9 (1) (March), 1–28.

Mohnen, V. A. 1988: The challenge of acid rain. *Scientific American*, 259 (August), 30–8.

Repetto, Robert. 1993; Trade and environmental policies: achieving complementariites and avoiding conflicts. In *Issues and Ideas*, Washington, DC: World Resources Institute, July.

Rice, Faye. 1993: Who scores best on the environment. *Fortune* (July 26), 114–22.

Runge, C. Ford. 1987: Induced agricultural innovation and environmental quality: the case of groundwater regulation. *Land Economics*, 63 (3) (August).

Runge, C. Ford. 1990: Environmental risk and the world economy. *The American Prospect*, 1 (Spring), 114–18.

Runge C. Ford, Ortalo-Magné, François and Vande Kamp, Philip. 1994; *Free Trade, Protected Environment: Balancing Trade Liberalization and Environmental Interests*. New York: Council on Foreign Relations.

Samuelson, P. A. 1954: The pure theory of public expenditure. *Review of Economic Statistics*, 36 (November), 386–9.

Sandler, Todd. 1992: *Collective Action; Theory and Applications*, An Arbor, MI: University of Michigan Press, ch. 2, pp. 19–62.

Schapiro, Mark, 1993: Murder on the Orient: pricey travel lets U.S. hunters kill rare game. *Condé Nast Traveler* (August), 23–5.

Smith, Adam. 1976: *The Wealth of Nations*, ed. Edwin Cannan. Chicago, IL: University of Chicago Press (originally published 1776).

Sullivan, John B., Jr, Gonzales, Melissa, Krieger, Gary R. and Runge, C. Ford. 1992: Health-related hazards of agriculture. In John B. Sullivan, Jr, and Gary R. Kriefer (eds), *Hazardous Materials Toxicology: Clinical Principles of Environmental Health*, Baltimore, MD: Williams & Wilkins.

US Congress, Office of Technology Assessment 1992: *Trade and Environment: Conflicts and Opportunities*, ch. 3, pp. 42–6.

Wirth, David A. 1992; A matchmaker's challenge: marrying international law and American environmental law. *Virginia Journal of International Law*, 32 (2) (Winter), 377–420.

Part IV

Environmental Stocks and Flows

17

Optimal Timber Management Policies

Claire A. Montgomery and Darius M. Adams

Forests have long served as an example of the point-input point-output class of investment problems in capital theory. Given a tree (or, by extension, a stand of trees of the same age) that is growing in value, one must determine the timing of harvest, the optimal rotation, that maximizes some measure of net return. This model serves as the cornerstone for the economics of timber management. It assumes a particular stand management strategy called *even-age management* in which the trees in a stand are approximately the same age and are harvested at one point in time. While this model is rich in the insights it provides into timber supply behavior, its scope is narrow.

Methods of forest stand management can be broadly classed into two strategies, even-age and uneven-age, depending on whether all or only some portion of the trees are removed at harvest time. The choice between strategies is dictated in part by economics and in part by the biological characteristics of the tree species being managed. Species best suited to even-aged management are not tolerant of shade and do best after a major disturbance such as fire or clearcutting creates an opening in the forest. Species best suited to uneven-aged management benefit from the protection of an overstorey when they are young and do well in stand in which a canopy of mature trees is maintained. In some regions and forest types, either form of management is applicable; in other cases only one of the two approaches is feasible. Since the mid-1960s the practice of clearcutting (in even-age management) has been increasingly identified as a symbol of the worst failures of markets to achieve socially efficient management of forest resources. There has been growing support for widespread use of uneven-aged management and modified forms of even-age management on public forests and for providing incentives for such practice on private land.

This chapter addresses timber management by private landowners responding to market incentives. In the first section we examine the basic static optimal rotation model for even-age stands, its analytical history, its comparative statics, and its elaborations. We identify economic variables that have strong impacts on timber harvest behavior. These may be effectively used as forest policy tools or they may be used for other purposes with the unintended result that timber harvest behavior is altered. The second section presents a model of the optimal harvest and timber stock in uneven-aged management and its variations. In uneven-age stands, the stand is entered for harvest repeatedly and some minimum stock of trees is left standing after each entry. This approach can be modeled as a continuous investment–disinvestment problem. Hence the analysis of uneven-age stands bears a close relationship to that for other renewable resources such as ocean fisheries, groundwater, and big game animals.

Beyond the stand level, broader issues of timber supply policy require an understanding of the management of individual stands of trees in the context of the entire forest. This is the focus of the final section of this chapter. For some owners and forests, forest-level management is simply the sum of independent stand-level decisions. For others, considerations related to timber markets, costs, and personal preferences effectively link stand-level decisions. Intertemporal patterns of harvest flows may differ markedly between these types of owners, and we are particularly interested in any conditions that might lead to an even flow of harvest over time.

The Optimal Harvest Age for Even-Aged Stands

Choice of the optimal age at which to harvest an even-age stand has been central to traditional forest economics, and an array of competing criteria have been proposed over the past 150 years for selecting the optimal rotation. A partial list of participants in the controversy include Faustmann (1849), Gaffney (1957), Duerr (1960), and Bentley and Teeguarden (1965) in the forestry literature and such luminaries as Fisher (1930), Boulding (1966), and Samuelson (1976) from the ranks of mainstream economists. The debate is summarized and resolved in a concise manner by Bentley and Teeguarden and by Samuelson, with the observation that the original 1849 formulation of a German tax collector named Martin Faustmann is essentially correct.

The basic Faustmann model

In its simplest form, the Faustmann model assumes that the timber landowner chooses the harvest age that maximizes returns to the fixed factor of production which is taken to be the land. This return is variously known as bare land value or soil expectation value (SEV). Stumpage price[1] and interest rate are determined by market equilibrium and are taken as given by the landowner. The model is static in the sense that price and interest rate are assumed to be constant over time. As a result, if the current best use of the land is for timber production, its best use in the future will also be for timber production and the optimal harvest age will be the same for current and future stands. The model is

$$\max F(A) = \frac{PQ(A) - C}{e^{rA} - 1} - C \qquad (17.1)$$

where A is harvest age, P is the stumpage price, C is a fixed per-acre cost incurred at the beginning of the rotation (it includes the cost of cleanup and preparation of the site and establishment of a new stand), $Q(A)$ is the volume yield function for a stand of trees (giving volume of timber per unit area) with $Q_A > 0$ and $Q_{AA} < 0$ over the relevant range, and r is the interest rate. The necessary condition for the optimal rotation age is

$$PQ_A = r[PQ(A) + F(A)] \qquad (17.2)$$

Given that $Q_{AA} < 0$, the sufficient condition for maximization is satisfied as long as $F(A) \geq 0$ (see appendix 17A). Equation (17.2) says that landowners will postpone harvest as long as the value of the incremental growth of the stand, PQ_A, is greater than the opportunity cost of the timber and the land. The opportunity cost of the timber is the forgone interest earnings on the income from current harvest, $rPQ(A)$, while the opportunity cost of the land is the forgone interest earnings on the value of the bare land, $rF(A)$.

In this simple model, price, interest rate, and establishment cost are the sole exogenous influences on optimal harvest age. An increase in the interest rate r or a one-time unanticipated increase in the stumpage price P lead to shorter rotations. In both cases this is because the marginal opportunity cost of postponing harvest rises relative to the incremental gain. Intuitively, landowners face a tradeoff. Shorter rotations given a rising interest rate reduce the impact of discounting on future returns and maintain present value, but also subject costs in future rotations to a lower discount factor as well. Shorter rotations raise the present worth impact of higher prices but reduce the volume at harvest. An increase in the stand establishment cost C results in longer rotations as landowners try to reduce the present value of these costs by pushing them further into the future. Because $F(A)$ falls as C rises in equation (17.2) for any stand age, harvest age must increase to reduce PQ_A and raise Q to reestablish the equality. Details of the comparative statics analysis are presented in appendix 17B. For a good graphical exposition of the basic Faustmann model, see Pearse (1990).

These results can be used to speculate on private timber management response in today's changing investment environment. Both price and interest rate are affected by policies specific to the forest sector and (oftentimes inadvertently) by more general macroeconomic policies. In recent years, maintenance of a large national debt in a world of imperfect capital markets has meant upward pressure on interest rates. Additionally, increased volatility in pubic policies related to private forest practice has raised uncertainty about future restrictions on private harvest practices. Thus, the risk-adjusted interest rate for evaluating investment in timber has probably been relatively high. It also appears that changing priorities for public forest land management agencies will mean a substantial permanent reduction in public timber supply. To the degree that international trade in wood products is restricted, this has led to an increase in domestic stumpage price. The combined impact of all these policy changes is to reduce investment in the private timber stock, that is, to shorten rotations.

The traditional approach to public regulation of forest management on private lands has been through forest practice legislation directly limiting or requiring certain management actions. Recalling the "cut and run" behavior of some private owners in the early days of settlement in the Lake States and far west, the most common form of regulation is the requirement of some minimum level of regeneration following harvest. If the regulation requires more investment than would otherwise be observed, it is equivalent to an increase in establishment cost C which would act to lengthen optimal rotation. Higher mandatory investment costs could also drive the soil expectation value below zero for forestry and lead to a shift of the land into uses other than timber production. Beyond this basic limitation, some states are now considering regulations (termed "new forestry" in some cases) that would require leaving some minimum portion of the timber standing after harvest to serve as the base for wildlife habitat and as a biological inoculum for subsequent stands. This would be equivalent to a percentage reduction in yield, Q, and would also result in longer rotations.

Changing assumptions

The formulation of the Faustmann model used to this point has been simplified to focus attention on basic behavioral implications. Here we explore the effects on rotation and soil expectation value of adding such "real-world" complications as taxation, variable management intensity, and non-timber values. Because price trends lead us away from static analysis, we reserve treatment of price to the end of the section.

Timber taxation

Few topics in the economics of forestry have received as much attention as the impact of timber taxation on the extent and timing of harvest. There is a large body of traditional research examining issues of equity or tax fairness, specifically the relative burden of various tax schemes on annual yield properties such as agricultural holdings compared with periodic yield properties such as timber stands. As forest cover in urbanizing areas of the United States has decreased and the average age of remaining timber has declined, interest has also focused on the effects of taxation on the retention of land in forest use and the timing of harvest.

Three broad forms of timber taxation are commonly examined: (i) an *ad valorem* system in which a fixed percentage tax is levied against the market value of the stand (land plus timber) each year; (ii) yield taxation where a fixed percentage tax is levied on the value of timber harvested; and (iii) a site or land value tax levied annually on the market value of the land only. In the analysis of tax impact it is common to assume (as we do below) that the full effect of the tax is incorporated in reduced soil expectation value (full tax capitalization). This need not be the case, however, if tax-induced timber supply reductions raise market stumpage prices. In this way some portion of the tax burden may be passed along to timber consumers.

If the tax rate is T, the *ad valorem* tax effectively augments the interest rate (Fairchild, 1935). From the preceding comparative statics analysis we know that raising the interest rate reduces the optimal rotation. In light of this rotation-shortening effect and practical problems of paying an annual tax for a parcel that produces revenue only at lengthy intervals, some states have adopted instead a yield tax. The yield tax is comparable to a percentage reduction in the stumpage price, leading to a longer rotation. The third alternative, the site or land value tax, leads to a scale reduction in bare land value and is neutral with respect to rotation age. Appendix 17C demonstrates these tax effects.

Taxation of timber and/or timberland, regardless of the form, induces some reduction in site value. Unless comparable burdens are placed on land values in alternative uses, the tax may occasion a shift from forest to non-forest use. Taxes with forms like the *ad valorem* or yield tax can also influence both the extensive and intensive margins of forest use by driving the site value negative. At the extensive margin, existing stands of timber might be harvested but not replaced except by natural regeneration. At the intensive margin, some silvicultural investments designed to increase the volume or quality of harvests would become uneconomic.

Variable management intensity

Timber producers must also choose the level of intensity with which to manage a stand. Management inputs include varying the initial planting density (seedlings per unit area), use of genetically selected planting stock, fertilization, thinning of the young stand to adjust spacing, and thinning of the mature stand to improve stand growth and generate revenue. The level of management intensity influences stand growth and also has broader environmental implications. For example, more intensive management usually shortens the time stands spend in juvenile stages, reducing wildlife habitat in these classes, and may also alter both the suitability of older stands as habitat and their visual and amenity characteristics.

Suppose, for simplicity, that management intensity is a single variable input m at the start of the rotation that influences yields $Q(A, m)$ over the life of the stand. This input has a cost of E per unit. As before we assume that the yield function is convex, $Q_A > 0$ and $Q_{AA} < 0$, $Q_m > 0$ and $Q_{mm} < 0$, and $Q_{AA}Q_{mm} - Q_{Am}^2 > 0$, but we do not *a priori* specify the sign of the first cross-partial Q_{Am}. The basic Faustmann expression then becomes

$$\max F_1(A, m) = \frac{PQ(A) - C - Em}{e^{rA} - 1} - C - Em \qquad (17.3)$$

Derivation of comparative statics results is greatly complicated by the presence of the cross-partials Q_{Am} and F_{1Am} whose signs are not known (see Chang, 1983). Nautiyal and Williams (1990) give practical arguments that increased management intensity increases the growth rate of the stand $(Q_{Am} > 0)$ and that the marginal contribution of management intensity to land value is decreasing with age $(F_{Am} < 0)$ over the relevant range. With these assumptions, optimal rotation can be shown to rise as management costs (E) increase, while changes in stumpage price P and reforestation cost C have the same effect on optimal rotation as in the simple model (17.1). The optimal level of management intensity m, in turn, rises with timber price and falls with higher reforestation (C) and management (E) costs. The impact of rising interest rate on both rotation and management intensity cannot be unambiguously determined from this general formulation. Nautiyal and Williams argue heuristically, however, that both must be negative.

Non-timber values

Forests provide a wide array of benefits in addition to timber. Some, such as forage for domestic livestock, have prices established in markets. Most, including wildlife habitat, water yields, recreation opportunities, visual amenities, and the sequestration of atmospheric carbon, do not. If the value of these non-timber benefits were known and assignable to landowners, they would appear in the Faustman calculus (or in the landowner's intertemporal utility function). Where timberland owners deviate from the Faustmann rotation because of professed concern for non-timber outputs, the value of the non-timber outputs that accrue to landowners may be inferred as the opportunity cost of "suboptimal" timber management.

In general non-timber values are continuous and depend on the age of the stand. Following Hartman (1976), Strang (1983) and Snyder and Bhattacharyya (1990), denote the annual non-timber value derived from a stand of age A as $G(A)$. The behavior of G with stand age may differ markedly with the specific non-timber benefit, as noted by Calish et al. (1978), in some cases even exhibiting multiple peaks. Ignoring regeneration cost C, for simplicity, the basic Faustmann model is

$$\max F_2(A) = \frac{PQ(A) + e^{rA} \int_{a=0}^{A} G(a)e^{-ra}\, da}{e^{rA} - 1} \qquad (17.4)$$

The necessary conditions for a maximum can be written in two equivalent ways:

$$PQ_A + G(A) = r[PQ + F_2(A)] \qquad (17.5)$$

or

$$PQ_A = \left(rPQ + \frac{rPQ}{e^{rA} - 1} \right) + \left[\frac{re^{rA} \int_{a=0}^{A} G(a)\, e^{-ra}\, da}{e^{rA} - 1} - G(A) \right] \qquad (17.6)$$

From (17.5), landowners will hold the stand just to the point where the incremental benefits from both timber output, $PQ(A)$, and non-timber output, $G(A)$, are equal to the incremental opportunity costs of holding both timber and land (the latter now including non-timber outputs). Relation (17.6) gives some insight into the effect of non-timber values on the optimal rotation length. The term in the first set of parentheses is the opportunity cost of postponing harvest when establishment cost C is zero and there are no non-timber values. The term in the second set of brackets is the difference between the opportunity cost of postponing the non-timber values from future rotations and the marginal non-timber benefit, $G(A)$. If this term is negative, the net marginal non-timber benefit of postponing harvest is positive and optimal rotation is longer. If non-timber values rise rapidly with age (G_A is large) the term in the second set of brackets may be so negative as to preclude harvest at any time because the marginal benefit of postponing harvest always exceeds the marginal cost.

As noted above, however, non-timber benefits need not uniformly rise or fall with stand age. Thus the Faustmann objective function may not be convex and may have multiple local optima, necessitating consideration of total values (Swallow et al., 1990).

Price behavior and expectations

The static properties of the model will be preserved if price is either fixed, endogenous (e.g. a function of stand age) or if price is random and generated by a stationary stochastic process as we discuss below. Timber markets are characterized both by a quality premium structure (with higher prices paid for timber of preferred species with straighter boles, fewer branches, and narrower annual rings) and by marked short-term price variation. However, stumpage prices for some species and regions also show significant long-term trends.

Log quality usually increases with tree size, and hence age. Per-unit harvest cost usually decreases with tree size as fewer logs must be handled to remove the same volume of wood. Thus, stumpage price may be expressed as a simple function of age, $P = P(A)$, where $P_A > 0$ and P_{AA} may have any sign. The basic model of equation (17.1) becomes

$$\max F_3(A) = \frac{P(A)Q(A) - C}{e^{rA} - 1} - C \qquad (17.7)$$

The necessary conditions become

$$P_{AQ}Q + PQ_A = r[PQ + F_3(A)] \qquad (17.8)$$

All other conditions constant, the economic intuition here is that higher prices for older trees should motivate owners to adopt longer rotations. This is difficult to show for the general case, since prices increasing with age would raise both the left-hand and right-hand sides of (17.8). It is easily seen in two special cases, however. In the first, we assume zero establishment costs $(C = 0)$. We can rewrite (17.8) as

$$\frac{P_A}{P} + \frac{Q_A}{Q} = \frac{r\,e^{rA}}{e^{rA} - 1} \qquad (17.9)$$

Here the rate of stand value growth is the sum of price and quantity growth rates, both of which are positive. If there is no quality premium $(P_A/P = 0)$, the equality in (17.9) occurs at an earlier age (remember that $Q_{AA} < 0$). Second, if we assume an exponential form for $P(A)$ so that $P(A) = P_0 e^{gA}$, the optimal rotation will increase as long as the rate of price growth, g, is positive.[2]

The shape of the price function depends, in part, on derived demand for logs in the production of a variety of products, primarily lumber, plywood, and a variety of chip and particle boards. As technologies are developed for doing "more with less" (e.g. micro-veneers and stronger, more aesthetic chip boards) the demand for large logs will fall relative to demand for small logs and the quality premium associated with age will be smaller – resulting in shorter rotations. Supply effects may offset this trend as "old-growth" timber stands available for harvest are depleted and as higher real wood price induces the conversion of land into tree plantations. The reduction in the supply of old trees and the increase in the supply of young trees would cause a relative increase in the premium associated with age – leading to longer rotations. However, the price function is probably not globally concave, as we have described it, and so the optimal rotation age may not respond smoothly to these technology and supply changes (Nautiyal, 1983).

A markedly different view of timber prices recognizes their inherent variability and highly volatile nature. Brazee and Mendelsohn (1988) assume that managers are risk-neutral, expected present net worth maximizers and that prices are a strictly stationary stochastic process.[3] They define a "reservation price," both today and for all future periods, at which the owner would be indifferent between harvesting now or later – at which "today's revenue would equal the expected net present value of waiting...." If today's price is below the reservation price the owner delays harvest one period, if above the stand is harvested. Since future returns depend on stand volume growth, the reservation price is found to vary (decline) with stand age and in an empirical example Brazee and Mendelsohn found the expected value of the optimal rotation to be slightly longer than the Faustmann rotation computed at the mean of the stochastic price process.

Criticism of this approach to harvest timing centers on the nature of the fundamental stationary price process. Washburn and Binkley (1990) argue that, over periods of year or more, timber markets are "efficient." That is, if this approach could produce a positive expected gain over a traditional Faustmann scheme based on the mean of the distribution alone, sellers, in attempting to capture this gain, would shift the mean so as to eliminate the expected gain.

Unlike most other renewable resources, the real prices of timber and timber products in the United States have shown distinct upward trends over the past 150 years. If this behavior is expected to continue, prices would not only vary but they would do so independently of stand-level conditions (such as age or total volume). The conditions for static equilibrium analysis – where optimal rotations and management decision rules are fixed over time – are not met. Modifications in the basic Faustmann model are required to determine optimal rotation. In particular, the optimal rotation age must be allowed to vary over the duration of the planning horizon. The basic Faustmann model becomes (Newman et al., 1985)

$$\max F_4 = \sum_{i=1}^{N} [P(t_i)Q(t_i - t_{i-1}) - C]\,e^{-rt_i} - C \qquad (17.10)$$

where the t_i are calendar times, with $t_i > t_{i-1}$. The rotation length for the ith rotation period is the interval $t_i - t_{i-1}$.

With this model, the opportunity cost of postponing harvest is equivalently the cost of shortening the next rotation or the cost of postponing all future rotations. As time passes, if price is growing, both the value and the cost of postponing harvest increase. While we suspect that the harvest ages of successive rotations may change, it is difficult to draw general conclusions without a specific form for $P(t)$ (see, for example, McConnell et al., 1983). To investigate this process Newman et al. assume exponential price growth and show that rotations gradually decline over time when the rate of price growth is no larger than the rate of interest but greater than zero. In the long term, rotations approach a steady state length: (i) equal to the Faustmann rotation ignoring the planting cost (C) when price growth is strictly less than the interest rate, or (ii) equal to the age of maximum average volume growth as the price growth rate approaches the interest rate. This rotation *shortening* contrasts with the quality premium example where the pattern of price movement repeats every rotation. However, in this case, with exponential price growth unrelated to stand conditions, the marginal cost of postponing harvest grows faster than the marginal gain.

Optimal Management of Uneven-Aged Stands

In their natural state, the dynamic behavior of even-aged stands is characterized by a limited range of tree ages and sizes, continued growth in total stand volume and in the average size of individual trees, and little or no regeneration of new trees. Disturbances (such as fire) tend to be dramatic, destroying large portions of the stand and stimulating regeneration activity. Uneven-aged stands, in contrast, have a wide range of individual tree ages and sizes, demonstrate relative stability in stand volume and in the number and size distribution of individuals, and support continuous (though often episodic) regeneration of new trees. Disturbances are of a reduced scale, opening smaller portions of the stand for regeneration and leaving a larger residual. Emulating these natural processes, the key decision variables in uneven-aged timber management are the residual stock of trees following harvest, the distribution of this stock across tree sizes, and the length of time between harvests.

Limited attention has been given to optimal management of uneven-age stands in comparison to even-age stands. However, beginning in the 1960s with the controversy surrounding clearcutting on the Monongahela National Forest, the trend in forest management on federal lands has been away from even-age systems (which make heavy use of clearcutting) toward management strategies that maintain some forest cover. Growing interest in "new forestry" and "ecosystem management" will probably mean further limitations on the use of clearcutting and increasing use of uneven-aged systems.

The basic optimal harvest model

Like the Faustmann model for even-aged stands, the objective of management in uneven-aged stands is assumed to be maximization of returns to the land. In the simplest approach, an undifferentiated stock of trees, S_t, grows according to a simple growth function $g(S_t)$. For regularity $g_s > 0$ and $g_{ss} < 0$, so that growth rate is strictly decreasing in the level of the growing stock. Figure 17.1 depicts such a function. A natural equilibrium ($\dot{S}_t = g = 0$) occurs at S_{gMAX} where growth equals mortality. Maximum sustained yield occurs at S_{MSY}.

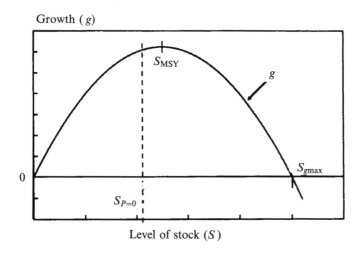

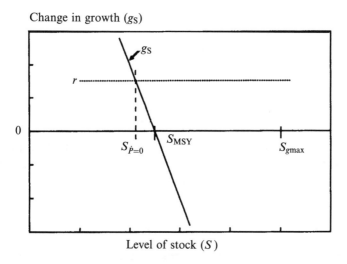

Figure 17.1 Growth (g) and change in growth (g_s) as functions of level of stock (S) in the uneven-aged management case, with optimal stocking for the case of no price growth ($S_{\dot{P}=0}$).

The methods of optimal control are particularly appealing in the analysis of the uneven-age case.[4] Since harvesting is an ongoing process, uneven-age management is analogous to the continuous investment/disinvestment problem of capital theory. Thus it is feasible to think of a steady state stand in which the rate of harvest and the level of the stock are constant over time. Because ownership of forest stands is defined and enforceable, there is no open access problem such as occurs in ocean fisheries and groundwater.

In its simplest formulation, landowners choose the volume to remove in each period (h_t) to maximize the present value of all future earnings. They are constrained by the initial stock and by the growth function. The intertemporal objective function for the uneven-aged forest stand owner is

$$\max \int_{t=0}^{\infty} P_t h_t \, e^{-rt} \, dt \tag{17.11}$$

subject to

$$\dot{S}_t = g(S_t) - t_t \tag{17.12}$$

$$S_t, h_t \geq 0 \quad \text{for all } t \tag{17.13}$$

$$S_0 \text{ given}$$

where P_t is the stumpage price, h_t is the control variable (the harvest volume at time t), r is the appropriate discount rate, S_t is the state variable (the stock of trees at time t), and $\dot{S}_t$ is the net instantaneous increment to the stock at time t. The objective function is maximized if, at each instant, landowners choose the value of the control variable h_t to

$$\max P_t h_t + \mu_t[g(S_t) - h_t] \tag{17.14}$$

The necessary conditions for a maximum are

$$P_t = \mu_t \tag{17.15}$$

and

$$\dot{\mu}_t = \mu_t(r - g_S) \tag{17.16}$$

where μ_t is the shadow price of unharvested timber. It represents the present value of the income forgone by harvesting now rather than later. Substituting (17.15) into (17.16) and rearranging yields

$$g_s = r - \frac{\dot{P}_t}{P_t} \tag{17.17}$$

A rational landowner will hold stock as long as the rate of return on the additional stock (g_s) exceeds the opportunity cost rate of holding the additional stock ($r - \dot{P}_t/P_t$).[5] A landowner will manage for maximum sustained yield ($g_s = 0$, $S_t = S_{MSY}$) if stumpage price is growing at the interest rate. If stumpage price is constant, a rational landowner will hold stock up to the point at which the marginal rate of return on the additional stock equals the interest rate ($S_{\dot{P}=0}$ in figure 17.1).[6] In the steady state, all the components of (17.17) are constant and $\dot{S} = 0$. The interpretation of these conditions is similar to the necessary conditions for the even-aged case. One postpones harvest of timber stock as long as the rate of return on investment (the additional stock in the uneven-aged case and the full value of the timber plus land in the even-aged case) exceeds the opportunity cost rate.

As in the even-aged case, we can also examine the impacts of changing exogenous elements of the optimization problem. Only price changes that affect the rate of price growth will influence the optimal stocking decision. Higher rates of price growth yield higher levels of optimal stock, because the opportunity cost of holding additional stock is lower. Lower interest rates increase optimal stock for the same reason. Changes in S_0 (for instance, destruction by fire) affect the optimal approach to a steady state, but do not affect the steady state conditions.

Changing assumptions

Characterizing an uneven-age stand solely in terms of volume is overly simple. The growth of the stand depends also on the distribution of trees by size class. Adams and Ek (1974) first examined the optimal distribution of volume by size class in a static analysis (prices vary with tree size but $\dot{P} = 0$ and $\dot{S} = 0$). They demonstrate substantial differences in potential harvest and present value depending on the distribution.

Quality premiums and multiple species
Quality premiums may be of considerable importance in uneven-aged management since harvesting often entails removal of stems across a wide range of sizes and hence qualities. It is also common for uneven-aged stands to include an array of tree species which may vary in price. The following reformulation of relations (17.11) and (17.12) can be used to model either price variation by size class or multiple species. Suppose the harvest h_{kt} of species of size class k in period t sells for price P_{kt}. If there are N species or size classes, the optimization problem is

$$\max \int_{t=0}^{\infty} \left[\sum_{k=1}^{N} P_{kt} h_{kt} \right] e^{-rt} \, dt \qquad (17.18)$$

subject to

$$\dot{S}_{kt} = g^k \left(\sum_{i=1}^{N} S_{it} \right) - h_{kt} \qquad \text{for all } k \text{ and } t \qquad (17.19)$$

Growth of the stock of the kth species or size class g^k depends on the total stock. Equation (17.17) becomes

$$\sum_{i=1}^{N} g^i_{S_{kt}} = r - \frac{\dot{P}_{kt}}{P_{kt}} \qquad \text{for } k = 1, \ldots, N \qquad (17.20)$$

indicating that an increment in the stock in the kth class affects the growth rate for all classes. Empirical studies show that, as the price gradient between small and large size classes increases, it is optimal in the steady state to hold more stock in total and to increase the proportion of stock in the larger classes (Adams and Ek, 1974; Haight et al., 1985).

Taxation
The three taxation schemes examined in the even-aged case are relevant in the uneven-aged case as well. For the *ad valorem* tax, (17.17) becomes

$$g_{S_t} = (r + T) - \frac{\dot{P}_t}{P_t} \qquad (17.21)$$

The effect is to augment the opportunity cost rate and hence less stock is held. The yield tax enters the objective as a simple multiple of harvest revenue and so is neutral. The land value tax, assessed instantaneously on the land value alone, is also neutral because there is no impact on the cost of holding stock. These results are shown in appendix 17D. Taxation does negatively affect the value of the land in timber production and so will distort the margin between timber production and other land uses unless other uses are similarly taxed (Klemperer, 1982; Stier and Chang, 1983).

Non-timber values
With uneven-aged management, yields of non-timber values will, in general, vary with the level of stock. While the aesthetic impacts of partial cutting are commonly held to be less than those of clearcutting, they are still negative. Partial harvests also act to increase habitat for early successional or edge-dependent wildlife species, perhaps to increase water flows, and to alter various recreational values. Thus the relation between the level of the stock and the yield of non-timber values may be positive for some values and negative for others. If $a(S_t)$ is a measure of the yield of non-timber values, the revised objective function is

$$\int_0^\infty [P_t h_t + a(S_t)] e^{-rt} \, dt \qquad (17.22)$$

Equation (17.17) becomes

$$g_{S_t} + \frac{a_{S_t}}{P_t} = r - \frac{\dot{P}_t}{P_t} \qquad (17.23)$$

If non-timber values increase at a decreasing rate with increasing stock ($a_s > 0$ and $a_{ss} < 0$), their presence augments the return from holding stock and more stock is held.

Optimal Timber Management at the Forest Level

In the traditional forestry literature, timber supply from the forest is set according to the principle of sustained yield: the ideal forest is to be "regulated" so as to produce a uniform harvest flow over time invariant to prices. Stands are harvested at the optimal (e.g. Faustmann) age and an equal proportion of the forest (1/rotation age) is harvested each year. The notion of sustainable harvest has reemerged in policy debates in recent years, and some states are considering laws requiring large forest owners to regulate their lands so as to ensure sustainable, even-flow harvests. But does even flow make economic sense? Are there any conditions under which it is optimal for private forest owners to regulate their forests and manage for an even flow of timber? This and an array of related timber supply questions are the concern of this section.

Forests comprising even-aged stands

The simplest case of forest-level timber supply is the owner whose sole objective is present-value maximization and whose costs and prices are fixed. The optimal strategy for this owner is to set the rotation according to the Faustmann model, harvest any stand that exceeds the optimal rotation age immediately, and thereafter harvest each stand just as it reaches the optimal age. Since individual stands have no biological interdependences (by assumption) and there are no other constraints, stands are treated as independent units. Timber supply at the forest level is simply the sum of stand-level harvest decisions. Aggregate supply response to market shifts is the sum of stand-level adjustments to changes in timber price, interest rate, and other determinants of rotation. The result at the forest level is the customary form of supply behavior. An unanticipated increase in timber price reduces the optimal rotation, more stands are eligible for harvest in the current period, and forest-level cut rises. An increase in the discount rate also reduces optimal rotation and acts to increase aggregate harvest.

The time path of forest-level harvest from a forest managed in this fashion depends on the initial age composition of the forest. It may be quite irregular, though with some cyclical pattern once all stands have been harvested one time, and may depart substantially from even flow.

For some forest landowners, however, stumpage price may depend on the volume harvested. They may supply a sufficiently large portion of logs to the mills in a region that they face a downward-sloping demand for logs. In this case stumpage price P_S is given by

$$P_S(h_t) = P_L(h_t) - C \tag{17.24}$$

where P_L is log price per unit, C is harvest cost per unit, and h_t is harvest volume. Alternatively, harvest cost may increase with harvest volume because of adjustment costs for capital such as roads and logging equipment, so that stumpage price is

$$P_S(h_t) = P_L - C(h_t) \tag{17.25}$$

Because the harvest of one stand influences the price received for all volumes harvested, decisions at the stand level are no longer independent. Owner welfare can be improved by coordinating harvest decisions across stands. The resulting flow of harvest is generally smoother than the case of fixed prices and costs.

To see why, consider the following highly simplified model. Suppose the forest consists of one uniform area of newly planted trees. Harvest volume at time t is the product of the fraction of the forest harvested, x_t, and the volume yield function, $Q(t)$:

$$h_t = x_t Q(t) \tag{17.26}$$

The entire forest is harvested by time T_{max}:

$$\sum_{t=0}^{T_{max}} x_t = 1 \tag{17.27}$$

and we ignore, for simplicity, any regeneration after harvest. Because of the nature of the stumpage price function, revenue $R(h_t)$ increases with the level of harvest at a decreasing rate, $(R_h > 0, R_{hh} < 0)$. The landowner chooses the fraction of the forest to harvest in each period to maximize the present value of the forest, ignoring the value of the land:

$$\max_{x_t} \sum_{t=0}^{T} \frac{R(h_t)}{(1+r)^t} + \mu\left(1 - \sum_{t=0}^{T} x_t\right) \tag{17.28}$$

The objective function is maximized when

$$R_h(h_t)(1+r) = R_h(h_{t+1})[1 + q(t)] \qquad \text{for } t = 0, \ldots, T-1 \tag{17.29}$$

where the volume growth rate is $q(t) = [Q(t+1) - Q(t)]/Q(t)$. Because $Q_{tt} < 0$, $q(t)$ falls with tree age. Early in the projection period the volume growth rate of the uncut forest exceeds the interest rate, $q(t) > r$. To satisfy (17.29) marginal revenue must be decreasing and hence the volume harvested must be increasing. When the volume growth rate falls to the point where $q(t) = r$, marginal revenue, and thus harvest volume, must be constant. As the remaining forest continues to age, the volume growth rate falls below the interest rate, $q(t) < r$. Marginal revenue must be increasing and hence the volume harvested must be decreasing over time. In the simple case of fixed prices, the owner's optimal strategy would have been to hold the forest to the Faustmann rotation and cut it all at one time. In this case the demand function generates economic incentives to smooth the flow of harvest volume.[7]

But will the harvest trajectory approach even flow regardless of the initial state of the forest? And if so, on what rotation will the forest be regulated? Mitra and Wan (1985, 1986) investigate optimal harvest trajectories in the general case in which land is used for timber production in perpetuity and the decision maker faces a general utility function. If the utility function is linear, their model reduces to the Faustmann model of present-value maximization and they demonstrate that the optimal management plan is to harvest each stand as it reaches the Faustmann rotation age with no tendency toward regulation of the forest. If the utility function is concave (representing a concave revenue function for a single landowner or a social utility function for a social planner) and there is no discounting, they demonstrate that the optimal harvest trajectory leads to regulation of the forest on a "golden rule" rotation age that corresponds to maximum sustained yield.[8] With discounting, however, they were unable to demonstrate either a unique optimal regulated forest or that an optimal harvest trajectory leads to regulation of the forest on any rotation.

Heaps (1984), Brazee and Mendelsohn (1990), Hellsten (1988) provide different perspectives on the characteristics of the optimally regulated forest. Heaps models long-term harvest decisions allowing for a U-shaped variable average harvest cost function that corresponds to the standard increasing marginal cost curve. Brazee and Mendelsohn examine harvest adjustments to a demand shift and the characteristics of the ensuing steady state forest. Hellsten explores the nature of a forest regulated so as to optimize social welfare. These studies all assume the dependence of stumpage price on harvest volume and share the conclusion that the Faustmann rotation is optimal for the regulated, steady state forest in the long term. Clear demonstration, however, that an optimal harvest trajectory leads directly to optimal regulation of the forest in the long run has proven elusive.

Forests comprising uneven-aged stands

For forests of uneven-aged stands, the distinction between stand and forest-level analysis is less clear. If all acres in a forest are treated as biologically identical, the model of equations (17.11)–(17.13) describes timber supply behavior from an uneven-aged forest. If stands of varying characteristics are recognized (at a minimum stands would be identified on the basis of different growth functions), the objective would simply involve the summation across these management units, as in the even-aged case, with no qualitative change in behavior.

Forest-level supply behavior is again of the conventional sort. From the discussion of the necessary conditions for an optimum of model (17.11)–(17.13), we found that harvest in the current period responds in a positive fashion to reductions in the rate of price growth (today's prices rise relative to future prices) and directly with changes in the interest rate (higher rates lead to higher current harvest). Over time if the rates of interest and of price change are constant, g_s in equation (17.17) must be constant and hence the level of stock must be constant as well. Thus supply in this case will follow an even-flow schedule, with harvest equal to growth.

Suppose that we generalize the owner's objective to recognize both the utility derived from the consumption of goods purchased with revenues from the sale of timber and the non-timber benefits derived (we assume) from the uncut stock itself. If we allow as well that the owner may obtain income from non-forest sources and either save or borrow at some fixed interest rate to modify intertemporal consumption patterns, the management problem in a simple two-period discrete form would appear as follows:

$$\max u(c_1) + v(S_1) + u(c_2) + v(S_2)$$

subject to

$$c_1 = P_1 h_1 + M - B$$

$$c_2 = P_2 h_2 + (1 + r)B$$

$$S_1 = S_0 - h_1$$

$$S_2 = S_1 + g(S_1) - h_2$$

(17.30)

where c_i is consumption in period i, h_i is harvest in period i, M is non-forest income, S_j is timber stock at time j, r is the discount rate, B is savings (if positive) or borrowing (if negative), g is the growth function, and u, v are utility functions for commodities and non-timber outputs respectively. To facilitate analysis we have assumed here that the utility function is additively separable between consumptive and non-consumptive uses of the forest and over time. We also assume $u', v' > 0$ and $u'', v'' < 0$.[9]

In this framework, if an owner does not recognize non-timber benefits, $v(S) = 0$, supply behavior again has the customary form. Current period timber supply will rise if the current price or interest rate rise and fall if next period's price rises. The timber supply decision is effectively decoupled from the intertemporal consumption decision (as a result of the lending/borrowing option) and the necessary conditions for optimal timber production are similar to those of equation (17.17) above.

If, however, the standing forest does have utility value to the owner, the harvesting decision cannot be separated from the consumption decision. The necessary conditions for an optimum in model (17.30) become

$$\frac{P_2}{P_1}(1 + g') = (1 + r) - \frac{v'(I_1)}{P_1 u'(c_2)} \tag{17.31}$$

Since u' and v' are both positive, the right-hand side of (17.31) is smaller than $1 + r$. This would require a higher level of stock (and hence lower g') relative to the case where $v = 0$ to bring about equality. The form of (17.31) does not allow us to determine the response of harvest to changes in current price; thus we can say little about supply behavior. The difficulty here is that desired harvest falls as owner income rises as a result of the utility value of the standing stock. Thus even though a higher current price raises utility from consumption and hence would evoke a positive harvest response, it also raises income which has a potentially offsetting effect.

Whether the standing forest has value or not, long-term harvest in this more general context reaches some even-flow level if price growth and interest rate are constant. The long-term steady state stock will be larger when the standing forest does have value, however, and hence the associated even-flow level will be lower.

Limitations and Extensions

Because this chapter addresses private forest management behavior, concerns for social optimality have received only peripheral reference. Here we wish to draw attention to two areas where the divergence between private and social optimality may provide legitimacy and direction for public involvement in forest management.

As demonstrated throughout the chapter, the intertemporal nature of forest management makes the interest rate a prominent determinant of timber harvest behavior. If capital markets were perfect and the future were known, private forest management would at least meet the criteria of intertemperol efficiency. Issues of intertemporal equity, however, would still require attention. The belief that the welfare of future generations is not adequately represented in markets and the belief that capital markets are indeed imperfect support the notion that the social rate of time preference (by which society expresses its intertemporal preferences) is lower than the market interest rate (by which private individuals assess investments). Public forest management agencies attempt to mitigate this failure explicitly by using discount rates for investment analysis that are not set in markets and implicitly by managing for maximum sustained yield (implying that the appropriate discount rate is zero).

The existence of forest products that are not readily exchanged in markets is a further source of inefficiency in forest management. Landowners manage for the production of non-market values only to the extent that these values accrue to them. Because many of these non-market goods have the character of public goods, their supply may be less than socially optimal. Again, public forest management agencies may attempt to mitigate this failure by constraining harvest flows over time or (equivalently) by explicitly recognizing the shadow price of these goods in their management decisions.[10]

Appendices

Appendix 17A   Second-order conditions for a maximum in the simplest even-age Faustmann problem

$$PQ_{AA}(e^{rA} - 1) - r^2 e^{rA} \frac{PQ(A) - C}{(e^{rA} - 1)^2} < 0 \qquad (A17.1)$$

if $PQ(A) \geq C$ since $Q_{AA} < 0$ by assumption.

Appendix 17B   Comparative statics results for the simplest Faustmann model

Treating the first-order conditions:

$$F_A = \frac{PQ_A}{e^{rA} - 1} - \frac{r[PQ(A) - C]e^{rA}}{(e^{rA} - 1)^2} = 0 \qquad (B17.1)$$

$F_A = 0$, as an implicit function of r, P, C, and A, we can write the total differential as

$$dF_A = \frac{\partial F_A}{\partial r} \, dr + \frac{\partial F_A}{\partial P} \, dP + \frac{\partial F_A}{\partial C} \, dC + \frac{\partial F_A}{\partial A} \, dA = 0 \qquad (B17.2)$$

Thus the response of optimal rotation to a change in any of the exogenous determinants x can be written as $dA/dx = -F_{Ax}/F_{AA}$. Since $F_{AA} < 0$ from the second-order conditions, the signs of the dA/dx and F_{Ax} are the same.

Interest rate: $dA/dr < 0$

After some simplification

$$F_{Ar} = (1 + rA - e^{rA}) \frac{PQ_A}{r(e^{rA} - 1)^2} \tag{B17.3}$$

To show that $1 + rA - e^{rA} < 0$, expand e^{rA} about $r = 0$ using a Taylor's series expansion. Since the remainder of the terms in (B17.3) are positive, $F_{Ar} < 0$ and $dA/dr < 0$.

Price: $dA/dP < 0$

$$F_{AP} = - \frac{rC e^{rA}}{P(e^{ra} - 1)^2} < 0 \tag{B17.4}$$

Establishment cost: $dA/dC > 0$

$$F_{AC} = \frac{r e^{rA}}{(e^{rA} - 1)^2} > 0 \tag{B17.5}$$

Appendix 17C   Taxation impacts on the Faustmann rotation

Ad valorem tax

Rewrite the objective function $F(A)$ as

$$F(A) = \frac{PQ(A) - \int_{s=0}^{A} [TPQ(s) e^{-rs}] ds \, e^{rA}}{e^{rA} - 1} - \frac{TF(A)}{r} \tag{C17.1}$$

The integral is the value of the tax on the timber stock for one rotation. The second term is the tax on the after-tax value of the land.

Solving for $F(A)$:

$$F(A) = \frac{r}{T + r} \left\{ \frac{PQ(A) - \int_{s=0}^{A} [TPQ(s) e^{-rs}] ds \, e^{rA}}{e^{rA} - 1} \right\} \tag{C17.2}$$

The first-order conditions for an optimum can be written as

$$PQ_A = (r + T)PQ(A) + r \left\{ \frac{PQ(A) - \int_{s=0}^{A} [TPQ(s) e^{-rs} \, ds] e^{rA}}{e^{rA} - 1} \right\} \tag{C17.3}$$

Multiplying and dividing the term in braces by $T + r$ and using the expression for $F(A)$ in (C17.2):

$$PQ_A = (r + T)[PQ(A) + F(A)] \tag{C17.4}$$

Thus $F(A)$ may be written as in equation (17.1) but with the interest rate term r replaced by $r + T$.

Yield tax
Here the tax acts as a multiplier for total revenue (or simply price):

$$\max F(A) = \frac{(1 - T)PQ(A) - C}{e^{rA} - 1} - C \qquad (C17.5)$$

Land tax
The tax is assumed to be levied on the (correctly estimated) soil expectation value each year.

$$\max F(A) = \frac{PQ(A) - C}{e^{rA} - 1} - C - \frac{TF(A)}{r} \qquad (C17.6)$$

Solving for $F(A)$:

$$F(A) = \frac{r}{r + T} \left[\frac{PQ(A) - C}{e^{rA} - 1} - C \right] \qquad (C17.7)$$

Appendix 17D   Tax impacts in uneven-age management

Ad valorem tax
The tax is paid as a proportion of the value of the timber and land. The objective function with tax is

$$F_0 = \int_{t=0}^{\infty} (P_t h_t - TH_t) e^{rt} \, dt \qquad (D17.1)$$

where F_t is the value of land and timber value at time t. This reduces to

$$F_0 = \int_{t=0}^{\infty} P_t h_t \, e^{-(r+T)t} \, dt \qquad (D17.2)$$

To see this, write F_0 in discrete form:

$$F_0 = \sum_{t=0}^{\infty} \frac{P_t h_t - TF_t}{(1 + r)^t} \qquad (D17.3)$$

Solve for F_n, $n = 0, \ldots$:

$$F_n = \frac{1}{1 + T} \left(P_n h_n + \sum_{t=n+1}^{\infty} \frac{P_t h_t - TF_t}{(1 + r)^{t-n}} \right) \qquad (D17.4)$$

Iteratively substitute F_{n+1} into F_n for $n = 0, \ldots$:

$$F_0 = \frac{1}{1+T} \sum_{t=0}^{\infty} \frac{P_t h_t}{(1+r)^t (1+T)^t} \qquad \text{for } n \to \infty \qquad \text{(D17.5)}$$

Thus, as in the even-age case, the discount rate is the sum of the interest rate and the tax rate, and less growing stock will be held as investment.

Land tax
The tax is a proportion of the value of the land only. The objective function is

$$F_0 = \int_{t=0}^{\infty} [P_t h_t - T(F_t - P_t S_t)] e^{-rt} \, dt \qquad \text{(D17.6)}$$

where $T(F_t - P_t S_t)$ is the tax and $P_t S_t$ is the value of the timber. This reduces (as with the *ad valorem* tax) to

$$F_0 = \int_{t=0}^{\infty} (P_t h_t + TP_t S_t) e^{-(r+T)t} \, dt \qquad \text{(D17.7)}$$

The current value Hamiltonian is

$$H_t = P_t h_t + TP_t S_t + \mu_t [g(S_t) - h_t] \qquad \text{(D17.8)}$$

Combining the first-order conditions H_h and $\dot{\mu}_t$ yields

$$\frac{\dot{P}_t}{P_t} = (r + T) - G_S - T \qquad \text{(D17.9)}$$

The tax cancels and thus the effect of land tax on optimal harvest trajectory is neutral.

Yield tax
The tax is levied as a percentage of harvest value.

$$F_0 = (1 - T) \int_{t=0}^{\infty} P_t h_t \, e^{-rt} \, dt \qquad \text{(D17.10)}$$

First-order conditions lead to

$$\frac{\dot{\mu}_t}{\mu_t} = \frac{\dot{P}_t(1 - T)}{P_t(1 - T)} = r - g_S \qquad \text{(D17.11)}$$

Thus the yield tax is neutral.

Notes

1 Stumpage refers to standing timber, as opposed to logs or other processed forms. Stumpage price is log price net of harvest cost.

2   In the comparative statics analysis of model F_3, rotation will increase with g if $P_0 e^{gA} V - r e^{rA} C/(e^{ra} - 1) > 0$ which is readily shown to be true if $F_3 > 0$.

3   Thus, prices have a constant mean and variance and a constant autocorrelation structure that depends only on the length of lag between observations (they assume zero autocorrelation at all lags). See also Lohmander (1988) and Norstrøm (1975).

4   While the optimal control approach can be applied to the rotation problem for even-aged stands, it yields no new insights and is awkward compared with the traditional present-value maximization approach (see, for example, Näslund, 1969; Anderson, 1976).

5   With a constant price, this solution is the same result as that obtained in analyses of equilibrium cases (Duerr and Bond, 1952; Adams, 1976; Chang, 1981).

6   In fact, real stumpage prices in the United States have appreciated, at an average rate of 5.3 percent for Douglas fir and 1.8 percent for southern pine sold from National Forests over the last 70 years. Moody's AAA corporate bond rate deflated by the rate of change in the consumer price index averaged 3 percent over the last 70 years. This suggests that managing for maximum sustained yield is not necessarily suboptimal.

7   This model is a more general version of Johnson and Scheurman's (1977) necessary condition for "simple financial maturity" under a quadratic objective function. Sessions (1977) discusses the empirical conditions for convergence to a long-run steady state in such a model.

8   As Bentley and Teeguarden (1965) note, the Faustmann model with constant stumpage price approaches maximum sustained yield as the interest rate approaches zero.

9   See Kuuluvainen (1990), Johansson and Löfgren (1985), and particularly Ovaskainen (1992) for detailed treatments of the two-period model, links to the continuous-time infinite horizon case, and necessary conditions for optima.

10 See Parades and Brodie (1989) for a discussion of the linkage between physical constraints in the harvest scheduling process and "correct" shadow prices in an unconstrained optimization.

References

Adams, D. M. 1976: A note on the interdependence of stand structure and best stocking in a selection forest. *Forest Science*, 22, 180–4.

Adams, D. M. and Ek, A. R. 1974: Optimizing the management of uneven-aged forest stands. *Canadian Journal of Forestry Research*, 4, 274–86.

Anderson, F. J. 1976: Control theory and the optimum timber rotation. *Forest Science*, 22, 242–6.

Bentley, W. R. and Teeguarden, D. E. 1965: Financial maturity: a theoretical review. *Forest Science*, 11, 76–87.

Boulding, K. E. 1966: *Economic Analysis*, 4th edn. New York: Harper.

Brazee, R. and Mendelsohn, R. 1988: Timber harvesting with fluctuating prices. *Forest Science*, 34, 359–72.

Brazee, R. and Mendelsohn, R. 1990: A dynamic model of timber markets. *Forest Science*, 36 (2), 255–64.

Calish, S., Fight, R. D. and Teeguarden, D. E. 1978: How do nontimber values affect Douglas-fir rotations? *Journal of Forestry*, 76, 217–21.

Chang, S. J. 1981: Determination of the optimal growing stock and cutting cycle for an uneven-aged stand. *Forest Science*, 27, 739–44.

Chang, S. J. 1982: An economic analysis of forest taxation's impact on optimal rotation age. *Land Economics*, 58, 310–23.

Chang, S. J. 1983: Rotation age, management intensity, and the economic factors of timber production: do changes in stumpage price, interest rate, regeneration cost, and forest taxation matter? *Forest Science*, 29, 267–77.

Duerr, W. A. 1960: *Fundamentals of Forestry Economics*. New York: McGraw-Hill.

Duerr, W. A. and Bond, W. E. 1952: Optimum stocking of a selection forest. *Journal of Forestry*, 50, 12–16.

Fairchild, F. 1935: Forest taxation in the United States. Misc. Publ. 218, US Department of Agriculture, Washington, DC.

Faustmann, M. 1849: On the determination of the value which forest land and immature stands possess for forestry. In M. Gane (ed.), *Martin Faustmann and the Evolution of Discounted Cash Flow*, Oxford: Oxford Institute Paper 42, 1968.

Fisher, I. 1930: *The Theory of Interest*. New York: Macmillan.

Gaffney, M. 1957: Concepts of financial maturity of timber and other assets. Agric. Econ. Series 62, North Carolina State College, Raleigh, NC.

Haight, R. G., Brodie, J. D. and Adams, D. M. 1985: Optimizing the sequence of diameter distributions and selection harvests for uneven-aged stand management. *Forest Science*, 31, 451–62.

Hartman, Richard. 1976: The harvesting decision when a standing forest has value. *Economic Inquiry*, 14, 52–68.

Heaps, Terry. 1984: The forestry maximum principle. *Journal of Economic Dynamics and Control*, 7, 131–51.

Hellsten, Martin. 1988: Socially optimal forestry. *Journal of Environmental Economics and Management*, 15, 387–94.

Johansson, P.-O. and Löfgren, K.-G. 1985: *The ~Economics of Forestry and Natural Resources*. Oxford: Basil Blackwell.

Johnson, K. N. and Scheurman, H. L. 1977: Techniques for prescribing optimal timber harvest and investment under different objectives. *Forest Science*, Monograph 18.

Klemperer, W. D. 1982: An analysis of selected property tax exemptions for timber. *Land Economics*, 58, 293–309.

Kuuluvainen, J. 1990: Virtual price approach to short-term timber supply under credit rationing. *Journal of Environmental Economics and Management*, 19 (2), 109–26.

Lohmander, P. 1988: Pulse extraction under risk and a numerical forestry example. *Systems Analysis, Modeling and Simulation*, 4, 339–54.

McConnell, K. E., Daberkow, J. N. and Hardie, I. W. 1983: Planning timber production with evolving prices and costs. *Land Economics*, 59, 292–304.

Mitra, T. and Wan, H. Y., Jr. 1985: Some theoretical results on the economics of forestry. *Review of Economic Studies*, 52, 263–82.

Mitra, T. and Wan, H. Y., Jr.1986: On the Faustmann solution to the forest management problem. *Journal of Economic Theory*, 40, 229–49.

Näslund, B. 1969: Optimal rotation and thinning. *Forest Science*, 15, 446–51.

Nautiyal, J. C. 1983: Towards a method of uneven-aged forest management based on the theory of financial maturity. *Forest Science*, 29, 47–58.

Nautiyal, J. C. and Pearse, P. H. 1967: Optimizing the conversion to sustained yield – a programming solution. *Forest Science*, 13, 131–9.

Nautiyal, J. C. and Williams, J. S. 1990: Response of optimal stand rotation and management intensity to one-time changes in stumpage price, management cost, and discount rate. *Forest Science*, 36, 21–23.

Newman, D. H., Gilbert, C. B. and Hyde, W. F. 1985: The optimal forest rotation with evolving prices. *Land Economics*, 61, 347–53.

Norstrøm, C. J. 1975: A stochastic model for the growth period decision in forestry. *Swedish Journal of Economics*, 77, 329–37.

Ovaskainen, Ville. 1992: Forest taxation; timber supply, and economic efficiency. *Acta Forestalia Fennica*, 233.

Pardes, V. G. L. and Brodie, J. D. 1989: Land value and the linkage between stand and forest level analyses. *Land Economics*, 65, 158–66.

Pearse, P. H. 1967: The optimum forest rotation. *Forestry Chronicle*, 43 (2), 178–95.

Pearse, P. H. 1990: *Introduction to Forest Economics*. Vancouver: University of British Columbia Press.

Samuelson, P. A. 1976: Economics of forestry in an evolving society. *Economic Inquiry*, 14, 466–91.

Sessions, J. 1977: Stability considerations in ECHO modeling. *Forest Science*, 23 (4), 446–9.

Snyder, D. L. and Bhattacharyya, R. N. 1990: A more general dynamic economic model of the optimal rotation of multiple-use forests. *Journal of Environmental Economics and Management, 18, 168–75.*

Stier, J. C. and Chang, S. J. 1983: Land use implications of the *ad valorem* property tax: the role of tax incidence. *Forest Science*, 29, 702–12.

Strang, W. J. 1983: On the optimal forest harvesting decision. *Economic Inquiry*, 21, 576–83.

Swallow, S. K., Parks, P. J. and Wear, D. N. 1990: Policy-relevant nonconvexities in the production of multiple forest benefits. *Journal of Environmental Economics and Management*, 19, 264–80.

Washburn, C. L. and Binkley, C. S. 1990: Information efficiency of markets for stumpage. *American Journal of Agricultural Economics*, 72 (2), 394–405.

Williams, J. S. and Nautiyal, J. C. 1990: The long-run timber supply function. *Forest Science*, 36, 77–86.

18

Bioeconomic Models of the Fishery

Jon M. Conrad

1   Introduction and Overview

> To the uninitiated, a study dealing with the economics of commercial fishing
> might appear to represent a routine application of the theory of the
> competitive industry. But by building upon such basic contributions as
> those of Lotka (1956), Gordon (1954), Scott (1955), and Crutchfield and
> Zellner (1962), the economics of fishing becomes almost unique in the
> breadth of its demands on modern economic concepts. The problems of
> stock–flow dynamics, externalities in production, the relation between man
> and his natural environment, social control or regulation, public investment,
> and the economic significance of property rights, all arise in an important
> and natural way in the economic analysis of fishing.
>
> (Quirk and Smith, 1969)

Since the mid-1950s there has been a steady increase in the number of
articles and books attempting to refine and extend the economic theory of
fishing. The core of this theory has provided a conceptual framework for
empirical studies into the dynamics of fish populations and the fishermen
who pursue them. Collectively, this literature had led to important changes
in the way coastal nations are managing the fishery resources within their
territorial waters.

The modern literature on fishery economics can trace its roots to the
classic article by H. Scott Gordon (1954) entitled "The economic theory of
a common property resource: the fishery." Gordon sought to explain why
established fisheries were often characterized by fleets of aging vessels,
earning little or no profit, from landings that were a fraction of their
historical record. Gordon's model explained why, after an initially
profitable period, commercial fisheries would usually struggle along with
too many vessels chasing too few fish.

This was followed by Tony Scott's (1955) paper, "The fishery: The objective of sole ownership." Building on Gordon's model, Scott examined the difference in the intensity of fishing depending on whether the resource was common property or owned by a single individual. He advocated measures that would restrict fishing "effort" (an aggregate measure of fishing inputs) to a level that maximized static profit.

The next important contribution, and the first to view fisheries management as a dynamic optimization problem amenable to solution by the calculus of variations, was the monograph by Jim Crutchfield and Arnold Zellner (1962) entitled "Economic aspects of the Pacific halibut fishery." This monograph did not initially receive the recognition it deserved, as it appeared in a relatively obscure series published by the Bureau of Commercial Fisheries (BCF), a predecessor of the present-day National Marine Fisheries Service (NMFS).

Vernon Smith (1968, 1969) published two important and somewhat controversial papers. The first was entitled "Economics of production from natural resources" and examined the possible dynamics that could arise from a competitive industry harvesting a common property resource. The second article was entitled "On models of commercial fishing." These two papers prompted a rather acrimonious exchange between Smith and Fullenbaum, Carlson, and Bell (1971, 1972) who, at the time, were economists with the BCF. Their comments and Smith's replies appeared in the *American Economic Review* (in June of 1971) and in the *Journal of Political Economy* (in July–August 1972), and centered on the validity of Smith's cost function for a representative vessel. Smith posited that the operating cost of a vessel depended on its catch rate and the stock of fish. Fullenbaum, Carlson, and Bell maintained that in the long run costs are not influenced by the catch rate. In retrospect, it would appear that Smith's formulation is valid, since it is possible to derive such an operating cost function from a neoclassical production function for the fishing firm and a cost equation.

At about this time Colin Clark was beginning work which would culminate in his influential text *Mathematical Bioeconomics: The Optimal Management of Renewable Resources* (1st edn, 1976). Clark, an applied mathematician, published two widely cited papers in 1973. The first (1973a) appeared in *Science* and was entitled "The economics of overexploitation." The second (1973b) appeared in the *Journal of Political Economy* and was entitled "Profit maximization and the extinction of animal species." Clark identified the importance of the discount rate (relative to a resource's intrinsic rate of growth) and stock-dependent harvest cost (relative to the market price) as crucial to determining the risk of extinction. He was also the first to note that the open access nature of many renewable resources *may* induce competitive harvestors to behave as if they had an infinitely high rate of discount.

Clark's text on mathematical bioeconomics (the second edition appeared in 1990) and his book entitled *Bioeconomic Modelling and Fisheries Management* (1985) firmly established the conceptual merit of treating resource management as an exercise in dynamic optimization. In this chapter we will define a bioeconomic model as one that seeks to maximize some measure of economic value, subject to resource dynamics.

Mathematical models of open access and optimal management helped to clarify the notion of "user cost," the dynamic cost of harvesting an additional unit of the resource today. This, in turn, allowed economists to better define the policy instruments that might move a competitive fishing industry toward optimal harvest. Gardner Brown Jr (1974) published a paper entitled "An optimal program for managing common property resources with congestion externalities" that focused on the potential role of variable input and landings taxes to account for the static (congestion) and user cost externalities that can arise in a commercial fishery. In addition to landings taxes, economists proposed individual transferable quotas (ITQs), often within a program of "limited entry," as a potential policy to rationalize fishery management (see Christy, 1973; Rettig and Ginter, 1978). The latter policy instrument had been previously proposed by Dales (1968) as a way to control pollution. In this context ITQs are called "tradable emission permits."

The discussion of management policies was to become of great practical importance in the mid- and late-1970s, given the widespread depletion of near-shore and pelagic fish stocks and the extension of territorial waters, outward to 200 miles, by coastal nations. The opportunities and challenges of extended jurisdiction (or the 200-mile "economic zone") were presented in an edited volume by Lee Anderson (1977) entitled *Economic Impacts of Extended Fisheries Jurisdiction*. In the introduction to that volume, Anderson notes:

> introducing extended jurisdiction by itself will not immediately restore fish stocks off our coasts, nor will it necessarily inject new vigor into our fishing industry. The ability to restrict foreign vessels from fishing off our coasts will be only a stopgap measure if proper management of national boats is lacking. Extended jurisdiction authority is an important first step, but it will be meaningless unless proper management is instituted.

In the United States, extended jurisdiction was codified in 1976 with the passage of the Magnuson Fisheries Conservation and Management Act (MFCMA). This Act created eight regional management councils that were charged with preparing management plans for species of commercial and recreational importance. The regional councils generally relied on a series of traditional management policies (such as aggregate quotas, season or area closures, and gear restrictions) that attempted to protect and conserve the resource, but had little effect on the economic incentives influencing a fisherman's decision of "if, when, where and how" to fish. There is now considerable evidence to suggest that these policies have *not* been particularly effective in restoring or maintaining coastal fish stocks at levels that anyone would regard as optimal (see Conrad, 1987). The United States is now considering the wider use of ITQs, which have been employed in New Zealand, Iceland, and Canada.

The rest of this chapter is organized as follows. In the next section we review the model of open access which established the *raison d'être* for fishery management. In the third section, two models of optimal management are presented. The first uses total catch as the control (regulatory) variable, while the second assumes that fishing effort can be regulated. In the fourth section two numerical examples are presented to show how the models of open access and optimal management might be used to describe the economic history of a fishery, in one case, and improve its future net value, in a second case. The final section concludes with a brief discussion of traditional management policies such as season closures, gear restrictions, limited entry and aggregate quotas, as well as the bioeconomic-based policies of landings taxes and ITQs. It is hoped that this chapter provides a foundation from which to approach the extant and growing literature in fisheries economics.

2   Open Access

A fishery is open access when the fish stock is harvested by a large number of unregulated, competitive fishermen with no barrier to entry or exit. In a strict sense, there a few, if any, open access fisheries in the world today. Most commercially valuable fisheries have come under some form of regulation. There are also instances where what might appear to be an open access fishery is actually one that is regulated through informal agreement by members of a fishing community. That said, there are also many examples where open access conditions are approximated. *De facto* open access can arise if management regulations are ineffective. This might occur, over time, if fishermen are adaptive and can reduce or eliminate the effect of regulations which previously restricted catch.

For students of economic or natural resource history, an understanding of open access dynamics is useful for descriptive and empirical studies of resource-based industries. This is particularly true for whaling and sealing, as conducted in the eighteenth, nineteenth and twentieth centuries (see, for example, Wilen, 1976; Clark and Lamberson, 1982; Busch, 1985; Bockstoce, 1986).

Let X_t denote the biomass or number of individuals in a fish stock or population, E_t the level of fishing effort expended in harvesting the stock, and Y_t the level of harvest, all in year t. A deterministic production process might be described by $Y_t = H(X_t, E_t)$, where fish stock and effort are inputs and $H(\cdot)$ is a concave function. Two possible forms for $H(\cdot)$ are the familiar Cobb–Douglas, where $Y_t = \alpha X_t^{\beta} E_t^{\gamma}$, and the exponential, where $Y_t = X_t(1 - e^{-qE_t})$, with the parameters α, β, γ, and q being positive, and $1 \geq \beta + \gamma$.

Suppose that the change in the fish stock can be described by the first-order difference equation

$$X_{t+1} - X_t = F(X_t) - H(X_t, E_t) \tag{18.1}$$

where $F(X_t)$ is a net growth function describing net biological recruitment to the fish stock, prior to harvest. The stock in year $t + 1$ will increase $(X_{t+1} - X_t > 0)$ if net growth exceeds harvest in year t, remain unchanged $(X_{t+1} - X_t = 0)$ if net growth equals harvest, or decrease $(X_{t+1} - X_t < 0)$ if net growth is less than harvest. Two possible forms for $F(X_t)$ are $F(X_t) = rX_t(1 - X_t/K)$ and $F(X_t) = X_t e^{r(1 - X_t/K)}$, where r is called the intrinsic growth rate and K is the environmental carrying capacity. Both functional forms have been called the discrete-time analogue of the logistic function. (See May (1975) for a discussion of the dynamics of the unharvested resource.)

Equation (18.1) describes the response of the resource to harvest. To describe the behavioral response of fishermen, it is assumed that effort will expand if rent (profit) is positive and contract if rent (profit) is negative. For simplicity let p denote a constant price per unit for the harvested resource, and c the constant unit cost of effort. If fishing effort adjusts based on profit or loss in the previous year, then

$$E_{t+1} - E_t = \eta[pH(X_t, E_t) - cE_t] \tag{18.2}$$

where $\eta > 0$ is an adjustment parameter measuring the responsiveness of effort to profit and loss.

Taken together, equations (18.1) and (18.2) constitute a dynamical system. Given an initial condition (X_0, E_0), equations (18.1) and (18.2) can be "iterated" forward in time generating trajectories X_t and E_t. It is sometimes possible to determine, in advance, how a dynamical system will behave based on mathematical analysis. The analysis is similar whether one is dealing with two first-order, nonlinear difference equations (such as we have here) or two first-order, nonlinear differential equations. (A discussion of the appropriate analysis for a system of two first-order, nonlinear difference equations may be found in Edelstein-Keshet (1988, ch. 2), while the analysis of two first-order, nonlinear differential equations is summarized in Clark (1990, ch. 6). While the analysis is similar, the system of first-order difference equations is capable of richer dynamic behavior, including deterministic chaos.)

The mathematical analysis, in either case, requires the determination of all steady state equilibria (or fixed points). Depending on the forms for

$H(\cdot)$ and $F(\cdot)$ there may be a unique, nonzero, open access equilibrium, which we will denote as (X_∞, E_∞). To keep things simple and consistent with the early analysis of Gordon (1954) and Scott (1955), we will adopt the forms $H(\cdot) = qX_tE_t$ and $F(\cdot) = rX_t(1 - X_t/K)$, where $q > 0$ is called the "catchability coefficient."

With the above forms for $H(\cdot)$ and $F(\cdot)$ the open access system may be rewritten as

$$X_{t+1} = [1 + r(1 - X_t/K) - qE_t]X_t$$
$$E_{t+1} = [1 + \eta(pqX_t - c)]E_t \tag{18.3}$$

It is now easier to see how to numerically iterate our open access system forward in time. Given parameter values for r, K, q, η, p, and c, along with an initial condition (X_0, E_0), the first iteration will determine (X_1, E_1). Substituting (X_1, E_1) back into the right-hand side, one can next determine (X_2, E_2), and so on. It would then be possible to plot the points (X_t, E_t) in X–E or "phase" space for $t = 0, 1, 2, \ldots, T$.

Might it ever happen that (X_t, E_t) would converge to a point, after which time X_t and E_t are unchanging? This, of course, is the concept of a steady state equilibrium or fixed point. At such an equilibrium $X_{t+1} = X_t = X$ and $E_{t+1} = E_t = E$. At a non-zero steady state equilibrium, equation (18.1) requires that net growth equals harvest and equation (18.2) requires that profit or rent equals zero. Given the specific functional forms in system (18.3) steady implies $E = r(1 - X/K)/q$ and $X = c/pq$. These lines are sometimes called "isoclines," since points on the first line imply that X is unchanging while points on the second (vertical) line imply that E is unchanging. These isoclines are drawn in figure 18.1 and they divide the phase space into four "isosectors."

Depending on the parameter values for r, K, q, η, p, and c, and the initial condition (X_0, E_0), system (18.3) is capable of a rich set of dynamic behavior. Two sample trajectories are drawn in figure 18.1 to illustrate what might dynamically happen. Trajectory (1) shows a spiral convergence to open access equilibrium at $X_\infty = c/pq$ and $E_\infty = r(1 - c/pqK)/q$. Note that X_∞ defines a "breakeven" stock size. For $X_t > X_\infty$, profit is positive and effort increases. For $X_t < X_\infty$, profit is negative and effort decreases. If exit from the fishing industry is rapid enough, harvest falls below net growth, the stock begins to increase, and spiral convergence to an open access equilibrium is possible.

Trajectory (2) depicts open access extinction. This might occur if exit is slow from the unprofitable industry and the remaining vessels find it economically advantageous to harvest the remaining stock before the species, and then the industry, ceases to exist.

A third possibility, not shown in figure 18.1, is a "limit cycle," where stock and effort cycle in a counterclockwise fashion around an open access equilibrium (X_∞, E_∞) but never reach it. This behavior is *not* possible in

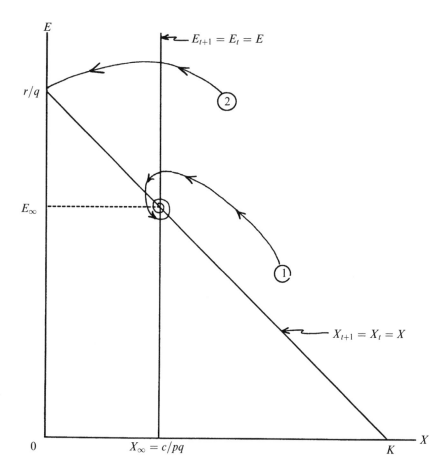

Figure 18.1 Open access: dynamics and equilibrium.

the continuous-time, differential equation, analogue to system (18.3). Clark (1990, pp. 189–90) shows that (X_∞, E_∞) will be a stable node or stable spiral.

The open access dynamics in figure 18.1 are drawn assuming that the parameters r, K, q, η, p, and c are constant. In an actual, empirical study these parameters are likely to be changing and there will not be an open access equilibrium. Additional outcomes could occur, including "industrial extinction," which is a reasonable description of what happened in the open access bowhead whale fishery (1848–1914) in the western Arctic when the market for baleen collapsed (see Bockstoce, 1986; Conrad, 1989).

Even if extinction or severe stock depletion is avoided, economists were quick to point out that open access equilibrium is suboptimal. There is overcapitalization in the fishery. Under effective management it is theoretically possible to have fewer vessels fishing a larger stock, generating positive net revenues, a portion of which could be used to compensate those vessel owners asked (or bribed) to leave the fishery. There have been examples of vessel buyout programs to reduce excessive capital. Care must be taken, however, since the remaining vessels in the now profitable fishery will have an incentive to expand *de facto* effort through vessel replacement, bigger engines, or better electronics. These aspects will be discussed in greater detail in section 5.

If open access is suboptimal, what is the preferred state for our stylized fishery? What policies would help establish and maintain such an optimal state?

3   Bioeconomics and Optimal Management

We have previously defined a bioeconomic model as one which seeks to maximize some measure of economic value subject to resource dynamics. We might consider "discounted social net benefit" as a reasonably general (and admittedly vague) measure of economic value. Suppose that net benefit in period t is given by $\pi_t = \pi(X_t, Y_t)$, where $\pi(\cdot)$ is a concave net benefit function. Net benefit would increase with an increase in X_t or Y_t. Increases in X_t would presumably lower the cost of harvest, while increments in Y_t have a positive value to producers and consumers.

Consider a candidate harvest schedule Y_t, $t = 0, 1, 2, \ldots, T$. Rewriting equation (18.1) as $X_{t+1} = X_t + F(X_t) - Y_t$, and given an initial condition X_0, we could iterate to obtain the resulting time path for X_t. Discounted social net benefit would be calculated according to

$$\pi = \sum_{t=0}^{T} \rho^t \pi(X_t, Y_t) \tag{18.4}$$

where $\rho = 1/(1 + \delta)$ is a discount factor and δ is the annual discount rate. Typically, there will be an infinite number of candidate harvest schedules. Suppose we wish to find the schedule Y_t which will

$$\text{maximize} \quad \pi = \sum_{t=0}^{\infty} \rho_t \pi(X_t, Y_t)$$

$$\text{subject to} \quad X_{t+1} - X_t = F(X_t) - Y_t \tag{18.5}$$

$$X_0 \text{ given}$$

This problem is called an infinite horizon problem and with $\pi(\cdot)$ and $F(\cdot)$ concave there will exist a steady state optimum (X^*, Y^*).

Recall from calculus that, when seeking the extremum (maximum, minimum, or inflection point) of a single variable function, a necessary condition requires that the first derivative of the function, when evaluated at a candidate extremum, be equal to zero. Out optimization problem is more complex because we have, in essence, an infinite number of variables Y_t and X_t, and we have constraints in the form of our first-order difference equation and the initial condition X_0. We can follow a similar procedure, however, after forming the appropriate Lagrangian expression for our problem. This is done by introducing a set of new variables, denote λ_t, called Lagrange multipliers.

The Lagrangian expression for our problem may be written

$$L = \sum_{t=0}^{\infty} \rho^t \{\pi(X_t, Y_t) + \rho\lambda_{t+1}[X_t + F(X_t) - Y_t - X_{t+1}]\} \quad (18.6)$$

The Lagrange multipliers may be interpreted as *current-value shadow prices*, which indicate the value of an additional unit of the resource when made available in a particular year. In our problem we can think of the difference equation as defining the level of X_{t+1} that will be available in period $t + 1$. The value of an additional (marginal) unit of X_{t+1} in period $t + 1$ will be λ_{t+1}. This reflects the value not only in period $t + 1$ but over the remainder of the horizon, assuming the resource is optimally managed.

After forming the Lagrangian expression we take a series of first-order partial derivatives and set them equal to zero. Collectively, they define the first-order necessary conditions, analogous to the first-order condition for a single variable function. They might be used to solve for the optimal levels of Y_t, X_t, and λ_t in transition *and* at the steady state, bioeconomic optimum. For our problem these necessary conditions require

$$\frac{\partial L}{\partial Y_t} = \rho^t \left[\frac{\partial \pi(\cdot)}{\partial Y_t} - \rho\lambda_{t+1}\right] = 0 \quad (18.7)$$

$$\frac{\partial L}{\partial X_t} = \rho^t \left\{\frac{\partial \pi(\cdot)}{\partial X_t} + \rho\lambda_{t+1}[1 + F'(\cdot)]\right\} - \rho^t\lambda_t = 0 \quad (18.8)$$

$$\frac{\partial L}{\partial(\rho\lambda_{t+1})} = \rho^t[X_t + F(X_t) - Y_t - X_{t+1}] = 0 \quad (18.9)$$

The partial of the Lagrangian with respect to X_t is a bit tricky. When we examine the representative term in period t, we observe X_t as an argument of the net benefit function and in the terms $X_t + F(X_t)$ in the difference equation. The partials of these terms appear in the braces in equation (18.8). Where did the last term, $-\rho^t\lambda_t$, come from? If we think of the Lagrangian as a long (infinite) sum of expressions, and if we wish to take the partial with respect to X_t we need to find *all* the terms involving X_t. When we back up one period, from t to $t - 1$, most of the terms are subscripted $t - 1$ with the notable exception of the last term, which becomes $-\rho^t\lambda_t X_t$ with a partial derivative $-\rho^t\lambda_t$.

We can simplify and rewrite the first-order conditions to facilitate interpretation. They become

$$\frac{\partial \pi(\cdot)}{\partial Y_t} = \rho \lambda_{t+1} \tag{18.10}$$

$$\lambda_t = \frac{\partial \pi(\cdot)}{\partial X_t} + \rho \lambda_{t+1}[1 + F'(\cdot)] \tag{18.11}$$

$$X_{t+1} - X_t = F(X_t) - Y_t \tag{18.12}$$

The left-hand side of equation (18.10) is the marginal net benefit of an additional unit of the resource, harvested in year t. For a harvest strategy to be optimal, this marginal net benefit must equal the discounted shadow price (also called user cost) of an additional unit of the resource in period $t + 1$, denoted $\rho \lambda_{t+1}$. Thus equation (18.10) requires that we account for *two* types of costs, the standard marginal cost of current harvest, which has already been accounted for in the partial of the net benefit function, *and* the future (user) cost that results from the decision to harvest an additional unit of the resource today.

On the left-hand side of equation (18.11) we have λ_t, the value of an additional unit of the resource in period t. When optimally managed, the marginal value of an additional unit of the resource in period t equals the current period marginal net benefit $\partial \pi(\cdot)/\partial X_t$ plus the marginal benefit that an unharvested unit will convey in the next period. This term is the discounted value of the marginal unit itself plus its marginal growth, or $\rho \lambda_{t+1}[1 = F'(\cdot)]$.

Equation (18.12) is simply our equation for resource dynamics, obtained from the partial of the Lagrangian with respect to $\rho \lambda_{t+1}$. This should occur in general; that is, the partial of the Lagrangian with respect to a discounted multiplier should yield the difference equation for the resource stock.

To use equations (18.10)–(18.12) to solve for the optimal values of Y_t, X_t, and λ_t we actually need two boundary conditions. We have one boundary condition in the form of our initial condition X_0, which will equal some value, say $X_0 = a$. The other boundary condition, in an infinite horizon problem, is a bit more difficult to explain and use. It is called a *transversality condition* and requires $\rho^t \lambda_t X_t \rightarrow 0$ as $t \rightarrow \infty$. A metaphysical interpretation might be "as we approach the end of time, the resource stock or its discounted value must go to zero." This seemingly arcane condition is actually of practical assistance. If we wish to solve numerically an infinite horizon problem, then we might approximate the solution by solving a "long" *finite* horizon problem (say, $T = 200$ or $T = 500$ years) with $\lambda_T = 0$.

In steady state, when X_t, Y_t, and λ_t are unchanging, equations (18.10)–(18.12) imply

$$\rho\lambda = \frac{\partial\pi(\cdot)}{\partial Y} \tag{18.13}$$

$$\lambda[1 + F'(X) - (1 + \delta)] = -\frac{\partial\pi(\cdot)}{\partial X} \tag{18.14}$$

$$Y = F(X) \tag{18.15}$$

Substituting the expression for $\rho\lambda$ from equation (18.13) into equation (18.14) and isolating δ on the right-hand side yields

$$F'(X) + \frac{\partial\pi(\cdot)/\partial X}{\partial\pi(\cdot)/\partial Y} = \delta \tag{18.16}$$

Equation (18.16) has been called the "fundamental equation of renewable resources." Along with equation (18.15) it will define the optimal steady state values for X and Y.

Equation (18.16) has an interesting economic interpretation. On the left-hand side the term $F'(X)$ may be interpreted as the marginal net growth rate. The second term has been called the "marginal stock effect" by Clark and Munro (1975) and measures the marginal value of the stock relative to the marginal value of harvest. The two terms on the left-hand side sum to what might be interpreted as the resource's internal rate of return. Equation (18.16) then implies that the optimal steady state values of X and Y will cause the resource's internal rate of return to equal the rate of discount, δ, which presumably equals the rate of return on investments elsewhere in the economy. From this "capital-theoretic" point of view, the renewable resource is viewed as an asset which, under optimal management, will yield a rate of return comparable with other capital assets. Equation (18.16) presumes an interior optimum, with X and Y positive. There may be instances where equation (18.16) cannot hold as an equality, and our bioeconomic model would need to be modified to allow for inequality constraints and the possibility that extinction or zero fishing would be optimal.

Equation (18.16), by the implicit function theorem, will imply a curve in X–Y space. Under our concavity assumptions for $F(X)$ and $\pi(X, Y)$, the slope of this curve will be positive. Its exact shape and placement in X–Y space will depend on all the bioeconomic parameters in the functions $F(X)$ and $\pi(X, Y)$, *and* on the discount rate. Several possible curves (for different underlying parameters) are labeled ϕ_1, ϕ_2, and ϕ_3 in figure 18.2. The case when the net growth is given by $Y = F(X) = rX(1 - X/K)$ is also drawn. The intersection of $F(X)$ and a particular ϕ would represent the solution of equations (18.15) and (18.16) and therefore depict a steady state, bioeconomic optimum.

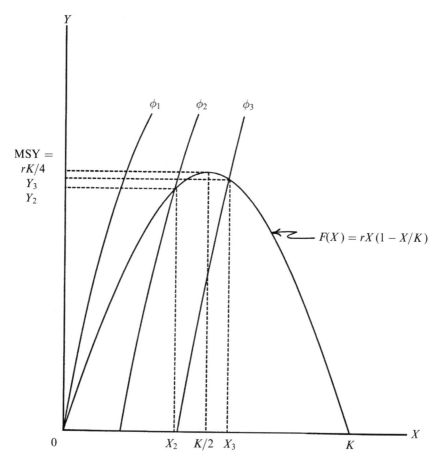

Figure 18.2 Maximum sustainable yield (MSY) and three bioeconomic optima.

Figure 18.2 shows four equilibria; three bioeconomic optima and maximum sustainable yield (MSY). The bioeconomic optimum at the intersection of ϕ_1 and $F(X)$ would imply that extinction is optimal! Such an equilibrium might result if a slow growing resource were confronted by a high rate of discount and if harvesting costs for the last members of the species were less than their market price.

The intersection of $F(X)$ and ϕ_2 implies an optimal resource stock at X_2, positive, but less than $K/2$ which supports MSY $= rK/4$. This would be the case if the marginal stock effect is less than the discount rate. (Look at equation (18.16) and see if you can figure out why this is true.)

The curve ϕ_3 implies a large marginal stock effect, greater in magnitude than the discount rate δ. This would occur if smaller fishable stocks significantly increased cost. In such a case it is optimal to maintain a relatively large stock at the bioeconomic optimum, even greater than the maximum sustainable yield stock $X_{MSY} = K/2$. The conclusion to be drawn from figure 18.2 is that the optimal stock, from a bioeconomic perspective, may be less than or greater than the stock level supporting maximum sustainable yield. Its precise location will depend on the function forms for $\pi(X, Y)$ and $F(X)$ and all of the bioeconomic parameters.

Equation (18.16) was originally derived by Clark (1990, pp. 39–40) for a continuous-time model where $\pi = [p - c(X)]Y$. Clark initially used the calculus of variations. The function $c(X)$ is a stock-dependent average cost function, with $c'(X) < 0$ (a larger stock lowers average cost). In steady state, $\partial\pi(\cdot)/\partial X = -c'(X)Y = -c'(X)F(X)$ and $\partial\pi(\cdot)/\partial X = p - c(X)$, and equation (18.16) becomes

$$F'(X) - \frac{c'(X)F(X)}{p - c(X)} = \delta \qquad (18.17)$$

Equation (18.17) *implicitly* defines the optimal fish stock, which is also called a "singular" solution. When $F(X) = rX(1 - X/K)$ and $c(X) = (c/q)X$, equation (18.17) implies an *explicit* solution for the optimal stock X^*. A fair amount of messy algebra and use of the quadratic formula will show that

$$X^* = \frac{K}{4}\left\{\left(\frac{c}{pqK} + 1 - \frac{\delta}{r}\right) + \left[\left(\frac{c}{pqK} + 1 - \frac{\delta}{r}\right)^2 + \frac{8c\delta}{pqKr}\right]^{1/2}\right\} \qquad (18.18)$$

One can use equation (18.18) to numerically observe that an increase in the cost–price ratio c/p, r or K will increase X^*, while an increase in δ will lower X^*.

To complete this section on bioeconomic models, we develop one last model where fishing effort E_t is the control variable. Consider once again the production function $Y_t = H(X_t, E_t)$. We will denote the partial derivatives of $H(X_t, E_t)$ with subscripts and assume $H_X > 0$, $H_E > 0$, $H_{X,E} = H_{E,X} > 0$, $H_{X,X} < 0$, $H_{E,E} < 0$. (Knowledge of the signs of these partial derivatives will be important in determining the effects of changes in the bioeconomic parameters and the slope of curves in X–E space.)

Let p again denote the per-unit price of the harvested resource and c the per-unit cost of effort. Then profit or net revenue in year t may be written as

$$\pi_t = pH(X_t, E_t) - cE_t \qquad (18.19)$$

Suppose now, however, that the dynamics of the fish population are given by

$$X_{t+1} = (1 - M)[X_t - H(X_t, E_t)] + F(X_t) \qquad (18.20)$$

where M is the annual natural mortality rate. In equation (18.20) the term $X_t - H(X_t, E_t)$ is sometimes called escapement because it represents the biomass, or number of individuals, that escape harvest. Escapement is then subject to natural mortality. The biomass surviving both harvest and natural mortality is augmented by recruitment, $F(X_t)$, to give the biomass at the beginning of year $t+1$.

Maximization of the present value of net revenue may be mathematically stated as

$$\text{maximize} \quad \sum_{t=0}^{\infty} \rho^t[pH(X_t, E_t) - cE_t]$$

$$\text{subject to} \quad X_{t+1} = (1 - M)[X_t - H(X_t, E_t)] + F(X_t) \qquad (18.21)$$

$$X_0 \text{ given}$$

The Lagrangian expression for this problem may be written

$$L = \sum_{t=0}^{\infty} \rho^t \bigg(pH(X_t, E_t) - cE_t$$

$$+ \rho\lambda_{t+1}\{(1 - M)[X_t - H(X_t, E_t)] + F(X_t) - X_{t+1}\bigg) \qquad (18.22)$$

The first-order conditions for this problem include

$$\frac{\partial L}{\partial E_t} = \rho^t[pH_E - c - \rho\lambda_{t+1}(1 - M)H_E] = 0 \qquad (18.23)$$

$$\frac{\partial L}{\partial X_t} = \rho^t\{pH_X + \rho\lambda_{t+1}[(1 - M)(1 - H_X) + F'(X_t)]\} - \rho^t\lambda_t = 0 \quad (18.24)$$

$$\frac{\partial L}{\partial(\rho\lambda_{t+1})} = \rho^t\{(1 - M)[X_t - H(X_t, E_t)] + F(X_t) - X_{t+1}\} = 0 \qquad (18.25)$$

Equations (18.23)–(18.25), and the boundary and transversality condition, might be used to solve for the optimal time path for effort, the resource stock, and the Lagrange multipliers. We will skip some of the details of this problem and proceed directly to the steady state optimum.

When evaluated in steady state, equations (18.23)–(18.25) will imply

$$\rho\lambda = \frac{pH_E - c}{(1 - M)H_E} \qquad (18.26)$$

$$\rho\lambda[(\delta + M) + (1 - M)H_X - F'(X)] = pH_X \qquad (18.27)$$

$$F(X) = MX + (1 - M)H(X, E) \qquad (18.28)$$

We have used equation (18.23) to obtain the expression for $\rho\lambda$ in equation (18.26). Equation (18.27) is derived from equation (18.24), but again requires a bit of algebra to get there. Equation (18.28) results from equation (18.25), and has a logical interpretation: in steady state recruitment $F(X)$ must equal natural mortality MX plus that portion of harvest that would have survived had it not been harvested, $(1 - M)H(X, E)$.

As in the first problem, equations (18.26)–(18.28) can be thought of as three equations in three unknowns. Collectively they define the bioeconomic optimum (X^*, E^*, λ^*). If you substitute (18.26) into (18.27) and simplify you can obtain the following expression which is a slightly different version of the fundamental equation.

$$F'(X) + \frac{c(1 - M)H_X}{pH_E - c} = \delta + M \tag{18.29}$$

Compare equation (18.16) with equation (18.29). In the first problem natural mortality was presumably incorporated into the net growth function $F(X)$. In the second problem, natural mortality was explicitly introduced, and we see that it has the same effect as an increase in the discount rate, as seen on the right-hand side of equation (18.29). The marginal stock effect explicitly involves the partial derivatives of the production function, H_X and H_E, along with the bioeconomic parameters c, M, and p. This variation on the fundamental equation results in a curve in X–E space. Given the signs for the partial derivatives of $H(X, E)$, this curve will be positively sloped. It is labeled $E(X)$ in figure 18.3.

Equation (18.28) can be shown to imply a downward-sloping curve in X–E space (provided $F'(X) - M - (1 - M)H_X < 0$). It is labeled $R(X)$ in figure 18.3. The intersection of $E(X)$ and $R(X)$ determines the optimal values for biomass and effort. Changes in c, δ, and p will shift the positively sloped curve, $E(X)$, but not the negatively sloped curve, $R(X)$.

To set the stage for one of the numerical examples in the next section, consider the case where *net growth is random and independent of the stock level X*. In this case $F'(X) = 0$. If the production function takes the form $H(X, E) = X(1 - e^{-qE})$, equation (18.29) becomes

$$\frac{c(1 - M)(1 - e^{-qE})}{pqXe^{-qE} - c} = \delta + M \tag{18.30}$$

It is possible to solve equation (18.30) for E as a function of c, δ, M, p, q, and X. This expression takes the form

$$E = \ln\left[\frac{c(1 - M) + (\delta + M)pqX}{c(1 + \delta)}\right] \Big/ q \tag{18.31}$$

Equation (18.31) is an example of what is called an *approximately optimal feedback control policy* (AOFCP). It is a current-period decision

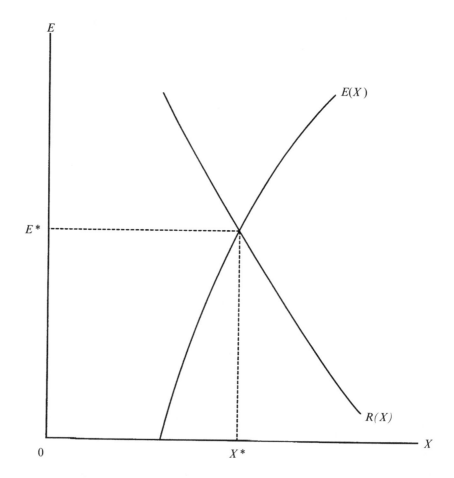

Figure 18.3 Optimal steady state stock and effort.

rule, requiring an assessment of X at the beginning of each period, which, along with updates of the other bioeconomic parameters, would allow fishery managers to set current-period effort. This approximation was first proposed by Burt (1964, 1967), who was concerned with identifying the optimal pumping rate from an aquifer that was subject to stochastic recharge. In comparing the AOFCP to an optimal policy derived from stochastic dynamic programming, Burt found that the optimal and approximately optimal pumping rates differed by no more than 4 percent for values of X within 40 percent of the long-run optimal groundwater stock. The usefulness of this approximation was reexamined by Burt and Cummings (1977) and subsequently applied to a model of the northern anchovy by Kolberg (1992) and the Pacific whiting by Conrad (1992). We will discuss some of the details of the latter study in the next section.

4   Some Numerical Examples

The North Sea herring fishery presents an interesting case study in open access dynamics. The stock has been traditionally harvested by several western European countries and the transboundary nature of the resource has resulted in a difficult management problem. The lack of cooperation between countries harvesting herring led to a situation of *de facto* open access, with the collapse of the fishery and its closure in 1977.

Table 18.1 is an amalgam of two tables from Bjørndal and Conrad (1987a). It shows estimates of the North Sea herring stock (in metric tons), Norwegian harvest (in metric tons), the number of Norwegian purse seiners, and the cost–price ratio for the years 1963–77. The data on yield, stock, and effort was used to estimate a production function for the Norwegian fleet, which was then assumed to hold for the *entire* fishery (comprising purse seiners from all countries). Time series data on the cost–price ratio were obtained from secondary data on the operating cost of Norwegian purse seiners and the ex-vessel price of herring landed in Norway. It was assumed that all countries participating in the fishery would face a similar cost–price ratio.

Table 18.1   Harvest of North Sea herring by the Norwegian purse seine fleet (Y_t, in metric tons), estimated stock of North Sea herring (X_t, in metric tons), number of participating purse seine vessels (E_T), and the cost–price ratio ($(c/p)_t$)

Year (t)	Y_t	X_t	E_t	$(c/p)_t$
1963	3,454	2,325,000	8	820.60
1964	147,933	2,529,000	121	964.73
1965	586,318	2,348,000	209	969.65
1966	448,511	1,871,000	298	939.53
1967	334,449	1,434,000	319	1,453.05
1968	286,198	1,056,000	352	1,615.63
1969	134,886	696,000	253	1,163.24
1970	220,854	717,000	201	1,060.38
1971	210,733	501,000	230	1,569.18
1972	136,969	509,000	203	2,127.76
1973	135,338	521,000	153	1,473.39
1974	66,236	345,000	165	1,377.99
1975	34,221	259,000	102	757.25
1976	33,057	276,000	92	846.00
1977	3,911	166,000	24	605.63

Several production functions were fitted to the data in table 18.1. The best fit was for a Cobb–Douglas form, with regression results

$$\ln Y_t = -2.7876 + 0.5621 \ln X_t + 1.3556 \ln E_t \qquad (18.32)$$
$$(2.11) \quad (5.84) \qquad (16.39)$$

The t statistics are given in parentheses below the coefficients. Adjusted $R^2 = 0.96$, and autocorrelation was not indicated. These results imply $Y_t = \alpha X_t^\beta E_t^\gamma$, with $\alpha = 0.06157$, $\beta = 0.562$, and $\gamma = 1.356$.

The open access system was specified as

$$X_{t+1} = \left[1 + r \left(1 - \frac{X_t}{K} \right) - \alpha X_t^{\beta-1} E_t^\gamma \right] X_t$$

$$(18.33)$$

$$E_{t+1} = E_t + \eta \left[\alpha X_t^\beta E_t^{\gamma-1} - \left(\frac{c}{p} \right)_t \right]$$

where the equation for effort dynamics assumes that effort changes according to normalized profit per vessel; that is, $E_{t+1} - E_t = \eta \pi_t / p E_t$. From previous analysis of this fishery, Bjørndal (1984) estimated that $r = 0.8$ and $K = 3,200,000$ metric tons while, in a companion study, Bjørndal and Conrad (1987b) obtained a point estimate of $\eta = 0.1$.

With the cost–price ratio varying from year to year, this open access system is said to be "nonautonomous." A steady state, open access equilibrium would *not* exist with time-varying parameters. If c/p were constant, it would be possible to solve for two simultaneous equations that would, in turn, define open access equilibrium, (X_∞, E_∞). These equations cannot be solved explicitly for X_∞ or E_∞ but could be solved numerically. For 1975, when $c/p = 757.25$, the open access equilibrium would be $X_\infty = 430,191$ metric tons, with $E_\infty = 393$ vessels. This point served as a reference point for the nonautonomous simulation from the initial conditions $X_{1963} = 2,325,000$ metric tons, $E_{1963} = 120$ vessels, and $(c/p)_t$ given in table 18.1. These results are given in table 18.2 and plotted in figure 18.4.

This simulation would presumably describe the dynamics of the *entire* fishery, comprising purse seiners from Norway and other Western European countries. Thus, the vessel numbers in table 18.2 would include the Norwegian vessels from table 18.1 The estimates of herring biomass differ from those in table 18.1, but they are not too far off. When we plot (X_t, E_t) in figure 18.4 we observe a partial, counterclockwise loop which shoots past the (X_∞, E_∞) for 1975, coming perilously close to the E axis and extinction. On the basis of this piece of analysis, the 1977 moratorium seemed quite appropriate.

As a postscript, the North Sea herring fishery did recover, with fishing allowed to resume in the southwestern sector in 1981 and in the central and northern sectors in 1984.

Table 18.2 Results of the nonautonomous, open access simulation for the entire North Sea herring fishery

Year (t)	Herring stock (X_t)	Total vessels (E_t)
1963	2,325,000	120
1964	2,679,895	166
1965	2,769,819	225
1966	2,669,322	305
1967	2,434,584	404
1968	2,081,884	461
1969	1,766,752	494
1970	1,501,775	559
1971	1,169,360	626
1972	779,946	626
1973	469,071	538
1974	310,092	480
1975	209,069	410
1976	155,111	385
1977	109,608	343

Our second numerical example will make use of the AOFCP discussed at the end of the previous section. The model which gave rise to the AOFCP, as specified in equation (18.31), was developed to describe the Pacific whiting fishery (see Conrad, 1992). This fishery takes place off the west coast of North America, from northern California to Vancouver Island, in Canada. The whiting spawns in January off southern California and Mexico, and in spring the population migrates northward, with older and larger fish crossing into Canadian waters in August. Random oceanographic conditions seem to play a dominant role in the survival of juveniles and their ultimate recruitment to the fishable population at about age 2. Analysis, over a time series of reconstructed recruitment and spawning biomass does not reveal a statistical relationship. This is not uncommon for many fish and shellfish, and thus we assume $F'(X) = 0$ and that recruitment is an independent and identically distributed random variable R_t.

Whiting are harvested by mid-water trawl and must be processed quickly if they are to be marketed for human consumption (and a higher price). The need for quick handling and processing meant that there was little economic interest in the resource until the formation of a joint-venture fishery around 1980. Under joint-venture agreements, US-owned catcher vessels would offload their catch of whiting onto foreign factory

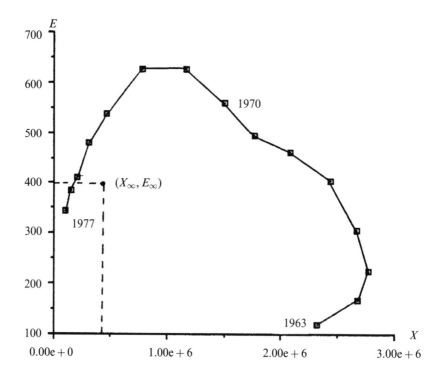

Figure 18.4   A plot of estimated herring stock and vessel numbers for the entire North Sea herring fishery.

vessels that would process and flash freeze the fish for sale in their domestic markets. The US vessels would be paid a previously agreed price per metric ton and the season would be closed when total harvest reached the "Allowable Biological Catch" (ABC) as specified by the Pacific Fishery Management Council.

Table 18.3 shows the data on harvest, estimated biomass, and the number of participating vessels for 1981 through 1989. Note the rapid increase in the number of participating vessels and harvest after 1985, and the decline in mean annual biomass. Cobb–Douglas and exponential production functions were fitted to the data. The regression for exponential form gave the following results:

$$\ln\left(1 - Y_t/X_t\right) = 0.0215 - 0.0028E_t \quad \text{(adjusted } R^2 = 0.9568) \quad (18.34)$$
$$(3.1732)\ (13.35) \quad (\text{DW} = 1.1146)$$

(DW, Durbin–Watson statistic). The t statistics are again given in parentheses below the coefficient. Unsuccessful attempts were made to correct for autocorrelation. In the process the intercept became insignificant, while the coefficient on effort was essentially unchanged

Table 18.3 Data on harvest (metric tons), mean annual biomass (metric tons), and vessels in the US Pacific Whiting Fishery

Year (t)	Harvest (Y_t)	Biomass (X_t)	Vessels (E_t)
1981	44,395	1,384,000	21
1982	68,488	2,000,000	17
1983	73,150	1,805,000	19
1984	81,610	1,742,000	21
1985	35,586	1,685,000	17
1986	85,103	2,225,000	25
1987	110,792	2,012,000	31
1988	142,657	1,688,000	42
1989	204,038	1,315,000	65

and remained highly significant. The coefficient on effort ranged from about -0.0022 to -0.0028. For the base-case parameter set we adopt $q = 0.25E\text{-}2$

Other parameters needed for adaptive management are the seasonal operating cost c, the discount rate δ, the average annual natural mortality rate M, and the price p, per metric ton received by US catchers. If one wished to calculate the long-run (stochastic) equilibrium one would need to know long-run, expected recruitment, denoted by R. At a long-run stochastic equilibrium, equation (18.28) becomes

$$R = MX + (1 - M)X(1 - e^{-qE}) \qquad (18.35)$$

Eliminating effort from equations (18.31) and (18.35) will lead to an explicit solution for long-run optimal biomass (X^*) which turns out to be the positive root of a quadratic (see Conrad, 1992, p. 231).

Seasonal operating cost, as estimated from the tax returns of 13 vessel-owners, was approximately $250,000 per season. The discount rate was initially set at 4 percent ($\delta = 0.04$). Population biologists at the NMFS have estimated the average annual mortality to be $M = 0.25$, while the price p for whiting in 1989 was $110 per metric ton. Recruitment, as noted earlier, is highly variable. An imprecise point estimate of average, annual, long-run recruitment is $R = 250,000$ metric tons.

Table 18.4 reproduces some of the calculations from Conrad (1992, table 4). It contains estimates of vessel numbers and harvest in long-run equilibrium and under adaptive management for the base-case parameter set, as well as for selective changes in q, c, δ, M, and p.

In the base case, the long-run optimal biomass would be 957,748 metric tons, supporting a fleet of only six vessels harvesting 14,083 metric tons.

Table 18.4 Long-run (stochastic) equilibria and adaptive management in the Pacific Whiting Fishery

---

(a) Base-case parameter set
$q = 0.25\text{E-}2$, $c = \$250{,}000$, $\delta = 0.04$, $M = 0.25$, $p = \$110$, $R = 250{,}000$ mt

| | $X^* = 957{,}748$ mt | $E^* = 6$ vessels | $Y^* = 14{,}083$ mt |

When

(i)	$X = 1{,}000{,}000$ mt	$E = 11$ vessels	$Y = 27{,}128$ mt
(ii)	$X = 1{,}500{,}000$ mt	$E = 67$ vessels	$Y = 230{,}159$ mt
(iii)	$X = 2{,}000{,}000$ mt	$E = 115$ vessels	$Y = 501{,}441$ mt

(b) When $q = 0.20\text{E-}2$, *ceteris paribus*
No commercial fishery in the long run. Vessels not sufficiently productive
When

(i)	$X = 1{,}000{,}000$ mt	No fishery in the short run stock too low	
(ii)	$X = 1{,}500{,}000$ mt	$E = 43$ vessels	$Y = 122{,}881$ mt
(iii)	$X = 2{,}000{,}000$ mt	$E = 96$ vessels	$Y = 349{,}730$ mt

(c) When $c = \$200{,}000$, *ceteris paribus*

| | $X^* = 867{,}361$ mt | $E^* = 21$ vessels | $Y^* = 44{,}213$ mt |

When

(i)	$X = 1{,}000{,}000$ mt	$E = 40$ vessels	$Y = 94{,}668$ mt
(ii)	$X = 1{,}500{,}000$ mt	$E = 104$ vessels	$Y = 342{,}837$ mt
(iii)	$X = 2{,}000{,}000$ mt	$E = 159$ vessels	$Y = 655{,}897$ mt

(d) When $\delta = 0.06$, *ceteris paribus*

| | $X^* = 956{,}702$ mt | $E^* = 6$ vessels | $Y^* = 14{,}432$ mt |

When

(i)	$X = 1{,}000{,}000$ mt	$E = 12$ vessels	$Y = 28{,}414$ mt
(ii)	$X = 1{,}500{,}000$ mt	$E = 70$ vessels	$Y = 239{,}956$ mt
(iii)	$X = 2{,}000{,}000$ mt	$E = 120$ vessels	$Y = 519{,}553$ mt

(e) When $M = 0.20$, *ceteis paribus*

| | $X^* = 1{,}075{,}564$ mt | $E^* = 17$ vessels | $Y^* = 43{,}609$ mt |

When

(i)	$X = 1{,}000{,}000$ mt	$E = 9$ vessels	$Y = 22{,}556$ mt
(ii)	$X = 1{,}500{,}000$ mt	$E = 56$ vessels	$Y = 195{,}652$ mt
(iii)	$X = 2{,}000{,}000$ mt	$E = 98$ vessels	$Y = 433{,}735$ mt

(f) When $p = \$100$, *ceteris paribus*
No viable commercial fishery in the long run. Price too low
When

(i)	$X = 1{,}000{,}000$ mt	$E = 0$ vessels	$Y = 0$ mt
(ii)	$X = 1{,}500{,}000$ mt	$E = 52$ vessels	$Y = 183{,}544$ mt
(iii)	$X = 2{,}000{,}000$ mt	$E = 98$ vessels	$Y = 436{,}090$ mt

---

Because of the highly variable nature of recruitment, the long-run (stochastic) equilibrium is not like to be of practical significance. More important is the AOFCP used for adaptive management. To use equation (18.31) we need an estimate of current period X. Under each subcase (a)–(f), we show the approximately optimal fleet and catch for $X = 1.0$, 1.5, and 2.0 million metric tons. In the base case, if $X = 1.0E6$ metric tons, $E = 11$ vessels, harvesting 27,128 metric tons. If the estimated stock is $X = 1.5E6$ metric tons, the optimal fleet is 67 vessels, harvesting 230,159 metric tons, and if $X = 2.0E6$, $E = 115$ vessels, harvesting $Y = 501,441$ metric tons. From this single bit of analysis, it would appear that the whiting fishery should be opportunistically managed, with multipurpose vessels entering and exiting the fishery depending on recent recruitment.

Another interesting aspect emerges from table 18.4. It is possible that the fishery may not be viable in the long run, under the prevailing economic conditions, but because of relatively high current abundance it may be profitable to fish in the short run. This is shown in case (b) where q has declined by 20 percent (from 0.25E-2 to 0.20E-2).

Careful examination of the other cases in table 18.4 will reveal (a) that a reduction in cost will reduce long-run biomass while increasing effort and harvest in the adaptive, short run, (b) an increase in δ from 0.04 to 0.06 will also reduce long-run biomass while increasing short-run effort and harvest but these changes are relatively small compared with the base case, (c) a decrease in mortality acts like a reduction in the discount rate (see equation (18.30)), increasing long-run biomass while reducing short-run effort and harvest, and finally (d) a reduction in price from \$110 to \$100 will make the fishery nonviable in the long run and in the short run for stock size less than or equal to 1 million metric tons, while it would be profitable in the short run if current-period biomass were 1.5 million metric tons ($E = 52$ vessels), or at $X = 2.0$ million metric tons ($E = 98$ vessels).

5   Management Issue

The preceding sections have hopefully provided a clear and concise introduction to the models that economists use to describe open access and to derive optimal management policies. Optimality, of course, must be defined in terms of an objective, and people may differ in what they regard as the appropriate objective of fisheries management. The debate over appropriate management policies is frequently made more difficult by the use of imprecise terms such as "preservation" and "conservation." Some interpret the term preservation to mean "no use" or "no consumptive use" of a resource. Preservation to the various species of baleen whale would therefore be synonymous with no harvest (or perhaps only harvest by indigenous peoples). Conservation might be defined as "wise use," which presumably would allow harvest in a manner that did not pose an undue risk of extinction. (We will assume that harvest schedules that result in extinction are "unwise.")

Even if resource conservation is the philosophical operative, agreement on the precise measure of "wise use" is likely to be controversial. When would the maximization of the present value of net revenue be appropriate? When is the discounted sum of consumer and producer surplus appropriate? When and how should we include nonmarket values, such as the value of observation and photography of marine mammals? How can we assess the risk of extinction posed by alternative harvest schedules?

These questions are important in understanding the traditional policies used to manage renewable resources and the "incentive-based" policies advocated by economists. Of particular interest are policies that (a) remain effective over time and across a broad range of objectives and (b) are adaptable in the face of stochastic changes to the resource or its environment.

There are at least four management policies which might be regarded as traditional: (a) closed seasons, (b) gear restrictions, (c) limited entry, and (d) aggregate catch quotas. The first three policies were often imposed in an attempt to restrict or reduce the effectiveness of fishing effort. The fourth policy is an attempt to restrict harvest to some target amount. Often these policies are biologically motivated, with little cognizance or concern for the economic forces which might work to mitigate and ultimately reduce their effectiveness,.

Closed seasons were often adopted to protect a fish stock during a critical stage in its life-cycle. An example might be the prohibition of salmon fishing by nonnatives, in the State of Washington, on rivers where the fish congregate en route to their spawning streams.

Gear restrictions have the effect of increasing the cost of harvest. They may also have a biological or ecological basis. For example, the groundfishery for cod, haddock, and flounder off the coast of New England is subject to a minimum mesh size, in the hope that smaller/younger fish will escape harvest and provide the necessary growth and recruitment to the fishery in later years. On Chesapeake Bay, in Maryland state waters, watermen dredging for oysters are restricted to sail-powered vessels. On Great South Bay, on Long Island, New York, baymen are restricted to hand tongs and rakes when harvesting hard clams. In the latter two cases, the use smaller, sail-powered dredges or hand-hauled rakes and tongs is thought to preserve better the benthic habitat for future generations of oysters or clams.

Limited entry, often used in conjunction with an aggregate quota, attempts to limit the number of vessels in a fishery. The State of Alaska and Province of British Columbia have both employed programs of limited entry in their salmon fisheries. The use of an aggregate quote still perpetuates a "race for the fish," prompting fishermen to engage in intensive and often dangerous effort in an attempt to maximize *their* share of the quota before the fishery is shut down. Aggregate quotas often lead to a shortening of the fishing season to a few weeks or even a few days. This, in turn, will result in a flood of fish to the market, lowering price, and often forcing the freezing and storage of fish which would have commanded a higher price on the fresh market had the quota been spread over a longer season.

For the latter three policies, lax enforcement and the underlying forces of open access may ultimately render the policy ineffective. For example, in the New England groundfishery it is thought that many boats switch to smaller-meshed nets once they reach the fishing grounds. Such behavior is difficult to detect by the limited number of coast guard vessels that are also responsible for rescue operations, marine pollution detection, and drug enforcement.

Even if limited entry and aggregate quotas are initially successful, increased profits by "rent-seeking" vessels might lead to "capital-stuffing." In this situation, vessels within a limited entry fishery have an incentive to replace older, smaller engines with newer, larger engines (capable of pulling a larger net). Alternatively, they may add new or more precise electronics to aid in navigation and finding schools of fish. Ultimately, the effective effort of a limited set of vessels can increase, resulting in a larger catch or a shortened season.

It was noted in the introduction to this chapter that landings taxes or ITQs might contribute to a more rational management policy. Recall from the first bioeconomic model that the optimal level of harvest in period t must satisfy the equation $\partial\pi(\cdot)/\partial Y_t = \rho\lambda_{t+1}$, where $\partial\pi(\cdot)/Y_t$ is the marginal net benefit of current-period harvest and might be written as $\partial\pi(\cdot)/Y_t = p - \text{MC}_t$, where p is the price per unit of harvested fish and MC_t is marginal cost (see equation (18.10)). Thus, we seek a policy which would induce fishermen to collectively equate price to the sum of marginal cost plus user cost; that is $p = \text{MC}_t + \rho\lambda_{t+1}$. In theory, either a landings tax (a tax per unit of fish landed) or a system if ITQs can approximate $\rho\lambda_{t+1}$ and induce optimal harvest. ITQs introduced into a limited entry fishery are likely to be more palatable to the fishing industry and may be easier to administer than a system of landings taxes. Such a system might operate as follows.

Each vessel-owner within a limited entry fishery is endowed with a certificate entitling him to harvest up to a specified fraction of the allowable catch in a particular year. For example, if a vessel were entitled to harvest 2 percent of the allowable catch, and if the allowable catch (which might vary from year to year) was 200,000 metric tons, then the vessel could harvest up to 4000 metric tons *anytime* during the year. The vessel-owner, however, would have the option of leasing all or a part of his ITQ during a particular year or selling the ITQ completely and leaving the fishery. The Ministry of Fisheries or another appropriate agency would be charged with recording ITQ ownership, rentals, and sales and also might serve as a broker, facilitating transactions by the electronic posting of bid–ask prices. With a large number of quota-holders and potential buyers, a quote price P_Q representing the per-unit price at which a lease takes place would emerge. This price would reflect the current market price of fish and the cost of fishing which, in turn, would depend on the size of the fish stock. The price for permanent acquisition of an additional unit of ITQ would presumably reflect the industry's expectations about future prices, harvest cost, stock size, and the efficacy of fisheries management.

The fact that all or part of an ITQ could be leased or sold creates an opportunity cost which, by adjusting total allowable catch, could induce the price per unit of quote in the quota market to equal user cost; that is, $P_Q = \rho\lambda_{t+1}$. At the margin, the net value to a fisherman of an additional unit of quota would equal what it would fetch on the quota market; thus $p - MC_t = P_Q = \rho\lambda_{t+1}$, satisfying the necessary condition for optimal harvest.

In practice, it is unlikely that fishery managers would have solved even a simple, deterministic bioeconomic model, and therefore they are unlikely to have an optimal biomass and harvest in mind. This does not raise any serious difficulties so long as fisheries scientists can agree on an appropriate, current-period, allowable catch that may be used to define the metric ton values of the ITQ shares. By monitoring landings and conducting research that produces time series estimates of the fish stock, they will at least be able to move and maintain the fish stock in some interval of "optimal" size. ITQs seem well suited to management even in the face of ill-defined management objectives. They also meet our second criterion; adaptability in the face of stochastic changes to the resource or its environment. Provided that random failures or windfalls in recruitment can be detected, allowable catch can be adjusted accordingly. In fact, the AOFCP discussed in the previous two sections could be used to set allowable catch within an ITQ program, provided that fisheries scientists can update their estimate of fishable biomass on an annual basis.

References

Anderson, L. G. 1977: *Economic Impacts of Extended Fisheries Jurisdiction.* Ann Arbor, MI: Ann Arbor Science.
Bjørndal, T. 1984: The optimal management of an ocean fishery. Unpublished Ph.D. Dissertation, Department of Economics, University of British Columbia, Vancouver.
Bjørndal, T. and Conrad, J. M. 1987a: The dynamics of an open access fishery. *Canadian Journal of Economics,* 20 (1), 74–85.

Bjørndal, T. and Conrad, J. M. 1987b: Capital dynamics in the North Sea herring fishery. *Marine Resource Economics*, 4, 63–74.

Bockstoce, J. R. 1986: *Whales, Ice, and Men: The History of Whaling in the Western Arctic.* Seattle, WA: University of Washington Press.

Brown, G. M. Jr. 1974: An optimal program for managing common property resources with congestion externalities. *Journal of Political Economy*, 82 (January–February), 163–74.

Burt, O. 1964: Optimal resource use over time with an application to groundwater. *Management Science*, 11, 80–93.

Burt, O. 1967: Temporal allocation of groundwater. *Water Resources Research*, 3, 45–56.

Burt, O. and Cummings, R. G. 1977: Natural resource management, the steady state, and approximately optimal decision rules. *Land Economics*, 53 (1), 1–22.

Busch, B. C. 1985; *The War Against the Seals: A History of the North American Seal Fishery.* Montreal and Kingston, Canada: McGill-Queens University Press.

Christy, F. T., Jr. 1973: Fisherman quotas: a tentative suggestion for domestic management. Occasional Paper 19, Law of the Sea Institute, Honolulu, Hawaii.

Clark, C. W. 1973a: The economics of overexploitation. *Science*, 181, 630–4.

Clark, C. W. 1973b: Profit maximization and the extinction of animal species. *Journal of Political Economy*, 81, 950–61.

Clark, C. W. 1976, 1990: *Mathematical Bioeconomics: The Optimal Management of Renewable Resources.* New York: Wiley (2nd edn 1990).

Clark, C. W. 1985: *Bioeconomic Modelling and Fisheries Management.* New York: Wiley.

Clark, C. W. and Lamberson, R. 1982: An economic history and analysis of pelagic whaling. *Marine Policy*, 6 (April), 103–20.

Clark, C. W. and Munro, G. R. 1975: The economics of fishing and modern capital theory; a simplified approach. *Journal of Environmental Economics and Management*, 2, 92–106.

Conrad, J. M. 1987: The Magnuson Fisheries Conservation and Management Act: an economic assessment of the first 10 years. *Marine Fisheries Review*, 49 (3), 3–12.

Conrad, J. M. 1989: Bioeconomics and the bowhead whale. *Journal of Political Economy*, 97 (4), 974–87.

Conrad, J. M. 1992: A bioeconomic model of the Pacific whiting. *Bulletin of Mathematical Biology*, 54 (2–3), 219–39.

Crutchfield, J. A. and Zellner, A. 1962: Economic aspects of the Pacific halibut fishery. *Fisher Industrial Research*, 1 (1).

Dales, J. H. 1968: *Pollution, Property and Prices.* Toronto: University of Toronto Press.

Edelstein-Keshet, L. 1988: *Mathematical Models in Biology.* New York: Random House.

Fullenbaum, R. F., Carlson, E. W. and Bell, F. W. 1971: Economics of production from natural resources: comment. *American Economic Review*, 61 (3), 483–7.

Fullenbaum, R. F., Carlson, E. W. and Bell, F. W. 1972: On models of commercial fishing: a defense of the traditional literature. *Journal of Political Economy*, 80 (4), 761–8.

Gordon, H. S. 1954: The economic theory of a common property resource: the fishery. *Journal of Political Economy*, 62, 124–42.

Kolberg, W. C. 1992: Approach paths to the steady state: a performance test of current period decision rule solution methods for models of renewable resource management. *Land Economics*, 68 (1), 11–27.

Lotka, A. 1956: *Elements of Mathematical Biology.* New York: Dover Publications.

May, R. M. 1975: Biological populations obeying difference equations: stable points, stable cycles and chaos. *Journal of Theoretical Biology*, 51, 511–24.

Quirk, J. P. and Smith, V. L. 1969: Dynamic economic models of fishing. Research Paper 22, Department of Economics, University of Kansas, Lawrence.

Rettig, R. B. and Ginter, J. J. C. 1978: *Limited Entry as a Fishery Management Tool.* Seattle, WA: University of Washington Press.

Scott, A. D. 1955: The fishery: the objective of sole ownership. *Journal of Political Economy*, 63, 116–24.

Smith, V. L. 1968: Economics of production from natural resources. *American Economic Review*, 58 (3), 409–31.

Smith, V. L. 1969: On models of commercial fishing. *Journal of Political Economy*, 77 (March–April), 181–98.

Wilen, J. 1976: Common property resources and the dynamics of overexploitation: the case of the North Pacific fur seal. Department of Economics, Programme in Natural Resource Economics, Paper 3, University of British Columbia, Vancouver.

19

Management Regimes in Ocean Fisheries

R. Bruce Rettig

Introduction

Why are some fishery management approaches, such as licence limitation and individual transferable quotas, adopted at about the same time and in about the same form in some countries? Why do these approaches emerge much later, not at all, or in radically different forms in other countries? Why are the responses by fishers so similar among some groups and so different among others? Standard bioeconomic models respond weakly to these questions. The limitations arise from the pervasiveness of phenomena excluded from the simplest models so that mathematical solutions can be obtained. Overcoming these challenges requires different methodologies, data collection, and collaboration among researchers in several disciplines.

The chapter begins with a response derived from conventional bioeconomic analyses. Next, trends in international fishery regimes are summarized, and a discussion follows of factors affecting the choice of management regime and the portfolio of alternative management tools. A brief review of analytical approaches pursued by neoinstitutional economists and scholars in related disciplines provides the basis for an expanded neoclassical analysis of management regimes in ocean fisheries. In closing, priorities for future research are discussed.

The neoclassical economic approach: a first approximation

Among the most critical assumptions in simple bioeconomic models is that information is available on key physical, biological, and economic phenomena. Although perfect knowledge is not assumed, the models do presume that functional forms are known and that uncertainty (or, more accurately, risk) takes the form of random variability in selected parameters. Perhaps most bothersome is the assumption that fishers, fish buyers, managers, and other involved parties do not undertake strategic decision making, whereas strategic decision making is central to ocean fisheries. Fortunately, there is a large and growing literature on the analytics of uncertainty and information, including strategic decision making (Hirshleifer and Riley, 1992).

Clark (1990) explains how game theory can be used to introduce strategic decision making into bioeconomic models of fishery management. Section 5.5 of Clark's classic text, entitled "Transboundary fishery resources: a further application of the theory" (Clark, 1990, pp. 158–64), was prepared by Munro. Munro used the theory of cooperative games to explain international negotiations over fish stocks.

Munro observes that negotiations over most transboundary stocks begin with formulas for sharing those stocks. He argues that fishery management could be simpler and cost less if managers would approach the negotiation process as if it were a cooperative game. Each country would be portrayed as a "player" who calculates the "payoffs" from alternative negotiation strategies. Each player calculates the present value of its net benefits given its fishery management actions and fishery management approaches taken by its neighbor. These net benefits include the willingness to pay for fish harvested locally less the opportunity costs of harvesting those fish (i.e. the sum of consumer and producer surplus in the domestic fishing industry) plus any surplus associated with the international trade in fishery products plus any transfer payment made between the two countries. Each player calculates its benefits both with international cooperation strategies and without cooperation. Only if both players expect their outcomes to be greater with cooperation that without would negotiations be successful.

Munro admits that the prevailing practice of predetermining harvest shares among countries before beginning negotiations and the failure to consider monetary compensation for concessions does permit negotiated (cooperative) solutions. However, he argues that these second-best solutions are complex and difficult to implement. His "second conclusion is that where differences in perceived optimal management strategies arise, it appears invariably to be related to the fact that for a number of reasons, one joint owner values the fishery more highly than the other. The optimal outcome is one appealing to common sense, namely, that of permitting the joint owner valuing the fishery most highly to determine the management program and then having that joint owner to compensate its fellow owner(s) through transfer payments" (Clark, 1990, p. 164). Among the sources of different value considered by Munro are different fishing costs, different market opportunities (translated into different landed value per unit harvested), and different time discount rates.

What issues need to be addressed?

Although Clark and Munro use game theory only to develop limited insights and do not make large claims for it, one can conceive of other useful results. Later in this chapter, a neoinstitutional economics approach will be adopted; that approach can be portrayed as a series of repeated cooperative games. However, a full analysis must address problems arising from limited information, large transaction costs, and the limits of human cognition in dealing with uncertainty. The next section summarizes selected aspects of international fishery management.

The International Law of the Sea

Fishery management regimes in most parts of the world differ fundamentally from those found two decades ago. This is true for measures used by the different nations to manage their own citizens, for management measures imposed by countries on foreigners, and for internationally managed biological populations. Perhaps the most important development has been the extension of coastal fishery jurisdiction.

Coastal jurisdiction

For many years, coastal nations controlled only those fisheries within a narrow territorial sea and a small contiguous fishing zone. Most nations limited this jurisdiction to an area that ranged from their internal waters to an outer limit somewhere between 3 and 12 miles from shore. The United Nations Convention on the Law of the Sea that was signed in 1982 incorporated a 200-nautical-mile extended economic zone (EEZ) which placed substantial fishery management authority in the hands of adjacent coastal nations. Although the Convention was not ratified by enough nations in the subsequent decade to come into force, many of its provisions, including the 200-mile EEZ, are widely accepted through unilateral assertion of rights and through the customary practice of EEZ fishery management.

The nationalization of adjacent stocks and anadromous stocks

Many nations modeled the language in their unilateral proclamations of extended jurisdiction on that found in the United Nations Convention.

Awarding jurisdiction for stocks that are found predominantly within the EEZ of a nation to the coastal nation is consistent with economic reasoning. The failure to define property rights over the fish stocks was viewed widely as a cause of the decline in those stocks. Who is more interested in the sustainable exploitation of fish stocks adjacent to a coastal nation than that coastal nation? And who can monitor and enforce sustainable management more effectively than the closest nation? Reversing this reasoning, who is more capable of depleting fish stocks and evading fish conservation measures than the coastal nation if that coastal nation has nothing at stake?

Shared access to coastal stocks

Coastal fishing nations choose one of three options to manage the populations found within their EEZs: (1) harvest the fish themselves and land the catch in domestic ports for consumption or subsequent export; (2) harvest the fish themselves, but transfer the catch to foreign processing vessels at sea; (3) allow foreign fishing fleets to capture the fish. In fisheries with historic participation by domestic harvesters and processors, the first option is preferred. The second option is a simplified version of a pattern of cooperation known as joint ventures. In many countries, including the United States, the joint venture is a temporary device to convert those stocks historically caught by distant-water fishing fleets to domestic harvest and processing. The third option is pursued by developed countries such as the United States to allow reciprocal access into other countries' fishing waters or to gain another diplomatic or political advantage. In less developed countries, and in some circumstances in developed countries, the third option is carried out in exchange for monetary payments or other considerations. In the late 1970s, the United States gave preferential access to countries for a variety of interests including access to those other countries' markets. US fishing zone access was swapped for the "chips" of access to Japanese and other markets; hence the name – fish and chips policy.

Transboundary stocks

The fishing jurisdiction for many valuable fish stocks is not easily assigned to adjacent coastal fishing nations. Responses, in terms of both applicable international fishery regime and approach taken within each member nation, vary depending on the ways that fish cross national boundaries. Three forms which have captured much attention have been straddling stocks, fish shared among the EEZs of more than one nation, and highly migratory stocks.

Straddling stocks

Some fish are found both within and just outside a nation's EEZ. For example, the stocks of the Grand Banks off the eastern coast of Canada are found predominantly within Canada's EEZ, but enough are captured more than 200 miles from the Canadian coast to raise conservation concerns. When coastal jurisdiction stopped 12 miles from shore, massive amounts of time and other resources went into international treaty organizations. These groups, such as the International Convention for the Northwest Atlantic Fisheries, made up of the United States, Canada, and many European nations, had limited success in controlling the excessive harvest of Atlantic Ocean fish stocks near the United States and Canada. After fishery jurisdiction was extended, the number of straddling stocks decreased while the expectations of coastal nations that something should be done rose; old crises affecting poor Canadian coastal fishers have been succeeded by new crises affecting poor Canadian coastal fishers. Some nations want coastal fishing jurisdiction extended farther than 200 miles for important straddling stocks, some are trying to deal with the issue through bilateral negotiations between coastal nations and distant-water fishing nations, and some argue that nothing can be done for straddling stocks independently of a new regime to handle high seas stocks (fish found predominantly outside coastal fishing jurisdiction).

Shared economic zones

One of the most troublesome circumstances for international fishery regimes occurs when fish stocks straddle the EEZs of adjacent fishing nations or when the fish migrate among the EEZs of more than one coastal fishing nation. This migration can be seasonal in response to spawning cycles or variation in the location of the prey of the fish stock; or it can reflect shifts in climatic conditions. An example of the latter is the poleward shift of stocks when low latitude waters become warmer. For example, northern anchovy populations migrate between Mexico and California. Their relative abundance in the ocean off the United States and California is influenced by the appearance of unusually warm water masses moving northward from the Equator.

Allocation of shared stocks among adjacent EEZs is often based on international quotas based on the amount of time the fish live in each EEZ, the critical importance of a particular EEZ to the survival of the fish (e.g. which EEZ provides the spawning habitat), and other factors. Complex and difficult international negotiations were necessary for a European Common Fishery Policy, both to manage the transboundary shared stocks and to provide consistency with other European Union policies.

Shared stocks – highly migratory

The United Nations Convention on the Law of the Sea left management of highly migratory stocks to international treaty organizations. To reduce uncertainty the applicable species were identified explicitly: seven species of tuna; frigate mackerel; pomfrets; marlins; sail-fishes; swordfish; sauries; dolphin; ocean sharks; and seven families of cetaceans. International treaties for highly migratory species are particularly difficult to enforce, but international management is possible. One circumstance is where the number of fishing nations is small and those nations feel strong pressure to negotiate agreements (such as the negotiations among the Japanese, Australians, and New Zealanders for southern bluefin tuna). Another example is where migratory species are taken largely within someone's EEZ and the harvest of that species is critically important to the local economy (as is true for small island states in the South Pacific).

Factors affecting the choice of management regime

Within each country, a portfolio of management tools forms a management regime. What influences each nation's perception of the appropriate methods for management measures to be included in international negotiations? A short review of some of the most common factors, abstracted from a longer paper (Rettig, 1992), may provide perspective for the discussion of management tools.

Biological considerations

To avoid recruitment failures (inability of the biomass to replenish itself), managers favor techniques that generate good information about the size of stock and allow for quick closures when problems are identified. Fishers have an interest in avoiding recruitment failures; management approaches that embody this interest meet with wider approval and are easier to enforce. The more fishers expect that protecting fish stocks now will increase their fishing opportunities in the future, the more they support conservation measures.

Several fisheries, especially trawl fisheries, capture assemblages that include many species at once. If fishers exploit some stocks to their maximum sustainable yields, others maybe overexploited. A related concern is that many fishing gears kill more fish than they harvest. For example, some fish drop out of nets after they die and before they are brought on board. Also, some regulations either require or encourage fishers to discard a part of the catch. Recognizing these realities, managers either favor fisheries with selective gear or abandon commitments to maintain productivity of all stocks.

Social equity and cultural heritage

Perceptions of unfair or inequitable treatment make some options politically unacceptable or difficult and expensive to administer. Because principles of justice and morality are grounded in religious practice, customs, ethnic preferences etc. and because these vary from place to place, restrictions on fishery management approaches based on morality issues will also vary widely (McGoodwin, 1990).

Whether a fishery regulation is fair and equitable varies from culture to culture, but a few themes are widespread. Some groups have higher standing before fishery managers than others. Often, managers favor local fishers over people from outside the decision-making area. Full-time fishers are often favored over part-time fishers in spite of good reasons for part-time fishing. Part-time fishing may be an example of occupational pluralism (McGoodwin, 1990): where no single year-round job can support families, workers may fish part of the year, farm part of the year, and work at one more other jobs the rest of the time. Other fishing groups given special consideration are defined by ethnicity, age, national origin, and wealth.

Administrative feasibility and political acceptability
The more costly and difficult regulations are to administer and enforce, the less desirable they are. In most fisheries, enforcement capacities are limited. Many nations never did much at-sea monitoring and enforcement. Even where enforcement vessels and planes are available, governments are increasingly concerned about their cost. Regulations that create incentives to carry out avoidance measures create additional costs to fishers. The less reason fishers have to work to offset the intent of regulations, the lower the costs of fishing and the greater the economic benefits from fisheries. Some regulations lead to wasteful and unwanted behavior even when fishers are not breaking rules, as when shifts in fishing patterns reduce the scientific value derived from catch and landing statistics.

Because fishery managers require approval from groups of fishers, their superiors in the government bureaucracy, or both, regulations are created and administered in a legal system driven by political concerns. Thus, management must be politically acceptable. If a management approach triggers unacceptable outcomes such as migration away from thinly populated areas and toward overpopulated cities, it is often either changed to meet the concerns or abandoned.

Management Tools

The natural resource and environmental economics literature stresses the exciting possibilities for use of monetary instruments and regulatory instruments that mimic property rights, and it dismisses other methods as wasteful. As Conrad and Anderson suggest in chapters 18 and 20, market-like approaches are not without problems. A reflective examination of fishery management measures should suggest that other approaches also are not without merit. The categorization of management approaches in this chapter follows Beddington and Rettig (1984).

Catch limits

Harvesting fish at levels greater than the biomass can sustain creates international concern. So, most international discussions begin by setting an overall catch limit, which may lead directly to a regulatory instrument or may provide a benchmark for testing the effectiveness of alternative management approaches.

International allocation

Before extended jurisdiction, international organizations met regularly to set the total allowable catch (TAC) for one or more stocks. Sometimes, approaches to restrain the fleets from overharvesting the TACs were also negotiated. Since extended jurisdiction, the process has been followed roughly as follows.

The coastal nation determines the allowable catch of living resources in its EEZ. To do this, scientists estimate the maximum sustainable yield (MSY) from major stocks. Either a scientific or a management group then estimates optimum yield by adjusting MSY for environmental and economic reasons. Subtracting the expected harvest by fishers from the coastal nation may yield a surplus. Coastal nations are supposed to allocate this surplus among other interested nations. Although the law of the sea language suggested that landlocked and geographically disadvantaged states should be favored, with special consideration for developing countries, access often goes to developed nations with a history of distant-water fisheries. The principal reason is that the coastal nation often is interested in getting something in return for granting access, commonly cash payments or assistance in developing the capability to harvest coastal stocks more fully. Joint ventures involve both fishers or processors from the coastal nation and their counterparts from a distant-water fishing nation. Another consideration is market access. For example, the value placed on access to Japanese markets and the sophistication of Japanese fishing and processing technology often leads to preferred treatment to Japanese fleets.

The pattern just described is common, but not uniform. Important variations depend on multilateral planning organizations, such as an advisory body to the fishery managers within the European Union, and availability of resources, as when less developed countries lack resources for complete planning, negotiation, and enforcement.

International allocation

Why did many nations model their fishery management regimes on guidelines rising from the most recent law of the sea treaty? Perhaps because treaty negotiations convinced them of the value of the guidelines, perhaps because the guidelines reflected what they had already decided to do, or perhaps because the treaty is now customary international law.

After adjusting for economic, social, and environmental factors, a TAC is set for many fish stocks. Frequently, allocation of the TAC among fishers is an unintended by-product of indirect methods of fishery management such as time and area closures and gear restrictions. Indirect methods are supplemented by restrictive licensing, monetary measures, and rights-based management measures.

Under any institutional arrangement, some groups catch more fish, catch them earlier, catch them in a more valuable condition, or otherwise appear to be favored in the eyes of fellow fishers. Fishery managers sometimes try to offset these perceived advantages by allocating allowable catch to each group. For example, the judicial system in the United States decided that members of certain American Indian tribes have rights to harvest 50 percent of selected fish stocks (primarily salmon that historically returned to the lands occupied by the tribes). Several restrictive measures are imposed on all other fishers to give the treaty tribes their share.

Other examples of allocating TAC within the United States include splits between recreational fishers and commercial fishers, between fixed and mobile gear groups, and between inshore fleets and offshore fleets. Although economic analysis is sometimes used to decide how to allocate stocks among the competing groups, the common practice is to divide the TAC in proportion to the historic shares received by the various groups. However the allocation is done, techniques are needed to restrict the harvest to meet the quotas.

Indirect methods

Once managers set catch limits, techniques are needed to limit the total catch and to influence the attributes of the catch. If the purpose of the limit is to maintain the stock over time, restrictions must ensure that adequate recruitment of future generations will occur and that the recruited fish grow to an acceptable size, weight, and quality. The most common methods are gear restrictions and time and area closures.

Seasonal closures, which protect very young fish or spawning fish, play a critical role in ensuring adequate recruitment. When fishing pressure increases, seasonal closures become a common way to enforce a TAC. Several problems arise when seasonal closures are used to restrict overfishing. Using seasonal closures to choke back excessive fishing effort blunts the effectiveness of seasonal closures as conservation tools.

Area closures are often combined with seasonal closures to achieve conservation goals. Since extended jurisdiction, they have been used in different ways as well. Area closures may separate competing fishing groups and reduce troublesome conflicts. Closing all fishing in an area makes surveillance cost effective (Chappell, 1984). Licensing gear for a specific area is an effective tool where monitoring and enforcement problems are not severe (MacGillivray, 1986).

Gear restrictions are also valuable conservation tools. Minimum mesh sizes let small fish with great growth potential escape while trawlers keep more mature fish. Requiring barbless hooks increases the survival of fish that are returned to the sea. Also, like time and area closures, gear restrictions are sometimes used to control overfishing. Restricting new technologies to reduce fishing pressures needlessly increases costs and sacrifices the comfort and safety of fishers. Finally, like time and area closures, gear restrictions combine with direct controls to create innovative fishery management systems.

Monetary measures

Monetary measures are commonly used, but rarely to achieve goals of economic efficiency. Royalties (taxes, fees etc.) are levied to rise money according to tax equity principles. Financial support (subsidies, public expenditure on infrastructure etc.) also is aimed more at equity goals than economic efficiency. Nonetheless, both approaches can significantly affect domestic and international fishery management regimes.

Although taxes are often levied in fisheries in developed nations, they are seldom intended to act as a fishery management tool. This is particularly true of a landings tax, that is, a tax where the size of the payment is proportional to the weight landed. Fishing vessel licence fees may vary in proportion to vessel size or fishing power. While this may modestly influence fishing effort, the taxation principle is apt to be an equity one: the fishers who receive the greatest value from the fishery should pay the largest shares of public costs.

Taxes are limited in their effectiveness in allocating fishing effort, and they are often inflexible. The abundance of many fish stocks varies widely over time. Consider a fish stock that falls in abundance owing to changing ocean conditions. Because such shifts are unpredictable, biologists need time to document the decline in abundance and to make their case strong enough that a fishery management body will take steps to curtail fishing effort.

Much excess fishing capacity, in developed and developing countries alike, can be traced to government subsidy programs. Some argue that the solution is to stop financial support programs (Brochmann, 1983). On the other hand, existence of excess capacity does not eliminate the need to improve fish quality so as to provide a better price, to improve the health and safety of fishers at sea, and to maintain infrastructure such as port facilities.

Restrictive licensing (input quotas)

Most restrictive licensing programs fall into three broad categories. Licences may be (i) freely available subject to the agreement to follow rules, (ii) available to individuals who meet certain qualifications, or (iii) limited in number and available only by following procedures such as bidding for the licences at periodic auctions or purchasing a licence from someone who already has one.

Qualified entry is a very old and widely accepted practice. Commonly used qualifications include belonging to a fishing family; having worked on a fishing boat as a crew member; living in a fishing community; and absence of a criminal record, especially with respect to violations of fishing laws. Although qualified entry plays a minor role in reducing the growth in fishing effort, it can reduce destructive and undesirable fishing practices.

A basic difference between licence limitation programs is how difficult it is to receive a licence, both initially and after the program comes into existence. Programs that reduce the number of fishers create more profits but cost more to administer and are more frequently challenged in court (Rettig, 1984). Licence limitation programs often have an announcement effect that increases rather than reduces effort. Because capping initial licences is so difficult, and because of the speculative surge caused by announcements, many nations try vessel reduction (buyback, buyout, scrapping) programs. Many countries planned major vessel reduction programs but made little progress as public funds grew scarce and political will weakened. Although restrictive licensing programs may, or may not, make large economic efficiency gains, they do bring a semblance of order to an otherwise chaotic fishery.

Property rights (and quasi-rights)

With a few noteworthy exceptions, governments do not allocate marine fishery resources directly (Mollett, 1986; Neher et al., 1989). Estuarine and riverine fisheries, especially for cultured fish, are often based on property rights. In contrast, marine fishery management is accidental and incidental in its creation of more fishing opportunities for some fishers than others.

Because other ways to reduce fleet capacity face so much difficulty, the success of programs based on individual transferable quotas and the historical success with most private property rights systems at lowering costs provide powerful arguments in their favor. Fishery managers have shown little interest in or aptitude for reducing excessive effort through administrative approaches. Thus, as Anderson notes in chapter 20, market approaches are being considered carefully for many overcapitalized fisheries.

Territorial use rights

Some relatively immobile fish species can be managed by controlling parts of the water column. For these species, regulations restricting fishing opportunities resemble property rights used on adjacent land areas. The term "territorial use rights in fisheries" describes this old and valuable approach (Christy, 1982).

The most elaborate modern system of property rights as a tool for managing marine fish populations evolved in Japan (Asada et al., 1983; Yamamoto and Short, 1992). While the historical roots for these programs go back to feudal times, a large and sophisticated bureaucracy evolved after the Second World War. The Japanese system places the stamp of national law on allocation decisions made at the local level, usually by a fishers' cooperative. Because the Japanese system is not easily transferable to other cultures, other types of property rights approaches have been expanding more rapidly in other developed countries.

Quota allocations

Rather than allocating fishing areas as is the case with territorial use rights, most rights-based programs allocate shares of a TAC. Although many observers are most interested in individual transferable quota programs, discussed extensively by Anderson in chapter 20, that approach faces many problems (Copes, 1986). Other forms of TAC allocation may turn out to be more common in practice.

In some fisheries, separate quotas are assigned to foreign fishing fleets, joint ventures (domestic fishers delivering their catch at sea to foreign processing vessels), and domestic fishers delivering to domestic processors. As fisheries become nationalized, TAC is allocated among competing domestic groups. When each group reaches its allocation, its fishery closes unless special provisions are made for continuation.

In fisheries where methods explicitly called individual transferable quotas (ITQs) may be unacceptable, a fishery management technique known as trip limits, with many attributes of ITQ programs, is commonly used. A maximum TAC is set for each vessel for each trip. Sometimes the maximum number of trips per week or month is set also. Trip limits, although not designed to do so, can serve as individual non-transferable quotas. Much of the basis for ITQ programs arises from fishers' perceived hardships with a non-transferable individual quota program. Norton and McConnell's criticism of individual quota programs may be based on problems encountered in New England under non-transferable quota programs (McConnell and Norton, 1980).

Individual transferable quotas
ITQ programs are being adopted or seriously considered in many fisheries. Many examples are fisheries where jurisdiction clearly falls to a specific nation, and sometimes to specific groups within that nation. An interesting exception, which suggests the potential value of individual quotas in international fishery regimes, is the southern bluefin tuna fishery which is shared by Japan, Australia, and New Zealand, and where Australia rations its TAC by ITQs (Lilburn, 1986). Because Anderson discusses ITQs at length in the following chapter, they are not discussed here. Interested readers should consult, among other sources, the comprehensive volume edited by Neher and others (1989).

A Neoinstitutional Analysis of Fishery Management Regimes

What does a revised fishery economics paradigm need to explain? First, most regimes consist of a complex portfolio of approaches including most of the management tools discussed in this chapter. Second, the portfolio varies by fishery. This variability includes variations from one country to another, from one area to another within each country, and from one point in time to another. Third, there are some consistent patterns associated with the biology of the fishery, the geography of the coastal nations closest to the fisheries, the cultures of the fishing nations, and other factors.

Toward a revision (expansion) of the neoclassical model

Ostrom (1990) argues that policy analysts try to make sense of complex systems through one or more metaphors, with the most famous being "the tragedy of the commons" popularized by Hardin (1968). Modern bioeconomic models draw heavily on the metaphor of the "single owner" offered by Scott (1955). Unfortunately, the "tragedy of the commons," as manifested in the standard bioeconomic portrayal of a perfectly competitive economy without ownership of the fish stock, omits the efforts of people to engage in cooperation. And the conception of the "single owner," simplistically described as a small-scale owner of a fishing ground exerting exclusive control, omits the need to develop cooperation among the people involved.

What is missing from many bioeconomic models is that fisheries pursued by more than one person involve both cooperation and competition. To develop cooperation, someone must develop background information helpful to negotiating agreements, someone must monitor these agreements, and someone must enforce the agreements. Borrowing legal terminology, contracts must be negotiated, procedures must be developed to address issues not initially negotiated (to anticipate fully all possible outcomes in advance usually is prohibitively expensive), and enforcement procedures must be developed to apprehend violators and remove the tendency to defect from accepted behaviors. To choose the preferred portfolio of management approaches, the policy analyst must consider transaction costs. A full discussion of this analytical approach must consider the size and nature of risk and uncertainty, decision rules used by people to address risk and uncertainty, and the special problem of incomplete information. Before developing this argument further, what special factors exist in fisheries that make negotiation of agreements specially difficult?

Fishing is constrained both formally, by fishery regulations, and informally, by social conventions and codes of behavior. The concept of informal constraints is related to what McGoodwin (1990) calls indigenous regulations. Thus fishing activities are constrained by available capital and technology, costly or difficult access to markets, cultural traditions, customs and beliefs, limited information and skills, and other forces. Even if formal fishery management were absent, informal constraints would limit the amount and type of fishing effort. The political and economic organizations that influence both fishing activities and fishery management are also a product of institutional arrangements – both formal and informal. In turn, changes in institutional arrangements alter the destinies of political and economic organizations.

To illustrate, consider fishery management in the United States. Marine fishery management, although the responsibility of state and federal agencies, is based on regional fishery management councils, which include both public officials and private individuals; the latter are often leaders of fishers' organizations and other groups managed by the public agencies. Since the system was introduced in 1976, the character of fishing organizations and fishery management agencies has changed dramatically. Fishing organizations created the planning process. Implementation of the planning process then changed the organizations. As time goes on, the organizations continue to change the planning process and the planning process continues to change the organizations, providing an example of what North (1990) calls the path dependency of institutional change.

What does this suggest about the transferability of the New Zealand individual transferable quota program to the United States, Chile, or other countries? Any newly introduced formal constraints (ITQs) must interact with a different set of informal constraints and a different set of organizations in each country. Very different outcomes would be found everywhere even if an identical set of formal constraints were adopted. To understand this more completely, consider the ways that transaction costs alter the evolution of fishery management.

Transaction costs and property rights

Although there are many definitions of property rights and transaction costs, a few concepts are found in most statements. For example, "Property rights of individuals over assets consist of the rights, or the powers, to consume, obtain income from, and alienate these assets" (Barzel, 1989, p. 2). Fishery management regimes are, in large part, methods for regulating access and proscribing certain methods of obtaining income from and alienating fish assets. One can race to fishing grounds and compete with others or one can agree to more orderly procedures; these procedures should provide answers to questions about when, where, and how fishing will take place and who can fish.

Fishing regulations and other social rules are solutions to bargaining problems analogous to contract law, tort law, and criminal law (Coleman, 1992). Sometimes, fish harvesters can negotiate, administer, and enforce their own rules. When this is cost effective and meets other resource management goals, local management is to be preferred (Bromley, 1992). Alternatively, when local negotiations are too difficult or costly, management rules are asserted by a "higher" authority such as a state, provincial, prefectural, or national government. In complex, intermediate cases, collaborative approaches which cede specified powers and authority to local groups, subject to the ultimate authority residing with outside government authority, may be preferred (Pinkerton, 1989).

Why do economists portray fishery management as a choice between open access and single owner control? "Economists' past failure to exploit the property rights notion in the analysis of behavior probably stems from their tendency to consider rights as absolute" (Barzel, 1989, p. 2). The reason that property rights are not absolute is that they are costly. "Transaction costs [are] the costs associated with the transfer, capture, and protection of rights" (Barzel, 1989, p. 2). If one uses the lawyers' metaphor of property as a "bundle of rights," one sees that some rights are defined and claimed through management rules while other rights are retained by other parties such as the government. Once the conception of divided bundle of rights is understood, the distinction between common property and private property becomes fuzzy. What many economist call common property, Barzel would describe as cases where defining rights costs more than it is worth, thus leaving the rights in the public domain. That is, anyone can take the "common property" subject to tort law, criminal law, and relevant social restrictions.

Transaction resources, often costly, are shared among fishers, other interests in the community, and local, regional, and national governments. Not only are the property rights divided among competing parties, but claims are often contingent on the state of nature. Fishers have certain rights and can transfer them, but other rights are controlled by others or depend on external circumstances including the state of the natural environment. Transaction costs are especially large for international fishery agreements where each nation duplicates some research information to prepare its negotiating position, where other interests confound and complicate fishery negotiations (as happened when the United States denied Soviet fleet access to US coastal waters after the USSR invaded Afghanistan), and where coordination of enforcement efforts among different policing agencies increases enforcement costs. Some international agencies, such as the International Council for the Exploration of the Seas, received support from many nations in northern Europe because their stock assessment advice was needed to make international negotiation of fishing agreements in the North Sea possible.

Enforceability
Among the most costly parts of transaction costs are expenditures to keep fishers from violating both formal and informal constraints. Consider this further. Suppose, after careful biological analysis, a government agency concludes that fishers should operate with nets with large mesh size in some areas but with small mesh gear in other areas, yet regulations require the same size mesh in all areas. Alternatively, suppose that biological considerations suggest that fishers should harvest a certain species of fish in one area, harvest other species in other areas, and land the combined catch ashore, yet the regulations relate only to the species composition of landings. Why are certain types of ITQ programs somewhat effective in Iceland where a few ports are used but rejected as unworkable in the US Gulf shrimp fishery, where shrimp can be transferred to small trucks in a vast number of bayous? The answer to all this is that fishery regulations are costly and difficult to enforce, and that these enforcement costs vary among fisheries.

The choice of fishery management regime depends on enforcement costs, the amount of avoidance of regulations by fishers, and the ability to transform penalties into deterrence against future violations. Although one may explain some behavior by a rational model of expected benefits and costs, fishers are classic cases of people for whom it is rational to be irrational (Frank, 1988). That is, fishers who rationally comply using cold hard logic may not be the types of people most likely to survive and do well in commercial fishing.

Much of the discussion to this point has related to trends in fishery management regimes, including side references to systems based on property rights. Turn to the question of the emergence of such programs. How do property rights emerge and what does this tell us about evolving rights-based programs?

The emergence of property rights

What Eggertsson (1990) calls the naive model of property rights emergence provides a helpful framework for discussing international differences in fishery management, such as those set out in a recent volume edited by Yamamoto and Short (1992). According to Demsetz,

> Property rights develop to internalize externalities when the gains of internalization become larger than the cost of internalization. Increased internalization, in the main, results from changes in economic values, changes that stem from the development of new technology and the opening of new markets, changes to which old property rights are poorly attuned . . . [G]iven a community's taste . . . [for private versus state ownership], the emergence of new private or state-owned property rights will be in response to changes in technology and relative prices.
>
> (Demsetz, 1967, p. 350)

This model can be expanded, for example by considering the difficulties that arise when moral values such as desires to share with starving or poor people make the process of exclusion costly. Exclusion costs, implicit in the work of McManus (1972), were formally introduced by Anderson and Hill (1975), who noted that defining and enforcing property rights is costly. Everything else being equal, this analysis suggests that, the lower the cost of defining or enforcing individual transferable fisherman's quotas, the more completely they will be defined and enforced. This is consistent with the observation that ITQs have been adopted in New Zealand and Iceland where there are few landing sites, but not in Louisiana where many landing sites are available.

Field (1986) extended the Anderson–Hill model to include internal governance costs. The more people who participate in a management unit the greater the internal governance costs. Assuming that internal governance costs rise with the number of members, the alternative is to break into more units. The more units, the more time will be spent in defending rights from other units. The more homogeneous the members of a group, the lower the internal governance costs. The lower the costs of exclusion, the more tempting it is to expand the size of the group. Libecap (1978) extended Field's work to look not only at what resources are granted rights but also at the precision of the definition of rights. These approaches suggested by economists parallel the models of other social scientists (McCay and Acheson, 1987; Ostrom, 1990).

The model of property rights formation helps explain why the Japanese have been so effective in defining and enforcing property rights over finfish, shellfish, and aquatic plants and over territories in which these resources are found. Japanese coastal fishing communities are homogeneous and little migration takes place between fishing communities (Yamamoto and Short, 1992). The historical influence of fishing cooperatives in fishing communities helps explain why internal governance costs are low. This may also explain why Japan has been much more successful in resolving disputes among fishers where the fish migrate very little and less successful where stocks migrate between the water assigned to one fishing community to the waters assigned to another fishing community.

A Research Agenda

The thesis of this chapter is that neoinstitutional economics provides the framework needed to address questions left unanswered by the more conventional neoclassical economics. This conclusion is not original:

> The edifice of contemporary microeconomics is elegant, even gorgeous, and it can sometimes solve specific predictive problems. But its empirical difficulties are legion, and . . . it will never conquer them. Furthermore, concerns about rationality are unavoidable, and normative policy implications will always be close at hand to generate bias. So the case of economics might seem hopeless. But there are better ways forward. Although some theorists should keep pushing the current strategy as hard as they can, I would urge economists to be more electric, more opportunistic, more willing to gather data, more willing to work with generalizations with narrow scope, and more willing to collaborate with other social scientists.
>
> (Hausman, 1992, p. 280)

The suggestion that some should continue to expand conventional bioeconomics is supported ably by Conrad in chapter 18 and the theoretical parts of Anderson's chapter 20. Hausman's other recommendations also apply to fishery economics.

Data deficiencies are more devastating for empirical analyses than missing analytical techniques. Although biologists continue to make strides in population dynamics including incorporation of environmental variability and consequences of cyclical and secular changes in the physical environment, they always face the challenge of staring into a dark and glassy sea and making the best inferences they can. As great as the challenge to understanding the physical and natural environment, the economic, social, and political environments are even harder to grasp. Few fishers keep accurate data records and those who do are reluctant to share this information with anyone associated with the government (often including academia and consulting firms). Nonetheless, our understanding of fishery economics must be confronted with real data if it is to be considered valid.

Finally, the common reluctance of economists to work with other social scientists must be overcome. True, sociologists, anthropologists, political scientists, and other scholars do see the world differently, but these different viewpoints can be as much an opportunity as a threat for the economists who choose to pursue them.

References

Anderson, Terry L. and Hill, P. J. 1975: The evolution of property rights: a study of the American West. *Journal of Law and Economics*, 18, 163–79.

Asada, Y., Hirasawa, Y. and Nagasaki, F. 1983: *Fishery Management in Japan*. FAO Fisheries Technical Paper 238.

Barzel, Yoram. 1989: *Economic Analysis of Property Rights*. New York: Cambridge University Press.

Beddington, J. R. and Retting, R. B. 1984: *Approaches to the Regulation of Fishing Effort*. FAO Fisheries Technical Paper 243, 39 pp.

Brochmann, B. S. 1983: Fishery policy in Norway experiences from the period 1920–82. In *Case Studies and Working Papers Presented at the Expert Consultation on Strategies for Fisheries Development (With Particular Reference to Small-scale Fisheries)*. Rome, May 10–14 1983, FAO Fishery, Report 295, Suppl, pp. 108–22.

Bromley, Daniel W. 1992: *Making the Commons Work*. San Francisco, CA: ICS (Institute for Contemporary Studies) Press.

Chappell, W. D. 1984: United States fishing effort restrictions and fishing vessel licensing under the 200-mile limit. In *Papers Presented at the Expert Consultation on the Regulation of Fishing Effort (Fishing Mortality)*, FAO Fishery Report 289, Suppl. 3, pp. 275–81.

Christy, F. T., Jr. 1982: *Territorial Use Rights in Fisheries*. FAO Fisheries Technical Paper 227, 10 pp.

Clark, Colin. 1990: *Mathematical Bioeconomics*, 2nd edn. New York: Wiley Interscience.

Coleman, Jules L. 1992: *Risks and Wrongs*. New York: Cambridge University Press.

Copes, P. 1986: A critical review of the individual quota as a device in fisheries management. *Land Economics*, 62, 278–91.

Demsetz, Harold. 1967: Toward a theory of property rights. *American Economic Review*, 57, 347–59.

Eggertsson, Thráinn. 1990: *Economic Behavior and Institutions*. New York: Cambridge University Press.

Field, Barry C. 1986: Induced changes in property rights institution. Research Paper, Department of Agricultural and Resource Economics, University of Massachusetts, Amherst, MA.

Frank, Robert. 1988: *Passions Within Reason*. New York: Norton.

Hardin, Garrett. 1968: The tragedy of the commons. *Science*, 162, 1243–8.

Hausman, Daniel M. 1992: *The Inexact and Separate Science of Economics*. New York: Cambridge University Press.

Hirshleifer, Jack, and Riley, John G. 1992: *The Analytics of Uncertainty and Information*. New York: Cambridge University Press.

Libecap, Gary. 1978: Economic variables and the development of the law: the case of Western mineral rights. *Journal of Economic History,* 38, 399–58.

Lilburn, B. 1986: Management of Australian fisheries: broad developments and alternative strategies. In N. Mollett (ed.), *Fishery Access Control Programs Worldwide: Proceedings of the Workshop on Management Options for the North Pacific Longline Fisheries,* Fairbanks, AK: Alaska Sea Grant College Program.

MacGillivray, P. 1986: Evaluation of area licensing in the British Columbia roe herring fishery: 1981–1985. In N. Mollett (ed.) *Fishery Access Control Programs Worldwide: Proceedings of the Workshop on Management Options for the North Pacific Longline Fisheries,* Fairbanks, AK: Alaska Sea Grant College Program.

McCay, Bonnie M. and Acheson, James M. 1987: *The Question of the Commons.* Tucson, AZ: University of Arizona Press.

McConnell, K. E. and Norton, V. J. 1980: An evaluation of limited entry and alternative fishery management schemes. In R. B. Rettig and Jay J. C. Ginter (eds), *Limited Entry as a Fishery Management Tool,* Seattle, WA: University of Washington Press, 188–200.

McGoodwin, J. R. 1990: *Crisis in the World's Fisheries: People, Problems, and Policies.* Stanford, CA: Stanford University Press.

McManus, John C. 1972: An economic analysis of Indian behavior in the North American fur trade. *Journal of Economic History,* 32, 36–53.

Mollett, N. (ed.) 1986: *Fishery Access Control Programs Worldwide: Proceedings of the Workshop on Management Options for the North Pacific Longline Fisheries,* April 21–25, Orcas Island, Washington. Fairbanks, AK: Alaska Sea Grant Report 86–4.

Neher, P. A., Arnason, R. and Mollett, N. (eds) 1989: *Rights Based Fishing.* Dordrecht: Kluwer.

North, Douglass C. 1990: *Institutions, Institutional Change and Economic Performance.* New York: Cambridge University Press.

Ostrom, Elinor. 1990: *Governing the Commons: The Evolution of Institutions for Collective Action.* Cambridge, MA: Harvard University Press.

Pinkerton, Evelyn. 1989: *Co-operative Management of Local Fisheries.* Vancouver: University of British Columbia Press.

Rettig, R. B. 1984: License limitation in the United States and Canada: an assessment. *North American Journal of Fisheries Management,* 4, 231–48.

Rettig, R. B. 1992: Recent changes in fishery management in developed countries. In T. Yamamoto and K. Short (eds), *International Perspectives on Fisheries Management with Special Emphasis on Community-Based Management Systems Developed in Japan,* Tokyo: National Federation of Fisheries Cooperative Associations (ZENGYOREN).

Scott, Anthony D. 1955: The fishery: the objectives of sole ownership. *Journal of Political Economy,* 63, 116–24.

Yamamoto, Tadashi, and Short, Kevin. 1992: *International Perspectives on Fisheries Management with Special Emphasis on Community-Based Management Systems Developed in Japan.* Tokyo: National Federation of Fisheries Cooperative Associations (ZENGYOREN).

20

Privatizing Open Access Fisheries: Individual Transferable Quotas

Lee G. Anderson

1 Introduction

The purpose of this chapter is to discuss management schemes which create property rights. Such schemes have the potential to solve many of the problems of open access fisheries or those regulated by traditional means. The focus will be on individual transferable quota (ITQ) schemes which have some advantages over other property right systems and which have been successfully implemented in many fisheries in the last decade. The first section will compare traditional management with property right schemes showing how the latter can provide incentives to improve resource utilization. This will be followed by a formal economic model of ITQ management. The discussion will then turn to the implementation of ITQs. It will be shown that in the real-world application of economic theory the move from models with simplifying assumptions to complex realities can be rather tenuous. Nevertheless, the models do provide very useful insights, which if applied bearing the basic economic principles in mind can generate programs that address open access utilization problems.

2 Open Access versus Controlled Access Regulation

The losses from open access and open access regulation

As was demonstrated in chapter 18 open access exploitation of a fishery will often lead to suboptimal utilization. There will be too many boats and fish stocks will be too small.[1] Over the years many methods have been used to correct for this, but unfortunately many traditional techniques have failed to address the economic aspects of the problem.

Traditionally managers have reduced fishing pressure by restricting the activities of current participants. Closed seasons limit when they can fish, closed areas limit where they can fish, and gear restrictions limit how they can fish. Total allowable catches (total quotas) specify how much can be taken in the aggregate before fishing must cease. Basically traditional methods control when, where, or how participants can fish, or the total amount that can be taken. They do nothing to restrict open access.

While these measures have sometimes proved useful, especially in the short run, they have not been universally successful. Restrictions on individual actors can be a losing battle if their number can increase. The ultimate example is the North Pacific halibut fishery which has been regulated by closed seasons. The fleet has grown such that fishing is restricted to several twenty-four hour periods per year. The result is a hectic race which results in a waste of fish, high processing and storage costs, and frequent injury or death for the fishermen. In addition it is sometimes not sufficient to restrict harvests to the desired level.[2]

Open access techniques can be seen as a game between the manager and the industry where the industry always has the last move. It the managers cut the season by one-third, the industry tries to increase effort during the open season. In the short run they may not be able to do much, but over time they can build bigger and more powerful boats. And, to the extent that the short-run reduction in effort is successful in increasing stock size, each individual fisherman will see the increased productivity as a way of justifying the extra expenses. Unfortunately, what is beneficial for one harms the fleet as a whole; the increase in the effectiveness of the fleet offsets the gains of the reduced season.

The same sort of thing can happen with closed areas or gear restrictions. If the managers restrict the used of one type of gear, to the extent that it is successful in improving the stock, fishermen will have incentives to increase the use of other non-restricted gear. Closed seasons, closed areas, and gear restrictions suffer the same weakness. They often are not effective in reducing fishing mortality in the long run. At the same time they force the fishermen to fish in ways that result in a higher cost of harvest than would otherwise be the case.

Total quotas can be effective biologically, to the extent that they can be enforced, but they also encourage an overcapitalized fleet, and hence higher than necessary costs, because the fishermen each want to be in a position to take as much of the quota as they can before the fishery is closed down.

Controlled access regulation

Open access and controlled access regulation can be distinguished as follows. The former controls the activities of participants but not their number. The latter controls, explicitly or implicitly, the number of participants, the number of fishing units (i.e. boats or traps), or the amount of a crucial element of fishing power (i.e. horse power or gross tonnage). A controlled access program may also control the activities of the restricted number of participants. For example, a program which limits the number of boats may not be enough to address all conservation issues. It may be necessary to forbid fishing in nursery areas.

Controlled access programs can be divided into two basic categories: input restriction and output restriction. Examples of the former are limits on the number of boats, participants, nets, or traps, etc., or on the total amount of hull displacement, gross tonnage, or total horsepower. Some of these limits are more binding than others. A limit on the number of boats can be a rather elastic constraint if there are no controls on size or the types and amounts of gear that can be used. ITQs are an output restriction. The right to harvest a certain amount, or a share of a total quota, is allocated to selected participants. ITQs only place an implicit restriction on the number of participants. But it is controlled access nonetheless. While there is no direct limit on the number of boats, individuals cannot legally operate if they do not have an individual quota. The flexibility in the number of boats is not a conservation problem, because there is a cap on total harvest.

Although both types have their advantages, those based on output restrictions have two advantages. First, to the extent that they can be enforced, they put a binding constraint on fishing mortality. There is no "rubber yardstick" as there is with many input controls. In addition, by leaving operational decisions to participants, the chances of obtaining efficient harvest techniques are increased. For these reasons, this chapter will focus on ITQs.

The basic idea of an ITQ program is quite simple. The three words – individual, transferable, and quota – which comprise the term ITQ tell the whole story, although it is most useful to describe them in a different order.

An ITQ program is based on an annual quota or total allowable catch (TAC). Biological concerns for the current size of the fish stock and for how it will change over time are addressed by limiting the total amount of annual fishing mortality.

Instead of an open race for the TAC, however, an ITQ program allocates shares to individual participants. Each participant is given the right to harvest a certain amount of fish each year, usually as a percentage of the TAC. The basic premise of ITQs is to regulate the amount each participant can take but to allow them to catch where, when, and how they want.

To increase the flexibility of the participants, the individual quota shares are transferable. The ITQ owners can produce the catch themselves, combine activities with others, rent or sell the right to harvest, or hire someone to fish on their behalf. Instead of pitting the ingenuity of the fishermen against regulatory constraints, the incentive is to encourage them to decrease harvest costs. In the same way, the ITQ owners will be motivated to increase the quality of their catch and to find higher valued markets because this will also increase profits. At the same time, new participants can enter the fishery by buying fishing rights.

In summary, ITQs are a regulation tool that can simultaneously address the necessary biological aspects of management and avoid some of the problems of traditional management techniques. They can provide operators with the flexibility to increase their profits by lowering their costs (by finding the most efficient way to harvest fish) and by increasing their revenues (by selling their products at those times and in those markets where prices are higher). By facing the allocation decision at the outset, the dual questions of how much to catch and who can catch it are separated. This separation leads to a system which can provide incentives matching the fishing power of the fleet to the productivity of the fish stocks.

3   A Formal Economic Model of Individual Transferable Quotas

Fundamentals

The capital-theoretic approach to fisheries economics is described in chapter 18. The purpose here is to demonstrate the workings of an ITQ system in the context of this model in order to provide a standard for the design of real-world programs and for evaluating their success.

In equations (18.19) through (18.31) (chapter 18) Conrad uses a bioeconomic model with effort as the control variable to describe the dynamic optimal utilization of a fish stock. The first-order condition for effort in that analysis, equation (18.23), states that the following must hold in every period.

$$pH_E - c = \rho\lambda_{t+1}(1 - M)H_E \equiv \Phi(t) \tag{20.1}$$

To review Conrad's notation, p is the price of fish, c is the cost of effort, H_E is the marginal yield, ρ is the discount factor, λ_{t+1} is the value of an additional unit of stock in the next period, and M is the natural mortality rate of the fish stock.

The left-hand side is the net marginal value product of effort. The right-hand side is the current value marginal user cost of effort. To understand the concept of marginal user cost of effort note that $H_E(1 - m)$ is the amount of fish killed by the marginal unit of effort that would not have died a natural death. Also $\rho\lambda_{t+1}$ is the current value of a fish in place next period. Therefore, the product represents the current value of the fish that will not be in place next period as a result of applying the marginal unit of effort. This is the marginal user cost of effort. For simplicity, denote this user cost as $\Phi(t)$. Note that $\Phi(t)$ is a decreasing function of effort. In summary, condition (20.1) says that, if fish stocks are to be optimally allocated, the net value of fish on the dock produced by the last unit of effort must be equal to the resultant loss in value of fish in the water.

It will be useful to derive the annual tax that will drive the open access fishery to achieve this condition. Open access equilibrium occurs where industry revenue equals industry costs. Expressed in average terms this is

$$P(H/E) - c = 0 \qquad (20.2)$$

The tax on effort that will turn equation (20.2) into (20.1) can be obtained from

$$P(H/E) - c - t = pH_E - c - \Phi \qquad (20.3)$$

The solution is

$$t = P(H/E - H_E) + \Phi \qquad (20.4)$$

The first term is a correction for the intra-period open access problem where participants use average rather than marginal output values. The second is to correct for the inter-period open access problem where firms do not consider user costs. See Anderson (1986, p. 226).

Before proceeding with the remainder of the analysis, it will be necessary to introduce the concept of sustainable yield. The production function $H(X, E)$ is a short-run production function in that it shows how output varies with effort for any given stock size. The stock growth function is $F(X)$. By equating the growth and the short-term yield function, an equation for the equilibrium stock size as a function of effort can be obtained. Substituting this for X in the short-run yield equation will result in the sustainable yield as a function of effort. Denote this as

$$Y = Y(E) \qquad (20.5)$$

A graphical interpretation of the annual optimizing condition is possible using figure 20.1 which plots average revenues and average costs of the fishery. It is assumed that this is a long-run constant cost industry (fishery) with homogeneous firms (boats). Industry long-run average cost of effort will equal industry long-run marginal cost and both will equal the minimum average cost of the firms. The open access equilibrium will occur at E_{oa}, the intersection of the sustainable average revenue of effort curve LAR_E, which is derived from equation (20.5) and the long-run average cost of effort curve LAC_E.

Given the equilibrium stock size at this point, the short-run average revenue and short-run marginal revenue curves for the fishery are SAR_E

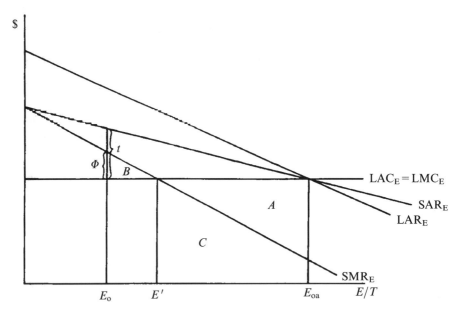

Figure 20.1   Equilibrium in the fishery.

and SMR_E. These curves are derived using the short-term yield curve $H(X, E)$. The short-run optimal level of effort, which is the first in the time path of optimal effort production, will occur at E_o, the level of effort where the distance between the SMR_E and the LMC curves is equal to Φ (see equation (20.1)).

Note that if Φ is high enough the optimal amount for effort for a given year may be zero. The value of fish in the sea in terms of future values of harvest is so high that the net present value of harvests will be increased by harvesting nothing now to leave more for the future.

The reduction in effort from E_oa to E' corrects for the intra-period open access waste because at this point costs are compared with industry marginal rather than average returns. Note that such a move will increase the net value of current output by an amount equal to area A. The reduction in effort will reduce costs by an amount equal to areas $A + C$, but will only reduce the value of output by an amount equal to area C. By the same line of reasoning, the further reduction in effort to E_o will reduce the net current value of output by an amount equal to area B. The purpose of this reduction is to correct for the inter-period open access waste. There may be a reduction in the net value of current output; however, the logic of the model tells us that this is an optimal investment in the stock and, at the margin, the reduction in net current value is just matched by an increase in the total net present value of output.

The combination of E_o units of effort with the open access stock size will produce a new stock size for the next period,[3] and the optimal level of effort for that year can be graphed in an analogous fashion. It will be necessary to draw in the new short-run marginal revenue curve using the new stock size and find the level of effort where the difference between SMR and LMC_E is equal to the user cost. Note that the value of λ and hence of Φ will change from year to year. The optimal amount of effort for every year along the optimal time path can be derived in the same manner. However, the solution of the maximization problem is simultaneous and not sequential as may be interpreted from the above discussion. It is important to note that, if costs, price, or the discount rate change, the optimal time path will change as well.

The tax that will force the open access fishery to operate at the short-run optimal level of effort is indicated in the diagram as the distance t. Note that it is equal to Φ plus the distance between the SAR_E and the SMR_E (see equation (20.4)).

The market for individual transferable quotas with a malleable homogeneous fleet

The purpose of this section is to describe how a market for effort ITQs (i.e. rights to produce a unit of effort) will have to work in order to achieve an optimal time path. Assume a fishery as described above that is exploited by a fleet of identical malleable vessels; that is, the vessels can be easily transferred into other fisheries or other uses in the economy. Under this assumption, all costs are variable to the fishery. The problem of non-malleable fleets is more complex (see Clark et al., 1979). See Anderson (1989) for a discussion of ITQs with heterogeneous fleets.

Figure 20.2(b) is analogous to figure 20.1, while figure 20.2(a) shows the cost curves of effort of a representative vessel. Together the two form the traditional firm–industry diagram in terms of a fishery (see Anderson, 1976). The LAR_E shows the sustainable return per unit of effort to boats for varying amounts of aggregate effort. The open access equilibrium will occur where the number of boats is such that the sum of the vessel marginal cost curve is equal to ΣMC_{oa}. At that point the return per unit of effort is R_1 and each boat will operate at e_o.

Assume that the fisheries authority wishes to move the fishery from the open access equilibrium position to an optimal time path of harvest and elect to do so by using effort ITQs. Further, assume that the agency will sell the appropriate amount of quotas each year on the open market. In the first year the agency will sell the rights to produce E_o units of effort during that year. Given the standing fish stock and that level of effort, the annual return per unit of effort will equal R_2.

Following Anderson (1989), the firm's demand curve for these annual effort ITQs is the difference between the return per unit of effort and the

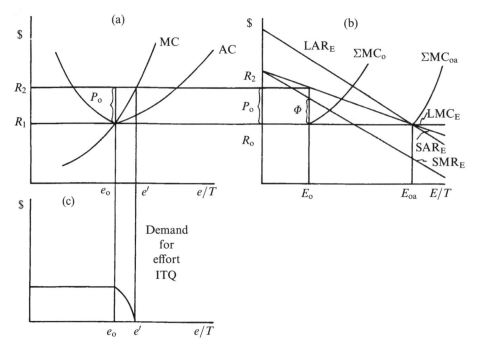

Figure 20.2   Demand for transferable quotas.

marginal cost of producing effort (see figure 20.2(c)). That is, if the effort ITQs were given away (but could not be resold), each firm would desire to hold e' units because at that point the marginal cost of effort equals R_2. The most they could afford to pay would be P_0, the distance between R_2 and the minimum of the average cost curve. At that price they would choose to operate at e_0.

Given a competitive market with perfect information, the price for the right to produce one unit of effort in the first year will equal P_0, and the number of firms that will be able to purchase sufficient quota to operate at e_0 will be such that the sum of the marginal cost curves will shift back to ΣMC_0. Those vessels which do not obtain quotas will move into other fisheries.

Note that the equilibrium price for annual quotas for the first year is equal to the optimal tax for the first year (see Clark, 1982, p. 283). Therefore the optimal ITQ program must consider both the intra-period and inter-period open access waste. The revenue earned by selling the ITQs equals the rent from the first year of that stream of rents which maximizes net present value. In this case, though it is probably smaller than annual rents to be earned after the stock increases, the current rent is positive.

To maintain the optimal time path of harvest, the agency will have to offer for sale annual quota such that the optimal amount of harvest is taken during the second and all remaining years. The equilibrium price will vary according to the movements of the SAR_E (as stock size changes) and the optimal annual level of effort which will partly be determined by the annual size of Φ.

Since the agency must know what the optimal time path of harvest will be from the outset (which means that it must have good estimates of price and cost changes to say nothing of a perfect knowledge of the population dynamics of the fish stock) it could announce a sale of a time stream of effort ITQs. Given a competitive harvesting sector with perfect knowledge, the prices for effort quota in the various years would be analogous to P_o in the first year. The value of revenues collected would equal the present value of rents to the optimally managed fishery. Alternatively the agency could give the quotas for the various years away in which case the total rent from the fishery will be distributed according to the amounts obtained of each year's allowable effort.

The amount of effort used each year would be optimal, and changes in annual production could be easily obtained from the malleable fleet. There are no problems of long-term investment. Or, to look at it from another perspective, there are no problems of disinvestment either because excess vessels can easily be absorbed in other industries. In the real world, fishing boats are often specialized and cannot be easily transferred into other fisheries. If such is the case, the process will be more complicated. In the first instance, when there is an excess number of boats, firms will use their average variable cost curve rather than average total cost in determining their demand curve for ITQs. The prices of ITQs will be higher in the short run as firms compete to gain enough rights to continue operating and at least make a contribution toward covering their fixed costs.

The market for individual transferable quotas with fixed annual quotas

For reasons described in detail in Anderson (1989), there are effectively no fisheries in the world where there are sufficient economic or biological data to derive an optimal harvest time path as described above. As Pearse (1980) notes, from an economic perspective, the best that can be achieved is to allow a safe catch to be determined and then to institute a regulation program that allows that harvest to be obtained as efficiently as possible.

In the proposed and operating ITQ programs in the world today, annual quotas (in terms of catch) are determined from biological assessments of the status of the stocks. Using figure 20.3 it is possible to analyze a market for ITQs when the annual quota is set on biological information and is

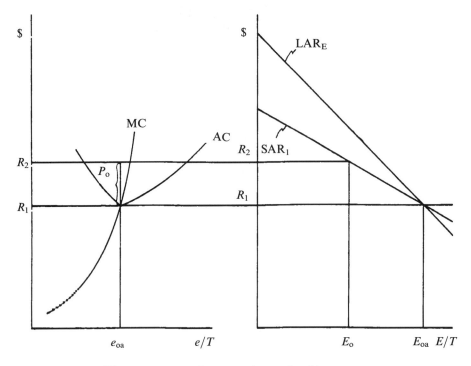

Figure 20.3   Willingness to pay for annual transferable quota.

assumed to remain constant. Although quotas will be in terms of harvest, the graph is still in terms of effort in order to describe the actions of the fleet.

Assume that a fishery with homogeneous vessels is in an open access equilibrium at E_{oa}. The return per unit of effort will be R_1 and each vessel will operate at e_{oa}. Assume that a catch quota which is smaller than the open access harvest is determined. Given the open access equilibrium stock size, there is a specific amount of effort that is required to harvest that amount of catch. Let E_o represent this amount of effort. In the first period, the rent per unit of effort, and hence the amount participants will be willing to pay to purchase effort ITQs, will be P_o. The price of the catch quota can be determined by dividing E_o by the catch per unit of effort. Regardless of how the harvest level, and hence E_o, is determined, the market signals which push the ITQs to the most efficient producers will still be there.

If the quota is not changed in the next period, the amount of effort that will be required to catch it will decrease because the stock size will have increased. Therefore the catch per unit of effort will go up and the price of the quota will increase. As this process continues, the level of effort required to take the quota will decrease and the price of harvest ITQs will increase until a biological equilibrium is established. If the quota is changed, the same general analysis applies; the only difference is that the actual amount of effort used in successive years will be a function of the existing standing stock of fish and the new quotas.

It can be seen that, by keeping all of the assumptions of the simple biological model but assuming that the quota is set on biological grounds, the time path of harvest will be non-optimal. There will probably be varying levels of effort through time, but that will be the result of changes in stock size and not the direct result of management policy. Except under the rarest of circumstances the time path of harvest will not be optimal. This will not be a failure of ITQ markets, however; it will be the result of insufficient management information to determine the amount of quota to sell each year.

However, even though the harvest path will be non-optimal, the reduction in effort can lead to an increase in rents over the open access situation. Further, the operation of the ITQ market will provide the potential of producing the harvest as efficiently as possible. As described above, that potential will be realized to the extent that the market allows for easy transfer of rights between well-informed participants.

4   Individual Transferable Quotas in the Real World

The previous section described the theoretical aspects of ITQs and demonstrated that, because of data constraints, real-world applications do not mimic an optimal control solution to dynamic fisheries utilization. Nonetheless, in the several dozen fisheries around the world which use some for of individual quota management program, many of the benefits predicted by the models have been achieved (see Muse, 1991; Crowley and Palsson, 1992; Sutinen et al., 1992). These programs have provided a natural laboratory for developing better applications of the results of rigorous but necessarily simple models to complex real-world situations. The remainder of this chapter will describe these more down-to-earth aspects of establishing property rights in fisheries. The next section will describe issues related to design and implementation of ITQ programs which will be followed by a discussion of potential problems and likely solutions. The aspiring economist should note how the application of basic economic principles can clarify many of the issues.

Design and implementation issues

The nature of the property right
The basic difference between an ITQ program and traditional management is the creation of a property right. The nature of the right can be changed

or limited to accomplish biological, managerial, or cultural objectives. However, it is important to compare what is being gained by limiting the nature of the property right to what is being lost by the diminished flexibility. The elements of the basic right are eligibility, duration, transferability, and ownership limits.

Eligibility can extend to any legal entity or ownership can be restricted to natural persons. Preventing corporations from participating may help maintain industry and community structure in small-scale or community-based fisheries. However, the limited flexibility may prevent ITQ owners from organizing their activities to their best advantage which may adversely affect efficiency.

The ownership right can be permanent or for a limited period. With permanent rights, the ITQ owner will have a secure planning horizon and will have better incentives to make efficient investments in harvesting and processing equipment and to develop market channels. However, some argue that term limits may help to maintain some long-term control over the fishery. By setting a specific term, the opportunity remains to reassign rights if current owners do not abide by all rules. Term limits will require that right be reallocated at regular intervals, which can be a very difficult distributional task.

A fundamental issue in real-world applications is whether ITQs should be transferable. Some would argue that an individual quota makes sense, but that making the rights transferable is not appropriate because it is a permanent consignment of a public resource to a private individual. Further, transferability may affect industry structure in ways that some people deem inappropriate. However, restrictions on transferability will constrain the flexibility of owners and the ability to achieve efficiency enhancing transfers or rentals which is one of the potential advantages of ITQs. Additionally, with no transferability, it is necessary to reallocate the ITQs once an owner has died or retired from fishing.

Even if ITQs are transferable, some have argued for limits. An initial allocation may include individuals who differ by gear type, boat size, firm size, type of final product, home port, etc. Unrestricted transferability between all such individuals may result in changes in the industrial or cultural aspects of the fishery. Restrictions on transfers between specified groups may help prevent such changes. However, they will also limit the flexibility of owners and in the long term could become a stifling influence on the development and utilization of the fishery as a whole.

An ITQ program could conceivably lead to excessive market power for ex-vessel fish, final product, or even ITQ shares (see Anderson, 1991). Current anti-trust law addresses problems of excess market power in any industry, including fisheries, and this may be adequate to prevent abuses. Alternatively these issues can be addressed directly in the ITQ program by placing individual limits on ownership.

Management units

Defining the management unit or units is an important part of any fisheries regulation program. This is no less true with an ITQ program. A management unit is the species, stocks, or aggregation of either for which a TAC is specified and for which harvesting rights are distributed. There are two questions pertaining to the definition of management units. First, how many species should be included in the program? If different species are biologically or commercially related, it may be wise to manage them jointly under an ITQ program. Second, how should each of the included species be classified? There may be several stocks or geographically distinct units of the same species, and it may be appropriate to have a separate TAC for each. At the other extreme, there may be certain groups that may be treated as aggregations for management purposes even though they are technically made up of separate species.

There is definitely a tradeoff in answering these two questions. The larger the number of stocks that are included in the program, the more inclusive the system will be and the lower will be the need for separate management programs to handle species and stocks not included. And, the more finely the quota share stocks are geographically defined, the easier it will be to focus management on more narrowly defined species or species groups if there are biological, technological, or distributional reasons for doing so. However, the larger the number of area divisions, the more difficult it will be to manage the ITQ program. There will be more TACs, and the monitoring program will have to be able to distinguish landings according to the stock from which they were harvested.

Monitoring and enforcement

A fisheries management program is only as good as its monitoring and enforcement system. However, there are fundamental differences in the required monitoring and enforcement system for an ITQ program. They are similar to other TAC-based programs because total harvest must be monitored to ensure that it does not surpass the TAC. In addition, however, it is necessary to monitor the harvest of each participant and to ensure that it does not surpass his or her current individual quota level. With transferability, it is also necessary to keep track of the current amount of individual quota owned by, or otherwise under the control of, each participant. While these extra burdens may seem formidable, it is necessary to evaluate the management and enforcement system relative to those of other types of management and relative to the potential benefits of an ITQ program. Will overall monitoring and enforcement costs by higher or lower? Even if the costs are higher, are the benefits of ITQ management worth it?

An ITQ monitoring system must be seen as being capable of detecting abuse. Participants must be confident that others cannot beat the system and thus diminish the value of their rights. In addition the participants must also know that the system will detect any misconduct on their own part so incentives to cheat will be small. However, this does not necessarily mean that every fish brought to the dock and every landings report filed must be personally inspected by an enforcement officer.

In-person inspections will be important in an ITQ monitoring system, but ultimate success will require a computerized system of electronic reporting and data management. In addition, there must be dual-entry reporting; both the harvester and the first fish receiver must fill out independent landing forms that can be double checked against each other. Similarly a transfer of an individual quota from one person to another must be verified in writing by both parties. The computer system should have a series of tests that can be run frequently to verify the accuracy and consistency of reported landings and trades.

The work of monitoring agents will change under an ITQ program. The emphasis will shift from checking the day-to-day fleet operations to monitoring catch levels. It is unclear whether the actual amount of monitoring activity or its cost will increase or decrease. Depending upon the circumstances, it is likely that at-sea monitoring, which can be very expensive, can be reduced. On the other hand, the amount of bookkeeping type activities will probably be increased. Concurrently, because participants have a long-term interest in protecting their harvest rights, they will be more inclined to adhere to the rules and to assist agents in detecting abuse from others.

Requiring permits for both harvesters and processors may strengthen the program. These permits should be available to any interested party at a nominal fee. A fisherman would be required to obtain a harvesting permit in order to own or lease ITQs. Any harvesting activity would be recorded against the harvesting permit number. Processors would be required to obtain a fish receiver's permit in order to buy fish landed under the ITQ program. All purchasing and processing activity wold be recorded against the fish receiver's permit number. The idea behind a permit program for processors is twofold. First, it provides for the double-entry system that is necessary to establish proper supervision. Second, it provides for a broader based enforcement program. If processors have to show that fish in their possession were legally harvested, they will be very careful from whom they buy. If they will not buy illegal fish, there will less incentive for ITQ owners and non-owners alike to bring in non-quota fish.

Penalties for non-compliance should be firmly established, rigorously enforced and severe enough to encourage compliance. For intentional and rampant cheating, there should be provision to revoke harvesting or fish receiving permits and even to confiscate the basic ITQ harvesting right.

Other regulations

The heart of an ITQ program is the TAC. If properly enforced, it will ideally address all conservation issues. However, this may not always be the case. For example, fishing in nursery grounds may affect future recruitment. Or, a stock may be especially vulnerable to exploitation in a particular location or during a particular season. If so, there may be incentives for ITQ owners to gear up to harvest at these times or locations so as to lower their costs. There will still be a race for catch, although it will be limited to fewer participants. In such cases, it may be necessary to use supplemental regulations such as closed seasons or ITQs defined by area or season.

The additional measures which will be worthwhile to implement, if any, will depend upon the particular circumstances of the fishery. The basic issues is to make sure that the modifications do not introduce problems worse than those they are meant to solve.

Units of measure for individual transferable quotas

ITQs can be measured in terms of tons of fish or as a percentage of the TAC. It is generally agreed that percentage ITQs are superior. In a percentage ITQ program, individuals would own a share of the allowable catch. How many tons they could catch in any year would be determined by multiplying the percentage share by the annual TAC.

Fish stocks are inherently variable in nature. Further, it is impossible to track their growth accurately and predict changes in stock size, especially on a newly exploited stock. To be successful, management programs should be able to adapt readily to the stochasticity of the stocks, and to profitably utilize existing biological information. In simple terms, both industry and fisheries agencies must be able to adapt to the patterns of change in fisheries production over time. Management must be flexible enough to allow the industry to get the most it can, over the long run, from the changing fish stock. Incentives should be such that harvesting capacity is large enough to harvest larger amounts in good years without having too much idle capacity in bad times. Under a percentage ITQ system, fishermen would be motivated to study the vagaries of the particular stocks they fish in order to plan their activities so that they could react to changes in the stock size, and hence changes in their yearly allowable catch, in the most profitable manner. The risk associated with harvesting a variable resource would fall squarely on the fishermen, not on the government.

ITQs can also be measured in terms of tons of fish. Use of tonnage ITQs is justified as providing better security for fishermen. A property right stated in percentage terms would be a less stable asset upon which to secure bank loans. With a tonnage ITQ, the government must enter the ITQ market to change the outstanding TAC. When fish stocks increase, the government can lease or sell, and when stocks decline they must buy and hold a sufficient number of ITQs to reduce actual catch to safe levels. The theory is that in the long run purchases will just match sales and so the role of the government will be that of an honest middleman.

The claim that purchases and sales will balance out requires further thought, however (see Hannesson, 1989). When the stock falls, necessitating government purchases, ITQ prices are likely to be high. The intent of the purchases is to prevent overharvest which should mean that the value of the ITQs left in private hands will be higher than they otherwise would be. At the same time, the reduction in the number of ITQs (i.e. total harvest) could mean an increase in the price of fish which will also increase the value of remaining ITQs.

The opposite will occur when the government has the opportunity to sell extra ITQs due to stock expansion. Extra output will tend to lower market prices and, unless this is compensated by an increase in catch per unit of effort, ITQ prices will fall. Therefore, even if the actual amount of quota sold or purchased balances out in the long run, the government will be buying dear and selling cheap which means that it will probably incur a long-run deficit. With a percentage ITQ system, changes in TACs (which are a necessary part of fisheries management) can be based purely on biological or bioeconomic information and not on budgetary circumstances.

Initial allocation
The initial allocation of quota shares to individuals is obviously very important. It will determine for the most part, who obtains the benefits from an ITQ program. It will determine the initial participants in the fishery. The future participants will be determined by the rules for transferability and the duration of the ownership rights. Important as these distributional issues are, for the most part the initial allocation issue is independent of other components of an ITQ program. It is a once-and-for-all step. Given flexible transferability rules and non-expiring ownership rights, allocation decisions only have to be made once. In order to maintain a balanced focus when considering ITQs, the independence of the initial allocation question from the other issues should be highlighted. Otherwise, it is possible that the distributional issues will unnecessarily cloud discussions of other important but basically independent issues.

There are two ways of making initial allocations. They can be sold or given away to historical participants. Under existing laws, rights can only be given away in the United States. Auctions or other means of collecting some of the rents that may be created with ITQs are currently prohibited. The pool of recipients has typically been chosen on the basis of past participation in the fishery. Historical catch and vessel size or other indicators of investment are the most common basis of distributing quota shares among this pool.

Potential problems of individual transferable quota programs

Setting total allowable catch

Some have argued that ITQ programs will not work in salmon or shrimp fisheries where it is difficult to set a TAC (see Copes, 1986). However, consideration of basic economic principles will demonstrate that there is more to this problem than is apparent. Take shrimp for example. It is an annual crop, the size of which is not directly related to the harvesting pressure in previous years. A natural question is therefore why there should be a limit of on harvest in any given year. Limiting harvest in one year will reduce benefits that year and yet will probably not have a positive effect on catch next year. Will not TACs lead to waste? To answer this question it important to look to the problem of waste from a broader perspective. On the one hand, a system which may allow some shrimp to die unharvested undoubtedly involves a waste of fish. On the other, a system which can harvest the very last shrimp even in peak years will also have waste. When average years come, the fleet cannot be fully utilized and that is a waste of fishing capacity.

An advantage of an ITQ system is that it can address both types of waste. If individuals know that they have a right to a share of the available harvest, they will be motivated to build their harvesting capacity such that they can make the most of the good years and at the same time not suffer large losses in medium or bad years.

Assuming that a TAC program may be justified with a short-lived species, Griffin et al. (1992) developed a method for specifying a TAC for Gulf of Mexico shrimp and for making mid-season upward adjustments when appropriate. The method is based on a weighted average of historical catches. Using hind-casting, the TACs determined by this method were very close to actual catches in previous years.

Recovery rates

While individual quotas are in terms of total biomass, fish are sometimes landed after some form of at-sea processing. Therefore, in order to prevent individuals from harvesting more than their legal quotas, provision must be made to convert the landed weight to a live weight. This can be a very complicated problem. For example, assume boats A and B with individual quotas of 100 tons have recovery rates of 20 percent and 30 percent respectively. Boat A will therefore land 20 tons of product while boat B will land 30. A recovery rate is the percentage of live weight that is landed as marketable product. If the government assumes the recovery rate is 25 percent, both boats will be permitted to land 25 tons. Boat A will be able to overharvest its quota and boat B will not be able to land its full quota. If more quota is held by boats with recovery rates lower than the government uses, the TAC will be surpassed.

The problem is to achieve a practical and cost-effective way of ensuring that individuals remain within their respective quotas. There is no problem if all firms have the same fixed recovery rate since a simple conversion factor will convert landed weight to green weight.

But more often than not, firms will have different recovery rates, due to different productivities in at-sea processing or in the market served which affects the required type of landed weight product. Setting standard recovery rates in these instances is inexpensive and easy to enforce but it can lead to inefficiencies in at-sea processing and potential quota busting.[4] On the other hand, at-sea monitoring to measure actual recovery rates eliminates the problems of standard rates, but it may require great effort and expense. The items to be considered in the selection of an overall optimum policy are fairly simple. There are two ways to ensure that the overall quota is not surpassed. First, each boat can be required to carry a suitably trained on-board observer to monitor the recovery rate for use in making that boat's conversion factor. The cost of such a program will be the opportunity costs of having the observers on board, which could include both lost production on land as well as the potential for reduced output as a result of fitting an extra person in a restricted space. Second, the government can use a recovery rate which is a weighted average of the rates of all boats calculating that the overcatches by some boats are matched by undercatches in others.[5] The costs of this would be the value of the lost marketable fish plus the effects of the redistribution of harvest among the fleet. Which policy is best will depend on the size of these items in particular fisheries.

Highgrading

One of the benefits of ITQs is the motivation to use the right to catch each ton of fish as profitably as possible. On the positive side, this means that firms will strive to harvest them as cheaply as possible and to sell in the market with the highest net price. This incentive can also have a negative effect. If there are differences in the prices of different sizes or different qualities of a particular fish, fishermen may discard the lowered valued fish. The decision to do so will depend upon the gain of the difference in price and the cost of sorting the fish, discarding, and replacing the discarded fish. A similar phenomenon occurs in non-ITQ fisheries if ice capacity or hold size are binding constraints on the operation of a boat.

If an ITQ program does lead to highgrading, the total mortality to the fish stock will be higher than the TAC. This could have long-term implications for the stock. There are ways to correct for this problem, however. On the macro scale, the TAC could be adjusted. For example if 1 ton of small fish is discarded for every 10 tons of fish landed, and the safe TAC is 110 tons, the operational TAC could be set at 100 tons. Or at a micro level, ITQ owners could be charged for 1 ton of small fish for every 10 tons of large fish landed. The fishermen would then have an incentive to land the small fish rather than discard it.

Multi-species fisheries

While an ITQ program in a single-species fishery would be relatively simple to implement and administer, things could be much more complex in a fishery where several types of fish are caught simultaneously. For one thing, the ratio of the TACs for the various species may not be the same as the ratio at which they are caught. For example, if the TACs for two species were 100 tons and 70 tons respectively, but they came up in the net in a 5 to 4 ratio, the total catch of the second would be 80 tons if the TAC for the first were achieved.

In addition, participants may have trouble building up a portfolio of ITQs of various species that matches their actual harvests. By-catch ratios vary for different boats, and will change seasonally and under different weather conditions. Fishermen may be forced to discard fish for which no ITQ rights are held.

There are ways to address these issues and they have been used with varying degrees of success. Quotas can be changed to match by-catch ratios. Retroactive trading may be allowed where participants have a certain amount of time to lease catch rights for fish already landed. Fishermen may be allowed to fish 110 percent of their ITQ in one year with any overages being deduced from their allowable catch in the following year. In some instances area or season closures may be helpful if by-catch rates are particularly high in certain areas or at certain times (see Clark and Duncan, 1986; Clark et al., 1988).

5   Conclusions

The discussion has focused on the theoretical and practical aspects of ITQ management. Although ITQs have only recently been used in real-world fisheries, preliminary evidence indicates that they produce the intended results. Several studies which provide more detail on ITQ management and the results they produce are listed in the references. It should not be concluded, however, that ITQs are a panacea nor that they should be implemented in every fishery. They are a tool which has great potential and which should be considered.

One way of comparing ITQs and other types of management is to see how each can address the important issues of the particular fishery.

Controlling discards, by-catch, mortality in nursery areas, and maintaining product quality and industry viability are just a few of the many problems that must be addressed. Likewise, the introduction of a property right system where no rights existed before can create an income distribution dilemma. It is frequently the case that potential management tools are dismissed because of a perceived weakness in addressing one of these issues. Since there is no perfect management tool, the important question in comparing various techniques is not which one has weaknesses, but which one can be adopted, implemented, and enforced such that the stated management objectives can be most nearly achieved.

Notes

1 Although the terms are sometimes used interchangeably, there is a difference between open access and common property. In the latter case, there are a limited number of participants with access to the stocks. In these instance mutually agreed upon rules can be implemented which might prevent economic and biological over-exploitation. See Ostrom (1990).
2 An ITQ program has recently been approved for this fishery and is scheduled to be implemented in 1995.
3 The fish stock will increase in this case because E_o is less than E_{oa}, the equilibrium level of effort for the existing stock size. It is possible that in some phases of the optimal harvest path that stock size will decrease. There will necessarily be decreases in stock size if the optimal path is derived starting with a virgin biomass. A steady state optimum will occur when the optimal harvest in a period is equal to the natural growth of the stock.
4 The proof that standardized recovery rates for enforcement papers will lead to inefficiencies in processing can be found in Anderson (1991b) which contains a much more detailed analysis of this problem. Briefly, however, the change from a green weight to a landed weight quota changes the incentives of individual processors. With a green weight quota, there is a motivation to increase the landed weight per fish as long as the marginal revenue from the extra sales equals the marginal cost of the more refined processing. With a landed weight quota, however, the motivation is to minimize the cost of achieving the allowable landed weight. At the margin therefore it will be profitable to trade off the extra landed weight that comes from more refined (and more expensive) processing procedures for extra landed weight that comes from catching more fish.
5 The procedure for calculating this weight average is described in Anderson (1991b).

Bibliography

Anderson, L. G. 1976: The relationship between firm and fishery in common property fisheries. *Land Economics*, 52, 180–91.
Anderson, L. G. 1985: Potential economic benefits from gear restrictions and license limitation in fisheries regulation. *Land Economics*, 64 (4), 409–18.
Anderson, Lee G. 1986: *The Economics of Fisheries Management*, revised and enlarged edition. Baltimore, MD: Johns Hopkins University Press.
Anderson, Lee G. 1989: Conceptual constructs for practical ITQ management policies. In P. Neher, R. Arnason and N. Mollett (eds), *Rights Based Fishing*, NATO ASI Series E: Applied Sciences 169, Dordrecht: Kluwer, 191–209.

Anderson, Lee G. 1991a: A note on market power in ITQ fisheries. *Journal of Environmental Economics and Management*, 21, 291–6.

Anderson, Lee G. 1991b: Efficient policies to maintain total allowable catches in ITQ fisheries with at-sea processing. *Land Economics*, 67 (2), 141–57.

Anderson, Lee G. 1992: Consideration of the potential use of individual transferable quotas in the U.S. fisheries: overview document. National ITQ Study Report 1992, vol. 1. Report prepared under a contract to National Oceanic and Atmospheric Administration, National Marine Fisheries Service, Silver Spring, MD.

Brown, G. J. 1974: An optimal program for managing common property resources with congestion externalities. *Journal of Political Economy*, 82, 163–74.

Clark, C. W. 1982: Models of fishery regulation. In L. J. Mirman and D. F. Spulber (eds), *Essays in the Economics of Renewable Resources*, Amsterdam: North-Holland.

Clark, C. W. and Munro, G. R. 1975: The economics of fishing and modern capital theory: a simplified approach. *Journal of Environmental Economics and Management*, 2, 92–106.

Clark, C. W., Clarke, F. and Munro, G. R. 1979: The optimal exploitation of renewable resource stocks: problems of irreversible investment. *Econometrica*, 47 (1), 25–47.

Clark, Ian N. and Duncan, Alexander J. 1986: New Zealand's fisheries management policies: the implications of an ITQ-based management system. In N. Mollett (ed.), *Fishery Access Control Programs Worldwide*, Fairbanks, AK: Alaska Sea Grant Report 86–4.

Clark, Ian N., Major, P. and Mollett, N. 1988: Development and implementation of New Zealand's ITQ management system. *Marine Resource Economics*, 5, 325–49.

Copes, Parcival. 1986: A critical review of individual quotas as a device in fisheries management. *Land Economics*, 62 (3), 278–91.

Crowley, R. W. and Palsson, H. 1992: Rights based fisheries management in Canada. *Marine Resource Economics*, 7, 1–21.

Crutchfield, J. A. 1961: An economic evaluation of alternative methods of fishery regulations. *Journal of Law and Economics*, 4 (October), 131–43.

Dasgupta, P. and Heal, G. M. 1979: *Economic theory and Exhaustible Resources*. Cambridge: Cambridge University Press.

DeWees, C. M. 199: Assessment of the implementation of individual transferable quotas in New Zealand's inshore fishery. *North American Journal of Fisheries Management*, 9 (2), 131–9.

Fraser, C. and Jones J. 1989: Enterprise allocations: the Atlantic Canadian experience. In P. Neher, R. Arnason and N. Mollett (eds), *Rights Based Fishing*, NATO ASI Series E: Applied Sciences 169, Dordrecht: Kluwer, 267–88.

Gardner, M. 1988: Enterprise allocation system in the offshore groundfish sector in Atlantic Canada. *Marine Resource Economics*, 5 (4), 389–414.

Geen, G. and Nayer, M. 1988: Individual transferable quotas in the southern bluefin tuna fishery: an economic appraisal. *Marine Resource Economics*, 5 (4), 365–88.

Griffin, Wade L, Roberts, Kenneth, Lamberte, Antonio B., Ward, John M. and Henderson, Holly M. 1992: Considerations for the potential use of individual transferable quotas in the Gulf of Mexico shrimp fishery. National ITQ Study Report 1992, Vol. 3. Report prepared under a contract to National Oceanic and Atmospheric Administration, National Marine Fisheries Service, Silver Spring, MD.

Hannesson, Rogvaldur. 1989: Catch quotas and the variability of allowable catch. In P. Neher, R. Arnason and N. Mollett (eds), *Rights Based Fishing*, NATO ASI Series E: Applied Sciences 169, Dordrecht: Kluwer, 467–83.

Joeres, E. F. and David, M. H. (eds) 1983: Buying a better environment: cost-effective regulation through permit trading. University of Wisconsin Sea Grant College Program Technical Report 239, Madison, WI.

Karpoff, J. M. 1984: Insights from the markets for limited entry permits in Alaska. *Canadian Journal of Fisheries and Aquatic Sciences*, 41, 1160–6.

Levhari, D., Michiner, R.and Mirman, L. J. 1981: Dynamic programming models of fisheries. *American Economic Review*, 71, 649–61.

Meany, T. 1979: Limited entry in the Western Australian rock lobster and prawn fisheries: an economic evaluation. *Journal of the Fisheries Research Board of Canada*, 36 (7), 789–96.

Munro, G. R. and Scott, A. D. 1985: The economics of fisheries management. In *Handbook of Natural Resource and Energy Economics*, vol. 2, Amsterdam: North-Holland, 623–74.

Muse, B. 1991: survey of individual quota programs. Alaska Commercial Fisheries Entry Commission, Juneau, Alaska.

Neher, P. A. 1974: Notes on the Volterra quadratic fishery. *Journal of Economic Theory*, 6, 39–49.

Ostrom, Elinor. 1990: *Governing the Commons*. Cambridge: Cambridge University Press.

Pearse, Peter H. 1972: Rationalization of Canada's West Coast salmon fishery: an economic evaluation. In *Economic Aspects of Fish Production*, Paris: Organization for Economic Co-operation and Development, 172–202.

Pearse, Peter H. (ed.) 1979: Symposium on policies for economic rationalization of commercial fisheries. *Journal of the Fisheries Research Board of Canada*, 36 (7), 711–866.

Pearse, Peter H. 1980: Property rights and regulation of commercial fisheries. *Journal of Business Administration*, 11 (1–2), 185–209.

Pearse, Peter H. 1991: Building on progress: fisheries policy development in New Zealand. Report to the Minister of Fisheries, Wellington, New Zealand.

Peterson, F. M. and Fisher, A. C. 1977: The exploitation of extractive resources: a survey. *Economic Journal*, 87, 681–721.

Reggig, R. Bruce, and Ginter, Jay J. C. (Eds) 1978: *Limited Entry as a Fishery Management Tool*. Seattle, WA: University of Washington Press.

Scott, A. 1988: Development of property in the fishery. *Marine Resource Economics*, 5 (4), 289–313.

Smith, V. L. 1977: Control theory applied to natural and environmental resources: an exposition. *Journal of Environmental Economics and Management*, 4, 1–24.

Sturgess, N. and Meany, T. 1982: *Policy and practice in Fisheries Management*. Proceedings of the National Fisheries Seminar held in Melbourne, 1980. Canberra: Australian Government Publishing Service.

Sutinen, Jon G., Mace, Pamela, Kirkley, James, DuPaul, William, and Edwards, Steve. 1992: considerations for the potential use of individual transferable quotas in the Atlantic sea scallops fishery. National ITQ Study Report 1992, vol. 5. Report prepared under a contract to National Oceanic and Atmospheric Administration, National Marine Fisheries Service, Silver Spring, Maryland.

21

Regulation, Imperfect Markets, and Transaction Costs: The Elusive Quest for Efficiency in Water Allocation

Bonnie G. Colby

The history of the West is a study of a place undergoing conquest and never fully escaping its consequences . . . conquest involving the drawing of lines on a map, the definition and allocation of ownership, . . . the pursuit of legitimacy in property . . .

(Limerick, *The Legacy of Conquest*, 1987)

1 Introduction

The pursuit of legitimacy in property rights over water in the American West continues to generate conflict more than a century after the California gold rush, when the prior appropriations doctrine evolved as the dominant form of rights to use water. Rights to use and to transfer water resources are highly regulated in the western United States. Market transactions, when they occur, often resemble complex diplomatic negotiations rather than commodity exchanges (Sax, 1991). The degree of regulation, the types of impacts considered in evaluating transfer proposals and the regulatory procedures adopted by states vary considerably, providing an opportunity to evaluate the consequences of differing policy approaches. This chapter explores the role of state regulations in markets for water rights, focusing on the impacts of transaction costs associated with state policies.

Transaction costs, viewed by some as an inefficient consequence of regulation, are incurred to comply with policies designed to account for externalities. Rather than assuming that regulations and consequent transaction costs are an impediment to efficiency, this chapter analyzes the incentives they provide for bargaining among affected parties and for mitigation of externalities. Transaction costs reflect the absence of "free" information and the need for hydrologic, legal, and economic data to address externalities in an efficient manner. The presence of significant transaction costs creates rent-seeking opportunities and the distribution of these costs among transacting parties, third parties, and public agencies is examined.

Public policies play an essential role in establishing property rights (and thus bargaining power), and in defining the parameters within which bargaining over access to water occurs. Tension between market-oriented and regulatory approaches to resource allocation has become increasingly evident in water policies. At their heart, these controversies are disagreements over the appropriate balance between market forces and laws promulgated to protect or enhance broader social values in water. Public policy could err, on the one hand, by "over-regulation," so that too few desirable transactions occur, or by "under-regulation," so that excessive external costs are imposed on third parties and the net social benefits of a transfer are negative. Striking an efficient balance requires evaluation of the costs of regulation, including the benefits of market transactions forgone due to regulatory costs and the costs of externalities generated by "under-regulated" transactions.

This chapter argues that by giving third parties who may be affected by transfers the ability to impose transaction costs on transfer proponents, state policies encourage consideration of externalities that otherwise would not be accounted by the parties to a water transaction. Drawing on data from several western states with active water markets, the economic incentives and distributional implications of transaction costs stemming from state policies are analyzed. The chapter concludes with a discussion of desirable changes in regulatory policies.

2   The Institutional Context for Water Transfers

> The enormous complexity of water laws can in part be understood as reflecting conscious public action to affirm and protect the entitlements of potentially affected third parties.
>
> (Young, 1986, p. 1146)

In western US water markets, transaction costs are incurred in searching for trading partners, ascertaining the characteristics of water commodities, negotiating price and other terms of transfer, and obtaining legal approval for the proposed change in water use (Crouter, 1987). This chapter focuses on the latter category of transaction costs, policy-induced transaction costs. Transferors incur these costs as they seek to obtain state approval to transfer a water right to a new place and purpose of use. Transaction costs induced by public policies may include attorneys' fees, engineering and hydrologic studies, court costs, and fees paid to state agencies. Policy-induced transaction costs specifically exclude the price paid for the water right and the costs of implementing a transfer once it has been approved. Transacting parties are the buyer and seller who directly negotiate the terms of a transfer. Third parties include neighboring water users, recreationists, environmental interests, businesses, and communities whose interests may be affected by a transfer and who have varying degrees of rights to intervene in the transfer review process and demand mitigation of externalities or outright denial of the transfer application.

Economic characteristics of water: public goods, externalities, and uncertainty

> Though officially inanimate, water gives all the signs of having a life of its own – and a mobile, restless and irrational life at that.
>
> (Limerick, 1987, p. 72)

Water resources have a number of characteristics which defy fully specified assignment of property rights. Water seeps, flows, evaporates, and precipitates without regard to private, state, and national boundaries. Water supplies are renewed by nature in a stochastic and seasonal manner so that policymakers and water users cannot predict river flows far in advance. This uncertainty has prompter investment in infrastructure to store and convey surface water and to recharge groundwater so that supplies are available in a more predictable manner. Public and private expenditures to reduce variability in water supplies have been immense. Federal subsidies for irrigation projects in the western states exceed $20 billion, about $2000 for each acre irrigated with water from federal projects (Wahl, 1989, p. 38). Federal taxpayers have subsidized 86 percent of the costs of providing irrigation water to these lands. Municipal and industrial recipients of water from federal projects also receive significant subsidies, with approximately 30 percent of the costs being borne by US taxpayers.

Streams and groundwater aquifers simultaneously provide multiple benefits, with varying degrees of tradeoffs between *in situ* uses (kayaking, wetlands preservation) and out-of-stream or off-site uses (gold course irrigation, power plant cooling, residential water service, and so on). Tradeoffs among the benefits provided are further complicated by the public good nature of some benefits. Water for recreation and wildlife habitat provides non-rival benefits for which beneficiaries cannot readily be charged a user fee corresponding to the benefits received (Daubert and Young, 1979; Loomis, 1987; Ward, 1987). Streamflows also provide non-rival and nonexcludable benefits through dilution and water quality enhancement. Water providers and wastewater discharges rely on the assimilative capacity of river flows and marshes to comply with water quality standards. These public good aspects of water resources are neglected when private water transfer agreements are negotiated and private transactions generally will not provide an efficient level of streamflows.

Market exchanges enhance flexibility, allowing water allocations to adapt to changing economic conditions and new social values. Water transfers also can generate externalities. While transfers create positive externalities in the area to which water is being moved, this chapter focuses on negative impacts since these lie at the heart of controversies over regulating water transfers. Negative externalities include reduced water supplies for other water right holders, diminished economic activity in areas from which water is taken, lower river flows and groundwater tables, and consequent degradation of water quality, fish and wildlife habitat, and recreation opportunities (Saliba and Bush, 1987; Kapaloski, 1988).

The institutional framework

A great deal of western property rights rest on narrow margin of timing . . . even though the years might give those property rights an aura of venerability, they none the less relied on a principle still in vogue in playground disputes: "It's mine, I got here first."

(Limerick, 1987, p. 67)

Property rights in water

Property rights in water are defined primarily by state law in terms of the quantity of water that may be diverted from a stream or pumped from underground over a specific time period and the relative priority of rights, that is, which rights must be curtailed first during times of shortage. The prior appropriate doctrine, common to western states' water law, gives first priority to the older, most senior water rights with lower priority going to the rights established at later points in time.

Mining was paramount to all other interests in the early days and its followers could wash away roads, undermine houses . . . and remove entire towns.

(Bancroft, 1888, p. 387)

The prior appropriation doctrine evolved in the gold mining camps of California and was affirmed by the California Supreme Court in 1855 (Irvin v. Phillips, 1855). The appropriation doctrine spread to other western states with some variations and was uniquely suited to this time in history. It facilitated rapid mining and agricultural development, consistent with the national imperative to settle the West with a populace loyal to the US government and to solidify US control over territories recently acquired by treaty and conquest from Spain, Mexico, France, and Native American nations.

Even though over a dozen decades have passed since the institutional framework for water rights emerged, some characteristics of a water right are not fully defined until an application to transfer the right is submitted to a state agency. Buyers and sellers typically face uncertainty regarding the quantity of water that may be transferred and conditions and costs that may be imposed. In addition, water rights have quality attributes (based on the quality of the streams, aquifers, and reservoirs which provide for the rights) that significantly affect their economic value, but which have been almost entirely disregarded as property rights have been defined. Laws and agencies governing water quality originated and generally operate independently of those governing rights to use water, and this creates uncertainties and conflicts when water transfers are proposed.

State policies governing transfers of water rights

> ... the administrative officer, like a gypsy fortuneteller, must foretell the future effects of the proposed appropriation or change.
>
> (Schaab describing state administrative procedures for evaluating proposed changes in the use of water, 1983, pp. 25–50)

While federal policies create strong incentives (and disincentives) for water transactions (Wahl, 1989), states primarily are responsible for regulating transfers of water rights. Those seeking to transfer a water right (the applicant) to a new use must file an application with the state water agency (Colby et al., 1989). Applicants often hire attorneys and engineers to help prepare the application. All states require public notice to alert parties who may be affected by the transfer. Parties who object to the proposed transfer (objectors or protestants) may file a protest with the state. However, not everyone who may be adversely affected can legally file a protest. The earliest, and still the most common, legal basis for protesting a proposed transfer is impairment of existing water rights.

When protests are filed, transfer approval is delayed as the applicant and protestants argue over the magnitude of transfer impacts and the extent of mitigation or compensation. If the applicant and objectors can negotiate a compromise, their negotiated modifications of the transfer proposal are submitted to the state agency and transfer approval normally follows. When unresolved protests remain, the state agency will hold hearings and rule on the transfer application. The ruling may approve the transfer as requested by the applicant, grant conditional approval with modifications to satisfy protestants' concerns, or deny the transfer altogether. Parties dissatisfied with the state's decision may appeal to the courts. This regulatory process varies somewhat from state to state and is summarized generically in figure 21.1.

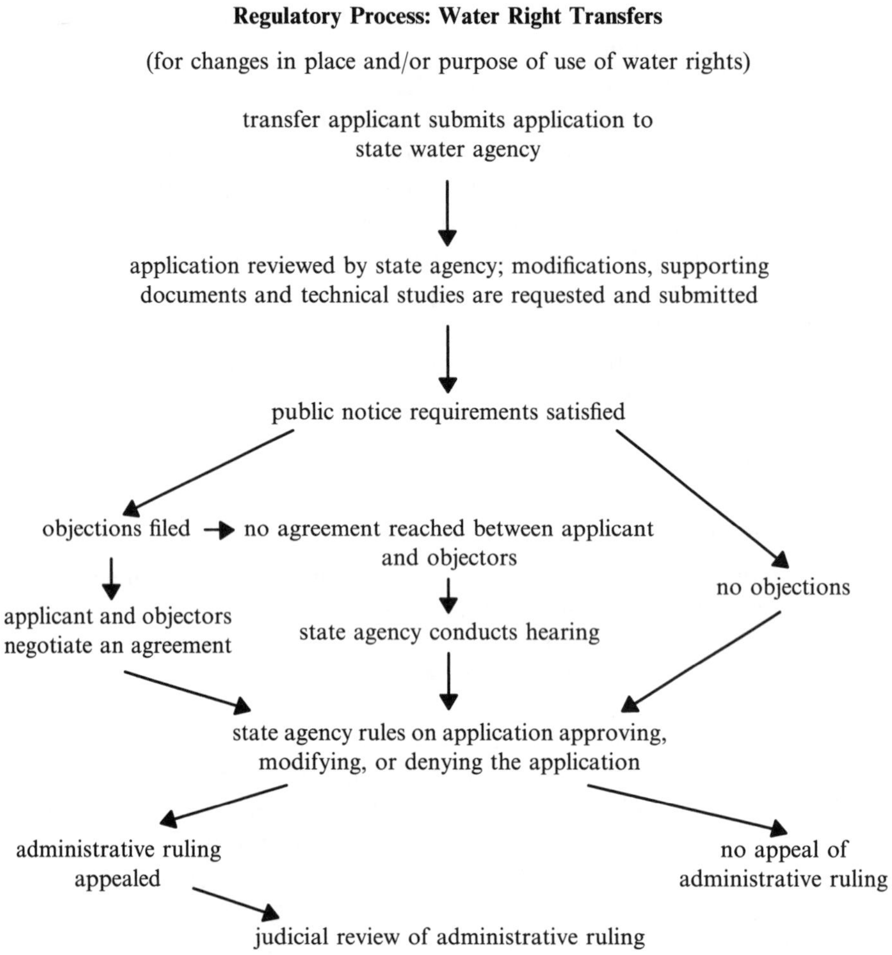

Regulatory Process: Water Right Transfers

(for changes in place and/or purpose of use of water rights)

transfer applicant submits application to
state water agency

application reviewed by state agency; modifications, supporting
documents and technical studies are requested and submitted

public notice requirements satisfied

objections filed → no agreement reached between applicant
and objectors

no objections

applicant and objectors
negotiate an agreement

state agency conducts hearing

state agency rules on application approving,
modifying, or denying the application

administrative ruling
appealed

no appeal of
administrative ruling

judicial review of administrative ruling

Figure 21.1   Regulatory process: water right transfers (for changes in place and/
or purpose of use of water rights).

The threat of a costly, protracted hearing followed by an unpredictable
ruling on the transfer application provides incentives for the parties to
negotiate a settlement. The ability to impose transaction costs, conferred
by legal standing to file a protest, is crucial in determining which impacts
will be considered when compromises are negotiated. Those interests that
have no legal standing to file a protest generally do not have a seat at the
bargaining table.

Despite the costs and uncertainties of the regulatory process,
MacDonnell (1990) finds that over 80 percent of change applications are
approved in Colorado, New Mexico, and Utah (the three western states
with the most applications to transfer water). However, one of the reasons

that approval rates are high is that many types of externalities are not considered when a water transfer is evaluated.

Externalities, changing values, and institutions

> To function well, institutions must have the flexibility to adapt to new opportunities. The agents of change are the political and economic entrepreneurs who perceive opportunities in change . . . . New statues and court decisions, which produce change, are formulated at the most pliable margin of the existing institutional framework.
>
> (North, 1992, p. 1)

Recreationists, wildlife advocates, and rafting outfitters all have an economic interest in maintaining streamflows but generally cannot obtain water rights or file a protest to protect their interests. Further, water quality is poorly integrated into most states' water allocation laws. In most western states water rights cannot be acquired for protecting water quality and impairment of water quality is not a valid basis for protesting a water transfer (Kapaloski, 1988). States limit the externalities which are considered when a transfer proposal is evaluated through policies which limit the purposes for which water rights may be held, which disallow protests by those who do not hold water rights, and which otherwise constrain the basis on which a valid protest may be filed.

While all western states review transfer applications before approval is granted for changes in the purpose and place of use of a water right (Colby et al., 1989a), different types of externalities are accorded markedly different degrees of importance. Foremost among the externalities considered is reduced water supplies for other water right holders. Other impacts are poorly considered in most states. Western state laws historically emphasized protection of existing water rights so that water users would have secure incentives to make the investments necessary to develop the West. However, water right holders do not fully represent the multiple interests who benefit from water resources and who experience losses as a result of water transfers.

> I am persuaded that to transfer water rights devoted for over a century to agricultural purposes, in order to construct a playground for those who can pay is a poor trade indeed. I find that the proposed transfer of water rights is clearly contrary to the public interest and . . . the Application should be denied.
>
> (Judge Encinias, ruling on application to transfer water rights from a
> community irrigation ditch to ski resort development in northern New
> Mexico, Sleeper case, 1985)

During the last decade, changing social values and consequent changes in property rights have become evident. The judge in the Sleeper case held that impacts on local culture and community cohesion should be considered in evaluating proposed transfers, though his decision was later reversed by a higher court. Most western states now allow state agencies to acquire water rights for maintaining streamflows, though private parties generally may hot hold rights for instream purposes. The National Audubon ruling (1983) required the City of Los Angeles to decrease its diversions from the Mono Lake area in order to protect that ecosystem, even though its diversions were based on valid, long-standing water rights. The Endangered Species Act, wilderness water rights, and changing water quality policies all are altering the nature of established property rights in water. Native American water claims, which have been affirmed by the courts and are now being quantified, are another threat to the security of established water rights in many areas of the West.

Role of markets in reallocating western water

> The market is the structure within which faceless buyers and sellers . . . meet for an instant to exchange standardized goods at equilibrium prices.
>
> (Yoram Ben-Porath, 1978)

The heterogeneous nature of water rights and the changing social values associated with water make instantaneous, faceless, and standardized transactions in water improbable and undesirable. Nevertheless, many economists argue that market incentives can and should play a greater role in water allocation.

In the western United States water has been reallocated from one use to another throughout the 1900s, though typically not through voluntary market transactions. Through the first half of the century, water development projects reallocated vast amounts of water from streams, to the detriment of recreation, fish, wildlife, and water quality, for offstream irrigation, mining, and urban uses. At the time these water development projects were conceived, they were not regarded as reallocations since the benefits associated with water left instream were largely unacknowledged. Indeed, water remaining in streams was widely regarded as water wasted. Moreover, flows in their natural watercourses often benefited Native American and Hispanic communities rather than economically mainstream Anglo towns and irrigators. Since instream uses and users were not recognized as having property rights in water, water development was viewed as a new claim on an unused resource, and irrigation districts, mining companies, ranchers and towns were accorded property rights in the resource.

Agriculture accounts for 85–95 percent of water use in most western states, and the opportunity cost of reducing irrigated acreage so that water can be available for other uses generally is far less than the cost of developing new water supplies (Young, 1984). The West's economic transition from ranching, irrigated farming, and mining to urban growth, services, tourism, and industry has brought strong pressure to transfer some water out of agriculture. Western cities pioneered the era of water marketing by purchasing irrigated land, sometimes entire irrigation districts, to acquire water rights for urban development (Saliba and Bush, 1987). The City of Los Angeles' acquisitions of irrigated lands in the Owens Valley, beginning in the 1920s, are often cited as a model of how *not* to transfer water out of agriculture, due to the decades of lawsuits and political backlash generated by the Owens Valley transfers. Denver area cities began acquiring and transferring water from the West slope of the Rockies in the 1930s to accommodate new industry and urban growth and continue to do so. Cities and developers in Arizona bought tens of thousands of acres of irrigated land in the 1980s to acquire water for urban growth. While urban growth still is the driving force behind water markets, water transfers to support wildlife, fisheries, and recreation have become more common (Colby, 1993). The *Water Strategist* (Smith, 1992) notes that transfers have become progressively more complex and innovative as drought, environmental, and community concerns have had increasing influence on transfers.

While market transfers have become a more common means to reallocate water, nowhere could such transactions be characterized as a "free market." Every western state imposes conditions on water transfers. Such policies generate uncertainties and costs for transferors and have been described as inefficient and unnecessary impositions on the market (Tregarthen, 1983; Anderson and Johnson, 1986). This chapter argues that public policy should not necessarily seek to minimize the cost of reallocating water and suggests that appropriately structured transaction costs may facilitate efficient reallocation by giving transacting parties an incentive to account for social costs of transfers.

Enduring suspicion of market mechanisms

> The economic function is but one of the many vital functions of land. It invests man's life with stability, it is the site of his habitation; it is a condition of his physical safety; it is the landscape and the seasons.
>
> (Polanyi, 1944, p. 178)

Polanyi did not object to market transactions in land (and water, by inference) *per se*, but to a market *system* under which all economic activity is governed by price-making markets. Western policymakers apparently share these apprehensions and seem to regard policies to encourage market reallocation as a last resort, an act of desperation, rather than a first resort as many economists would suggest. Tregarthen (1983) captured this hostility toward markets succinctly in his essay "Water in Colorado: fear and loathing of the marketplace," and the state of Colorado has more market transactions per year than the rest of the western states combined! (Smith, 1989–93).

Policymakers cautiously explore markets only after the inefficiencies arising from their absence become unacceptable. This has occurred in California, where millions of acre feet of subsidized public project water have been locked into agricultural uses while growing cities build desalinization plants and other expensive projects to acquire more water, and while wildlife refuges and popular fishing streams go dry. Only after decades of litigation and lobbying are market transactions being given a chance to transfer some of that public project water out of agriculture. Congress passed the Central Valley Project Improvement Act late in 1992, over the bitter opposition of many California agricultural interests. California cities and environmental advocates, for the first time, can acquire federal project water from willing agricultural sellers.

Arizona has developed complex regulations to reduce groundwater overdraft, creating impressive costs for developers and growing cities who cannot use local groundwater to support growth. Meanwhile, hundreds of thousands of acre feet of subsidized federal project water are allocated to the agricultural sector. Discussions about reallocating these under-utilized agricultural allocations through market transactions raise concerns about windfall profits for farmers, if they are above to sell federally subsidized water at market prices. Government agencies also fear loss of their control if water users can make their own arrangements instead of turning under-utilized water allocations back to a public agency, which will make it available to some other "deserving" party. Partly as a consequence of this distrust of the market mechanism, water in the West continues to be reallocated through involuntary as well as voluntary transactions.

Voluntary and involuntary reallocation – a paradoxical complementarity

> I witnessed that legal mechanism by which water is prepared for its eventual pumping toward money. It has to be adjudicated, its claims of ownership documented, its title quieted, to be made merchantable, saleable, which is what enables it to be freed up from land, acequia, community and tradition.
>
> (Stanley Crawford, referring to adjudication proceedings in northern
> New Mexico, 1990)

Complex legal proceedings, termed adjudications, are taking place in many areas to quantify and prioritize the competing claims of Native Americans, wilderness areas, cities, and farms. The Arizona General Stream Adjudication seeks to clarify water claims for most of Arizona and is the largest judicial proceeding ever undertaken in the United States, with over 100,000 claimants, including 20 Indian tribes and several wilderness areas. In the Big Horn Basin of Wyoming, a decade-long adjudication and a series of court rulings have reallocated water from irrigation districts and farmers to Indian tribes which are seeking to use the water instream for fisheries, recreation, and for reservation agricultural development. Many western tribes currently do not have access to water, but have strong legal claims to high priority water rights. Unless these tribes can be persuaded to accept money in lieu of their senior water rights, a reduction in the quantity and reliability of supplies for non-Indian cities and farms is inevitable.

Involuntary approaches sometimes are used to acquire water for environmental purposes. Litigation based on the Endangered Species act, the Clean Water Act, federal reserved rights, and the public trust doctrine has successfully forced reallocation of water to preserve streamflows. Water also has been reallocated to environmental purposes through voluntary transactions (Colby, 1993). However, voluntary transfers acknowledge the existing property right structure and fully compensate water right holders for selling or leasing their water. Moreover, the costs of providing water for rivers and streams are borne by organizations and agencies advocating instream values. The involuntary approach is more appealing to some environmental advocates because it seeks to change the distribution of property rights. The costs of reallocating water through litigation and new legislation are spread among the parties to the conflict that ensues as changes in water allocations and policies are contemplated and as established water users and institutions lobby and litigate to protect their interests. While the voluntary and involuntary strategies are quite different, they often work in a complementary manner. There is no incentive quite so effective in stimulating voluntary transfers as the looming threat of a protracted and costly court battle. The threat of judicial and administrative reallocations has provided impetus for numerous voluntary reallocations among the parties to adjudication proceedings and other conflicts over water (Colby et al., 1991).

Defining property rights: adjudications versus a case-by-case approach
A common prescription for improving efficiency in water allocation is to fully define transferable property rights in water (Anderson, 1983; Tregarthen, 1983). Certainly, substantial improvements are needed in this regard. However, characteristics of the resource itself combined with changing social values for competing water uses confound attempts to define property rights in water "once and for all." While state transfer procedures often are criticized for the uncertainty they present to

transactors, the incremental approach that clarifies attributes of water rights when a transfer is proposed may be preferable to the massive, lengthy adjudications unfolding in various western river basins. When a water right is reviewed as a part of a transfer proceeding, affected parties have an incentive to appear and their interests. Hydrologic and legal information is gathered, scrutinized, and debated by the various parties. Disputes over the nature, magnitude, and transferability of the property rights in question often are settled through negotiation among affected parties. This approach takes advantage of the dispersed information that affected parties possess and provides incentives for all participants to weigh carefully the advantages and disadvantages of their own participation. The costs of objecting to a proposed transfer mitigate against frivolous claims. The transaction costs created by objectors provide incentives for transfer proponents to consider potential externalities and resolve conflicts over the proposed transfer.

3 Previous Studies and Theoretical Considerations

> Transaction costs have a deservedly bad name as a theoretical device . . . partly because there is a suspicion that almost anything can be rationalized by invoking suitably specified transaction costs.
>
> (Fischer, 1977, p. 317)

Transaction costs in the externalities literature

Transaction costs have been central to the externalities literature for several decades. Coase, Cheung, and Demsetz each emphasized the importance of transaction costs. Coase (1960), in examining the reciprocal nature of externalities and the prospects for resolution through bargaining among affected parties, observed that identifying relevant parties, collecting pertinent information, conducting negotiations, enforcing agreements, and so on can be sufficiently costly to prevent many transactions from being achieved. Coase explored the role of private firms, courts, and government agencies in lowering transaction costs and resolving conflicts. Demsetz (1964), in developing a theory of property rights and their relationship to externalities, identified negotiating costs as a key component in determining whether a given externality would become internalized through voluntary rearrangements of property rights, such as "buying out" affected parties or making an agreement to reduce the level of external impacts. Cheung (1975) addressed transaction costs in the context of agricultural land markets and emphasized the influence of differing legal arrangements on transaction costs and thus on negotiations and contractual behavior.

These and other early authors developed a rich and colorful literature, replete with externality examples involving fishing lodges, bees, apple orchards, factories, laundromats, and the like (Meade, 1952; Coase, 1960; Demsetz, 1964; Samuels, 1971, Buchanan, 1972; Cheung, 1975). Throughout this literature there is a sense that, while some transaction costs are inevitable, they should be minimized so that market transactions can proceed unencumbered.

Randall (1975, p. 734), in clarifying relationships between property rights, incentive structures and institutions, provides the following definition of transaction costs: "the costs of resolving situations where involved parties have conflicting interest . . . including the costs to each party of gathering information, determining their position and strategy; the costs of the bargaining, negotiating, arbitration, judicial or any other process by which an agreement is reached . . . and the costs of enforcing the agreement made." Randall observes that "The existence of transaction costs *per se* does not necessitate a second best solution . . . . Surely prices will be different from what they would be in a transaction cost free fairyland, but that does not imply inefficiencies" (p. 741).

Williamson (1979) argues that transaction costs are what make economics interesting. "If transaction costs are negligible, the organization of economic activity is irrelevant, since any advantages of one mode of organization appears to hold over another will simply be eliminated by costless transacting" (p. 233). Williamson notes that "idiosyncratic" transactions, in which the identity of the buyer and the seller matter and the commodity is highly specialized and heterogeneous, necessarily involve high transaction costs.

Bromley (1991) incorporates transaction costs into a two-party externality model to analyze the impacts of alternative property rights assignments when transaction costs are non-zero. He observes that "it is the party *not* protected by the extant legal structure who must initiate action to deal with the other party. Information and contacting are expensive, and these costs are, for the most part, borne by the party that is vulnerable to unwanted costs in the status quo" (p. 77). Bromley illustrates how the outcome of bargaining between two parties differs given differing property rights structures and distributions of transaction costs, each outcome seemingly efficient given the property rights that led to that outcome.

Crocker (1971) provided an early, and still one of few, empirical analysis of the role of transaction costs in natural resource transfers. Using data on Florida land transactions to analyze the impacts of air pollution on agricultural land use, Crocker concluded that the transaction costs for affected farmland owners to bargain with polluters were very high, as were the costs of demanding compensatory damages through a judicial process. In Crocker's case study, the landowners eventually succeeding in shifting the property rights structure through obtaining a new state law creating air pollution control districts. With that law, farmers commenced to negotiate with polluters from a much stronger bargaining position, receiving better prices to be "bought out" and obtaining agreements for reduced emissions levels.

Leffler and Rucker (1990) applied transaction costs analysis to the structure of timber harvesting contracts and established empirical evidence for the influence of specific types of transaction costs on contractual provisions. In particular, this chapter highlights the role of measurement costs in reducing uncertainty regarding the value of the timber resources which are the subject of a transaction.

Previous studies on transaction costs and water transfers

In the water resources literature one finds frequent reference to transaction costs stemming from regulation of water use and transfer. Transaction costs often are characterized as factors that prevent markets from operating efficiently, or that prevent markets from developing altogether (Tregarthen, 1983; Crouter, 1987).

Tregarthen observes that Colorado procedures for regulating water transfers create considerable uncertainty and legal costs of several hundreds of thousands of dollars for transfer proponents. Anderson, in discussing western water resources, states: "Restrictions on transferability are restrictions on efficiency" (p. 4). Burness and Quirk argue that "Ultimately, the cause of inefficiency in the appropriative doctrine [the body of law that defines property rights in water in the West] is the restriction on the transfer of water rights" (p. 123). Crouter, analyzing the market for agricultural land and water in northeastern Colorado, concludes that "The presence of high transaction costs can impede the development of a separate [from land] and competitive water market" (pp. 262–3).

Saleth et al. (1991) model water market transactions as a multilateral bargaining game in order to understand the efficiency implications of "thin" markets, markets in which there are only one or a few buyers and sellers – not an uncommon situation in the western United States. The authors find that thin markets are more susceptible to efficiency losses due to strategic bargaining and asymmetric information. They note that carefully designed bargaining rules are necessary to avoid market distortions and diminishment of the social gains from water transactions.

Brookshire et al. (1993) used experimental markets to examine the effect of differing policies on third parties' rights to object a proposed water transfer. They note that a successful intervention (one that succeeded in blocking or modifying a "harmful" transfer) becomes a public good because it sets a precedent for protection in future cases, the probability of successful intervention for other parties increases, and their costs of intervention decrease. They conclude that court decisions and other policies that broaden the class of interests who may intervene to block a transfer will decrease market activity and increase the costs to water market transactors.

A few previous studies have quantified the magnitude of transaction costs incurred when transferring water rights. Anderson et al. (1983) analyzed water rights in the Tehachapi Basin of southern California and found that the five-year judicial process to clarify property rights in groundwater for the 100 groundwater users in the basin cost $55 per acre foot of water adjudicated (p. 243). The authors anticipated that transfers could occur at low cost once these rights were clarified. The transaction costs reported in Anderson et al. (1983) appear to be comparatively low in light of recent studies on transaction costs, due to the small number of groundwater users and the small size of the basin.

Khoshakhlagh et al. (1977, pp. 50–4) found that transaction costs per acre foot transferable to the proposed new use ranged from under $1 to $758, with an average of $4, for 20 transactions occurring in the period 1963–75. Costs are reported in nominal dollars for the year the transaction occurred. This study found that applicant transaction costs were significantly lower for those water rights that had been adjudicated previously and thus for which uncertainties regarding quantity and priority date had already been addressed.

Nunn (1989, p. 16 to end) found that for 87 transfers in New Mexico over the period 1975–87 applicants' transaction costs per acre foot of water transferable (typically the consumptive use associated with the right) averaged $191 (in 1988 dollars), with high variability across river basins and over time. Nunn observed an increase in average transaction costs per acre foot over the 12-year study period from $16 in the mid-1970s to $328 in the mid-1980s. Nunn also found economies of scale, as unit transaction costs decreased with the quantity of water transferred.

MacDonnell (1990, pp. 55–6) reports transaction cost figures and some statistical analysis based on data collected in Colorado and New Mexico in the late 1980s. The Colorado sample is based on nine observations on applicant transaction costs. The average transaction cost in Colorado was $380 per acre foot and includes both objector and applicant transaction costs. Statistical analysis indicates significant economies of scale and that the entering of an objection to the proposed transfer increased costs by over $600 per acre foot. The analysis reported for New Mexico (p. 56) is based on applicant transaction cost data for 201 cases. The average cost to applicants was £135 per acre foot. Economies of scale also were evident from the New Mexico data.

Transaction costs as a policy instrument

From a public policy perspective, the ability to impose transaction costs is an important determinant of different interests' influence on resource allocation. For instance, it is one thing for wildlife advocates to complain in the press about the impact of a development project on a particular species. It is another level of influence entirely for those same advocates to be able to initiate litigation that will delay the development and impose additional costs on the developers. In the second scenario, the developers have a genuine incentive to bargain with the wildlife advocates – because of the threat of substantial transaction costs. The Endangered Species Act is one example of an institutional change that shifted the bargaining positions of environmental interests. The Clean Water Act, the National Environmental Policy Act, and many other laws provided a new legal basis for imposing transaction costs and provided new incentives for negotiations between environmental interests and developers. The power to impose costs, a power conferred by institutional arrangements, represents an entrée into decisions about resource use, grants a seat at the bargaining table, and provides the "chips" with which to threaten and bribe other parties to behave in the desired manner. This role of transaction costs in policy is clearly evident in the western water arena.

The ability to impose transaction costs on those proposing to transfer water is conferred by state laws governing who may hold water rights and who may file protests. Market transactions are undertaken for economic gain, based on the perception that water supplies will generate higher returns in their new use than in their former use. The power to erode this expected gain through imposing transaction costs gives third parties leverage with transfer proponents and a role in the water reallocation process. The property rights structure determines how transaction costs are distributed and which party must bear the costs of initiating action to protect their interests. Adapting a diagram used by Bromley (1991) to illustrate the effect of property rights on bargaining to resolve externalities, the quantity of water transferred is directly related to which party bears the transaction costs.

In figure 21.2, Q on the horizontal axis measures the quantity of water transferred as a proportion of the quantity of applicant requested, from 0 to 100 percent. Zero implies the transfer was denied altogether by regulators. One hundred percent indicates that the full quantity requested by the applicant was approved for transfer. The MB_A function measures the applicant's benefits from the transfer as a function of the quantity transferred. The MD_O function measures the damages imposed on the objector as a function of quantity transferred. The efficient quantity in the absence of transaction costs is Q^*. However, these MB_A and MC_O functions are not observable to the regulator who must determine Q. The

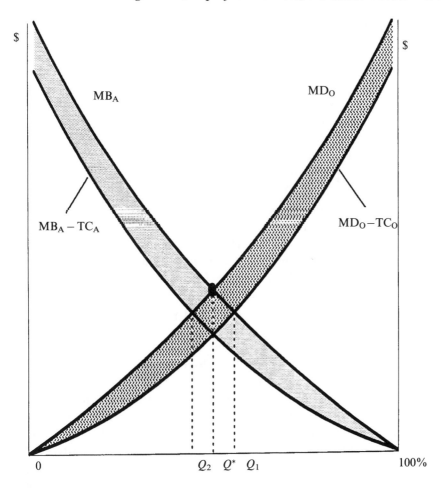

Figure 21.2 Q is the percentage approved of applicant's request to transfer a specific quantity of water.

affected parties themselves may have only imperfect information on MD_O. Suppose that the objector must bear all of the costs of documenting the externalities associated with the transfer, so that their willingness to pay to avoid damages is reduced by these transactions costs, denoted TC_O. Now it appears that the optimal quantity to be transferred is Q_1. Alternatively, if the transfer applicant bears the entire burden of "defending" the transfer against objectors, then the applicants' willingness to pay is reduced by these costs, denoted TC_A in the diagram. Now it seems that Q_2 is the efficient quantity to be transferred. The outcome clearly varies with the institutions that determine who has the burden of proof with regard to documenting transfer benefits and costs and persuading the state agency to adjust the quantity that may be transferred.

Conceptual model for transaction cost expenditures

The model developed here is highly simplified given the complex nature of benefits and costs, uncertainties, and risk preferences associated with water transfers and state regulations. Howe and Butler (1988), Brookshire et al. (1993), Leffler and Rucker (1990), and Crouter (1987) have incorporated some of these complexities into resource transfer models that incorporate transaction costs. However, the model serves to illuminate the incentives facing transfer applicants, who stand to benefit from obtaining approval to transfer a larger proportion of the total quantity requested, and objectors who stand to lose as the size of the transfer increases.

Benefits to the transfer applicant (B) and losses imposed on the objector (L) both are a function of the quantity of water transferred, Q. Each party must determine its own optimal level of effort to influence the quantity of water that can be transferred. Q is jointly a function of efforts by the applicant (E_A) and by the objector (E_O) to influence the state agency's ruling on the quantity of water that can be transferred. These efforts include attorney and expert witness fees, hydrologic modeling, and other preparation of evidence to influence the state agency who must determine Q. Each party may influence the other's level of effort by offering bribes, threats, and other forms of persuasion (denoted P_A and P_O) that influence the level of effort undertaken by the other party. Thus each party has two choice variables, level of effort to influence the state and persuasion directed at the other party, which affect the other party's level of effort.

Transfer applicants are assumed to maximize the net benefits of a water transfer. Benefits to the applicant are modeled as a positive concave function of the quantity of water transferred, Q. Objectors' losses (L) depend on the quantity transferred, and objectors seeks to minimize their losses. Applicant efforts positively influence Q ($\partial Q/\partial E_A > 0$) and efforts by the objector decrease Q ($\partial Q/\partial E_O < 0$).

The applicant's objective function (net benefit function) with effort E_A and persuasion P_A as the choice variables can thus be written as

$$\max NB_A = B\{Q[E_A, E_O, (P_A)]\} - P_O E_A - C_A(E_A, P_A) \qquad (21.1)$$

The first-order conditions are

$$\frac{\partial NB_A}{\partial E_A} = 0 \Rightarrow \frac{\partial B}{\partial Q}\frac{\partial Q}{\partial E_A} - P_O - \frac{\partial C_A}{\partial E_A} = 0 \qquad (21.2)$$

$$\frac{\partial NB_A}{\partial P_A} = 0 \Rightarrow \frac{\partial B}{\partial Q}\frac{\partial Q}{\partial E_O}\frac{\partial E_O}{\partial P_A} - \frac{\partial C_A}{\partial P_A} = 0 \qquad (21.3)$$

That is, the larger the marginal benefit of water transferred ($\partial B/\partial Q$), the more effective the applicant's efforts in influencing Q ($\partial Q/\partial E_A$), the lower the marginal cost of effort; and the lower the persuasion offered by the other party (P_O), the larger the optimal effort (E_A) to influence the outcome of the state agency review. Where water is more valuable, one would expect to see higher applicant expenditures to obtain state approval, since these expenditures are justified by the benefits received.

The optimal level of persuasion applied to influence the objector's efforts (P_A) depends on the effectiveness of the objector in influencing the state agency $(\partial Q/\partial E_A)$ and the marginal cost of persuasion $(\partial CA/\partial P_A)$.

For the objector (also called an intervenor or protestant in some states), the objective is to minimize the net losses associated with the transfer and the costs associated with objecting to the transfer by expending the appropriate amount of effort E_O to reduce the quantity transferred and the appropriate amount of persuasion P_O to reduce the applicant's efforts. The objective function with E_O as the choice variable is

$$\min NL_O = L\{Q[E_A(P_O), E_O]\} - P_A E_O + C_O(E_O, P_O) \qquad (21.4)$$

The first-order conditions are

$$\frac{\partial NL_O}{\partial E_O} = 0 \Rightarrow \frac{\partial L}{\partial Q} \frac{\partial Q}{\partial E_O} - P_A + \frac{\partial C_O}{\partial E_O} = 0 \qquad (21.5)$$

$$\frac{\partial NL_O}{\partial P_O} = 0 \Rightarrow \frac{\partial L}{\partial Q} \frac{\partial Q}{\partial E_A} \frac{\partial E_A}{\partial P_O} + \frac{\partial C_O}{\partial P_O} = 0 \qquad (21.6)$$

One would expect higher expenditures by applicants where the marginal losses $\partial L/\partial Q$ imposed by transfers are larger. The effectiveness of objectors' efforts in influencing quantity $(\partial Q/\partial E_O)$ will vary among different types of objectors, depending on the prominence their concerns are accorded in the property rights structure. Water right holders who object to a proposed transfer should have high $\partial Q/\partial E_O$, while environmental or community interests may have low or zero $\partial Q/\partial E_O$. In addition, the persuasion offered by the applicant (P_A) and the marginal cost of effort $(\partial C/\partial P_O)$ influence the optimal E_O.

The optimal level of persuasion directed at the applicant (P_O) depends on the effectiveness of the applicant's efforts in influencing quantity $(\partial Q/\partial E_A)$ and the marginal costs of persuasion to the objector $(\partial C_O/\partial P_O)$.

State agencies encourage resolution of conflicts among the parties and generally will approve an agreement that has been reached by the applicant and objectors. Incentives to bargain are a function of marginal losses and benefits associated with the transferable quantity and each party's relative effectiveness in influencing the state. Each party's effectiveness and bargaining power is a function of the policies and property rights that govern review of proposed transfers and right to intervene and influence regulatory decisions.

The model highlights the interdependences between the transfer applicant and objector. The value of each party's objective function depends jointly on their own choices and on choices of the other party.

4   Transaction Costs and Water Transfers – Empirical Analysis

Colby et al. (1989) analyzed applicant, protestant, and state agency costs for water transfers in several states with active water markets based on transaction cost data collected for transfers initiated in the 1980s. MacDonnell (1990) analyzed characteristics of all transfer applications filed in Colorado, New Mexico, and Utah over a ten-year time period. These two studies focus on Utah, New Mexico, and Colorado because these states each have several decades of experience with water markets, have public records on changes in water rights that are useful for analysis, and have legal frameworks governing water transfers that differ somewhat from one another, providing an opportunity for comparing alternative regulatory approaches.

Comparisons among states

Water transfers occur regularly in the three states for which transaction cost data were collected, with an average of 70, 100 and 350 water transfers approved each year over the period 1975–84 in Colorado, New Mexico, and Utah, respectively. Transaction costs incurred by applicants to satisfy state regulations averaged a small fraction (6 percent) of the prices paid for water rights (Colby et al., 1989). Applicants' policy-related transaction costs averaged $91 per acre foot of water transferred with considerable variation among states. Colorado applicants' transaction costs averaged $187 per acre foot. The average policy-related transaction costs for applicants was $54 in New Mexico and $66 in Utah. Another measure of policy-related transaction costs involves the opportunity costs to transfer applicants of time delays while waiting for state agency approval of a transfer proposal. This time period is measured in months from the time a transfer application is filed to the date of the state agency division. Time delays varied considerably by state: 20 months in Colorado, 6 months in New Mexico, and 9 months in Utah (MacDonnell, 1990).

Transfers of water rights in New Mexico are seldom protested. Only 6 percent of transfer applications were protested during the ten-year period (1975–84). New Mexico transfers typically involve small amounts of water; 51 percent of transfers involve less than 10 acre feet of water.

About one-third of transfers moved water out of agriculture to some other use, another one-third involved transfers within agriculture and the remainder were transfers among non-agricultural uses. Ninety-five percent of transfer applications were approved over the ten-year period studied.

Colorado water transfer applications involve a median of 12 acre feet of water, are approved for about 80 percent of the cases and are concentrated in the most rapidly urbanizing and populous areas of the state. Two-thirds of Colorado transfers involve moving water from agricultural to non-agricultural uses. Sixty percent of all Colorado transfers were protested over the ten-year study period.

In Utah, where transfers have also occurred routinely for decades, 61 percent of transfers involve less than 10 acre feet of water. Less than one-third of Utah transfers involve movement of water out of agricultural use. Only 9 percent applications in Utah were protested over the ten-year period 1974–84, and 90 percent of the applications were approved.

Empirical model and results

Econometric analysis reveals that larger transfers have lower applicant transaction costs per acre foot transferred, indicating some economies of scale. The filing of a protest has a significant and positive impact on applicant costs per acre foot. Time delay, a measure of applicants' opportunity costs, also is significantly and positively related to whether or not protests were filed.

Empirical results are summarized in table 21.1 for twenty-five transactions occurring in the mid- to late-1980s in Colorado, New Mexico, and Utah. Two different measures of applicant costs were used as dependent variables in multiple linear regression . The variable "months," in the first equation, is a proxy for the opportunity costs of time delays (deferred benefits) while awaiting transfer approval. The variable is

Table 21.1 Transaction costs: empirical results

(1) Months $= 21.78 - 3.77$(ln acre feet) $+ 39.7$(protest)
   t statistics (2.6)   (−2.3)   (5.5)
   F ratio $= 15.09$, adjusted $R^2 = 0.53$, $N = 26$

(2) Applicant unit costs $= 216.91 - 44.2$(ln acre feet) $+ 329.8$(protest)
   t statistics   (2.06)   (−2.2)   (3.5)
   F ratio $= 6.7$, adjusted $R^2 = 0.32$, $N = 25$

measured in months, or fractions of months, from the date an application is filed to the date of a decision on the application by the estate agency. The filing of a protest significantly increases time delays. The dependent variable in the second equation, applicant costs per acre foot, is significantly increased by protests and large transfers have somewhat lower per-unit costs. Both independent variables were significant at the 5 percent level in both equations and the *F* ratios indicate a relationship between the dependent and independent variables that is significant at the 0.005 level.

Implications of empirical findings

The large positive coefficients on the protest variable in table 21.1 confirm that those parties who have legal standing to file a protest strongly influence the costs incurred by a transfer applicant. Neighboring water right holders who object to a proposed transfer have significant bargaining power in the water reallocation process.

Colby (1989) and MacDonnell (1990) both observe systematic differences in applicant transaction costs, frequency of protests, and time delays among states. One explanation for the variation among states lies in the different *types* of transfers occurring in each state. Transfers out of agriculture generally are more controversial than transfers among farmers. Transfers out of agriculture account for 76 percent of transfers in Colorado and only 35–42 percent of the transfers that have occurred in New Mexico and Utah over the last ten years (MacDonnell, 1990). Further 67 percent of Colorado transfers involve surface water, while only 17 percent of Utah transfers and 30 percent of New Mexico transfers involve surface water. Externalities involved in transferring surface water rights to new uses and locations include lower streamflows and a reduction in water availability for other users of the stream. These impacts are more obvious and immediate than externalities involved in groundwater pumping, which include altered rates and locations of groundwater decline and gradual changes in pumping lifts for nearby groundwater users.

The MacDonnell (1990) and Nunn (1989) data indicate instructive variations in transaction costs and time delays within states. In Colorado, 84 percent of transfer proposals in the most populous and "water scarce" basin in Colorado were protested, compared with only 40 percent in the least competitive basins in the state. Colorado transfers involving water rights in the most "water scarce" area of the state had significantly higher applicant unit costs and time delays than elsewhere. In New Mexico, larger transfers took much longer to win state approval – the average volume of New Mexico transfers approved in less than three months was 79 acre feet, compared to more than four years to approve transfers with an average volume of 312 acre feet. Nunn found large differences in transaction costs for different regions of New Mexico. Significant regional differences across regions of the state reflect varying degrees of water scarcity and conflict over transfers. Transaction costs per acre foot averaged $1084 (in 1988 dollars) in the Rio Grande Basin north of Albuquerque, where the City of Santa Fe, developers, pueblos, outlying villages, and traditional community ditch associations (acequias) vie for limited supplies. The transaction costs in this region are nearly ten times greater than the state-wide average.

In Utah, one basin accounts for a disproportionately large number of all protests filed in the state. In this basin, which is experiencing high growth rates and has no remaining unclaimed water supplies, approval time delays are twice as long as those typical elsewhere in Utah.

These intra-state comparisons indicate that policy-induced transaction costs are higher in areas where water is more scarce and more valuable, transfers are more controversial, and the externalities of water transfers are more likely to be significant. These data support the hypothesis that the magnitude of transaction costs reflect externalities associated with transfers and the relative value of water supplies.

Colorado has much higher transaction costs and longer time delays for approval than other western states. Some of these higher costs are due to higher water values in Colorado, as evidenced by significantly higher market prices than are typical in other states (Saliba and Bush, 1987). However, Colorado transaction costs are out of proportion with market values, compared with other states. Colby et al. (1989) found that while transaction costs average 6 percent of the price the transfer applicant paid for the water rights involved in the transfer for all three states studied, they average 12 percent for Colorado transactions. One might hypothesize that transaction costs are higher in Colorado because a broader range of externalities is considered when transfer proposals are evaluated in that state. However, Colorado actually lags behind many other states in considering instream and public interest impacts.

In Colorado, changes in water use are evaluated in the state water court system in formal judicial proceedings and attorneys' fees account for well over half of transaction costs. A small proportion of transaction cost expenditures are paid for engineering and hydrologic studies to measures transfer impacts and to injured third parties as compensation. There are rents to be captured as water is reallocated from lower-valued to higher-valued uses and current policies redistribute the rents from water transfers in a manner that raises equity concerns. When policymakers have considered taxation and redistribution of profits from water transfers, the intended beneficiaries have been rural communities, wildlife preserves, and stream protection program – not attorneys.

5 Summary and Policy Implications

Overall, transaction costs do not appear to be excessive, given water values in the areas studied. Costs incurred by applicants appear to reflect the differing economic value of water in different regions. Transaction costs are significantly higher in areas where existing water supplies are fully appropriated, importation or development of new supplies is expensive, and demand for water is increasing. In these areas, the value of water is high and high transaction costs are not necessarily an indication of inefficiency and overregulation. Transaction costs are "well-behaved," and roughly consistent with the incentives that would be created by a Pigovian tax on water transfers. The higher the value of water and the greater the externalities associated with transfers, the higher the "tax" on transfers in the form of transaction costs incurred in satisfying state policies.

Why not tax water transfers directly to account for external impacts? Determining the optimal rate for such a tax would require complete centralized information on all parties' marginal costs and benefits. Existing information regarding externalities is dispersed among affected parties and hydrologic and economic studies to identify the magnitude and distribution of impacts are costly. Few would argue that state agencies could efficiently collect the marginal benefit and marginal damage information needed to impose a credible Pigovian tax. The current institutional framework relies on autonomous, self-interested transfer applicants and protestants to incur costs to the point where it is no longer worthwhile to do so. The benefits and external impacts of transfers are considered as each party determines the expenses they will incur to pursue or oppose a particular water transfer and the "payoffs" they are willing to make or to accept in order to reach a settlement. However, to the extent that state laws exclude some of those who have real economic interests from participating in the process, some social costs are being ignored.

One goal of policy reforms should be to generate information on the externalities that accompany water transfers in a least-cost manner. Most disputes between applicants and protestants involve the *quantity* of water that should be transferable. States could establish a presumptive transferable quantity per irrigated acre. New Mexico, with the lowest transaction costs of the three states studied, sets a standard quantity of water that may be transferred per unit of irrigated land. Parties who disagree with this quantity bear the costs of proving that some other amount is appropriate. In contrast, the Colorado system invites all parties to provide evidence on transferable quantity, with considerably higher cumulative costs incurred for engineering and legal studies.

Judicial proceedings should not be the first forum for evaluating a transfer proposal, as they are in Colorado where the adversarial nature of court proceedings prompts "overinvestment" in attorneys and other experts. In a litigation setting, much technical information developed by experts representing the parties is proprietary and thus is not available to build up a cumulative knowledge base for future public use. Data developed for previous transfers (river basin and groundwater models, engineering reports, crop consumptive use studies, etc.) should be publicly available for evaluating impacts of future transfer proposals, with the goal of reducing information costs.

Policy reforms also should seek to broaden the types of externalities considered. State laws specifically exclude some parties who may experience significant externalities from filing protests and from influencing the conditions of transfer approval. In general, only water right holders can force their concerns to be accounted for. Wastewater treatment plant managers, recreationists, environmental interest, and persons who take their living in water-based recreation typically have no bargaining power in the regulatory process.

Those who *do* have legal basis to protest a transfer, other water right holders, act in their own self-interest to protect the benefits they receive from their water right. It is costly to file a protest and prospective objectors must weigh these costs against the potential payoffs, which take the form of externalities avoided through modifications in the transfer proposal or monetary compensation for damages. Colby (1989) found that objectors spent an average of $7052 per protest filed for a sample of transfers in Colorado, New Mexico, and Utah. The costs of protesting serve to inhibit (though probably not eliminate) frivolous protests filed purely to obtain payments from transfer applicants.

States need to define the public goods attributes of water that they wish to protect and to incorporate these into their transfer policies. Broader access to property rights in water and to the transfer approval process can allow a wider array of externalities to be considered. This will make water transfers more expensive than previously, as a broader group of interests can formally object to a proposed transfer. However, given externalities generated by transfers, is there a sound economic rationale for making water transfers as inexpensive as possible? Higher transaction costs reflect the substantial and multiple economic benefits associated with water in various uses, benefits which can be impaired by a transfer. Transaction costs are high in areas where new water supplies are locally unavailable and expensive to import, where demand for water is increasing, and where water rights are valuable property. Transaction costs are lower in states and in river basins where unclaimed water still is available and the market value of water rights is lower.

Transaction costs generated by state policies are a reasonable means to account for social costs of water transfers, given the immense information requirements for optimality taxing transfers. The present institutional structure gives affected parties, each weighing their own costs and benefits, an incentive to generate information on transfer impacts and to negotiate transfer conditions and mitigation of externalities. State water transfer criteria are not arbitrary hindrances imposed upon the marketplace. These policies protect existing investments by water right holders and, as they are broadened to include other interests, they can reflect other social values affected by water use and transfer. By giving objectors the ability to impose transaction costs, state policies provide incentives for transfer applicants to consider externalities that otherwise would not be accounted for in private negotiations between water buyers and sellers.

References

Anderson, T. L. 1983: *Water Rights*. San Francisco, CA: Pacific Institute for Public Policy.
Anderson, T. L. and Johnson, R. 1986: The problem of instream flows. *Economic Inquiry*, 24, 535–54.
Anderson, T. L., Burt, O. R. and Fractor, D. 1983; Privating groundwater basins. In T. L. Anderson (ed.), *Water Rights*, San Francisco, CA: Pacific Institute for Public Policy.
Bancroft, H. H. 1888: *History of California*. San Francisco, CA: The History Company.
Ben-Porath, Yoram. 1978: The F connection: families, friends and firms and the organization of exchange. Report published by the Hebrew University of Jerusalem.
Bromley, D. W. 1991: *Environment and Economy: Property Rights and Public Policy*. Oxford: Basil Blackwell.
Brookshire, D., McKee, M. and Ganderton, P. 1993: Intervening to prevent a collective harm. Unpublished manuscript, Department of Economics, University of New Mexico, Albuquerque.
Buchanan, J. M. 1972: Politics, property and the law . . . . *Journal of Law and Economics*, 15, 439–52.
Burness, H. S. and Quirk, J. P. 1980: Water law transfers and economic efficiency: the Colorado River. *Journal of Law and Economics*, 23, 111-34.
Central Valley Improvement Act. 1992: Title 34 of Public Law 102–575.
Cheung, S. N. 1973: The fable of the bees: an economic investigation. *Journal of Law and Economics*, 16, 11–33.
Cheung, S. N. 1975: Transactions costs, risk aversion and the choice of contractual arrangements. *Journal of Law and Economics*, 18, 535–54.
Coase, R. 1960: the problem of social cost. *Journal of Law and Economics*, 3, 1–44.
Colby, B. G. 1989. *Water Transfers and Transaction Costs: Case Studies in Colorado, New Mexico, Utah and Nevada*. Tucson, AZ: University of Arizona, Department of Agricultural Economics.
Colby, B. G. 1993: Benefits, costs and water acquisition strategies: economic considerations in instream flow protection. In L. Macdonnell (ed.), *Instream Flow Law and Policy*, Boulder, CO: University of Colorado Press.
Colby, Bonnie G., McGinnis, M. and Rait, K. 1989. Procedural aspects of State water law: transferring water rights in the Western States. *Arizona Law Review*, 31, 697–720.
Colby, Bonnie G., McGinnis, M. and Rait, K. 1991: Mitigating environmental externalities through voluntary and involuntary water allocation: Nevada's Truckee-Carson River basin. *Natural Resources Journal*, 31 (4), 757–84.
Crawford, Stanley. 1990: Dancing for water. *Journal of the Southwest*, 32, 265–7.

Crocker, T. D. 1971: Externalities, property rights and transaction costs: an empirical study. *Journal of Law and Economics*, 14, 451-64.

Crouter, J. P. 1987: Hedonic estimation applied to a water rights market. *Land Economics*, 563, 259–71.

Daubert, J. and Young, Robert. 1979: Economic benefits from instream flow in Colorado. Colorado State University Water Resources Research Report 91, Fort Collins.

Demsetz, H. 1964: The exchange and enforcement of property rights. *Journal of Law and Economics*, 7, 11–26.

Fischer, S. 1977: Longterm contracting, sticky prices and monetary policy. *Journal Monetary Economics*, 3, 317.

Howe, C. and Butler, P. 1988: An analytic framework for understanding water transfers. Unpublished paper, University of Colorado Department of Economics, Boulder, CO.

Irvin v. Phillips, 5 Cal. 140, 147 (1855).

Johnson, N. K. and Du Mars, C. T. 1989: Survey of the evolution of Western water law in response to changing economic and public interest demands. *Natural Resources Journal*, 29, 347–88.

Kapaloski, Lee. 1988: Effects of upstream transfers on water quality formatting. In *Water Quality Control: Integrating Beneficial Uses and Environmental Protection*. Boulder, CO: University of Colorado, Natural Resources Law Center.

Khoshakhlagh, R., Brown, Lee and Du Mars, Charles. 1977: Forecasting future market values of water rights in New Mexico. Final Report to New Mexico Water Resources Research Institute, University of New Mexico Department of Economics.

Leffler, K. and Rucker, R. 1990: Transaction costs and the efficient organization of production: a study of timber harvesting contracts. *Journal of Political Economy*, 99, 1060–87.

Limerick, P. N. 1987: *The Legacy of Conquest*. New York: Norton.

Loomis, J. 1987: The economic value of instream flow: methodology and benefit estimates. *Journal of Environmental Management*, 24, 169–79.

MacDonnell, Larry (ed.) 1989: *Instream Flow Protection: Law and Policy*. Boulder, CO: University of Colorado Press.

MacDonnell, L. 1990: The water transfer process as a management option for meeting changing water demands. Natural Resources Law Center Report, University of Colorado, Boulder, CO.

Meade, J. E. 1952: External economics and diseconomies in a competitive situation. *Economic Journal*, 54, 52–67.

National Audubon Society v. Superior Court, 33 Cal. 3d 419, 658 P.2d 709, 189 Cal. Rptr. 346 (1983).

North, Douglass. 1992: Transaction costs, institutions, and economic performance. Occasional Paper 30, International Center for Economic Growth.

Nunn, S. C. 1989: Transfers of New Mexico water: a survey of changes in place and purpose of use, 1975–1987. Unpublished manuscript, University of New Mexico, Department of Economics, Albuquerque.

Polanyi, Karl. 1944: *The Great Transformation*. Boston, MA: Beacon Press.

Polanyi, Karl. 1947: Our obsolete market mentality. *Commentary*, 3, 109-17.

Randall, A. 1975: Property rights and social microeconomics. *Natural Resources Journal*, 15, 729–45.

Saleth, R. M., Braden, J. and Eheart, J. 1991: Bargaining rules for a thin spot water market. *Land Economics*, 67, 326–39.

Saliba, B. C. and Bush, D. B. 1987: *Water Marketing in Theory and Practice: Market Transfers, Water Values and Public Policy*. Boulder, CO: Westview Press.

Samuels, W. J. 1971: Interrelations between legal and economic processes. *Journal of Law and Economics*, 14, 435–50.

Sax, Joseph. 1990–1: Personal communication with author.

Schaab, William. 1983: Prior appropriation, impairment, replacements, models and markets. *Natural Resources Journal,* 23, 25–50.

Sleeper, 1985: In the matter of Howard Sleeper et al., Rio Arriba County Court Case No. RA 84-53(c). Ruling issued by New Mexico District Court Judge Art Encinias. Reversed in 1988 by New Mexico Court of Appeals.

Smith, Rodney (ed.) 1989–93: *Water Strategist.* Claremont, VA: Stratecon.

Tregarthen, T. D. 1983: Water in Colorado: fear and loathing of the marketplace. In T. L. Anderson (ed.), *Water Rights,* San Francisco, CA: Pacific Institute for Public Policy.

Wahl, Richard. 1989: *Markets for Federal Water.* Washington, DC: Resources for the Future.

Ward, F. A. 1987: Economics of water allocation to instream uses in a fully appropriated river basin. *Water Resources Research,* 23, 381–92.

Williamson, O. E. 1979: Transactions-cost economics: the governance of contractual relations. *Journal of Law and Economics,* 22, 233–61.

Young, R. 1984: Direct and indirect regional impacts of competition for irrigation water. In E. Englebert and A. Scheurming (eds), *Water Scarcity: Impacts on Western Agriculture,* Berkeley, CA: University of California Press.

Young, Robert. 1986: Why are there so few transactions among water users? *American Journal of Agricultural Economics,* 68, 1143–51.

22

Issues in the Conjunctive Use of Surface Water and Groundwater

Bill Provencher

1 Introduction

The value of groundwater resources in regions where surface water inflows are the primary source of water is perhaps never more apparent than when drought strikes California. At a conference on groundwater in the middle of one such drought, Howitt and M'Marete (1990, 45) observed:

> The drought years of 1976 and 1977 were the worst since the early 1930's, and, with a large agricultural and urban productive base developed and dependent on water, the predictions of economic loss to irrigated agriculture were severe and compelling. As the second year of the drought commenced, the California Department of Water Resources issued the following predictions for drought-related economic loss in the agricultural sector: A pessimistic view predicted losses of $2.1 billion, a moderate and "most likely" view put losses at $1.4 billion while an optimistic prediction showed losses of $800 million to the sector.

In fact, however, these warnings of impending doom fell far from the mark. The authors continue,

> A year later, the California Crop and Livestock Reporting service reported that net farm income in the worst drought year of 1977 was at its second highest value ever recorded, and 4 percent higher than the pre-drought 1975 net farm income. What did California's irrigated agricultural industry do to adjust so successfully to a two-year drought, that had not been anticipated by the experts?

What farmers did was pump groundwater. Howitt and M'Marete report that in 1975, just prior to the drought, irrigated agriculture in the Central

Valley (the large agricultural region of the state) used 15.25 million acre feet of surface water, and 11.65 million acre feet of groundwater, for a total of 26.90 million acre feet and a net farm income of $2.44 billion. At the height of the drought in 1977, total water used in agriculture *rose* slightly to 27.26 million acre feet, and net farm income rose to $2.53 billion, even as surface water consumption fell 70 percent to 8.97 million acre feet. The indisputable conclusion is that groundwater saved the state's agricultural industry from disaster.

This chapter presents material from the recent literature on the conjunctive use of surface water and groundwater. It focuses especially on the allocation of groundwater when stochastic surface water inflows are the primary source of water. As evident by the presence of conferences like the one at which Howitt and M'Marete presented their paper (aptly titled, "Coping with water scarcity: the role of groundwater"), this issue is a practical concern in the western United States and arid regions throughout the world; water managers continue to grapple with the question of how to jointly manage surface water and groundwater, and economists have something to say about this. Moreover, it is an inherently interesting resource issue, and thinking about it in broad terms provides insights to larger questions of resource management. In arid and semi-arid regions, surface water is best cast as a flow resource, the variability of which causes water users to adjust their behavior from season to season. Farmers, for instance, respond to the variability of surface water supply via decisions about how many acres of a crop to grow and how to irrigate the crop. Surface water can be stored in reservoirs to reduce the variability of supply, but storage capacity is usually relatively small, and in extended droughts, seasonal supplies eventually fall. On the other hand, groundwater is often best understood to be a stock resource mined by water users. The groundwater stock may increase due to natural and artificial recharge, but recharge is usually small relative to the capacity of the groundwater aquifer, and so often its variability is not a significant consideration in the allocation decision. Given the natural constancy of the groundwater resource, clearly a primary consideration in the joint use of surface water and groundwater is the role of the groundwater resource as a contingent source of water; the groundwater resource serves to buffer seasonal revenues against the vicissitudes of surface water supply.

Implicit in the concern about the conjunctive use of surface water and groundwater is the belief – prominent among resource economists – that in the absence of government intervention the groundwater resource is misallocated. Put another way, discussions about the role of government in groundwater management must begin with an understanding of the consequences of doing nothing. The next section develops the standard model of the efficient use of groundwater to investigate the inefficiency of groundwater pumping in the absence of central (optimal) control. The discussion emphasizes that estimates of the welfare loss under the common property regime depend on the particular model of firm behavior enlisted in the analysis. Section 3 examines two distinct notions of the buffer value of groundwater – that is, the value of the resource as a buffer against the vicissitudes of surface water inflows. The significance of the discussion lies in the potentially severe economic consequences of not correctly casting the management of groundwater and surface water as a problem involving the joint management of substitute resources in an uncertain world. The final section argues that some forms of decentralized groundwater management are practical alternatives to the control regimes usually prescribed for conjunctive management.

2 Models of Groundwater Use

Burt (1964a) examined the problem of the conjunctive use of surface water and groundwater in a seminal monograph that remains the most lucid and comprehensive discussion available of the economics of conjunctive use. Numerous other papers have added to the understanding of the groundwater extraction problem under a variety of circumstances; these are included in the references at the end of the chapter. To date, most studies concerning the benefit of groundwater management – whether in conjunctive use situations or otherwise – involve a comparison of the solution of a dynamic optimization problem to the rate of groundwater pumping arising instead under the *common property arrangement*, where government does not intervene in the allocation of groundwater and access to the resource is limited, either institutionally or by virtue of the high cost of pumping and moving groundwater around, to those individuals or firms with land overlying the resource. Usually left implicit in these comparisons is the extraction behavior of firms under the common property arrangement. This section develops a simple deterministic model of the water planner's problem to briefly examine the inefficiency of the common property arrangement for two models of extraction behavior.

Suppose M firms exploit an aquifer characterized by a flat bottom and perpendicular sides. At each time t all of the M firms receive the same amount of surface water, s. Moreover, the firms are identical in the sense that the water revenue function $\pi(w_t)$ and the per-unit cost of pumping groundwater, $c(x_t)$, are the same for all firms, where w_t is the total volume of water consumed at time t and x_t is the stock of groundwater.[1] The water revenue function is increasing and concave.[2] The concavity of the water function implies that the derived demand for water, $\pi_w^{-1}(\cdot)$ is downward sloping. Typically the cost of extraction is decreasing and convex in the stock of groundwater.

For simplicity, we assume consumption of surface water is costless. Firms consume all available surface water before pumping groundwater, and so, letting q_t denote the firm's extraction of groundwater at time t, each firm's net revenue from water consumption is

$$\pi(q_t + s) - c(x_t)q_t$$

Suppose the water planner's objective is to maximize the present value of net revenues. Then because all firms are identical, the total amount of groundwater extracted at time t must be Mq_t. The state equation governing the evolution of the groundwater stock is thus

$$x_{t+1} = x_1 - Mq_t + r \tag{22.1}$$

where r is recharge. A more realistic model would cast recharge as a stochastic variable dependent upon the amount of water extracted – normally, some of the water applied in irrigation returns to the groundwater aquifer. Here we simplify the model to simplify the exposition.

Let $v(x_t)$ denote each firm's present value of net revenues from groundwater consumption, given an infinite planning horizon and *optimal* current and future extraction decisions. In the lexicon of dynamic programming, $v(\cdot)$ is a *value function* (see, for instance, Bellman, 1957, or Bertsekas, 1976). It is conceptually equivalent to the static indirect profit function in so far as it represents the value of an objective function at the optimum. In this case, however, the optimum involves a *sequence* of optimal pumping decisions, $\{q_t^*, q_{t-1}^*, q_{t+2}^*, \dots\}$, and the state of nature is defined not by input and output prices, as with the indirect profit function, but by the observed stock of groundwater (input and output prices remain implicit – and fixed – in the revenue function $\pi(\cdot)$). Note from (22.1) that the value function $v(x_{t+1})$ can be expressed as conditional on the pumping decision in period t: $v(x_{t+1}) \equiv v(x_t - Mq_t + r)$. With this result in mind, the water planner's problem is given by the functional equation[3]

$$Mv(x_t) = \max_{q_t} M[\pi(q_t + s) - c(x_t)q_t + \beta v(x_t - Mq_t + r)] \tag{22.2}$$

where β is a discount factor. This equation is known as Bellman's equation; it reduces an infinite horizon problem to a static one, but clearly (22.2) is more complex than the usual static problem, in so far as the value function appears on the right-hand side. Solving Bellman's equation is a task that has received considerable attention since Bellman introduced the concept of dynamic programming in 1957.[4] Here we simply note that the solution to (22.2) must satisfy the necessary condition

$$\pi_w(q_t + s) - c(x_t) = \beta Mv_x(x_{t+1}) \tag{22.3}$$

where subscripts on functions denote partial derivatives and arguments of derivatives indicate the point at which the function is evaluated. The term on the right-hand side of (22.3) is the *social marginal user cost* of groundwater pumping (note that it is evaluated at x_{t+1}). This term reflects the fact that pumping the marginal unit of groundwater in the current period reduces the future welfare of all M firms by increasing the future cost of groundwater pumping.[5]

Two models of behavior under the common property arrangement

Myopic behavior
Typically economists concerned with the welfare loss associated with the common property arrangement characterize this arrangement as one in which the firms using the groundwater resource execute myopic pumping decisions; that is, each firm pumps groundwater until the current marginal net benefit of groundwater equals zero, as reflected by the result

$$\pi_w(q_t + s) - c(x_t) = 0 \qquad (22.4)$$

This is the model of behavior used in most empirical studies (see, for instance, Gisser and Sanchez, 1980; Feinerman and Knapp, 1983; Llop and Howitt, 1983; Allen and Gisser, 1984; Nieswiodomy, 1985; Worthington et al., 1985). The assumption implicit in all of these models is that firms do not recognize the effect of their groundwater pumping on the state of the groundwater resource. Formally, the state equation (22.1) – or some form of it – does not enter the firm's decision problem. At first glance this assumption seems rather peculiar. One could argue that a rational firm will eventually learn that its pumping decisions do affect the stock of groundwater and will bring this information to bear in its pumping decision. On the other hand, one might expect this model of behavior to perform reasonably well when the groundwater resource is exploited by a large number of small firms. In this case, each firm's groundwater extraction is a sufficiently small part of the total extraction that the assumption of "stock-taking" behavior may well represent the reality of the situation, just as the assumption of competitive "price-taking" behavior no doubt accurately depicts the situation in many input and output markets. This analogy is explicit in the series of papers by Gisser and his coauthors (Gisser and Sanchez, 1980; Gisser, 1983; Allen and Gisser, 1984), who refer to this case of the common property arrangement as the "competitive arrangement." In other words, each firm is too small a part of the whole to give serious consideration to how its pumping decision affects future water supplies. Support for this model comes from a survey of farmers in Kern County, California, conducted by Dixon (1989). He found that, in the absence of government control, farmers are apparently unconcerned with how their groundwater pumping affects the future availability of the resource.

In the usual case where $\pi(\cdot)$ is concave in groundwater pumping and firm welfare increases with an increase in the groundwater stock ($v_x > 0$), a comparison of conditions (22.4) and (22.3) confirms the intuition that the "tragedy of the commons" is characterized by a rate of groundwater extraction greater than the efficient rate. Interestingly, some empirical analyses suggest that "tragedy" is a hyperbole when describing the effect of myopic pumping. The question of the size of the welfare loss associated with myopic groundwater pumping is examined in some detail in the concluding section.

Closed loop pumping strategies

Although myopic groundwater pumping may be a good approximation of behavior when the groundwater resource is exploited by a large number of small firms, and although this may be the typical case, the appropriate characterization of pumping behavior when the number of firms is small remains an interesting theoretical question. In two of the models that have emerged in the literature, firm behavior is "memoryless," in the sense that each firm's pumping behavior depends only on the current state of nature (in our simple model, the current size of the groundwater stock). Firm behavior is distinguished in the two models by the type of strategy employed by firms. Firms pursuing *open loop (path)* strategies take the extraction paths of their rivals as given. On the other hand, firms pursuing *closed loop (feedback)* strategies take the state-dependent extraction *rules* of their rivals as given, where an extraction rule expresses the groundwater pumping decision as a function of the observed groundwater stock. An equilibrium in open loop strategies is a set of M extraction paths, the jth element of which is the extraction path maximizing the welfare of firm j, given the other $M - 1$ extraction paths of the set. An equilibrium in closed loop strategies is a set of M state-dependent extraction rules, the jth element of which is the extraction rule maximizing the welfare of firm j, given the other $M - 1$ extraction rules of the set.

Dixon (1989), Negri (1989), and Provencher and Burt (1993) all discuss the open and closed loop models of pumping behavior under the common property arrangement. The closed loop model appears the more realistic of the two because usually firms do not commit to particular paths of groundwater extraction, instead basing their extraction decisions on the observed state of nature. With this in mind, and in light of space limitations, here we investigate only the closed loop model. Let $q^{cp}(x_t)$ denote the equilibrium extraction rule employed by each of the identical firms. Firm j perceives the state equation governing the groundwater stock to be

$$x_{t+1} = x_t - (M - 1)q^{cp}(x_t) - q_{jt} + r \qquad (22.5)$$

Firm j "knows" the state-dependent extraction rules of its rivals; in particular, it knows that its rivals ultimately react to its own extraction behavior. This is readily apparent by forward substituting in (22.5). Forward substituting to period $t + 2$ yields

$$x_{t+2} = x_t - (M - 1)q^{cp}(x_t) - (M - 1)q^{cp}[x_t - (M - 1)q^{cp}(x_t) - q_{jt} + r]$$
$$-q_{j,t+1} - q_{jt} + 2r \qquad (22.6)$$

The firm's extraction decision in period t affects the state of the groundwater resource in period $t + 2$ directly; each unit of groundwater extracted in period t is one less unit available for extraction in period $t + 2$. This direct effect is accompanied by an indirect effect arising because the firm's extraction decision in period t influences the state-dependent extraction decisions of its rivals in period $t + 1$ (note that q_{jt} is an argument in q^{cp}). In light of (22.5), the firm's problem can be stated:

$$v^{cp}(x_t) = \max\{\pi(q_t + s) - c(x_t)q_t$$
$$+ \beta v^{cp}[x_t - (M - 1)q^{cp}(x_t) - q_t + r]\} \qquad (22.7)$$

where the superscript on the value function serves to distinguish the present value of the firm's net revenue stream from that arising under the control solution. The necessary condition for an optimum is

$$\pi_w(s + q_t) - c(x_t) = \beta v_x^{cp}(x_{t+1}) \qquad (22.8)$$

The inefficiency of the common property arrangement under the closed loop behavioral model is readily apparent by comparing (22.8) with (22.3). In the closed loop model, firms consider only the *private* marginal user cost of groundwater extraction; that is, firms recognize that their current extraction of groundwater increases the cost of extracting groundwater in the future (by lowering the groundwater table), but they internalize only the private opportunity cost implied by this relationship.

This private marginal user cost reflects strategic interactions between firms. Given the solution to (22.7), and in light of (22.6), the envelope theorem yields

$$v_x^{cp}(x_{t+1}) \equiv -c_x(x_{t+1})q^{cp}(x_{t+1}) + \beta v_x^{cp}(x_{t+2})[1 - (M - 1)q_x^{cp}(x_{t+1})] \qquad (22.9)$$

The identity in (22.9) reveals that the private marginal user cost of extracting groundwater in period t is a linear combination of two costs: (a) the cost arising because extracting the marginal unit of groundwater stock increases the cost of groundwater extraction in period $t + 1$, and (b) the discounted marginal user cost in period $t + 1$. The latter cost is reduced by the term $(M - 1)q_x^{\text{cp}}(x_{t+1})$, which reflects the pumping response of all other firms to an increase in the groundwater stock in period $t + 1$. One can now tell a simple story. In the closed loop model the firm recognizes that leaving the marginal unit of water in the ground in period t stimulates the groundwater extraction of its $M - 1$ rivals by making extraction in period $t + 1$ somewhat cheaper. Accordingly, the firm's evaluation of the private marginal user cost of current groundwater extraction is lower than it would be otherwise, and it pumps more groundwater. This strategic behavior, where a firm pumps more groundwater to induce its rivals to pump less in future periods, distinguishes the closed loop model from the open loop model.

Other models of behavior are possible. For instance, a small number of firms or individuals may cooperate to achieve the economically efficient allocation of a groundwater resource over time.[6] The above discussion is intended to provide a sense of the diversity of behavioral models relevant to the common property arrangement, and to emphasize that myopic behavior represents the "worst case scenario" under the common property arrangement, in so far as the firm internalizes none of the social marginal user cost in its groundwater extraction decision, while in other behavioral models the firm internalizes at least part of this cost (for instance, the part which is private).

3 The Role of Groundwater in a Stochastic Setting

The most interesting issues concerning conjunctive use arise when surface water inflows are stochastic. Two such issues are briefly discussed below. Both emphasize the role of groundwater as a buffer against the uncertainty of surface water supply. Both also serve to caution resource managers that the failure to correctly frame the management of groundwater and surface water as a matter involving the joint use of substitute resources in an uncertain world can lead to bad management decisions and large economic losses.

The first issue is whether a groundwater resource is more valuable in a stochastic setting than in a deterministic one where random variables are fixed at their means.[7] This question is addressed by Tsur (1990) and Tsur and Graham-Tomasi (1991). As the authors argue, the significance of the question lies in the propensity of planners to simplify the analysis of groundwater projects by evaluating the projects in a deterministic setting. Economic intuition suggests that groundwater is undervalued in a deterministic setting, because such a setting fails to consider the role of the resource as a buffer against surface water drought. This intuition is supported by simulations for the Negev Desert in Israel reported in Tsur and Graham-Tomasi. The authors found that the *buffer value* of groundwater – the difference between the actual value of the Negev's groundwater resource and its value as calculated in a deterministic setting – ranged from 5 to 84 percent of the total value of the resource, depending on extraction costs, the variability of surface water inflows, and aquifer size. Interestingly, however, the positive sign on the buffer value is apparently an empirical result, not a theoretical one. That is, one cannot rely solely on microeconomic "first principles" to prove that the groundwater resource is undervalued in a deterministic analysis; additional assumptions are necessary. Suppose, for instance, that the model developed in the previous section is modified by assuming that surface water inflow is an independent, identically distributed random variable with mean $\bar{s}$. The water planner's problem is modified appropriately:

$$Mv(x_t, s_t) \equiv \max_{q_t} M\{\pi(q_t + s_t) - c(x_t)q_t$$

$$+ \beta E[v(x_t - Mq_t + r, s_{t+1})]\} \qquad (22.10)$$

where E is the expectation operator. Under central (optimal) control the buffer value is positive if the firm-level *unconditional* expected present value of net revenues from groundwater consumption, $Ev(x_t, s_t)$, is greater than the firm-level *conditional* expected present value of net revenues at $\bar{s}, v(x_t, \bar{s})$, for all feasible values of the state variable x. By Jensen's inequality, this relationship holds if the value function is convex in s for all feasible values of x. In the model above, such is the case if (a) net revenues are concave in x_t and w_t, and (b) the third derivative of $\pi(\cdot)$ is non-negative over the economically relevant range of w.[8] These conditions for positive buffer values are similar to those found by Tsur and Graham-Tomasi (1991). The second condition is not sustained by "first principles" alone. Recalling that $\pi_w^{-1}(\cdot)$ is the derived demand for water, this condition requires that the demand for water is convex. Although this is certainly plausible, and perhaps empirically prevalent, its violation does not violate the standard assumptions of the neoclassical paradigm.

If we accept that in the real world the buffer value of groundwater is usually positive, then deterministic analyses usually underestimate the value of the resource. Consider now a related issue: is the return to groundwater management also underestimated in a deterministic setting? Here the return to groundwater management is measured as the difference between the expected present value of net revenues under optimal control and the expected present value of net revenues under the common property arrangement. The answer to this question turns on the relative magnitude of the buffer values under central (optimal) control and the common property arrangement.[9] To see this, let $v(x_t, \bar{s})$ represent the firm-level present value for net revenues under optimal control in the deterministic setting, and let $\bar{v}^{cp}(x_t, \bar{s})$ represent its counterpart for the common property arrangement.[10] Then with buffer values denoted by $b(x_t)$ and $b^{cp}(x_t)$, respectively, the unconditional expected return to groundwater management at stock level x_t is

$$Ev(x_t, s_t) - Ev^{cp}(x_t, s_t) = [\bar{v}(x_t, \bar{s}) - \bar{v}^{cp}(x_t, \bar{s})] + [b(x_t) - b^{cp}(x_t)] \qquad (22.11)$$

If the buffer value of the groundwater resource is about the same under the common property arrangement as under central control, the usual practice of calculating the return to groundwater management in a deterministic setting provides a good estimate of the "true" return to management, even in the case where $\bar{v}(\cdot)$ severely underestimates $Ev(\cdot)$. Still, this is once again an empirical question, and to date there apparently exist no studies comparing the calculation of returns to management obtained in a deterministic analysis with that obtained from the correct stochastic one.

Surface water inflows are not necessarily purely exogenous; water managers can exert some control over inflows, and the optimal control of inflows depends on the availability of groundwater. A brief examination of this issue provides another view of the buffer role of groundwater. Note first that, because water revenue $\pi(\cdot)$ is concave in water consumption, surface water inflows are more valuable when fixed at the mean value $\bar{s}$ than when drawn from the natural distribution of inflows. That is, Jensen's inequality yields

$$\pi(\bar{s}) > E\pi(s_t)$$

and so

$$\pi(\bar{s}) \sum_{t=0}^{\infty} \beta^t > \sum_{t=0}^{\infty} \beta^t E\pi(s_t)$$

This result suggests the potential for welfare gains from "smoothing" surface water inflows. This, of course, is a significant rationale for the construction of surface water reservoirs. Note, however, that this rationale is diminished by the presence of groundwater, which is itself a source of water consumption "smoothing." In this context, the buffer value of groundwater is the welfare gain from postponing (perhaps indefinitely) those inflow-smoothing surface water projects which would prove economical to undertake immediately in the absence of groundwater.

Suppose, for instance, that such a project is the construction of a surface water reservoir with maximum capacity $\bar{S}$. Let I denote the state of nature concerning the availability of the reservoir, with $I_t = 1$ if the reservoir already exists at the start of the period t, and $I_t = 0$ otherwise. An additional state variable is required to track the volume of surface water in the reservoir; denote this state variable by S, with $S \leq \bar{S}, \forall t$. The state variable S evolves according to a state equation governed by natural inflows s and outflows chosen by the water planner. If the reservoir is constructed in period t, $I_t = 0$ and $S_t = \bar{S}$; if the reservoir is not constructed until some future date, $I_t = 0$ and $S_t = 0$. Construction of the reservoir is irreversible; once the reservoir is constructed, it remains in place forever.

In this new setting, the state of nature is defined by four state variables: x, s, I, and S. Let $\tilde{v}(x_t, s_t, I_t, S_t)$ represent the maximum expected present value of net water revenues given the state of nature at the start of period t. This value function is the outcome of a dynamic programming problem like the one in (22.2), where now the planner makes decisions about groundwater extraction, reservoir construction, and reservoir outflows. As before, implicit in the value function is that optimal decisions are made in all future periods. Suppose the reservoir is not yet constructed ($I_t = 0$) and so the water planner must decide whether to construct the reservoir immediately – that is, in period t – or postpone construction. Let $h^0(s_t)$ denote the expected net present value of surface water given that construction of the reservoir is postponed, and let $h^1(s_t)$ denote the expected net present value of surface water given that construction of the reservoir occurs immediately (the latter value includes construction and operating costs associated with the reservoir). Similarly, let $v^0(x_t, s_t)$ and $v^1(x_t, s_t)$ denote the expected net present value of groundwater given postponement and immediate construction, respectively. The decision to construct the reservoir may be stated as

$$\tilde{v}(\cdot)|_{I_t=0} = \max\ [h^0(\cdot) + v^0(\cdot),\ h^1(\cdot) + v^1(\cdot)] \qquad (22.12)$$

The only interesting case is where $h^1(\cdot) > h^0(\cdot)$; this is the case where the reservoir passes a benefit–cost test in the absence of groundwater. The buffer value of groundwater is defined as the difference $v^0(\cdot) - v^1(\cdot)$; note that $v^1(\cdot)$ is analogous to $\bar{v}(\cdot)$ in the previous discussion. We expect that the buffer value of groundwater is positive; quite simply, groundwater is more valuable in the absence of the reservoir because it serves a buffer role usurped by construction of the reservoir. It is thus immediately apparent from (22.12) that, even in the case where $h^1(\cdot) > h^0(\cdot)$, postponement of the reservoir may be optimal if the buffer value of groundwater is sufficiently large. In other words, because groundwater is available, costly projects to smooth surface water flows – projects which would otherwise pass a benefit–cost test – are optimally postponed.

The buffer role of groundwater is even more pronounced when the potential for using surface water inflows to recharge the groundwater resource is considered. In this case, the variability of net revenues can be further reduced by using the "excess" inflows in wet periods to recharge the groundwater resource, thereby reducing groundwater pumping costs in dry periods. Water managers have diverted surface water to groundwater aquifiers for many years, and no doubt the practice will become more commonplace in the future (see, for instance, Reichard and Bredehoeft, 1984; Danskin and Gorelick, 1985; Pyle, 1988; Danskin, 1990; Pyle and Iger, 1990). For instance, in the Central Valley of California, irrigation districts charged with the procurement and management of surface water supplies for member farmers have for years practiced *de facto* conjunctive use management, by artificially recharging underlying groundwater aquifiers in wet years when water delivered by the Central Valley Project – a system of reservoirs and aqueducts operated by the Bureau of Reclamation – exceeds the perceived "need" of district farmers. Future recharge projects promise to be large and complex, involving interbasin storage and transfer. In light of the high cost of pumping and moving water, some of these projects may ultimately prove uneconomical, despite their buffering effect.[11]

4   Concluding Remarks

The significance of proper modeling to address conjunctive use issues does not end with a discussion of how to model behavior under the common property arrangement, nor does it end with an examination of the buffer role of groundwater. Provencher and Burt (1993) discuss a risk externality present under the common property arrangement when firms are risk averse. In light of the buffer role of groundwater, it should come as no surprise that the riskiness of water revenues depends on the size of the groundwater stock. As the groundwater stock is depleted, extraction costs increase, and the buffer role of groundwater is diminished; firms find themselves less protected against the threat of drought. It stands to reason, then, that each unit of groundwater extracted by a firm increases the risk faced by *all* firms.   But of course, in its extraction decision the firm considers only the *private* marginal user cost associated with this risk effect, and so it consumes too much groundwater. In the absence of information about firm risk preferences, the significance of this risk externality is difficult to assess, and estimating the efficient inertemporal allocation of groundwater becomes a daunting task.

On a similar note, Allen and Gisser (1984) argue that imperfect estimation of the water demand function $\pi_w^{-1}(\cdot)$ used for central control may leave groundwater users worse off under central control than under the common property arrangement. They state, "since it is likely that optimal control and no control will yield close pumping trajectories, the strategy of no control may lead water users closer to the true optimal control when compared with a strategy of optimal control which relies on an estimated demand function" (p. 755). That control provides only trivial gains in economic welfare is a sobering possibility raised in several empirical studies. Gisser and Sanchez (1980) found that control of the Pecos Basin of New Mexico would yield virtually the same level of aggregate welfare as the "no-control" case; a follow-up study using a nonlinear specification for demand also found this result (Allen and Gisser, 1984).[12] In a study of the southern part of the Ogallala aquifer in Texas, Lee et al. (1981) found that control raised the net benefit of groundwater by only 0.3 percent. In a study of the Kern County, California, groundwater resource, Dixon (1989) also found that control raised the net benefit of groundwater by 0.3 percent. An examination of groundwater management in the Texas High Plains found that control raised the value of the resource by 1–3.7 percent, depending on the discount rate (Kim et al, 1989). In the only such study to recognize the stochastic nature of surface water inflows explicitly, Provencher (1991) found that control raised the value of the groundwater resource of Madera County, California, by 2–3 percent. Not all studies have found such modest returns to groundwater management. Among those studies to find that control increases the value of groundwater by at least 10 percent are Bredehoeft and Young (1970), Feinerman and Knapp (1983), Noel et al. (1980), and Worthington et al. (1985).

Groundwater management alternatives
Taken together, the issues raised above suggest that a water planner would be ill-prepared to determine the optimal allocation of ground-water over time, and that the costs of management may often exceed the benefits. Still, there are cases where some form of management is either clearly appropriate, or politically expedient. In this light, it is worthwhile to consider alternatives to central control which are either unintrusive, in the sense that they rely mostly on the private information held by firms, or relatively costless, or preferably both. Two such alternatives are control by local water districts, and a permit system in which a firm's entitlement to the groundwater resource is determined by the number of tradeable permits it holds. Local control might work well in the Central Valley of California, where the current patchwork of irrigation districts and water districts provides elements of the requisite infrastructure. Compared with a single, centralized regulator, these smaller units of control would prove more responsive to changing economic and hydrologic conditions, and more capable of obtaining the production and cost information necessary to make the appropriate allocative decisions. The disadvantage of local control is that in so far as a small number of independent entities extract groundwater from a common aquifer, the potential still exists for inefficient use of the resource. In particular, districts may behave in a manner described by the model of feedback strategies discussed in section 2, with each local district

considering the marginal user cost that its (collective) pumping imposes on its members, and ignoring the marginal user cost its pumping imposes on non-members. Even in this case, however, the broader perspective of a water district charged with maximizing the net present value of the water revenues of its members engenders a welfare improvement over the common property arrangement. Moreover, other forms of behavior which would yield the efficient outcome remain plausible (see note 6).

Another alternative to central control is a system of tradeable pumping permits in which the regulator determines a minimum groundwater stock $\bar{x}$, and allocates among firms tradeable pumping permits corresponding to the difference between the initial (current) stock level and $\bar{x}$. This allocative regime is discussed by Smith (1977), Anderson et al. (1983), and Provencher (1991, 1993a). In essence, each firm's bundle of permits represents its private stock of groundwater. This private stock declines due to groundwater pumping and increases to reflect the firm's share of periodic recharge. It also changes in response to the firm's activity in the market for groundwater stock permits, increasing when permits are purchased and decreasing when permits are sold. As a practical matter, the market price for permits serves to allocate groundwater over time. This particular regime is not economically efficient; both the pumping cost externality and the risk externality persist after the allocation of permits. Still, the regime is more capable than others of exploiting the private information held by firms, and the creation of the permit market provides unique opportunities for risk management. In an empirical application involving Madera County, California, the regime recovered 80–95 percent of the potential gain from groundwater management (Provencher, 1991).

Summary

The discussion in this chapter is intended to provide a sampling from the recent literature of the issues involved in the conjunctive use of groundwater and surface water. Both the discussion of the behavioral models characterizing the common property arrangement and the examination of the buffer role of groundwater emphasize the significance of developing realistic models for policy evaluation. Unfortunately, the difficulty of obtaining appropriate hydrologic and economic data, and the computational burden arising as state and decision variables are added to a model (as would occur, for instance, in efforts to capture the hydrogeologic variation in an aquifer), remain barriers to the development of sophisticated dynamic optimization models. At best, current models provide only a general sense of the economic effects of various management prescriptions. The inability of these models to provide more exact results suggests the need for creative, decentralized forms of surface water and groundwater management.

Notes

1 The water revenue function is simply the restricted profit function $\pi[w_t, p, x^*(w_t, p)]$, where p is a vector of input and output prices and x^* is a vector of conditional factor demands. In the analysis prices are fixed, and so the only explicit argument of $\pi(\cdot)$ is w_t.

2 Because land is fixed for each firm, it is possible to eventually reduce revenues by consuming too much water. Let w' represent the level of water consumption where marginal revenue becomes negative. Here we assume $s < w'$, and so the nonincreasing part of $\pi(\cdot)$ is not economically relevant.

3 The discussion assumes that the groundwater stock is never completely exhausted, because as the stock is drawn down, pumping costs increase to the point where it is not economical to reduce the groundwater stock further. This assumption simplifies the analysis, and is realistic in many instances. This case applies, for instance, where $x > 0$ at the optimal steady state. Provencher and Burt (1993) consider the case where pumping costs are positive and the groundwater stock is exhausted.

4 Kennedy (1986) provides a basic introduction to dynamic programming techniques, as well as a thorough review of dynamic programming applications in agricultural and natural resource economics.

5 Interpretation of v_x is apparent upon substitution. See, for instance, Provencher and Burt (1993).

6 Dixon (1989) discusses noncooperative behavior involving the use of "trigger" or "punishment" strategies, where the credible threat of retaliation keeps all firms pumping groundwater at the efficient rate. Bromley (1991) and Schlager and Ostrom (1992) discuss the prevalence of cooperative behavior to allocate the commons.

7 For the remainder of the discussion, a "deterministic" analysis or setting is one in which random surface water inflows are fixed at their means. This is the typical approach for removing uncertainty from a model.

8 This result is derived in Provencher (1993b).

9 The concept of buffer value is not unique to resources which are optimally managed. One would expect that under the common property arrangement, too, the value of the groundwater resource obtained in a deterministic analysis differs from that obtained when the stochastic nature of inflows is recognized.

10 Note that $\bar{v}(x_t, \bar{s}) \neq v(x_t, \bar{s})$ and $\bar{v}^{cp}(x_t, \bar{s}) \neq v^{cp}(x_t, \bar{s})$. In both inequalities, the function on the left-hand side implies $s = \bar{s}$ in *all* future periods, while the function on the right-hand side implies only that $s = \bar{s}$ in period t, and is otherwise a random variable with known distribution.

11 For instance, Pyle and Iger (1990) state that the new Kern Water Bank will provide the California State Water Project with an additional 144,000 acre feet per year in dry years, at an estimated cost (construction plus operating costs) of $70 per acre foot. This additional water represents a marginal increase in a total Project volume which even in dry years rarely falls below 2 million acre feet per year and comes at the opportunity cost of using the water in the wet years in which it originates. It seems improbable that the benefit of moving these marginal units of water from wet years to dry years will exceed the anticipated cost of $70 per acre foot.

12 The "no control" case refers to the common property arrangement where firms behave myopically.

References

Allen, R. C. and Gisser, M. 1984: Competition versus optimal control in groundwater pumping when demand is nonlinear. *Water Resources Research*, 20, 752–6.

Anderson, T. L., Burt, O. R. and Fractor, D. T. 1983: Privatizing groundwater basins: a model and its application. In Terry L. Anderson (ed.), *Water Rights: Scarce Resource Allocation, Bureaucracy, and the Environment*, San Francisco, CA: Pacific Institute for Public Policy Research.

Andrews, B. T. and Fairfax, S. K. 1984: Groundwater and intergovernmental relations in the southern San Joaquin Valley of California: what are all these cooks doing in the broth? *University of Colorado Law Review*, 55, 149–269.

Bellman, R. 1957: *Dynamic Programming*. Princeton, NJ: Princeton University Press.

Bertsekas, D. P. 1976: *Dynamic Programming and Stochastic Control*. New York: Academic Press.

Bredehoeft, J. D. and Young, R. A. 1970: The temporal allocation of ground water – a simulation approach. *Water Resources Research*, 6, 3–21.

Bredehoeft, J. D. and Young, R. A. 1983: Conjunctive use of groundwater and surface water: risk aversion. *Water Resources Research*, 19, 1111–21.

Bromley, D. W. 1991: *Environment and Economy: Property Rights and Public Policy*. Oxford: Basil Blackwell.

Brown, G. and Deacon, R. 1972: Economic optimization of a single-cell aquifer. *Water Resources Research*, 8, 557–64.

Brown, G. and McGuire, C. B. 1967: A socially optimum policy for a public water agency. *Water Resources Research*, 3, 33–44.

Burness, H. S. and Martin, W. E. 1988: Management of a tributary aquifer. *Water Resources Research*, 24, 1339–44.

Burt, O. R. 1964a: The economics of conjunctive use of ground and surface water. *Hilagardia*, 36, 110pp.

Burt, O. R. 1964b: Optimal resource use over time with an application to groundwater. *Management Science*, 11, 80–93.

Burt, O. R. 1967a: Groundwater management under quadratic criterion functions. *Water Resources Research*, 3, 673–82.

Burt, O. R. 1967b: Temporal allocation of groundwater. *Water Resources Research*, 3, 45–56.

Cummings, R. G. and McFarland, J. W. 1974: Groundwater management and salinity control. *Water Resources Research*, 10, 909–15.

Danskin, W. R. 1990: The role of ground water in ameliorating long-term water scarcity. In Johannes J. Devries (ed.) *Proceedings of the Seventeenth Biennial Conference on Ground Water*, Water Resources Center, University of California, Report 72.

Danskin, W. R. and Gorelick, S. M. 1985: A policy evaluation tool: management of a multiaquifer system using controlled stream recharge. *Water Resources Research*, 21, 1731–47.

Dixon, L. S. 1989: Models of groundwater extraction with an examination of agricultural water use in Kern County, California. Ph.D. Dissertation, University of California.

Dudley, N. J. 1988: Capacity sharing of water resources. *Water Resources Research*, 24, 649–58.

Feinerman, E. and Knapp, K. C. 1983: Benefits from groundwater management: magnitude, sensitivity, and distribution. *American Journal of Agricultural Economics*, 65, 703–10.

Gisser, M. 1983: Groundwater: focusing on the real issue. *Journal of Political Economy*, 91, 1001–27.

Gisser, M. and Sanchez, D. A. 1980: Competition versus optimal control in groundwater pumping. *Water Resources Research*, 16, 638–42.

Howitt, R. E. and M'Marete, M. 1990: The value of groundwater in adapting to drought: lessons from 1976–1977. In Johannes J. Devries (ed.), *Proceedings of the Seventeenth Biennial Conference on Ground Water*, Water Resources Center, University of California, Report 72.

Kennedy, J. O. S. 1986: *Dynamic Programming: Applications to Agriculture and Natural Resources.* New York: Elsevier.

Kim, C. S., Moore, M. R., Hanchar, J. J. and Nieswiodomy, M. 1989: A dynamic model of adaptation to resource depletion: theory and application to groundwater mining. *Journal of Environmental Economics and Management,* 17, 66–82.

Lee, K. C., Short, C. and Heady, E. O. 1981: Optimal groundwater mining in the Ogallala Aquifer: estimation of economic losses and excessive depletion due to commonality. Unpublished manuscript, Center for Agricultural and Rural Development, Iowa State University.

Llop, A. and Howitt, R. 1983: On the social cost of groundwater management: the role of hydrologic and economic parameters on policy actions. Unpublished manuscript, University of California, Davis.

Negri, D. H. 1989: The common property aquifer as a differential game. *Water Resources Research*, 25, 9–15.

Nieswiodomy, M. 1985: The demand for irrigation water in the high plains of Texas, 1957–80. *American Journal of Agricultural Economics*, 67, 619–26.

Noel, J. E., Gardner, B. D. and Moore, C. V. 1980: Optimal regional conjunctive water management. *American Journal of Agricultural Economics*, 62, 489–98.

Provencher, B. 1991: A quantitative analysis of private property rights in groundwater. Ph.D. Dissertation, University of California.

Provencher, B. 1993a: A private property rights regime to replenish a groundwater aquifer. *Land Economics,* forthcoming.

Provencher, B. 1993b: Discussion of the buffer role of groundwater. Unpublished manuscript, University of Wisconsin-Madison.

Provencher, B. and Burt, O. 1993: The externalities associated with the common property exploitation of groundwater. *Journal of Environmental Economics and Management*, 24, 139–58.

Pyle, S. 1988: The role of water banking. In Johannes J. Devries (ed.), *Proceedings of the Sixteenth Biennial Conference on Ground Water*, California Water Resources Center, University of California.

Pyle, S. and Iger, R. B. 1990: The promise of water banking: a quantity and quality issue – update on Kern water bank. In Johannes J. Devries (ed.), *Proceedings of the Seventeenth Biennial Conference on Ground Water*, Water Resources Center, University of California, Report 72.

Reichard, E. G. and Bredehoeft, J. D. 1984: An engineering economic analysis of a program for artificial groundwater recharge. *Water Resources Bulletin,* 20, 929-39.

Schlager, E. and Ostrom, E. 1992: Property rights regimes and natural resources: a conceptual analysis. *Land Economics,* 68, 249–62.

Smith, V. L. 1977: Water deeds: a proposed solution to the water valuation problem. *Arizona Review,* 26, 7–10.

Tsur, Y. 1990: The stabilization role of groundwater when surface water supplies are uncertain: implications for groundwater development. *Water Resources Research,* 26, 811–18.

Tsur, Y. and Graham-Tomasi, T. 1991: The buffer value of groundwater with stochastic surface water supplies. *Journal of Environmental Economics and Management,* 21, 201–24.

Worthington, V. E., Burt, O. R. and Brustkern, R. L. 1985: Optimal management of a confined groundwater system. *Journal of Environmental Economics and Management,* 12, 229–45.

23

Minerals Policy

Richard L. Gordon

Governments throughout the world employ extensive programs directly and indirectly affecting mineral supply. This is true whether or not the definition of minerals includes energy.[1] The interventions involve using all the main policy tools – taxation (of wildly different types), property right laws, subsidies, controls of many sorts over pricing decisions, and nationalization.

The present chapter centers on two aspects of mineral policy – controls by land policy and controls by price and tax regulation. Mineral land policy, particularly in the United States, is part of overall land use policy. Thus, perspectives are given on the framework into which mineral policy fits.

Since explicitly environmental policies affecting minerals are the subject of several other chapters in this book, they are ignored here. However, another way to attain environmental goals is through rigorous enforcement of policies designed to limit supply for nonenvironmental reasons. This indirect approach to environmental goals is widely employed and thus commented upon here.

As often occurs with public policies, totally contradictory forces influence practice. Natural resources are routinely considered national treasures, but disagreement prevails about what this implies. Concerns exist that the resources will be overdeveloped and that, whether or not the development is excessive, private profits will be too high. Others worry that the outcome will be insufficient or at least inappropriately located operations.

Some policies are designed to squeeze out more than all of the excess profits earned in the industry. Other programs seek to subsidize (in the broadest sense of the term). Not only are different industries treated dissimilarly, but the accretion of programs in a given sector may simultaneously subject the same sector to procedures with opposed objectives. Frequently, revenues raised from mineral production are used to subsidize government projects in which mineral producers share the benefits.

Fears of excesses inspire governments to regulate usage and to extract revenues from those using the resources. As shown here, the practice rarely employs the efficient taxes of rents stressed in natural resource theory. Often, an effort is made to transfer the rents to consumers through some form of price controls. The apprehensions of inadequate development lead to implementing the many types of interventions that can aid industry progress.

Neither the tendency to intervene nor the ambivalence about goals are unique to minerals. Indeed, many important mineral interventions are part of broader policies such as the US government's heavy involvement in land ownership and management. Mineral regulation may be rationalized by national security industry arguments to a greater degree than actions elsewhere.

However, agricultural policies are worse examples of other faults. In particular, intervention is more expensive. In addition, farm policy is also a more clear-cut example of the stress on aiding sunset – rather than emerging – industries and of mindless invocation of a "basic industry" concept to justify aid. Economic theory gives many rationales for regulation, but importance to the economy is not among these justifications.

In this chapter, discussion begins by indicating the different ways in which each key policy goal can be attained. Then, study turns to examples. Rather than attempt detailed discussions of the many programs that arose, the essence of key cases is given. Typically, the specifics are of interest only to those directly involved.

Review begins with experience with US federal land management. This is contrasted with ventures into price controls that have arisen. Attention is given the way in which tax and international trade policies were used to stimulate US mineral production. Examples are given of experience in other countries with both rent taxation and industry promotion. Note is taken of how nationalization elsewhere often proved more an output-stimulating than a government income-raising action. Finally, attention is given to the periodically revived efforts to develop schemes to stabilize the prices of minerals and other commodities.

Conceptual Background

Much of the concern over mineral and other natural resources involves economic rents, particularly those attributable to the economic superiority of a given property. Rents are incomes in excess of that needed to recover all economic costs including that of using equity capital. The main categories are those mentioned due to access to a superior resource and those emanating from monopoly.

Some writers imprecisely talk of Hotelling rents, the excess of revenues over current production costs that rewards saving resources for later generations. (Hotelling is the author of a 1931 article that at least sketched all the critical elements of exhaustible resource theory.) Care should be taken to distinguish between the rent portion and the interest earned from waiting. A mineral property may be more valuable if some immediate profits are sacrificed for higher gains in future generations. A fast literature, most recently surveyed by Sweeney, deals with the consequences of exhaustion.

Many discussions, moreover, suggest that the benefits of saving for future generations are a major influence on mineral decision making. However, strong criticism has been expressed by many practitioners of applied mineral market analysis – starting at least with Orris Herfindahl. Adelman (1993) asserted that the ultimate stock of resources is economically irrelevant. Markets behave as if the stock was effectively infinite (or, if you prefer, the availability constraints are for some reason nonbinding).

One great tradition in economics is that rents are a desirable revenue source. Since rents by definition are incomes in excess of those needed to sustain operations, taxing rents in principle can raise revenue without affecting output. Annexing, in turn, can be effected in at least three ways. The state can make itself the landowner and secure the rents through charges on the leasing or sale of rights to use the resource. Alternatively, the state may choose, whether or not it owns the resources, to impose taxation to extract the rents. Finally, the state might try to own the organizations that exploit the resources and operate them to maximize profits (in a competitive world economy).

Several problems arise with the implementation of any of these schemes. Determination of rents is possible in principle when extensive trading occurs and is well reported. Efficient markets by definition lead to land selling for the present value of the excess over cost the bidder expects to realize when utilizing the land. Government ownership facilitates but certainly does not guarantee maintenance of frequent, publicly reported sales.

As long has been at least tacitly recognized, nationalization is a risky way to collect rents. If the national industry is fully independent, it may possess and utilize monopoly power. (It was for this reason that Lange tried to "save" socialism by redefining it as central planning designed to develop prices more efficient than those employed in the marketplace. The widespread acceptance of his assertion that this could be done looks very silly in 1993.)

In practice, the nationalized firms lack independence and must pursue inefficient policies. Again, the inefficiency can lie in either direction. One danger is that profits are drained into excess hiring and other inefficient uses. Moreover, constraints are imposed that lessen the ability to maximize profits. Conversely, by design or ineptitude, monopoly power may be exercised.

Yet another fruitful conjecture of Ronald Coase (1972) concerns the problems faced by the owner of a durable resource such as public lands in restricting sales to utilize monopoly power. Since land is retained, confidence must be established that further sales will not glut the market. One proposed solution is retention of ownership and limited leasing. While stressing leasing may have other rationales, its popularity may be due to a desire to establish a credible monopoly. A practice of leasing that concentrates on "adequacy" of revenues to government may produce monopolistic behavior.

In particular, governments either as owners or taxers can and regularly do use approaches that restrict output. This is often done by limiting public or private sales or imposing taxes or utilization charges that vary with revenue or output. Such charges have the identical distorting effect, discussed in many textbooks, of sales taxes. Thus, in land management, nationalization involves the same monopolization danger widely noted in general discussions of public ownership.

In practice, another major problem is that actual profits are a return to both the land and past efforts to make it usable. This is what may be called the John Locke problem. In 1690, Locke noted, "Whatsoever then he removes out of the State that Nature hath provided, and left in, he hath mixed his *Labour* with, and joyned to it something that is his own, and thereby makes it his *Property*."[2]

Moreover, another classic criticism of imposition of rent taxes on properties that have been held for a long time is that the present owner may not be earning any rents. The rights may have been resold, and on the basis of the argument just stated, the seller will receive a payment equal to the present value of the economic rents. The relevance of this point is examined below.

A more subtle issue is the fixation over optimal efficient timing of sales. In efficient markets, one can only sell too late. The only consequence of a sale before the optimal time to start operations is that the payments are reduced by the cost to the buyer of waiting longer to receive a payoff. The seller can tolerate the reduction because the earlier receipt enables earlier reinvestment to recover the initial reduction in receipts.

The economic considerations that affect the intrinsic ability to compete are inherent in the existence of the land and independent of its ownership. A profit-seeking buyer will not develop before the optimal time. A failure of government to release the land would foreclose timely development.

Delay is unlikely to have clear equity advantages. A systematic examination of the classic market failures indicates that changing timing will not directly cure the problem. Any monopoly problems or failures to internalize environmental externalities will persist; time might or might not eliminate the failures. Even if capital market and foresight problems exist, it is unclear what they are and how limiting sales at any time would cure them. Thus, optimal timing is a dubious concept.

Another policy tradition is to seek rent suppression instead of rent collection. Suppression involves various forms of price controls.These may be imposed by legislation as was done for oil in the 1970s or by establishing a regulatory agency such as those that regulated natural gas prices from the 1950s to the 1990s. In either case, the rent reduction usually is effected by reducing supply and creating an excess demand. The regulators then must undertake further programs to determine the basis on which the supplies are allocated.

If the industry is monopolized, it can be shown that price controls can be used to reduce prices to a more efficient level and increase supplies. Energy economists generally argued that this argument had no practical relevance in the United States. The US oil price control system avoided the excess supply problem by adding special features discussed below.

All this suggests that efficient rent taxation is not the true goal of public policy. It also illustrates the problem that "public utility" regulation as practiced extends far beyond what can reasonably be considered natural monopolies. The deregulation efforts of the 1970s and 1980s sought to remove controls from the more competitive industries.

Governments can and do aid industries in many ways – direct subsidies including ones to maintain prices above market-clearing levels, more favorable tax treatment, owning the industry and tacitly subsidizing inefficiently high production, provision of government-produced goods at subsidized prices, implementing programs to limit output, imposing limits on entry of domestic competitors, and imposing tariffs and quotas on foreign competition. Every one of these policies except nationalization of mineral production has been employed towards some US minerals. Nationalization is widespread elsewhere.

Federal Land – the Last Battleground in the United States

While many of the worst US mineral policies have been dismantled, those involving federal land remain critical. The federal government is a major land owner in the Mountain and Pacific states and Alaska. In addition, mineral rights are held on much of the lands transferred to private ownership, and underseas minerals outside the historical limits of state jurisdiction are also federally owned (see table 23.1).

The federal government has moved to decrease the ability of private parties to secure ownership of the land and increase regulation of private use. This follows a worldwide pattern of government exertion of ownership and control of land. The oddity of US experience is the

Table 23.1   Federal share of landownership in selected states, fiscal year 1989

	Federal share
Alaska	67.802
Arizona	43.324
California	45.111
Colorado	34.064
Idaho	62.573
Montana	27.728
Nevada	82.265
New Mexico	33.109
Oregon	48.165
Utah	63.782
Washington	28.981
Wyoming	48.774

Source: US Bureau of Land Management, *Public Land Statistics 1991*, Washington, DC: US Government Printing Office, 1992, p. 5 with correction of an error for California. (Checking showed a large disparity between the figure for California in various prior reports and that in the fiscal year 1990 *Public Land Statistics* report of the Bureau of Land Management (the latest available issue for 1991 reprints the 1990 table without any updatings including a correction). Calls to the Bureau of Land Management led me to Richard Barber of the Sacramento office who determined that the 1989 figure was erroneous and secured the corrected figure usd here.)

conflict between historical practice of private ownership that is strongly endorsed for the rest of the US economy. A country purporting to stress private enterprise continues to keep almost 30 percent of its land in public hands. Every aspect of the federal government's effort to manage this land is severely criticized. Environmentalists call for tighter controls on the inefficiency. Market liberals advocate return to the tradition of encouraging privatization.[3]

Broadly, public policy since the late nineteenth century followed the premise that overly permissive land law was leading to inefficient land use. The US government has moved to retain land ownership and regulate its utilization. Economists specializing in public land (e.g. Clawson, 1983) counter that, in fact, land law was inadequately responsive to the difference between the territory east of the Mississippi and that in the West. Law that led to the nearly total disposal of eastern land failed in the West. The emphasis in the law on encouraging small homesteads for farming was inappropriate for the arid West. Different activities such as ranching requiring much larger acreage were appropriate for the West.

Numerous laws enacted at various times during American history govern the management of this land for different purposes. Instead of crafting a law that allowed land to go to its most profitable use, Congress took a piecemeal approach and designed laws for individual sectors. Associated with these laws are numerous federal management programs.

The core of criticism of this approach is that no rationale exists for retaining so much land in public ownership. Large amounts of the land are used for purely private purposes such as ranching, farming, and timber growing. Except perhaps in the last case, the environmental amenities are limited and certainly not obviously greater than those associated with farming, ranching, and timber growing on private lands.

The retention is a glaring contrast to the general stress on private ownership in US public policy. The record indicates that the standard reasons for this preference are validated. The key federal agencies – the Bureau of Land Management (BLM), the Mineral Management Service (MMS), the Forest Service, and the National Park Service – display all the shortcomings that cause distrust of government ownership. Their responsibilities greatly exceed the resources provided to attain them.

Thus, privatization has wide support among the observers. The difference from a moderate such as Clawson and an ideologue such as Hanke is of degrees. Clawson would start with the land with no obvious amenity value. Hanke would dispose of everything.

Among the special programs are those governing mining. The mineral situation since 1920 involves a sharp division of resources into two categories. The Mining Law of 1872 still governs rights to metal deposits. Under the law, it was effectively presumed that mineral exploitation invariably was the best use of land and had unqualified preference. Anyone who found a valuable mineral deposit and undertook work to develop it was qualified to obtain ownership.

Differences in the nature of finding and exploiting metals compared with other minerals led to the Mineral Leasing Act of 1920. The later Act established a basic distinction between locatable and leasable minerals. The former, mostly metals, are governed under the 1872 system by which the person who first locates the deposit enters a claim which if granted allows the transfer of ownership to that claimant.

Those minerals made leasable were principally oil, gas, and coal but also include other minerals such as sulfur and other fertilizer minerals. Presumably the rationale for oil and gas are that their extraction is of limited duration and does not materially obstruct surface uses. For some of the more common materials, the concern is that mining claims were often used to secure access for other uses. With coal, the main issue may have been the large amount of land in which the government had retained coal resource ownership when selling the surface.

Leasing might have seemed a preferable way to limit the extent to which acquisition of coal rights caused difficult-to-resolve conflicts with surface owners. In fact, the change perpetuated the tensions. This is a case in which Coase's celebrated analysis of social costs clearly applies. Given the right laws, an efficient private solution could emerge. What is needed is a system by which the coal rights can be freely obtained and be used or sterilized as the owner prefers.

Leasing has the intrinsic drawback that the rights are of limited duration. The situation is aggravated by provisions that preclude sterilization. Leases are lost if they are not exploited.

Originally, further distinctions were made for leasable minerals between those properties on which the existence of minerals was known and those on which it was not. When existence was known, competitive bidding was required; otherwise priority was given to the discoverer. As the difficulties of distinguishing which properties had "known" minerals became more evident, a shift to only competitive bidding arose. The criteria for deciding whether a property has clear economic potential are inherently unclear. The BLM lacks the resources fully to monitor the information available on different locations.

Moreover, increasing efforts were made to ensure that greater revenues were secured from production of leasable minerals. This produces formidable problems. Close scrutiny is exercised over BLM and MMS to avoid the appearance of giveaways. Some members of Congress specialize in searching for giveaways. The environmental movement has found that claims of inadequate payment are another way to block development.

The problem has been more effectively surmounted in oil and gas than in coal. A long history of oil and gas leasing has established a record of securing high payments for leases. Despite this record, the DOI must regularly meet charges of giveaways and has developed elaborate methods for evaluating the adequacy of bids. The reliance on royalties creates the additional administrative burden of ensuring that accurate metering of output is effected.

Another complication is the use of administrative discretion and legislation to restrict offshore exploration on environmental grounds. Such restrictions are more sweeping than typically adopted. Moreover, the actions probably are harmful to the environment. Oil spills of all sorts tend to have small and transitory effects. Tanker accidents are more frequent than field blowouts. A drilling ban is likely to increase tanker imports of oil and thus produce more rather than less damage.

Competitive bidding for coal leases began in earnest only in 1981, and the problems of evaluating the outcomes produced such a furor that leasing was suspended in 1983 and by 1993 had not resumed.

To date, the old system remains in force for metals. The system had an initial major drawback of giving mineral use unqualified priority. As often occurs in public land law, the correction was not undertaken in the most direct possible fashion. The ideal would have allocated access by allowing potential users for all activities to compete for the rights. Instead, exclusions of land from mining claims were adopted.

Those concerned with rent collection object to the absence of access charges. The existence of state taxes on production, however, is ignored in these assertions. Further problems arise with all public land operations from the effects of the long duration of many of the access rights. As a result, many of the rents were collected by long-dead original owners. The transferability of mineral rights is assured by the grant of ownership. The system has features that often allow effective transfer of rights to leases. For example, with grazing, the rights to federal land use are typically given the owners of adjacent private lands. The access to federal land is sufficiently well assured that sellers of the private lands can charge for the benefits of these entitlements.

In the early 1990s, efforts were mounted to reform the mining law. The emphasis is on rent collection, limiting favoritism of mining use, and controlling environmental impacts. Questions then arise of whether these changes will be as limiting as those in coal.

Land Law Around the World – Controlled Private Use and Public Operation

Intervention in land law, particularly that related to mineral rights, prevails throughout the world. Private activity is widely restricted and in many cases prohibited. The record is vast but variably documented. Among the most studied regimes involving restricting private uses is the development of oil and gas resources in the North Sea – particularly in the British and Norwegian portions. Initial British policy was severely criticized for inefficiencies, notably the efforts to overstimulate exploration drilling. (Bidders could trade off additional drilling outlays for lease payments.) The Norwegians are used as examples of the chronic tendency to demand unrealistically high payments. Gas development was delayed until payment demands were lowered.

Similarly, the formidable problems of ensuring the competitiveness of waterborne shipment of natural gas were aggravated by demands for high tax payments. Ocean transport can be made economic only if the gas is liquefied at low temperatures. Heavy investments then are needed to effect the liquefaction, to construct ships that maintain the liquefaction, and to receive and decompress the gas. Gas in a field far from the seashore and separated from major markets by sea is far less valuable than gas delivered to major industrial centers. Establishing a tax regime that treats the economics realistically has aggravated the difficulties.

In practice, the problem was mainly overestimation of how valuable gas would be when delivered. Demands were driven by exaggeration of both the prospects of rising energy prices and the relationship between oil and gas prices. Traditionally, the marginal use of gas was in industry in which it competed with heavy fuel oil – the cheapest major oil product – and sold at prices competitive with those of heavy fuel oil. Expectations arose that gas would become too scarce to compete in these markets and would be competitive in retail markets that use the more expensive lighter distillate oil and sell at distillate oil parity.

However, even greater problems arose with nationalization. It proves all too often to be another way for the government to promote inefficiency. The possibilities for feather bedding and inefficiency noted above are realized very frequently. Here as with most of the criticisms, nationalization is only one of many ways that defects can arise. Governments can impose restrictions on private firms that force overstaffing.

Complaints are widespread of overstaffed nationalized companies forced by political pressures to make inefficient decisions. This can involve underdevelopment of potentially profitable ventures, the perpetuation of unprofitable activities, or even both simultaneously.

At least two barriers arise to efficient development of potentially attractive opportunities. First, limits may be imposed upon how resources are developed. Adelman (1993) suggests that national oil companies universally are restrained from securing the services of the foreign private firms most experienced in resource development – the large established oil companies plus the leading drilling service firms.

A special problem of nationalization is that being part of government can be a curse. Another Coase principle (expressed in several places in Coase, 1988), that the state appropriation process may divert funds to less efficient uses than mineral supply development, applies. Moreover, many governments have so badly mismanaged their finances that the ability to borrow for all purposes including mineral development is drastically limited. In many cases, the mismanagement is closely associated with imprudent borrowing in anticipation that commodity booms would last forever.

The last problem is somewhat unfairly labeled the Dutch disease because of frictions in the Dutch reaction to discovery of large natural gas deposits. All indications are that these impacts were far smaller than those of such countries as Mexico and Nigeria that still are shaking off the effects of borrowing so large and unprofitable that their ability to raise money is severely restricted.

The proposed North American Free Trade Area among the United States, Canada, and Mexico is criticized because it does little to overcome the problems of the prevailing Mexican energy situation. The nationalized Mexican petroleum industry suffers from all the problems noted – overstaffing, constraints on the use of foreign firms in development, competition for funds, and a government debt management problem.

Similarly, many examples can be given of nationalized industries supporting inefficient operations. The best documented cases involve coal in the United Kingdom. However, subsidies preserve the nominally private coal industry of Germany. (The creation of a supercorporation with private stockholders, *Ruhrkohle,* to manage most of the industry and serve as a funnel for state aid may be *de facto* socialization.) Suggestions arise that unprofitable metal mines in Africa and South America are kept operating.

Depletion Allowances

Another way to promote mineral production is to adopt tax incentives instead of rent taxes. The United States is notorious for its long-standing devotion to such incentives. In particular, percentage depletion allowances long have been a feature of US tax law. The provision was originally confined to oil and gas production, then extended to other minerals, and later withdrawn in stages from oil and gas production.

A depletion allowance is simply an allowed "expense" deducted in computing taxable income. The allowance was set at some percentage of gross revenues such as the initial 27.5 percent figure initially adopted for oil and gas with a limit of no more than half of new income before the allowance. (The percentages for other minerals were lower.)

Industry apologists for the allowances talked about the need to recapture capital values. However, the only capital values recovered would be earned economic rents. Ordinary depreciation allows for (partial) recapture of both the cost of investment in facilities and any payments to the original owners. Stephen McDonald (1963) examined a more sophisticated argument that the allowance overcomes deficiencies in the tax code that prevent tax-free recapture of past investment. He concluded that these were pervasive deficiencies that justified general tax reform rather than special provisions for minerals.

Pro-rationing

Yet another Coase-type problem is the appropriate property law for oil and gas. Oil and gas, unlike solid minerals, can be extracted by operating wells outside the land above the oil or gas. American law took the unfortunate step of allowing landowners to remove all the oil and gas they desired. This produced various inefficiencies including incentives for drilling wells that transferred ownership rather than added to productive capacity.

An answer to the question of how best to ensure that the efficient outcome occurs remains unclear. In the oil and gas case, the goal is to organize operations so that each field is managed as a unified entity; this outcome is termed unitization. Some evidence suggests that the incentives to private solutions are so great that government need only refrain from creating any obstacles to unitization. Other evidence suggests that large-number bargaining problems require the state to force agreements to unitize.

Whatever the correct answer, actual practice involved first trying an administrative alternative to unitization and then moving to require unitization. The administrative approach was to attempt to regulate production. The rules were complex and varied from state to state and over time in each state. What caused particular concern was the effort in several key states such as Texas to employ what was termed marked demand pro-rationing.

The approach went beyond limiting output to levels that would have occurred under unitization. An effort was made to limit output to market demand. Clearly, a tacit target price must be assumed in determining demand, but that assumption was never disclosed. Texas, for example, adopted the legal fiction that market demand should be defined without considering price.

Experience in the 1960s suggested a tacit accord between the states and the federal government to keep nominal oil prices stable. With large supplies of then cheap oil available abroad, import controls were needed – and provided – to lessen pressures on prices. The US government tended to vary import levels to prevent rises in nominal prices.

Pro-rotationing, like many actual cartels, was designed more to protect the weak than to maximize joint profits. To lessen the severe regulatory problems, the states exempted small producers from controls. Thus, a fringe of exempt operators arose. Buy their nature, their numbers were greater and thus more politically potent than efficient producers. (Consider a case in which it takes 100 small wells to produce what the average large well produces. If the small wells supplied 10 percent of output, small-well output is then a ninth, about 11 percent, of large-well output. The 100-to-1 per-well production ratio implies 11 times as many small wells as large.) The main objective of pro-rotationing was to preserve as many small wells as possible.

Entry Restrictions

The main way that countries explicitly restrict entry into mineral production is by giving a nationalized company a monopoly. Controls on performance such as safety and reclamation requirements restrict entry; a fringe of operators who operate in violation of the standards can then emerge. Milton Friedman has forcefully argued that often entry restriction is the primary rationale for such regulations. Later writings such as by Savel and Spilber have indicated the weaknesses of the theoretic case for government intervention into transactions on health and safety grounds. The belief that the government has superior understanding of the hazards involved in the transactions does not survive theoretic or practical scrutiny.

Another type of entry restriction, and of efforts to evade it, is a by-product of output-restricting schemes. Meseroll's study of tin production in Thailand examines the rise of a sector of initially illegal operators who used small boats to pump tin ore from underwater deposits. The government has worked to legalize the activity while limiting its scope.

Minimum Prices and Other Maximum Prices

As noted, rent suppression through price controls is a widely employed policy in minerals and elsewhere. The United States has two notorious cases – the protracted experiment with gas price controls from 1954 to the early 1990s, and the venture into oil price controls between 1973 and 1982. The United States stumbled into gas price regulation. The Natural Gas Act of 1938 was apparently designed to bring gas pipelines under the "public utility" controls to which all transportation had been subjected. The scope of the law was sufficiently ambiguous that Congress long debated clarification. Twice – in 1950 and 1956 – the Act was amended to exempt production from control, and two Presidents vetoed the change and were not overridden. The first, Truman, favored controls; the second, Eisenhower, opposed control but felt that offers of financial aid to at least one member of Congress tainted the bill.

In 1954, the Supreme Court decided that the Act required regulation of prices charged by gas producers. The initial effort employ the standard in public utility regulation of regulating each operation produced a massive backlog of cases. To break this jam, the Federal Power Commission devised a system of area prices. The country was divided into producing regions and, for each, two tiers of prices were established. Gas produced from newly drilled wells into fields containing no oil received a higher price than gas from older wells or from wells in fields in which oil was also produced.

The Natural Gas Act of 1978 complicated the processes by establishing many more categories of gas. Each category was subjected to a different initial ceiling price. Differences also prevailed in both the formulas for adjusting ceilings and how long the ceilings were to be imposed. Some were supposed to be perpetual but were repealed in 1989.

The oil controls started as part of the Nixon administration's experiment with price controls (as an anti-inflation device) but were continued in energy-specific programs. Again, many distinctions were made of types of wells – and with each distinction came different initial ceilings and formulas for change. The controls were scheduled to end in the early 1980s; one of the first acts of the Reagan administration was to end the controls immediately.

A standard price control system creates an excess demand and the need to devise nonprice rationing methods (figure 23.1). This occurred with natural gas control and led to a system of priorities with households having the highest priority and electric utilities the lowest.

Close substitutes are those commodities on which those whose desire to spend is frustrated by a price control system redirect their expenditures. This is most interesting in cases such as oil and gas in which the identity of substitutes is well known. As suggested above, the oil system was designed to take advantage of the tendency of frustrated buyers of domestic oil to turn to imports. A tax and rebate system eliminated most of any advantage of access to cheap domestic crude and mot disadvantage of heavy importing. Those with cheap average crude oil costs made a payment that was largely used to compensate those with above-average costs. (Following practices employed with oil import controls, some of the revenues were drained off to subsidize small refineries. These then proliferated.)

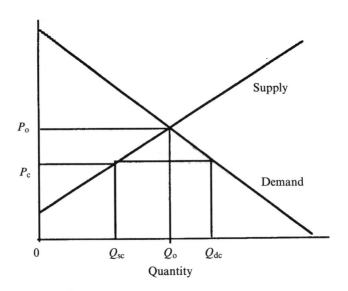

Figure 23.1   Excess demand under conventional price controls.

Effectively then the supply curve seen by domestic refiners started out as the domestic supply curve under ceilings. When output reached the maximum producible under ceilings, imports augmented the supply. The price-averaging method meant that, rather than pay the world price for this oil, refiners paid the weighted average of domestic and foreign prices. As imports gained a greater weight in total supplies, this weighted average rose. Nevertheless, the market could clear at the weighted average price at which the quantity demanded equaled the quantity supplied. Since the weighted average was below world prices, the amount of oil consumed was higher. Given the normal production-suppressing effects of a ceiling, the higher consumption and lower domestic output meant higher imports than without price controls.

The effects of a multitiered price control system complicate the appraisal. With sufficient cleverness and luck, domestic supplies could be increased. The minimum requirement to attain this outcome is that the highest tiers get ceilings above world prices. A further, unlikely requirement is that the incentives to production in the higher tier are not offset by disincentives of the lower tier ceilings. This was how energy independence was pursued.

Minimum prices cannot be sustained without supporting government programs to suppress excess supply. The usual methods are import controls sufficient to make domestic output salable at target prices, and government purchase programs. A more difficult-to-implement alternative is to pay potential producers not to produce.

Government Services – Dams and Aquifers

Having created its convoluted system of outright land sales, long-term leases, and management plans for every activity, the US government decided to spend heavily on infrastructure in the West, principally hydroelectric dams and irregation projects. While various electric projects were undertaken, the largest by far in the West is the collection of dams on the Colombia river. The US Army Corps of Engineers and the Bureau of Reclamation of the Interior Department both built dams. An independent marketing agency, the Bonneville Power Authority, has the responsibility of dividing up the windfalls from these dams. At a minimum, the dams differ in production cost and tend to be cheaper than the marginal sources of power – coal and nuclear plants. Critics argue that additional subsidies are provided because Bonneville has not adequately repaid its investment.

Bonneville aggravated the situation by appointing itself the coordinator of power planning for the northwest. It devised an elaborate expansion scheme, the core of which was that a newly created Washington

Public Power Supply System was to build five nuclear-powered units. Bonneville guaranteed that the first three units would recover their costs from Bonneville revenues; the remaining units were supposed to be self-supporting. Only one of the five was completed; the cancellation of the last two units was accompanied by what was said to be the largest municipal bond default in US history.

The water projects are less visible but no less problem prone, Again the problem is pricing below market-clearing levels, and the need to decide who gets access. With both power and water resources, many vested interests have arisen with the beneficiaries often those who secured ownership or leases over public land.

Commodity Price Agreements: Cartels or Stabilizers

Commodity agreements greatly resemble in rationale and form farm price-support programs. Intervention is supposedly needed to prevent both undesirable long-term declines in incomes from commodity prices and allegedly excessive cyclical swings in prices. Efforts to support such agreements were among the post-Second World War policy innovations ultimately rejected. The Argentine economist, Raul Prebisch, made a career of advocating stabilization schemes from his United Nations posts – first the Economic Commission for Latin America and later the United Nations Commission for Trade and Development.

However, the concept attracted little support from other international trade and development economists, and the efforts to implement the idea have reinforced the skepticism. No efficiency arguments, and dubious equity arguments, arise from continually keeping commodity prices above their market-clearing levels. If any market failures arise in commodities, they are more likely to be those of monopoly. The time is long past, if it ever existed, when mining companies from abroad could pay countries less than the present value of the economic rents from mining deposits.

Many complications, such as extensive mining output in developed countries and the danger that governments will divert the revenues to other sectors, make questionable whether the transfers truly will aid the victims. Macbean (1966) warned that so many commodities are not dominantly produced by poor countries and, on a weighted basis, not many poor countries are heavily dependent on commodities.

In essence, the criticism reflects a general tendency of economists to object to industry protection as a method of social policy. Resources get trapped for many decades. The advanced industrialized countries have not rescued their farmers from the 1929–33 crash while other sectors have moved ahead. The invariable experience is that the money spent in delaying the adjustment could more profitably have been spent on aiding adjustment. The cost of assisting the most marginal workers aided often turns out to be more costly than immediately granting a lifetime pension.

Stabilization is problematic enough if it could be separated from the effort to maintain high prices at all times. Nothing in theory or practice creates confidence that stabilization fund managers can out perform professional speculators. Indeed, the opposite may be true. Another standard distinction between public and private activities applies. The public sector can cover losses by taxation or, if it has not dissipated it, its borrowing power. Private speculators go bankrupt. Thus, the latter have powerful incentives to anticipate prices as accurately as possible. Persistent errors mean persistent losses and ruin.

The most sustained mineral commodity price stabilization scheme – the international Tin Agreement – eventually collapsed because it could not avoid the pressures to keep prices perpetually above market-clearing levels. Thus, the manager ran out of money in 1985 trying to keep prices at sustainable levels, and at that point the agreement went into limbo.

Conclusion

This sampling of mineral policy experience suggests that many inefficiencies were created. The examples unfortunately are quite representative of the full mineral situation. Throttling of competition and aid to the unworthy are the principal themes.

Notes

The review deliberately draws on general knowledge of policies around the world and seeks not to reiterate my prior extensive writings on intervention in coal. This goal was met more successfully in the examples provided than in the concepts stressed. The latter have universality that necessitated their inclusion.

1 The separation in economics of energy from minerals is fairly recent. From the late nineteenth century until the 1977 transfer of responsibility for selected energy programs to a newly created Department of Energy (DOE), the Department of the Interior (DOI) was the lead agency for policy and data gathering for minerals broadly defined. Moreover, while the DOE took over data gathering and energy research, the DOI retained most of its other responsibilities for energy including the continued commitment to managing federal land resources. Similarly, the broader field of mineral economics was organized long before energy specialists sought a separate identity.

2 Two editions of Locke were consulted – a 1947 Oxford University Press book containing Locke's second essay, Hume's "Of the original contract," and Rousseau's *The Social Contract*, and the 1965 New American Library reprint of the critical edition initially issued by the Cambridge University Press in 1960 and revised in 1963. The wording and spelling of the cited sentence are identical in both, but the later edition adds the italics and capitalizations shown.

3   The latter have generated many appraisals of failures in public land management that suggest the desirability of privatization.

References

Adelman, M. A. 1993: Modelling world oil supply. *Energy Journal*, 14 (1), 1–32.

Baden, John A. and Leal, Donald (eds) 1990: *The Yellowstone Primer: Land and Resource Management in the Greater Yellowstone Ecosystem*. San Francisco, CA: Pacific Institute for Public Policy Research.

Barnett, Harold J. and Morse, Chandler. 1963: *Scarcity and Growth: The Economics of Natural Resource Availability*. Baltimore, MD: Johns Hopkins University Press for Resources for the Future.

Bohi, Douglas R. 1990: *Energy Price Shocks and Macroeconomic Performance*. Washington, DC: Resources for the Future.

Bohi, Douglas R. and Montgomery, W. David. 1982: *Oil Prices, Energy Security, and Import Policy*. Washington, DC: Resources for the Future.

Bradley, Robert L., Jr. 1989: *The Mirage of Oil Protection*. Lanham, NY: University Press of America.

Brubaker, Sterling (ed) 1984: *Rethinking the Federal Lands*. Washington, DC: Resources for the Future.

Carlton, Dennis. W. 1984: Futures markets: their purpose, their history, their growth, their successes and failures. *Journal of Futures Markets*, 4 (3), 237–71.

Clawson, Marion. 1983: *The Federal Lands Revisited*. Baltimore, MD: Resources for the Future.

Coase, Ronald H. 1937: The nature of the firm. *Economica, NS*, 4 (4) (November), 386–405. Reprinted in George J. Stigler and Kenneth E. Boulding (eds), *Readings in Price Theory*, Homewood, IL: Richard D. Irwin, 1952, pp. 331–51; in Ronald H. Coase, *The Firm, the Market and the Law*, Chicago, IL: University of Chicago Press, 1988; and in Oliver E. Wiliamson and Sidney G. Winter (eds), *The Nature of the Firm: Origins, Evolution and Development*, New York: Oxford University Press, 1991.

Coase, Ronald H. 1960: The problem of social costs. *Journal of Law and Economics*, 3 (October), 1–44. Reprinted in Ronald H. Coase, *The Firm, the Market and the Law*, Chicago, IL: University of Chicago Press, 1988.

Coase, Ronald H. 1972: Durability and monopoly. *Journal of Law and Economics*, 15 (1) (April), 143–9.

Coase, Ronald H. 1988: *The Firm, the Market and the Law*. Chicago, IL: University of Chicago Press.

Deacon, Robert T. and Johnson, M. Bruce (eds) 1985: *Forestlands: Public and Private*. Cambridge, MA: Ballinger for Pacific Institute for Public Policy Research.

Deese, David A. and Nye, Joseph S. (eds) 1981: *Energy and Security*. Cambridge, MA.: Ballinger.

Friedman, Milton. 1962: *Capitalism and Freedom*. Chicago, IL: University of Chicago Press.

Globerman, Steven, and Walker, Michael (eds) 1993: *Assessing NAFTA: A Trinational Analysis*. Vancouver: The Fraser Institute.

Gordon, Richard L. 1976: Government policies for mineral development and trade. In William A. Vogely (ed.), *Economics of the Mineral Industries*, 3rd edn, completely revised and rewritten. New York: American Institute of Mining, Metallurgical, and Petroleum Engineers, 735–78.

Gordon, Richard L. 1981a: *An Economic Analysis of World Energy Problems.* Cambridge, MA: MIT Press, 282 pp.

Gordon, Richard L. 1981b: *Federal Coal Leasing Policy, Competition in the Energy Industries.* Washington, DC: American Enterprise Institute for Public Policy Research.

Gordon, Richard L. 1984: Access to federal lands for profit making purposes – an economic overview. *Materials and Society,* 8 (4), 699–718.

Gordon, Richard L. 1985a: Energy policy issues. In William A. Vogely (ed.), *Economics of the Mineral Industries,* 4th edn, New York: American Institute of Mining, Metallurgical, and Petroleum Engineers, 535–91.

Gordon, Richard L. 1985b: Levies on U.S. coal production. *Energy Journal, Special Tax Issue,* 6, 241–54.

Gordon, Richard L. 1987: Coal in U.S. land policy. In John Byrne and Daniel Rich (eds), *Planning for Changing Energy Conditions,* New Brunswick, NJ: Transaction Books, 139–72.

Gordon, Richard L. 1988: Federal coal leasing: an analysis of the economic issues. Discussion Paper EM88-01, Energy and Materials Division, Resources for the Future, Washington, DC, July.

Gordon, Richard L. 1992: Energy intervention after Desert Storm. *Energy Journal,* 13 (3), 1–15.

Hanke, Steve H. 1982: The privatization debate: an insider's view. *Cato Journal,* 2 (3) (Winter), 652–62.

Herfindahl, Orris C. 1967: Depletion and economic theory. In Mason Gaffney (ed.), *Extractive Resources and Taxation,* Madison, WI: University of Wisconsin Press, 63–90.

Hufbauer, Gary Clide, and Schott, Jeffrey J. 1992: *North American Free Trade: Issues and Recommendations.* Washington, DC: Institute for International Economics.

Hufbauer, Gary Clide, and Schott, Jeffrey J. 1993: *NAFTA: An Assessment.* Washington, DC: Institute for International Economics.

Leshy, John D. 1987: *The Mining Law: A Study in Perpetual Motion.* Washington, DC: Resources for the Future.

Libecap, Gary D. 1981: *Locking Up the Range: Federal Land Controls and Grazing.* Cambridge, MA: Ballinger for Pacific Institute for Public Policy Research.

Libecap, Gary D. and Wiggins, Steven N. 1984: Contractual response to the common pool problem: prorationing of crude oil production. *American Economic Review,* 74 (1) (March), 87–98.

Libecap, Gary D. and Wiggins, Steven N. 1985: The influence of private contractual failure on regulation: the case of oil field unitization. *Journal of Political Economy,* 93 (4), 690–714.

Lovejoy, Wallace F. and Homan, Paul T. 1967: *Economic Aspects of Oil Conservation Regulation.* Baltimore, MD: Johns Hopkins University Press for Resources for the Future.

Macbean, Alasdair I. 1966: *Export Instability and Economic Development.* Cambridge, MA: Harvard University Press; London: George Allen & Unwin.

Mancke, Richard B. 1974: *The Failure of U.S. Energy Policy.* New York: Columbia University Press.

Mancke, Richard B. 1976: *Squeaking By: U.S. Energy Policy Since the Embargo.* New York: Columbia University Press.

McDonald, Stephen L. 1963: *Federal Tax Treatment of Income from Oil and Gas.* Washington, DC: Brookings Institution.

McDonald, Steven, 1971: *Petroleum Conservation in the United State: An Economic Analysis.* Baltimore, MD: Johns Hopkins University Press for Resources for the Future.

McDonald, Steven, 1979: *The Leasing of Federal Lands for Fossil Fuels Production.* Baltimore, MD: Johns Hopkins University Press for Resources for the Future.

Mead, Walter J., Sorensen, Philip E. Jones, Russell and Moseidjord, Asbjorn. 1980: *Competition and Performance in OCS Oil and Gas Lease Sales and Lease Development, 1954–1969*. Reston, VA: US Geological Survey.

Mead, Walter J., Moseidjord, Asbjorn, Muraoka, Dennis D. and Sorensen, Philip E. 1985: *Offshore Lands: Oil and Gas Leasing and Conservation on the Outer Continental Shelf*. San Francisco, CA: Pacific Institute for Public Policy Research.

Meseroll, Dennis J. 1992: Structural change in the tin mining industry of Thailand and its implications. Unpublished M.S. Thesis in Mineral Economics, Pennsylvania State University, University Park, PA.

Nelson, Robert H. 1983: *The Making of Federal Coal Policy*. Durham, NC: Duke University Press.

Newbery, David M. G. and Stiglitz, Joseph E. 1981: *The Theory of Commodity Price Stabilization: A Study in the Economics of Risk*. Oxford: Oxford University Press.

Newlon, Daniel H. and Breckner, Norman V. 1975: *The Oil Security System: An Import Strategy for Achieving Oil Security and Reducing Oil Prices*. Lexington, MA: Lexington Books, D. C. Heath.

Plummer, James L. (ed.) 1982: *Energy Vulnerability*. Cambridge, MA.: Ballinger.

Portney, Paul R. (ed.) 1990: *Public Policies for Environmental Protection*. Washington, DC: Resources for the Future.

Shavell, Steven. 1987: *Economic Analysis of Accident Law*. Cambridge, MA: Harvard University Press.

Shwadran, Benjamin. 1973: *The Middle East, Oil and the Great Powers*, 3rd edn. Jerusalem: Israel Universities Press.

Spulber, Daniel F. 1989: *Regulation and Markets*. Cambridge, MA: MIT Press.

Sweeney, James L. 1993: Economic theory of depletable resources: an introduction. In Allen V. Kneese and James L Sweeney (eds), *Handbook of Natural Resource and Energy Economics*, vol. 3, Amsterdam: Elsevier, 759–854.

Tyson, Laura d'Andrea. 1992: *Who's Bashing Whom?: Trade Conflict in High-Technology Industries*. Washington, DC: Institute for International Economics.

US Commission on Fair Market Value Policy for Federal Coal Leasing. 1984: *Report of the Commission*. Washington, DC: US Government Printing Office.

US Congress. 1976: *Federal Coal Leasing Amendments Act of 1975*. Washington, DC: US Government Printing Office.

US Public Land Law Review Commission. 1970: *One Third of the Nation's Land*. Washington, DC: US Government Printing Office.

Verleger, Philip K., Jr. 1982: *Oil Market in Turmoil*. Cambridge, MA: Ballinger for Pacific Institute for Public Policy Research.

Watkins, G. Campbell. 1993: NAFTA and energy: a bridge not far enough? In Steven Globerman and Michael Walker (eds), *Assessing NAFTA: A Trinational Analysis*, Vancouver: The Fraser Institute, 193–225.

Weaver, Jacqueline Lang. 1986: *Unitization of Oil and Gas Fields in Texas: A Study of Legislative, Administrative, and Judicial Policies*. Washington, DC: Resources for the Future.

Weintraub, Sidney. 1993: The North American Free Trade Agreement as negotiated: a U.S. perspective. In Steven Globerman and Michael Walker (eds), *Assessing NAFTA: A Trinational Analysis*, Vancouver: The Fraser Institute, 1–31.

Wiggins, Steven N. and Libecap, Gary D. 1985: Oil field unitization: contractual failure in the presence of imperfect information. *American Economic Review*, 75, 3 (June), 368–85.

Williamson, Oliver E. and Winter, Sidney G. (eds) 1991: *The Nature of the Firm: Origins, Evolution and Development*. New York: Oxford University Press.

Part V

The Valuation Problem

24

Valuation of Environmental Quality under Certainty

Richard C. Bishop and Richard T. Woodward

Theory plays a central role in valuation. It dictates the data that are gathered, how those data are analyzed, and how the results are interpreted. This is equally true whether the study involves valuation of a conventional economic good or service or an environmental amenity. In studies involving the environment, theory governs whether estimated values for environmental amenities can be compared in a meaningful way with more conventional economic values or whether attempting such comparisons will involve the proverbial fallacy of comparing "apples and oranges." Our goal here is to explain the theory of environmental valuation needed to support "apples-and-apples" comparisons. Theoretically sound values are needed if environmental effects are to be incorporated into benefit–cost analyses and related work in such areas as natural resource damage assessment.

For conventional goods and services, markets provide important information about values. Environmental amenities, however, are often not directly purchased and sold in markets. One cannot purchase cleaner air or protection of biological diversity in a store. In fact, because environmental services frequently take on public goods characteristics, effective markets for them may be difficult or impossible to establish in most cases. Hence theoretical research on environmental valuation has focused on non-market valuation.

The starting point for this chapter is a traditional neoclassical model of the consumer except that environmental quality, as well as conventional goods and services, provides utility. Because non-market valuation is tightly linked to the theory of valuation of price changes, a rather detailed review of price change valuation is presented. The theory for price changes is then extended to environmental quality changes. From the theoretical perspective, environmental amenities take on values that are fully analogous to values for market goods.

Though easy to conceptualize, environmental values are difficult to observe. There are basically two choices. One is to ask people directly, through surveys and interviews, about the values they place on changes in environmental quality. This is the so-called contingent valuation method. The other option is to try to capitalize on links between environmental quality and market goods. While many amenities cannot be purchased in markets, gaining access to them involves the purchase of market goods. In such cases, environmental quality changes may *shift* demand functions for associated market goods. For example, improvements in water quality may shift the demand for boats or the demand for gasoline to visit affected beaches. Much of this chapter will be devoted to understanding what can and cannot be inferred about the values of environmental quality changes from observing these shifts.

All conventional approaches to environmental quality valuation except contingent valuation can be linked to the concept of weak complementarity. This concept has been the key to unlocking the conditions under which changes in environmental quality can be valued based on shifts in demand for market goods, and it will be discussed at some length. While the logic of weak complementarity appears to be strong, two important amendments are emerging in the literature that will warrant some attention toward the end of the chapter. First, as demonstrated in a recent paper by Bockstael and McConnell (1993), past applications of weak complementarity have been rather simplistic in their implicit assumptions about the possible relationships that could exist between environmental quality and market goods and about the relative magnitudes of alternative value measures. Second, an important class of values known as existence values may be present for environmental amenities. If so, then weak complementarity conditions are violated, with important implications for the choice of empirical valuation methods and for the interpretation of values based on market demand shifts.

The Problem

Including environmental quality in a theoretical consumer's maximization problem is not difficult. Consider this only slightly modified version of the standard problem:

$$\max_{q} u(q, b) \text{ subject to } p * q = y \tag{24.1}$$

where q is a vector of market goods of known dimension, b is a vector of environmental quality levels of known dimension, $u(\cdot)$ is a quasi-concave utility function with all the standard properties, p is a vector of prices, one for each market good, the asterisk signifies vector multiplication, and y is income. We assume that all market goods are "goods," and not "bads," that is,

$$\partial u / \partial q_i > 0$$

for all elements i in q. Likewise, we assume that environmental quality yields positive marginal utility:

$$\partial u / \partial b_j > 0$$

for all elements j in b.

Environmental quality b incorporates all aspects of the environment that affect the consumer's well-being. Though we refer to it as "quality," obviously it would often be expressed in quantitative terms. Miles of visibility at certain locations, biological oxygen demand (BOD) in specified water bodies, average catch rates of trout from a stream, and any other such measures relevant to the consumer could be included in b. More qualitative measures for, let us say, bad odors or noise could also be present.

Environmental quality is assumed to be provided without ramifications in the budget constraint. That is, b has no price *per se*, and provision of b at various levels will be assumed to have no implications (e.g. through taxes) for y. To simplify the analysis still further, we assume non-satiation for both q and b.

At this point, a review of the standard theory for valuation of price changes for market goods will provide a foundation on which to build a theory for valuing changes in elements of b. For the moment, b will remain constant, but we shall want to pause often and consider the significance of including b.

Valuation of Price Changes

Solving the problem stated in (24.1) yields a Marshallian demand function for each of the market goods in q:

$$q_i = q_i(p, b, y)$$

This seemingly normal, straightforward step reveals one of the theoretical keys to non-market valuation. Elements of the environmental vector b are potentially relevant parameters in the market demand for q_i. Unless

$$\partial q_i / \partial b_j = 0$$

for relevant possible values of b_j, changes in b_j will shift the Marshallian demand function for q_i. This offers a possible avenue for inferring something about the value of changes in b_j from the effects of such changes on the market demand for q_i.

Before attempting to exploit this observation, let us set forth some standard definitions and results. Following standard steps (see Kreps, 1990, p. 45), the Marshallian demand functions are substituted into the utility function, some simplifying is done, and the result is the indirect utility function $v(p, b, y)$. The indirect utility function tells us directly the maximum utility level that can be achieved given some set of prices, some levels for environmental amenities, and income. Note that environmental quality is once again simply carried along as a set of parameters like prices and income.

Likewise, solution of the dual to (24.1) yields the consumer's expenditure function $m(p, b, u^o)$, where u^o is maximum utility as determined from (24.1). The expenditure function defines the minimum expenditure required to reach utility level u^o, given prices and environmental quality. Note next that one would normally expect

$$\partial v / \partial p_i < 0$$

and

$$\partial m / \partial p_i > 0$$

On the other hand, it is quite intuitive to expect that increasing some dimension of environmental quality has the opposite effects:

$$\partial v / \partial b_j > 0$$

and

$$\partial m / \partial b_j < 0$$

Given the way the utility function was set up at the outset, increasing an element of b while holding all else constant would increases utility or, stating the same result from another perspective, increasing environmental quality reduces the expenditure needed to reach a specified level of utility.

As usual,

$$\partial m / \partial p_i = h_i(p, b, u)$$

the Hicksian compensated demand function for the ith market commodity (Kreps, 1990, pp. 54–8). Again, it is relevant to note that levels of environmental quality are potentially relevant parameters. Here, they could act as shifters of the compensated demand functions.

Let us refer to a proposed new governmental policy, program, regulation, or project as the "intervention." Suppose that a proposed intervention would result in a price of p_i^w, where superscript w represents the price "with" the intervention. The price "without" the intervention would be p_i^o. Let p' be the price vector with p_i extracted for separate treatment. All prices in p' are the same with and without the intervention. Let u^o equal the level of utility attainable without the intervention. It would then be defined as follows:

$$u^o = v(p_i^o, p', b, y)$$

"Compensating variation" for the price change, which we shall symbolize as cv, is defined as the amount of compensation, paid or received, that will hold the consumer to the pre-intervention level of utility, given that the intervention occurs. Using the expenditure function, cv can be defined formally in the following way:

$$cv = m(p_i^o, p', b, u^o) - m(p_i^w, p', b, u^o)$$

If the price change is favorable (i.e. $p_i^w < p_i^o$), then cv is positive and reflects the consumer's "willingness to pay" (WTP) for the improved situation. If the "with intervention price" is higher, then the change will be disadvantageous from the consumer's point of view. In that case, cv is negative and represents the minimum compensation required to return the consumer to u^o once the intervention is adopted. Minimum compensation demand will be symbolized by CD, and it will occasionally be useful to express it as an absolute value, $|CD|$.

Using the relationship between the expenditure function and the Hickstead compensated demand function for the good in question, a synonymous definition is

$$cv = -\int_{p_i^o}^{p_i^w} h_i(p_i, p', b, u^o) \, dp_i$$

The minus sign is needed to make the sign of the integral conform with the convention adopted here that WTP values be positive and CD values be negative.

Compensating variation bases value on the level of utility that would have been attained without the intervention. That is, cv is defined using u^o as the *reference level* of utility. We can also define value using the "with-intervention" level of utility, u^w, as the reference point, where

$$u^w = v(p_i^w, p', b, y)$$

Values that arise from price changes based on u^w are referred to as "equivalent variation," which we will symbolize as ev. In other words, ev is the compensation paid or received that will allow the consumer to reach the post-intervention level of utility, given that the intervention is not implemented. In a fashion fully parallel to cv, ev can be defined as

$$ev = m(p_i^w, p', b, u^w) - m(p_i^o, p', b, u^w)$$

or, equivalently, as

$$\mathrm{ev} = \int_{p_i^0}^{p_i^w} h_i(p_i, p', b, u^o)\, \mathrm{d}p_i$$

Interpretation here is parallel to that for cv. If the price change would be favorable (i.e. $p_i^w < p_i^o$), then ev represents the CD (negative) required to achieve u^w in the absence of the intervention. If the opposite holds (i.e. $p_i^w > p_i^o$), then ev represents WTP to avoid the price increase. Hence, it is always the case that, if cv > 0, ev < 0, and vice versa.

Next, consider the relationships between the change in traditional consumer surplus, what we shall call "Marshallian surplus" and cv and ev. Let us symbolize Marshallian surplus by

$$ms = -\int_{p_i^0}^{p_i^w} q_i(p_i, p', b, y)\, \mathrm{d}p_i$$

That is, consumer surplus is the area under the Marshallian demand function and between p_i^o and p_i^w. As we have seen, cv and ev are alternative ways of measuring the value of the price change that would be induced by the intervention. How then is ms to be interpreted? This is a central issue because the Hicksian compensated demand functions needed to measure cv and ev are not readily observable in the real world, while Marshallian demand functions needed to determine ms are observable from market data.

The most direct route to addressing this question is to consider the relationships between the Marshallian demand function and two Hicksian compensated demand functions:

$$h_i(p_i^o, p', b, u^o) = q_i(p_i^o, p', b, y) \tag{24.2}$$

and

$$h_i(p_i^w, p', b, u^w) = q_i(p_i^w, p', b, y) \tag{24.3}$$

This follows directly from duality. For any given set of parameters, the expenditure-minimizing quantity of the good as expressed by $h_i(\cdot)$ must equal the utility-maximizing quantity of the good as expressed by $q_i(\cdot)$.

This correspondence between Hicksian and Marshallian demand functions is important enough in what comes later to warrant some additional discussion. Consider the usual price–quantity diagram, in this case for the ith good, as pictured in figure 24.1. Across a wide range of points in the diagram, each combination of price and quantity will have two demand functions passing through it, a Marshallian and a Hickson demand function. For example, at p_i^o and q_i^o, we have the intersection between Marshallian function $q_i(p_i, p', b, y)$ and the Hicksian function $h_i(p_i, p', b, u^o)$ when each is evaluated at p_i^o.

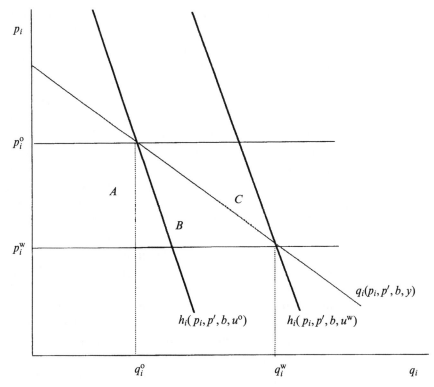

Figure 24.1 Hicksian and Marshallian demands and the corresponding compensating variation, equivalent variation and change in consumer surplus.

The next step in exploring the relationships between ms, ev, and cv is to compare the slopes of Hicksian and Marshallian demand functions. Notice that $y = m(p_i^o, p', b, u^o)$ and hence that

$$q_i(p_i^o, p', b, y) = q[p_i^o, p', b, m(p_i^o, p', b, u^o)]$$

Bearing this relationship in mind, differentiate either (24.2) or (24.3) with respect to price and get

$$\frac{\partial h_i(\cdot)}{\partial p_i} = \frac{\partial q_i(\cdot)}{\partial p_i} + \frac{\partial q_i(\cdot)}{\partial y}\frac{\partial m(\cdot)}{\partial p_i} \qquad (24.4)$$

This is the well-known Slutsky equation for a marginal change in the good's own price.[1] To focus on the slope of the Hicksian demand function, equation (24.4) is written with the "substitution effect" on the left-hand side, the slope of the Marshallian demand function as the first term on the right-hand side, and the "income effect" as the second term on the right-hand side. At any given price for the good in question, the slope of the Hicksian demand function (negative) equals the slope of the corresponding Marshallian demand function (also negative) plus the income effect. If the income effect is zero (i.e. a change in income would have no effect on the Marshallian demand for the commodity) then the slopes of the two demand functions are equal. If the normal relationship holds, where $\partial q_i(\cdot)/\partial y > 0$, then the income effect is positive. The slope of the Hicksian demand function will be smaller (more negative) than the slope of the Marshallian demand function at the same point. Stated less abstrusely, at any given point the Marshallian demand function will normally be "flatter" than the Hicksian demand function passing through that point.

This relationship can be used to compare cv, ev, and ms. Consider the case where the intervention causes a price decrease, as pictured in figure 24.1. The Mashallian demand function $q_i(p, b, y)$ and two corresponding Hicksian demand functions, one through the point (q_i^o, p_i^o) and the other through the point (q_i^w, p_i^w), as shown. In keeping with expression (24.4) both the Hicksian functions are steeper than the Marshallian. The two measures of value can also be seen in the figure. The value of cv is represented by area A.[2] It is interpreted as the consumer's WTP for the price change,. The value of ev is equal to the negative of areas $A + B + C$ and should be interpreted as CD for the assumed intervention.

Marshallian surplus ms is represented by areas $A + B$. The Marshallian measure may be thought of as "inexact" measure of value compared with the "exact" measures, cv and ev. Market data could be used to estimate the Marshallian demand function and ms could be evaluated, but ms would not be an exact measure of either cv or ev. It will overestimate cv by area B. It will also be an underestimate of the absolute value of ev.[3] This is a general result. If the income is positive, then for all price reductions

$$\text{cv} < \text{ms} < |\text{ev}|$$

Likewise, for all price increases

$$\text{ev} < |\text{ms}| < |\text{cv}|$$

The terminology from Hicks (1943) is a bit more cumbersome than is necessary here. By way of summary, it will suffice to say theory predicts the following relationships for a normal good:

$$\text{WTP} < |\text{ms}| < |\text{CD}|$$

For price changes where the income effect is positive, Marshallian surplus (expressed as an absolute value) will always exceed WTP and fall below compensation demanded (expressed as an absolute value).

If ms is an inexact measure of cv and ev, how inexact is it? In a very widely cited article, Willig (1976) argued that in many practical applications the difference is small enough to be ignored. Obviously, the error involved in using ms as a measure of value depends on the magnitude of the income effect. Willig developed a way of viewing this magnitude based on the ratio of ms to y and the income elasticity of demand, parameters that can be estimated from market data. He showed that for many (or even most) practical cases, the error in using ms as a measure of cv and ev will be less than 5 percent. In those cases where the ratio of ms to y in combination with the income elasticity of demand is sufficiently large to make large errors a concern, ms can be adjusted to approximate cv or ev or both more closely. Because this chapter is directed toward non-market valuation, further technical details on Willig's results as they relate to market goods will be left to standard references, including not only Willig's seminal piece but also Hausman (1981) and Mckenzie (1983) and expositional treatments by Just et al. (1982, pp. 97–111) and Boadway and Bruce (1984, pp. 216–21). Randall and Stoll (1980) extended Willig's results to cover cases where interventions affect quantities of publicly provided commodities rather than prices.

Before leaving price changes, reviewing one other aspect will prove useful later on. We have just considered the effects of a good's own price on its quantity demanded. Now consider the so-called "cross-price effects." Let us consider some other market good, say the kth good, where k is not equal to i. If an increase in the price of q_k shifts the *Marshallian* demand function for the ith good to the left (i.e. for marginal changes, $\partial q_i(\cdot)/\partial p_k < 0$) the two goods are said to be *gross* complements. If the opposite holds ($\partial q_i(\cdot)/\partial p_k > 0$), they are gross substitutes. Likewise, if such a price increase shifts the *Hicksian* demand function to the left ($\partial h_i(\cdot)/\partial p_k < 0$), then the two goods are *net* complements and, if the opposite holds, they are net substitutes.[4]

Having kept it in the background in order to review the basics of valuation for price changes, the time has come for environmental quality to take center-stage. Suppose that, rather than causing a price change, the intervention causes some element of the vector b to change. How might the value of the change be defined and measured?

Toward Valuation of Environmental Quality

Suppose that the intervention will affect b_j, the jth element of b. Suppose that, without the intervention, it will stand at b_j^o and with the intervention it will stand at b_j^w. Let b' equal the vector of environmental quality levels with b_j extracted. Since it will be held constant throughout the analysis, b' can be suppressed for notational convenience. Let cs equal the "compensating surplus" associated with the change in environmental quality and es the "equivalent surplus." The convention is to call such measures compensating and equivalent *surplus* rather than compensating and equivalent *variation*. Hicks (1943) originally developed the terminology and he dealt only with price changes. His compensating and equivalent *surplus* measures (as opposed to compensating and equivalent *variation*) restricted the consumer's ability to adjust consumptions levels once compensation was actually paid or received. Likewise, here the consumer has no choice about the level of b_j. For example, if noise from an airport affects a neighborhood, residents of that neighborhood presumably cannot adjust the level of noise if they are compensated for their losses. Hence, to call the value measure here compensating surplus is more or less in keeping with the spirit of Hick's definitions.

Following the same logic as we did for price changes, cs for the quality change can be defined using the expenditure function

$$cs = m(p, b_j^o, u^o) - m(p, b_j^w, u^o) \tag{24.5}$$

where now $u^o = v(p, b_j^o, y)$.

A useful result is obtained by differentiating the expenditure function with respect to b_j, which yields a function reflecting the marginal value of environmental quality of the form

$$h_j(p, b_j, u) = -\partial m/\partial b_j$$

This function, which we shall term the "marginal valuation function," is very much the analogue of a Hicksian compensated demand function for market goods. The minus sign on the left-hand side allows us to portray this function in the usual quadrant. As long as the marginal utility of b_j is decreasing in b_j, $h_j(\cdot)$ will be downward sloping as in figure 24.2.[5] Now cs can be expressed as the integral of the marginal value function:

$$cs = - \int_{b_j^o}^{b_j^w} h_j(p, b_j, u^o)\, db_j$$

If the intervention will have a positive effect on environmental quality from the consumer's perspective, cs is WTP for the change. This is the area depicted as cs in figure 24.2. If the effect of the intervention is negative, cs represents CD, the minimum compensation required to cover the consumer's loss. Equivalent surplus (es) is also easily defined, an exercise that will be left to the reader.

In the way we have just demonstrated, environmental quality can easily be added to standard consumer theory and the results manipulated to define standard measures of value. Even an analogue to the Hicksian compensated demand function exists in the marginal valuation function. No theoretical issues that have arisen thus far need detain us. Rather, the problem is an empirical one. The marginal valuation function for environmental quality is even less observable than the Hicksian demand functions for conventional goods and services. Furthermore, the lack of markets where environmental amenities are bought and sold rules out

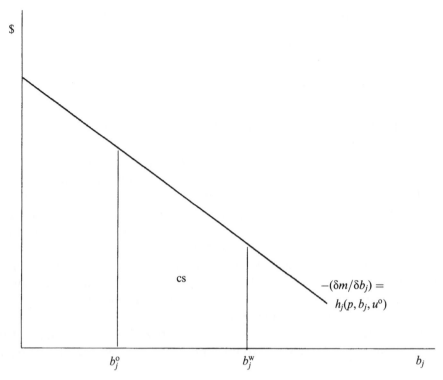

Figure 24.2 The compensating surplus (cs) associated with a quality change from b_j^o to b_j^w.

direct observation of some sort of analogue of ms for environmental quality. Thus, measuring environmental values represents a substantial challenge.

Researchers who would va!ue environmental amenities for consumers have two alternatives. One would be to do a contingent valuation study or some such procedure. Here, a scenario would be developed in the context of an interview or survey describing the change from b_j^o to b_j^w and a sample of affected individuals would be asked to consider the scenario and reveal their values of cs (or equivalent surplus if desired). Contingent valuation does not normally try to estimate demand functions. Instead it asks respondents to calculate their cs or es directly. For this reason, none of the additional issues raised in this chapter arises for contingent valuation. Further discussion of it will be postponed to chapter 28. The alternative to contingent valuation is to try to exploit the fact that b is an argument in the demand functions for q. That is, changes in b may shift the demand functions for some elements of q. For example, improvements in air quality in a central city may increase the demand for properties there. The researcher might be able, through analysis of such shifts, to gain an estimate of cs or es for the quality-improving intervention. This possibility raises issues that are treated under the general heading of "weak complementarity," to which we now turn.

Weak Complementarity

Consider figure 24.3. Suppose that q_i is a market good and that the Hicksian compensated demand function for it in the absence of some quality-improving intervention is given by $h_i(p_i, p', b_j^o, u^o)$. Assume that, if environmental quality is improved to b_j^w, the demand for q_i will shift to the right to $h_i(p_i, p', b_j^w, u^o)$. Continuing to build on the foundation of market-price-change valuation, q_i and b_j will be referred to as net complements in this case, since the improvement in b_j shifts the Hicksian demand function for q_i to the right. Let p_i^e be the market price of q_i and suppose that $p_i^m(b_j^o)$ is a price sufficiently high that Hicksian demand for q_i will be zero if the intervention does not occur. Likewise, $p_i^m(b_j^w)$ will be the "choke price" after the intervention shifts the Hicksian demand function.

Consider a simple example. Suppose q_i is visits to a private fishing site where the admission price is p_i^e per visit. Suppose b_j is water quality at the site and that the intervention would control pollution upstream, causing an

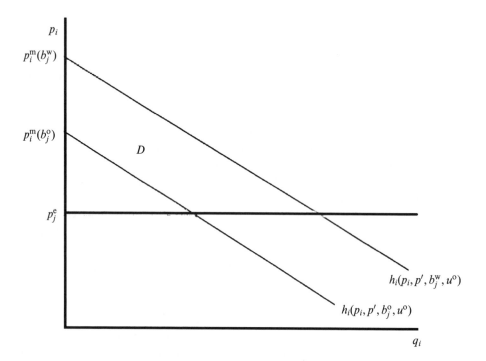

Figure 24.3 Hicksian demand curves and the corresponding compensating surplus (cs) assuming non-essentiality and weak complementarity.

increase in the Hicksian demand for visits. This exogenous improvement in fishing causes the consumer's compensating variation associated with visits to the site to increase by an amount equal to area D in figure 24.3. The question is, what is the relationship between area D and cs?

Drawing on Maler (1974) and following the specific exposition of Bockstael and McConnell (1993), the answer is that area D measures cs exactly if two conditions are met:

Condition 1 q_i must be non-essential. Let $q_i^a > 0$ be some specific value for q_i and let q^a be a vector of goods other than q_i. Then q_i is non-essential if there exists some second bundle of other goods, q^c, such that $u(q_i^a, q^a, b) = u(0, q^c, b)$ for all q_i^a and q^a.

Condition 2 q_i and b_i must be weak complements. Weak complementarity holds if, over relevant ranges of the variables,

$$\frac{\partial u(0, q', b_j)}{\partial b_j} = 0$$

Suppose the consumer is deprived of q_i. Then, condition 1 requires that it is possible to fully compensate him or her with some bundle of other goods. Condition 2 requires that, if q_i is not consumed, utility will be unaffected by changes in b. In terms of the example, suppose our consumer does not choose to visit the fishing site (say, because $p_i > p_i^m(b_j^w)$). Condition 1 requires that it be possible, given sufficient income, for her to reach u^o anyway. Condition 2 requires that, if our consumer does not choose to purchase any visits to the site, then she cares not a wit about water quality there.

A full formal proof will not be presented (see Maler, 1974, pp. 183–91), but an intuitive grasp of the logic of weak complementarity is straightforward. Referring to figure 24.3, area D can be defined as

$$D = \int_{p_i^e}^{p_i^m(b_j^w)} h_i(p_i, p', b_j^w, u^o)\, dp_i - \int_{p_i^e}^{p_i^m(b_j^o)} h_i(p_i, p', b_j^o, u^o)\, dp_i \qquad (24.6)$$

That is, in the example, area D equals the triangle of compensating variation for q_i with the pollution control intervention minus the comparable triangle without the intervention, as can be seen in the graph. Completing the integration yields

$$D = m[p_i^m(b_j^w), p', b_j^w, u^o] - m(p_i^e, p', b_j^w, u^o)$$
$$- m[p_i^m(b_j^o), p', b_j^o, u^o] + m(p_i^e, p', b_j^o, u^o)$$

The second and fourth terms can be combined to equal cs based on the definition of cs given in equation (24.5), so that

$$D = cs + \{m[p_i^m(b_j^w), p', b_j^w, u^a] - m[p_i^m(b_j^o), p', b_j^o, u^o]\} \qquad (24.7)$$

If condition 2 holds, then changes in b_j have no effect on the minimum expenditure required to reach u^o, the terms in braces cancel, and

$$D = \text{cs} \tag{24.8}$$

Next, notice that thus far we have dealt only with Hicksian demand functions, which cannot be observed directly. At first glance, at least, an easy extension of what has already been said can be expanded to addresses this problem. Why not simply estimate the Marshallian demand function for the market good and, based on Willig (1976), use the change in Marshallian surplus that would occur if the intervention to improve environmental quality is activated as a close approximation of cs? Unfortunately for those of us who were comfortable with it, this neat solution has been challenged theoretically in a recent article by Bockstael and McConnell (1993). Basically, results for valuation of price changes have been extended to valuation of quality changes without carefully thinking through the theoretical implications of doing so. Let us see what is involved.

Theoretical Issues Associated with the Approach

The Bockstael and McConnell paper makes three basic points. First, the assumption that improvements in environmental quality will always shift demand functions for market goods to the right may not be justified. Even if environmental improvements increase the marginal utility of a market good, it would not follow automatically that the market good and environmental quality are either gross or net complements. Second, while the error associated with using Marshallian surplus is likely to be small for market price changes, this result does not necessarily carry over to environmental quality changes. Using the environmental-quality-induced change in Marshallian demand as an estimate of either compensating or equivalent surplus involves potential errors that are uncertain in sign and magnitude. Third, and this point is related to the second, one does not dare assume, based on the price change analysis, that the change in Marshallian surplus from an environmental improvement is bounded by WTP and |CD| for that change.

Let us begin to examine these results by supposing that the environmental quality improvement will enhance the enjoyment of only one market good. That is, we assume that

$$\partial^2 u / \partial q_i \partial b_j > 0 \tag{24.9}$$

and

$$\partial^2 u / \partial q_k \partial b_j = 0 \qquad \text{all } k \neq i \tag{24.10}$$

What would be the implication for Marshallian demand of an environmental quality improvement? Using comparative statics, Bockstael and McConnell (1993) show that

$$\partial q_i(\cdot)/\partial b_j \geq 0$$

would hold. In other words, expressions (24.9) and (24.10) are sufficient to ensure that q_i and b_j are gross complements. However, they argue that q_i and b_j are not necessarily net complements under these assumptions. Apparently, it is conceivable that the environmental improvement could shift the Marshallian demand to the right, yet the Hicksian compensated demand would shift to the left!

As before, a Slutsky-like equation can show why this is possible. Recall the relationship between the Hicksian and Marshallian demand functions at the consumer's optimum for all values of b:

$$h_i(p, b, u) = q_i[p, b, m(p, b, u)]$$

Differentiating with respect to b_j reveals that

$$\frac{\partial h_i(\cdot)}{\partial b_j} = \frac{\partial q_i(\cdot)}{\partial b_j} + \left[\frac{\partial q_i(\cdot)}{\partial y} \frac{\partial m(\cdot)}{\partial b_j} \right] \tag{24.11}$$

If the assumptions of equations (24.9) and (24.10) hold, environmental quality and the market good are gross complements. Thus, the first term on the right-hand side is positive. The second term (i.e. the term in brackets) is analogous to the income effect in this context. For a normal good, this term is negative, since income changes would have a positive effect on Marshallian demand and environmental quality has a negative effect on the minimum expenditure needed to reach any specified level of utility. Thus, the sign of the shift in Hicksian demand depends on the relative strength of these two effects. Even though environmental quality enhances enjoyment of the market good and sufficient assumptions have been made to justify concluding that quality and the market good are gross complements, the sign of $\partial h_i(\cdot)/\partial b_j$ could be negative, that is, they could be net substitutes.

This mathematical possibility raises economic issues that have not been resolved at the time of this writing. When we constructed figure 24.3, we assumed the environmental quality and q_i were net complements. This led to area D being positive. If instead they are net substitutes, then D is negative, and as long as weak complementarity holds, the improvement is environmental quality leads to a negative value for cs. However, the way we constructed the problem makes this impossible; cs must be positive. No doubt further theoretical work will resolve this apparent paradox.

Once the assumption in expression (24.10) is dropped and environmental quality affects the marginal utility of goods other than q_i, even gross complementarity is assured only under fairly strong assumptions. In place of expression (24.10), for example, Bockstael and McConnell show that environmental quality and q_i are gross complements if any effect of an improvement in environmental quality on demand for the kth market good will increase $\partial u / \partial q_k$ if q_i and q_k are net complements and decrease $\partial u / \partial q_k$ if they are net substitutes (Bockstael and McConnell, 1993, p. 4). Some such *a priori* restriction on preferences will apparently be necessary to justify the expectation that environmental quality and market goods are gross complements. Even under such assumptions, theoretical expectations about the sign of effects on Hicksian demand are elusive.

This result calls attention to a potentially relevant point about the effects of environmental quality on the demand for market goods. Suppose an environmental improvement will enhance enjoyment of a market good in the sense portrayed in equation (24.9). How could an increase in quality cause the Marshallian and/or Hicksian demand for that good to shift downward? Part of the intuition behind such a result lies in the possibility that the improvement in environmental quality may enhance the enjoyment not only of q_i but also of other goods. If the effects on other goods is stronger than the effect on q_i, then perhaps it will cause the consumer to demand more of the other goods and less of q_i. For example, suppose that we consider two beaches, Alpha and Beta, to be imperfect substitutes. A water quality improvement enhances our potential enjoyment of both beaches. However, it could so enhance our enjoyment of Alpha Beach that we would demand fewer visits to Beta Beach than we would have if water quality had remained at b_j^o. Started more succinctly, water quality and visits to Beta Beach could be both gross and net substitutes.

Questions arise, however, about the applicability of weak complementarity once expression (24.10) fails to hold. Suppose that b_j does affect enjoyment of both q_i and q_k, and that the demand for q_i is to be used to estimate the value of an improvement in b_j. Condition 2 will hold only if the marginal utility of q_k is unaffected by improvements in b_j when q_i is at its choke price.[6] The two-beach example shows how this could be implausible in many practical cases. Would it be plausible to assume that the consumer no longer cares about water quality at Beta Beach if Alpha Beach were closed. As this example shows, the assumption of weak complementarity may be harder to justify *a priori* than has been generally recognized.

A second problem related to the uncritical, informal application of Willig's (1976) arguments regarding price changes to cases of quality changes. To see what is involved, let us assume for the sake of argument that the quality change does in fact shift the Marshallian demand function for a market good to the right. However large might the error be from using the change in Marshallian surplus as an estimate of cs instead of the change in Hicksian surplus? Bockstael and McConnell (1993, p. 10) summarize the traditional wisdom roughly as follows. Willig (1976) has shown that, under plausible conditions, using |ms| to estimate cv or ev will lead to errors that are relatively small and the estimate will always lie between the true values of WTP and |CD|. Since this result holds for price changes, why should not similar results apply to quality changes?

To understand why this chain of reasoning is flawed, reconsider figure 24.1. Bockstael and McConnell point out that Willig's approach works for price changes because the Marshallian and Hicksian demand functions intersect at known points, such as (q_i^o, p_i^o) or (q_i^w, p_i^w).

Now consider figure 24.4, where a quality change has shifted the Hicksian demand for the market good from $h_i(p, b_j^o, u^o)$ to $h_i(p, b_j^w, u^o)$. This part of the new graph is identical to figure 24.3 except that the notation has been simplified slightly for convenience. Figure 24.4 now adds two Marshallian demand functions, $q_i(p, b_j^o, y)$ and $q_i(p, b_j^w, y)$. The "without intervention" Marshallian and Hicksian demand functions in figure 24.4 intersect at a predictable point, namely (q_i^e, p_i^e). However, while the position of the shifted Marshallian demand function might be

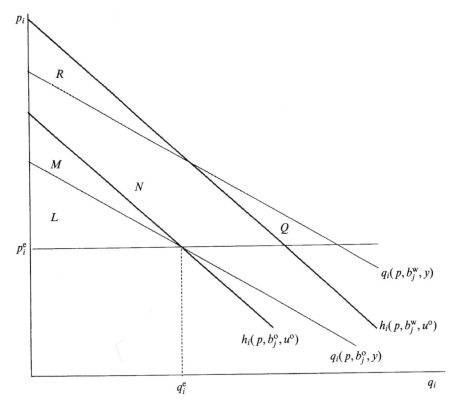

Figure 24.4 The compensating surplus (area $N + R$) and the change in consumer surplus (area $M + N + Q$) arising from a change in quality.

predictable from observable data, the position of the shifted Hicksian demand function would not be. Equation (24.11) indicates that for a normal good the shifted Hicksian and Marshallian demand functions will not intersect at p_i^e but at some other price greater than p_i^e. Where the shifted Hicksian demand function would intersect the shifted Marshallian demand function is impossible to predict without further restrictions on preferences.[7]

This result greatly complicates the error from using Marshallian demand functions to estimate welfare changes. Assuming non-essentially and weak complementarity, the exact measure of the change in compensating variation resulting from the quality change is given by areas $N + R$. The change in Marshallian surplus is areas $M + N + Q$. Using the change in Marshallian surplus as a proxy for the change in compensating variation would therefore be in error by area $M + Q - R$. Based on Willig (1976) one might be tempted to argue that area M is small. However, even here, being too cavalier is not warranted. The price of the good is being pushed to its choke level, which could involve enough Marshallian surplus (as a proportion of income) to make Willig's bounds rather wise if the income effect is relatively strong. The sign and potential magnitude of area $Q - R$ remains impossible to estimate unless the shifted Hicksian demand function can somehow be estimated. Area R is particularly troubling. While Q is within the shifted Marshallian demand function, R is out in *"terra incognita"* from the standpoint of empirical data.

Two conclusions follow. First, this weakens the justification for assuming that a small error results from using the change in Marshallian surplus as the value measure. Second, expectations about relative magnitudes are clouded. To calculate the equivalent surplus associated with the quality change, one would begin with a new reference level of utility given by

$$u^w = v(p_i^e, p', b_j^w, y)$$

and follow the same logic as before to arrive at

$$es = m(p_i^e, p', b_j^w, u^w) - m(p_i^e, p', b_j^o, u^w)$$

Here, es measures the CD that would be required to place the consumer at utility level u^w without the environmental-quality-improving intervention. Assuming that b_j is a normal "good," WTP $< |CD|$ would still hold, but because of the problems just raised in judging how the Hicksian compensated demand function would shift, we cannot predict whether the change in Marshallian surplus for the quality change would be bounded by WTP and $|CD|$.

We must conclude that theoretical guidance for empirical work will be substantially less clear than was generally believed prior to the Bockstael and McConnell paper. That environmental quality enhances consumption of market goods is plausible, but the inference that improved quality will shift demand for that market good to the right has been lost. Furthermore, evidence that the Marshallian demand function will shift in response to a quality improvement should not be taken as definite evidence that the Hicksian demand function would also be affected or that the Hicksian shift would be in the same direction as the Marshallian shift. Finally, concerns about the income effect confusing the analysis are intensified by the fact that a strong income effect can lead to estimates of the welfare effects of a quality change that exceed both |CD| and WTP. The full implications of all this for approaches like the hedonic price method are yet to be explored.

Applied researchers can take one of two directions, given current understanding of this problem. One would be to hope that income effect is sufficiently "small" so that the error from using Marshallian demands will not be large enough to worry about. So long as the change in quality is not too dramatic and the income elasticity of demand for q_i is large, one would be on relatively safe ground. Alternatively, one could estimate a Marshallian demand function of a form that can be "integrated back" to get the expenditure function from which cs can be directly calculated. Bockstael and McConnell, drawing on Willig (1978), discuss some theoretical assumptions about preferences that would make this possible. For better or worse, most researchers will probably take the first course, but without the confidence they incorrectly drew from Willig (1976) prior to the Bockstael and McConnell's insights.

Despite these difficulties, economists will no doubt continue to estimate values for environmental quality changes by examining the effects of those changes on the Marshallian demand functions for associated market goods. In chapter 29, travel and other costs associated with recreational visits will be used as proxies for admission prices to estimate Marshallian demand functions for publicly provided recreational opportunities. Applications of the travel-cost method are not limited to the evaluation of quality changes, but such applications are certainly one of the main motivations. If visits to recreation sites are non-essential and weak complementarity holds between an amenity and the recreational activity in question, then shifts in such travel-cost demand functions might be used to estimate the compensating or equivalent surplus associated with the change. In chapter 30, the relationship between environmental quality and housing values will be used, with hedonic price models, to explore the values associated with changes in environmental quality. Again, if the housing in a given neighborhood is non-essential and the amenity and housing in the neighborhood are weak complements, then shifts in the demand for housing resulting from changes in amenity provision could be used to estimate the value homeowners would place on the amenity change.[8]

It is not necessarily disastrous for non-market valuation if weak complementarity does not hold. Suppose, for example, that data are available to estimate the Marshallian demand function for a market good and that the demand for this good will shift with a change in environmental quality. Assume that the income effect is small in the case in question so that the change in Marshallian surplus for the market good can be taken as a good approximation of the change in compensating and equivalent surplus. Finally assume that a choke price exists so that condition 1 is satisfied. Nevertheless, what are the implications if evidence shows that consumers would still be made better off by an improvement in environmental quality even if they could not afford this market good? If condition 2 is violated, how then is the estimated value to be interpreted? So long as environmental quality is a "good" (rather than a "bad"), the change in Marshallian surplus would represent an approximate lower bound on cs. All that the violation of weak complementarity would mean is that consumers would receive additional benefits from the improvement in environmental quality beyond those associated with the shift in demand for the market good in question.

Weak complementarity might be violated for many reasons. One of the most interesting and potentially important cases where weak complementarity will be violated is existence value.

Existence Value

Existence values are values associated with changes in amenities above and beyond the values associated with personal use of the amenity by the consumer in question. Suppose that weak complementarity (condition 2) is violated for market good q_i. Under our assumptions this would mean that

$$\frac{\partial m[\,p_i^{\mathrm{m}}(b_j^{\mathrm{w}}), p', b_j, u^{\mathrm{o}}]}{\partial b_j} < 0$$

implying that, even though the ith market good has such a high price that it is unaffordable to this consumer, an increase in the environmental amenity would lower the expenditure required to achieve u^{o}. Suppose that this held for all the goods in q. That is, a thorough search through all possible market goods turns up not a single good satisfying condition 2. Such a situation might exist for an amenity, such as a national park or wilderness area, personal enjoyment of which requires travel by car. Let p_i be the price of gasoline.[9] Violation of condition 2 by gasoline in such a case would mean that the consumer's welfare would be affected by changes in the amenity even if she or he could not afford the gasoline to travel to it. Here, the amenity would be said to have an "existence value" to the consumer.

A more formal definition of existence value can be stated by first rearranging equation (24.7) as

$$\text{cs} = D + \{m[p_i^m(b_j^o), p', b_j^o, u^o] - m[p_i^m(b_j^w), p', b_j^w, u^o]\} \qquad (24.7a)$$

Following Randall and Stoll (1983), cs would be referred to as the "total value" of the quality change. Assume that when p_i is at its choke price, the demand for all other market goods is not affected by changes in b_j. The area between the two compensated demand functions for q_i in figure 24.3 (i.e. area D), then, would identify the change in value associated with market goods. Since purchase of goods such as gasoline in the example just given usually involves use of the environmental amenity, this area is referred to as the change in "use value" associated with the change in the amenity. The term in braces is existence value.

Why, one may ask, might the welfare of consumers be affected by changes in the amenities that they do not consume? A number of possible motives might be involved. Altruism toward friends and relatives or toward members of the general public who do use the resource might lead to positive existence values.[10] Altruism toward future generations, either in general or toward one's personal heirs, might be involved. Sympathy for animals that live there and general benevolence toward nature could lead to positive values for natural environments that a given individual never personally uses. Feelings of responsibility for possible environmental harm could lead to positive existence values for maintaining environmental resources.

Existence value is still a relatively new concept.[11] There is still substantial disagreement regarding appropriate terminology. Some (e.g. Walsh et al., 1984; Sutherland and Walsh, 1985; Loomis, 1987, 1989) distinguish between bequest value (the value one places on leaving a legacy to future generations) and existence value, where the latter is defined as the value of simply knowing that the amenity still exists. Here, however, we shall use the term in the broader sense to include all values, under certainty, stemming from motivations other than personal use. Existence values so defined are one component of what are termed "non-use" or "intrinsic" or "passive use" values. The other component that is sometimes included in non-use values is option value or option price, as discussed in the next chapter.

The fact that existence value is incompatible with weak complementarity has important implications. Suppose the travel cost or hedonic price method is being applied to a resource and someone argues that weak complementarity is violated because existence value is present. This challenge would not rule out such an application provided that results were properly interpreted as representing use values alone. Once weak complementarity is violated, however, neither of these approaches can be assumed to fully measure the total values of amenities to which they are applied. So long as existence values are positive, estimates of the value of an environmental quality change from studies of markets for related conventional goods and services must be viewed as approximate lower bounds on total values.

Though it is convenient to pretend that existence values can be totally separated from the use values of market goods, this is probably not completely true (Larson, 1991). That people could care about an amenity and yet not alter their behavior in any way seems unlikely. If nothing else, they may buy a newspaper to keep informed. In a more complex model of the consumer that includes time allocation, surely amenities that affect welfare would influence time devoted to information gathering? Still, such preference-revealing behavior is likely to be difficult to trace and use in valuation. Where existence values are potentially significant, most researchers argue that the only method to estimate total values for environmental amenities is contingent valuation.

Overview and Final Thoughts

Until recently, the theory of valuation has focused primarily on price changes. Environmental economists have made significant progress toward extending the theory to environmental quality changes. On the abstract level, where expenditure functions and associated Hicksian demand functions can be used directly, the scope of value theory has been easily widened to include the environment. The seminal contribution here was Maler's (1974) combined concepts of non-essentiality and weak complementarity. Where these concepts hold, exact measures of the values of environmental quality changes can be measured as changes in the areas under compensated demand functions for market goods that are either complements to or substitutes for environmental quality. Even where the weak complementarity assumption does not apply, as in the case of existence values, it helps to clarify and interpret areas between demand functions as lower bounds on total values.

Despite progress on an abstract level, there are still substantial unresolved issues in actual applications. The transition from Hicksian demand functions for associated market goods, which cannot be observed directly, to Marshallian demand functions, which can be observed, continues to be difficult. In fact, the very recent contribution by Bockstael and McConnell is likely to generate increasing debate, rather that resolve long-standing concerns. Nearly all of us thought we could expect environmental quality and market goods to be both gross and net complements. Now, unless someone comes forward with new, general, widely acceptable assumptions that resolve the matter, theory will provide much less guidance about the direction of shifts in demand functions as environmental quality changes. Furthermore, results relating to the size and relative magnitudes of exact and inexact value measures that are well understood for price changes are now doubtful for quality changes. Researchers will continue to try to resolve these issues, but in the meantime, empirical results will be less credible.

Stepping back from what was done in this chapter, we need to acknowledge that there are bigger issues, even within the confines of neoclassical economic theory. Mainstream theory begins with individuals, using them as the building blocks from which to construct a concept of social welfare. Thus, the focus on the individual consumer throughout this chapter is fitting. Nevertheless, once individual welfare has been considered, it is necessary to aggregate over individuals. This is normally a simple problem in addition, and nothing we have run into in this chapter would make us fear that aggregation over individuals will be more complicated for environmental improvements than for price changes.

Standard theory also involves aggregation across commodities to account for cases where interventions affect prices of more that one good. Aggregation over several environmental parameters has not been considered, but necessary procedures would parallel those needed for multiple price changes. The enquiry presented here has been conducted in a partial equilibrium context, but again, once the building blocks of this chapter are assembled, the transition to general equilibrium welfare analyses follows a well-established path.

It is also worth noting that we have dealt only with consumers. Producers and resource owners are also affected by environmental quality. Effects on producers and resource owners (under certainty) are generally valued as changes in rents and quasi-rents measured in monetary terms. Once more, extension of standard approaches is straightforward.

Among the many treatments of the general theoretical principles needed to address all these issues, Boadway and Bruce (1984) and Just et al. (1982) stand out as particularly thorough and clear. Freeman (1979) also treats topics related specially to environmental evaluation. Finally, uncertainty has not been considered here but will be addressed in the following chapter.

It is impossible to overlook the extent to which people's welfare is affected by environmental resources. The applicability of economic tools associated with public decision making, such as benefit–cost analysis, cost-effectiveness analysis, and natural resource damage assessment procedures, would be extremely limited if environmental values were excluded because of the kinds of theoretical issues raised here or for other reasons. Valuation techniques based on Marshallian demand shifts promise useful, though inexact, insights into people's relative values for environmental amenities. More application can be expected as societies around the world continue to struggle with the tradeoff between quality and market goods and services.

Notes

Nancy Bockstael was generous with her time in helping us understand recent theoretical work. Patricia Champ and Daniel Mullarkey made many helpful comments on an earlier draft.

The research was supported by the College of Agricultural and Life Sciences, University of Wisconsin-Madison; and by the University of Wisconsin Sea Grant College Program through grants from the National Oceanic and Atmospheric Administration, US Department of Commerce, and from the State of Wisconsin Federal Grant NA 80 AA-DD00086, Project R/PS-33.

1   For reviews of the Slutsky equation that may prove helpful throughout this chapter (they certainly proved helpful to its authors), see Silberberg (1990, pp. 323–33) and Kreps (1990, p. 59).
2   As a matter of convention, areas indicated with capital letters in the figures in this chapter are used to identify the area between solid lines.
3   Recall that ev for this change will be negative since it measures CD.
4   If any of these partial derivatives is zero, the two goods are said to be neutral on a gross or net basis as the case may be.
5   Recall that the derivative of expenditure with respect to environmental quality is negative. Hence the minus sign makes it positive, so that WTP can be stated as a positive number and the function itself can be drawn in the northeast quadrant.
6   Nancy Bockstael in a personal communication suggests the following utility function which would satisfy weak complementarity but would not satisfy the restriction imposed by equation (24.10): $u(x_1, x_2, b) = x_1 x_2 b + g(x_1) + h(x_2)$.
7   For example, if the demand function is specified in such a manner that the income effect is zero, the Hicksian and Marshallian functions would exactly coincide. Bockstael and McConnell (1993), drawing on Willig (1978), explore other conditions which would allow the intersection of the shifted Hicksian and Marshallian functions to be determined.
8   As we shall see in chapter 30, non-marginal changes in the amenity may alter the equilibrium in the market for real property in ways that will greatly complicate a full analysis of the effects of the change on a given consumer and all property owner and renters combined. In our terms, various elements of the price vector relating to substitutes in the housing market may be altered. If so, the analysis will be more complex than portrayed here, but the link between the value of the amenity change and the prices of housing based on weak complementarity will continue to hold.
9   We assume that none of the other goods in q satisfies the weak complementarity conditions either.
10   Certain theoretical questions do arise when one considers possible aggregation of intra-generational existence values. See Madariaga and McConnell (1987).
11   It can be traced back to Krutilla (1967).

References

Boadway, Robin W. and Bruce, Neil. 1984: *Welfare Economics*. New York: Basil Blackwell.
Bockstael, N. E. and McConnell, K. E. 1993: Public goods as characteristics of non-market commodities. *Economic Journal*, forthcoming.
Freeman, A. Myrick. 1979: *The Benefits of Environmental Improvement: Theory and Practice*. Baltimore, MD: Johns Hopkins University Press.
Hausman, Jerry A. 1981: Exact consumer's surplus and deadweight loss. *American Economic Review*, 71 (4), 662–76.

Hicks, J. R. 1943: The four consumers' surpluses. *Review of Economic Studies*, 11 (1), 31–41.

Just, Darrell, Hueth, L. and Schmitz, Andrew. 1982: *Applied Welfare Economics and Public Policy*. Englewood Cliffs, NJ: Prentice Hall.

Kreps, David M. 1990: *A Course in Microeconomic Theory*. Princeton, NJ: Princeton University Press.

Krutilla, John. 1967: Conservation reconsidered. *American Economic Review*, 57, 777-86.

Larson, Douglas M. 1991: Recovering weakly complementary preferences. *Journal of Environmental Economics and Management*, 21 (2), 97–108.

Loomis, John B. 1987: Balancing public trust resources of Mono Lake and Los Angeles' water right: an economic approach. *Water Resources Research*, 23 (8), 1449–56.

Loomis, John, B. 1989: Test–retest reliability of the contingent valuation method: a comparison of general population and visitor responses. *American Journal of Agricultural Economics*, 71 (1), 76–84.

Madariaga, Bruce and McConnell, Kenneth E. 1987: Exploring existence value. *Water Resources Research*, 23 (5), 936–42.

Maler, Karl Goran. 1974: *Environmental Economics; A Theoretical Inquiry*. Baltimore, MD: Johns Hopkins University Press.

Mckenzie, George W. 1983: *Measuring Economic Welfare: New Methods*. New York: Cambridge University Press.

Randall, Alan and Stoll, John R. 1980: Consumer's surplus in commodity space. *American Economic Review*, 70 (3), 449–55.

Randall, Alan and Stoll, John R. 1983: Existence value in a total valuation framework. In R. D. Rowe and L. G. Chestnut (eds), *Managing Air Quality and Scenic Resources at National Parks and Wilderness Areas*, Boulder, CO: Westview Press.

Silberberg, Eugene. 1990: *The Structure of Economics: A Mathematical Analysis*. New York: McGraw-Hill.

Sutherland, Ronald J. and Walsh, Richard G. 1985: Effect of distance on the preservation value of water quality. *Land Economics*, 61 (August), 281–91.

Walsh, Richard G., Loomis, John B. and Gillman, Richard A. 1984: Valuing option, existence and bequest demands for wilderness. *Land Economics*, 60 (February), 15–29.

Willig, Robert D. 1976: Consumer's surplus without apology. *American Economic Review*, 66 (4), 589–97.

Willig, Robert D. 1978: Incremental consumer's surplus and hedonic price adjustments. *Journal of Economic Theory*, 17, 227–53.

25

Environmental Valuation under Uncertainty

Richard C. Ready

In the previous chapter we saw a theoretical framework for evaluating welfare changes in a world with no uncertainty. Compensating surplus (CS) was identified as the measure of the benefits and costs to individuals of a certain change in environmental quality.[1] The range of environmental policy problems includes many issues where uncertainty plays a central role, however. Natural systems are inherently variable, across space and across time. This variability, combined with our own lack of knowledge over natural processes, means that we can never predict with certainty the physical and biological impacts of an environmental policy change. Along with uncertainty over the natural system, economic agents face uncertainty over their economic situations, so that the economic impacts of a policy change will also be uncertain.

The goal of this chapter is to identify a welfare measure that logically and consistently measures the benefits and costs from a policy change whose impacts are uncertain. The search for such a measure has generated a large literature, organized around two proposed welfare measures, option price (Weisbrod, 1964) and the willingness-to-pay locus (Graham, 1981). The option price literature will be briefly reviewed here to give the reader a feeling for the evolution of thinking that has occurred. More detailed reviews of early works on option price are available elsewhere (Bishop, 1982; Smith, 1983). Authors writing on the willingness-to-pay locus have not yet reached a consensus view. This chapter will explore some of the issues that remain unresolved. The chapter concludes with a discussion of issues related to estimation of either of these measures.

Option Value and Option Price

The early history of the concepts of option value and option price are an interesting case study where intuition preceded more rigorous treatments.

Weisbrod (1964) was the first to argue that consumer surplus[2] might not accurately measure benefits in the face of uncertainty. He was concerned with the decision of whether to shut down a facility such as a national park. The prevailing view at that time was that if the consumer surplus for the park, defined as the largest amount that a price-discriminating monopolist could extract from the park visitors, was less than the costs of operating the park, then economic efficiency would be promoted by closing the park. Weisbrod believed that this approach would undercount the total benefit from keeping the park open.

Weisbrod saw two distinct groups of people who benefited from keeping the park open. The benefit to the current visitors is correctly measure by the consumer surplus for the park. Current non-visitors may also receive a benefit if the park is kept open, however, because they may want to visit the park in the future. Keeping the park open would provide a benefit to current non-visitors because it would ensure that the park would be available should they decide to visit it in the future. This additional benefit from keeping the park open, which Weisbrod called an option value, would not be included in the consumer surplus estimated from current visitors.

Unfortunately, Weisbrod was not very precise in his definitions, and his arguments were intuitive rather than theoretically rigorous. This led to some confusion among subsequent authors regarding the definition and interpretation of option value.[3] Long (1967), Lindsay (1969), and Byerlee (1971) each reacted to Weisbrod's article with intuitive arguments of their own. Long argued that Weisbrod's option value is simply another motivation for consumer surplus, so that adding the two together would result in double counting. Lindsay, like Weisbrod, argued that consumer surplus would underestimate total benefits, and drew analogy to the purchase of insurance. A risk-averse uncertain demander would be willing to pay a risk premium to eliminate the risk of wanting to visit the park but being unable to do so. In contrast, Byerlee viewed keeping the park open as a risky investment for an uncertain demander that should therefore be valued at less than its expected value, so that consumer surplus would overestimate benefits for an uncertain demander.

The problem with intuitive arguments is that it is difficult to reconcile contrasting results. To complicate matters, these first four articles used terminology in conflicting and ambiguous ways. Cicchetti and Freeman (1971) established terminology that differs from that used by Weisbrod, Long, Lindsay, or Byerlee, but is unambiguous and has come to be widely used. They considered an individual who is uncertain about whether to visit the park. Option price (OP) is defined as the maximum amount that the uncertain individual would be willing to pay to purchase an option to visit the park in the future. Consumer surplus (CS) is the amount that the individual would be willing to pay to visit the park after the individual has decided to be a demander. Expected consumer surplus (E(CS)) is then equal to CS multiplied by the probability of wanting to visit the park. Finally, Cicchetti and Freeman defined option value (OV) as the difference between option price and expected consumer surplus;

$$OP = E(CS) + OV \tag{25.1}$$

These definitions have been adopted as standard in subsequent articles.

Put into the context of Cicchetti and Freeman's terminology, Weisbrod's intuition was that E(CS) would underestimate the benefits of keeping the park open. This conclusion relies on two assumptions: first that option price is the benefit measure that should be used in policy analysis and second that option value is positive for a risk-averse individual. While these assumptions may be intuitive, they need to be reexamined. Is it true that OP is the correct benefit measure for policy analysis, and, if so, are we sure that OV will be positive? These questions need to be answered not just for Weisbrod's park example but in more general contexts as well.

We will turn to these two questions shortly, but first we need a general model of the policy decision problem, and how environmental policy affects individual utility. The model present in the next section uses a state-preference approach that was first used for this purpose by Schmalensee (1972).[4]

A framework for policy analysis under uncertainty

The environmental valuation problem is to measure the benefits and costs from a change in environmental quality. In an uncertain world, however, it may not make sense to view the government as choosing a particular level of environmental quality and attaining that level with certainty. More generally, the government chooses an environmental policy which results in a particular level of environmental quality. This distinction is important because the relationship between environmental policy and environmental quality can be complex and uncertain.

The relevant valuation problem is then to measure the benefits and costs of a change in environmental policy. The myriad dimensions of environmental policy will be represented by a vector δ, called the policy vector. For example, for a pollution control policy, components of δ could include ambient air or water quality standards, the process for granting pollution permits, and inspection and enforcement efforts used to ensure compliance with the permits. The proposed change in environmental policy would change the value of δ from some baseline value δ_0 to some new value δ_1. The two policy vectors δ_0 and δ_1 could represent a decision regarding any government action including granting a permit, construction of a water project, protection of a wilderness area, or the closing of a national park. This is the decision problem for which we are conducting a policy analysis. This framework can still accommodate environmental valuation problems. We would simply include the level of environmental quality as components of δ. Weisbrod's park problem can also easily be accommodated. In that example, the two policies would be $\delta_0 \equiv$ "close park" and $\delta_1 \equiv$ "keep park open."

At the time when the government must choose between δ_0 and δ_1, there is uncertainty over a number of factors that will influence the outcome from the policy. All of the future factors over which there is uncertainty are collectively described by the state of the world, s. There are many possible states of the world that could occur, $s = s_1, \ldots, s_M$. At some time after the decision is made, the state of the world is revealed. The vector s could contain information about the future state of natural variables, such as weather or birth and death rates in a wildlife population, or information about future economic variables such as prices or individual incomes and preferences. In Weisbrod's park example, there is uncertainty over future preferences. Each individual has two possible future states, $s_1 \equiv$ "wants to visit the park" and $s_2 \equiv$ "does not want to visit the park."

The terms *ex ante* and *ex post* refer to the amount of information that is available to the decision maker. *Ex ante* refers to the situation where the state of the world is still unknown. *Ex post* refers to the situation after the state has been revealed. The policy decision must be made *ex ante*. While we do not know, *ex ante*, which state will occur, the *ex ante* probability that any given state s_k will occur is given by π_k, with $\sum_{k=1}^{M} \pi_k = 1$. These probabilities may or may not depend on the policy option chosen, that is they may be a function of δ; however, we will assume that the individuals affected by the policy decision cannot influence the probabilities. This last assumption ensures no complications due to moral hazard.

Notice that the state of the world as defined here is policy independent. Combining knowledge of the state with the knowledge of the policy option chosen gives complete information about the outcome, which is defined by the pair (δ, s). For Weisbrod's park example, if an uncertain visitor to the park experiences state s_1 and the policy chosen is δ_0 then the outcome is that the individual wants to visit the park but it has been closed. Three other possible outcome exist, corresponding to the three other possible combinations of s and δ.

Ex post, each individual ranks possible outcomes according to an *ex post* utility function $V(Y, \delta, s)$, where Y is income. We can use this *ex post* utility function to measure the *ex post* benefit that an individual receives from the policy change. If $V(y, \delta_1, s_k) > V(Y, \delta_0, s_k)$, then the individual is an *ex post* winner in state s_k. That individual's compensating surplus for the policy change is defined as the maximum amount that the individual would be willing to pay to get δ_1 rather than δ_0, given that he or she knows that state s_k will occur with certainty. If $V(Y, \delta_1, s_k) < V(y, \delta_0, s_k)$, then the individual is an *ex post* loser in that state and compensating surplus is defined as the minimum amount that the individual would require in compensation to allow δ_1 rather than δ_0, given knowledge that state s_k will occur with certainty. In either case, compensating surplus in state s_k (CS_k) is defined by

$$V(Y - CS_k, \delta_1, s_k) = V(Y, \delta_0, s_k) \tag{25.2}$$

Note that the same individual could be an *ex post* winner in some states and an *ex post* loser in other states, that is, CS_k could be positive for some states and negative for others. Expected compensating surplus ($E(CS)$) is then defined by

$$E(CS) = \sum_{k=1}^{M} \pi_k CS_k \tag{25.3}$$

To continue with Weisbrod's park, CS_1 would represent the amount that an individual would be willing to pay to see the park kept open, given that the individual wants to visit the park. Absent some non-use value for the park, this amount could be collected by a price-discriminating monopolist running the park. CS_2 would measure how much someone wold be willing to pay to keep the park open, given that he or she is certain not to want to visit the park. Absent some non-use value, that amount would presumably be zero. If so, then expected compensating surplus would equal $\pi_1 CS_1$. Notice that if there are a large number of potential park visitors, N, and the probabilities of their wanting to visit the park are independent, then approximately $\pi_1 N$ will choose to visit the park, and the price-discriminating monopolist will be able to collect $\pi_1 N CS(s_1) = N E(CS)$ in revenues.

Ex ante, individual utility depends on the potential *ex post* outcomes and their probabilities. Here it will be assumed that individuals maximize expected *ex post* utility, so that *ex ante* utility is defined by

$$U(Y, \delta) = \sum_{i=1}^{M} \pi_k V(Y, \delta, s_k) \tag{25.4}$$

The expected utility assumption is used for notational convenience but is not necessary. Any *ex ante* utility specifications could be used.

With the *ex ante* utility function, we can identify *ex ante* winners and losers from the policy change. Following Bishop (1986) *ex ante* winners, defined as those for whom $U(Y, \delta_1) > U(Y, \delta_0)$, would *ex ante* prefer that δ_1 is chosen rather than δ_0. *Ex ante* losers are those for whom the opposite is true. For an *ex ante* winner, option price is defined as the maximum amount the individual would be willing to pay, *ex ante*, to get δ_1 rather than δ_0. For an *ex ante* loser, option price is the minimum amount the individual would need to be compensated to accept δ_1. In either case, option price is defined by

$$\sum_{k=1}^{M} \pi_k V(Y - OP, \delta_1, s_k) = \sum_{k=1}^{M} \pi_k V(Y, \delta_0, s_k) \tag{25.5}$$

or equivalently by

$$U(Y - OP, \delta_1) = U(Y, \delta_0) \tag{25.6}$$

The right-hand sides of these equations represent baseline *ex ante* utility. On the left-hand sides, the policy change has been adopted, and income is either increased (OP negative) or decreased (OP positive) until the individual is left as well off, *ex ante*, as under the baseline. To complete the park example, OP measures the maximum amount that an uncertain park demander would pay, *ex ante*, for retaining the option to visit the park in the future.

Ex ante and *ex post* compensation tests

Having defined option price and compensating surplus in the context of the above framework, we can more clearly see why they might differ. Compensating surplus is an *ex post* welfare measure, in that it measures the amount of money that must be added or subtracted from an individual's income to leave that person as well off, according to his/her *ex post* utility function, as he/she would be under the baseline. Option price is an *ex ante* welfare measure, using the *ex ante* utility function to measure willingness to pay. Option value does not represent a separate category of benefits but is simply the difference between an *ex ante* measure of benefits and the expected value of an *ex post* measure. Before resolving the issue of whether OV is positive, negative, or zero, first let us investigate which type of benefit measure, *ex ante* or *ex post*, we desire for policy analysis.

The conceptual foundation for a measure of benefits and costs is the potential Pareto-improvement criterion. In a certain world, that criterion states that if it is possible for the winners from a policy change to compensate the losers such that everyone is made better off, then the policy change increases social welfare.[5] In an uncertain world, we must first determine whether compensation should take place *ex ante* or *ex post* (Ulph, 1982; Hammond, 1981). Bishop (1986) identified three possible forms the compensation test could take, two *ex post* forms and one *ex ante* form.

Bishop's *ex post* compensation test requires that the *ex post* winners be able to compensate the *ex post* losers in every state, i.e. $\sum_{i=1}^{N} CS_k^i > 0$ for all states s_k.[6] The attraction of the *ex post* compensation test is that, if δ_1

passes the test, there is no possibility that we will regret, *ex post*, having chosen it over δ_0. Regardless of which state occurs, the net *ex post* benefits will be positive. The disadvantage of this compensation test is that it is extremely conservative. Even if the potential net *ex post* benefits from δ_1 are very large, and the probability of positive net *ex post* benefits is very high, any slight probability of negative net *ex post* benefits would result in the rejection of δ_1. This approach results in a very strong bias toward the baseline policy.

Society will probably be willing to accept some risk of negative net *ex post* benefits when considering a policy change. A second *ex post* compensation test is the expected *ex post* compensation test. This test requires that the expected value of the net *ex post* benefits be positive, i.e. $\sum_{i=1}^{N} CS_k^i > 0$. The expected *ex post* compensation test does not require positive net *ex post* benefits in every state. Some risk of negative net *ex post* benefits is allowable as long as the expected net *ex post* benefit is positive.

One concern of early authors about the expected *ex post* compensation test is that it does not adequately incorporate the cost of risk bearing. Among others, Eckstein (1965) argued that uncertain future benefits should be discounted at a higher rate than certain benefits, to reflect the costs of risk bearing. Subsequent authors provided arguments against using a "risky" discount rate. Arrow and Lind (1970) argued that, if risk is spread across enough people, then the risk can be ignored. Samuelson and Vickrey (1964) argued that if the government makes a large number of policy decisions that each satisfy the expected *ex post* compensation test, and the risks associated with each decision are independent, then those risks will be pooled such that the aggregate *ex post* benefit from all decisions will be riskless. These arguments were made in the context of decisions whose outcomes are purely financial, however. They give no guidance for situations where risk is over a non-financial argument of individual utility, such as environmental quality (Ulph, 1982).

A more direct way to incorporate the costs of risk bearing on individuals is to measure welfare *ex ante*. The *ex ante* compensation test requires that the *ex ante* winners are able to compensate the *ex ante* losers, using *ex ante* compensation payments. This test will be satisfied if $\sum_{i=1}^{N} OP^i > 0$. This approach uses the individual *ex ante* utility function to assess the costs of risk bearing. If the individual negatively views the risk associated with the outcome from a policy, that risk aversion will be reflected in his OP for that policy.

Which type of compensation test, *ex ante* or *ex post*, is more appropriate for policy analysis? Most current authors seem to agree that policy analysis should be conducted using *ex ante* preferences (Ulph, 1982; Bishop, 1986; Freeman, 1986). Put yourself in the position of an individual who will be impacted by a proposed policy change, where the impact is uncertain. How would you want your preferences to be measured? In particular, what adjustment would you like to see made to your expected *ex post* benefit to account for your risk aversion? At the time of the decision, the best measure of your preferences, and of your view of the risks involved, is your own *ex ante* utility function.

Accepting this argument, option price is the correct measure of benefits and costs under uncertainty. Unfortunately, option price is often difficult to measure. In Weisbrod's park example, $E(CS)$, or at least a close approximation of $E(CS)$ (Willig, 1976), can be measured from a demand curve for the park. Such a demand curve could be estimated from observable behavior using the travel-cost method. Our preferred welfare measure, option price, cannot be estimated from observable behavior. If, however, we could show that OP will always be close to $E(CS)$, or that the difference between them is predictable, we could use $E(CS)$ as a proxy measure of OP.

The size and sign of option value

Weisbrod's original intuition was that OV in the park example would be positive. If this is generally true, then we could use $E(CS)$ for purposes of policy analysis, recognizing the bias in our measure. Lindsay agreed with Weisbrod, but Byerlee's argument would imply that OV would be negative. Long argued that OV should equal zero. None of these authors used a welfare-theoretic model to support their contentions, however.

Cicchetti and Freeman were the first to attempt a rigorous analysis of the sign of OV. They concluded that option value would indeed be positive, but their result depended on some rather restrictive assumptions regarding individual utility functions. Schmalensee (1972), using a more general framework, concluded that for a risk-averse individual whose preferences are uncertain the OP for a price change may be larger or smaller than $E(CS)$, so that the sign of OV is indeterminate. Bohm (1975) took issue with Schmalensee's definition of risk aversion, but came to the same conclusion using a different definition, that OV could be positive or negative (see also Anderson, 1981).

A brief review of the arguments made in these papers, using the context of the park example, can give some insight into why the sign of OV is interdeterminate. Assume that an individual who *ex post* does not want to visit the park places no value on the park, that is, $CS_2 = 0$. Combining our definitions of OP and CS gives

$$\pi_1 V(Y - OP, \delta_1, s_1) + \pi_2 V(Y - OP, \delta_1, s_2)$$

$$= \pi_1 V(Y - CS_1, \delta_1, s_1) + \pi_2 V(Y, \delta_1, s_2) \qquad (25.7)$$

Rearranging gives

$$\pi_1[V(Y - \text{OP}, \delta_1, s_1) - V(Y - \text{CS}_1, \delta_1, s_2)]$$
$$+ \pi_2[V(Y - \text{OP}, \delta_1, s_2) - V(Y - \text{OP}, \delta_1, s_2)] = 0 \qquad (25.8)$$

If the individual is risk averse, then the *ex post* utility function will be concave,[7] and a liner approximate to the utility differences will place a lower bound on the true utility differences:

$$\pi_1[(\text{CS}_1 - \text{OP})V_Y(Y - \text{OP}, \delta_1, s_1)]$$
$$+ \pi_2[(-\text{OP})V_Y(Y - \text{OP}, \delta_1, s_2)] \le 0 \qquad (25.9)$$

where $V_Y(\cdot)$ is the marginal utility of income. Rearranging gives

$$E(\text{CS}) = \pi_1 \text{CS}_1 \le \frac{\pi_1 \text{OP} V_Y(Y - \text{OP}, \delta_1, s_1) + \pi_2 \text{OP} V_Y(Y - \text{OP}, \delta_1, s_2)}{V_Y(Y - \text{OP}, \delta_1, s_2)}$$

$$(25.10)$$

If the marginal utility of income is equal in both states, that is, $V_Y(Y - \text{OP}, \delta_1, s_1) = V_Y(Y - \text{OP}, \delta_1, s_2)$, then the right-hand side of this inequality will simplify to equal OP, and we get that $\text{OP} \ge E(\text{CS})$. In that case, we can reliably say that OV will be positive, confirming Lindsay's intuition. OP is larger than $E(\text{CS})$ because of the individual's desire to avoid the risk of wanting to visit the park but being unable to do so.

If the marginal utility of income is different across the two states, this result can break down. If the marginal utility of income is greater in states s_1 than in state s_2, we are still assured that OV will be positive. If, however, the marginal utility of income is greater in state s_2 than in state s_1, then it is possible for OP to be smaller than $E(\text{CS})$, so that OV is negative. What is the intuition behind this result. Consider why the maginal utility of income might be high in state s_2. It could be because the individual's income is very low, or there is some pressing need for that income, such as an expensive illness. If so, then the individual will want to protect that income in state s_2. OP requires a payment to keep the park open in both states, but CS requires payment only in state s_1. The desire to preserve income in state s_2 will tend to drive OP down, but will not affect CS_1 and will therefore not affect $E(\text{CS})$. If the marginal utility of income in state s_2 is high enough, this effect will overcome the risk aversion effect and OP will be smaller than $E(\text{CS})$.

This result is discouraging. Even for the park example, where intuition suggested a predictable result, we cannot claim that $E(\text{CS})$ represents a reliable upper or lower bound on our preferred benefit measure, option price. Bishop (1982) provided some hope by showing that, for an important class of environmental policy problems, the sign of OV can be unambiguously determined. Previous authors had been concerned with the problem of demand-side uncertainty, where individuals are uncertain over their future demand due to stochastic preferences. Bishop considered a problem with supply-side uncertainty. He envisioned a situation where pollution is entering a body of water. *Ex ante*, it is not known whether the pollution will negatively impact an important recreational fishery. Two states are possible. In state s_1, the pollution impacts the fishery. In state s_2, it does not. Absent a change in environmental policy, the *ex ante* probability that the pollution will damage the fishery is $\pi_1(\delta_0)$. A stricter environmental policy, δ_1, that reduces pollution loadings would reduce to zero the probability that the fishery would be damaged, that is, $\pi_1(\delta_0) = 0$. Bishop showed that option value for this problem will always be positive.

Why is this result predictable, when the demand-side result was not? In the demand-side problem, there were two competing effects, the risk reduction effect and the effect caused by differences between the states in the marginal utility of income. In Bishop's supply-side problem, the individual's utility is not stochastic, so the second effect does not come into play. Because the policy eliminates risk, individuals include a risk premium in their *ex ante* value for the policy. This risk premium, acting alone, generates the result that OP will be greater than $E(CS)$, and that supply-side OV is unambiguously positive.

Bishop's result regarding supply-side option value is not very robust, unfortunately. If income or preferences are uncertain, or if the proposed policy does not completely eliminate the risk of damage, then the sign of supply-side option value is again indeterminate (Freeman, 1985b; Plummer, 1986; Wilman, 1987; Bishop, 1988; Johansson, 1988). Other sources of uncertainty have also been considered, including uncertainty over income, over prices, and over the quality of an environmental amenity (Freeman, 1984; Chavas et al., 1986; Plummer and Hartman, 1986; Hartman and Plummer, 1987). While for some specific sources of uncertainty the sign of OV can be determined, in real-world policy problems there will usually be many sources of uncertainty, and the sign of option value will typically be indeterminate. The hoped-for result, that option value would represent a consistent bias if $E(CS)$ is used in place of option price, cannot be confirmed.

Being unable to assign a consistent sign to option value, several authors took a different tack, attempting to determine whether option value will be small enough that it can be ignored in applied work (Freeman, 1984; Smith, 1984; Freeman, 1985a; Plummer, 1985). This work suggested that for problems where OP is small relative to income, individuals are not highly risk averse, and the policy decision does not involve unique and irreplaceable resources, OV will typically be small relative to OP, and $E(CS)$ will be close to OP. These conditions are commonly met for market goods, implying that we can use $E(CS)$ as a reasonable measure of OP when considering price or quantity changes in markets. For many important environmental policy problems, however, they will not be met, and OV can be large relative to OP.

Because we cannot depend on OV to be small, or even to be of predictable sign, for important valuation problems, the research focus has in more recent years turned towards estimating OP directly in situations where uncertainty plays an important role. Issues surrounding estimation of OP will be addressed in a later section.

The Willingness-to-Pay Locus

We turn now to discussion of a second *ex ante* benefit measure, the willingness-to-pay locus (Graham, 1981). Earlier, we accepted the arguments in favor of using an *ex ante* compensation test. This does not necessarily imply that compensation has to be accomplished *ex ante*. The relevant distinction between the *ex ante* and *ex post* compensation test is whether utility is measured *ex ante* or *ex post*, not the timing of compensation. Graham accepted the arguments in favor of an *ex ante* compensation test, but recognized that we could compensate an individual so that *ex ante* utility was maintained, but do so using *ex post* compensation.

Suppose we approached someone who is an *ex ante* winner from the policy change and wanted to strike a deal whereby we would provide the policy change in return for a monetary payment. If we limit ourselves to considering only those deals where money could be collected at the time that δ_1 is adopted, then option price represents the largest amount of money that we could persuade the individual to agree to. If, however, we structured the deal such that payment was not due until after the state of the world is revealed, then we could make that payment conditional on which state occurs.

Such a contract would specify the amount of money that the individual would have to pay in each state: if state s_1 occurs, g_1 will have to be paid; if state s_2 occurs, g_2 will have to be paid, etc. The vector $g = (g_1, \ldots, g_M)$ is called a contingent compensation payment, because the compensation payment that must be made is contingent on the state of the world. Similarly, we could approach an *ex ante* loser from the policy change and offer compensation in the form of a contingent compensation payment. This contract would specify how large the compensation payment will be in each state.

In either case, the individual will be willing to sign the contract if *ex ante* utility under the terms of the contract is higher than baseline utility, that is, if the contingent compensation payment g satisfies

$$\sum_{k=1}^{M} \pi_k V(Y - g_k, \delta_1, s_k) \geq \sum_{k=1}^{M} \pi_k V(Y, \delta_0, s_k) \qquad (25.11)$$

Two points should be noted about these contingent compensation payments. First, g can contain both positive and negative elements, even for the same individual. Second, for any individual there will be an infinite number of vectors g that satisfy (25.11). For example, if an individual is willing to commit to a particular contingent payment g, then that individual will also be willing to commit to any contingent payment to which an individual will be willing to commit. Here, because g is an M-vector, no single g can be called the "largest" contingent compensation payment. Rather, we identify all contingent compensation payments that satisfy equation (25.11) with equality. This set of contingent payments is called the willingness-to-pay (WTP) locus for the policy change.

Graham presented a simple example of a policy change that involved the construction of a dam to illustrate these concepts. The *ex ante* winner from the policy change is a farmer who lives downstream from the dam. *Ex ante* there is uncertainty over the amount of rain that will fall, with two states of nature possible, $s_1 \equiv$ "wet year" and $s_2 \equiv$ "dry year," with probabilities π_1 and π_2. The *ex post* benefit that the farmer gets from the dam is state dependent. If it is a wet year, the farmer benefits from flood control. If it is a dry year, the farmer benefits from irrigation.

In this context, with only two possible states of nature, the farmer's WTP locus can be represented graphically. In figure 25.1, the axes represent the contingent payment amounts g_1 and g_2, so that each point in the resulting x–y space represents a different contingent payment vector $g = (g_1, g_2)$. The broken line running at a 45° slope form the origin includes all contingent payments with $g_1 = g_2$. These are the sure payments, that could be made *ex ante*. The farmer's WTP locus will include all contingent payments that satisfy

$$\pi_1 V(Y - g_1, \delta_1, s_1) + \pi_2 V(Y - g_2, \delta_1, s_2)$$

$$= \pi_1 V(Y, \delta_0, s_1) + \pi_2 V(Y, \delta_0, s_2) \tag{25.12}$$

These form a downward-sloping curved line in figure 25.1.

We have already identified two particular contingent payment vectors on the farmer's WTP locus. Option price represents the largest sure payment that the farmer would be willing to pay to get the dam. The farmer will therefore be willing to sign a contract that requires contingent payments $g_1 = OP$ and $g_2 = OP$. Similarly, the contingent payment with $g_1 = CS_1$ and $g_1 = CS_2$ will also lie on the WTP locus. Either contract will leave the farmer with the same *ex ante* utility as under the baseline. Because the farmer is an *ex ante* winner from the policy change, OP is positive and the WTP locus passes through the positive quadrant of (g_1, g_2) space. The WTP locus for an *ex ante* loser would pass through the third quadrant.

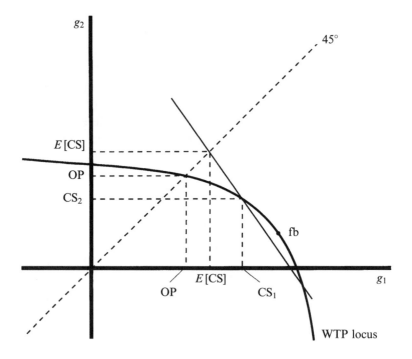

Figure 25.1   Graham's WTP locus with negative OV.

It may be helpful to thick of the WTP locus as an *ex ante* indifference curve. The farmer's *ex ante* utility is held constant at the baseline utility. Compensation payments g_1 and g_2 are both "bads" for the farmer. Different points along the WTP locus represent different combinations of g_1 and g_2 that produce that baseline utility. Accordingly, the slope of the WTP locus can be interpreted as the farmer's marginal rate of substitution between g_1 and g_2. Totally differentiating equation (25.12) gives

$$-\pi_1 \frac{\partial V(Y - g_1, \delta_1, s_1)}{\partial Y} dg_1 - \pi_2 \frac{\partial V(Y - g_2, \delta_1, s_2)}{\partial Y} dg_2 = 0 \qquad (25.13)$$

The slope of the WTP locus is therefore given by

$$\frac{dg_1}{dg_2} = -\frac{\pi_1 V_Y(Y - g_1, \delta_1, s_1)}{\pi_2 V_Y(Y - g_2, \delta_1, s_2)} \qquad (25.14)$$

where $V_Y(\cdot)$ is the *ex post* marginal utility of income. A movement along the WTP locus involve's the farmer giving up income in one state to get extra income in the other state. The *ex ante* marginal utility of an income change in one state is equal to the *ex post* marginal utility multiplied by the state probability. The farmer is willing to trade off income between states

s_1 and s_2 as long as the *ex ante* utility decrease from decreasing income in one state equals the *ex ante* utility increase from increasing income in the other state.

Two assumptions about the farmer's *ex post* utility function generate the WTP locus shown in figure 25.1. If we assume that the *ex post* marginal utility of income is always positive in both states, then the WTP locus will be everywhere downward sloping. Second, if the farmer is risk averse, that is, the *ex post* marginal utility of income is decreasing in income in each state, then the WTP locus will be concave to the origin. As g_1 is increased along the WTP locus, net income in state s_1 decreases and $V_Y(Y - g_2, \delta_1, s_1)$ increases, making the WTP locus more steeply sloped. A risk-loving individual's WTP locus would be convex to the origin.

Using the WTP locus, we can demonstrate the earlier result that option value can be positive or negative. In figure 25.1, a straight line has been drawn passing through the point (CS_1, CS_2) with a slope of $-\pi_1/\pi_2$. Every point on this line will have the same expected value. The line is described by the equation

$$\pi_1 g_1 = \pi_2 g_2 = E(CS) \tag{25.15}$$

We can measure $E(CS)$ by looking for the point on the line where $g_1 = g_2$. This occurs where the line crosses the 45° line. In this particular case, $E(CS)$ is larger than OP, so that OV is negative. It is just as easy to show a case where OV is positive, however. Such an example is shown graphically in figure 25.2.

Finally, Graham specifically identified one more point on the WTP locus. The fair-bet point is the point on the WTP locus that has the highest expected value. In figures 25.1 and 25.2, the fair-bet point is labeled fb and is located where the WTP locus has a slope equal to $-\pi_1/\pi_2$.

Cost–benefit analysis using the willingness-to-pay locus

Our *ex ante* compensation test stated that it is possible for the *ex ante* winners from the policy to compensate the *ex ante* losers, such that everyone is better off *ex ante* under δ_1 than under δ_0, then the policy change increases social welfare. It was implicitly assumed that this compensation would take place *ex ante*, i.e. compensation would be accomplished using state-independent compensation payments. Graham's WTP locus allows us to consider state-dependent compensation.

A state-dependent *ex ante* compensation test would require that the *ex ante* winners can compensate the *ex ante* losers using state-dependent (contingent) compensation. Formally, there must exist a contingent compensation payment g^i for each individual that satisfies equation (25.11), and the sum of those contingent payments must be positive in all

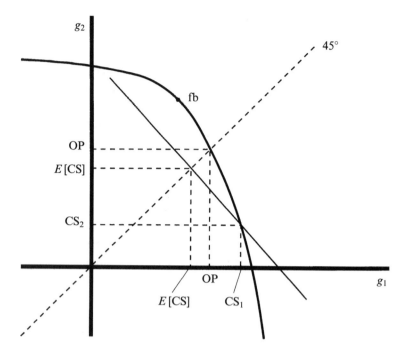

Figure 25.2   Graham's WTP locus with positive OV.

states, that is, $\sum_{i=1}^{N} g_k^i \geq 0$ for all states s_k. If such contingent compensation payments exist, then we know that it is at least theoretically possible to make everyone better off under policy δ_1 than under the baseline δ_0.

Again, for the dam example with two states, this test can be presented graphically. In figure 25.3, there are two individuals impacted by the dam. The farmer is an *ex ante* winner and has a WTP locus shown as WTP^A. The second individual is an *ex ante* loser from the dam. This individual might be a fisherman who suffers from the loss of the free-flowing river. The WTP locus, shown as WTP^B, passes through the third quadrant. As constructed, the farmer's positive option price for the dam, OP^A, is smaller in magnitude than the fisherman's negative option price, OP^B. If we restrict ourselves to sure compensation payments, the farmer cannot compensate the fisherman.

Graham's approach allows us to consider contingent compensation payments. To evaluate whether the dam passes Graham's state-dependent *ex ante* compensation test, we first construct the aggregate WTP locus (AWTP locus) for the dam. Because it lies on his WTP locus, we know that the farmer would be willing to sign a contract that requires him to pay the contingent compensation payment (g_1^A, g_2^A) in figure 25.3. Under that contract, the farmer would pay compensation if state s_2 occurs, but would receive money if state s_1 occurs. Likewise, the fisherman would be willing

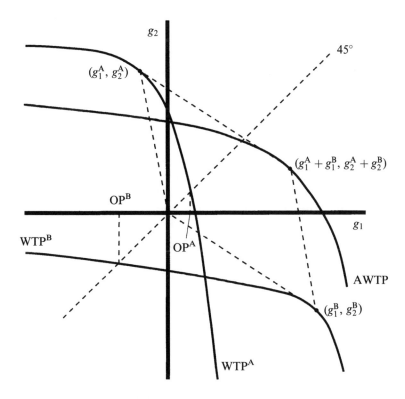

Figure 25.3 Construction of an aggregate WTP locus.

to sign a contract that binds him to the contingent compensation payment (g_1^B, g_2^B), which pays him compensation is state s_2 occurs but requires him to pay if states s_1 occurs. If the farmer and the fisherman commit to paying these two contingent payments, how much money, in total, would be collected? If state s_1 occurs, the net amount of money that the government will collect will be $g_1^A + g_1^B$. If state s_2 occurs, the net money collected by the government will be $g_2^A + g_2^B$. These two contracts therefore provide the government with an aggregate contingent payment of $(g_1^A + g_1^B, g_2^A + g_2^B)$.

The AWTP locus is constructed by repeating this summation using every possible combination of contingent payments on WTP^A and WTP^B. This process generates a set of aggregate contingent payments that the government could collect and still leave both the farmer and the fisherman at their baseline utilities.[8] The AWTP locus is then defined as the upper boundary of this set of feasible aggregate contingent payments. It represents all of the "largest" aggregate contingent payments that the government could collect.

Not all combinations of contingent payments on WTP^A and WTB^B will yield an aggregate contingent payment that lies on the AWTP locus. The particular combination of contingent payments shown in figure 25.3

does, because the payments were chosen such that, at their respective payments, the WTP loci for the farmer and the fisherman have the same slope. If payments were chosen at points on the two loci with different slopes, the resulting aggregate contingent payment would lie inside the AWTP locus.

The state-dependent *ex ante* compensation test then asks whether there is an aggregate contingent payment on the AWTP locus that is larger than zero in every state. If so, then we know that the farmer could compensate the fisherman using contingent compensation payments. For this example, the AWTP locus does contain points that are greater than zero in every state. Point $(g_1^A + g_1^B, g_2^A + g_2^B)$ is one example of such a point. The dam therefore does pass the state-dependent *ex ante* compensation test.

Construction of the entire AWTP locus is a cumbersome process. Luckily, there are some special cases where it is not necessary. Graham shows that if individuals are identical, and face common risks, then the point $(\sum_{i=1}^{N} OP^i, \sum_{i=1}^{N} OP^i)$ will lie on the AWTP locus. In that special case, the state-dependent *ex ante* compensation test is identical to the state-independent test. A second special case exists where the risks faced by individuals are independent. Suppose that each individual faces uncertainty over their own future situation, and that the state probabilities for any one individual are independent from the probabilities for any other individual. For example, it might be reasonable to assume that the uncertainty individuals face regarding their own future income is independent of the uncertainty faced by any other individual. Suppose that, in such a situation, the government required individuals to commit to paying their fair-bet point contingent compensation payment. We can use a large numbers argument to show that in such a case the government would collect $\sum_{i=1}^{N} E(fb^i)$ with certainty. The state-dependent compensation test would than whether $\sum_{i=1}^{N} E(fb^i)$ is larger than zero.

Should compensation be state dependent or state independent?

Graham's approach is interesting but leaves us with a problem: which form of the *ex ante* compensation test should we use for policy analysis? This question is important because the two tests can give different recommendations regarding the same policy change. Because the state-dependent test places one less restriction on the form of compensation, any policy change that passes the state-independent *ex ante* compensation test will also pass the state-dependent *ex ante* compensation test. However, some policy changes, including the dam example presented above, will pass the state-dependent tests but fail the state-independent test.

Should the dam be built? Here, a consensus view has not been reached. According to Graham, the answer depends on whether the implementation of state-dependent compensation is feasible (see also Graham, 1984). If the government could realistically carry out state-dependent compensation, then the analysis using the WTP locus as a benefit measure assures us that, if we chose to implement compensation, we could make everyone better off with the dam than they would be without the dam. In that sense, the dam represents a potential Pareto improvement over the baseline. If state-dependent compensation is not feasible, however, but state-independent compensation is, then Graham supports the state-independent compensation test, and OP is the correct benefit measure. Smith (1990) and Meier and Randall (1991) come to similar conclusions.

Others support the state-dependent test even more strongly; they (Cory and Saliba, 1987; Colby and Cory, 1989) point out that compensation is rarely, if ever, actually paid. There is therefore no reason to place a restriction on the form that the compensation must take. As long as compensation is hypothetical, why not assume that the payments are state dependent. Similarly, Freeman (1991) argues that if society decides that compensation need not be paid, then hypothetical compensation payments can take any form. Their argument, that the feasibility of compensation should not matter, is consistent with our view of compensation in a certain world. There, if compensation will not actually occur, we do not consider the costs associated with implementing compensation, such as the information, contracting, and enforcement costs that would be incurred. It is enough that compensation is conceptually possible. We do not require that it be realistically possible.

Support for the state-dependent test is not universal, however. I have argued (Ready, 1993) that the AWTP locus will overvalue a policy change, and that too many policy changes will pass the state-dependent test. To understand this argument, we must first get an intuitive understanding of why the state-dependent and state-independent compensation tests can lead to different conclusions. The ultimate reason has to do with the opportunities that exist to reallocate risks among individuals in society. Unless complete markets exist for contingent claims on income,[9] the existing allocation of risk among individuals will typically be inefficient. Efficiency in exchange for any two commodities requires that the marginal rate of substitution between the commodities be equal for all individuals. Similar, efficiency in risk allocation requires that the *ex ante* marginal rate of substitution between income in one state and income in another state be equal for all individuals. If this is not the case, there will be opportunities for individuals to insure each other or otherwise reallocate risk by trading contingent claims. Such a reallocation could make everyone better off, and therefore would represent a Pareto improvement over the status quo.

If the policy change is adopted, and compensation is accomplished using state-independent payments, the allocation of risk that results would still be inefficient. This can be seen graphically for the dam example in figure 25.3. Suppose that the dam is built, and the farmer and fisherman each pay (receive) their option price. Recall that the slope of the WTP locus reflects the individual's *ex ante* marginal rate of substitution between income in the two states. The WTL locus for the farmer at his option price is steeper than the WTP locus for the fisherman at his option price, meaning that their marginal rates of substitution are not equal and the allocation of risk is inefficient.

In contrast, it is possible to choose a set of contingent compensation payments that results in an efficient allocation of risk (Graham, 1981). If we contract with the farmer to pay (g_1^A, g_2^A) and contract with the fisherman to pay (g_1^B, g_2^B), the slopes of their WTP loci will be equal, and an efficient allocation of risk will result. In fact, collection and payment of the contingent contracts that underlay any point on the AWTP locus would result in an efficient allocation of risk. By collecting and paying such contingent compensation payments, we mimic the existence of complete contingent claims markets. State-dependent compensation therefore generates an additional benefit, the benefit from moving an inefficient allocation of risk to an efficient allocation.

The issue, then, is whether this additional benefit should be included as a social benefit from the policy change. Doing so can generate perverse situations. Consider a slight modification to the dam example. In figure 25.4, the fisherman's WTP locus, WTP^B, is the same as before. The fisherman is still an *ex ante* loser from the dam. Now, however, the farmer's WTP locus, WTP^C, has shifted down and the left. Perhaps the farmer would lose some arable land due to construction of the dam. The farmer is now also an *ex ante* loser from the dam. Common sense tells us that if both individuals would be made worse off by the dam, then the dam should not be built. However, the AWTP locus constructed from WTP^B and WTP^C still contains a point that is greater than zero in both states. Even though both individuals would prefer, *ex ante*, that the dam not be built, movement to an efficient allocation of risk would generate enough benefits that the dam passes the state-dependent compensation test.

The problem with this result is that unless we require actual state-dependent compensation, we will not move to an efficient allocation of risk. Here there are three possible situations. The baseline situation, where the dam is not built, will be called situation A. In situation B, the dam is built, but compensation is not paid. In situation C, the dam is built and appropriate state-dependent compensation payments are paid and received, resulting in an efficient allocation of risk. Situation B is clearly the least desirable of the three. Situation A is Pareto superior to B, since

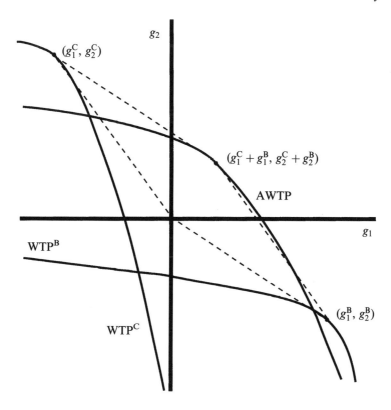

Figure 25.4 AWTP locus for two *ex ante* losers.

both the farmer and the fisherman prefer that the dam not be built. Situation C is also Pareto superior to B, since it involves moving to an efficient allocation of risk.

The state-independent compensation test correctly determines that a move from situation A to situation B does not increase social welfare. The state-dependent compensation test, however, claims that, because situation C is Pareto superior to situation B, a move from situation A to situation B does increase social welfare. The benefit from moving to an efficient allocation of risk is included, even though that efficient allocation of risk is not achieved. The distinction between situations B and C appears to be a restatement of the familiar question, should actual compensation be required? In a world without uncertainty, this issue is sidestepped as being a question regarding the distribution of wealth. Because alternative distributions of wealth are Pareto non-comparable, we cannot judge on efficiency grounds whether compensation should or should not be paid. In an uncertain world, however, payment of compensation can have efficiency implications. State-dependent compensation affects not only the distribution of wealth but also the allocation of risk.

Should the dam be built? If compensation is not paid, or if compensation is paid using state-independent payments, then the dam should not be built. If compensation is paid using appropriate state-dependent compensation payments, then the dam should be built. In general, unless the proposed policy change will be implemented in a way that actually results in an efficient allocation of risk, the state-independent *ex ante* compensation test is the correct test for policy analysis. The implication is that option price is the correct benefit measure under uncertainty, not the WTP locus. This conclusion is consistent with that of Mendelsohn and Strang (1984). They argued that the extra benefit that arises from risk reallocation should be counted as a benefit from the policy change only if such a reallocation will actually occur. They further argued that because the government will rarely be able to implement state-dependent compensation, option price will typically be the correct benefit measure.

One more possibility needs to be considered. It may be that the amount that each individual pays or receives as a result of the policy change will be state dependent but will not result in an efficient allocation of risk. For our dam example, it is common for farmers to pay some amount for irrigation water. The amount the farmer pays could be conditional on how much water he uses, which will in turn depend on the weather. The fisherman might be required to pay a boat launch fee, should he decide to fish in the lake. It would be extremely lucky if these state-dependent payments resulted in an efficient allocation of risk. In addition, we need to worry about dead weight losses associated with any price distortions that the water charges and entry fee would introduce. In such situations, the best approach is to incorporate the fees and charges into the description of the policy, δ, and to measure OP for this more completely described policy (Ready, 1993).

Empirical Issues and Future Directions

If we accept that option price is the appropriate measure of the benefits and costs of a policy change under uncertainty, the next issue that arises is, how can it be measured? Where market prices are available, common practice in applied work is to calculate welfare triangles from observed *ex post* demand curves, and ignore uncertainty. Will this approach result in serious errors? We saw earlier that option value should tend to be small under conditions that are often satisfied for market goods. This theoretical result needs to be confirmed empirically for a range of market goods.

Empirical estimates of option value are therefore still of some interest. One interesting new approach that may help provide such estimates is that of Larson and Flacco (1992). They show how option price can be calculated from *ex post* demand data for a market good. Their approach requires full knowledge of the distributions of the random variables involved, as well as of the structure of individual utility functions. Unfortunately, such information will rarely be available for applied problems. Still, where such information is available, this approach can be used to estimate the error associated with simply calculating the *ex post* welfare triangle. Larson (1991) applied this approach to recreation data, and found that option value was negligibly small relative to option price. If this result is replicated in a variety of contexts, we may justified in ignoring uncertainty when an *ex post* demand curve can be estimated.

But is the demand curve that we observe necessarily an *ex post* demand curve? In Weisbrod's park example, visitors show up at the park only after they have decided to visit the park. A demand curve estimated using the travel-cost method will therefore be *ex post* relative to uncertainty over the desire to visit the park. But what about uncertainty over the quality of the experience at the park? Suppose that a visitor is uncertain whether the scenic views at the park will be obscured by haze. The decision to visit the park must be made *ex ante* to obtaining information about the quality of the views on the day of the visit. The demand curve for visits to the park is therefore *ex ante* to this source of uncertainty, and the welfare triangle measured from the demand curve will provide an estimate of option price. Similarly, Smith (1985) showed that the hedonic pricing approach to amenity valuation can generate an estimate of option price if the related market good is purchased *ex ante* to the source of the uncertainty. In general, every decision is made *ex post* to some sources of uncertainty and *ex ante* to others. To complicate matters further, we have until now assumed that the welfare triangle calculated from an *ex post* utility function will necessarily measure $E(CS)$. While this will be true for situations where individuals face independent risks, if all individuals face some collective risk, the *ex post* demand curve will only include information regarding preferences in one state of nature. A welfare triangle estimated from observed behavior could therefore represent compensating surplus for one state, expected compensating surplus, or option price.

Where preferences for environmental quality do not influence behavior, such as for resources with significant non-use value, the only possible approach to estimating option price or compensating surplus will be contingent valuation.[10] Ideally, in such situations, option price would be estimated directly. Information about compensating surplus or about option value will serve no purpose if a contingent valuation estimate of OP is possible. Such an approach requires that a credible *ex ante* contingent scenario be constructed, however, which may be difficult in some contexts. For example, we might ask a hunter his willingness to pay for an increase in the probability of success during a hunt. If the question is asked as part of an on-site survey, the hunter's response will be *ex post* to uncertainty over participation in the hunt. There is therefore still a need for contingent valuation estimates of option value. Boyle et al. (1992) recently reviewed and critiqued empirical attempts to estimate option value using the contingent valuation method. They found that only a few such studies have been done, and that each of those studies have flaws, some serious.

If we do not accept the argument that option price is the appropriate welfare measure, then we must consider ways to estimate the WTP locus. Here, the task is more difficult, because it requires estimation of more than one point on the locus. A contingent valuation estimate of option price will provide one point on the WTP locus. Estimates of compensating surplus will provide a second point. Other points on the WTP locus could be estimated using contingent valuation, by offering the respondent a dichotomous choice involving state-dependent payments. Care must be taken that the uncertainty is truly exogenous, however, or the respondent may consider possible adjustments of the state probabilities when responding to a contingent payment.

Still, the empirical importance of estimating a complete WTP locus may be small. Cameron and Englin (1991) used contingent valuation to estimate a WTP locus for reductions in acid rain damages, where individuals are uncertain visitors of damaged lakes. They found that estimated WTP loci were only very slightly curved, so that the difference between OP and the expected value of the fair-bet point was relatively small. For this particular problem, the opportunities for risk reallocation were not very important empirically.

While the empirical importance of the difference between $E(CS)$, OP, and the WTP locus has not yet been convincingly demonstrated, we should not at this point conclude that the theoretical issues can be ignored in applied work. More empirical research is needed to determine under what conditions we can ignore uncertainty in benefit estimation. We may find that for situations like those investigated by Larson and by Cameron and Englin, where uncertainty is over economic parameters such as prices or preferences, the issues surrounding uncertainty may be empirically unimportant. It is likely, however, that for some environmental policy changes, such as those that affect health risks, correct treatment of uncertainty will be very important.

Notes

1   In this chapter we restrict attention to compensating welfare measures. All of the material presented in this chapter is equally applicable to equivalent welfare measures.
2   As used by Weisbrod and other early authors, the term "consumer surplus" is synonymous with compensating surplus.

3   Some authors have also given Weisbrod's article credit for the first articulation of the concept of quasi-option value. Quasi-option value relates to the benefit that society gets from collecting information over time and using that information to make better decisions. Quasi-option value is discussed in chapter 26.

4   In the model presented here, welfare measures are defined using indirect utility functions. Smith (1987) provides an alternative framework that uses the planned expenditure function.

5   Throughout this discussion, it will be assumed that adoption of the policy change does not require any monetary outlays by the government, so that positive net benefits are sufficient for the policy change to be a potential Pareto improvement.

6   The superscript *i* will refer to individuals in the population, while the subscript *k* continues to refer to alternative states of nature.

7   This is the definition of risk aversion used by Bohm.

8   Here *ex ante* winners and losers are combined to form one AWTP locus. Freeman (1991) separates winners from losers and constructs an aggregate willingness-to-accept locus for the losers. The two approaches are mathematically identical.

9   It will be assumed here that such markets do not exist. If they did, then the difference between the state-dependent and the state-independent tests would disappear. An individual who has access to complete contingent claims markets would be willing to commit to any contingent payment that costs the same, at the prevailing prices in the contingent claims market, as his option price. Each individual's WTP locus would therefore be linear with a common slope, and the AWTP locus would include the point $(\sum_{i=1}^{N} OP^i, \sum_{i=1}^{N} OP^i)$.

10 The validity of contingent valuation estimates has been called into question recently, particularly for non-use values (Desvousges et al., 1992; NOAA, 1993). Unfortunately, it is precisely those situations where contingent valuation is most needed, that is, where market information is unavailable, that its validity is most suspect. These issues are discussed in more detail in chapter 28.

References

Anderson, Robert J., Jr. 1981: A note an option value and the expected value of consumer's surplus. *Journal of Environmental Economics and Management*, 8 (June), 187–91.

Arrow, Kenneth J. and Lind, Robert C.. 1970: Uncertainty and the evaluation of public investment decisions. *American Economic Review*, 60 (June), 364–78.

Bishop, Richard C. 1982: Option value: an exposition and extension. *Land Economics,* 58 (February), 1–15.

Bishop, Richard C. 1986: Resource valuation under uncertainty: theoretical principles for empirical research. In V. K. Smith (ed.), *Advances in Applied Microeconomics*, vol. 4, Greenwich, CT: JAI Press.

Bishop, Richard C. 1988: Option value: reply. *Land Economics*, 64 (February), 88–93.

Bohm, Peter. 1975: Option demand and consumer's surplus: comment. *American Economic Review*, 65 (September), 733–6.

Boyle, Kevin, J., McCollum, Daniel W. and Teisl, Mario F. 1992: Empirical evidence on the sign and size of option value. In Bruce Rettig (ed.), *Benefits and Costs in Natural Resources Planning: Fifth Interim Report of Regional Project W-133* Corvallis, OR: Oregon State University Press.

Byerlee, D. R. 1971: Option demand and consumer's surplus: comment. *Quarterly Journal of Economics*, 85 (August), 523–7.

Cameron, Trudy Ann, and Englin, Jeffrey, 1991: Cost–benefit analysis for non-market resources: a utility theoretic empirical model incorporating demand uncertainty. In Catherine Kling (ed.), *Benefits and Costs in Natural Resources Planning: Fourth Interim Report of Regional Project W-133*, Davis, CA: University of California Press.

Chavas, Jean-Paul, Bishop, Richard C. and Segerson, Kathleen. 1986: Ex Ante consumer welfare evaluation in cost–benefit analysis. *Journal of Environmental Economics and Management*, 13 (December), 255–68.

Cicchetti, Charles J. and Freeman, A. Myrick III. 1971: Option demand and consumer surplus: further comment. *Quarterly Journal of Economics*, 85 (August), 538–39.

Colby, Bonnie G. and Cory, Dennis C. 1989: Valuing amenity resources under uncertainty: does the existence of fair contingent claims markets matter? *Journal of Environmental Economics and Management*, 16 (March), 149–55.

Cory, Dennis C. and Saliba, Bonnie Colby. 1987: Requiem for option value. *Land Economics*, 63 (February), 1–10.

Desvousges, William H., Johnson, F. Reed, Dunford, Richard W., Boyle, Kevin J., Hudson, Sara P. and Wilson, K. Nicole. 1992: Measuring nonuse damages using contingent valuation: an experimental evaluation of accuracy. Research Triangle Park, NC: Research Triangle Institute Monograph 92-1.

Eckstein, Otto. 1965: *Water Resource Development: The Economics of Project Evaluation.* Cambridge, MA: Harvard University Press.

Freeman, A. Myrick III. 1984: The sign and size of optional value: *Land Economics*, 60 (February), 1–13.

Freeman, A. Myrick III. 1985a: The sign and size of optional value: Reply. *Land Economics*, 61 (February), 78.

Freeman, A. Myrick III. 1985b: Supply uncertainty, option price and option value. *Land Economics*, 61 (May), 176–81.

Freeman, A. Myrick III. 1986:Uncertainty and environmental policy: the role of option and quasi-option values. In V. K. Smith (ed.), *Advances in Applied Microeconomics*, vol. 4, Greenwich, CT: JAI Press.

Freeman, A. Myrick, III. 1991: Welfare measurement and the benefit–cost analysis of projects affecting risk. *Southern Economic Journal*, 58 (July), 65–76.

Graham, Daniel A. 1981: Cost–benefit analysis under uncertainty. *American Economic Review*, 71 (September), 715–25.

Graham, Daniel, A. 1984: Cost–benefit analysis under uncertainty: reply. *American Economic Review*, 74 (December), 1100–2.

Hammond, Peter J. 1981: *Ex-ante* and *ex-post* welfare optimality under uncertainty. *Economica*, 48 (August), 235–50.

Hartman, Richard and Plummer, Mark. L. 1987: Option value under income and price uncertainty. *Journal of Environmental Economics and Management*, 14 (May), 212–25.

Johansson, Per-Olav. 1988: Option value: comment,. *Land Economics*, 64 (February), 86–7.

Larson, Douglas M. 1991: Option prices and option values from market data. In Catherine Kling (ed.), *Benefits and Costs in Natural Resources Planning: Fourth Interim Report of Regional Project W-133*, Davis, CA: University of California Press.

Larson, Douglas, M. and Flacco, Paul R. 1992: Measuring option prices from market behavior. *Journal of Environmental Economics and Management*, 22 (March), 178–98.

Lindsay, Cotton M. 1969: Option demand and consumer's surplus. *Quarterly Journal of Economics*, 83 (May), 344–6.

Long, Millard F. 1967: Collective consumption services of individual consumption goods: comment. *Quarterly Journal of Economics*, 81 (May), 351–2.

Meier, Charles E. and Randall, Alan. 1991: Evaluating use benefits under uncertainty: is there a "correct" measure? *Land Economics*, 67 (November), 379–89.

Mendelsohn, Robert and Strang, William J. 1984: Cost–benefit analysis under uncertainty: comment. *American Economic Review*, 74 (December), 1096–1100.

NOAA. 1993: Natural resource damage assessments under the Oil Pollution Act of 1990. *Federal Register*, 58 (January 15), 4601–14.

Plummer, Mark L. 1985: The size and sign of option value: comment. *Land Economics*, 61 (February), 76–7.

Plummer, Mark L. 1986: Supply uncertainty, option price, and option value. *Land Economics*, 62 (August), 313–18.

Plummer, Mark L. and Hartman, Richard C. 1986: Option value: a general approach. *Economic Inquiry*, 24 (July), 455–71.

Ready, Richard C. 1993: The choice of a welfare measure under uncertainty. *American Journal of Agricultural Economics*, 75 (November), forthcoming.

Samuelson, Paul A. and Vickrey, William. 1964: Discussion. *American Economic Review*, 59 (May), 88–96.

Schmalensee, Richard. 1972: Option demand and consumer's surplus: valuing price changes under uncertainty. *American Economic Review*, 62 (December), 813–24.

Smith, V. Kerry. 1983: Option value: a conceptual overview. *Southern Economic Journal*, 49 (January), 654–8.

Smith V. Kerry. 1984: A bound for option value. *Land Economics*, 60 (August), 292–6.

Smith, V. Kerry. 1985: Supply uncertainty, option price, and indirect benefit estimation. *Land Economics*, 61 (August), 303–7.

Smith, V. Kerry. 1987: Uncertainty, benefit–cost analysis, and the treatment of option value. *Journal of Environmental Economics and Management*, 14 (May), 283-92.

Smith, V. Kerry. 1990: Valuing amenity resources under uncertainty: a skeptical view of recent resolutions. *Journal of Environmental Economics and Management*, 19 (September), 193–202.

Ulph, Alistair. 1982: The role of *ex ante* and *ex post* decisions in the valuation of Life. *Journal of Public Economics*, 18 (July), 265–76.

Weisbrod, Burton A. 1964: Collective-consumption services of individual consumption goods. *Quarterly Journal of Economics*, 78 (August), 471–7.

Willig, Robert D. 1976: Consumer surplus without apology. *American Economic Review*, 66 (September), 589–97.

Wilman, Elizabeth A. 1987: Supply side option value. *Land Economics*, 63 (August), 284–9.

26

Quasi-Option Value

Theodore Graham-Tomasi

1 Introduction

In 1964 Burton Weisbrod introduced the concept of option value (OV). OV is an additional value, over and above the expected value of a good's consumption, that is attached to maintaining a good's future availability when faced with uncertainty about its future demand or supply. Research on OV has shown that it derives from risk aversion (see, for example, Graham, 1981; Bishop, 1982; Smith, 1983; Graham-Tomasi and Myers, 1990). Generally speaking, the OV literature addresses the correct measurement of welfare change under uncertainty, with alternative institutional structures for managing risk.

In 1974, Arrow and Fisher forwarded a different approach to option value, derived under risk neutrality, and based on a dynamic formulation. Arrow and Fisher examined the effects of learning more over time about the uncertain benefits of preserving an area of wilderness land when its development would be irreversible. These authors demonstrated that, relative to a situation in which the decision-maker ignores opportunities for learning, an extra value is attached to preservation when it is realized that one may learn the true benefits of preservation. This extra value they called quasi-option value (QOV).

In this chapter, QOV will be investigated and some of the literature in this area reviewed. Naturally, the basic insight that recognizing opportunities for learning may change decision criteria is applicable beyond the wildland development/preservation scenario investigated by Arrow and Fisher. Hence, levels of general capital investment may be altered in response to learning opportunities (Epstein, 1980; Bernanke, 1983; Demers, 1991). Here, the natural resource connection will be stressed, but the literature is broader than the natural resource examples discussed.

The basic results will establish conditions under which the prospect of receiving "better information" in the future led one to adopt "more flexible" decisions today. The intuitive reasoning is clear: if one is in an inflexible situation, so that any alterations of it are costly (or impossible), then one is less willing to respond to changes in beliefs induced by receipt of information. Hence, being in an inflexible position undermines the value of the information to be received. As the information to be received improves, the incentive to remain flexible and take advantage of it increases.

Clearly, the situation studied by Arrow and Fisher is a special case of this more general concern. Undertaking a completely irreversible action, such as the development of a wildland area, results in a more inflexible position than does leaving the area undeveloped today and having a choice of development or preservation tomorrow. And receipt of perfect information about the true value of wilderness is an extreme version of obtaining "more information."

A resource problem that illustrates most of the issues is the depletion of moist tropical rainforests. The resource stock has value both for its timber and the agricultural land (or other uses) it may be converted to, as well as for the ecosystem services it provides and the biodiversity it contains. The values of the goods and services provided by a tropical forest in its natural state are not well known in comparison with our understanding of the value of harvested timber and agricultural products. The harvest of trees from such forests may result in destruction of the forests, or harvest may be done in a manner (e.g. using helicopters) which preserves much of the standing forest and its ability to provide ecological services. Through scientific research, we can come to learn more about the value of standing forest ecosystems. More informative research is based on larger sample sizes and better procedures. The basic idea of QOV, then, is that the mere prospect of improved research programs on the value of moist tropic forest ecosystems, even allowing for the possibility that they may find that such forests are less valuable than we now believe, should lead to greater conservation of such forests.

2   A General Resource Decision Model

As discussed above, the basic idea of QOV regards the relationship between information and choices that are costly to reverse. In this section we define these ideas in terms of a simple natural resource model with uncertainty.

The resource system

Let the state of a resource system at time t be given by x_t. This could be the amount of land area in an undeveloped state, or the amount of an exhaustible or renewable resource on hand. Let q_t be a control that is applied to the system by a decision maker (DM). Examples are new development of land for roads, harvest of timber, or extraction of fossil fuels. The control is constrained to lie in a set Q_t, which may depend on the state of the system. For example, you cannot extract more resource, or develop more wilderness, than you have.

Uncertainty is represented by a random variable s, taking values in the (time-invariant) set $S = \{s_1, \ldots, s_n\}$. A realization of s at time t is s_t. Important special cases are where (i) there is just one true state of nature $s°$ in S, rather than a sequence of realizations, and (ii) the sequence of realizations s_t forms a Markov process. This uncertainty could arise in a number of ways, affecting the resource itself, or payoffs from its use, or both. Examples would be uncertainty about the demand for wilderness experiences, where s is a parameter of the demand system, or about the value of species in a forest for medicinal purposes, or about a threshold point in the growth function for a renewable resource below which the population is bound for extinction.

If the system is in state x_t, control q_t is applied, and s_t arises, then the system moves to a new state x_{t+1} according to the transition equation

$$x_{t+1} = g(x_t, q_t, s_t) \tag{26.1}$$

Payoffs to the DM depend on where the system is, what is done to it, and the realization of s. Letting $z_t = (x_t, q_t, s_t)$, payoffs take the additively separable, discounted form

$$U = \sum_t \alpha^t u(z_t) \tag{26.2}$$

where $\alpha = 1/(1 + r)$ is a discount factor. Here, we will assume that this general payoff function takes the particular form

$$u(z_t) = w(x_t, s_t) + v(x_0 - x_t, s_t) + (p_t - c_t)q_t \tag{26.3}$$

Thus, the benefits are given by the uncertain value of the resource stock, the uncertain value of the cumulative extraction, and the value of the current extraction. In the case of forests, $w(\cdot)$ is the value of the standing trees, $v(\cdot)$ is the value of the land freed up from forests for alternative uses such as pasture, and $p - c$ is the net value of today's harvested material. In the case of fossil fuels, $w(\cdot)$ may be zero, while $v(\cdot)$ represents uncertain environmental effects, such as global warming, stemming from burning such fuels. In the case of a renewable resource, such as harvest of whales, $v(\cdot)$ may be zero, while $w(\cdot)$ represents non-use values attached to these creatures.

The decision maker's problem is to maximize the expected present value of payoffs, based on one's information about s.

Beliefs and information

The DM's beliefs at time t about the random event are summarized by a probability mass function $\pi_t = (\pi_{1,t}, \ldots, \pi_{n,t})$, where π_{it} is the probability that the realized event at t is s_i. The DM knows that she will receive information over time which can be used to revise her beliefs. The most common representation of this idea is that the DM can observe a "signal" in the form of a random variable y_t, sometimes called the outcome of an "experiment," which is correlated with s_{t+1}. Let Y_t be a set of signals or messages that the DM could receive, where $Y_t = \{y_{1,t}, \ldots, y_{m,t}\}$.

If the DM's current beliefs about the random event are π_t, and the message received is $y_{j,t}$, then the DM's new beliefs are given by the transformation

$$\pi_{t+1} = B(\pi_t, y_{j,t}, t) \qquad (26.4)$$

The DM faces a sequence of experimental outcomes. Let $\{Y\}_t$ denote the sequence of experiments and associated probabilities the DM faces from date t onward. Note that in much of the literature on sequential experimentation (see, for example DeGroot, 1970) it is supposed that there is one control decision to be made after observing the outcomes of a sequence of experiments, where the number of observations to be made, as well as the experiments to be conducted, are choices. Here, a control decision is made each period, and the sequence of experiments is exogenous.

An important case is when $B(\cdot)$ is the map implied by Bayes's rule. To develop this a little further, let β^t be the matrix of joint probabilities, with typical element β_{ij}^t, that is, this is the probability that $s_{t+1} = s_{i,t+1}$ and $y_t = y_{j,t}$. The likelihood matrix of conditional probabilities is $\varDelta^t = [\delta_{ji}^t] = \mathrm{pr}\,(y_t = y_{j,t} | s_{t+1} = s_{i,t+1})$. Thus, δ gives the probability of observing a particular signal y, given that the true state to arise is s. Let the Θ^t be the posterior probabilities, the matrix of probabilities on s, conditional on having observed a particular y. A typical element of Θ^t is $\theta_{ij}^t = \mathrm{pr}(s_{t+1} = s_{i,t+1} | y_t = y_{j,t})$. Having observed the signal $y_{j,t}$, the conditional distribution on next period's random event is given by the jth column of Θ^t. Finally, let λ^t be the predictive distribution of y_t, that is, the marginal distribution regarding which message will be received, given current beliefs.

Then the linkage between the experiment and the random event is summarized by the following relationships (dropping the time notation):

$$\lambda_j = \sum_i \beta_{ij} = \sum_i \pi_i \delta_{ji}$$

$$\beta_{ij} = \theta_{ij} \lambda_j \qquad (26.5)$$

Thus, the map $B(\cdot)$ when the DM is using Bayes's rule is

$$\pi_{i,t+1} = \frac{\delta_{ji}^t \pi_{i,t}}{\sum_k \delta_{jk}^t \pi_{k,t}} \tag{26.6}$$

If there is just one true state of nature s (rather than a sequence of realizations), or if the draws s_t are independent and identically distributed (i.i.d.), then the transformation $B(\cdot)$ does not itself depend on time when Bayes's rule is being used. In these situations the sequence of beliefs $\{\pi_t\}_t$ has the Markov property. That is, all that matters to the revision of beliefs is the current state of beliefs π_t, and not the whole history. In the case of a sequence of i.i.d. realizations s_t, the sequence of beliefs also is i.i.d.

The decision problem

The DM maximizes the expected present value of payoffs, subject to the transition equation on the resource state, as well as the transition equation on beliefs. Let the state of the system be $(x_t, \pi_t) \equiv Z_t$. The system evolves according to (26.1) and (26.5). The DM solves

$$\max_q E \sum_t \alpha^t u(x_t, q_t, s_t) \tag{26.7}$$

subject to

$$x_{t+1} = g(x_t, q_t, s_t)$$
$$\pi_{t+1} = B(\pi_t, y_{j,t}, t)$$
$$q_t \in Q_t(x_t)$$
$$x_o = x^0(=1) \qquad \pi_0, \{Y\}_0 \text{ given}$$

It is important to note that the experiment here is exogenous to the DM. There is no choice among experiments to be made and, in particular, the information to be received does not depend on the control chosen. We will comment on this below.

At each date, the DM chooses the control q as a function of the current state (x_t, π_t); this function is called a plan. Given a plan $q(Z)$, the expected discounted payoffs are

$$J[q(Z)] = E\{u[x_0, q(Z_0), s_0] + \sum_{t=1} \alpha^t u[x_t, q(Z_t), s_t]\} \tag{26.8}$$

where Z_t evolves according to (26.1) and (26.6) and the expectation is relative to the information the DM expects to receive via the experiments.

The problem is to find the best plan from the set of all feasible plans. A plan is feasible if it specifies a control that lies in Q_t for all t. Thus, letting F

be the set of all feasible plans, the problem is to find

$$V(x_0, \pi_0; \{Y\}_0) = \sup_{q(Z) \in F} J[q(Z)] \qquad (26.9)$$

Under some technical conditions, the optimal plan can be characterized using dynamic programming methods. A full treatment of these issues is beyond the scope of this chapter (see, for example, Blackwell, 1965; Maitra, 1968; Blume et al., 1982). We assume here that the problem is stationary, so that $B(\cdot)$ does not depend on time. The constraint set Q_t is given by a fixed function of the state, that is, $Q_t = Q(x_t)$. It is further assumed that $Q(x)$ satisfies the following condition:

$$q^1 \in Q(x^1), q^2 \in Q(x^2) \Rightarrow kq^1 + (1-k)q^2 \in Q[kx^1 + (1-k)x^2]$$
$$k \in [0, 1] \qquad (26.10)$$

In the resource context, such a condition would be satisfied if $Q(x) = [0, x]$ (e.g. you cannot extract more of a resource than you have). Finally, we assume that, for each s, the transition equation is twice differentiable and concave in (x, q), and the reward function is twice differentiable and strictly concave in (x, q).

By well-known results (e.g. Blume et al., 1982) we know that the DM's maximization problem has a solution $q(Z)$, and that the solution is unique. Also, $V(Z_0; \{Y\}_0)$, the optimized objective function, is differentiable, concave in x, and satisfies the recursive relationship

$$V(Z_t; \{Y\}_t) = \max_q \ [E_t(u[x_t, q(Z_t), s_t]$$
$$+ \alpha V\{g[x_t, q(Z_t), s_t], B(\pi_t, y_t); \{Y\}_{t+1}\}) | \ q \in Q(x_t)] \qquad (26.11)$$

where the expectation is with respect to the DM's current information.

The timing of the observation of the experiment relative to the choice of q and realization of s is important. It is assumed that the DM enters each period in state Z_t, that is, with x_t on hand and with current beliefs about s of π_t. Then, she must choose current action q. Based on the current resource state and the action q, the resource moves to a new state x_{t+1}, perhaps stochastically. The DM also observes the outcome of the experiment Y_t, and revises her beliefs about next period's random events according to the map $B(\pi_t, y_t)$.

Being more explicit about the expectations operator, (26.11) can be written as

$$V(Z_t; \{Y\}_t) = \max_{q \in Q} \sum_i \pi_{i,t} u(x_t, q, s_{i,t})$$
$$+ \alpha \sum_j \sum_k \pi_{k,t} \delta_{jk}^t V[g(x_t, q, s_{i,t}), B(\pi_t, y_{j,t}); \{Y\}_{t+1}] \qquad (26.12)$$

Of course, $\sum_k \pi_{k,t} \delta_{jk}$ is just $\lambda_{j,t}$, the probability that one observes signal y_j and time t.

Our task now is to make explicit what is meant by an "irreversibility effect" such that receiving better information induces one to take more flexible positions.

Information

We wish to compare the resource decisions that get made when the DM is to receive information over time from one set of signals to those decisions that are made when improved information is available. There are a number of ways that the idea of improved information has been represented in the literature. Not necessarily referring to the above decision problem, let $W(x, q, s_i)$ be the payoffs from taking action q when the true state is s_i and the resource is in state x. If the DM has just received the message y_j, which arrives with (predictive) probability λ_j, she uses the posterior probabilities θ_{ij} in assessing the chance that s_i will arise. Let Y and Y' denote two different message systems, with corresponding probabilities (λ, Θ) and (λ', Θ'). We have the following definition.

The message system Y is more valuable than the message system Y' (written $Y \succeq_V Y'$) if

$$\sum_j \lambda_j \max_{q \in Q} \sum_i \theta_{ij} W(x, q, s_i) \geq \sum_j \lambda'_j \max_{q \in Q} \sum_i \theta'_{ij} W(x, q, s_i) \qquad (26.13)$$

Thus, we have the $Y \succeq_V Y'$ if a maximizing DM attains higher expected payoffs observing signals from Y than she does observing signals from Y'. This holds regardless of the risk preferences embodied in $W(\cdot)$.

This definition is equivalent to another, which proves to be extremely useful analytically. Let $\Delta^m \equiv \{(\xi_1, \ldots, \xi_m) | \xi_i \geq 0, \Sigma_i \xi_i = 1\}$, i.e. Δ_m is the set of m-dimensional probability vectors. Let $\Phi(\xi)$ be any convex function defined on Δ_m. We have the following definition

Y is more informative than Y' (written $Y \succeq_I Y'$) if

$$\sum_j \lambda_j \Phi(\theta_{ij}) \geq \sum_j \lambda'_j \Phi(\theta'_{ij}) \qquad \forall \text{ convex } \Phi : \Delta_n \to \mathbb{R} \qquad (26.14)$$

The following lemma shows the usefulness of the definition of "more informative."

Lemma 1 $Y \succeq_I Y' \to Y \succeq_V Y'$.

Thus, more informative message systems are more valuable. Lemma 1 was proved by Bohenblust et al. (1949) (see also Marschak and Miyasawa,

1968, theorem 12.1).[1]

These approaches say that, when one has access to better information, then one's initial beliefs are subject to greater revision. Similarly, one can show that if one's initial beliefs are more uncertain then the same information will lead to greater revision of the initial beliefs. Thus, Jones and Ostroy (1984) prefer to use the terminology "greater variability of beliefs" rather than "improvement in information."

The above definitions are stated as if there is only a single observation on the experiment. But our general decision problem above involves multiple time periods. The first definition of "more valuable" experiments in (26.12) is obtained by replacing W by V appropriately. Hence, we have

$$\{Y\}_t \succeq_V \{Y'\}_t \text{ if}$$

$$V(Z_t; \{Y\}_t) \geq V(Z_t; \{Y'\}_t) \tag{26.15}$$

This definition can be written more suggestively by noting that

$$V(Z_t; \{Y\}_t) = \max_{q \in Q(x)} \left\{ \sum_i \pi_{i,t} u(x_t, q, s_{i,t}) \right.$$

$$+ \alpha \left[\sum_j \lambda_{j,t} \max_{q' \in Q[g(x,q,s)]} \left(\sum_k \theta_{kj} u[g(x_t, q, s_{i,t}), q', s_{k,t+1}] \right.\right.$$

$$+ \alpha \sum_j \sum_k \delta_j^{t+1} \pi_{k,t+1} V\{g[g(x_t, q, s_{i,t}), q', s_{k,t+1}],$$

$$\left.\left.\left. B[B(\pi_i, y_{j,t}), y_{m,t+1}]; \{Y\}_{t+2} \right) \right] \right\} \tag{26.16}$$

This definition of "more informative" in (26.13) does not need to be altered at all if it is understood that Φ is defined on a vector given by sequences $\{\theta_{ij,t}\}_t$.

More informative experiments lead to increases in the value function for the optimization program. The difference between the value function for the improved information structure and the value function for the base information structure equals the expected value of information (VOI) in the improved information. Thus, we offer

The VOI for structure $\{Y\}_t$ relative to that of structure $\{Y'\}_t$ is
$$\text{VOI}(Y, Y') = V(Z_t; \{Y\}_t) - V(Z_t; \{Y'\}_t)$$

The result on the VOI is recorded in

Theorem 1 If $Y \succeq_I Y'$, then $\text{VOI}(Y, Y') \geq 0$

Proof This follows immediately from lemma 1 applied to (26.16).

Examples of "more informative" experiments readily can be provided in particular resource situations. Thus, if we have a wilderness area, then travel-cost or contingent valuation studies of the area's value could be based on larger sample sizes. Or, the value of biodiversity could be assessed using a clinical trial of a plant's usefulness as a drug, rather than using laboratory rats, etc.

Flexibility and irreversibility

The previous section set forth relationships between information structures. In this section we set forth relationships between choices regarding the extent to which they are flexible and preserving of future options.

One way to do this (Freixas and Laffont, 1984) is to consider the size of the constraint set one faces in the next period as it depends on current choices. Consider two decisions, q and q'. In terms of our above model we have

q is more options preserving than $q'(q \succeq_o q')$ if $Q[g(x,q,s)] \supseteq Q[g(x,q',s)]$ for every x and s

Jones and Ostroy (1984) focus on the costs of getting from one position to another. They decompose $u(x, q, s)$ into a payoff from being in situation x and a switching cost to get from x_t to x_{t+1}, $C(x, x_{t+1}, s_t)$.[2] Jones and Ostroy say that position x is more flexible than position $x' (x \succeq_f x')$ if the set of new positions reachable at a given cost from x is bigger than the set reachable form x' at that cost. Formally, define

$$G(x_t, s_t, k) \equiv \{x_{t+1} | C(x, x_{t+1}, s_t) \leq k\}$$

Then we have

$$x \succeq_f x' \text{ if } G(x_t, s_t, k) \supseteq G(x'_t, s_t, k) \quad \text{for all } s, k$$

The definition here is based on positions of the resource state x, rather than on choices q. This can be translated into a definition for q by applying the ordering $\succeq_f$ to positions reached from q, that is, by a new ordering $\succeq_F$ defined by

$$q \succeq_F q' \Leftrightarrow g(x_t, q, s_t) \succeq_f g(x_t, q', s_t) \text{ for all } x, s$$

It obviously is the case that, as long as the utility function is decomposable as specified above, then the two definitions of flexibility of choices, $\succeq_o$ and $\succeq_F$, are equivalent.

A special case of the idea of flexibility is perfect irreversibility, a case with which most of the literature is concerned. A perfectly irreversible position is one from which nothing can happen except movement to a new time period. That is, no control can be applied which would move the resource system except to where it would move by itself. Thus, we have

A position x^i is irreversible if $x^i_{t+1} = g(x^i, q, s)$ for all q in $Q(x^i)$

Note that this does not necessarily mean that next period's state must bear any particular relationship to this period's state, but it does mean that there is nothing that the DM can do to alter the evolution of the resource state.

Note that there is some reversibility in the case of renewable resources, so we do not require strictly irreversible processes in the above definition. Naturally, in the case of exhaustible resources, where $g(x, q, s) = x - q$ and $Q(x) = [0, x]$, any extraction is absolutely irreversible. In the case of forests or wilderness, we may allow some "reversion to the wild" in $G(\cdot)$, or we allow the growth of renewable resources. In these cases, irreversibility is captured by a constraint $q \geq 0$, so that the resource stock cannot be augmented faster than its natural rate of regeneration.

The above definitions regarding flexibility were stated as if they pertained to a two-period model; they applied to a single control decision at one point in time. However, our basic decision model outlined earlier is a multi-time model. Thus, the above definitions need to be extended to include whole sequences of choices. The most obvious extension is

The sequence $\{q_t\}_t \succeq_o \{q'_t\}$ if $q_t \succeq_o q'_t$ for all t

Thus, one sequence is more options preserving than another if each if its elements is more options preserving.

3 Irreversibility Effects and Quasi-Option Values

We now are in a position to state the central results of this literature. These are obtained by applying the above definitions of orderings on information and flexibility of positions (or special cases of them) to the general decision problem stated earlier (or special cases of it).

Some writers in this area study what we call the "irreversibility effect." This is a relationship between better information and the flexibility of initial positions. Establishing the existence of an irreversibility effect requires establishing that an ordering on information induces an ordering on flexibility. This is the approach taken by Freixas and Laffont (1984) and by Jones and Ostroy (1984) among others. In this sense, there is no "quasi-option value" derived explicitly. Formally stated, we have

The irreversibility effect (IE) holds if $\{Y\}_t \succeq_I \{Y'\}_t \Rightarrow \{q_t\}_t \succeq_F \{q'_t\}$

Another approach is to derive values, the QOVs, as a sequence of taxes which would induce a DM who "ignores the improved information" to choose the same control as that used by a DM who builds the receipt of better information into the decision problem (Arrow and Fisher, 1974). But what does it mean to ignore information? And what kinds of taxes should one consider?

Naturally, there is an intimate tie between the existence of an irreversibility effect and the sign of the approximately defined tax on controls. For example, suppose that the IE implies that less of the resource is extracted at some date. Then, a tax could be placed on extraction such that a DM facing worse information would use the same control as a DM obtaining the improved information. Thus, if the IE exists, the associated QOV, conceived of as a tax on the control, is positive.

Still another approach identifies the QOV as an expected value of information (VOI), rather than as a tax on development (Hanemann, 1989). This VOI approach looks at the benefits realized from incorporating information instead of ignoring it. In some circumstances the VOI equals the QOV given by a tax on the control; for example, if $Q(x) = \{0, x\}$. However, in other cases of relevance (e.g. $Q = [0, x]$), this equivalence does not hold (see Hanemann, 1989). Here, because of its close relationship to the IE, we submit that the appropriate concept of QOV is the tax on the control.

Finally, some authors have restricted their attention to a situation where a given decision will be implemented, and the issue is how much information to obtain before doing this, where information is accumulated through time. This is more in line with the literature on sequential experimentation (e.g. DeGroot, 1970) and will not be discussed further here.

In most of the literature on the irreversibility effect and QOV, it is supposed that there are just two time periods and that either one receives perfect information, or no information at all. It is further supposed that the decision space is $Q = \{0, x\}$ or, equivalently, a linear benefit function is imposed with $Q = [0, x]$, in which case either q is set equal to zero or all of the available resource is extracted. This allows sharper results (Hanemann, 1989), but we take the more general approach of allowing continuous choices with nonlinear payoffs.

In this chapter, we will examine two resource problems. The first, which we shall call case E, represents exhaustible resource extraction. The extraction of fossil fuels and irreversible land development examples are in this class. The transition equation in case E is $g(x, q, s) = x - q$. The second case is called case R, for renewable resource extraction. The transition equation in this instance is $g(x, q, s) = F(x) - q$, where $F(x) = x + G(x)$ and G is the growth function for the resourse. Of course, case R becomes case E when $G(x) = 0$ for all x. In both these cases we suppose that $Q(x_t) = [0, x_t]$. Note that uncertainty has been expunged from the transition equation for the resource stock, thereby limiting somewhat the scope of our analysis here.

It is straightforward to show that, for either of these cases, smaller extractions are more options preserving. We state this as

Lemma 2 In either case E or case R, $\{q_t\}_t \succeq_0 \{q'_t\}$ if $q_t \leq q'_t$ for all t.

Of course, in the case of renewable resources, this cannot be an "if and only if" statement. This lemma does not characterize all the interesting issues. For example let G be concave, first rising and then falling. Let x^m be the maximum sustained yield (MSY) biomass level, and take $\{q\}_t$ to be a constant equal to the maximum sustainable harvest, $q^m = G(x^m)$. Consider some alternative $\{q'\}_t$ set equal to a constant level of harvest $q' < q_m$ and associated steady state stock x' on the upward-sloping portion of the growth function. Relative to q', a larger stock can be obtained, and a more flexible position reached, via the control sequence composed of $q_t = 0$ until $x_t = x^m$ and $q_t = q^m$ thereafter. So the reverse implication of lemma 2 does not hold. Moreover, this example shows that, with multiple time periods and renewable resources, determining the more flexible positions will require some work (see Fisher and Hanemann (1985) for an investigation along these lines).

Unless the general decision model is restricted further, the irreversibility effect does not hold and the QOV can be positive or negative. This, in some ways, is rather surprising, since it makes intuitive sense that the prospect of learning more should lead one to adopt more flexible positions. After all, information is valuable; if one is in an inflexible position, one cannot make use of the information to revise one's actions and the benefit of learning is forgone. What is required to demonstrate the irreversibility effect is that the gain in the value of information from taking a more flexible position outweighs the opportunity costs of this position.

We assume that the utility function takes the form in (26.3), that is, that

$$u(x, q, s) = w(x, s) + v(1 - x, s) + (p - c)q$$

where $u(\cdot)$ and $v(\cdot)$ are concave in their first argument for each s. Holding the resource stock may involve maintenance costs implicit in w. In some papers (e.g. Epstein, 1980; Freixas and Laffont, 1984; Graham-Tomasi, 1984) it is supposed that utility is a function of stocks of developed and undeveloped resource alone, with no benefits and/or costs of current development.

The first-order necessary condition for a maximum of (26.16) is

$$(p - c) + \alpha \sum_j \sum_k \pi_{k,t} \delta^t_{jk} \frac{\partial V(Z_{t+1})}{\partial x_{t+1}} \frac{\partial g[x_t, q(Z), s_{i,t}]}{\partial q} \leq 0 \qquad \text{if } q(Z) \leq 0$$

$$= 0 \qquad \text{if } q(Z) > 0$$

$$(26.17)$$

Condition (26.17) generalizes, by incorporating uncertainty and receipt of information, the usual discrete-time version of the renewable resource problem.

In either case R or case E, $\partial g[x_t, q(Z), s_{i,t}]/\partial q = -1$. Thus,

$$(p - c) = \alpha \sum_j \sum_k \pi_{k,t} \delta_{ji}^t \frac{\partial V[x + F(x) - q(x_t, \pi_t), \pi_{t+1}]}{\partial x_{t+1}} \quad \text{if } q(Z) > 0$$

$$(26.18)$$

$$(p - c) \le \alpha \sum_j \sum_k \pi_{k,t} \delta_{ji}^t \frac{\partial V[x + F(x) - q(x_t, \pi_t), \pi_{t+1}]}{\partial x_{t+1}} \quad \text{if } q(Z) = 0$$

Hence, if the expected marginal shadow value of the resource stock exceeds the value of a unit of extracted stock, then extraction will be zero. However, if extraction is to be positive, it is carried out to the point which balances the current marginal gains from extraction and the expected shadow value of the resource *in situ*. Naturally, if the problem were reversible, so that the resource stock could *actively* be augmented (i.e. q could be negative), then (26.18) would hold as an equality for all t. It is the second line of (26.18) where irreversibility is realized.

We see immediately that if the term on the right-hand side of (26.18) is convex in π_{t+1}, then an improvement in information leads to increases in flexibility by reducing the current extraction of the resource. This is so by lemmas 1 and 2, and the assumed concavity of w and v in their arguments. We state this as follows.

Theorem 2   If payoffs are concave in x for all (x, s) and $\partial V(Z_{t+1})/\partial x_{t+1}$ is convex in π_{t+1}, then the irreversibility effect holds, that is, an improvement in information leads to an increase in flexibility.

Proof   If the value function is convex in π for given x, an improvement in information increases the right-hand side of (26.18), by lemma 1. In order to maintain the equality in (26.18), by the concavity of $V(\cdot)$ in x, x_{t+1} must increase, requiring a decrease in $q(Z_t)$. This corresponds to an increase in flexibility, according lemma 2.

This is an application of Epstein's theorem 1 to a multi-time resource extraction problem. It is also a reformulation of the result in Freixas and Laffont (1984). They show that, if the derivative with respect to the state variable of the expected value of information (conditional on the choices with inferior information) is positive, then the irreversibility effect holds in their model. But this will hold if the expected shadow value function is convex in beliefs. The result extends both of these papers to include net values for current extraction.

To define the QOV and its relationship to the irreversibility effect, suppose that a DM operates using information system $\{Y'\}_t$ and ignores the availability of an improved information system $\{Y^0\}_t$. In order to induce the same choice of extraction, a unit tax can be placed on extraction. The appropriate tax is the expected shadow value of the resource with the improved information, less its expected value with the inferior information. That is, we have the following definition.

Suppose that $\{Y^0\}_t \succeq_I \{Y'\}_t$. Then

$$\text{QOV}(\{Y^0\}, \{Y'\}) = \alpha \sum_j \sum_k \pi^0_{k,t} \delta^{0t}_{ji} \frac{\partial V[x + F(x) - q(x_t, \pi^0_t), \pi^0_{t+1}]}{\partial x_{t+1}}$$

$$-\alpha \sum_j \sum_k \pi'_{k,t} \delta''_{ji} \frac{\partial V[x + F(x) - q(x_t, \pi'_t), \pi'_{t+1}]}{\partial x_{t+1}}$$

(26.19)

Thus, the QOV equals the difference between two shadow prices of the stock. It is not given by a value of information, which is the difference between two value functions. An immediate corollary to theorem 2 is that, under the stipulated conditions, an improvement in information leads to a positive QOV. Formally, we have the following.

Corollary Under the conditions of theorem 2, QOV ≥ 0.

The trick, of course, is to determine conditions under which the derivative of the value function with respect to the state variable is convex in beliefs. We show that, under the conditions stipulated so far, the expected shadow value of the stock is in fact a convex function of beliefs in case E and case R.

Theorem 3 For case E or case R, the expected shadow value of the stock, $E[\partial V(x, \pi; \{Y\})/\partial x]$, is convex in π.

Proof See the appendix.

In the proof it is revealed that the result depends on information which might provide both "good" and "bad" news. That is, if all the information that one might receive leads to an expected shadow value of the stock which exceeds the current value of extraction, then a positive level of extraction is undertaken under all beliefs. In this case of only good news, being obtained in the sense that it is not discovered that pat extraction was excessive, then improved information has no effect, the irreversibility effect does not hold, and the QOV is zero. Similarly, if all the information leads to bad news, so that the constraint is always binding, then the IE does not hold and QOV is zero. Only if some messages lead to good news and some to bad does the prospect of improved information imply an increase in flexibility and a positive QOV.[3]

Bernanke–Graham-Tomasi quasi-option value

As discussed briefly above, different authors treat the scenario of ignoring the improved information differently. Bernanke assumed that the ignorance case involves maximizing each period's payoffs separately, in a sequence of myopic optimization problems. Thus, each period, the DM who ignores information solves

$$\max_q E([p - c]q + \alpha\{w[g(x, q), s] + v[1 - g(x, q), s]\}) \qquad q \in Q(x)$$

Imposing the separable utility function as in (26.3), we see that the solution to this problem is characterized by the condition

$$\alpha \sum_i \pi_{i,t} \frac{\partial w(x_t, s_{i,t})}{\partial x} - \frac{\partial v(1 - x_t, s_{i,t})}{\partial x} = p - c \qquad (26.20)$$

Thus, the DM in this version sets the discounted expected net marginal benefits of increasing the resource stock (by decreasing q) equal to the net benefits forgone from the decrease in q.

Suppose that the improved information scenario involves applying condition (26.19). To deduce the QOV we need an expression for $\partial V/\partial x$. Using the envelope theorem, we find that

$$\frac{\partial V(Z_t)}{\partial x} = \sum_i \pi_{i,t} \left[\frac{\partial w(x_t, s_{i,t})}{\partial x} - \frac{\partial v(1 - x_t, s_{i,t})}{\partial x} \right]$$
$$+ \frac{1 + G'(x)}{1 + r} \sum_j \sum_k \pi_{k,t} \partial_{ji}^t \left[\frac{\partial V(Z_{t+1})}{\partial x} \right] \qquad (26.21)$$

Combining this with (26.20) we can see that the QOV for this comparison is

$$\frac{1 + G'(x)}{1 + r} \sum_j \sum_k \pi_{k,t} \delta_{ji}^t \frac{\partial V(Z_{t+1})}{\partial x} \qquad (26.22)$$

This is proportional to the term on the right-hand side of (26.19). Bernanke's QOV is positive.

Why would a DM ignore the future and act myopically as Bernanke supposes? In an independent derivation of the same result as Bernanke's, Graham-tomasi considered a model of wilderness development in which new development is costless and confers no direct benefit. Then, if one is not considering the receipt of information, the optimal dynamic policy is to behave myopically, that is, assume no revisionof beliefs, so that a dynamic optimization problem is solved,but using $\pi_t = \pi_0$ for all t. We have $x_t = 1 - \sum_{s \leq t} q_t$ and $U = u(\sum_{s \leq t} q_t, 1 - \sum_{s \leq t} q_t, s_t)$. It is easy to show that the optimal policy is $\{q\}_t = (q^m, 0, 0, \ldots)$, where q^m solves $u_1 - u_2 = 0$ and u_i is the derivative of u with respect to its ith argument. This is the equivalent of the Bernanke approach in this model. Then, introducing information leads to setting $u_1 - u_2 = \text{QOV}$, defined as above. Graham-Tomasi shows that, in this model, the shadow price function is convex in beliefs. Thus, the IE holds and QOV is positive.

4 Discussion

There are a variety of ways that QOV has been discussed. Originally, the motivation was that decision makers, such as government agencies, appeared to ignore possibilities for learning in their natural resource decisions. Cost–benefit analysts typically employ simplified procedures when uncertainty is present, and use current information to replace random variables by their means or to compute expected future benefits and costs. A concern then arises that such incomplete decision rules lead to decisions biased in a particular direction. The demonstration that QOV is positive implies that typical benefit–cost decision rules are biased in favor if irreversible investments.

This chapter has applied these ideas to a more general set of concerns. This more general framework reveals the wide applicability of the notion of QOV. It seems that the concept is fundamental to problems of resource use. The difficulty, of course, lies in empirical treatments which might establish the magnitude of the bias in particular situations. In fact, few such empirical applications of the idea have been attempted (see Fisher and Hanemann (1986) for one effort).

There are three extensions of the above analysis that warrant discussion. First, the approach removed uncertainty from the transition equation. Some of the arguments of environmentalists pertain to the difficulty of undertaking decisions when the laws governing ecosystem function are poorly understood. The model above can handle some of these concerns. For example, we should not be cavalier about substitution of capital for resources, since we know little about which are the necessary resources. This introduces uncertainty into the demand for the resource stock, as above. However, there needs to be uncertainty in the transition equation to handle problems of hysteresis and uncertain thresholds below which extinction occurs.

Second, the basic arguments could be applied to more general equilibrium, macro-oriented concerns. Adding capital to the model would allow this. It would be reasonable, then, to introduce uncertainty in the production function relating capital to resource stocks of various kinds. The value function would play the role of an appropriate national income equation, and the shadow prices appropriately would consider uncertainty. Thus, national income accounts augmented to include resources should employ shadow values which include recognition of uncertainty as well as opportunities for learning.

Finally, the information structure here was taken as exogenous. But the amount to be learned obviously depends on research expenditures, taken out of current output. Moreover, as Miller and Lad (1984) pointed out, the amount learned may depend on extraction decisions themselves. Thus, with oil exploration in wilderness, to learn more about the oil stock requires some development of wilderness. In this case, the QOV results derived are undermined. However, in many circumstances, learning will increase with conservation, which will only serve to reinforce the irreversibility effect. Perhaps more importantly, the amount to be learned via research effort should be made endogenous.

Appendix

Here, we prove theorem 3, which states that the value function is convex in beliefs. First, we consider a finite-horizon problem and show that each value function is convex using an induction argument. Then, we use a result that the infinite-horizon value function retains the features of the finite-horizon value function in the limit as the time horizon becomes arbitrarily long. The proof is based on one by Demers (1991).

Step 1

Consider a finite time horizon version of the above problem (26.7), with end-date T. Let $V^N(Z_{T-N})$ be the value function with N dates remaining. Define an operator

$$\Gamma[V(x, \pi)] = \max_{q \geq 0} \sum_i \pi_i \{w(x, s_i) + v(1 - x, s_i)\}$$

$$+ (p - c)q + \alpha \sum_j \sum_k \delta_{jk} \pi_k V[x + F(x) - q, B(\pi, y_j)]$$

If $C(S)$ is the space of bounded, continuous functions $V: S \to \mathbb{R}$, with S compact, previous assumptions ensure that $\Gamma C(S) \to C(S)$. Give $C(S)$ the sup norm, under which $C(S)$ is a complete metric space. Then Γ satisfies the properties of a contraction mapping on a complete metric space, due to arguments in Blackwell (1965). Every contraction map on a complete metric space has a unique fixed point (Rodin, 1976). Thus, the equation $\Gamma V = V$ has a unique solution, which is the infinite-horizon value function for (26.7). Moreover, letting Γ^m be the application of Γ m times, $\| \Gamma^m V^0 - V \|$ goes to zero uniformly (since it is convergence in the sup norm) as m goes to infinity, for any initial V^0. Concavity and differentiability are established by Blume et al. (1982).

Let $V^N(x, \pi) = \Gamma V^{N-1}(x, \pi)$. Since V^N is differentiable and converges to V uniformly, assuming that $\partial V^N(x, \pi)/\partial x$ converges, it does so uniformly to

$\partial V(x, \pi)/\partial x$ (Rodin, 1976). Since the limit of a sequence of convex functions is convex, it suffices to show that $\partial V^N(x, \pi)/\partial x$ is convex in π for every N.

Step 2

We need to show that $V^N(x, \pi)/\partial x$ is convex. Pick two beliefs, π^0 and π^1, and let $\pi^\mu = \mu\pi^0 + (1 - \mu)\pi^1$, for $\mu \in [0, 1]$. Thus, we need to show that

$$\frac{V^N(x, \pi^\mu)}{\partial x} \leq \mu\frac{\partial V^N(x, \pi^0)}{\partial x} + (1 - \mu)\frac{\partial V^N(x, \pi^1)}{\partial x} \tag{A26.1}$$

From equation (26.21)

$$\frac{\partial V^N(x, \pi^\mu)}{\partial x} = \sum_i \pi_{i,t}^\mu \left[\frac{\partial w(x_t, s_{i,t})}{\partial x} - \frac{\partial v(x_t, s_{i,t})}{\partial x}\right] + \frac{1 + G'(x)}{1 + r}$$

$$\times \sum_j \sum_k \pi_{k,t}^\mu \delta_{ji}^t \frac{\partial V^{N-1}[x + G(x) - q(x, \pi^\mu), \pi_{t+1}^\mu]}{\partial x} \tag{A26.2}$$

Since $V^0 = 0$, $\partial V^1(x, \pi^\mu)/\partial x$ is linear in π and hence convex. Using an induction argument, we know that $\partial V^1/\partial x$ is convex in π, and will assume that $\partial V^2/\partial x$, $\partial V^3/\partial x, \ldots, \partial V^{N-1}/\partial x$ are all convex in π; we shall then show that $\partial V^N/\partial x$ is convex in π.

Use $\pi^\mu = \mu\pi^0 + (1 - \mu)\pi^1$ in the first summation in (A26.2) and add and subtract

$$\mu\frac{1 + G'(x)}{1 + r}\sum_j \sum_k \pi_{k,t}^0 \delta_{ji}^t \frac{\partial V^{N-1}[x + G(x) - q(x, \pi^0), \pi_{t+1}^0]}{\partial x}$$

and

$$1 - \mu\frac{1 + G'(x)}{1 + r}\sum_j \sum_k \pi_{k,t}^1 \delta_{ji}^t \frac{\partial V^{N-1}[x + G(x) - q(x, \pi^1), \pi_{t+1}^1]}{\partial x}$$

This yields

$$\frac{\partial V^N(x, \pi^\mu)}{\partial x} = \mu\frac{\partial V^N(x, \pi^0)}{\partial x} + (1 - \mu)\frac{\partial V^N(x, \pi^1)}{\partial x}$$

$$+ \frac{1 + G'(x)}{1 + r}\sum_j \sum_k \pi_{k,t}^\mu \delta_{ji}^t \frac{\partial V^{N-1}[x + G(x) - q(x, \pi^\mu), \pi_{t+1}^\mu]}{\partial x}$$

$$- \mu\frac{1 + G'(x)}{1 + r}\sum_j \sum_k \pi_{k,t}^0 \delta_{ji}^t \frac{\partial V^{N-1}[x + G(x) - q(x, \pi^0), \pi_{t+1}^0]}{\partial x}$$

$$- \mu\frac{1 + G'(x)}{1 + r}\sum_j \sum_k \pi_{k,t}^1 \delta_{ji}^t \frac{\partial V^{N-1}[x + G(x) - q(x, \pi^1), \pi_{t+1}^1]}{\partial x}$$

$$\tag{A26.3}$$

Thus, we need to show that the sum of the last three lines is non-positive. Divide through these terms by $(1 + G')/(1 + r)$. Then the terms are related to the first-order conditions for a maximizing choice of q in (26.18). We must consider whether the alternative beliefs π^μ, π^0, and π^1 lead to corner solutions or interior solutions. We shall consider the alternatives in turn.

1   Suppose first that the three beliefs all lead to interior solutions. By the first-order condition for q, the first term is $p - c$, while the second and third terms are $\mu(p - c)$ and $(1 - \mu)(p - c)$. Thus, the sum of these is zero. In this case, the expected shadow value of the resource is linear in beliefs and it does not respond to improvements in information. Then, too, neither does extraction respond to improvements in information, so there is no irreversibility effect and QOV is zero.

2   Suppose that all three beliefs lead to a corner solution. We cannot say what happens to the expected shadow value of the resource, since it generally will be nonlinear in π. But, since all three extractions are zero, there is no irreversibility effect and QOV again is zero.

3   Suppose now, without loss of generality, that π^0 leads to an interior solution, while π^1 leads to a corner solution. We must consider two further cases regarding π^μ: (i) π^μ leads to an interior solution and (ii) π^μ leads to a corner solution.

In case (i), we have that the second line in equation (A26.3) equals $p - c$, and the third equals $\mu(p - c)$. Since π^1 leads to a corner solution the fourth line does not fall short of $(1 - \mu)(p - c)$, as shown in (26.18). Assume that it exceeds it. Then in case (i), the sum of these terms is negative, and the expected shadow price is convex.

For case (ii), the second line exceeds $p - c$, the third line equals $\mu(p - c)$, while the fourth line exceeds $(1 - \mu)(p - c)$. We use the induction assumption that $\partial V^{N-1}/\partial x$ is convex in π. Taking the summation term by term and dividing through by π^μ, the sum of these three lines would be non-positive if all these derivatives were evaluated at the same stock, namely, with $q = 0$. However, setting $q > 0$ in the third line in (A26.3) increases this term above even more, by the concavity of V^{N-1} in x. Hence, by the induction hypothesis, the sum of these three lines is negative and the expected shadow price is convex.

Notes

1   Another definition of informativeness of experiments was provided by Blackwell (1951). Let M be a matrix M with nonnegative elements and columns that sum to 1. Then we have that Y is sufficient for the experiment Y' if there is a matrix M such that $\Theta' = M\Theta$ and $\lambda = M\lambda'$. It was proven by Blackwell that sufficient experiments are more informative in the above sense. The result says that, if we can get to the experiment Y' by taking the experiment Y and subjecting it to the noise induced by M, then Y is more informative than Y', and also more valuable.

A final approach to comparing information is to use partitions of the event space S. This is employed by Freixas and Laffont (1984). Recall that a partition $\mathcal{F}$ of a set S is a collection of subsets $\{S_k\}$ such that $S_k \cap S_z = \varnothing$ for all k and z, and $\cup S_k = S$. Suppose that the information to be received is that the true state lies in one element of a partition of S. Clearly, if one information structure is represented by one partition $\mathcal{F}'$, and a second by another $\mathcal{F}$ which is finer than $\mathcal{F}'$ (in the sense that any element of $\mathcal{F}$ is contained in one element of $\mathcal{F}'$), then the finer partition provides better information. It was shown by Green and Stokey (1978) that finer partitions represent sufficient experiments.

2   In terms of our model, this is defined as follows. For any given state and realization of the random event, by our previous assumptions there is a unique control required to move the system to a given new state x_{t+1}. This control is $q(x_{t+1}; x_t, s_t)$, defined implicitly by $g[x_t, q(x_{t+1}; x_t, s_t), s_t] = x_{t+1}$. Suppose that the utility $u(x, q, s)$ takes the separable form

$$u(x, q, s) = u(1 - x, s) + w(x, s) + (p - c)q$$

Define

$$C(x, x_{t+1}, s_t) \equiv c[q(x_{t+1}; x_t, s_t), s_t]$$

3   A different question is the effect of an increase in the riskiness of the decision environment, holding fixed the information to be received. Rothschild and Stiglitz (1970) have shown that, if a distribution of a random variable is subjected to a mean-preserving spread, then the expected value of any convex function of the random variable increases. It is the curvature of the shadow value function in s that is important to determining the impact of an increase in risk. This is not the same as curvature in beliefs, so the above proof in theorem 3 implies nothing about increases in risk. The above analysis examined the effect of an increase in the quality of information on resource extraction decisions.

References

Arrow, K. 1969: Optimal capital policy with irreversible investment. In J. Wolfe (ed.), *Value Capital and Growth*, Edinburgh: Edinburgh University Press.

Arrow, K. and Fisher, A. 1974: Environmental preservation, uncertainty, and irreversibility. *Quarterly Journal of Economics*, 98, 85–106.

Bernanke, B. 1983; Irreversibility, uncertainty, and cyclical investment. *Quarterly Journal of Economics*, 98, 85–106.

Bishop, R. 1982: Option value: an exposition and extension. *Land Economics*, 58, 1–15.

Blackwell, D. 1951: Comparison of experiments. In J. Neyman (ed.), *Proceedings of the Second Berkeley Symposium on Mathematical Statistics and Probability*, Berkeley, CA: University of California Press.

Blackwell, D. 1965: Discounted dynamic programming. *Annals of Mathematical Statistics*, 36, 226–35.

Blume, L. Easley, D. and O'Hara, M. 1982: Characterization of optimal plans for stochastic dynamic programs. *Journal of Economic Theory*, 28, 221–34.

Bohenblust, H., Shapley, L. and Sherman, S. 1949: Reconnaissance in game theory. Rm-208, Rand Corporation.

DeGroot, M. 1970: *Optimal Statistical Decisions*. New York: McGraw-Hill.

Demers, M. 1991: Investment under uncertainty, irreversibility, and the arrival of information over time. *Review of Economic Studies*, 58, 333–50.

Epstein, L. 1980: Decision making and the temporal resolution of uncertainty. *International Economic Review*, 21, 264–83.

Fisher, A. and Hanemann, W. M. 1985: Valuing pollution control: hysteresis phenomenon in aquatic ecosystems. Working Paper 361, Department of Agricultural Economics, University of California, Berkeley

Fisher, A. and Hanemann, W. M. 1986: Option value and the extinction of species. In V. K. Smith (ed.), *Advances in Applied Microeconomics*, vol. 4, Greenwich, CT: JAI Press.

Freixas, Z. and Laffont, J. J. 1984: On the irreversibility effect. In M. Boyer and R. Kihlstrom (eds), *Bayesian Models in Economic Theory*, Amsterdam: Elsevier.

Graham, D. 1981: Cost–benefit analysis under uncertainty. *American Economic Review*, 71, 715–25.

Graham-Tomasi, T. 1984: The economics of wilderness preservation and timber supply problems in dynamic optimization and uncertainty. Unpublished Dissertation, University of Michigan.

Graham-Tomasi, T. and Myers, R. 1990: Supply-side option value: further discussion. *Land Economics*, 66, 425–9.

Green, J. and Stokey, N. 1978: Two representations of information structures and their comparisons. Technical Report 271, IMSS, Stanford University.

Hanemann, M. 1989: Information and the concept of option value. *Journal of Environmental Economics and Management*, 16, 23–7.

Jones, R. and Ostroy, J. 1984: Flexibility and uncertainty. *Review of Economic Studies*, 51, 13–32.

Maitra, A. 1968: Discounted dynamic programming on compact metric spaces. *Sankhya, Series A*, 30 (2), 211–16.

Marschak, J. and Miyasawa, K. 1968: Economic comparability of information systems. *International Economic Review*, 9, 137–74.

Miller, J. and Lad, F. 1984: Flexibility, learning, and irreversibility in environmental decisions: a Bayesian approach. Journal of Environmental Economics and Management, 11, 161–72.

Rodin, W. 1976: *Principles of Mathematical Analysis*, 3rd edn. New York: McGraw-Hill.

Rothschild, M. and Stiglitz, J. 1970: Increases in risk I: a definition. *Journal of Economic Theory*, 2, 225–43.

Smith, V. K. 1983: Option value: a conceptual overview. *Southern Economic Journal*, 49, 654–68.

27

Evaluating Changes in Risk and Risk Perceptions by Revealed Preference

A. Myrick Freeman III

Many environmental externalities take the form of increases in the risks that people face. examples include the risk of cancer or chronic lung disease associated with emissions of airborne carcinogens or other pollutants and the risk of illness due to drinking contaminated water. In order to evaluate policies to regulate these externalities, it is necessary to obtain estimates of people's economic value or willingness to pay for controlling risks. In this chapter, I describe how models of individual choice can be used to derive measures of the value of risk changes from observed choices or revealed preference. These models are based on the assumption of expected utility maximization; but I show that the models can be adapted to accommodate alternative models of choice, for example the prospect theory of Kahneman and Tversky (1979) or the regret theory of Loomes and Sugden (1982).

I first establish a model of individual preference and choice in which an environmental risk is one argument in the individual's preference function and the individual can affect the level of risk by her choices of other variables. I then derive measures of willingness to pay for changes in risk and show that these measures are functions or observable variables, meaning that individual's values can be inferred from data on the choices that they make.

Individual Preferences, Risk, and Value

Consider some environmentally transmitted risk such as that of developing a cancer or finding a thick haze of pollution at a scenic vista. Risks such as these can be described in terms of two characteristics: the range of possible adverse consequences or severity, and the probability distribution across consequences. For cancer, there may be two alternative consequences: it is treatable with no loss of life expectancy, or it is not treatable. For the haze of pollution, severity might be measured by loss of visual range in miles. To keep the exposition simple, I will consider only one possible adverse consequence and two states of the world: the event occurs with a given severity, or the event does not occur.

Assume that an individual facing an environmental risk has a well-behaved preference ordering over bundles of goods, X, and the adverse event over which he has no control. Let the variable A measure the severity of the adverse event. A takes the value A^* with probability π and 0 with the probability $1 - \pi$. In any state of nature, this preference ordering can be represented by the indirect utility function

$$U = V(M, P, A) \qquad (27.1)$$

with

$$V(M, P, 0) > V(M, P, A^*)$$

where M and P represent income and prices (both assumed constant); and

$$V_M > 0 \qquad V_{MM} < 0 \qquad V_A < 0 \qquad V_{AA} < 0$$

where subscripts indicate partial derivatives. Assume that the individual knows the severity of the adverse event A^* and the probability of its occurrence. Also, for simplicity, assume that there are no opportunities for insurance or purchase of contingent claims.

Suppose there is some public policy action which has the effect of reducing the severity of the adverse event, reducing its probability, or both. For example, a regulation that restricts emissions of sulfates and particulates from power plants can result in a smaller reduction in visual range when meteorological conditions favor the formation of haze. This form of policy will be referred to as a "risk reduction" policy. An example of a policy to reduce the probability of an adverse event is the control of emissions of carcinogens, since the risk of cancer is a function of the dose received by the individual. This form of policy will be referred to as a "risk prevention" policy.

Many risk reduction and risk prevention policies are public goods in that they have the characteristics of nonrivalry and nonexcludability. The public good character of these policies means that a private market system will fail to provide these protective measures in efficient quantities. Thus there is a case for governmental intervention to improve the efficiency of resource allocation. In order to determine whether risk reduction and risk prevention policies result in improvements in welfare, it is necessary to define and measure the benefits and costs of changes in risks.

If individuals maximize expected utility, their behavior can be described as the solution to the following maximization problem:

$$\max E(U) = \pi V(M, A^*) + (1 - \pi)V(M, 0) \tag{27.2}$$

where the price term is omitted for simplicity. By taking the total differential of this expression, setting it equal to zero, and rearranging terms, we obtain measures of the tradeoff between income and some other argument in the function holding expected utility constant. These expressions are marginal willingnesses to pay.

For example, the *ex ante* marginal value for a change in π is

$$\frac{dM}{d\pi} = \frac{V(M, 0) - V(M, A^*)}{\pi V_{M^*} + (1 - \pi)V_{M^\circ}} \tag{27.3}$$

where V_{M^*} is the marginal utility of income given $A = A^*$, etc. Willingness to pay is the change in the expected value of the utility loss with a small change in probability, converted to monetary units by a weighted average of the marginal utilities of income in the two states of the world. This is a standard result in the literature (Jones-Lee, 1974; Cook and Graham, 1977; Machina, 1983).

Similarly, the *ex ante* value of a marginal reduction in A^* given that the event occurs is

$$\frac{dM}{dA^*} = \frac{\pi V_{A^*}}{\pi V_{M^*} + (1 - \pi)V_{M^\circ}} \tag{27.4}$$

The marginal willingness to pay for a change in A^* is equal to the expected marginal disutility of A^* converted to a money measure by the expected value of the marginal utility of income.

Models of Choice and Value

Generally speaking, the use of models of individual choice to infer values involves three steps. The first step is to derive the expression for willingness to pay as a function of the environmental variable either from the indirect utility function or the expenditure function. This step results in expressions such as equations (27.3) and (27.4) above. In the second step, a model of individual-optimizing or utility-maximizing behavior is developed which relates the individual's choices or observed behavior to the relevant prices and constraints. The first-order conditions for optimization are derived. The third step involves an examination of the model to see whether the first-order conditions include a relationship between the desired marginal value and some observable variable. If they do, then the observable variable can be taken as a measure of the welfare change.

Theoretical models for estimating individuals' values for sure changes in some environmental quality parameter from revealed preferences are well developed. Broadly speaking, these models are based on some form of substitution relationship between environmental quality and a private good (e.g. the defensive expenditure or averting behavior models of Courant and Porter, 1981, and Harrington and Portney, 1987), on hedonic price theory where environmental quality is a characteristic of a differentiated product such as housing (Rosen, 1974), or on the model of weak complementarity. In this section, I describe how the substitution and hedonic price models can be applied to the valuation of changes in risk given expected utility preferences. In the next two sections, I generalize these models to non-expected utility preferences and show how these results can also be applied to the weak complementarity model.

The substitution model

In the case of the substitution model, the relevant first-order condition governs the optimal purchase of some good that substitutes for the environmental good or defends against the environmental bad in the production of some final good that affects utility (e.g. health or cleanliness). As long as the environmental characteristic and the substitute or defensive good affect utility only indirectly through the production of the final good and do not enter the utility function directly, then the marginal value of the environmental characteristic can be estimated from knowledge of the technical relationship between the environmental characteristic and the private good in the production of the final good. This technical relationship is observable in principle.

Suppose that *ex ante* an individual can select a level of private spending R that will reduce the magnitude of A^* given that the event occurs according to the relationship $A^* = A(R, G)$, where G is the level of government protective spending. An example would be the purchase of medicine to reduce the severity of the symptoms of lung disease. Assume that this function has the following properties:

$$A(0, 0) = A^* \qquad A_R^* < 0 \qquad A_G^* < 0$$

The individual chooses R, given G so as to maximize expected utility:

$$E(U) = \pi V[M - R, A(R, G)] + (1 - \pi)V(M - R, 0) \qquad (27.5)$$

The first-order conditions include

$$\frac{1}{A_R^*} = \frac{\pi V_A}{\pi V_{M^*} + (1 - \pi)V_{M^\circ}} \qquad (27.6)$$

where V_{M^*} is the marginal utility of income evaluated at the level of A associated with the given level of G. The term $1/A_R^*$ is the reciprocal of the marginal productivity of expenditure on risk reduction, or equivalently, the marginal private cost of reducing A^*. The right-hand side is the marginal value of reducing A^* that was derived above.

The relevant value for policymakers is the value to the individual of dG, a marginal increase in public spending on risk reduction. To find this *ex ante* value, take the total differential of (27.5), set it equal to zero, and substitute in the first-order condition for the choice of private protective spending (equation (27.6)). After some simplification, we have

$$\frac{\mathrm{d}M}{\mathrm{d}G} = -\frac{A_G^*}{A_R^*} = \frac{\partial R}{\partial G} \tag{27.7}$$

This means that the individual's marginal willingness to pay for a small increase in government spending is the ratio of the marginal productivities of private spending and public spending in reducing A^* or the marginal rate of technical substitution between R and G in reducing A^*. This measure can be calculated if the technical relationship $A(R, G)$ is known. This relationship is observable in principle.

The welfare change is also given by the marginal rate of substitution between private and public spending holding expected utility constant. This is not the same as the observed change in private spending. For example, if G increases, the individual will reduce R but will also attain a higher level of expected utility. If R enters the utility function directly, then the welfare measure will include unobservable marginal utility terms, and the measure derived here will be an underestimate (overestimate) if R provides positive (negative) utility.

Similar results can be obtained for the case where individual *ex ante* spending has the effect of reducing the probability of the adverse event. Now let the production function relating private and public expenditures to the probability of the adverse event be

$$\pi = \pi(R, G)$$

where

$$\pi(0, 0) = \pi^*$$

$$\pi_R < 0 \qquad \pi_G < 0$$

The individual chooses R so as to maximize expected utility given by

$$E(U) = \pi(R, G)V(M - R, A^*) + [1 - \pi(R, G)]V(M - R, 0) \tag{27.8}$$

The first-order conditions include

$$\frac{1}{\pi_R} = \frac{V(M - R, 0) - V(M - R, A^*)}{\pi(R, G)V_{M^*} + [1 - \pi(R, G)]V_{M^\circ}} \tag{27.9}$$

The left-hand side of (27.9) is the reciprocal of the marginal productivity of private expenditure on reducing the probability, or, equivalently, the marginal private cost of reducing π. The right-hand side is the marginal value of reducing π as given by equation (27.3).

The marginal value of an increase in public spending to reduce the probability of the event is found by totally differentiating (27.8), setting the result equal to zero, and substituting the first-order condition where appropriate. The result is

$$\frac{\mathrm{d}M}{\mathrm{d}G} = -\frac{\pi_G}{\pi_R} = \frac{\partial R}{\partial G} \tag{27.10}$$

This result is similar to the case of public spending to reduce A^*. The individual's marginal willingness to pay for public spending at the margin is equal to the ratio of the marginal productivities of private and public spending to reduce π or to the marginal rate of technical substitution between R and G, holding A^* constant. Again, this result is analogous to those derived in the existing literature on protective spending in the absence of uncertainty.

Unfortunately, these results do not carry over to the case where the averting activity jointly produces reductions in π and A^*. Repeating the steps described above but making both A^* and π functions of R and G leads to the following expression:

$$\frac{\mathrm{d}M}{\mathrm{d}G} = \frac{\pi V_{A^*} A_G + \pi_G (V^* - V^\circ)}{\pi V_{A^*} A_R + \pi_R (V^* - V^\circ)} \tag{27.11}$$

The unobservable utility terms do not cancel out of this expression, so marginal willingness to pay cannot be inferred from information on the averting technology. The inability to use the averting technology. The inability to use the averting behavior model in this case is due to the jointness of the implicit production technology.

Hedonic prices

In the case of the standard hedonic price model, the first-order conditions for utility maximization require equality between the individual's marginal willingness to pay for the characteristic in question and the marginal implicit price of that characteristic. As long as the environmental characteristic affects utility only through consumption of the differentiated product, its marginal implicit price can be taken as a measure of marginal welfare change or marginal value.

If either the probability or the magnitude of a risk (or both) is a characteristic of heterogeneous goods such as housing or jobs, hedonic price estimation can be used to obtain the relevant *ex ante* marginal values for risk changes. The following discussion is based on the market for housing. For discussions of the application of hedonic theory to the labor market, see Cropper and Freeman (1991) and Freeman (1993).

Suppose that the magnitude of the adverse event varies across the space used for residential housing. For example, the dose of a toxic chemical from an accidental release could depend on the distance from the source of the release. If people are aware of this spatial variation, then they should be willing to pay more for houses in those areas where risks are lower. Competition for these more attractive houses would result in a systematic inverse relationship between the price of housing, P_h, and A_i^*, where i indexes the spatial location of the house.

For simplicity suppose that the magnitude of the event is the only relevant characteristic of housing. Then the price of a house at location i can be found from the hedonic price function $P_h(A_i^*)$. Given income, the probability of the event, and the magnitude of the event, the individual chooses a location so as to maximize expected utility:

$$E(U) = \pi V[M - P_h(A_i^*), A_i^*] + (1 - \pi)V[M - P_h(A_i^*), 0] \qquad (27.12)$$

The first-order condition is

$$\frac{dP_h}{dA_i^*} = \frac{\pi V_{A_i^*}}{\pi V_{M^*} + (1 - \pi)V_{M^\circ}} \qquad (27.13)$$

Since the right-hand side of this condition is the *ex ante* marginal value of a reduction in A_i^* (see equation (27.4)), this condition says that expected utility maximization calls for setting the marginal value of risk reduction equal to its marginal implicit price, which is the slope of the hedonic price function. Thus if individuals and the housing market are in equilibrium, the estimated marginal implicit price of risk reduction for each individual reveals that individual's marginal *ex ante* valuation for risk reduction. However, since a house is a long-lived asset, and P_h is an asset price, equation (27.13) yields a compensating wealth measure of the lifetime welfare change associated with a permanent change in π.

If the relevant housing characteristic that varies across space is the probability of the adverse event and housing prices reflect differences in π_i, the results are similar. The expression for expected utility is

$$E(U) = \pi_i V[M - P_h(\pi_i), A^*] + (1 - \pi_i)V[M - P_h(\pi_i), 0] \qquad (27.14)$$

and the first-order condition is

$$\frac{\partial P_h}{\partial \pi_i} = -\frac{V[M - P_h(\pi_i)] - V[M - P_h(\pi_i), A^*]}{\pi_i V_{M^*} + (1 - \pi_i)V_{M^\circ}} \qquad (27.15)$$

Again, the right-hand side is the *ex ante* marginal value of the probability change (equation (27.3)). Thus the observed implicit price of the probability reduction also reveals the individual's marginal *ex ante* value of risk prevention. If both the probability and magnitude of the event vary independently across space, housing prices will be a function of both characteristics. Both equations (27.13) and (27.15) must be satisfied in equilibrium. Hedonic price functions that do not include both characteristics as explanatory variables will be misspecified.

Values with Nonexpected Utility Preferences

The models described above for indirect benefit measurement are based on expected utility as a representation of individuals' preferences under uncertainty. There is substantial evidence that individuals' choices frequently violate expected utility theory. For examples of this evidence and discussions of its implications for the theory of preferences under uncertainty, see for example Kahneman and Tversky (1979), Arrow (1982), Grether and Plott (1979), Machina (1987), and Thaler (1987). An important question, therefore, is whether models of value of the sort described here can be modified for use with nonexpected utility preferences.

It turns out that revising these models to reflect other forms of preferences is straightforward and involves no additional complications, at least in certain circumstances. This follows from the key features of the indirect methods for estimating individuals' values from data on behavior. As described above, these models involve deriving the expression for welfare change, finding the first-order conditions for optimization, and substituting them into the expression for welfare change. Given the assumptions of the models described here, this substitution allows for the cancelling out of any observable utility terms. It turns out that, at least for many nonexpected utility representations of preferences, the same result occurs, so that the derived observable welfare measures are independent of the particular form of preferences. This is a straightforward consequence of the envelope theorem. I first show this for the general case and then for one specific form of nonexpected utility preferences, the prospect theory of Kahneman and Tversky (1979).

Let I be some general index of preferences where the preferences depend on income, prices (implicitly), the probabilities of different states of the world, and the magnitudes of the adverse event in different states:

$$I = f(M, A, \pi) \tag{27.16}$$

I assume that this function is convex and twice differentiable. This expression could be nonlinear in the probabilities and/or incorporate regret and rejoice terms or other deviations from the standard expected utility function. Expected utility preferences also fit this general formulation.

Consider the substitution model where $A^* = A(R, G)$. The first-order condition for the optimum R is

$$\frac{\partial I}{\partial R} = -f_{M^*} + f_{A^*} A_R^* = 0 \tag{27.17}$$

or

$$f_M = F_{A^*} A_R^*$$

To find the marginal welfare measure for a policy that reduces A^*, totally differentiate (27.16), rearrange terms, and substitute in the first-order condition to obtain

$$dI = f_{M^*}\, dM + (f_{A^*} A_R^* - f_M)dR + f_{A^*} A_G^*\, dG = 0 \tag{27.18}$$

and

$$\frac{dM}{dG} = -\frac{f_{A^*} A_G^*}{f_{M^*}} = -\frac{A_G^*}{A_R^*} \tag{27.19}$$

The marginal willingness to pay for publicly supplied risk reduction is equal to the marginal rate of technical substitution between public and private risk reduction.

Consider, next, the hedonic model. Suppose that the probabilities of the adverse event vary across space. Then the general index of preferences would be

$$I = f[M - P_h(\pi_i), A, \pi_i] \tag{27.20}$$

The first-order condition for the selection of the risk characteristic of housing is

$$\frac{\partial I}{\partial \pi_i} = -f_M \frac{\partial P_h}{\partial \pi_i} + f_{\pi_i} = 0 \tag{27.21}$$

or

$$f_{\pi_i} = f_M \frac{\partial P_h}{\partial \pi_i} \tag{27.22}$$

Totally differentiating (27.20) to obtain the welfare measure for the change in π_i and substituting the first-order condition gives

$$dI = f_M\, dM + \left(f_{\pi_i} - f_M \frac{\partial P_h}{\partial \pi_i}\right) d\pi_i + f_{\pi_i}\, dG = 0 \tag{27.23}$$

$$\frac{dM}{dG} = -f \frac{f_{\pi_i}}{f_M} = \frac{\partial P_h}{\partial \pi_i} \tag{27.24}$$

The marginal willingness to pay for publicly supplied risk prevention is equal to the observable marginal implicit price of the risk characteristic of housing.

To illustrate this general result, consider the prospect theory model of Kahneman and Tversky (1979). In the two-state model based on the indirect utility function, the index of preferences takes the following form:

$$I = g(\pi)V(M, A^*) + g(1 - \pi)V(M, 0) \tag{27.25}$$

where

$$g(0) = 0 \qquad g(1) = 1$$

and

$$g(\pi) + g(1 - \pi) < 1 \text{ for } 0 < \pi < 1$$

Assume that the magnitude of the adverse event depends both on the level of expenditure on a private averting activity, R, and public expenditure G. The value of reducing A^* is

$$\frac{dM}{dA^*} = \frac{g(\pi)V_{A^*}}{g(\pi)V_{M^*} + g(1 - \pi)V_{M^\circ}} \tag{27.26}$$

which is not directly observable because of the utility and probability weighting terms. But it can be inferred. Given the level of G, the individual's optimal level of the private averting activity is given by

$$\frac{\partial I}{\partial R} = -g(\pi)V_{M^*} + g(\pi)V_A A_R^* - g(1 - \pi)V_{M^\circ} = 0 \tag{27.27}$$

Thus

$$\frac{1}{A_R^*} = \frac{g(\pi)}{g(\pi)V_{M^*} + g(1 - \pi)V_{M^\circ}} V_{A^*} \tag{27.28}$$

The marginal value to the individual of a change in G is found by totally differentiating (27.25), setting it equal to zero, and solving for

$$\frac{dM}{dG} = \frac{dR}{dG} - \frac{g(\pi)\,dR}{g(\pi)V_{M^*} + g(1 - \pi)V_{M^\circ}} V_{A^*} A_R^* \frac{dR}{dG}$$

$$- \frac{g(\pi)}{g(\pi)V_{M^*} + g(1 - \pi)V_{M^\circ}} V_{A^*} A_G^* \tag{27.29}$$

After substituting in (27.28), this becomes

$$\frac{dM}{dG} = -\frac{A_G^*}{A_R^*} \tag{27.30}$$

Similarly, if it is π that can be reduced by private and public expenditure, the value of a reduction in π is

$$\frac{\mathrm{d}M}{\mathrm{d}\pi} = \frac{g(1-\pi)V(M-R,0) - g(\pi)V(M-R,A^*)}{g(\pi)V_{M^*} + g(1-\pi)V_{M^\circ}} \qquad (27.31)$$

The first-order condition for private averting expenditure is

$$-\frac{1}{\pi_R} = \frac{V(M-R,0) - V(M-R,A^*)}{g(\pi)V_{M^*} + g(1-\pi)V_{M^\circ}} \qquad (27.32)$$

And after substitution, the value of the public risk prevention expenditure is

$$\frac{\mathrm{d}M}{\mathrm{d}G} = -\frac{\pi_G}{\pi_R} \qquad (27.33)$$

Similar results can be derived for other forms of preferences, for example the regret theory of Loomes and Sugden (1982). See Freeman (1991).

Weak Complementarity

In the case of weak complementarity, the environmental characteristic affects utility (either positively or negatively) only when the consumption of the private complementary good is positive. An improvement in the environmental quality characteristic shifts the private good's demand curve out. the welfare measure is the area between the two compensated demand curves, which, in principle, are observable from econometric estimates of the demand function.

Extending the results of our analysis of nonexpected utility preferences to the case of weak complementarity is straightforward. Suppose that the consumption of some market good x_i increases the probability of occurrence of some adverse event for the purchaser so that $\pi = \pi(x_i)$. Suppose further that there is some public policy action represented by G that can reduce the risk associated with consuming x_i for all consumers. So

$$\pi = \pi(x_i, G) \qquad (27.34)$$

with

$$\frac{\partial \pi}{\partial x_i} > 0$$

and

$$\frac{\partial \pi}{\partial G} < 0$$

This policy will increase the general preference index for all consumers of x_i and will cause the demand curve for x_i to shift out. formally, the general preference index can be written as

$$I = f(M, A, \pi, p_i)$$

where p_i is the price of the complementary good. The general form of the expenditure function is

$$E = E(p_i, A, \pi, I^*)$$

Weak complementarity requires that there be a choke price for x_i and that at the choke price

$$\frac{\partial E}{\partial \pi} = 0$$

When the conditions for weak complementarity are satisfied, the monetary equivalent of the increase in well-being is the area between the compensated demand curves for the good before and after the public policy change. Similarly, if the market good affects the severity of the adverse event, weak complementarity requires that $\partial E / \partial A^*$ or $\partial I / \partial A^*$ be zero when the good is not purchased. Since these results are independent of any particular specification of the preference function (other than the conditions of weak complementarity), they will hold for expected utility and nonexpected utility preferences as well as in the case of certainty.

Conclusions

I have shown that the three broad classes of models which have been developed to measure the benefits of environmental change from revealed preferences under certainty can be easily generalized to apply to valuing changes in risk. This generalization of the models does not require that individual preferences take the expected utility form. The principal requirement is that individuals be maximizing some objective function. By the envelope theorem, welfare measures that contain unobservable preference terms can be reduced to functions of observable relationships by substitution of the first-order conditions for preference maximization. Thus if the conditions for utilizing these models are satisfied, there is no particular need to be concerned with how people make their choices under uncertainty.

The analysis up to this point has been based on the implicit assumption that the probability assessments of the individuals making choices have been accurate. Suppose, however, that individuals systematically overestimate the probability of the adverse event. Portney (1992) has posed a particularly stark version of the problem. In his hypothetical town of Happyville, the experts are utterly convinced that the chemical found in the drinking water supply is benign. But the citizens believe that the chemical is responsible for the above-average incidence of cancer observed in their town; and they each say that they are willing to pay $1000 for what the experts say will be unnecessary and costly treatment to remove the chemical.

On the information given, it is not possible to determine whether the people have misperceived the risk of cancer (errors in probabilities) or if they place a very high value on preventing a very small but catastrophic risk (preferences). All that is known is that each person has expressed a willingness to pay $1000 for treatment. So if that sum will cover the cost, it seems to be welfare enhancing to build the treatment plant.

When indirect methods such as the substitution and hedonic price models are used to infer values of risk changes, it is not generally possible for the researcher to determine whether an observed high marginal value results from the subject's overestimate of the risk change or her high valuation of a correctly perceived change. All that is observed is the risk–dollar tradeoff. The possibility of differences between individuals' perceived risks and objective risks may not be important in situations where policy decisions are being based on individuals' responses to the risks being evaluated. But it is often the case that individuals' responses to one kind of risk are used to assign values to changes in some other form of risk (a form of benefits or value transfer). In these cases, it will be very important to know what individuals think they are getting in return for their expenditures on risk reduction and risk prevention. This means that the investigator must learn about the individuals' own subjective probabilities.

Notes

This chapter is adapted, with permission, from my book, *The Measurement of Environmental and Resource Values; Theory and Method*, Washington, DC: Resources for the Future, 1993.

References

Arrow, Kenneth J. 1982: Risk perception in psychology and economics. *Economic Inquiry*, 20 (January), 1–9.

Cook, Philip H. and Graham, Daniel A. 1977: The demand for insurance and protection: the case of irreplaceable commodities. *Quarterly Journal of Economics*, 91 (February), 143–56.

Courant, Paul N. and Porter, Richard. 1981: Averting expenditure and the cost of pollution. *Journal of Environmental Economics and Management*, 8 (December), 321–9.

Cropper, Maureen L. and Freeman, A. Myrick, III. 1991: Valuing environmental health effects. In John Braden and Charles Kolstad (eds), *Measuring the Demand for Environmental Quality*, Amsterdam: North-Holland.

Freeman, A. Myrick, III. 1991: Indirect methods for valuing changes in environmental risks with non-expected utility preferences. *Journal of Risk and Uncertainty*, 4 (April), 153–65.

Freeman, A. Myrick, III. 1993: *The Measurement of Environmental and Resource Values: Theory and Methods*. Washington, DC: Resources for the Future.

Grether, David M. and Plott, Charles R. 1979: The economic theory of choice and the preference reversal phenomena. *American Economic Review*, 69 (September), 623–48.

Harrington, Winston, and Portney, Paul R. 1987: Valuing the benefits of health and safety regulations. *Journal of Urban Economics*, 22 (July), 101–12.

Jones-Lee, Michael W. 1974: The value of changes in the probability of death or injury. *Journal of Political Economy*, 99 (August), 835–49.

Kahneman, Daniel, and Tversky, Amos. 1979: Prospect theory: an analysis of decisions under risk. *Econometrica*, 47 (February), 263–91.

Loomes, Graham, and Sugden, Robert. 1982: Regret theory: an alternative theory of rationale choice under uncertainty. *Economic Journal*, 92 (December), 805–24.

Machina, Mark J. 1983: Generalized expected utility analysis and the nature of observed violations of the independence axiom. In B. T. Stigum and F. Wenstop (eds), *New Foundations of Utility and Risk Theory with Applications*, Dordrecht: Reidel.

Machina, Mark J. 1987: Choice under uncertainty: problems solved and unsolved. *Economic Perspectives*, 1 (Winter), 121–54.

Portney, Paul R. 1992: Trouble in Happyville. *Journal of Policy Analysis and Management*, 11 (Winter), 131–2.

Rosen, Sherwin. 1974: Hedonic prices and implicit markets: product differentiation in perfect competition. *Journal of Political Economy*, 82 (February),34–55.

Thaler, Richard. 1987: The psychology of choice and the assumptions of economics. In Alvin E. Roth (ed.), *Laboratory Experimentation In Economics: Six Points of View*, Cambridge: Cambridge University Press.

28

Contingent Valuation

Richard C. Bishop, Patricia A. Champ, and Daniel J. Mullarkey

The contingent valuation method (CVM) is used to estimate values for environmental amenities and other non-market goods and services. Surveys are used to ask respondents about their monetary values for non-market goods *contingent* upon the creation of a market or other means of payment. Therefore, all transactions are hypothetical. CVM has been applied in hundreds of studies, many of which have been designed to further develop the method. As a result of this research, CVM has received considerable acceptance in the United States as a tool for measuring values to be used in benefit–cost analysis. It was authorized for the valuation of outdoor recreation in the *Economic and Environmental Principles and Guidelines for Water and Related Land Resources Implementation Studies* (US Water Resources Council, 1983). Later, the US Army Corps of Engineers prepared its own manual for applying the method (Moser and Dunning, 1986) and has conducted many CVM studies (Mitchell and Carson, 1989, p. 13). CVM has also been deemed acceptable by the US Fish and Wildlife Service for human use and evaluation studies (US Fish and Wildlife Service, 1985). In addition, the US Environmental Protection Agency, in its *Guidelines for Performing Regulatory Impact Analysis*, lists CVM as one of the four basic methods for valuing the environmental benefits of proposed regulations (US Environmental Protection Agency, 1983). CVM has gained international attention and is now being applied in many countries.

Nevertheless, the accuracy of contingent valuation continues to be a subject of debate. Other valuation methods, including market valuation and applications of non-market valuation techniques such as the travel-cost method (chapter 29) and the hedonic price method (chapter 30), depend on evidence generated as economic actors reveal their preferences through market transactions and other behavior. Preferences revealed through actual behavior have great credibility in economics. Statements by economic actors about how they would act under hypothetical circumstances continue to be viewed with great suspicion.

The scientific issue here can be framed in terms of the concept of *validity*. Mitchell and Carson (1989, p. 190) explain validity and apply it to CVM in this way:

> The validity of a measure is the degree to which it measures the theoretical construct under investigation. This construct is, in the nature of things, unobservable; all we can do is to obtain imperfect measures of that entity. In the contingent valuation context the theoretical construct is the maximum amount of money the respondents would actually pay for the public good if the appropriate market for the public good existed.

To this we would only add that the concept of validity could also be applied to compensation demanded. Though we shall want to elaborate a bit as we go, roughly speaking CVM is valid to the extent that it accurately measures people's "true values." True values here refer to people's compensating surplus or equivalent surplus[1] for changes in environmental resources.[2]

In order for CVM to yield valid economic values, study participants must be both willing and able to reveal their values. They may be unwilling to reveal such values either because they perceive strategic responses to be in their best interest or because they see little incentive to take the valuation process seriously. Even if they are willing to respond accurately, they may be unable to do so. Chances are that participants have never before been asked to express their preferences for environmental goods in monetary terms. Even if they are quite willing to do so, they may be unable to predict how much they would willingly pay or how much they would demand in compensation if a market or other mode of payment were created. From a psychological perspective, it is a very different thing to fill out a survey than to enter a market to buy or sell something. For all these reasons, many economists continue to voice reservations about values estimated using CVM. As we shall see toward the end of the chapter, this issue has been addressed empirically, but so far the results of empirical studies have not been sufficient to build toward consensus about the validity of the method.

The intensity of the controversy in the United States over the validity of CVM increased tremendously when steps were taken to apply it in assessing damages from spills of oil and toxics in the context of litigation. As of this writing, rules for damage assessments under the Comprehensive Environmental Response, Compensation, and Liability Act of 1980 (CERCLA) and the Oil Pollution Act of 1990 are being considered by US federal agencies. Whether CVM should be allowed under those rules is the subject of a raging debate among academics, industry representatives, and government officials. Other countries are watching this debate with considerable interest and, in the cases of insurers and business interests, with considerable trepidation.

In the first section of this chapter, we develop a theoretical framework for assessing the validity of CVM. This framework defines three types of validity – content, construct, and criterion. The second section of the chapter deals with developing content validity. We focus rather intensively on the heart of the matter, the so-called *scenario*. In the scenario, participants in contingent valuation surveys learn about the environmental amenities to be valued and the terms under which the hypothetical transaction will be considered. The first step toward achieving a valid CVM measure – if validity is achievable at all – is to develop a high quality scenario. People need to know what they are being asked to value and how they would pay or receive compensation before they can express valid values. Of course, other aspects of the study design will also affect its validity and we shall touch on these briefly. The last two sections discuss construct and criterion validity.

Even well-designed and well-executed CVM studies may lack validity. In the end, respondents may still be unwilling or unable to reveal good approximations of their true values no matter how well the study is designed. This possibility will lead us, toward the end of the chapter, to examine other kinds of evidence on validity. There is not enough empirical evidence available at this time to arrive at definitive conclusions about the validity of CVM. A full review of the evidence now available would be a substantial research undertaking in its own right. We can, nevertheless, give the reader a preview of the kinds of evidence that are available before drawing conclusions about the current state of the art for CVM.

A Framework for assessing the Validity of the Contingent Valuation Method

Assessing the validity of CVM would be easy if it were possible to observe true values. This is difficult or impossible in principle, however.[3] Rather than drawing categorical conclusions about the validity of CVM, conclusions must be more tentative and dependent on the weight of the combined evidence from all available sources. Heavy dependence on subjective judgment about the weight of evidence makes strong conclusions about the validity of CVM difficult to justify and potentially controversial.

In attempting to measure concepts like intelligence, psychologists face problems that, if anything, are, more difficult than those faced by economists attempting to measure compensating or equivalent surplus for non-market environmental amenities. In evaluating the accuracy of their measurement tools, psychologists have found it useful to distinguish between three kinds of validity: content validity, construct validity, and criterion validity. Content validity deals with whether a measure adequately covers all the aspects of the theoretical construct. Construct validity is concerned with the degree to which the measure under scrutiny is related to other measures as predicted by theory. Criterion validity considers the relationship between the measure and an alternative measure that is closer to the underlying construct. Each of these concepts involves a different approach to evaluating the validity of a measure. As such, they provide a useful framework for assessing the overall validity of CVM.

One issue needs to be raised in order to fully adapt the psychological concepts of validity to CVM. Psychologists nearly always have an interest in the validity of their measures at the level of the individual subject, while economists are mainly interested in aggregates and averages. In studies of intelligence, for example, a psychologist is interested in how individuals perform on IQ tests. Average scores across subjects may also be of some interest, but a great deal of attention is focused on the accuracy of IQ tests at the individual level. An economist would be happy with an accurate measure of average willingness to pay (WTP) or compensation demanded (CD) over a sample from the population of interest, even if there was a good deal of random inaccuracy at the individual level. In general, economists can live with more random error in their measures than can psychologists.

Content Validity

A measurement instrument has content validity if it accurately measures the aspects of the theoretical construct that are to be quantified. In the case of CVM, evaluating the content validity of a study involves examining the content of the survey instrument and related materials, such as letters and visual aids to be sent to would-be respondents. The goal is to determine whether, in all their various dimensions, materials to be used in the survey are conductive to the revelation of true values. For example, to the extent that a valuation question creates incentives to answer strategically, this would reduce its content validity. Mitchell and Carson (1989, p. 192) suggest that one should ask the following questions when assessing the content validity of a contingent valuation scenario:

> Does the description of the good and how it is to be paid for appear to be unambiguous? Is it likely to be meaningful to the respondents? Is there anything in the scenario that might suggest to some respondents that the good would not be paid for? Are the property rights and the market for the good defined in such a way that the respondents will accept the WTP format as plausible? Does the scenario appear to force reluctant respondents to come up with WTP amounts?

In a sense, any evaluation of CVM begins with the content validity of the specific applications. If the content validity of an application seems highly suspect, there would appear to be little point in debating its construct or criterion validity. Therefore, we will now focus on how to design a scenario that has content validity.

Designing a contingent valuation scenario with content validity

The valuation problem takes as its point of departure a change in the status or characteristics of some environmental amenity. Where results from the CVM application are to be used in benefit–cost analysis, the change will normally be linked to some sort of governmental intervention that will affect the quantity or quality of the environmental services derived from the amenity. The task then is to estimate the change in either compensating or equivalent surplus associated with the change in service flows. If a study involves damage assessment, then presumably there has already been a change in the status or condition of some environmental resource that was precipitated by a spill of oil or toxics. In this case, the task of the analyst is to evaluate how the compensating or equivalent surplus of relevant members of the public for the affected amenity has changed as a result of the spill. In either case, the objective of the researcher is to design a scenario that provides participants with all the information they would need to value the amenity in question.

While this may seem simple in theory, it is a complicated task in practice, particularly in applications where study participants have had little or no experience with the environmental amenity in question. The more novel the good, the more important the clarity and completeness of the scenario (Fischoff and Furby, 1988). Complicating the matter further is the limit on the amount of new information that participants are willing and/or able to absorb and process at one time. There is a delicate balance between providing too little and too much information. If the scenario is too long, the participant may become bored or impatient and stop absorbing new and potentially relevant information. Similarly, if too much information is presented, the participant may become confused. This phenomenon is referred to as "information overload" and is problematic in that the resulting confusion may lead the participant to ignore or misinterpret important information (Grether and Wilde, 1983; Bergstrom and Stoll, 1990).

The provision of sufficient information is only half of the issue here. It is equally important to ensure that participants understand this information. In personal interviews and mail surveys, visual aids such as maps, photographs, charts, and graphs may help participants understand the change. Even in telephone interviews, such aids could be sent out in advance. While one can never be completely certain that all the information has been absorbed, procedures are evolving to assess the effectiveness of communications. Such procedures are referred to as "qualitative research."[4]

"Focus groups" are an important tool of qualitative research. Eight to 12 people are recruited from the population of potential survey participants. A moderator then conducts a structured group discussion focusing on the proposed scenario and related issues of survey design. Early in the study design, focus group participants may be asked to evaluate the adequacy of verbal descriptions of resources presented by the moderator or very preliminary versions of written materials or visual aids. Later focus groups may be asked to read and comment on the scenario in its nearly final form. Further fine tuning of the instrument can be accomplished in intensive one-to-one interviews between a moderator and potential survey respondents. Throughout the process, the goal is to find effective ways to communicate relevant information. Words the participants themselves would use to describe relevant phenomena are carefully noted. Language unfamiliar to the person on the street is eliminated. Phrasing that future respondents may misinterpret is identified and fixed. Information that participants find unnecessary is removed.

Careful attention needs to be given to incentives throughout the process of designing the scenario. The goal is to create a setting for valuation that is not only understandable to the participants but also "incentive compatible." That is, the participants should be placed in an economic situation that is conducive to revealing their true compensating or equivalent surplus values. Qualitative research in the design stage and follow-up questions in the final survey can both be used to identify incentives to behave strategically.

Effective scenario design need not follow a rigid formula, but rather should tailored to fit the specific application. There are three principal components, however, that a complete scenario should describe: the good, the payment mechanism, and the context for valuation (Fischoff and Furby, 1988). Each component has various elements that need to be incorporated into the scenario. here again, qualitative research can help the researcher determine which features of the scenario need more clarity. The discussion below follows Fischoff and Furby (1988), which contains an excellent discussion of the basic elements of the scenario.

The good

The complexity of the task of defining the good depends on the nature of the resource or policy being considered. It is a far simpler task to define increased or decreased hunting opportunities to experienced, informed hunters than to quantitatively describe changes in the levels of the various services provided by wetlands to the general populace. Nevertheless, some guidelines can be stated for defining any good. Ideally, the scenario should explicitly define the following aspects of the good: (i) its attributes, (ii) reference and target levels, (iii) the source of the changes, (iv) the extent and timing of changes, and (v) the certainty of changes.

Attributes The good can be thought of as a bundle of attributes (Fischoff and Furby, 1988). For example, wetlands provide a number of different services, such as wildlife habitat, flood flow alteration, and nutrient cycling. Attributes can be contextual as well as physical. For example, the site or sites in question may be locally, regionally, or globally unique; or they may be sites of historical, cultural, religious, educational, or archaeological significance. The researcher needs to determine, based on common sense and qualitative research, which attributes potentially affect individuals' values for the good. Each such attribute must then be explicitly described. A complex good may have many attributes that need to be described. The omission of any such attribute will present the participant with an incomplete picture. Even if an individual attribute will not be affected by the change, this may need to be noted in order to avoid confusion.

Reference and target levels Reference and target levels need to be specified for each attribute of the good. Reference levels are the levels that will be obtained without the intervention, and target levels are the levels that would result from the intervention. Note that this does not follow a strictly before and after framework, but rather depends upon the nature of the intervention in question. For example, if the intervention would maintain the current quality of a resource (e.g. water quality) that would otherwise deteriorate, the reference level is the future deteriorated state (after), and the target level is the level of quality supported by the intervention (before). Alternatively, if the policy question is whether or not to allow clear cutting of a forest, the reference level is the existing stock of forest services (before), and the target level is the resulting level of forest services (before), and the target level is the resulting level of forest services (after). In damage assessment, if damages are to be estimated in terms of WTP to avoid injury to the resources, then the reference level will normally be the condition of the resources as they are affected by the spill and the target level will be their condition in the absence of the spill. If CD is to be the measure of damages, then the reference level is the undergraded state and the target level the degraded state.

Source of change How a change is to occur, or has occurred, may legitimately influence the value a participant places on a change in an amenity. Whether the change is or was anthropomorphic in origin, as opposed to having natural causes, may affect the value of the change. It may also be the case that, for environmental improvements, the methods by which the change occurs could influence values. For example, a study on which we are currently working involves a program to remove obsolete roads from a national park. It is clear from focus groups that participants value the program differently if the work is to be done by volunteers rather than by government employees.

Extent and timing   The change being valued needs to be pinpointed in both space and time. The geographical location of the change should be fully described. For example, in the case of air quality changes, the range of visibility should be specified for all affected areas (Fischoff and Furby, 1988). Visual aids of various sorts are always worth considering. A second dimension is the temporal extent of the change. How long the change will last should be made clear. Temporal information is particularly vital to non-use values. Existence values, for example, may depend in part on the knowledge that a resource has been preserved for some extended period of time. The timing of changes in attributes also needs to be specified. People may discount changes that will occur in the future, so it is important to specify whether the change will occur at the time of payment or at some time in the future.

Certainty   The degree of certainty regarding reference and target levels of attributes should also be made explicit. If there is uncertainty about the level of provision of any individual attribute, the value of the amenity will probably be different than if a high degree of certainty exists. For example, the filling of 100 acres of wetlands will probably entail the loss of various wetland functions, but it may be impossible to determine the extent of the loss before it occurs (or even after!). This uncertainty must be conveyed to the participant. When possible, this should be done quantitatively, using numbers instead of descriptive terms such as "very likely" or "a slight loss" (Fischoff and Furby, 1988). How participants deal with uncertainty in a CVM scenario is not well understood, but theoretically speaking, as we learned in chapter 11, uncertainty is potentially highly relevant to how economic agents value possible changes in environmental resources.

Payment mechanism

As with defining the good, definition of the payment component requires explicit, careful description of each aspect of the payment mechanism, including (i) the payment vehicle, (ii) the decision-making unit for which the value is to be expressed, (iii) the timing of the payment or payments, and (iv) the relevant prices of other goods.

Payment vehicle   The payment vehicle defines the structure or mechanism through which the monetary payment will be transferred. There are many possible payment vehicles. For example, WTP could be expressed in terms of income taxes, property axes, sales taxes, "special tax funds," licensing fees, entrance fees, utility bills, or changes in the prices of market goods. The payment vehicle should relate naturally to the amenity or policy issue in question. Choice of a vehicle that does not fit the situation may seem artificial to participants and therefore lead to confusion. Choice of a controversial or unpopular vehicle may also affect the measured values in undesirable ways. For example, Americans may have negative reactions to higher property taxes. If so, their responses to a CVM scenario that uses property taxes as a payment vehicle may more a reflection of their attitudes toward the tax and less a reflection of their preferences regarding the environmental amenity that is the intended subject of the study. Ideally, a good payment vehicle will be one that is both neutral and plausible. Mitchell and Carson (1989) advocate the use of a fairly general statement like "higher prices and taxes." Qualitative research can be useful for evaluating alternative payment vehicles.

Decision-making unit   The choice of a decision-making unit is typically between the individual or the household. The decision here depends to some extent on the environmental asset being valued. For example, valuing a hunting opportunity would more naturally lend itself to individual valuation, while neighborhood air quality might more naturally use the household. The scenario should clearly convey to participants whether they are speaking for themselves alone or for their households.

Timing   The timing of the payments or receipts needs to be clearly defined. Is the payment a one-time expense? If so, when is it to be paid? Does the payment structure involve more than one payment? If so, how frequent are the payments, what is the duration of the payment schedule, and when does it begin and end? Is the amount or rate of the payment the same throughout its duration? The scenario must clearly answer such questions to avoid misunderstandings.

Relevant prices   In a benefit–cost analysis, if the prices of market goods and services that respondents may purchase will change depending on the intervention, these changes need to be specified. In many cases it may be appropriate to assume that any such changes would be negligible, but this too should be stated.

The context of valuation

Scenarios typically specify either a market context or a political context for valuation. The choice of which valuation context to employ should be dictated in part by the amenity or policy to be valued. A political context is appropriate in cases where the good is mainly public in nature, such as air quality. In the United States, people are familiar with the idea of voting in referenda to make decisions pertaining to public goods, so this model will seem natural. Participants might find use of the private market model in such cases rather artificial. Alternatively, if the good has strong private good characteristics, such as allocation of sites in campgrounds with differing levels of amenities, it may be more appropriate to select the private market model. A thorough discussion of valuation contexts can be found in Mitchell and Carson (1989). In describing the valuation context in a CVM scenario, three elements must be explicitly defined: (i) who the other participants are, (ii) whether the measure of value will be WTP or CD, and (iii) the value elicitation device.

Participants   A participant's valuation of a resource or policy change may not be independent of who the other participants are. This possibility should be recognized in CVM studies. While economists assume rational, self-interested consumers, participants may place value on who else will benefit and who else will bear the costs of the policy change. Therefore, a carefully designed scenario should explicitly describe all the other participants in the market. In cases modeled after the private goods market, this entails defining the supplier(s) of the good and all other potential demanders. It may also be important to answer the question, who else will have access to the good? For example, if the study seeks to estimate how much a hunting opportunity is worth, the scenario should state who will be eligible to purchase or receive hunting licences, and how many such licences will be available. If the political context is chosen, other voters and all those who will pay for the change or receive compensation represent potentially relevant pieces of information

Willingness to pay or compensation demanded   Once amenities to be valued and the payment mechanism have been introduced, respondents will normally be confronted with the valuation question. Either WTP or CD or both would be elicited. For reasons that will become clearer as we review the evidence on validity, the decision in most recent studies has been in favor of WTP measures. Nevertheless, CD remains a more theoretically desirable measure in some contexts (e.g. damage assessment) and be expected to continue to attract the attention of researchers who will try to improve upon existing measurement techniques. For a detailed discussion of the WTP versus CD issue, the reader is encouraged to consult Mitchell and Carson (1989).

The value elicitation device   Various modes for actually asking the valuation question have been developed. Traditionally, so-called bidding games have been used to elicit values in many studies. Here, respondents are asked whether they would be willing to pay or receive a fixed amount, the "starting bid." Depending on their response, they are asked about successively higher or lower amounts until their maximum WTP or minimum CD is expressed. Open-ended questions simply ask participants to express their maximum WTP or minimum CD directly, without being prompted through a bidding game or other procedure. "Payment cards" are sometimes presented showing various amounts that respondents could choose to pay or receive. Dichotomous choice techniques involve asking respondents whether they would be willing to pay (or receive) specific amounts and the amount is varied across respondents so that "yes" and "no" answers are elicited for a full range of values. A special type of dichotomous choice involves scenarios that ask people to vote on a referendum. The decision rule for determining whether or not the change in attributes will occur is linked to the choice of the value elicitation device. For example, the standard decision rule for a referendum is a majority vote. It is important for the scenario to explicitly state the decision rule since it may affect people's responses.

Some modes of soliciting values may be better than others from a psychological perspective. for example, open-ended questions tend to yield lower values than the other methods, all else equal, perhaps because respondents tend to focus on a "reasonable" first bid rather than their maximum WTP. Dichotomous choice questions are thought to be easier for study subjects. Other methods try to force respondents to express maximum values, whereas dichotomous choice questions ask them only for responses to specific amounts, much as they would consider prices in a store. Each of the methods has its proponents in the research community, with referenda and payment cards dominating in recent studies.

Other Issues in Study Design

In addition to designing the scenario, many other issues must be resolved as a CVM study proceeds. Researchers designing CVM studies are fortunate to have an excellent treatment of many aspects of CVM in the book by Mitchell and Carson (1989). Only a brief overview will be possible here.

One set of issues revolves around population definition and sampling. To the extent that the study deals only with use values, the population may consist only of users and possibly potential future users of the resources in question. If total values are to be estimated and there are reasons to believe that substantial non-use values are present,[5] then the general population of a given geographic region may serve as a sampling frame. Once the population for the study has been defined, a sampling strategy must be developed that will assure a sufficiently large and representative sample to support statistical inferences about study population.

A choice must be made early on about whether to use personal interviews, telephone interviews, or a mail survey. From a methodological perspective, each of these modes of surveying people has advantages and disadvantages that require careful consideration in the context of the specific study being designed. Standard reference works here include Mitchell and Carson (1989) and Dillman (1978).

The design of the survey instrument itself presents scores of issues, large and small. In addition to designing a suitable scenario, the survey may gather data useful in satisfying several goals. First, additional data to be used in evaluating construct validity can be gathered. Examples of the types of data relevant here will become evident in the next section. Second, in applied studies, policymakers may have questions that can be addressed from survey data. For example, policymakers may want to know about the attitudes of respondents toward the alternative policies under consideration.

In developing the scenario and building the rest of the survey around it, we should bear in mind that economists traditionally have little training in survey research methods. There is a great deal more to effective survey research than writing down a few questions *ad hoc* and mailing them. Economists are usually well trained in analyzing data that are already in hand, but training in primary data gathering in general and survey methodology in particular are not parts of the normal curriculum. Some (e.g. Bishop and Ervin, 1992) are calling for change in this regard. In the meantime, consultation with survey specialists or, better yet, true interdisciplinary teamwork can greatly improve the chances for success of studies attempting to apply CVM.

As noted above, qualitative research is important in the early stages of designing a CVM study. As a study progresses, steps are taken to become increasingly quantitative and these steps need to be carefully planned in advance. After the survey instrument has been developed using qualitative research methods, the instrument should be pre-tested on a small but representative sample of the population. The pre-test might identify additional problems that did not become apparent in the qualitative phase. The pre-test can also be used to test the research procedures. For example, if the final study is to involve a mail survey, the pre-test will be mailed to study subjects. Problems such as low overall response rates or high item non-response rates, which might not have been apparent from focus groups, may emerge and require further work. After pre-testing, pilot studies with sufficient sample sizes to support statistical analysis may be required. For example, if one wanted to compare two payment vehicles or two alternative descriptions of an attribute, this could be done in a pilot study with a sufficient sample size to support hypothesis testing.

Execution of a final survey must also be carefully planned. For example, participants in a mail survey might first receive an advance letter telling them about the study and encouraging their cooperation. A week later, the survey itself, with a cover letter and any other materials such as visual aids would arrive. The following week a postcard would arrive, reminding them of the importance of their participation and thanking them if their response is already in the mail. Two weeks and four weeks after receiving the first survey, additional sets of survey forms and associated materials would be received by those who had yet to reply.[6] Comparable steps must be planned to execute telephone and personal interviews.

The overall goal is a "high" response rate. For a mail survey, the attainable response rate relative to deliverable surveys depends on the silence of the study topic to the participants. For studies on environmental issues of direct interest to a specialized group, like anglers, a response rate of 75–80 percent is a reasonable goal. For a general population where silence of the issue under study is likely to be highly variable across the population, one should still hope for between 65 and 70 percent. There are numerous CVM studies that report response rates below 50 percent on mail surveys. This may be sign of problems with the survey design. Perhaps careful follow-up procedures were not followed, or maybe the survey was poorly constructed and failed to attract and hold the interest of potential respondents. In the extreme, many members of the sample may even have been angered by the survey, because they correctly or incorrectly perceive that the researcher is attempting to justify preconceived conclusions that are contrary to their own views. Throughout the design and execution of a survey, researchers would do well to remember that people are most likely to participate when they see that it is clearly in their self-interest to do so. An attitude expressed in a statement like "I am doing a research project and want you to help me" will not do much to encourage response.

Actual refusals are normally less frequent for personal interviews. In one recent study of the US population as a whole (Carson et al., 1992), sampling involved enumeration of all dwelling units in preselected census tracts and then random selection from those units. Interviews were ultimately completed with 75 percent of the sample. In most cases where interviews were not completed, repeated efforts failed to find anyone at home. Many of the non-responses probably involved units that were at least temporarily unoccupied. Unfortunately, a high response rate for personal interviews can cost hundred of dollars per observation.

Once the data are collected, care must be taken to accurately encode them for analysis. The analysis itself should be relatively straightforward for economists. Simple statistics (e.g. mean, median, standard errors) for WTP or CD can be calculated for responses to bidding games, payment cards, and open-ended questions. Bid equations, which regress expressed values on socioeconomic variables, are often estimated. Responses to referenda and other dichotomous choice questions require use of qualitative-response models such as logit and probit.

Such analysis can be used to assess both the construct and criterion validity of CVM. A survey of all the literature that bears in one way or another on the construct and criterion validity of CVM would be a major undertaking, far beyond the scope of this introduction to the topic. Our goal in the next two sections is the more limited one of presenting selected studies that illustrate how the issue has been addressed to date. Four studies dealing with construct validity and two with criterion validity will be briefly summarized.

Construct Validity

Construct validity deals with the degree to which the measure under scrutiny is related to other measures as predicted by theory. Mitchell and Carson (1989) discuss two forms of construct validity, convergent and theoretical. Evidence regarding the convergent validity of a measure would be provided when the measure in question and a second measure "converge" in a manner predicted by theory. In the case of CVM, convergent validity could be assessed, for example, by comparing values estimated from a CVM study to values for the same amenity estimated using a travel cost model or a hedonic price model. If convergence is not observed, then at least one of the measures of value is wrong and the comparison would not support the validity of the contingent value.[7] Whether or not the contingent value is invalid is not established. The travel cost or Hedonic value could be invalid.

Assessment of the theoretical form of construct validity involves examining the relationship between the measure under scrutiny and other variables that ought, on the basis of theory, to be related to it in some specified way. For example, one way of assessing the theoretical validity of a contingent value would be to examine the signs on variables in a so-called bid equation, where contingent values expressed by respondents are regressed against explanatory variables that theory suggests should be related to them in certain ways. Theory suggests, for instance, that income and the value measure should be positively correlated. Theoretical validity of the contingent values would be supported to the extent that this relationship holds true in bid equations. If a positive relationship to income cannot be demonstrated with statistical precision or the coefficient on income is negative, this would cast some doubt on the theoretical validity of the results. This would not be considered definitive evidence of invalidity, however, since it might simply indicate that the environmental amenity in question has a weak income effect or is an inferior good.

In the general area of construct validity, studies providing evidence on convergent validity will be considered first. We will examine studies that compare CVM values with values from travel cost and hedonic price studies. Sellar et al. (1985) evaluated boating opportunities on four lakes in Texas. Their contingent valuation efforts were thwarted for one lake, but they did succeed in comparing travel cost and dichotomous choice contingent values at the other three. In all three cases 95 percent confidence intervals around the travel cost values and corresponding contingent values overlapped.[8] Furthermore, in two out of the three comparisons, mean estimates were quite close. In one of the cases, for example, the mean estimate of the travel cost value for an annual permit was $32.06, while the contingent value was $39.38. In the third case, Lake Livingston, mean values were substantially different, with a travel cost value of $102.09 and a contingent value of $35.21. Even here, however, 95 percent confidence intervals overlapped ($68.06 to $204.19 compared with $13.04 to $76.01, respectively).

Several other studies[9] have compared travel cost and contingent values with roughly similar results. The conclusion would seem to be that travel cost and CVM studies tend to yield roughly comparable values. Such results are not very satisfying, however, for two reasons. First, parameter estimates tend to have rather large standard errors. This is illustrated by the large confidence intervals from the study just summarized. One often ends up wondering if differences in final results are really just noise or whether there is so much noise that fundamental differences are masked. Second, just as designing a CVM study involves a large number of judgment calls, questions always seem to arise about the judgment calls involved in designing the travel cost study used in the comparisons. For example, Sellar et al. (1985) used no allowance for travel time, a feature which many travel cost practitioners would question. Would the confidence intervals for Lake Livingston in particular still have over-lapped if a more standard allowance for travel time had been included in the model?

Brookshire et al. (1982) investigated the convergent validity of CVM by comparing the contingent values for an improvement in air quality at the study subject's current area of residence in the Los Angeles metropolitan area to a hedonic analysis of the property value data for the same metropolitan area.[10] They argue that, based on economic theory, "the rent differential associated with air quality improvement from hedonic analysis of the property value data must exceed household willingness to pay for the survey responses, if the survey responses are a valid measure of the value of air quality improvements" (Brookshire et al., 1982, p. 166). The logic for this hypothesis is quite intuitive. The property value differential from the hedonic price model should reflect opportunities to purchase housing with varying levels of air quality. Respondents' true WTP should be less than this differential. Otherwise they should move to a neighborhood with a higher level of air quality. Therefore, if an individual's contingent value for an air quality improvement exceeds the corresponding property value differential from the hedonic price equation, it must also exceed her or his true value. Eleven different comparisons of contingent WTP for air quality improvements with corresponding property value results showed the latter to be higher in every case. The null hypothesis that the property value differential was higher could not be rejected at the 10 percent level for all cases. While such results clearly support the validity of CVM, they do so only in a qualitative way. CVM could be off by an order of magnitude or more and still support such a validity test.

One example of a theoretical validity test is presented in a study of the non-use damages associated with the Exxon Valdez oil spill. Carson et al. (1992) conducted a national survey to measure the loss of passive use values that resulted from damage to natural resources by the Exxon Valdez oil spill. Carson et al. assess the theoretical validity of the contingent values for a ship escort service which would reduce the risk of future spills by estimating a valuation function (bid equation). Table 28.1 shows the estimated coefficients of the predictor variables. In general, the valuation function shows statistically significant relationships that are consistent with economic theory. Factors that were positively related to the amount individuals indicated they were willing to pay for the ship escort service included the following: expectations that "a great deal more" or "more" damage would occur without the escort service, if an individual mentioned the Exxon spill as a major environmental accident caused by humans, if the individual thought protecting coastal areas from oil spills was "extremely important" or "very important," if the respondent indicated that the government should set aside a "very large amount" or a "large amount" of land as wilderness, self-identification as a strong environmentalist, indication that the household is "very likely" or "somewhat likely" to visit Alaska in the future, having a high income, and being white. Individuals who thought the ship escort service would prevent "less than a great deal of damage" were willing to pay less than the average respondent for the escort service. Likewise, respondents who thought that without the escort plan there would be "less" or "no" damage were also willing to pay less than the average respondent. Finally, individuals who said that Exxon should pay all the costs of the escort ship service were also willing to pay less on average. All of the predictor variables were significant at the 10 percent level, with the exception of whether or not individuals mentioned that Exxon should pay all the costs of the escort ship service.

We will draw on a study by Desvousages et al. (1992) for a second example of a theoretical validity test. They tested the hypothesis that WTP estimates would increase as the level of natural resource services increased for two goods. The first good was prevention of three levels of migratory waterfowl deaths in oil waste ponds. In particular, independent shopping-mall intercept samples were asked to express their WTP for preventing 2000, 20,000, or 200,000 deaths. Desvousges et al. hypothesized that the amount individuals were willing to pay would be higher for the higher levels of death. They also tested this hypothesis by asking independent

Table 28.1 Weibull valuation function for ship escort service[a]

Parameter	Estimate	Standard error	Asymptotic t value
Location	1.684	1.66	1.01
Scale	0.670	0.029	22.98
Great deal more damage will occur without the escort service[b]	0.859	0.279	3.08
More damage will occur without the escort service[b]	0.664	0.162	4.11
Less damage will occur without the escort service[b]	−0.270	0.143	−1.88
No damage will occur without the escort service[b]	−0.783	0.426	−1.84
Escort service will prevent some damage[b]	−0.855	0.129	−6.62
Escort service will not reduce damage at all[b]	−1.735	0.196	−8.85
Mentioned Exxon Valdez spill as one of the major environmental accidents caused by humans[b]	0.202	0.132	1.53
Protecting coastal areas from oil spills is extremely or very important[b]	0.408	0.141	2.90
Government should set set aside a very large or large amount of new land as wilderness[b]	0.259	0.117	2.21
Self-identification as a strong environmentalist[b]	0.468	0.226	2.08
One's household is very or somewhat likely to visit Alaska in the future[b]	0.238	0.136	1.76
Income	0.282	0.098	2.88
White[b]	0.418	0.148	2.82
Exxon should pay all the costs of the escort service[b]	−1.214	0.143	−8.50
Log-likelihood -1198.793			

[a]This table is a reproduction of table 5.13 in Carson et al. (1992).
[b]Dummy variable.

shopping-mall intercept samples about preventing two different levels of oil spills. Their results failed to support the hypothesis that WTP estimates would increase as the level of natural resource services increased.

Using the terms developed here, Randall (1993) questioned the content validity of the Desvousges et al. research for a number of different reasons, including the use of a mall-intercept survey and use of the open-ended format for the contingent valuation question. Also, Randall noted that "economic theory is unclear about how much inter-treatment difference in WTP there *should* be" (Randall, 1993, p. 14). In other words, the hypothesis Desvousges et al. put forth as a test of theoretical validity is not, according to Randall, justifiable on the basis of economic theory. The number of birds killed might or might not be an argument in utility functions of participants. For example, people may simply be concerned about solving the problem regardless of the number of birds killed.

Too many studies have estimated bid equations for us to hope to give a complete set of citations, but recent examples include Adamowicz et al. (1989), Edwards and Anderson (1987), Milon (1988), and Viscusi and Evans (1990). About all that can be said by way of summarizing these studies is that they often show that hypothesized relationships between value and socioeconomic variables do hold for specific applications. Other studies dealing with theoretical validity in ways similar to Desvousges et al. (1992) include Diamond and Hausman (1992) and Kahneman and Knetsch (1992). Such studies demonstrate that it is easy enough to conduct CVM studies that fail to meet theoretical expectations. Whether such results are sufficient to conclude that *in general* CVM lacks theoretical validity seems doubtful. More research using CVM exercises that would be widely accepted as having a high degree of content validity should prove helpful.

Criterion Validity

The third concept of validity is criterion validity. In the context of psychological testing, Sundberg (1977) defines criterion validity as "the relation of the [psychological] test to criteria outside the test itself" (Sundberg, 1977, p. 44). Adapting this approach to CVM, Mitchell and Carson (1989) say that in order to evaluate the criterion validity of a contingent value it is "necessary to have in hand a criterion which is unequivocally closer to the theoretical construct than the measure whose validity is being assessed" (Mitchell and Carson, 1989, p. 192).

Actual market prices would be ideal measures to use in assessing the criterion validity of CVM. However, market prices do not usually exist for environmental amenities being valued in a contingent valuation question. "Simulated markets" provide one way to establish criteria for judging the validity of CVM. Simulated markets involve creating situations in the field or laboratory where subjects have the opportunity to actually pay for an item being valued or receive compensation for giving it up. Such markets should be fully parallel to the proposed hypothetical transactions in all ways except for the actual exchange of money. Simulated markets differ from real markets in several ways. First, each individual may be involved in only one transaction. Second, the mechanism by which the price is determined may seem somewhat artificial to participants. Nevertheless, since simulated markets involve actual transactions, they should provide values that are more closely related to true WTP or CD than contingent values, and thus should be capable of serving as criteria for evaluating the validity of CVM. Kealy et al. (1990, p. 247) state the point this way:

> The WTP values measured in a simulated market are the best available criterion to evaluate the self-reports of WTP from the corresponding hypothetical situation posed by the contingent valuation method.

Bohrnstedt (1983) has defined two types of criterion validity: predictive validity and concurrent validity. Predictive validity involves "an assessment of an individual's future standing on a criterion variable and can be predicted from present standing on measure" (Bohrnstedt, 1983, p. 97). One way to measure predictive validity would be to ask an individual a contingent valuation question at one point in time and later give the same individual a chance to actually purchase the good in a simulated market. "Concurrent validity," on the other hand, "is assessed by correlating a measure and a criterion of interest at the same point in time" (Bohrnstedt, 1983, p. 97). In other words, the measure and the criterion against which the measure is to be assessed are measured simultaneously.

The relationship between convergent construct validity and criterion validity can be subtle. For example, we have already suggested that comparison of contingent values and travel cost or hedonic values is a test of construct validity. If there were reasons to believe that travel cost or hedonic values were inherently more accurate than CVM values, then such comparisons would be considered tests of criterion validity. For several previously expressed reasons, we do not accept *a priori* arguments for the inherent superiority of travel cost and hedonic approaches and thus view comparisons between the three major approaches as tests of convergent validity.

On the other hand, comparisons of contingent values and simulated market values are viewed as tests of criterion validity provided that the experimental design of the test meets minimum standards of content validity for both the CVM and the simulated market components. Two examples of simulated-market based tests of criterion validity (Bishop et al., 1988, 1992; Kealy et al., 1990) will illustrate the approach. In the case of Bishop et al. (1988), the environmental amenity was opportunities to participate in a special deer hunt in the Sandhill Wildlife Demonstration Area in Wisconsin. Simulated markets and CVM exercises were conducted to test concurrent validity in both 1983 and 1984. In 1983, four Sandhill deer hunting permits were bought and sold in simulated markets. Permits were purchases from the four lowest bidders in an auction among hunters who received them in a state lottery. Results were used as criteria for evaluating contingent measures of CD. Also, four permits were sold to the highest bidders in an auction among hunters who applied for permits but were not allocated one in the state lottery. The simulated markets for the permits were set up as four different types of auctions so that both open-ended questions and bidding games could be evaluated on the WTP side of the experiment.[11] A contingent valuation survey was mailed to hunters who did not participate in the auction. Hypothetical auctions used in the survey were constructed to parallel the simulated market auctions. The CD offers in the simulated and hypothetical markets were not statistically different. However, the mean cash offer was $1184 and the mean hypothetical offer was $833; such values were deemed implausible for a one-day hunt of this kind. Therefore, Bishop et al. (1988) concluded that neither the simulated nor the contingent valuation market measured CD for the hunting permits accurately. On the WTP side, in three of the four cases the contingent bids were statistically different from the cash bids. In all cases the contingent values were larger.

In the 1984 treatments, up to 75 Sandhill deer hunting permits could be bought and sold. This allowed testing of the dichotomous choice format for measures of both WTP and CD. Bishop et al. (1988) concluded that "respondents behaved differently on the willingness-to-accept-compensation [CD] side depending on whether the offers were real or hypothetical. No such difference could be detected on the willingness-to-pay side" (Bishop et al., 1988, p. 7). The expected values of a permit estimated for CD from the simulated and hypothetical market data were $153 and $432, respectively. The coefficients in the logit equations used to estimate these values were significantly different at the 10 percent level. On the WTP side, the expected value of a permit estimated using simulated market data was smaller than the value estimated using the contingent value data ($31 and $41, respectively) but this difference was not statistically significant (Bishop et al., 1992).

Kealy et al. (1990) conducted simulated market experiments to test the predictive validity of the contingent valuation method. A CVM measure has high predictive validity when there is a high correlation between contingent values expressed at one point in time and actual behavior by the same respondents at another point in time. The authors looked at values obtained for both a private good (a candy bar) and a public good (reduction of damage to the Adirondack region aquatic system from acid rain). They conducted the study in two periods with two weeks between each period. For the private good, part of the sample participated in the hypothetical market in both periods. The other part of the sample participated in a hypothetical market in the first period, not knowing that they would participate in a simulated market in the second. For the public good, one group of individuals participated in the hypothetical market both periods. A second group participated in a hypothetical market the first period without knowing that they would participate in a simulated market the second period, whereas a third group participated in a hypothetical market in the first period knowing that they would be participating in a simulated market in the second period.

The predictive validity of the contingent valuation method, which the authors define as "the power of a verbal report of behavioral intention to predict actual behavior" (Kealy et al., 1990, p. 256), was found to be high for both the public and the private good. They found that "verbal reports acknowledging an intention to pay for each of the commodities are reasonably correlated with actual behavior in the simulated market" (Kealy et al., 1990, p. 258). The results from the public good experiment where individuals were told about the second period simulated market suggest that prior knowledge of a future obligation to pay may reduce the tendency of individuals to overstate their WTP, which was found in the treatments where such prior knowledge was not present.

A few other simulated market studies now exist in the literature (Bishop et al., 1983; Brookshire and Coursey, 1987; Coursey et al., 1987; Dickie et al., 1987; Boyce et al., 1989; Duffield and Patterson, 1992). Our interpretation of their results is that, on the whole, they are encouraging for contingent WTP. Contingent values for WTP are rather consistently strong in predicting simulated market values, although, as we saw in the Sandhill case, contingent values are sometimes higher. Contingent CD has yet to show much promise. In cases where it has been tested (again, as the Sandhill results illustrate) it tends to have a rather strong upward bias. Generalization about the criterion validity of CVM based on comparisons with simulated market data is not yet possible. Too few studies are available at this point to justify sweeping conclusions about the validity of CVM. In particular, skepticism remains high about generalizing the results of currently available studies to public goods (Diamond and Hausman, 1992) and especially to non-use values.

Concluding Remarks

We have focused a great deal of attention on the validity issue because CVM has been and continues to be controversial. In closing, we might step back from the debate and reflect on what researchers working on the CVM approach have and have not accomplished. The need to establish values for non-market services like those from environmental resources is real. Without such measures, benefit–cost analysis, the major tool in the arsenal of applied economics, is crippled. Surely, to be relevant to public policy, economics cannot limit itself to the *market* allocation of scarce resources among unlimited wants. Human welfare is affected in too many ways by allocations of scarce resources outside the market. This is particularly true in the case of environmental amenities.

CVM is not the only method of assessing non-market values in monetary terms, but if it can be made to work satisfactorily it is the most versatile. Travel cost methods are useful only for measuring recreational use values. Hedonic price methods are limited to use values as they are reflected in real estate, wage, or other markets. Other approaches are available (see Freeman, 1979), but these approaches are invariably limited in the scope of their applicability and are usually subject to theoretical misgivings. CVM could conceivably be applied to a very wide range of resource use values and to date is the only known approach that can hope to capture the full non-use values associated with environmental assets.

We would argue that those who have set out to develop CVM and test its validity have made considerable progress in creating a tool that is useful for measuring non-market values. Perhaps the views of a distinguished panel of experts will help to support this conclusion. This panel was organized by the National Oceanic and Atmospheric Administration (NOAA) of the US Department of Commerce, the agency that is assigned to promulgate rules for assessing the damages from oil spills in US waters. NOAA asked the panel, which was co-chaired by Nobel laureates in economics Kenneth Arrow and Robert Solow, to consider whether CVM is sufficiently valid to be used in assessing damages from oil spills, including the non-use damages. The NOAA Panel used slightly different terminology than we have here, employing "reliability" in place of what we have called "validity" and "passive-use value" for what we termed "non-use value." In its conclusions, the panel stated (US Department of Commerce, 1993, p. 4610):

> It has been argued in the literature and in comments addressed to the Panel that the results of CV studies are variable, sensitive to details of the survey instrument used, and vulnerable to upward bias. These arguments are plausible. However, some antagonists of the CV approach go so far as to suggest that there can be no useful information content to CV results. The Panel is unpersuaded by these extreme arguments.

In the body of its report, the Panel identified a number of guidelines for CVM applications. If they are done with adequate attention to these guidelines, the Panel concluded (US Department of Commerce, 1993, p. 4610):

CV studies convey useful information. We think it is fair to describe such information as reliable by the standards that seem to be implicit in similar contexts, like market analysis for new and innovative products and the assessment of other damages normally allowed in court proceedings . . . . Thus, the Panel concludes that CV studies can produce estimates reliable enough to be the starting point of a judicial process of damage assessment, including lost passive-use values.

The panel also outlined many potential directions for research to improve our understanding of CVM.

Without necessarily endorsing each and every guideline for CVM studies or the research priorities that it advanced, we would conclude that the NOAA panel succeeded in capturing three essential points about the current state of the art. First, there is too much evidence to the contrary to warrant dismissal of the method. CVM is capable of providing useful, if possibly imperfect, information about values. Second, CVM studies do not automatically provide such information. To be taken seriously, a CVM study must have a high degree of content validity at the outset. To the extent that evidence supporting construct and/or criterion validity is also accumulated, credibility of results is further enhanced. Third, more research to learn how to enhance the validity of CVM applications is badly needed. As the NOAA Panel recognized, CVM is not a perfected technique. Instead, it should be viewed as a new approach to non-market valuation that has demonstrated some promise but that badly needs further testing and refinement if it is eventually to receive the degree of acceptance among economists that it ultimately deserves on the basis of careful scientific scrutiny.

Notes

1 Compensating and equivalent surplus are defined in chapter 24.
2 Given the subject matter of this volume and for convenience, we will focus on environmental amenities, but it is worth noting that CVM can be applied to other non-market goods and services as well.
3 It is worth noting that this difficulty is not limited to non-market goods and services. Even for market goods, true values are unobservable in principle.
4 "Qualitative" here is not meant to imply that measurement in quantitative terms is totally absent. Rather, it refers to the fact that sample sizes are not usually large and samples may not be fully representative of the population. In qualitative research, the goal is not to develop quantitative estimates of parameter of the population, but to develop a "respondent-friendly" survey instrument, including the scenario, and to identify and repair glaring problems in it.
5 Chapter 24 contains a discussion of the concepts of non-use values and total valuation.
6 Those who are brave (or desperate) may send the last mailing as Certified Mail, a procedure that requires the addressee to sign upon receipt of the package. Hopefully, this is a way of underscoring the importance of the would-be respondent's participation. It can draw considerable criticism from disgruntled

members of one's sample, however. Those who are not at home when the postal worker tries to deliver the package must go to the post office, which may be miles away, to claim an apparently important piece of mail. Once there, they learn that they have expended time and trouble to retrieve yet another copy of a survey that they have already ignored. For obvious reasons, this procedure has been discontinued by many researchers, even those who are relatively zealous about response rates.

7   The reader may be wondering why we do not simply say that contingent and other values should be equal. As we shall see later on, it turns out that hedonic values should, in theory, be less than or equal to the contingent value. Thus, the null hypothesis in a test of convergent validity would involve an inequality.

8   Using confidence intervals in this way has been criticized in a recent paper by Poe et al. (1993).

9   An incomplete list would include Cameron (1992), Bishop et al. (1983), and Desvousges et al. (1983).

10 See Pommerehne (1988) for another assessment of the convergent validity of CVM and the hedonic price method.

11 There were two treatments with open-ended questions, one involving a structure where auction winners pay their bids and the other involving a structure where winners would pay the highest unsuccessful bid. The latter has certain desirable incentive properties. Bidding games involved predetermined starting bids and starting bids set by respondents.

References

Adamowicz, Wiktor L., Fletcher, Jerald J. and Graham-Tomasi, Theodore. 1989: Functional form and the statistical properties of welfare measures. *American Journal of Agricultural Economics*, 71, 414–20.

Bergstrom, John C. and Stoll, John R. 1990: An analysis of information overload with implications for survey design research. *Leisure Sciences*, 12, 265–80.

Bishop, R. C. and Ervin, D. E. 1992: Natural resources and the environment. In Rueben C. Buse and James Driscoll (eds), *Rural Information Systems: New Directions in Data Collection and Retrieval* Ames, IA: Iowa State University Press.

Bishop, R. C., Heberlein, T. A. and Kealy, M. J. 1983: Contingent valuation of environmental assets: comparisons with a simulated market. *Natural Resources Journal*, 23, 619–33.

Bishop, R. C., Heberlein, T. A., McCollum, D. W. and Welsh, M. P. 1988: A validation experiment for valuation techniques. Draft Report to Center for Resource Policy Studies, School of Natural Resources, College of Agricultural and Life Sciences, University of Wisconsin-Madison.

Bishop, R. C., Welsh, M. P. and Heberlein, T. A. 1992: Some experimental evidence on the validity of contingent valuation. Unpublished manuscript.

Bohrnstedt, George W. 1983: Measurement. In P. H. Rossi, J. D. Wright and A. B. Anderson (eds), *Handbook of Survey Research*, New York: Academic Press.

Boyce, R. R., Brown, T. C., McClelland, G. D., Peterson, G. L. and Schulze, W. D. 1989: Experimental evidence of existence value in payment and compensation contexts. Paper presented at the joint meetings of the Western Committee on the Benefits and Costs of Natural Resource Planning (W133) and the Western Regional Science Association, San Diego, CA.

Brookshire, David S. and Coursey, Don L. 1987: Measuring the value of a public good: an empirical comparison of elicitation procedures. *American Economic Review*, 77, 554–6.

Brookshire, David S., Thayer, Mark A., Shulze, William P. and d'Arge, Ralph C. 1982: Valuing public goods: a comparison of survey and hedonic approaches. *American Economic Review*, 72 (1), 165–76.

Cameron, Trudy Ann. 1992: Combining contingent valuation and travel cost data for the valuation of nonmarket goods. *Land Economics*, 68 (3), 302–17.

Carson, Richard T., Mitchell, Robert C., Hanemann, W. Michael, Kopp, Raymond J., Presser, Stanley and Ruud, Paul A. 1992: A contingent valuation study of lost passive use values resulting from the Exxon Valdez oil spill. Report submitted to the Attorney General of the State of Alaska. Reprinted by Natural Resource Damage Assessment.

Coursey, D. L., Hovis, J. J. and Schulze, W. D. 1987: The disparity between willingness to accept and willingness to pay measures of value. *Quarterly Journal of Economics*, 102, 679–90.

Desvousges, W. H., Smith, V. Kerry and McGiveny, Matthew P. 1983: A comparison of alternative approaches for estimating recreation and related benefits of water quality improvements. EPA-230-05-83-001, Office of Policy Analysis, US Environmental Protection Agency, Washington, DC.

Desvousges, W. H., Johnson, F. R., Dunford, R. W., Boyle, K. J., Hudson, S. P. and Wilson, K. N. 1992: Measuring natural resource damages with contingent valuation: tests of validity and reliability. Paper presented at the Cambridge Economics Symposium titled "Contingent Valuation: A Critical Assessment," Washington, DC, April 2–3.

Diamond, P. A. and Hausman, J. A. 1992: On contingent valuation measurement of nonuse values. Paper presented at the Cambridge Economics Symposium titled "Contingent Valuation: A Critical Assessment," Washington, DC, April 2–3.

Dickie, M., Fisher, A. and Gerking, S. 1987: Market transactions and hypothetical demand data: a comparative study. *Journal of the American Statistical Association*, 82, 69–75.

Dillman, D. A. 1978: *Mail and Telephone Surveys – The Total Design Method*. New York: Wiley.

Duffield, John W. and Patterson, David A. 1992: Field testing existence values: comparison of hypothetical and cash transaction values. Paper presented at the joint meetings of the Western Committee on the Benefits and Costs of Natural Resource Planning (W133) and the Western Regional Science Association, South Lake Tahoe, Nevada.

Edwards, Steven F. and Anderson, Glen D. 1987: Overlooked biases in contingent valuation surveys: some considerations. *Land Economics*, 63 (2), 168–78.

Fischoff, Baruch, and Furby, Lita. 1988: Measuring values: a conceptual framework for interpreting transactions with special reference to contingent valuation of visibility. *Journal of Risk and Uncertainty*, 1, 147–84.

Freeman, Myrick, III. 1979: Approaches to measuring public goods demands. *American Journal of Agricultural Economics*, 61, 915–20.

Grether, D. M. and Wilde, L. L. 1983: Consumer choice and information: new experimental evidence. *Information Economics and Policy*, 1, 115–44.

Kahneman, Daniel, and Knetsch, Jack L. 1992: Valuing public goods: the purchase of moral satisfaction. *Journal of Environmental Economics and Management*, 22, 57–70.

Kealy, M. J., Montgomery, M. and Dovidio, J. F. 1990: Reliability and predictive validity of contingent values: does the nature of the good matter? *Journal of Environmental Economics and Management*, 19, 244–63.

Milon, J. Walter. 1988: Travel cost methods for estimating the recreational use benefits of artificial marine habitat. *Southern Journal of Agricultural Economics*, 20 (1), 87–101.

Mitchell, Robert Cameron, and Carson, Richard T. 1989: *Using Surveys to Value Public Goods: The Contingent Valuation Method*. Washington, DC: Resources for the Future.

Moser, David A. and Dunning, C. Mark. 1986: *A Guide for Using the Contingent Valuation Methodology in Recreational Studies, National Economic Development Procedures Manual – Recreation*, vol. 2. IWR Report 86-R-5, Fort Belvoir, VA: Institute for Water Resources.

Poe, G. L., Lossin, E. K. and Welsh, M. P. 1993: A convolutions approach to measuring the differences in simulated distributions: application to dichotomous choice contingent valuation. Agricultural Economics Working Paper 93-03, Cornell University, Ithaca, NY.

Pommerehne, Werner W. 1988: Measuring environmental benefits: a comparison of hedonic technique and contingent valuation. In Dieter Bos, Manfred Rose, and Christian Seidl (eds), *Welfare and Efficiency in Public Economics*, New York: Springer.

Randall, A. 1993: Passive-use values and contingent valuation – valid for damage assessment. *Choices*, 2, 12–15.

Seller, C., Stoll, J. R. and Chavas, J.-P. 1985: Validation of empirical measures of welfare change: a comparison of non-market techniques. *Land Economics,* 61, 156–75.

Sundberg, N. D. 1977: *Assessment of Persons*. Englewood Cliffs, NJ: Prentice-Hall.

US Department of Commerce, National Oceanic and Atmospheric Administration. 1993: Natural resource damage assessments under the Oil Pollution Act of 1990. *Federal Register*, 58 (10), 4601–14.

US Environmental Protection Agency. 1983: *Guidelines for Performing Regulatory Impact Analysis*.

US Fish and Wildlife Service. 1985: Human use and economic procedures. *Ecological Services Manual* (104 ESM).

US Water Resources Council. 1983: *Economic and Environmental Principles and Guidelines for Water and Related Land Resources Implementation Studies*. Washington, DC: US Government Printing Office.

Viscusi, W. K. and Evans, W. N. 1990: Utility functions that depend on health status: estimates and economics implications. *American Economic Review*, 80 (3), 353–74.

29

Travel Cost Models

Nancy E. Bockstael

Introduction

Revealed preference approaches to environmental valuation use information derived from observed behavior, rather than responses to hypothetical questions, to derive welfare measures of policy changes. While more in line with conventional economics techniques, these approaches cannot be used for as wide a variety of valuation tasks as can contingent valuation. They depend on the existence of observable behavior that is connected in some clearly defined way with the amenity to be valued.

This chapter deals with a subset of these revealed preference models that can be defined by the following criteria:

1   individuals are observed to incur costs in order to consume commodities related to the environmental amenity of interest;
2   the consumed commodities are non-market goods, that is, they are not purchased in a market setting with prices determined by supply and demand.

The term "travel cost" model characterizes a feature of the most prevalent type of application, where the non-market commodity is outdoor recreation and the cost of consuming the commodity includes the travel costs to the recreational site. At least in recent times, these models have most frequently been applied to valuing environmental amenities as quality dimensions of recreation trips, although early applications focused on the losses associated with the elimination of a recreational site or activity. Other overviews of the travel cost model can be found in Smith (1989) and Bockstael et al. (1991); and Smith and Kaoru (1990) provide a meta-analysis of travel cost empirical studies.

A Theoretical Framework for the General "Travel Cost" Model

Because we are interested in the consumption of commodities not exchanged on the market, the household production model of Becker (1965) provides a rich framework for presentation of the travel cost model and one that highlights important features of the underlying decision process.

The household production motivation for the travel cost model

Consider the household that gains utility from a vector of commodities, z. A vector of market goods, q, are purchased at prices p and combined with household members' time t_z to produce the commodities according to the production process $s(z, q, t_2) = 0$. Many of the elements of z will be identical to elements of the q vector, because the goods purchased on the market will themselves be utility-generating commodities. But other commodities, such as children in Becker's models or recreational experiences in ours, will result from combining purchased inputs and household time.

The household's decision process, in its most general form, is characterized by the maximization of utility subject to two potentially interrelated constraints: one on household income and one on household time. The income constraint now embodies a cost function implied by the household technology which may exhibit non-constant returns and joint production. Additionally, income may be a decision of the household if work time is a choice variable in the framework. Finally, there will be a constraint on the allocation of time among the household-produced commodities and between these and the labor market.

The general problem is given by

$$\max u(z) \quad \text{subject to} \, [K + W(t_w)](1 - \tau) - c(z, T_z, p) = 0$$
$$\text{and} \, T - t_w - t_z' z = 0 \tag{29.1}$$

In the above, K is non-wage income, t_w is the hours worked, $W(t_w)$ is earned income, τ is the marginal tax rate, t_z is a vector of per-unit household time costs for producing the vector of commodities, T is the total time available, and $C(\cdot)$ is the joint cost function implied by the household technology.[1]

The general case is complex and too cumbersome to have useful application. In particular, the cost function may not be linearly homogeneous in z, in which case Marshallian demand functions for the

zs will not exist, complicating welfare measurement (Bockstael and McConnell, 1983). The usual practice of estimating the demand for trips to a site as a function of a constructed cost per trip can be made consistent with the above household production model either by viewing trips to the site as an essential input in the production of the commodity "recreational experience" or by interpreting the trips themselves as commodities that have constant marginal costs.

The household production framework encourages some interesting insights, such as the inclusion of durable recreational goods that might enter into the production technology and therefore the cost function. It also serves to highlight aspects of the problem that are critical for empirical modeling.

The role of time

Even before recognizing the applicability of the household production framework, economists realized the importance of accounting for the time cost of access in the recreational trips demand function. Time and monetary costs of travel can be expected to be highly correlated, so that omission of time costs biases the travel cost coefficient upward, thus biasing consumer surplus estimates downward (Cesario and Knetsch, 1970).

Returning to (29.1), simplify the problem by assuming a wage rate of ω and a vector of constant (and parametric) marginal money costs for each commodity, p_z. Now the problem becomes

$$\max u(z) \quad \text{subject to } [K + \omega^* t_w](1 - \tau) - p_z' z = 0$$
$$\text{and } T - t_w - t_z' z = 0 \tag{29.2}$$

It t_w (work time) is a choice variable, then the two constraints can be collapsed into one and the resulting demand functions will have the form

$$z = z[p_z + (1 - \tau)\omega t_z, (1 - \tau)(K + \omega T)] \tag{29.3}$$

The first term in (29.3) is a vector of "prices" equalling each z's constant marginal monetary cost plus its time cost valued at the after-tax wage rate. The second term is Becker's "full income," the after-tax income should the individual use all available time for work.

The demand function in (29.3) suggests "pricing" the time spent accessing the recreational site at some fraction of the individual's wage rate (Nichols et al., 1978). McConnell and Strand (1981) suggested estimating that fraction as a parameter in the demand function.

Implicit in these approaches is the assumption that individuals can freely substitute work time and leisure, but for individuals with fixed work weeks, recreation takes place on weekends or during pre-designated annual vacation and cannot be traded for leisure at the margin. In such cases, the opportunity cost of time will be non-zero, but it need no longer be related to the wage rate (Bockstael et al., 1987b; Shaw, 1992). One way of approaching the problem is to elicit from individuals information as to whether or not they can substitute work for leisure and to model the two groups differently. Another is to assume that the relevant trade-off is among recreational uses of time, not between work and leisure (Smith et al., 1983).

Most applications have ignored on-site time because of its complicated role as both a cost and a measure of quality (duration) of experience. As long as on-site time is constant over the sample and is either valued at a constant "price" or is not correlated with other explanatory variables in the model, its omission is relatively harmless. McConnell (1992) shows that even when on-site time varies but is a choice variable of the individual, the correct demand function for trips will be the usual one estimated. It will be a function of the "price" of on-site time (the opportunity cost per unit of time) but not of the amount of time on-site, since the latter is endogenous.

The definition of the commodity

The recreational trip, being produced internally by the household, is "custom made." Recreational trips are heterogeneous commodities that may vary in description over households and over trips for any household. When trips to a site vary in length, i.e. a site attracts both single and multiple day visitors, the research strategy has often involved separate modeling of the decision processes and estimation of different demand functions for the different "commodities." Heterogeneity may also take the form of multiple destination trips with no clear way of allocating the fixed trip costs over sites. Mendelsohn et al. (1992) have suggested modeling the demands for all single and multiple destination combinations as separate, but substitute, commodities.

The valuation question

In revealed preference models behavior and welfare measurement are inextricably linked. Well-defined valuation *questions* must be posed as changes in parameters exogenous to the individual; welfare *effects* (willingness-to-pay measures or their approximations) are then revealed through individuals' responses to these parameter changes. Policy actions change the context in which individuals make decisions, and its this change in context that is being valued.

In the household production framework, the welfare effects of any policy action that alters an input price or a technology-related parameter in the production function could be measured. Likewise, we could value the availability of a recreational site or activity by measuring the welfare losses that would occur if its implicit price were driven high enough to drive the individual out of the "market." Most often, however, economists have been interested in using recreational demand models to measure the welfare effects of changes in environmental amenities that can be viewed as quality characteristics of the recreational experience. These amenities have included water quality (e.g. Binkley, 1978; Caulkins et al., 1986; Smith and Desvousges, 1986; Bockstael et al., 1987a), wildlife catch and bag rates (e.g. Loomis, 1982; Samples and Bishop, 1985; Milon, 1988), and landscape amenities (Garrod and Willis, 1992) to name just a few.

The commonly accepted welfare measure is the change in the expenditure function brought about by the change in the parameter. To illustrate this consider the simplified model in (29.2), but call the after-tax wage rate w the after-tax "full income" y and assume that the commodities all have constant marginal costs so that they can be treated as though they were goods q with parametric prices p. We must now add a parameter b for the level of an environmental amenity that individuals view as a quality dimension of the recreational good. Except for the treatment of time, the utility maximization problem is now identical to the one posed in chapter 24:

$$v(p, wt_q, b, y) = \max u(q, b) \quad \text{subject to } y - (p + wt_q)'q = 0 \quad (29.4)$$

as is the related expenditure function

$$m(p, wt_q, b, u^0) = \min (p + wt_q)'q \quad \text{subject to } u(q, b) = u^0 \quad (29.5)$$

The compensating variation measure of a change in the environmental amenity from b^0 to b^1 is then $m(p, wt_q, b^0, u^0) - m(p, wt_q, b^1, u^0)$. The remainder of the chapter illustrates how information on observable behavior can be used to extract approximations to the above Hicksian measures of welfare in different estimation frameworks.

The Practice of Estimating "Traditional" Travel Cost Demand Models

Traditional travel cost models explain the demand for number of trips over a specified time horizon (generally a season or year) for the either one or several recreational sites or activities. Implicitly, the decision-maker is viewed as deciding on the number of trips within a planning horizon where diminishing marginal utility is associated with increasing frequency of trips.

Single and multiple site models, single and multiple parameter valuations

Traditional travel cost models have been estimated for single sites; demand systems have been estimated for multiple sites; and multiple sites have been accommodated in the estimation of a single equation which incorporates characteristics that vary over sites. The form the "travel cost" model takes is driven by the valuation question being posed and the availability of behavioral data.

When the valuation question is one of a price change at a single site (or, as a special case, elimination of that site), then estimation of a single demand function for trips to the site is sufficient because the welfare measure can be made solely on the basis of the single site's demand curve. Omission of the prices of important substitute sites, however, can bias the estimate of the own-price coefficient if the substitute prices are correlated with the own-site price over the sample (Caulkins et al., 1985; McKean and Revier, 1990). This is indeed troublesome since, no matter what the functional form, welfare measures will be dependent on the own-price coefficient. Correlation of this sort will be devastating when individuals relatively close to (far from) one site will be relatively close to (far from) all sites. Unfortunately, inclusion of substitute site prices, when prices are highly correlated, is equally unsatisfying as coefficients cannot be estimated with any precision.

Obviously, attention to substitute sites becomes particularly important if policy actions affect price at more than one site. Multiple price changes appear to require the estimation of systems of demands as functions of all substitute prices so that price changes can be evaluated sequentially, as suggested in chapter 29. But once again prices may be highly correlated, precluding successful estimation.

In one special case, Kling (1989) has shown that the correlation among prices may actually help the researcher. If prices at substitute sites are highly correlated and the policy action preserves that correlation, then welfare measures extracted from integrating over price in each market will be correct because they will be equivalent to integrating over a particular path of price changes, where substitute price changes are implicitly functionally related to own price change. In generalizing Kling's results, Smith (1993b) points out that in this case a site's misspecified demand function serves as a general equilibrium demand function.

So far we have dealt only with price changes, but behavioral models that capture the substitution among recreational sites are often necessary if environmental quality changes are to be valued, because the necessary variation in quality can be found by looking across sites with varying quality dimensions. Systems of demand equations for different sites do not work well in this context because objective measures of quality at any given site do not vary over individuals visiting that site. Exceptions occur when information is available on individuals' perceptions or expectations of quality. When policy actions relate to wildlife stocks and the quality characteristic affecting the individual is bag or catch rate, variation in quality across individuals is sometimes manageable because individuals with differing skills, experience, and equipment may expect different success rates.

Varying parameter models have been employed where variation in quality at any one site is not measurable (Vaughn and Russell, 1982; Smith and Desvousges, 1986). A system of n site demand equations is first estimated as functions of prices and income, and then the set of n parameters associated with the own-price variable is regressed on the quality characteristics at the n sites. A final alternative is to pool observations over all sites and estimate one demand function. Site demands are assumed to be identical except for the costs of access and the quality characteristics included as explanatory variables in the model. In these models substitute prices and qualities are restricted to those of the "next best" alternative, if included at all.

Sample selection models and count models

Recent attention to limited dependent variable models in the econometrics literature has led to a wholesale departure from ordinary least squares estimation of travel cost models.[2] When the data available to the researcher are collected "on-site," the sample will be conditioned on recreational participation at that site and are said to be "truncated" (see Shaw (1988) for issues related to estimation).[3] Data are available to estimate demand models of the form

$$q = f(x) + \epsilon$$

where

$$f(x) + \epsilon > 0$$

More interesting stories are possible when data include observations on non-participants as well. Such data are especially important if one wishes to use the results of the model to predict responses to policy changes where these changes might cause individuals to enter or leave the "market" for recreational good.

Modeling strategies such as the tobit adjust for the "censoring" of the data, but explain both the participation decision (zero or non-zero trips) and the trips demand decision (number of trips conditioned on non-zero trips) with the same function. The implicit model is

$$q = f(x) + \epsilon \qquad \text{when } f(x) + \epsilon > 0$$

and

$$q = 0 \qquad \text{when } f(x) + \epsilon \leq 0$$

Alternatively, other factors may affect whether an individual is a potential participant. For example, factors such as age, health, and swimming skills may preclude beach use for some individuals, irrespective of access costs and water quality. Sample select models allow for this additional participation "switch." We might hypothesize that

$$q = f(x_1) + \epsilon \qquad \text{when both } g(x_2) + v > 0 \text{ and } f(x_1) + \epsilon > 0$$

and

$$q = 0 \qquad \text{otherwise}$$

Different likelihood functions are associated with different assumptions on the error terms (Heckman, 1979). For a discussion of the relative merits of these models in recreation demand settings see Creel and Loomis (1989), Bockstael et al. (1990), and Bockstael et al. (1991).

Count models, that accommodate discrete integer values for the dependent variable, constitute the most recent econometric modification to travel cost demand estimation. The Poisson regression model is a common choice, where the probability that the dependent variable takes on some value y_i, where $y_i = 0, 1, 2, \ldots$ is given by

$$\exp(-\lambda_i) \frac{\lambda_i^{y_i}}{y_i!}$$

For the Poisson distribution, λ_i is both the mean and variance of y_i. This parameter is generally modeled such that the ln λ_i is a linear function of the explanatory variables of the travel cost model. The negative binomial regression model offers a generalization that allows the mean of y_i to differ from its variance. Applications to recreation can be found in Hellerstein and Mendelsohn (1992) and in the trip demand stage of the Hausman et al. (1992) model.

Welfare measurement problems

The empirical models discussed so far are Marshallian demand functions that produce estimates of consumer surplus, not compensating variation, so that all the caveats associated with this distinction must apply. It is possible to recover estimates of compensating variation only if estimated demand functions can be integrated back to quasi-expenditure functions, either analytically as suggested by Hausman (1981) or numerically as suggested by Vartia (1983). When welfare measures of quality changes are required, further restrictions on preferences must be imposed in the integration process (see Bockstael and McConnell, 1993). LaFrance and Hanemann (1989) and Hanemann and Morey (1992) examine the difficulties of obtaining compensating variation measures from systems of demands.

Several authors have argued the merits of utility theoretical demand specifications and Hicksian-defined welfare measures, but intuition suggests that a consumer surplus estimate obtained from a well-fitting Marshallian travel cost model may be more meaningful than compensating variation measures obtained from the few functional forms that are both easily estimated and integrable. Smith (1989) argues that, given all the approximations implicit in our characterization of behavior and measurement of variables, requiring models to follow from a specific utility function "overstretches" the power of the construct. This is especially true as preferences for and expenditures on recreational trips hold a minor place in the individual's decision context.

Welfare measures (whether consumer surplus or compensating variation) computed from estimated parameters of recreational demand models will themselves be random variables with nontrivial distributions. The estimated welfare measures are usually biased, and because their distributions are often unknown, confidence intervals frequently cannot be computed (Bockstael and Strand, 1987). Since it is the welfare estimate rather than the demand function parameters that typically matter for policy analysis, this outcome is unfortunate. Kling and Sexton (1990) show using simulation experiments that the bias can be considerable and the standard error can exceed the point estimates. These authors (as well as Adamowicz et al., 1989) suggest bootstrapping techniques for determining whether the bias is significant and for constructing confidence intervals around welfare estimates. Taking a different view, Smith (1990) proposes choosing an estimation strategy that minimizes the mean squared error of the consumer surplus estimate instead of optimizing on the properties of the demand function parameters.

The Practice of Estimating Random Utility Recreational Demand Models

In seeking to value changes in a quality dimension of recreational trip, researchers have found it convenient to focus attention on the individual's choice among alternative sites of differing quality. Intuitively, the extra time and money an individual is willing to spend to access a site with more desirable amenities yields useful information for valuation of those amenities. Of interest in this characterization is the discrete choice among a finite set of alternative sites on any given trip occasion rather than the continuous choice of how many recreational trips to take in an arbitrary period of time. Kling (1988) and Kling and Weinberg (1990) have used Monte Carlo methods to compare traditional and discrete choice random utility travel cost models using simulated data. They find that traditional models (e.g. varying parameters) provide better estimates when substitution is not an issue, but the reverse seems true when site substitution is an important element of the decision problem.

A reformulation of the travel cost model as a random utility discrete choice model

Random utility models of recreational demand are travel cost models with a different time horizon. These models do not assume that the individual plans at the beginning of the season how many trips will be taken to all possible sites. Instead, the simplest form of this model focuses on the decision of where to go on a given "choice occasion," conditioned on the decision to take a recreational trip.

An obvious conceptual framework for this decision is McFadden's random utility model (McFadden 1974, 1981). Consider an individual who derives utility $V_i(b_i, \tilde{y} - p_i - wt_i)$ from visiting site i on a given choice occasion, conditional on the prior decision of taking a recreational trip. In this formulation b_i reflects quality characteristics at site i, $p_i + wt_i$ is the cost of accessing site i, and $\tilde{y}$ is a sub-budget for the relevant time period, so that $\tilde{y} - p_j - wt_i$ is the income available for other purchases. Given the alternative set S, the individual will choose site i if

$$V_i(b_i, \tilde{y} - p_i - wt_i) = \max[V_s(b_s, \tilde{y} - p_s - wt_s) \quad \forall s \in S]$$

Conditioned as the problem is on taking a recreational trip, the approach avoids dealing directly with the time allocation problem, but the time as well as monetary travel costs of the recreational trip are critical in explaining choice among sites, as are quality measures of the sites.

For estimation purposes, the V_j are usually assumed linear in the above explanatory variables and a stochastic term. For example,

$$V_j(b_j, \tilde{y} - p_j - wt_j) = \theta_1 b_j + \theta_2(\tilde{y} - p_j - wt_j) + \eta_j$$

where in many cases b_j will be a vector. The assumption of independent extreme-value distributions for the η lead to McFadden's conditional logit model where the probability that the individual chooses alternative i is given by

$$\text{pr}(i) = \frac{\exp(\theta' x_i)}{\sum \exp(\theta' x_s)}$$

The x_i vector includes explanatory variables associated with the ith site and the summation in the denominator is over all sites in the individual's alternative set.

One drawback of the conditional logit is that it embodies the independence of irrelevant alternatives (IIA) property identified by Luce. This implies that the "odds" of choosing one alternative over another is independent of the other alternatives in the alternative set. Specifically, the ratio of the probabilities of two alternatives is a function only of the difference in the explanatory variables associated with the two alternatives:

$$\frac{\text{pr}(i)}{\text{pr}(k)} = \exp\left[\theta_1(b_j - b_k) + \theta_2(p_j + wt_j - p_k - wt_k)\right]$$

Because $\tilde{y}$ does not change over alternatives, it will not enter into the estimation.

In the recreational context, as in other decision environments, the alternative set frequently violates the IIA property. For example, if the recreational swimming alternatives available to an individual include a local lake and a saltwater beach, the addition of another local lake site would not be expected to reduce the probabilities of visiting the first lake site and the saltwater beach proportionately, producing a violation of the IIA property.

McFadden (1978) has shown that a generalized extreme-value distribution for the errors is consistent with a "nested" decision model that allows for a general pattern of dependence among the alternatives and thus provides a solution to the above dilemma. Suppose the individual has available two local lake sites and three ocean beach sites as alternatives. The decision may be viewed in two states: (i) the choice between local freshwater beaches and saltwater beaches, and (ii) the choice between the two local freshwater beaches or the three saltwater beaches. Denote x as a vector of characteristics that affect utility and vary over all beaches and z as a vector of characteristics that affect utility and vary between lake and ocean beaches. Then the utility associated with visiting the ith beach of the kth type will be

$$V_{ik} = \theta' x_{ik} + \gamma' z_k + \eta_{ik}$$

If the η_{ik} are distributed generalized extreme value, the probability of choosing beach i conditioned on choosing type of beach k is given by

$$\text{pr}(i|k) = \frac{\exp(\theta' x_{ik})}{\sum \exp(\theta' x_{sk})}$$

where the summation in the denominator is over all beaches of the kth type. The probability of choosing a beach of the kth type is given by

$$\text{pr}(k) = \frac{\exp(\gamma' z_k + \mu I_k)}{\sum \exp(\gamma' z_h + \mu I_h)}$$

where the summation in the denominator is over the two types of beach and

$$I_k = \ln \left[\sum \exp(\theta' x_{ik}) \right]$$

where the summation is over all beaches of type k. The above term is called the "inclusive value" and provides a means of carrying information, specifically the potential value of each type of beach alternative, to the higher stage of the decision process. McFadden has shown that the coefficient on the inclusive value may range between zero and one if a pattern of dependence among alternatives exists. Hanemann (1980) was the first to apply these models to environmental valuation and Hanemann and Carson (1987) have estimated the most extensive version of a multilevel nested discrete choice model.

While nesting resolves the IIA violations, the order of the nested decisions is not always obvious and little is known about the consequences of incorrect nesting (Smith and Kaoru, 1986). Additionally, the definition of the relevant alternative set is important and incorrect specification can lead to biased parameter estimates. This is a particular difficulty when the alternative set is large and aggregation over alternatives is necessary (Parsons and Kealy, 1992; Parsons and Needelman, 1992).

Welfare measurement

McFadden's motivation of the discrete choice model as a random utility model allows the calculation of "per choice occasion" welfare measures of parameter changes. The derivation of these measures is due to Small and Rosen (1981) with specific procedures for considering the stochastic nature of the measure suggested by Hanemann (1984, 1985). Consider a policy action that alters the quality at site i from b_i^0 to b_i^1. The compensating variation of this quality change, conditioned on the individual choosing site i, would be given by CV in the following:

$$V(b_i^1, \tilde{y} - p_i - wt_i - \text{CV}) = V(b_i^0, \tilde{y} - p_i - wt_i)$$

However, the measure is stochastic; the individual chooses site i with some probability less than one. An approximate closed form solution to CV can be derived as

$$\text{CV} \approx \frac{1}{\theta_*} \left\{ \ln \sum \exp[V_i(b_i^1)] - \ln \sum \exp[V_i(b_i^0)] \right\}$$

where the summation is over all alternatives and the θ_* is the coefficient on the price term and, implicitly, the coefficient on income. Intuitively, the expression $\ln \sum \exp[V_i(b_i)]$ is an approximation for the expected value of utility and the $1/\theta_*$ term converts the change in utility to a money measure of welfare.

The demand for trips dilemma

A policy action that alters the environmental quality at one or more recreational sites may affect the individual's choice of recreational site, but may also affect how many recreational trips (to all sites) are taken. The CV defined above measures the benefits or losses on one trip occasion. Researchers have tended to append a separate continuous choice decision model (censored or count-type traditional travel cost models) for the number of trips to all sites and have captured price and quality of trips, given that prices and qualities differ over sites, by an "inclusive value" measure obtained from the discrete choice model (Bockstael et al., 1987a; Hausman et al., 1992).

Except in special circumstances, no models have been developed that treat the stochastic elements of the continuous demand and the random utility model consistently. Hanemann and Carson (1987) is an exception. They model sportfishing trips taken per week during the sportfishing season and can include a decision level that captures the choice among 0, 1, 2, 3, . . . sportfishing trips per week-long choice period. Most recently Morey et al. (1991) have proposed a model that allows joint estimation of the number of trips and the choice of site. The model depends on the assumption that the season can be divided into T decision periods within which at most one trip can be taken and combines a binomial distribution on number of "successes" in T trials with a multinominal logit model of site choice. The model is developed for the case when the number of trips is known, but the destinations of only a subset of the trips are available. Extension to nested models can be found in Morey et al. (1993).

Concluding Remarks

The literature on "travel cost" models is voluminous and this chapter can provide only an overview of those issues receiving the most attention. Problems such as how to incorporate environmental quality measures into these models, how to determine the "extent of the market" for the environmental amenity, and how to aggregate results to the level of the population or generalize results to different geographical settings are demanding of attention but largely unresolved.

Notes

1 The discussion between the individual and the household is largely untreated in the literature. The term "individual" will be used to designate the decision-maker from here on, recognizing that we typically have no notion of the household's internal decision process.
2 For details of the maximum likelihood estimation of the models discussed in this section see, for example, Maddala (1984). Econometrics software such as LIMDEP (Econometric Software Inc.) is now available to estimate all of these models.
3 On-site sampling often requires reweighting since the sampling scheme yields a random sample of trips rather than of individuals. Individuals who take more trips will have a higher probability of being sampled. This is a choice-based sampling problem such as is discussed in Manski and McFadden (1981).

References

Adamowicz, Wictor L., Fletcher, Jerry L. and Graham-Tomaski, Theodore. 1989: Functional form and the statistical properties of welfare measures. *American Journal of Agricultural Economics*, 71 (May), 414–21.
Becker, Gary. 1965: A theory of the allocation of time. *Economic Journal*, 75, 493–517.
Binkley, Clark. 1978: *The Recreation Benefits of Water Quality Improvements: An Analysis of Day Trips in an Urban Setting*. Washington, DC: US Environmental Protection Agency.
Bockstael, Nancy E. and McConnell, Kenneth E. 1983: Welfare measurement in the household production framework. *American Economics Review*, 73 (September), 804–14.
Bockstael, Nancy E. and McConnell, Kenneth. 1993: Public goods as characteristics of non-market commodities. *Economic Journal*, forthcoming.
Bockstael, Nancy E and Strand, Ivar E. 1987: The effects of common sources of regression error on benefit estimates. *Land Economics*, 63 (February), 11–20.
Bockstael, N. E., Hanemann, W. M. and Strand, I. E. 1987a: *Measuring the Benefits of Water Quality Improvements Using Recreation Demand Models*. Environmental Protection Agency Cooperative Agreement CR-811043-01-0.
Bockstael, Nancy E., Strand, Ivar E. and Hanemann, W. Michael. 1987b: Time and the recreation demand model. *American Journal of Agricultural Economics*, 69 (May), 293–302.
Bockstael, N. E., Strand, I. E., McConnell, K. E. and Arsanjani, F. 1990: Sample selection bias in the estimation of recreation demand functions: an adaptation to sportfishing. *Land Economics*, 69 (February): 40–9.
Bockstael, Nancy E., McConnell, Kenneth E. and Strand, Ivar E. 1991: Recreation. In J. B. Braden and C. D. Kolstad (eds), *Measuring the Demand for Environmental Quality*, New York: North-Holland.
Caulkins, Peter P., Bishop, Richard C. and Bouwes, Nicolaas. 1985: Omitted cross-price variable biases in the travel cost model: correcting common misconceptions. *Land Economics*, 61 (May), 182–7.
Caulkins, Peter P., Bishop, Richard C. and Bouwes, Nicolaas W., Sr. 1986: The travel cost model for lake recreation: a comparison of two methods for incorporating site quality and substitution effects. *American Journal of Agricultural Economics*, 68 (May), 291–7.
Cesario, F. J. and Knetsch, J. L. 1970: Time bias in recreation benefit studies. *Water Resources Research*, 6, 700–4.
Creel, D. Michael, and Loomis, John B. 1989: Theoretical and empirical advantages of truncated count data estimators of analysis of deer hunting in California. In *Benefits and Costs in Natural Resources Planning*, Interim Report 2, Western Regional Research Publication W-133, 11–26.

Garrod, Guy, and Willis, Ken. 1992: The amenity value of woodland in Great Britain: a comparison of economic estimates. *Environmental and Resource Economics*, 2 (4), 415–34.

Hanemann, W. Michael. 1978: A methodological and empirical study of the recreation benefits from water quality improvement. Ph.D. Dissertation, Department of Economics, Harvard University, Cambridge, MA.

Hanemann, W. Michael. 1980: A methodological and empirical study of the recreation benefits from water quality improvements. Ph.D. Dissertation, Harvard University, Cambridge, MA.

Hanemann, W. Michael. 1984: Discrete/continuous models of consumer demand. *Econometrica*, 52 (May), 541–61.

Hanemann, W. Michael. 1985: Applied welfare analysis with discrete choice models. Working Paper, Department of Agricultural and Resource Economics, University of California, Berkeley.

Hanemann, W. Michael, and Carson, Richard. 1987: *Southcentral Alaska Sport Fishing Economic Study*. Report to Alaska Department of Fish and Game, Jones and Stokes Associates.

Hanemann, W. Michael, and Morey, Edward. 1992: Separability, partial demand systems, and consumer's surplus measures. *Journal of Environmental Economics and Management*, 22 (May), 241–58.

Hausman, Jerry A. 1981: Exact consumer's surplus and deadweight loss. *American Economic Review*, 81 (June), 635–47.

Hausman, Jerry A., Leonard, Gregory and McFadden, Daniel. 1992: A utility-consistent, combined discrete choice and count data model: assessing recreational use losses due to natural resource damage. Paper presented at the Cambridge Economics Symposium titled "Contingent Valuation: A Critical Assessment," Washington, DC, April 2–3.

Heckman, James. 1979: Sample selection bias as a specification error. *Econometrica*, 47 (January), 143–61.

Hellerstein, Daniel, and Mendelsohn, Robert. 1992: A theoretical foundation for applying count data models to measure recreation values. Working Paper, Economic Research Service, US Department of Agriculture.

Kling, Catherine L. 1988: Comparing welfare estimates of environmental benefits from recreation demand models. *Journal of Environmental Economics and Management*, 15 (September), 331–40.

Kling, Catherine L. 1989: A note on the welfare effects of omitting substitute prices and qualities from travel cost models. *Land Economics*, 65 (August), 290–6.

Kling, Catherine L. and Sexton, Richard. 1990: Bootstrapping in applied welfare analysis. *American Journal of Agricultural Economics*, 72 (May), 406–18.

Kling, Catherine L. and Weinberg, M. 1990: Evaluating estimates of environmental benefits based on multiple site demand models: a simulation approach. In Link and Smith (eds), *Advances in Applied Microeconomics*, vol. 5, Greenwich, CT: JAI Press.

LaFrance, Jeffrey, and Hanemann, W. Michael. 1989: The dual structure of incomplete demand systems. *American Journal of Agricultural Economics*, 71 (May), 262–74.

Loomis, John. 1982: Use of travel cost models for evaluating lottery rationed recreation: application to big game hunting. *Journal of Leisure Research*, 14, 117–24.

Maddala, G. S. 1984: *Limited-dependent and Qualitative Variables in Econometrics*. Econometrics Society Monographs in Quantitative Economics, Cambridge: Cambridge University Press.

Manski, C. F. and McFadden, D. (eds). 1981: *Structural Analysis of Discrete Data with Econometric Applications*. Cambridge, MA: MIT Press.

McConnell, K. E. 1992: On-site time in the demand for recreation. *American Journal of Agricultural Economics*, 74 (November), 918–25.

McConnnell, K. E. and Strand, I. E. 1981: Measuring the cost of time in recreational demand analysis: an application to sport fishing. *American Journal of Agricultural Economics*, 63 (February), 153–6.

McFadden, Daniel. 1974: Conditional logit analysis of qualitative choice behavior. In Zarambka (ed.), *Frontiers in Econometrics*, New York: Academic Press.

McFadden, D. 1978: Modeling the choice of residential location. In A. Karlquist et al. (eds), *Spatial Interaction Theory and Residential Location*, Amsterdam: North-Holland.

McFadden, Daniel. 1981: Econometric models of probabilistic choice. In C. F. Manski and D. McFadden (eds), *Structural Analysis of Discrete Data with Econometric Applications*, Cambridge: MIT Press.

McKean, J. R. and Revier, C. F. 1990: An extension of omitted cross-price variable biases in the linear travel cost model: correcting common misperceptions. *Land Economics*, 66 (November), 430–6.

Mendelsohn, Robert, Hof, John, Peterson, George, and Johnson, Reed. 1992: Measuring recreation values with multiple destination trips. *American Journal of Agricultural Economics*, 74 (November), 926–33.

Milon, J. W. 1988: Travel cost methods for estimating the recreational use benefits of artificial marine habitat. *Southern Journal of Agricultural Economics*, 20 (July), 87–101.

Morey, Edward, Shaw, W.,Douglass, and Rowe, Robert. 1991: A discrete-choice model of recreational participation, site choice, and activity valuation when complete trip data are not available. *Journal of Environmental Economics and Management*, 22 (March), 181–201.

Morey, Edward, Shaw, W., Douglass, and Watson, Michael. 1993: A repeated nested-logit model of Atlantic salmon fishing. *American Journal of Agricultural Economics*, 75 (August), 578–92.

Nichols, L. M., Bowes, M. and Dwyer, J. F. 1978: Reflecting travel time in travel-cost-based estimates of recreation use and value. Department of Forestry Research Report 78–12, University of Illinois.

Parsons, George R. and Kealy, Mart Jo. 1992: Randomly drawn opportunity sets in a random utility model of lake recreation. *Land Economics*, 68 (February), 93–106.

Parsons, George R. and Needelman, Michael S. 1992: Site aggregation in a random utility model of recreation. *Land Economics*, 68 (November), 418–33.

Ribaudo, Marc, and Epp, Donald. 1984: The importance of sample discrimination in using the travel cost demand method to estimate the benefits of improved water quality. *Land Economics*, 60 (February), 397–403.

Samples, K. C. and Bishop, R. C. 1985: Estimating the value of variations in anglers' success rates: an application of the multiple-site travel cost method. *Marine Resource Economics*, 2, 55–74.

Shaw, Daigee. 1988: On-site samples' regression: problems of non-negative integers, truncation and endogenous stratification. *Journal of Econometrics*, 37, 211–23.

Shaw, W. D. 1992: Searching for the opportunity cost of an individual's time. *Land Economics*, 68 (February), 107–15.

Small, Kenneth, and Rosen, Harvey. 1981: Applied welfare economics with discrete choice models. *Econometrica*, 49 (January), 105–30.

Smith, V. Kerry. 1989: Taking stock of progress with travel cost recreation demand methods: theory and implementation. *Marine Resource Economics*, 6, 279–310.

Smith, V. Kerry. 1990; Estimating recreation demand using the properties of the implied consumer surplus. *Land Economics*, 66 (May), 111–20.

Smith, V. Kerry. 1993a: Nonmarket valuation of environmental resources: an interpretative appraisal. *Land Economics*, 69 (February), 1–26.

Smith, V. Kerry. 1993b: Welfare effects, omitted variables, and the extent of the market. *Land Economics*, 69 (May), 121–31.

Smith, V. Kerry, and Desvousges, William H. 1986: *Measuring Water Quality Benefits.* Boston, MA: Kluwer-Nijhoff.

Smith, V. Kerry and Kaoru, Y. 1986: Modeling recreation demand within a random utility framework. *Economic Letters*, 22, 395–9.

Smith, V. Kerry and Kaoru, Y. 1990: Signals or noise: explaining the variation in recreation benefit estimates. *American Journal of Agricultural Economics*, 72 (May), 419–33.

Smith, V. Kerry, Deesvouger, William H., and McGivney, M. 1983. The opportunity cost of travel time in recreational demand models. *Land Economics*, 59 (August), 259–78.

Vartia, Y. 1983: Efficient methods of measuring welfare changes and compensated income in terms of orderly demand functions. *Economica*, 51 (January), 79–98.

Vaughn, William, and Russell, Clifford. 1982: Valuing a fishing day: an application of a systematic varying parameter model. *Land Economics*, 58 (November), 450–63.

30

Hedonic Pricing Methods

A. Myrick Freeman III*

Economists were providing evidence on the association between the prices of houses and environmental amenities such as air quality even before this relationship had been recognized as an application of the newly developed theory of hedonic prices.[1] In the past 20 years there has been a virtual explosion of both theoretical and empirical studies of the monetary values of non-market amenities and disamenities based on hedonic price theory.[2] The two questions which have been explored most extensively in this literature are the proper specification and estimation of the model relating housing prices to amenities and the development of measures of welfare change which make the best use of the available data and are consistent with the underlying economic theory. This chapter has two purposes. The first is to describe the evolution of economic thinking about property prices and environmental amenities. The second is to review the current state of knowledge concerning the two questions of model specification and welfare measurement.

Historical Background

According to the theory of rents, the equilibrium price for a parcel of land is the present value of the stream of rents produced by the land. Economic theory has long recognized that the productivity of land differs across sites. These productivity differentials will yield differential rents to land and therefore differential land values. Where land is a producer's good, competition and free entry are sufficient to ensure that productivity differentials are fully reflected in the land rent structure. For any property where the land rent is less than its productivity, the activity occupying that land must be earning a profit. Some potential entrant will be willing to bid above the going rent in order to occupy that site and reap the rewards of a superior productivity. It is this competition that assures that rent differentials will be equal to productivity differentials. And since the price at which a unit of land sells in the market is the present value of the stream of future rents, productivity differentials will also be reflected in land prices.

Some environmental characteristics such as air or water quality may affect the productivity of land as either a producer's good or a consumer's good. Where this is so, the structure of land rents and prices will reflect these environmentally determined productivity differentials. These results from classical rent theory aroused considerable interest among economists about the possibility of using data on land rent or land value for residential properties to measure the benefits to households brought about by improvements in environmental characteristics such as air or water quality. Ronald Ridker (1967) was the first economist to attempt to use residential property value data as the basis for estimating the benefits of changes in measures of environmental quality such as air pollution. He reasoned as follows.

> If the land market were to work perfectly, the price of a plot of land would equal the sum of the present discounted streams of benefits and costs derivable from it. If some of its costs rise . . . or if some of its benefits fall . . . the property will be discounted in the market to reflect people's evaluation of these changes . . . . We should therefore expect to find the majority of effects reflected in this market, and we can measure them by observing associated changes in property values.
>
> (Ridker, 1967, p. 25)

The last sentence of this passage raises three questions. The first is whether environmental variables such as air pollution do systematically affect land prices. Assuming an affirmative answer to this question, the second is whether knowledge of this relationship is sufficient to predict changes in land prices when, say, air pollution levels change. And the third question is whether changes in land prices accurately measure the underlying welfare changes.

As for the first question, Ridker and Henning regressed median census tract property values on a measure of sulfate air pollution and found a significant inverse relationship. They then went on simply to assert affirmative answers to the second and third questions. Specifically they argued that the coefficient on the air pollution variable in the regression equation could be used to predict the change in the price of any residence conditional on a change in its air pollution level and that the sum of all such changes could be taken as a measure of the benefit of improving air quality in the urban area (Ridker and Henning, 1967, p. 254).

Subsequent efforts to provide a sound theoretical basis for interpreting the air pollution–property value relationship have taken one of two paths. The first was to develop models of the urban land market to determine whether and under what circumstances changes in aggregate land values accurately measure the benefits associated with environmental improvements (Strotz, 1968; Lind, 1973; Pines and Weiss, 1976; Polinsky and Shavell, 1976). The second path drew on hedonic price theory to interpret the derivative of the cross-section regression equation with respect to air pollution as a marginal implicit price and therefore a marginal value for the air quality improvement (Freeman, 1974; Rosen, 1974). In this chapter I will describe the latter approach to welfare measurement.

The Model of Individual Choice

Assume that each individual's utility is a function of her consumption of a composite commodity X, a vector of location of specific environmental amenities, Q, a vector of structural characteristics of housing such as size, number of rooms, age, type of construction denoted by S, and a vector of characteristics of the neighborhood in which the house is located such as quality of local schools, accessibility to parks, stores, and workplace, and crime rates, denoted by N.

Any large area has in it a wide variety of sizes and types of housing with different locational, neighborhood, and environmental characteristics. An important assumption of the hedonic technique is that the urban area as a whole can be treated as a single market for housing services. Individuals must have information on all alternatives and must be free to choose a house anywhere in the urban market. It is as if the urban area were one huge supermarket offering a wide selection of varieties. Of course, individuals cannot move their shopping carts through this supermarket. Rather their selections of residential locations fix for them the whole bundle of housing services. It is much as if shoppers were forced to make their choices from an array of already filled shopping carts. Individuals can increase the quantity of any characteristic by finding an alternative location alike in all other respects but offering more of the desired characteristic.

Since our interest is in the values of characteristics to buyers of houses, there is no need to model the supply side of this market formally. Let us simply assume that the housing market is in equilibrium, that is, that all individuals have made their utility-maximizing residential choices given the existing array of houses and their prices and that these prices just clear the market. Given these assumptions, the price of the ith residential location, P_i, can be taken to be a function of the structural, neighborhood, and environmental characteristics of that location:

$$P_i = P(S_i, N_i, Q_i)$$

This is termed the hedonic price function.

Assume that the hedonic price function has been estimated for an urban area. Its partial derivative with respect to any of its arguments, for example q_j, gives the marginal implicit price of that characteristic, that is, the additional amount that must be paid by any individual to move to a house with a higher level of that characteristic, other things being equal. If this function is nonlinear, the marginal implicit price of a characteristic is not constant but depends on its level and perhaps the levels of other characteristics as well.

To model the problem more formally, consider an individual who occupies house i. His utility is given by

$$u = u(X, Q_i, S_i, N_i)$$

Assume that preferences are weakly separable in housing and its characteristics. This assumption makes the demands for characteristics independent of the prices of other goods, a convenient property for empirical work. The individual maximizes utility subject to the budget constraint

$$M - P_i - X = 0$$

The first-order condition for the choice of environmental amenity, say q_j, is

$$\frac{\partial u / \partial q_j}{\partial u / \partial X} = \frac{\partial p_i}{\partial q_j}$$

If the individual is assumed to be a price taker in the housing market, he can be viewed as facing an array of marginal implicit price schedules for various characteristics. An individual maximizes utility by simultaneously moving along the marginal price schedules for each characteristic until he reaches a point where his marginal willingness to pay for an additional unit of that characteristic just equals the marginal implicit price of that characteristic. If an individual is in equilbrium, the marginal implicit prices associated with the housing bundle actually chosen must be equal to the corresponding marginal willingness to pay for those characteristics.

The analysis described here results in a measure of the price of and the marginal willingness to pay for q_j but does not directly reveal the marginal willingness-to-pay function. The second stage of the hedonic technique is to combine the quantity and implicit price information in an effort to identify the marginal willingness-to-pay function or bid function for q_j. This function gives the maximum willingness to pay or bid for an increase in q_j holding utility constant and given the optimally chosen levels of all other characteristics. It is convenient to assume that the utility function is weakly separable in housing so that prices of other goods can be omitted in the specification of the marginal willingness-to-pay function. Also, it is convenient to assume that each individual purchases only one housing bundle. If more than one were purchased, it would be necessary that they be identical or that the hedonic price function be linear in all characteristics. This is so that there can be only one marginal implicit price recorded for each individual for each characteristic.

Given these assumptions, for the individual who chooses the ith house, the bid function is

$$b_j = b_j(q_{ji}, Q_i^*, s_i, N_i, u^*)$$

where Q_i^* is all amenities except q_j and u^* is the reference level of utility. The task of identifying this function from observed choices will be addressed below. If this function can be identified, it can be used to estimate the welfare change of an individual associated with changes q_j, assuming other things are held equal. Specifically, if the quantities of other characteristics and amenities do not change, the welfare change can be found by integrating b_j over the relevant range of the change in q_j. However, a change in the quantity of one characteristic can result in changes in the quantities the individual chooses of other characteristics and changes in the hedonic price function itself. The task of welfare measurement when individuals can fully adjust to the new supply of amenities and characteristics will also be discussed below.

Identifying Characteristics Demands

The attractiveness of the hedonic price model for applied welfare analysis lies in the potential for using estimates of individuals' marginal implicit prices for a characteristic to recover information on the underlying structure of preferences, specifically the marginal willingness-to-pay function. Sherwin Rosen had argued that marginal willingness-to-pay and marginal supply price functions could be estimated from the information contained in the hedonic price function in the following manner:

> compute a set of implicit marginal prices . . . for each buyer and seller evaluated at the amounts of characteristics . . . actually bought or sold, as the case may be. Finally, use estimated marginal prices . . . as endogenous variables in the second-stage simultaneous estimation of [the marginal willingness-to-pay and supply price functions]. Estimation of marginal prices plays the same role here as do direct observations on prices in the standard theory and converts the second-stage estimation into a garden variety identification problem.
>
> (Rosen, 1974, p. 50)

This suggestion has been the source of a large literature over the past 15–20 years. Since the emphasis in this chapter is on models and basic economic method rather than econometric issues, I will only provide an overview of the sources of the identification problem and alternative approaches to solving it.[3]

The difficulties in identifying the marginal willingness-to-pay function from hedonic price data come in two forms. The first arises from the fact that the source of data for the dependent variable in the marginal willingness-to-pay function is not direct observation of b_j; rather it is the calculation of the marginal implicit price $\partial P_i / \partial q_j$ for the estimated hedonic price function. But this variable is itself computed as a function of the same characteristics that are explanatory variables in the marginal willingness-to-pay function. Brown and Rosen (1982) and Mendelsohn (1987) show that at least in some cases this procedure leads to parameter estimates for the marginal willingness-to-pay function that are identical to the estimated coefficients in the hedonic price function. In other words, since the second stage estimation procedure utilizes no additional data beyond those already contained in the hedonic price function, it can do no more than reproduce the coefficients estimated from the hedonic price function.

The second source of difficulty lies in the fact that both the quantity of the characteristic and its marginal implicit price are endogenous in the hedonic price model. Unlike the standard market model in which an individual faces an exogenously determined price and chooses a quantity, the individual chooses one point from a price schedule. The choice of that point simultaneously determines the marginal willingness to pay and the quantity of the characteristic. As Palmquist put it, "the other marginal prices [on the individual's marginal willingness-to-pay function] are only observed for other individuals with other socio-economic characteristics and provide no information on the original consumer's bid for different quantities of the characteristic" (1991, p. 96). This makes it very difficult to separate out the effects of demand shifters from the price–quantity relationship, itself.

One approach to identification is to find truly exogenous variables to be used as instruments. This appears to be a difficult task. Another approach is to impose sufficient structure on the problem by assumption to ensure that the conditions for identification of the marginal willingness-to-pay function are met. For example, Quigley (1982) assumed a functional form for preferences that included homotheticity as a property. By specifying the relationship between income and demand, this assumption made it possible to separate the effects of income and quantity change on the marginal willingness to pay for characteristics.

Probably the most reliable approach to solving the identification problem is to find cases where the marginal implicit prices of characteristics vary sufficiently independently of the other demand shift variables. Specifically this means cases where individuals with the same preferences, income, and so forth face different marginal implicit prices.

This can only occur if similar individuals must choose in markets with different hedonic price functions, which in turn implies either segmented markets within a city or observations taken from several different housing markets, for example, in different cities.

The first step in implementing this approach is to estimate separate hedonic price functions for each housing market using the same specification. The second step is to compute the marginal implicit price faced by each individual from the hedonic price function in that market. Then the computed marginal implicit prices can be regressed on the observed quantities of the characteristics and the exogenous demand shifters to obtain the uncompensated bid function. Assuming sufficient independent variation across markets and assuming that there are no unobserved differences in preferences across individuals, this approach will lead to reliable and properly identified bid functions.[4]

Measuring Welfare Changes

It has been established that in an equilibrium of the housing market utility-maximizing individuals equate their marginal willingness to pay for housing characteristics with the marginal implicit prices of these characteristics and that, in some circumstances, it may be possible to estimate marginal willingness-to-pay and uncompensated inverse demand functions on the basis of this information. We now ask the question: how can we use the information on prices and preferences which can be extracted from the hedonic housing market to calculate measures of welfare change for changes in environmental amenities? The basic concepts of welfare measurement at the level of the individual are straightforward. But welfare measurement in the aggregate may be more difficult because of induced price changes and the possibility that individuals will adjust their consumption positions in response to changes in prices and quantities. Also, in principle, it is necessary to consider changes in the supply side of the hedonic property market, as well.

In this section I will first define the basic welfare measure for marginal and nonmarginal changes in a characteristic or environmental amenity holding other things constant. This means, in effect, that people do not move to different housing sites with different bundles of characteristics in response to the change in the environmental characteristic or any induced changes in the hedonic price function. This measure also looks only at benefits to purchasers of housing bundles. I then consider a fully general measure of welfare change which includes possible changes in profits on the supply side of the hedonic market as well as the consequences of individuals' adjustments on the demand side of the market. Finally I describe some models which can be applied as special cases of the more general definition of welfare change or which can provide lower or upper bound approximations of the correct measure, at least in certain circumstances.

Also in this section, we must distinguish between the task of defining a conceptually correct welfare measure and identifying what must be known in order to implement such a measure. Some of the welfare measures identified in this section require knowledge of the marginal willingness-to-pay function for each individual. But even when the identification problems discussed above can be solved, our models generally provide only estimates of the uncompensated bid function. I will also include some discussion of how one might obtain the necessary marginal willingness-to-pay functions from data on inverse demands.

Basic principles

Since a change in an environmental amenity in an urban area is nonexcludable and nondepletable, it is, in effect, a public good. The marginal value of the change, then, is simply the sum of the marginal willingness to pay of each of the affected individuals evaluated at the existing housing equilibrium. In other words, for the amenity q_j:

$$w_q = \sum_{i=1}^{n} b_{ji} = \sum_{i=1}^{n} \frac{\partial P}{\partial q_{ji}} \tag{30.1}$$

where w_q is the aggregate marginal welfare change, i indexes both individuals and their houses, and n is the total population. Although most proposed environmental policy changes are nonmarginal in magnitude, the ease of calculating equation (30.1) still may make it useful for indicating whether some improvement is desirable, by comparing this measure with an estimate of the marginal cost of the improvement.

Similarly, in a partial equilibrium setting where there are no changes in other prices or characteristics, the welfare value of a change in an environmental amenity, say from q_j^0 to q_j^1, is given by

$$W_q = \sum_{i=1}^{n} \int_{q_j^0}^{q_j^1} b_{ji}(q_{ji}, Q_i^*, S_i, N_i, u_i^*) \, dq_j \tag{30.2}$$

where W_q is the aggregate benefit. Notice that this measure requires knowledge of the marginal willingness-to-pay functions of individuals. If the uncompensated bid functions from the second stage of the hedonic price estimation are used, the welfare gain (loss) will be overestimated (underestimated) for compensating measures of welfare change.

There is a method for calculating exact welfare measures for nonmarginal changes in a characteristic, holding all other things constant. It is based on an adaptation of Hausman's technique for exact welfare measurement for price changes (Hausman, 1981). This adaptation is due to Horowitz (1984). Suppose that an individual's uncompensated bid function

$$b_j^* = b_j^*(q_j, Q_i^*, M - P_i)$$

has been identified. In equilibrium,

$$\frac{\partial u / \partial q_j}{\partial u / \partial M} = b_j^* = \frac{\partial P_i}{\partial q_j} \tag{30.3}$$

The left-hand side of (30.3) is the slope of the indifference curve between the numeraire, M, and q_j. So, in equilibrium

$$\frac{\mathrm{d}M}{\mathrm{d}q_j} = b_j^*(\cdot)$$

This expression can be solved for

$$M = f(q_j, Q^*, C)$$

where C is a constant of integration. The benefit of an increase in q_j is

$$W_q = f(q_j^0, Q_i^*, C) - f(q_j^1, Q_i^*, C)$$

Horowitz (1984) presents a simple example where the inverse demand function is derived from a Cobb–Douglas utility function.

In principle at least, measures of welfare change based on equations (30.1) or (30.2) can be generalized to incorporate the effects of general equilibrium adjustments. At any location, the value of a nonmarginal change can be taken to be the integral of the values of a series of infinitesimal changes in the amenity (Bartik and Smith, 1987, p. 1223). The value of each small change is taken to be the willingness to pay of the occupant of that site at that point in the sequence of changes. The measures for all sites together is the sum of the values for each site. It is given by

$$W_q = \sum_{i=1}^{n} \int_{q_j^0}^{q_j^1} \frac{\partial P_i(q_j, Z)}{\partial q_j} \, \mathrm{d}q_j$$

where Z is the vector of all other site characteristics, which are held constant by assumption.

In principle this measure allows individuals to relocate in response to changes in the quantity and price of this amenity, since, in effect, it sums individuals' marginal values as the amenity changes at each site. This is important, since a major limitation of some of the measures to be described below is their inability to account for individual relocation decisions. Furthermore, this measure does not require knowledge of either the marginal willingness-to-pay or the bid function. It relies on the fact that at each point in the sequence of changes, each individual's marginal bid is revealed by the marginal implicit price of the characteristic.

However, the hedonic price function is likely to shift as a consequence of the change in the amenity level. Therefore, in order to implement this measure, it is necessary to know how the hedonic price function and the marginal implicit prices at each location change as the levels of the amenities at each location change along the path of integration. This, as a practical matter, is a major limitation of this measure.

A comprehensive measure of benefits

Suppose that there are increases in several environmental amenities in an urban area. These increases need not be uniform across the area. Specifically let us consider the case where the vector Q increases from Q^0 to Q^1. We will first look at the immediate welfare effects of this change and then examine how the welfare gains are magnified and redistributed by the rational adjustments of individuals and ensuing price changes in the hedonic market.[5]

First, assuming that individuals cannot move to new locations and that the hedonic price function does not change, the benefit to individuals is given by an expanded version of equation (30.2):

$$W_q = \sum_{i=1}^{n} \int_{Q_i^0}^{Q_i^1} b_i(Q_i, P_i, u_i^*) \, dQ_i \tag{30.4}$$

where each individual's welfare gain is computed from a path-independent line integral over the changes in the individual elements in Q_i and where $b_i(\cdot)$ is the vector of individual marginal willingness-to-pay functions for the characteristics.

At the existing hedonic price function, some people may wish to choose different bundles of characteristics. If they do change, it must be because they perceive themselves to be better off after the adjustment. This welfare gain is in addition to that given by equation (30.4). Furthermore, the effort to adjust to different characteristics bundles is likely to affect the hedonic price function unless the number of people wishing to do so is quite small relative to the market.

Also the suppliers of housing may respond to changes in the hedonic price function by offering different bundles of housing characteristics. This could have further repercussions on the hedonic price function. And it will increase the profits of housing suppliers.

When all of these adjustments have worked themselves out, the aggregate benefit to individuals can be defined in terms of each individual's total willingness to pay for a housing unit with given characteristics, holding utility constant. Let this total willingness to pay be given by

$$B_i(Q_i^{j*}, s_i^{j*} u^*)$$

where Q_i^{j*} and S_i^{j*} $(j = 0, 1)$ indicate the vectors of environmental and other characteristics actually chosen by the individual in the original and new equilibria. Each individual's total benefit is the increase in total willingness to pay for the characteristics actually chosen, holding utility constant, minus any increase in actual expenditure on housing. These increases in total willingness to pay can be summed across all individuals to obtain the total benefit to occupants of housing.

Turning to the supply side of the market, there may be benefits accruing to producers of housing. In aggregate, they realize a change in aggregate profits given by the algebraic sum of the change in expenditures on housing and the change in the cost of supplying housing. The change in spending can be derived from the hedonic price function. Any change in costs can be derived from the suppliers' cost functions.

The welfare change for society as a whole is the sum of the benefits to occupants and the changes in profits of suppliers of housing. Full implementation of this welfare measure would require enormous amounts of information. But this measure reduces to equation (30.4) if the hedonic price function does not change and if the change in environmental amenities does not affect the costs of supplying housing amenities for producers.

Even if this set of conditions is not satisfied, equation (30.2) can be interpreted as a lower bound on the true measure of benefits. This can be seen by decomposing the true benefit measure into a sequence of changes and adjustments. Consider first the change in amenity levels without any adjustment on the part of individuals or suppliers. The welfare change associated with this first step is given by equation (30.2) plus any reduction in the costs of supplying existing houses at the affected locations. Second, suppose hypothetically that the hedonic price function is shifted to its new equilibrium position but that no individual or supplier adjustments to the new price function are permitted. At this stage, although some individuals and suppliers may gain while others lose, on net, all of the price changes sum to zero. At this stage, there is no net change in welfare.

Finally, allow individuals and suppliers to respond to the new hedonic price function. Any adjustments that take place at this stage must represent welfare improvements for those responding. The total welfare change is the sum of equation (30.2), any costs reduction to suppliers, and the benefits of adjusting to the price change. The last two components are either zero or positive. Thus, equation (30.2) represents a lower bound on the true measure of benefits. And the error involved in using (30.2) is smaller, the smaller is the adjustment to the changes in the hedonic price function.

A special case

If the hedonic price function does not shift, then exact welfare measurement may be a relatively easy task. One situation in which the hedonic price function could be assumed to be constant is when the number of parcels experiencing a change in the amenity level is small relative to the total urban market. If this is the case, and if individuals can move without cost from one site to another in response to the change in environmental amenity levels, Palmquist (1992) has shown that exact welfare measurement is straightforward. The hedonic price function can be used to predict the changes in the prices of affected properties. Benefits are exactly measured by the increase in the values of the affected properties. And knowledge of the marginal bid functions is not required.

The change in the amenity level results in an increase in the price of each house which can be calculated from the hedonic price function. The owner of the property is better off by this increase in wealth. Even though the occupant of the property experiences the increase in amenity level, he or she is made worse off because of the increase in the cost occupying this property. The occupant will move to a different house. But with costless moving, the occupant can relocate to his or her original equilibrium position. So the net welfare change is the increase in wealth to the owner. If the owner and occupant are the same person, the result is still the same. This individual might choose to move to a property with an amenity level somewhat greater than the original level because of a wealth effect. But the increase in wealth fully captures the benefit of the amenity improvement to this individual.

Conclusions

It is now time to summarize the answers to the two questions raised at the beginning of this chapter. The first question concerned the specification and estimation of a model of housing prices for purposes of valuing environmental amenities. Hedonic price theory provides a coherent basis for explaining the prices of houses in an urban market as a function of the levels of characteristics embedded in each house. And there is a dynamic version of this model which relates changes in the prices of houses to changes in the levels of one or more characteristics, other things being equal. The major limitation of the hedonic model is its assumption that consumers of housing can select their most preferred bundle of characteristics from a complete range of levels of all characteristics.

The second question concerned the derivation of measures of economic value and welfare change for changes in the levels of environmental amenities. Measures of value for marginal and nonmarginal changes can be derived from a properly specified hedonic price model. Values for marginal changes in amenity levels are found simply by adding up the observed or computed marginal willingness to pay for all affected individuals. But nonmarginal amenity changes, welfare measurement requires knowledge of the inverse demand function or the income compensated bid function for the amenity. And this, in turn, requires a solution to the daunting identification problem.

There are some limitations to the property value models for estimating welfare effects. First, since the property value models are based on the consequences of individuals' choices of residence, they do not capture willingness to pay for improvements in environmental amenities at other points in the urban area, for example, the workplace, shopping areas, or parks and recreational area. Second, because the property value models are based on observing behavioral responses to differences in amenity levels across houses, they only capture willingness to pay for perceived differences in amenities and their consequences. For example, if there are subtle, long-term health effects associated with reduced environmental quality at some housing sites but people are unaware of their causal link to the housing site, their willingness to pay to avoid these effects will not be reflected in housing price differences.

On the other hand, property value measures have the capability of capturing the value of all of the possible effects of changes in environmental quality at a housing site in a single number. For example, if air pollution causes increases in the incidence of respiratory disease, damages ornamental vegetation, and reduces the quality of the view, the property value model summarizes these effects in a single number.

Notes

This chapter is adapted, with permission, from my book *The Measurement of Environmental and Resource Values: Theory and Method*, Washington, DC: Resources for the Future, 1993.
1   One of the principal early contributors to the development of the hedonic price theory was Griliches (1971). The first empirical study of housing prices and an environmental amenity was by Ridker and Henning (1967). The formal structure of hedonic models was first analyzed by Rosen (1974). And the relevance of hedonic price theory to interpreting the link between housing prices and air quality was pointed out by Freeman (1974).

2 For further discussion of this literature, see the surveys in Bartik and Smith (1987) and Palmquist (1991).
3 Readers interested in a more technical discussion, especially from an econometric perspective, should consult Brown and Rosen (1982), Epple (1987), Bartik (1987), and McConnell and Phipps (1987). Bartik and Smith (1987) and Palmquist (1991) also provide useful reviews of the issues.
4 Examples of this approach include Palmquist (1984) and Bartik (1987).
5 This section is based on the analysis of Bartik (1988).

References

Bartik, Timothy J. 1987: The estimation of demand parameters in hedonic price models. *Journal of Political Economy*, 95 (February), 81–8.
Bartik, Timothy J. 1988: Measuring the benefits of amenity improvements in hedonic price models. *Land Economics*, 64 (May), 172–83.
Bartik, Timothy J. and Smith, V. Kerry. 1987: Urban amenities and public policy. In E. S. Mills (ed.), *Handbook of Regional and Urban Economics*, Amsterdam: Elsevier.
Brown, James N. and Rosen, Harvey S. 1982: On the estimation of structural hedonic price models. *Econometrica*, 50 (May), 765–8.
Epple, Dennis. 1987: Hedonic prices and implicit markets: estimating demand and supply functions for differentiated products. *Journal of Political Economy*, 87 (February), 59–80.
Freeman, A. Myrick, III. 1974: On estimating air pollution control benefits from land value studies. *Journal of Environmental Economics and Management*, 1 (May), 74–83.
Griliches, Zvi (ed.) 1971: *Price Indexes and Quality Change*. Cambridge, MA: Harvard University Press.
Hausman, Jerry A. 1981: Exact consumer's surplus and dead weight loss. *American Economic Review*, 71 (September), 662–76.
Horowitz, Joel L. 1984: Estimating compensating and equivalent income variations from hedonic price models. *Economics Letters*, 14 (4), 303–8.
Lind, Robert C. 1973: Spatial equilibrium, the theory of rents, and the measurement of benefits from public programs. *Quarterly Journal of Economics*, 87 (May), 188–207.
McConnell, Kenneth E. and Phipps, T. T. 1987: Identification of preference parameters in hedonic models: consumer demands with nonlinear budgets. *Journal of Urban Economics*, 22 (July), 35–52.
Mendelsohn, Robert. 1987: A review of identification of hedonic supply and demand functions. *Growth and Change*, 18 (Winter), 82–92.
Palmquist, Raymond B. 1984: estimating the demand for characteristics of housing. *Review of Economics and Statistics*, 64 (August), 394–404.
Palmquist, Raymond B. 1991: Hedonic methods. In J. B. Braden and C. D. Kolstad (eds), *Measuring the Demand for Environmental Improvement*, Amsterdam: Elsevier.
Palmquist, Raymond B. 1992: Valuing localized externalities. *Journal of Urban Economics*, 31 (January), 359–68.
Pines, David, and Weiss, Yoram. 1976: Land improvement projects and land values. *Journal of Urban Economics*, 3 (January), 1–13.
Polinsky, A. Mitchell, and Shavell, Steven. 1976: Amenities and property values in a model of an urban area. *Journal of Public Economics*, 5 (January–February), 119–29.
Quigley, John M. 1982: Nonlinear budget constraints and consumer demand: an application to public programs for residential housing. *Journal of Urban Economics*, 12, 177–201.
Ridker, Ronald G. 1967: *Economic Costs of Air Pollution: Studies in Measurement*. New York: Praeger.

Ridker, Ronald G. and Henning, John A. 1967: The determinants of residential property values with special reference to air pollution. *Review of Economics and Statistics*, 49 (May), 246–57.

Rosen, Sherwin. 1974: Hedonic prices and implicit markets: product differentiation in perfect competition. *Journal of Political Economy*, 82 (February), 34–55.

Strotz, Robert H. 1968: The use of land value changes to measure the welfare benefits of land improvements. In J. E. Haring (ed.). *The New Economics of Regulated Industries*, Los Angeles, CA: Occidental College.

Index